W9-ACV-652

THE GLOBAL AGENDA

ISSUES AND PERSPECTIVES

FOURTH EDITION

EDITED BY

Charles W. Kegley, Jr.
University of South Carolina

Eugene R. Wittkopf
Louisiana State University

22, 23, 24, 25, 30

1, 12, 14

8, 9, 19, 45

32, 33, 35, 36, 59

McGRAW-HILL, INC.

New York   St. Louis   San Francisco   Auckland   Bogotá
Caracas   Lisbon   London   Madrid   Mexico City   Milan   Montreal
New Delhi   San Juan   Singapore   Sydney   Tokyo   Toronto

This book was set in Times Roman by The Clarinda Company.
The editors were Peter Labella and Fred H. Burns;
The production supervisor was Paula Keller.
The cover was designed by Carla Bauer.
R. R. Donnelley & Sons Company was printer and binder.

THE GLOBAL AGENDA
Issues and Perspectives

This book is printed on acid-free paper.

2 3 4 5 6 7 8 9 0   DOC   DOC   9 0 9 8 7 6 5

ISBN 0-07-034043-9

Library of Congress Cataloging-in-Publication Data
The global agenda: issues and perspectives / [edited by] Charles W.
    Kegley, Jr., Eugene R. Wittkopf. —4th ed.
        p.   cm.
    Includes bibliographical references and index.
    ISBN 0-07-034043-9
    1. International relations.   2. International economic relations.
    I. Kegley, Charles W.   II. Wittkopf, Eugene R., (date).
    JX1395.G575   1995
    327—dc20   94-30047

ABOUT THE EDITORS

CHARLES W. KEGLEY, JR., is Clarence Carter Visiting Professor at Rice University and Pearce Professor of International Relations at the University of South Carolina. Past president of the International Studies Association (1993–1994), Kegley has held appointments at Georgetown University and the University of Texas, Rutgers University. He is the editor of *Controversies in International Relations Theory: Realism and the Neoliberal Challenge* (St. Martin's Press, 1995) and *The Long Postwar Peace* (HarperCollins, 1991). With Gregory A. Raymond, Kegley is the coauthor of *A Multipolar Peace? Great-Power Politics in the Twenty-First Century* (St. Martin's Press, 1994).

EUGENE R. WITTKOPF is R. Downs Poindexter Professor of Political Science at Louisiana State University. A past president of the Florida Political Science Association and of the International Studies Association/South, he has also held appointments at the University of Florida and the University of North Carolina at Chapel Hill. Wittkopf is the author of *Faces of Internationalism: Public Opinion and American Foreign Policy* (Duke University Press, 1990) and the editor of the second editions of *The Future of American Foreign Policy* (St. Martin's Press, 1994) and *The Domestic Sources of American Foreign Policy* (St. Martin's Press, 1994).

Together, Kegley and Wittkopf have coauthored and edited many texts, including *World Politics: Trend and Transformation,* fifth edition (1995); *American Foreign Policy: Pattern and Process,* fourth edition (1991); *The Future of American Foreign Policy* (1992); *The Nuclear Reader: Strategy, Weapons, War,* second edition (1989); and *The Domestic Sources of American Foreign Policy* (1988), all with St. Martin's Press.

For Linda and Suzanne
CWK

For Barbara, Debra, and Jonathan
ERW

CONTENTS

PREFACE   ix

PART ONE   ARMS AND INFLUENCE   1

1   Power, Capability, and Influence
      in International Politics   11
      K. J. Holsti

2   Force or Trade: The Costs and Benefits
      of Two Paths to Global Influence   24
      Richard Rosecrance

3   The Future of Military Power:
      The Continuing Utility of Force   35
      Eliot A. Cohen

4   The Obsolescence of Major War   44
      John Mueller

5   Nuclear Myths and Political Realities   54
      Kenneth N. Waltz

6   War in the Post-Cold War Era: Structural
      Perspectives on the Causes of War   64
      Jack S. Levy

7 What Should Be Done with Nuclear Arsenals?
Disarmament and Weapons Proliferation 75
Michael Renner

8 Controlling the Global Trade in Arms 85
Michael T. Klare

9 Disorder in the New World Order?
The Future of Terrorism 95
Edward F. Mickolus

10 Sanctions: A Look at the Record 100
Kimberly Ann Elliott

11 The Changing Nature of World Power 105
Joseph S. Nye, Jr.

PART TWO DISCORD AND COLLABORATION 119

12 Models of International Relations:
Realist and Neoliberal Perspectives
on Conflict and Cooperation 129
Ole R. Holsti

13 Cold War, Chill Peace:
Prospects for Order and Disorder 144
Michael Howard

14 Great-Power Relations: Paths to Peace
in the Twenty-First Century 154
Charles W. Kegley, Jr., and Gregory A. Raymond

15 Southern Perspectives on World Order 166
Shahram Chubin

16 The Coming Clash of Civilizations
Or, the West against the Rest 179
Samuel P. Huntington

17 Islam and Liberal Democracy: Muslim
Perceptions and Western Reactions 183
Bernard Lewis

18 Human Rights in the New World Order 190
Jack Donnelly

19   Out of the Cold: Humanitarian
     Intervention in the 1990s   200
         Stanley Hoffmann

20   Wandering in the Void: Charting the UN's
     New Strategic Role   205
         John Gerard Ruggie

21   The Reality and Relevance of International
     Law in the Post-Cold War Era   211
         Christopher C. Joyner

22   Achieving Cooperation under Anarchy:
     Strategies and Institutions   225
         Robert Axelrod and Robert O. Keohane

PART THREE   POLITICS AND MARKETS   231

23   Three Ideologies of Political Economy   241
         Robert Gilpin

24   Looming Collision of Capitalisms?   259
         Erik R. Peterson

25   Trade Lessons from the World Economy   270
         Peter F. Drucker

26   No More NICs   277
         Robin Broad and John Cavanagh

27   The Regional Way to Global Order   289
         Robert D. Hormats

28   EC/EU: Confidence Lost   298
         Michael J. Brenner

29   After NAFTA: Global Village or Global Pillage?   303
         Jeremy Brecher

30   Mercantilism and Global Security   310
         *Michael Borrus, Steve Weber, and
         John Zysman, with Joseph Willihnganz*

31   Oil: Reopening the Door   322
         Joseph Stanislaw and Daniel Yergin

PART FOUR   ECOLOGY AND POLITICS   331

32   The Ecological Perspective on
       International Politics   341
       Dennis Pirages

33   The Earth Summit and Beyond   347
       Crispin Tickell

34   Agenda 21: Toward a Strategy to Save Our Planet   355
       Daniel Sitarz

35   Population Pressures and the Global Habitat   367
       Charles W. Kegley, Jr., and Eugene R. Wittkopf

36   Managing Migrations   381
       Doris Meissner

37   Hunger versus the Environment:
       A Recipe for Global Suicide   391
       Nabil Megalli

38   Agriculture and the Environment:
       Meeting Global Food Needs   396
       Orville L. Freeman

39   The Politics of Water   402
       Sandra Postel

40   The GATT: Environmental Menace or Ally?   412
       Hilary F. French

41   The Tragedy of the Commons
       in Global Perspective   422
       Marvin S. Soroos

42   The International State of Nature and
       the Politics of Scarcity   436
       William Ophuls and A. Stephen Boyan, Jr.

43   Environment and Security: Muddled Thinking   446
       Daniel Deudney

PREFACE

With the end of Cold War competition between the United States and the Soviet Union and their allies, the world for the third time in this century must confront the challenges and opportunities that the end of global conflict portends. Inevitably the transformation of world politics now taking place will confront nation-states and other world political actors with new issues that cry out for novel means of addressing them. Older issues, including those that may come packaged in new ways, will also demand attention. The competition between the new and the old will shape the global agenda for the remainder of this century and into the next.

With the dramatic changes the world has witnessed in recent years, it is not surprising that fresh perspectives now also vie with more traditional ones as scholars, political commentators, and policymakers alike seek to make sense of the often confusing and chaotic issues that populate the global agenda. Our purpose in preparing the fourth edition of *The Global Agenda: Issues and Perspectives* is to present incisive analytical perspectives and informed commentary on the policy issues that now animate the theory and practice of world politics. We believe that these analyses are critical to an understanding of the issues that inevitably will shape the world in which we all live and that today's students will inherit. We also continue to believe that there is a need for educational materials that treat description and theoretical exposition in a balanced manner and that expose a variety of normative interpretations without advocating any particular one. It seems to us that, to a greater or lesser degree, these purposes are rarely fulfilled in standard texts (by design and necessity) and that a supplementary anthology is the logical place for them.

The Global Agenda: Issues and Perspectives continues to categorize readings into four "baskets" that build on the distinction between *high politics*—peace and security issues—and *low politics*—issues of material and nonmaterial well-being. The distinction between high and low politics has never been entirely clear, and that is perhaps even more true with the end of the Cold War than previously. Still, the politics of peace and security often unfold differently than the politics of material and nonmaterial well-being. The conceptual distinction between high and low politics thus continues usefully to capture the elements of change and continuity that shape the contemporary global agenda. The criteria that guided the selection of particular articles and the rationale that underlies the organization of the book are made explicit in our introductions to each part. The introductions also help students connect individual readings to common themes.

Our editor at McGraw-Hill, Peter Labella, has been especially encouraging as we prepared the fourth edition of this book, and Fred Burns and Lisa V. Calberg have been helpful in seeing it to fruition. We thank them both. We also thank those who have contributed original articles to the book and the many others—from journal editors to permissions managers, from students to scholars and policymakers—who have contributed to our thinking about the issues and perspectives that animate the global agenda and who have kindly made important contributions, large and small, to the continuing appeal of this book.

Charles W. Kegley, Jr.

Eugene R. Wittkopf

PART ONE

ARMS AND INFLUENCE

The contemporary international political system began to acquire its present shape and definition more than three centuries ago with the emergence of a state system in Europe following the highly destructive Thirty Years War. As the 1648 Peace of Westphalia brought that war to an end and as political, economic, and social intercourse grew among the states of Europe, new legal norms were embraced in an effort to regulate interstate behavior. The doctrine of state sovereignty, according to which no legal authority is higher than the state, emerged supreme. Thus the nascent international system was based on the right of states to control their internal affairs without interference from others and to manage their relations with other states with whom they collaborated or competed as they saw fit. Foremost in this system was the belief, reinforced by law, that the state possessed the right—indeed, the obligation—to take whatever measures it deemed necessary to ensure its preservation.

Although the international system and patterns of interaction among its political actors have changed profoundly since the birth of the state system, contemporary world politics remains significantly colored by its legacy. International politics continues to be conducted in an atmosphere of anarchy. As in the past, the system remains fragmented and decentralized, with no higher authority above nation-states, which, as the principal actors in world politics, remain free to behave toward one another as they choose.

This is not meant to imply either that states exercise their freedom with abandon or that they are unconstrained in the choices they make. The political, legal, moral, and circumstantial constraints on states' freedom of choice are formida-

1

ble. Moreover, states' national interests are served best when they act in a manner that does not threaten the stability of their relations with others or of the global system that protects their autonomy. Hence, as the British political scientist Hedley Bull has pointedly observed, the international system may be an anarchical society, but it is nonetheless one of "ordered anarchy."

The world has grown increasingly complex and interdependent as contact, communication, and exchange have increased among the actors in the state system and as the number of nation-states and other non-state international actors has grown. Expanded interaction enlarges the range of potentially mutual beneficial exchanges between and among states. But just as opportunities for cooperation have expanded, so have the sources of disagreement. That we live in an age of conflict is a cliché that contains elements of truth, as differences of opinion and efforts to resolve disputes to one's advantage, often at the expense of others, are part of any relationship. Thus, as the world has grown smaller, the mutual dependence of nation-states and other transnational political actors on one another has grown and the number of potential rivalries and antagonisms has increased correspondingly. Friction and tension appear to be endemic to international politics. Even as the Cold War fades from memory, competition and conflict persist, as demonstrated by Iraq's brutal invasion of Kuwait in 1990, and the ubiquitous eruption of ethnic conflict in the Balkans, Africa, South Asia, and elsewhere.

Given the persistent characteristics of contemporary world politics, the number of *issues* that are at any one time in dispute among nation-states and other global actors appears to have increased greatly. The multitude of contentions renders the *global agenda*—the list of issues that force their way into consideration and command that they be addressed, peacefully or not—more crowded and complex. Because the responses that are made to the issues on the global agenda shape our lives both today and into the future, it is appropriate that we direct attention to those matters that animate world politics and stimulate the attention and activities of national decision makers. At the same time, as different state and non-state actors view global political issues from widely varying vantage points, it is fitting that we remain sensitive to the various perceptual lenses through which the items on the global agenda are viewed. Accordingly, *The Global Agenda: Issues and Perspectives* seeks to focus on the range of issues that dominates world politics as well as on the multitude of analytical and interpretive perspectives through which those issues are viewed.

The issues and perspectives discussed in *The Global Agenda* are grouped into four broad, somewhat overlapping, but analytically distinct issue areas: (1) arms and influence, (2) discord and collaboration, (3) politics and markets, and (4) ecology and politics. The first two deal with states' security interests, often referred to as matters of *high politics.* The latter two deal with the non-security issues, often referred to as matters of *low politics,* that increasingly have come to occupy, if not dominate, the attention of world political actors. In all four issue areas, we seek to convey not only the range of issues now facing those responsible for political choices but also the many vantage points from which they are typically viewed.

We begin in Part I by considering issues appropriately subsumed under the collective rubric *arms and influence*. As the term high politics suggests, the issues and perspectives treated here focus on the prospects for peace and security in a world of competitive nation-states armed with lethal weapons that can be used to inflict violence and destruction.

ARMS AND INFLUENCE

It is often argued that states strive for power, security, and domination in a global environment punctuated by the threat of violence and death. This viewpoint flows naturally from the characteristics of the international political system, which continue to be marked by the absence of central institutions able to manage and resolve conflict. Hence, preoccupation with preparations for defense is understandable, as the fear persists that one adversary might use force against another to realize its goals or to vent its frustrations. In such an environment, arms are widely perceived as useful not only to enhance security but also as a means to realize and extend one's influence. Moreover, nation-states frequently see their interests best served by a search for power, by whatever means. Thus *power* and *influence* remain the core concepts in the study of world politics.

Appropriately, our first essay, "Power, Capability, and Influence in International Politics," by K. J. Holsti, provides a thoughtful discussion of these core concepts in international politics as they relate to the foreign policy behavior of states in contemporary world politics. The essay provides insights important not only for evaluating the subsequent essays in this book but also for evaluating how these sometimes ambiguous terms typically inform interpretations of global issues—for almost invariably such discussions make reference, implicitly or explicitly, to the interrelationships among power, capability, and influence.

If the purpose of statecraft is the pursuit of political power, then a critical question is, What are the most appropriate means that might propel states to positions of prominence in the international hierarchy? In "Force or Trade: The Costs and Benefits of Two Paths to Global Influence," Richard Rosecrance outlines rival approaches to the realization of that goal. The first encompasses the conventional path: the acquisition of military might. The United States and the Soviet Union exhibited steadfast dedication to this tradition throughout the Cold War, as did other participants in the post-World War II struggle for arms and influence. In contrast, other states—especially in Europe and Asia—chose a second path, which brought them global power through trade expansion, not territorial control and force.

Predicting that global leadership is destined to pass to what he calls "the new trading states," Rosecrance argues that those who remain wedded to the pursuit of power through territorial control and military spending will experience an erosion of their power and influence. States have a clear choice and must weigh the trade-off between economic and military power, according to Rosecrance, as prosperity through economic power and excessive military spending are incompatible. His conclusion—that trade instead of arms provides the most viable path to both prosperity and peace—finds a prominent place on the global agenda because it poses a dilemma no policy maker can ignore, especially now that the superpowers' military competition has ceased and the economic battleground arguably has become the primary locus in the struggle for power and influence. At issue is how security is to be realized and welfare assured.

Rosecrance's thesis is, of course, open to theoretical and empirical challenge. In the next selection, "The Future of Military Power: The Continuing Utility of Force," Eliot A. Cohen takes exception to the view that military force no longer plays a decisive role in world politics, even with the end of the Cold War and the spread of liberal democracy in Eastern Europe and elsewhere. Unlike Rosecrance, Cohen maintains that the usability and usefulness of military force have not diminished and that the threat and actual use of military force retain many of their traditional functions and advantages.

Although Cohen recognizes that preparation for war is costly and the use of force risky, he questions the view that "methods of commerce are displacing military methods." Moreover, he questions the validity of three popular neo-liberal theories: that in creating conditions of interdependence, "the horrific quality of modern military technology, the spread of democracy, and the rise of transnational issues and actors" will inhibit recourse to war and give birth to a new age of lasting peace. Cohen maintains that none of these so-called liberal arguments is persuasive, as the trends and conditions that make them plausible are unlikely to endure. Thus, the conclusion that military power is becoming obsolete is not warranted. Instead, "war, and potential war, will remain a feature of international politics." In short, Cohen concludes that the usefulness of military power endures and that military force will continue to occupy a central place in world politics.

Cohen's thesis is compelling. The picture and prescriptions he presents must, however, be balanced against the long-term implications of a profoundly important world political achievement: Since World War II the great powers have experienced the longest period of uninterrupted peace since the advent of the state system in 1648. The faces of war and international politics *have* been transformed. How this remarkable achievement occurred is, however, subject to diametrically opposed interpretations. One says that the existence of weapons of mass destruction produced the long peace. The other contends that the long peace occurred *despite* these weapons, not because of them.

In "The Obsolescence of Major War," John Mueller explores the policy and moral implications of the long peace. He argues that war has passed from a noble institution to one in which it is now widely regarded as illegal, immoral, and counterproductive. The steps to this global awakening are traced in an account that suggests nuclear weapons were essentially irrelevant to the preservation of the long postwar peace. Mueller recognizes that "war in the developed world . . . has not become impossible" and that war in the Third World remains frequent and increasingly deadly. Still, he sees hope for the future in the fact that "peoples and leaders in the developed world—where war was once endemic—have increasingly found war to be disgusting, ridiculous, and unwise." "If war begins in the minds of men, as the UNESCO Charter insists," then, Mueller maintains, "it can end there." That would indeed alter the way the world has conventionally thought about arms, influence, and peace. In such a world (Cohen's assessment notwithstanding), the utility of force would be certain to command less respect than in the past.

Nuclear weapons are doubtless the most lethal form of power and hence the most threatening instruments of influence. How to avoid their use has dominated strategic thinking ever since the atomic age began in 1945. *Deterrence*—preventing a potential adversary from launching a military attack—has long been a central concept in these considerations. The failure of deterrence, particularly in a war between nuclear powers, could, of course, ignite a global conflagration culminating in the destruction of humanity, which means that the entire world has a stake in the operation of a successful deterrent strategy.

For many years great faith was placed in the ability of nuclear weapons to keep the peace. Indeed, the most popular theory of the avoidance of general war since 1945 is the claim that nuclear weapons have made general war obsolete. But others endorse John Mueller's thesis that nuclear weapons are "essentially irrelevant" in the prevention of major war. As argued at length in his well-known 1989 book *Retreat from Doomsday,* the growing aversion to war in general, in conjunction with the inhibiting fear of another major *conventional* war in particular, explains the obsolescence of war in the developed world.

Kenneth N. Waltz, a neo-realist, disagrees. As argued in "Nuclear Myths and Political Realities," Waltz believes that nuclear weapons have had a pacifying impact on the course of world affairs since World War II. In a comprehensive review of thinking about nuclear weapons that outlines the evolution of nuclear doctrines, the efforts to construct a foolproof strategic defense, and efforts to bring about nuclear disarmament, Waltz advances the controversial conclusion that nuclear weapons have been "a tremendous force for peace" which "afford nations who possess them the possibility of security at reasonable cost." Without them, the post-World War II world would likely have been far less peaceful. Thus the peace and stability of the postwar world cannot be attributed to conventional deterrence. But, Waltz warns, scholars and policy makers have not understood the true strategic implications of nuclear weaponry and the reasons why nuclear weapons dominate strategy, with the result that the advantages of nuclear weapons have not been properly appreciated.

Because arms both threaten and protect, a congeries of rival hypotheses can be advanced about the causes of armed conflict and of peace in the nuclear age. In "War in the Post-Cold War Era: Structural Perspectives on the Causes of War," Jack S. Levy summarizes leading ideas embedded in the assumptions of contending theoretical foci to explain the role of force in world politics and the means of preserving peace. As Levy notes, the outbreak of war derives from a wide range of circumstantial and causal factors, some internal to individual states and many external to them. Both contribute to its occurrence.

Focusing primarily on "systemic" or "structural" factors—attributes of the international system writ large—Levy reviews three major explanations for the continuing outbreak of war: (1) international anarchy and the security dilemma it creates, (2) theories of international equilibrium such as the operation of a successful balance of power under the emerging conditions of multipolarity, and (3) "power transition" theories and the propositions associated with them. His review suggests that, because war clearly has multiple potential causes, its control is difficult to manage, inasmuch as control depends on a varied combination of tangible and intangible factors. He warns, moreover, that "the changing structures of power in international and regional systems that have influenced decisions for war or peace so often in the past will continue to play a central role in such decisions in the future."

Achieving international security is often confounded by changes in global conditions. One change that could inhibit realization of that objective is the probability that the number of members of the "nuclear club" may increase dramatically in the future. Thus managing *nuclear proliferation* is a major political issue.

As Michael Renner warns in "What Should Be Done with Nuclear Arsenals? Disarmament and Weapons Proliferation," the nuclear issue remains complex. Despite recent breakthroughs in the negotiated reduction of the nuclear arsenals of the United States, Russia, and other former Soviet states, many states have powerful incentives to join the nuclear club and are actively pursuing development of nuclear capabilities. Showing why "the laying down of arms is a tricky process," Renner inventories the problems and prospects confronting the world community on this global issue. He finds the obstacles to the further expansion of nuclear states insufficient. To contain the spread, Renner argues that "disarmament will require shutting down test sites, converting weapons design labs to civilian use, dismantling existing warheads, and devising solutions for disposal of fissionable materials."

Renner warns that the danger of current disarmament agreements being reversed or abused always exists in a world where many leaders continue to equate arms with influence. And, he reminds us, the reduction of nuclear arsenals has a long way to go, as illustrated by the fact that in 1994 "the remaining weapons still [contained] more than enough firepower to annihilate all life on Earth." To "nix the use of nukes," Renner advocates a multiple attack on preventing the clandestine diversion or theft of the huge stocks of plutonium and highly enriched uranium from which new nuclear weapons might be built.

Implicit in Renner's perspective is the belief (in contrast to Waltz) that nuclear weapons undermine international security and therefore need to be abolished. To Renner, faith in weapons is unwarranted. To reduce the danger, the ideology that equates military might with influence and security must be challenged: "The continued possession of nuclear weapons by a few countries— even small numbers—perpetuates the idea that they constitute a legitimate instrument for national defense. In so doing, it lends legitimacy to other countries' efforts to acquire them." Because the perceived faith in the legitimacy of nuclear weapons remains, the proliferation debate is likely to remain intense.

A dramatic increase in the capacity to destroy is among the inevitable consequences of states' efforts to enhance their influence. As Renner's analysis suggests, many political analysts see the prospects for peace dramatically reduced by these efforts. Michael T. Klare is among them. In "Controlling the Global Trade in Arms," he warns that even though the Cold War has ended, effective measures to arrest the sale of arms have not been implemented. Given the prevailing policies and practices of both arms suppliers and purchasers, the expansion of the trafficking in arms appears likely. Massive supplies of surplus weapons are being funneled into the arms inventories of emerging Third World powers, and barriers to this flow are inadequate. Focusing on the close connection between unconventional and conventional weapons, Klare identifies the key reasons why "controlling the conventional arms trade is essential" as "uncontrolled arms sales represent a very significant threat to international stability." To illustrate the magnitude of the threat, he reviews the Iraqi arms buildup and its aftermath, showing in the process how "many Third World states are now engaged in [similar] regional power struggles." Klare concludes that this outcome is not preordained. Instead, steps can be taken to control the problem, and Klare reviews the components necessary to build a comprehensive arms transfer control regime.

As noted, some analysts argue that weapons increase national security and that the most lethal arms deter their use. Nonetheless, other forms of violence— often referred to as "low-intensity conflict"—are unlikely to decline as the spread of arms continues.

The widespread evidence of low-intensity violence draws attention to perhaps its most conspicuous and threatening form: international terrorism. In "Disorder in the New World Order? The Future of Terrorism," Edward F. Mickolus offers a timely and illuminating discussion of international terrorism, recent trends in its occurrence, its old and new causes, and its probable future impact. Mickolus doubts that this terrifying force can be brought under control, even in the wake of the Cold War. The recent decline in the frequency of terrorism, Mickolus warns, "should not be misinterpreted as an end of terrorism." Accordingly, he contends that efforts to grapple with terrorism must begin with a sober account of its diverse purposes and changing character. Although "terrorism will not fundamentally change the direction of the new world order . . . , terrorism will continue to be an issue, but not a determinant, in the politics of nations and the conduct of world affairs."

Terrorism is practiced by those who are weak in an attempt to attempt to influence the strong (and, through "state terrorism," often by powerful governments to repress the powerless). More commonly, states engage in another practice in their hope to change the behavior of a target by methods short of the actual use of force: *sanctions*. Ranging from economic methods of punishment such as trade embargoes to collective international censorship to ostracize the target, the purpose of sanctions is generally the same: to modify the target's conduct so as to persuade it to do something it would not otherwise do (such as ceasing to pursue nuclear armament) or to convince it to stop some action in which it is currently engaging (such as persecution of minorities).

In "Sanctions: A Look at the Record," Kimberly Ann Elliott surveys the use of sanctions as an instrument of international influence from World War II until the 1990 United Nations embargo of Iraq. Based on an historical survey of more than one hundred sanction efforts, Elliott isolates the conditions under which such attempts to exercise influence have succeeded and why they have often failed.

Distressingly for those who would rely on sanctions as an instrument of statecraft, Elliott finds that only about one-third of previous sanction attempts were successful. Although their efficacy could improve as the world political economy continues its rapid globalization, Elliott predicts that such a change is unlikely because "changes in the international economy in recent decades have reduced the number of targets likely to succumb to unilateral economic coercion." As a consequence, Elliott concludes that "a more interdependent global economy means that the effectiveness of unilateral sanctions [will depend] increasingly on the subtlety, skill, and creativity with which they are imposed."

Finally, Part I concludes with an assessment of power and influence in light of the 1990s' turbulent transformations. In "The Changing Nature of World Power," Joseph S. Nye, Jr., provides the tools necessary to evaluate how the relationships between arms, influence, and world leadership are likely to change in the waning days of the twentieth century. He surveys and critiques current thinking about the changing sources of power, the balance of power, and hegemony in modern history. And, in comparing rival models (for example, realist interpretations of hegemonic transitions, the neo-Marxist view of hegemony, and the long-cycle theory of world leadership), Nye provides a theoretical foundation from which to predict the future of American power and to evaluate the risks of system-wide war as we approach the millennium.

The issues discussed in the eleven essays in Part I—capabilities and influence, trade power, the use of force, the frequency of war, the effects of nuclear weapons and effectiveness of strategies of nuclear deterrence, the causes of war, nuclear proliferation, the arms trade, terrorism, sanctions as a mode of coercive diplomacy, and the changing nature of world power—do not exhaust the range of security problems that populate the global agenda. However, in focusing attention on some of the many issues relating to the role of arms and influence in a world of interdependent and often competitive states, they offer insight into the complexities of the issues of high politics with which national decision makers must grapple. Part II, in which we shift attention to the nature of discord and collaboration in world politics, adds further insight into the politics of peace and security.

1

POWER, CAPABILITY, AND INFLUENCE IN INTERNATIONAL POLITICS

K. J. Holsti

In this essay K. J. Holsti clarifies the meaning of three concepts crucial to the conduct of international politics—power, capability, and influence—and examines the complexities of each as it relates to states' efforts to realize their foreign policy objectives. Holsti is professor of political science at the University of British Columbia. His publications include *Peace and War: Armed Conflicts and International Order, 1648–1989* **(1991).**

. . . [A foreign policy] act is basically a form of communication intended to change or sustain the behavior of those upon whom the acting government is dependent for achieving its own goals. It can also be viewed as a "signal" sent by one actor to influence the receiver's image of the sender.[1] In international politics, acts and signals take many different forms. The promise of granting foreign aid is an act, as are propaganda appeals, displays of military strength, wielding a veto in the Security Council, walking out of a conference, organizing a conference, issuing a warning in a diplomatic note, sending arms and money to a liberation movement, instituting a boycott on the goods of another state, or declaring war. These types of acts and signals, and the circumstances in which they are likely to succeed, will be discussed. . . . Our organizing principle will

---

[1]A comprehensive treatment of how governments "signal" each other is in Robert Jervis, *The Logic of Images in International Relations* (Princeton, N.J.: Princeton University Press, 1970).

Reprinted from K. J. Holsti, *International Politics: A Framework for Analysis,* 4th ed., pp. 114–59. © 1983. Reprinted by permission of the author. Some footnotes have been deleted.

be the amount of threat involved in the various techniques of influence. Diplomatic persuasion seemingly involves the least amount of threat; economic pressures, subversion, intervention, and various forms of warfare involve increasingly great amounts of threat and punishment. To help understand what all these types of action or techniques of influence have in common, however, we will discuss in a more abstract manner the behavior governments show when they turn toward each other to establish orientations, fulfill roles, or achieve and defend objectives.

The international political process commences when any state—let us say state A—seeks through various acts or signals to change or sustain the behavior (for instance, the acts, images, and policies) of other states. Power can thus be defined as the general capacity of a state to control the behavior of others. This definition can be illustrated as follows, where the solid line represents various acts:

A seeks to influence B because it has established certain objectives that cannot be achieved (it is perceived) unless B (and perhaps many other states as well) does X. If this is the basis of all international political processes, the capacity to control behavior can be viewed in several different ways:

1 Influence (an aspect of power) is essentially a *means* to an end. Some governments or statesmen may seek influence for its own sake, but for most it is instrumental, just like money. They use it primarily for achieving or defending other goals, which may include prestige, territory, souls, raw materials, security, or alliances.

2 State A, in its acts toward state B, uses or mobilizes certain *resources*. A resource is any physical or mental object or quality available as an instrument of inducement to persuade, reward, threaten, or punish. The concept of resource may be illustrated in the following example. Suppose an unarmed robber walks into a bank and asks the clerk to give up money. The clerk observes clearly that the robber has no weapon and refuses to comply with the order. The robber has sought to influence the behavior of the clerk, but has failed. The next time, however, the robber walks in armed with a pistol and threatens to shoot if the clerk does not give up the money. This time, the clerk complies. In this instance, the robber has mobilized certain resources or capabilities (the gun) and succeeds in influencing the clerk to comply. But other less tangible resources may be involved as well. The appearance of the person, particularly facial expression, may convey determination, threat, or weakness, all of which may subtly influence the behavior of the clerk. In international politics, the diplomatic gestures and words accompanying actions may be as important as the acts themselves. A government that places troops on alert but insists that it is doing so for domestic reasons will have an impact abroad quite different from the government that organizes a similar alert but accompanies it with threats to go to war. "Signals" or diplomatic "body language" may be as important as dramatic actions such as alerts and mobilizations.

3 The act of influencing B obviously involves a *relationship* between A and B, although, as will be seen later, the relationship may not even involve overt communication. If the relationship covers any period of time, we can also say that it is a *process*.

4 If A can get B to do something, but B cannot get A to do a similar thing, then we can say that A has more power than B regarding that particular issue. Power, therefore, can also be viewed as a *quantity*, but as a quantity it is only meaningful when compared to the power of others. Power is therefore relative.

To summarize, power may be viewed from several aspects: It is a means; it is based on resources; it is a relationship and a process; and it can be measured, at least crudely.

We can break down the concept of power into three distinct analytic elements: power comprises (1) the *acts* (process, relationship) of influencing other states; (2) the *resources* used to make the wielding of influence successful; and (3) the *responses* to the acts. The three elements must be kept distinct. Since this definition may seem too abstract, we can define the concept in the more operational terms of policy makers. In formulating policy and the strategy to achieve certain goals, they would explicitly or implicitly ask the five following questions:

1 Given our goals, what do we wish B to do or not to do? (X)

2 How shall we get B to do or not to do X? (implies a relationship and process)

3 What resources are at our disposal so that we can induce B to do or not to do X?

4 What is B's probable response to our attempts to influence its behavior?

5 What are the *costs* of taking actions 1, 2, or 3—as opposed to other alternatives?

Before discussing the problem of resources and responses, we have to fill out our model of the influence act to account for the many patterns of behavior that may be involved in an international relationship. First, the exercise of influence implies more than merely A's ability to *change* the behavior of B. Influence may also be seen when A attempts to get B to *continue* a course of action or policy that is useful to, or in the interests of, A.[2] The exercise of influence does not always cease, therefore, after B does X. It is often a continuing process of reinforcing B's behavior.

---

[2] J. David Singer, "Inter-Nation Influence: A Formal Model," *American Political Science Review,* 57 (1963), 420–30. State A might also wish state B to do W, Y, and Z, which may be incompatible with the achievement of X.

Second, it is almost impossible to find a situation where B does not also have some influence over A. Our model has suggested that influence is exercised only in one direction, by A over B. In reality, influence is multilateral. State A, for example, would seldom seek a particular goal unless it has been influenced in a particular direction by the actions of other states in the system. At a minimum, there is the problem of feedback in any relationship: If B complies with A's wishes and does X, that behavior may subsequently prompt A to change its own behavior, perhaps in the interest of B. The phenomenon of feedback may be illustrated as follows:

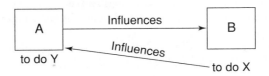

Third, there is the type of relationship that includes "anticipated reaction."[3] This is the situation where B, anticipating rewards or punishments from A, changes his behavior, perhaps even before A makes any "signals" about possible action. Deterrence theory clearly assumes that B—the potential aggressor against A—will not attack (where it might, were there no deterrent), knowing that an unacceptable level of punishment would surely result. A similar situation, but in reverse, is also common in international politics. This is where A might wish B to do X, but does not try to influence B for fear that B will do Y instead, which is an unfavorable response from A's point of view. In a hypothetical situation, the government of India might wish to obtain arms from the United States to build up its own defenses, but does not request such arms because it fears that the United States would insist on certain conditions for the sale of arms that might compromise India's nonalignment. This anticipated reaction may also be multilateral, where A wishes B to do X, but will not try to get B to do it because it fears that C, a third state, will do Y, which is unfavorable to A's interests. India wants to purchase American arms, but does not seek to influence the United States to sell them for fear that Pakistan (C) will then build up its own armaments and thus accelerate the arms race between the two countries. In this situation, Pakistan (C) has influence over the actions of the Indian government even though it has not deliberately sought to influence India on this particular matter or even communicated its position in any way. The Indian government has simply perceived that there is a relatively high probability that if it seeks to influence the United States, Pakistan will react in a manner contrary to India's interests.

[3]Herbert A. Simon, "Notes on the Observation and Measurement of Political Power," *Journal of Politics,* 15 (1953), 500–16. For further analysis, see David A. Baldwin, "Inter-Nation Influence Revisited," *Journal of Conflict Resolution,* 15 (December 1971), 478–79.

Fourth, power and influence may be measured by scholars, but what is important in international politics is the *perceptions* of influence and capabilities held by policy makers and the way they interpret another government's signals. The reason that governments invest millions of dollars for gathering intelligence is to develop a reasonably accurate picture of other states' capabilities and intentions. Where there is a great discrepancy between perceptions and reality, the results to a country's foreign policy may be disastrous. To take our example of the bank robber again, suppose that the person held a harmless toy pistol and threatened the clerk. The clerk perceived the gun to be real and deduced the robber's intention to use it. As a result, the clerk complied with the demand. In this case, the robber's influence was far greater than the "objective" character of the robber's capabilities and intentions; and distorted perception by the clerk led to an act which was unfavorable to the bank.

Finally, as our original model suggests, A may try to influence B *not to do* X. Sometimes this is called negative power, or deterrence, where A acts in a manner to *prevent* a certain action it deems undesirable to its interests. This is a typical relationship in international politics. By signing the Munich treaty, the British and French governments hoped to prevent Germany from invading Czechoslovakia; Israeli attacks on PLO facilities in Lebanon [were] designed to demonstrate that PLO guerrilla operations against Israel [would] be met by vast punishments, the costs of which to the PLO would far outweigh the gains of the terrorist acts. Such a cost-benefit analysis, the Israelis [hoped], would deter the PLO from undertaking further operations. The reader should keep in mind the distinction between compellence and deterrence.

RESOURCES

The second element of the concept of power consists of those resources that are mobilized in support of the acts taken to influence state B's behavior. It is difficult to assess the general capacity of a state to control the actions and policies of others unless we also have some knowledge of the capabilities involved.[4] Nevertheless, it should be acknowledged that social scientists do not understand all the reasons why some actors—whether people, groups, governments, or states—wield influence successfully, while others do not.

It is clear that, in political relationships, not everyone possesses equal influence. In domestic politics, it is possible to construct a lengthy list of capabilities and attributes that seemingly permit some to wield influence over large numbers of people and important public decisions. Robert Dahl lists such tangibles as money, wealth, information, time, political allies, official position, and control over jobs, and such intangibles as personality and leadership qualities.[5] But not

---

[4]We might assess influence for historical situations solely on the basis of whether A got B to do X, without our having knowledge of either A's or B's capabilities.

[5]Robert A. Dahl, *Who Governs?* (New Haven, Conn.: Yale University Press, 1961).

everyone who possesses these capabilities can command the obedience of other people. What is crucial in relating resources to influence, according to Dahl, is that one *mobilize them for one's political purposes* and possess the skill to mobilize them. One who uses wealth, time, information, friends, and personality for political purposes will probably be able to influence others on public issues. A person, on the other hand, who possesses the same capabilities but uses them to invent a new mousetrap is not apt to be important in politics. The same propositions also hold true in international politics. The amount of influence a state wields over others can be related to the capabilities *mobilized* in support of *specific* foreign-policy objectives. To put this proposition in another way, we can argue that resources do not determine the uses to which they will be put. Nuclear power can be used to provide electricity or to deter and perhaps destroy other nations. The use of resources depends less on their quality and quantity than on the external objectives a government formulates for itself.

The *variety* of foreign-policy instruments available to a nation for influencing others is partly a function of the quantity and quality of capabilities. What a government seeks to do—the type of objectives it formulates—and how it attempts to do it will depend at least partially on the resources it finds available. A country such as Thailand, which possesses relatively few resources, cannot, even if it would desire, construct intercontinental ballistic missiles with which to intimidate others, establish a worldwide propaganda network, or dispense several billion dollars annually for foreign aid to try to influence other countries. We can conclude, therefore, that how states *use* their resources depends on their external objectives, but the choice of objectives and the instruments to achieve those objectives are limited or influenced by the quality and quantity of available resources.

THE MEASUREMENT OF RESOURCES

For many years, students of international politics have made meticulous comparisons of the potential capabilities of various nations, assuming that a nation was powerful, or capable of achieving its objectives, to the extent that it possessed certain "elements of power." Comparative data relating to production of iron ore, coal, and hydroelectricity, economic growth rates, educational levels, population growth rates, military resources, transportation systems, and sources of raw materials are presented as indicators of a nation's power. Few have acknowledged that these comparisons do not measure a state's power or influence but only its potential capacity to wage war. Other resources, such as diplomatic or propaganda skills, are seldom measured; but surely they are as important as war-making potential. Measurements and assessments are not particularly useful anyway unless they are related to specific foreign-policy issues. Capability is always the capability to do something; its assessment is most meaningful when carried on within a framework of certain foreign-policy objectives.

The deduction of actual influence from the quantity and quality of potential and mobilized capabilities may, in some cases, give an approximation of reality, but historically there have been too many discrepancies between the basis of power and the amount of influence to warrant adopting this practice as a useful approach to international relations. One could have assumed, for example, on the basis of a comparative study of technological and educational levels and general standards of living in the 1920s and 1930s that the United States would have been one of the most influential states in international politics. A careful comparison of certain resources, called the "great essentials,"[6] revealed the United States to be in an enviable position. In the period 1925 to 1930, it was the only major country in the world that produced from its own resources adequate supplies of food, power, iron, machinery, chemicals, coal, iron ore, and petroleum. If actual diplomatic influence had been deduced from the quantities of "great essentials" possessed by the major nations, the following ranking of states would have resulted: (1) United States, (2) Germany, (3) Great Britain, (4) France, (5) Russia, (6) Italy, (7) Japan. However, the diplomatic history of the world from 1925 to 1930 would suggest that there was little correlation between the resources of these countries and their *actual influence*. If we measure influence by the impact these states made on the system and by the responses they could invoke when they sought to change the behavior of other states, we would find for this period quite a different ranking, such as the following: (1) France, (2) Great Britain, (3) Italy, (4) Germany, (5) Russia, (6) Japan, (7) United States.

Indeed, many contemporary international relationships reveal how often the "strong" states do not achieve their objectives—or at least have to settle for poor substitutes—even when attempting to influence the behavior of "weak" states. How, for instance, did Marshal Tito's Yugoslavia effectively resist all sorts of pressures and threats by the powerful Soviet Union after it was expelled from the Communist bloc? Why, despite its overwhelming superiority in capabilities, was the United States unable in the 1960s to achieve its major objectives against a weak Cuba and North Vietnam? How have "small" states gained trading privileges and all sorts of diplomatic concessions from those nations with great economic wealth and military power? The ability of state A to change the behavior of state B is, we would assume, enhanced if it possesses physical resources to use in the influence act; but B is by no means defenseless or vulnerable to diplomatic, economic, or military pressures because it fails to own a large modern army, raw materials, and money for foreign aid. The successful exercise of influence is also dependent upon such factors as personality, perceptions, friendships, and traditions, and, not being easy to measure, these factors have a way of rendering power calculations and equations difficult. . . .

---

[6]Frank H. Simonds and Brooks Emeny, *The Great Powers in World Politics* (New York: American Book, 1939).

VARIABLES AFFECTING THE EXERCISE OF INFLUENCE

One reason that gross quantities of resources cannot be equated with effective influence relates to the distinction between a state's overall capabilities and the *relevance* of resources to a particular diplomatic situation. A nuclear force, for example, is often thought to increase the diplomatic influence of those who possess it. No doubt nuclear weaponry is an important element in a state's general prestige abroad and may be an effective deterrent against a strategic attack on its homeland or "core" interests. Yet the most important aspect of a nuclear capability—or any military capability—is not its possession, but its relevance and the ability to signal one's determination to use it. Other governments must know that the capability is not of mere symbolic significance. The government of North Vietnam possessed a particular advantage over the United States (hence, influence) because it knew that in almost no circumstances would the American government use strategic nuclear weapons against its country. It therefore effectively broke through the significance of the American nuclear capability as far as the Vietnam War was concerned. A resource is useless unless it is both mobilized in support of foreign-policy objectives and made credible. Likewise, nuclear weapons would be irrelevant in negotiations on cultural exchanges, just as the Arab countries' vast oil resources could not be effectively mobilized to influence the outcome of international negotiations on satellite communications. Influence is always specific to a particular issue, and resources must be relevant to that issue.

A second variable that determines the success or failure of acts of influence is the extent to which there are *needs* between the two countries in any influence relationship. In general, a country that needs something from another is vulnerable to its acts of influence. This is the primary reason that states that are "weak" in many capabilities can nevertheless obtain concessions from "strong" countries. Consider the case of France and Germany and some of the "weak" states in the Middle East. Both European countries are highly dependent upon Arab lands for oil supplies. They have an important need, which only the Arab countries can satisfy at a reasonable cost. On the other hand, the Middle Eastern countries that control these oil resources may not be so dependent upon Germany and France, particularly if they can sell their oil easily elsewhere. Because, in this situation, needs are not equal on both sides, the independent states (in terms of needs) can make demands (or resist demands made against them) on the dependent great powers and obtain important concessions. The German and French governments know that if they do not make these concessions or if they press their own demands too hard, the Arab states can threaten to cut off oil supplies. Their dependence thus makes them vulnerable to the demands and influence acts of what would otherwise be considered "weak" states. To the Arab states, oil is much more important as a capability than military forces—at least in their relations with major powers. In the form of a general hypothesis, we can suggest that, regardless of the quantity, quality, and credibility of a state's capabilities, the more state B needs, or is dependent upon, state A, the more likely that state A's acts—threats, promises, rewards, or punishments—will succeed in changing or sustaining B's behavior.

A third variable that has assumed increasing importance in the past several decades, and one that can be considered an important resource, is level of technical expertise. An increasing number of issues on the international and foreign-policy agendas are highly technical in nature: law of the sea, satellite broadcasting, international monetary matters, and the like. Many of these issues are discussed in international fora, where leadership often depends more on knowledge of the technical issues than on other types of resources. Those governments which come armed with technical studies, have a full command of the nature of the problem, and are prepared to put forth realistic solutions are more likely to wield influence than are governments which have only rudimentary knowledge of the problem and no scientific studies to back their national positions. A number of recent case studies have demonstrated conclusively that the outcomes of negotiations on technical questions cannot be predicted from the gross power of the participants and that knowledge, among other factors, accounts for more than raw capabilities.[7]

Understanding the dynamics of power relationships at the international level would be relatively easy if resource relevance, credibility, need, and knowledge were the only variables involved. Unfortunately, political actions do not always conform to simple hypotheses, because human characteristics of pride, stubbornness, prestige, and friendship enter into all acts of influence as well. A government may be highly dependent upon some other state and still resist its demands; it may be willing to suffer all sorts of privations, and even physical destruction and loss of independence, simply for the sake of pride. The government of North Vietnam was willing to accept a very high level of destruction of lives and productive facilities by American bombers rather than make diplomatic or military concessions to the United States.

Additional variables affecting the exercise of influence can be observed in the situation where two small states of approximately equal capabilities make similar demands upon a "major" power and neither of the small states is dependent upon the large—or vice versa. Which will achieve its objectives? Will both exercise influence equally? Hypothetically, suppose that the ambassadors of Norway and Albania go to the British Foreign Office on the same day and ask the British government to lower tariffs on bicycles, a product that the two countries would like to export to England. Assume that the quality and price of the bicycles are approximately the same and that the British government does not wish to allow too many imports for fear of damaging the domestic bicycle

---

[7]See, for example, the case studies in Robert O. Keohane and Joseph S. Nye, *Power and Interdependence: World Politics in Transition* (Boston: Little, Brown and Company, 1977). See also David Baldwin's strong emphasis on the relevance of resources to particular situations in "Power Analysis and World Politics," *World Politics,* 31 (January 1979), 161–94.

industry. Assume further that both the Norwegian and Albanian ambassadors offer roughly equal concessions if the British will lower their tariffs on bicycles. Both claim they will lower their own tariffs on English automobiles. Which ambassador is most likely to succeed—that is, to achieve his government's objectives? Chances are that the British government would favor the request of the Norwegian ambassador and turn down the representation by the diplomat from Tirana. The explanation of this decision can probably not be found in the resources of either of the small countries (both offered approximately equal rewards) or in need, since in this hypothetical situation Britain needs neither of the small countries' automobile markets. Norway would get the favorable decision because British policy makers are more *responsive* to Norwegian interests than to those of Albania. Albania represents a Communist state whose government normally displays through its diplomacy and propaganda strong hostility toward England.

After relevant resources, need, and knowledge, the fourth variable that determines the effectiveness of acts of influence is thus the ephemeral quality of responsiveness.[8] Responsiveness can be seen as a disposition to receive another's requests with sympathy, even to the point where a government is willing to sacrifice some of its own values and interests in order to fulfill those requests; responsiveness is the willingness to be influenced. In one study, it was shown that members of the State Department in the United States may take considerable pains to promote the requests and interests of other governments among their superiors and in other government agencies, provided that the requesting government feels that the issue is important or that the need must be fulfilled.[9] In our hypothetical case, if the quality of responsiveness is present in the case of the Norwegian request, members of the British Foreign Office would probably work for the Norwegians and try to persuade other government agencies concerned with trade and commerce to agree to a lowering of the tariff on bicycles. In the British reaction to the Albanian request, it is not likely that the government would display much responsiveness. Suspicion, traditional animosities, lack of trust, and years of unfavorable diplomatic experience would probably prevent the development of much British sympathy for Albania's needs or interests. . . . When the other variables, such as resources or need, are held constant or made equal, the degree of responsiveness will determine the success or failure of acts taken to influence other states' behavior.

---

[8]The concept of responsiveness is introduced by Karl W. Deutsch et al., *Political Community and the North Atlantic Area* (Princeton, N.J.: Princeton University Press, 1957); developed by Dean G. Pruitt, "National Power and International Responsiveness" *Background,* 7 (1964), 165–78. See also Dean G. Pruitt, "Definition of the Situation as a Determinant of International Action," in *International Behavior: A Social-Psychological Analysis,* ed. Herbert C. Kelman (New York: Holt, Rinehart & Winston, 1965), pp. 393–432.

[9]Pruitt, "National Power," 175–76.

If effective influence cannot be deduced solely from the quantity and quality of physical capabilities, how do we proceed to measure influence? If we want to assess a situation that has already occurred, the easiest way to measure influence is to study the *responses* of those in the influence relationship.[10] If A can get B to do X, but C cannot get B to do the same thing, then in that particular issue, A has more influence. If B does X despite the protestations of A, then we can assume that A, in this circumstance, did not enjoy much influence over B. It is meaningless to argue that the Soviet Union [may have been] more powerful than the United States unless we cite how, for what purposes, and in relation to whom the Soviet Union and the United States [were] exerting influence. . . .

HOW INFLUENCE IS EXERCISED

Social scientists have noted several fundamental techniques that individuals and groups use to influence each other. In a political system that contains no one legitimate center of authority that can command the members of the group or society, bargaining has to be used among the sovereign entities to achieve or defend their objectives. Recalling that A seeks one of three courses of conduct from B (B to do X in the future, B not to do X in the future, or B to continue doing X), it may use six different tactics, involving acts of:

1 PERSUASION. By persuasion we mean simply initiating or discussing a proposal with another and eliciting a favorable response without explicitly holding out the possibility of rewards or punishments. We cannot assume that the exercise of influence is always *against* the wishes of others and that there are only two possible outcomes of the act, one favoring A, the other favoring B. For example, state A asks B to support it at a coming international conference on the control of narcotics. State B might not originally have any particular interest in the conference or its outcome; but it decides, on the basis of A's initiative, that something positive might be gained, not only by supporting A's proposals, but also by attending the conference. In this case, B might also expect to gain some type of reward in the future, although not necessarily from A. Persuasion would also include protests and denials that do not involve obvious threats.

2 THE OFFER OF REWARDS. This is the situation where A promises to do something favorable to B if B complies with the wishes of A. Rewards may be of almost any type in international relations. To gain the diplomatic support of B at the narcotics conference, A may offer to increase foreign-aid payments, lower tariffs on goods imported from B, support B at a later conference on communications facilities, or promise to remove a previous punishment. The last tactic is used often by negotiators. After having created an unfavorable situation, they promise to remove it in return for some concessions by their opponents.

---

[10]Robert A. Dahl, "The Concept of Power," *Behavioral Science,* 2 (1957), 201–15.

3 THE GRANTING OF REWARDS. In some instances, the credibility of a government is not very high, and state B, before complying with A's wishes, may insist that A actually give the reward in advance. Frequently, in armistice negotiations neither side will unilaterally take steps to demilitarize an area or demobilize troops until the other shows evidence of complying with the agreements. One of the clichés of . . . diplomacy holds that deeds, not words, are required for the granting of rewards and concessions.

4 THE THREAT OF PUNISHMENT. Threats of punishment may be further subdivided into two types: (a) positive threats, where, for example, state A threatens to increase tariffs, institute a boycott or embargo against trade with B, or use force; and (b) threats of deprivation, where A threatens to withdraw foreign aid or in other ways withhold rewards or other advantages that it already grants to B.

5 THE INFLICTION OF NONVIOLENT PUNISHMENT. In this situation, threats are carried out in the hope of altering B's behavior, which, in most cases, could not be altered by other means. The problem with this tactic is that it often results in reciprocal measures by the other side, thus inflicting damage on both, and not necessarily bringing about a desired state of affairs. If, for example, A threatens to increase its military capabilities if B does X and then proceeds to implement the threat, it is not often that B will comply with A's wishes, because it, too, can increase its military capabilities. In this type of situation, both sides indulge in the application of punishments that may escalate into more serious forms unless the conflict is resolved. Typical acts of nonviolent punishment include breaking diplomatic relations, raising tariffs, instituting boycotts and embargoes, holding hostages, organizing blockades, closing frontiers, or walking out of a diplomatic conference.

6 FORCE. In previous eras, when governments did not possess the variety of foreign-policy instruments available today, they frequently had to rely upon the use of force in the bargaining process. Force and violence were not only the most efficient tactics, but in many cases the only means possible for influencing. Today, the situation is different. As technological levels rise and dependencies develop, other means of inducement become available and can serve as substitutes for force.

PATTERNS OF INFLUENCE IN THE INTERNATIONAL SYSTEM

Most governments at some time use all their techniques for influencing others, but probably over 90 percent of all relations between states are based on simple persuasion and deal with relatively unimportant technical matters. Since such interactions seldom make the headlines, we often assume that most relations between states involve the making or carrying out of threats. But whether a government is communicating with another over an unimportant technical matter or over a subject of great consequence, it is likely to use a particular type of tactic in its attempts to influence, depending on the past tradition of friendship or hostility between those two governments and the amount of compatibility between their objectives and interests. Allies, for example, seldom threaten each other with force or even make blatant threats of punishment, but governments that disagree over a wide range of policy objectives and hold attitudes of suspicion and hostility toward each other are more likely to resort to threats and imposition of punishments. The methods of exerting influence between Great Britain and the United States are, typically, persuasion and rewards, whereas the methods of exerting influence between the Soviet Union and the United States in the early post–World War II era were typically threatening and inflicting punishments of various types. . . .

To summarize this analysis of power, we can suggest that power is an integral part of all political relationships; but in international politics we are interested primarily in one process: how one state influences the behavior of another in its own interests. The act of influencing becomes a central focus for the study of international politics, and it is from this act that we can best deduce a definition of power. If we observe the act of influencing, we can see that power is a process, a relationship, a means to an end, and even a quantity. Moreover, we can make an analytical distinction among the act of influencing, the basis, or resources, upon which the act relies, and the response to the act. Resources are an important determinant of how successful the wielding of influence will be, but they are by no means the only determinant. The nature of a country's foreign-policy objectives, the skill with which a state mobilizes its capabilities for foreign-policy purposes, its needs, responsiveness, costs, and commitments are equally important. Acts of influencing may take many forms, the most important of which are the offer and granting of rewards, the threat and imposition of punishments, and the application of force. The choice of means used to induce will depend, in turn, upon the general nature of relations between any two given governments, the degree of involvement between them, and the extent of their mutual responsiveness. . . .

2

FORCE OR TRADE: THE COSTS AND BENEFITS OF TWO PATHS TO GLOBAL INFLUENCE

Richard Rosecrance

Throughout history, states have pursued power through the acquisition of military capabilities and the use of force. This convention, argues Richard Rosecrance, has been challenged by post-World War II developments. "The trading state"—a nation that expands its resources through economic development and foreign trade—has demonstrated the advantages of economic approaches to world power and global influence. Trade, Rosecrance argues, has replaced territorial expansion and military might as the vehicle for prosperity and preeminence on the world stage. Rosecrance is professor of political science and director of the Center for International Relations at the University of California at Los Angeles. Among his many books are *America's Economic Resurgence* (1990).

The notion of the state as a sovereign unit, dependent in the final analysis only on itself, has largely captured intellectual fashion. But today, no state can aspire to the degree of independence that such concepts have entailed. Even the United States and [Russia] are dependent on other nations . . . for their continued existence. The theory of international exchange and trade gives a basis for mutual cooperation and mutual benefit, and it applies to the essence of what states do day by day. When noticed, trading is dismissed as "low politics," pejoratively contrasting it with the "high politics" of sovereignty, national interest, power, and military force. However, it is possible for relationships among states to be entirely transformed or even reversed by the low politics of trade. Through trade Japan has become the third industrial nation in the world, and it will soon become the second nation, surpassing [Russia]. It may in time exceed the United States of America. [Since this was written, Japan has surpassed the former Soviet Union to become the second largest industrial power.—Eds.]

Many have misunderstood the differences between Japan and America, believing that Japan is simply a youthful, smaller edition of the United States, a still not fully developed major power with political and economic interests that have yet to be defined on a world stage. Sooner or later, many feel, Japan too will become a world power with commensurate political and military interests. This is a misconception of the Japanese role in world affairs and a mistaken assimilation of a trading state to the military-political realm. Even if, at some distant future time, Japan increased her defense expenditure to 2 percent of gross national product, she would not follow the United States . . . strategy in international politics or try to become the world's leading naval or military power. As a trading state it would not be in her interest to dominate the world, control the sea lanes to the Persian Gulf, or guarantee military access to markets in Europe or the western hemisphere. She depends upon open trading and commercial routes to produce entry for her goods. It is not the American model that Japan will ultimately follow. Rather, it is the Japanese model that America may ultimately follow.

It is thus important to consider how states advance themselves and to bring the trading strategy into a regular and durable place in the theory of international politics. . . .

THE WORLDS OF INTERNATIONAL RELATIONS: THE MILITARY-POLITICAL WORLD, THE TRADING WORLD

The choice between territorial and trading means to national advancement has always lain before states. Most often, however, nations have selected a point between extremes though nearer the territorial end. In the early years of the modern period in the sixteenth and seventeenth centuries, that point was close to the territorial and military pole; at mid-nineteenth century it briefly moved toward the trading pole. In World Wars I and II the military and territorial orientation was chosen once again. Only after 1945 did a group of trading nations emerge in world politics. Over time this group has grown and its success, at least in economic terms, has been greater than that of either the United States or the [then] Soviet Union. . . .

The Military-Political World

In a military-political world nations are ranged in terms of power and territory from the greatest to the weakest. States in such a world are homogeneous in form; that is, they do not have differentiated objectives or perform a variety of functions. They all seek the same territorial objectives and each, at least among the major powers, strives to be the leading power in the system. None of the contenders wishes to depend upon any other for any vital function, from the provision of defense to economic resources. . . .

The military-political world involves a continual recourse to war because the units within it compete for primacy. None is content to accept the hegemony of one of their number if it can be prevented; each is afraid that the dominance of one power will undermine its domestic autonomy and perhaps its very existence. Hence the balance of power becomes a means of resistance to threatened hegemony. The means of constructing a balance ultimately involves a resort to force to discipline an ambitious pretender. Warfare may be stabilizing if it succeeds in restraining challenge, but it cannot be acceptable if the destruction it causes more than outweighs the evil it seeks to prevent. In addition, since every state in a political-military order seeks to be self-sufficient, each strives to grow larger in order to achieve full independence. This drive itself is a cause of war.

The Trading World

In contrast, the trading world is not composed of states ranked in order of their power and territory, all seeking preponderance. Instead, it is composed of nations differentiated in terms of function. Each may seek to improve its position, but because nations supply different services and products, in defense as well as economics, they come to depend upon each other. While some will be stronger than others, their functions give them a kind of equality of status. They may specialize in terms of particular defense functions: conventional or nuclear forces. They may offer raw materials or primary products to the international trading system as opposed to manufactured goods. Within the category of manufacturers, there may be intra-industry specialization in terms of technology. Certain industrial countries may concentrate, like Switzerland and Italy, on producing goods of very high quality and craftsmanship. Others, like Korea or Taiwan, may produce shoes, watches, textiles, steel, or ships on an efficient low-cost basis. Trading states will also normally form alliances as a precaution against sudden intrusion by military-political nations.

While trading states try to improve their position and their own domestic allocation of resources, they do so within a context of accepted interdependence. They recognize that the attempt to provide every service and fulfill every function of statehood on an independent and autonomous basis is extremely inefficient, and they prefer a situation which provides for specialization and division of labor among nations. One nation's attempt to improve its own access to products and resources, therefore, does not conflict with another state's attempt to do the same. The incentive to wage war is absent in such a system for war disrupts trade and the interdependence on which trade is based. Trading states recognize that they can do better through internal economic development sustained by a worldwide market for their goods and services than by trying to conquer and assimilate large tracts of land. . . .

In international society where government does not exist, nations will have power conflicts unless they can work out a system of interdependence to satisfy their needs. Only the reciprocal exchange and division of labor represented by the trading world can prevent conflict in such an anarchic environment. Industrial and population growth strengthen interdependence and make it harder to achieve national objectives autonomously. When technology was rudimentary and population sparse, states had little contact with one another and did not generally get in each other's way. With the commercial and industrial revolutions, however, they were brought into closer proximity. As the Industrial Revolution demanded energy resources—great quantities of food, coal, iron, water power, and petroleum—the number of states which could be fully independent declined. Those which sought complete autonomy and even autarchy had to conquer the lands which contained the materials they needed. The military-political and territorial system, then, required more war. Only a shift in direction toward an interdependent trading system, giving up autonomy in return for greater access to world resources and markets, could produce greater cooperation among nations.

The trading system does not require large, self-sufficient units. As the national objective is exchange and trade with other states, trading countries do not need large territories and populations. Like Singapore and Hong Kong, they may be small countries, little more than cities, which manufacture the raw materials of other nations into finished commodities, gaining a high return in foreign trade. . . .

The creation of the International Monetary Fund at Bretton Woods in 1944 was a giant step toward a trading system of international relations. The new regime called for an open world economy with low tariffs and strictly limited depreciation of currencies. Tariff hikes and competitive devaluation of currencies were to be restricted by the General Agreement on Tariffs and Trade (GATT) and by the Fund. Unlike the situation after World War I, nations were to be persuaded not to institute controls by offering them liquid funds to float over any period of imbalance in international payments. They would then have a grace period to get their economies in order, after which they could repay the loans.

The plethora of small nations created after the war by the decolonization process in Africa, Asia, the Middle East, and Oceania were generally not large or strong enough to rely on domestic resources, industry, agriculture, and markets for all their needs. Unless they could trade, they could not live. This meant that the markets of the major Western and industrial economies had to take their exports and they in return would need manufacturing exports from the developed countries. The open international economy was critical to their growth and stability. This is not to say that there were no other factors which supported the independence of new nations in the post–World War II period. Military factors and superpower rivalries made the reconquest of colonial areas very costly; ethnic and cultural differences limited the success of attempts to subdue one country or another. But political and military viability were not enough. Small states could not continue to exist as independent entities unless they could earn an economic livelihood. To some degree economic assistance from developed nations or from multilateral agencies met this need. If tariffs and restrictions had inhibited the trade of new nations, however, they would not have been able to function as independent units.

But the open economy of the trading world did not benefit only small nations. The growth of world trade, which increased faster than gross national product until 1980, attracted larger states as well. As the cost of using force increased and its benefits declined, other means of gaining national welfare had to be found. . . . Germany, following Hanseatic precedents, became more dependent on international trade than [pre-World War II] Germany had been. The United Kingdom, France, Italy, Norway, Switzerland, Germany, Belgium, Holland, and Denmark had imports and exports which equalled 30 percent or more of their gross national product, nearly three times the proportion attained in the United States. Japan's huge economy was fueled by foreign trade, which amounted to 20 percent of her GNP total.

The role of Japan and Germany in the trading world is exceedingly interesting because it represents a reversal of past policies in both the nineteenth century and the 1930s. It is correct to say that the two countries experimented with foreign trade because they had been disabused of military expansion by World War II. For a time they were incapable of fighting war on a major scale; their endorsement of the trading system was merely an adoption of the remaining policy alternative. But the endorsement did not change even when the economic strength of the two nations might have sustained a much more nationalistic and militaristic policy. Given the choice between military expansion to achieve self-sufficiency (a choice made more difficult by modern conventional and nuclear weapons in the hands of other powers) and the procurement of necessary markets and raw materials through international commerce, Japan and Germany chose the latter. . . .

The increasing prevalence of the trading option since 1945 raises peaceful possibilities that were neglected during the late nineteenth century and the 1930s. It seems safe to say that an international system composed of more than [190] states cannot continue to exist unless trade remains the primary vocation of most of its members. Were military and territorial orientations to dominate the scene, the trend to greater numbers of smaller states would be reversed, and larger states would conquer small and weak nations. . . .

The basic effect of World War II was to create much higher world interdependence as the average size of countries declined. The reversal of past trends toward a consolidation of states created instead a multitude of states that could not depend on themselves alone. They needed ties with other nations to prosper and remain viable as small entities. The trading system, as a result, was visible in defense relations as well as international commerce. Nations that could not stand on their own sought alliances or assistance from other powers, and they offered special defense contributions in fighting contingents, regional experience, or particular types of defense hardware. Dutch electronics, French aircraft, German guns and tanks, and British ships all made their independent contribution to an alliance in which no single power might be able to meet its defense needs on a self-sufficient basis. Israel developed a powerful and efficient small arms industry, as well as a great fund of experience combating terrorism. Israeli intelligence added considerably to the information available from Western sources, partly because of its understanding of Soviet weapons systems accumulated in several Arab-Israeli wars. . . .

At least among the developed and liberal countries, interdependent ties since 1945 have come to be accepted as a fundamental and unchangeable feature of the situation. This recognition dawned gradually, and the United States may perhaps have been the last to acknowledge it, which was not surprising. The most powerful economy is ready to make fewer adjustments, and America tried initially to pursue its domestic economic policies without taking into account the effect on others, on itself, and on the international financial system as a whole. Presidents Kennedy and Lyndon B. Johnson tried to detach American domestic growth strategies from the deteriorating United States balance of payments, but they left a legacy of needed economic change to their successors. Finally, in the 1980s two American administrations accepted lower United States growth in order to control inflation and began to focus on the international impact of United States policies. The delay in fashioning a strategy of adjustment to international economic realities almost certainly made it more difficult. Smaller countries actively sought to find a niche in the structure of international comparative advantage and in the demand for their goods. Larger countries with large internal markets postponed that reckoning as long as they could. By the 1980s, however, such change could no longer be avoided, and United States leaders embarked upon new industrial and tax policies designed to increase economic growth and enable America to compete more effectively abroad. . . .

FORCE OR TRADE: THE COSTS AND BENEFITS

The growing preference of states for a trading strategy in international relations stems not only from the benefits of commerce; it reflects the difficulties represented by the continuing stalemate in the military-political world. Since 1945 a few nations have borne the crushing weight of military expenditure, while others have gained a relative advantage by becoming military free-riders who primarily rely on the security provided by others. While the United States spent nearly 50 percent of its research and development budget on arms, Japan devoted 99 percent to civilian production. Meanwhile the Soviet Union's growth rate slowed from 6 to 4 to 2 percent per year and her industrial investment languished, as a result of the 12 to 14 percent of GNP per year which she [spent] on the military. Japan, with less than 1 percent of its GNP devoted to armaments, further enhanced its trillion dollar economy through trade and productivity gains. In the West, and particularly in the United States, large government deficits, caused in the most part by immense military spending of nearly $300 billion a year, generated high interest rates which slowed investment, hiked currency values, and limited American export competitiveness. All these expenditures raised the opportunity costs of a military-political and territorial system. . . .

The disadvantages of high military spending in sacrificing other economic opportunities, however, are not its only costs; direct costs are also involved. The industrialization of warfare, with concomitant acceleration in the expense of weapons, has imposed its own burdens. Until the mid-nineteenth century, the cost of uniforms and food for troops and horses was the main expense of war, and, as Russia showed, a populous power could be strong without a well-developed industry. But by World War I industrial strength had become a decisive factor in war, and it was production during the war that determined its outcome. It appeared that the machine age could produce weapons almost indefinitely, and the problem became finding soldiers who would fight. After the early battles of World War I, conscription brought in new recruits when needed, but these became less willing to sacrifice themselves as casualties mounted and the battle lines remained more or less fixed. New means of offensive war had to be found, or there would be a political resistance of great magnitude. The armored tank was then developed to protect men in the forward battle area. Increased protection, firepower, and maneuvering speed were heralded as substitutes for massed infantry attacks. But the new tanks, artillery, and airplanes that performed these functions became very expensive. In constant dollar terms, tanks went from less than $50,000 per unit in 1918 to more than $2,000,000 in 1980. Fighter planes that cost less than $100,000 in 1944 rose to at least $10,000,000 per copy forty years later. Paradoxically, as manpower became more expensive politically, the weapons that were to replace it became even more costly. This would not have been a major factor if weapons had lasted longer, but tanks and aircraft were subject to enormous rates of attrition on the battlefield. Ships became obsolescent and were rendered vulnerable to attack by surface missiles. In the end, all but the very strongest powers needed economic help to purchase armaments for long wars. Israel could not have continued to fight after two weeks in 1973 without shipments of arms from the United States. British rearmament would have ceased without Lend-Lease financial assistance from the United States in World War II, and the Soviet Union [never acknowledged] the enormous help it received from military equipment provided by Western powers. In wars after 1945, Vietnam, Israel, Egypt, Jordan, and Syria could not have fought without huge amounts of outside help.

Rapid innovation in weapons technology, producing AWACS (Airborne Warning and Control Systems), precision-guided munitions, and new forms of defense has made the battlefield a more hostile place for attacking tanks and planes. To survive, tanks must carry more armor and move faster, but this takes more fuel, which is expensive to transport. Enormous utilization rates in wartime require that large numbers of weapons and supplies be stockpiled beforehand. But powers hesitate to buy too many copies of any one weapon for fear that it will become outmoded. In modern war, there is no relatively fixed design, like the battleship *Dreadnought,* which could be bought, with minor improvements, by a decade of European naval ministers.

The conventional battlefield has become even more uncertain than its early-twentieth-century predecessor. Technology that might appear to give the advantage to a sudden offensive thrust—such as the tank and jet aircraft—could well be nullified by antitank and antiaircraft defenses. Defensive abilities to counter a tank attack by destroying second echelon forces, logistics, and supply bases behind the lines could transfer the initiative to a defender who might then be able to unleash a counteroffensive into enemy territory. Unlike the German Schlieffen Plan in 1914, which assumed that the surprise turning of the French left flank with a huge force would bring victory in six weeks, no contemporary commander can predict the outcome against a comparably equipped enemy force. Instead, uncertainties dominate the outcome.

The one outcome that is not uncertain is that the peacetime stockpiling of military hardware will become more expensive, rising at least 3–5 percent above inflation per year. This will progressively reduce the number of weapons that can be deployed and provide extra incentives for arms control. The economic costs of a military-political world are not its only defects; political costs are also rising. In Western states there has been a growing revulsion against fighting in overseas wars that are not quick and decisive. Ever since World War I and particularly since World War II, the political costs of military service have been increasing. Patriotism has been a fluctuating asset and one which declines with the length and indecisiveness of war. Political and international limits on conventional conflicts, dictating that they not violate nearby frontiers, have limited the scope, but probably increased the length of engagements. The results have typically been inconclusive, reflecting the political stamina of respective opponents. Often the same conflicts break out again and again. Futile wars have not inspired the loyalty of those who are forced to fight in them; only short, dynamic, and successful conflicts command approval and support.

The decline of military loyalty is also a product of political ineffectiveness and uncertainty. In an environment of growing interdependence, modern governments have been unable to fulfill the demands of their populations for economic welfare, security, and peace; domestic alienation has grown. Tax revolts have fed on governmental inefficiency and bureaucracy. If the government cannot provide for their needs with tax revenues, the people prefer to keep the money. In many countries, informed citizens resent military appropriations of billions per year, believing that such expenditures only feed the arms race as the opponent is forced to respond in kind. The security dilemma—where a defensive protection for one state means greater offensive power against another—suggests that more expenditure may actually mean less security. Western political support for arms reduction has grown greatly.

The pervasiveness of interdependence has another effect. As late as the 1930s, it was still possible for nations to calculate that they had a reasonable chance of seizing and holding by force territories containing needed raw materials and markets. In Japan's intervention in China in the 1930s she sought to conquer a vast market for her goods. This invasion was doomed to failure because she could never absorb China ethnically, politically, or militarily. But her move into Southeast Asia held some hope of success so long as the United States stayed out of the war. Hitler's drive into East Europe might have succeeded if he had not invaded the Soviet Union as well. In Rumania and Poland he sought the oil and coal that would enable Germany to ride out a long war with the Western powers. . . . Such ambitions are now beyond the reach of any major industrial nation. At present it is much easier to obtain needed access to raw materials and markets through trade than to try to control them territorially by force.

The defects of the military-political world do not stem only from its inherent weaknesses but also from the counterattractions of the trading world. However, despite its benefits, the trading strategy may not be elected by major and minor powers. Russia and to some degree the United States remain wedded to the older orientation. Borrowing precedents in the seventeenth and eighteenth centuries, Russia has westernized but has cut herself off from any significant dependence upon trade with European countries and the United States. . . .

In the past the military-political world was efficient. It was cheaper to seize another state's territory by force than to develop the sophisticated economic and trading apparatus needed to derive benefit from commercial exchange with it. Nomads and barbarians proved that lesser-developed nations could, by honing their military skills, defeat better-developed states and economies. Force made up the disadvantage and allowed peripheral nations to seize the benefits of Western economic systems. Rome gave way to the barbarian tribes on its borders. The trading world of the Mediterranean was interrupted once by Islam and again by the rise of the Ottoman Turks. Portugal's new naval skills allowed her to intercept Eastern Mediterranean trade at its source, and undercut the link between Venice and India. In their incursions into North Italy, France and Austria, the Hapsburgs hoped to seize the most developed and civilized region of Europe. Throughout history the excessive brightness of a civilization nearing sunset has tempted aggressors to seize what they could not emulate. In a similar way Western civilization has afforded a constant temptation to the Russians.

In one of those reversals to which history is prone, however, the pathway of aggression is no longer smooth. Western or Eastern riches do not lie at the feet of any organized power with fleets or horsemen. At least since the seventeenth century, economic development and cultural advancement have been associated with military power, and, as the record of imperialism shows, the better-developed initially subdued the lesser-developed regions of world politics. In the later twentieth century, the balance has become more even: Western weapons and technology . . . confronted Eastern numbers and ideological zeal. Where both sides [had] access to modern weapons, staying power [decided] the outcome. The very arms race [between the United States and the Soviet Union] itself complicated the seizure of new territory, for arms are now readily available in world markets, and defenders have as much access to them as aggressors. Both sides may spend more, but the result is still indecisive. The costs of the military-political world are not likely to decrease, and they may increase further. The trade-off between military-political and trading worlds will be more significant because the particular nations that might choose one can always choose the other. The great economic nations will have military choices. The great military nations will have trading choices.

Such decisions are also influenced by changes in domestic politics. As wars have become more difficult and costly to win, domestic support for such wars has declined. The size of the state may have peaked in 1914, but domestic cohesion and support for state policy continued to grow spasmodically until the 1930s, when it reached its coercive apogee with the National Socialist regime of Adolf Hitler. For a time it appeared that World War II might have provided a different lesson in the exemplary fighting of the "good war." But the campaigns afterward were neither so morally unambiguous nor decisive. The result was that citizens in democratic countries came to resent and oppose them. Wars had to be short and decisive like the Falklands or Grenada to gain approval. . . . Even the Soviet Union and the internal system of Communist repression [never] solved the problem of popular laxity, indifference, and lack of support. Such trends do not increase the benefits or reduce the costs of the military-political system.

. . . The very success of economic and trading nations might serve as a beacon to those who had traditionally pursued their great power callings through military rivalries, arms races, and nuclear crisis. . . . The trading world would then have transformed international politics. Which strategy will be dominant cannot presently be predicted, but if history is any guide, indecision and ambivalence is unlikely to endure. After the 1870s the territorial system reasserted itself against the British trading system, as it did later in the 1930s. Unless critical great powers agree to contend their struggles in different terms, such a transformation is possible once again.

3

THE FUTURE OF MILITARY POWER: THE CONTINUING UTILITY OF FORCE

Eliot A. Cohen

This essay questions the proposition that military force has lost its utility in contemporary world politics. Challenging three core arguments about the diminishing importance of force in world politics, Eliot A. Cohen suggests why "war, and potential war, will remain a feature of international politics," and why, accordingly, military force will retain its importance in the post-Cold War era of destructive weapons and burgeoning democracies. His thesis is supported by examples drawn from the events and experiences since World War II, and especially in the 1980s and early 1990s. Cohen is professor and director of strategic studies at the Nitze School of Advanced International Studies, the Johns Hopkins University. He has co-authored (with John Gouch) *Military Misfortunes: The Anatomy of Failure in War* (1990).

What direction should . . . strategy take? Indeed, does it have a future at all, or has the end of the Cold War and the apparent triumph of liberal democracy and capitalism in Eastern Europe rendered it obsolete? If the need for strategy—defined as the preparation and use of military power for the ends of policy—does persist, how should [the West] prepare . . . to meet the challenges of the last decade of this century? . . .

The revolutions of 1989 have by no means ended, but surely enough has occurred to make it obvious that international politics has undergone an epochal change. The Soviet empire has collapsed. The Kremlin has allowed its Eastern European glacis to crumble away even as the forces of dissent and hatred [undermined] the USSR itself. The multiple crises of [Russia] reinforce each other. Although by a combination of statecraft and luck [the Commonwealth of Independent States] may survive, it is equally likely that it will . . . collapse altogether.

For over forty years [Western] strategy and defense planning . . . focused on the Soviet threat. That threat [has disintegrated], and [the] military power [of the former Soviet Union] is undergoing a long-term and irreversible reduction. If so, one must ask where [Western] defense planning should concentrate its attention henceforth, and how it should adapt to new challenges. Such a mammoth practical and conceptual task would be complex enough in any circumstances. It is made more difficult, however, by a variety of arguments to the effect that military force is no longer an important factor in world politics, that traditional considerations of *Machtpolitik* will lose or have lost their primacy; that force, in other words, is finished.

A lively debate has already occurred . . . on this latter point, focusing on Francis Fukuyama's audacious argument that history has come to, or is coming to, an end. Others have advanced similar arguments for the obsolescence of force. Even an analyst of such impeccably hawkish credentials as Edward Luttwak has put forth the proposition that the "methods of commerce are displacing military methods," and that the "decay of the military grammar of geopolitics" is a central fact of contemporary international politics.[1] On the whole, those who argue that military force is becoming less important appeared to be gaining the day, at least until the invasion of Kuwait by Iraq. This debate, however, transcends the jolt delivered by Saddam Hussein, and merits examination on its own terms. . . .

There are three core arguments for the dwindling importance of force in international politics. First, it is maintained that the development of the techniques of warfare has made military power increasingly unappealing as a tool of international politics; or, more extreme, that modern weapons have made military power *unusable* for purposes of foreign policy. Nuclear weapons create the kind of stalemate that perversely but blessedly created the long peace of the Cold War; chemical weapons serve as the poor man's atomic bomb; conven-

---

[1]Fukuyama's essay, "The End of History?" appeared in *The National Interest,* No. 16 (Summer 1989). Responses to it in that issue and the next, most notably Samuel P. Huntington, "No Exit: The Errors of Endism" in the Fall 1989 issue, cover some of the same ground that are dealt with here, but with a rather different focus. See also John Mueller, *Retreat From Doomsday: The Obsolescence of Major War* (New York: Basic Books, 1989). Fred C. Iklé, "The Ghost in the Pentagon," *The National Interest,* No. 19 (Spring 1990), also deals with some of the issues covered in this essay. Edward Luttwak's "From Geopolitics to Geo-Economics" appeared in *The National Interest,* No. 20 (Summer 1990).

tional weaponry including such modern refinements as cluster bombs, fuel-air explosives, and multiple rocket launchers make even that form of conflict too difficult to control. Not man's virtue, but his diabolical ingenuity in creating engines of destruction, has brought peace. Or has it?

Nuclear weapons probably—one cannot be certain about events that did not happen—prevented an all-out U.S.-Soviet war. But nuclear weapons have most assuredly not prevented the launching of wars, some quite large, against nuclear-armed states. The North Koreans and Chinese in the Korean War, the Vietnamese Communists in the Indochina War, the Arabs in the Yom Kippur War, and the Argentines in the Falklands War did not let their opponents' nuclear weapons stop them from using a great deal of force to secure their political objectives. Vast disproportions in firepower attributable to nuclear weapons did not prevent the Vietnamese from fighting a bitter frontier war with China, Afghan mountaineers from harassing Soviet invaders, or Palestinian and Shiite terrorists from raiding Israeli border settlements. And the real or potential existence of nuclear weapons has come very close to *inducing* warfare, as indicated by Soviet feelers about preventive war against China in the Nixon administration and the Israeli raid on the Iraqi Osirak reactor. Nuclear weapons exercise certain kinds of inhibiting effects on conflict, but in other cases they may provoke it—would the United States, indeed *should* the United States stand idly by if Muammar Qaddafi were to acquire an atomic bomb?

In other cases, nuclear weapons clearly do not prevent warfare, although they may set certain limits to it. It would be a terrible mistake to think that the elaborate and arid logic of nuclear deterrence that operated between the superpowers will continue to hold elsewhere. The U.S.-Soviet confrontation took place between a stable, pacific, and contented democracy and a highly rational, cautious dictatorship that found nothing inherently shameful about retreating in the face of superior force. It was, in many ways, an ideal opposition, and one highly unlikely to be repeated.

Are chemical weapons the equivalent of nuclear weapons in their deterrent effects? One should not overdo the comparison, either in terms of destructiveness (bad weather can drastically reduce the impact of a chemical attack) or psychology. After Hiroshima and Nagasaki there was an altogether healthy taboo on the use of nuclear weapons, which we should attempt to preserve. Chemical weapons, in contrast, were used repeatedly during World War I and on many occasions since, including, it appears, in Southeast Asia. The Iraqi use of chemicals in the war with Iran was particularly chilling: chemical weapons were used openly and successfully (in both the tactical and strategic senses). No international sanctions followed their use. (Indeed, in that conflict the United States tilted toward the side that had used them.) Probably the day will come when the civilized nations will regret their failure to punish those who used such weapons. For we may be entering an age in which chemical weapons are used by more parties rather than fewer [despite the recent chemical weapons convention].

Has conventional conflict become so terrible that man cannot wage it? The view has been pressed so many times in the past—from Ivan Bloch's dire predictions before 1914 of the slaughter that would ensue, to the terrifying predictions of annihilation through aerial bombardment in the interwar period—that a certain skepticism is warranted. Some modern weapons—highly precise long-range cruise missiles for example—appear to make violence more controllable. And other modern weapons contribute to the persistence of war, because they give the underdog a fighting chance. The Soviets discovered this unpleasant fact in battles with Afghan tribesmen who, despite their poverty and rudimentary educations, managed to master the use of Stinger missiles in a few weeks. Certain kinds of conventional weapons are now much easier to acquire than ever before, since Chilean, Chinese, and South African suppliers, among many others, ask few embarrassing questions about the uses of their cluster bombs, ballistic missiles, and long-range artillery.

What is almost certain is that we are entering a period of technological change in warfare so dramatic that it justifies the [former Soviet Union's] description: "the revolution in military affairs," a term they . . . applied to the invention of nuclear weapons, and before that, the advent of the tank and airplane. It is a revolution brought about by a host of technologies, particularly those involving information processing. Although the Soviets . . . thought through some of its implications, neither [the Russians nor the Americans] can claim fully to understand it. What this means, however, is that war will take very different forms than it did in the past, not that it will cease to exist.

In the past, changes in technology and in politics drastically altered the destructiveness of war (compare the wars of religion in the seventeenth century with those of kings in the eighteenth and those of nations in the nineteenth). Similar changes may be expected in the future, but the essence of war—armed conflict between political entities—will not become impossible. In his *Memoirs: Fifty Years of Political Reflections,* Raymond Aron observes that "our century, in fact, presents simultaneously the most varied forms of combat, from the terrorist act to carpet bombing—war has never been so polymorphous, it has never been so omnipresent." The ambush in a Kashmiri village, the terrorist outrage in a London office building, the stone-throwing of masked youths in a West Bank village—these are battles in larger campaigns every bit as much as the set piece engagements of the battle for the Faw Peninsula in Iraq or the siege of Cuito Cuanavale in Angola.

The technological arguments for the obsolescence of war are thus either flimsy or partial. A more persuasive case is made by those who point to the spread of free enterprise and liberal democracy, and the death of communism. They rightly scoff at those who contend that in principle the United States and Canada, newly-united Germany, and France will be potential military opponents once the overarching fear of the USSR has vanished. Small-scale fighting may go on in obscure corners of the world, they argue, but the advanced, secure, and liberal democracies of North America, Europe, and Australia will never contemplate armed conflict with each other. As liberal regimes spread, so too will the zone of peace. Meanwhile, the overwhelming preponderance of military power residing in the free world, and its irrelevance to political and economic disputes within that world, will debase traditional strategy to only marginal importance.

But the argument for peace through democracy needs to be qualified in many ways. It was, after all, the democratization of conflict in the nineteenth century that restored a ferocity to warfare unknown since the seventeenth century; the bloodiest war in American history remains the one fought between two (by today's standards flawed) democracies—the Civil War. Concentration camps appeared during another conflict between two limited democracies, the Boer War. World War I was launched by two regimes—Wilhelmine Germany and Austria-Hungary—that had greater representation and more equitable legal systems than those of many important states today. And even when modern liberal democracies go to war they do not necessarily moderate the scope of the violence they apply; indeed, sensitivity to their own casualties sometimes leads to profligate uses of firepower or violent efforts to end wars quickly. Shaky democracies fight each other all the time. [In the spring of 1990] India and Pakistan came close, once again, to open warfare. We must remind ourselves just how peculiar the wealthy and secure democracies of the West are, how painful their evolution to stability and the horror of war with each other has been. Perhaps other countries will find short-cuts to those conditions, but it would be foolish to assume they will.

Moreover, although at the moment Western-style liberal democracy appears to be the most appealing form of government, we should not be complacent about its durability, especially where it is newly established. Will its global popularity withstand major economic setbacks, or even a prolonged failure to deliver the goods to developing nations eager to reach European, Japanese, and American standards of living? George Orwell observed in 1940:

> Nearly all Western thought since the last war, certainly all "progressive" thought, has assumed tacitly that human beings desire nothing beyond ease, security and avoidance of pain. . . . Hitler, because in his own joyless mind he feels it with exceptional strength, knows that human beings *don't* only want comfort, safety, short working-hours, hygiene, birth-control, and, in general, common sense; they also, at least intermittently, want struggle and self-sacrifice, not to mention drums, flags and loyalty parades. . . . Whereas socialism, and even capitalism in a more grudging way, have

said to people "I offer you a good time," Hitler has said to them "I offer you struggle, danger and death," and as a result, a whole nation flings itself at his feet.[2]

Can we disregard this entirely as a relic of far off times? Saddam Hussein's seizure of Kuwait [in 1990] initially made him more popular at home, not less. The "end of history" argument, intriguing though it is, has many flaws. One may sum up one critique of it by noting how much of its plausibility hinges on one's view of Auschwitz. If one believes that the mad slaughter of the Holocaust was merely a horrible blip in man's general progress to consumerism, one may accept the argument. If, however, one sees in Hitler's war proof that anything is possible, that history is not linear, and that evil, including the evil that breeds civilization-shattering wars, is a permanent part of man's makeup, one cannot think that history is at an end or ending.

Liberal democracy gained victory in the Cold War by showing a persistence and a courage that many did not expect, and by delivering a prosperity that few could have imagined a half century ago. But the collapse of the Soviet empire owes as much, and perhaps more, to the fundamental hollowness and self-destructive nature of Marxism-Leninism. But other ideologies, as yet dimly foreseen, may pose threats equivalent to those of communism in its heyday, as may organized religions. Secular Western intellectuals, themselves immune to religious passion, may underestimate the power such beliefs exert not only on backward cobblers and peasant farmers, but on computer programmers, engineers, professors, and generals.

Furthermore, democracy may come under assault from wholly novel angles of attack. Are we certain, for instance, that the biological bases of liberal democracy, which assume equality and free will, will remain secure? If it becomes possible, as it well might, to breed men and women as easily as cattle are now bred, can we be quite certain that no one will exploit such awful possibilities for political purposes? "The present nature of man is tough and resilient. It casts up its sparks of genius in the darkest and most unexpected places." Thus wrote Churchill as he wondered about this very question in a prescient essay entitled "Fifty Years Hence" (in *Amid These Storms*). But suppose, he asked, a political elite could alter that nature in the laboratory? How will democracies adapt to the possibility that, despite Jefferson's famous dictum, some men may indeed be born with spurs on their feet, and others with saddles on their backs?

A third and final argument for the obsolescence of force comes from the rise of global economic interdependence, and the general (or rather purported)

[2]George Orwell, "Review of *Mein Kampf* by Adolf Hitler," in Sonia Orwell and Ian Angus, ed., *The Collected Essays, Journalism and Letters of George Orwell, Vol. II, My Country Right or Left, 1940–1943* (New York: Harcourt Brace Jovanovich, 1968), p. 14. Orwell noted that "Perhaps later on they will get sick of it and change their minds, as at the end of the last war. After a few years of slaughter and starvation 'greatest happiness of the greatest number' is a good slogan, but at this moment 'better an end with horror than a horror without end' is a winner."

decline in the autonomy and importance of the nation-state. Here again, an awareness of history inclines one to skepticism. Norman Angell traced this kind of interdependence before World War I and proclaimed that it made war impossible. In the 1970s a band of academic theorists put forward the same arguments, which crumbled in the face of wars in the Middle East and Soviet-supported conflicts in Africa and Asia. Of course, the case should not be overstated: "geoeconomics," as Edward Luttwak terms it, *is* of rising importance, and so too are such novel problems as those of environmental pollution.

But just as it would be foolish to ignore the emergence of new transnational forces and agencies on the one hand, and difficult global problems on the other, it would be wrong to succumb to the fallacy of interpreting all international developments as portents of global peace. Political entities fight wars; indeed, it is the political character of warfare that distinguishes it from the violence of organized crime. War can do quite well in the absence of nation-states: empires, city-states, confederations, and aspiring subnational groups have all used warfare to preserve or aggrandize themselves. And as the Crown Prince of Jordan . . . warned [in 1990], we may see greater conflict because of the attempt to break up nation-states. Certainly, the crack-up of empires is rarely peaceful. . . . The fissiparous tendencies of modern ethnic strife—in the [Russian Federation], Yugoslavia, Ethiopia, South Asia, and Lebanon—carry an implicit threat of violence. International institutions such as the European [Union] may breed peace, although the rise of the [EU] is surely as much a consequence of peace as a cause of it. In any case, the [EU] is the exception, not the rule: other organizations such as ASEAN, the OAU, and the OAS have not had anything like the vigor of the European [Union].

It is unlikely that new collective security arrangements—directed not against a potential enemy but against any and all potential aggressors—can replace the traditional forms of armament and alliances. The history of such pacts, and most notably of the League of Nations, is that they simply do not work. When the crunch comes, states either cannot agree on the definition of aggression, do not find it in their interests to oppose the aggressor, or simply do not have the stomach to use force. Collective security pacts therefore become marginal talking shops (which is all the Conference on Security and Cooperation in Europe, for example, can ever be) or they scare off potential members. If the U.S. Senate, for instance, thought that by ratifying a treaty it would commit the country to military intervention in a border war between Hungary and Romania, say, would it ever go along with such a notion?

All three arguments for an era of peace—the horrific quality of modern military technology, the spread of democracy, and the rise of transnational issues and actors—contain important truths. But neither separately nor together do they warrant a general conclusion that military power is becoming obsolete, or that war will not be used by states and other political groups. The causes of war remain as they were described by Thucydides, namely fear, ambition, and the desire for gain. It is only appropriate to celebrate the spread of freedom in and the waning of the threat from the East. But it would be well to temper our optimism with Alexander Hamilton's unsparing assessment of human affairs. In the *Federalist Papers* No. 6, he warned those who would believe in the "paradox of perpetual peace" that men are "ambitious, vindictive, and rapacious." "Momentary passions, and immediate interests," he argued, "have a more active and imperious control over human conduct than general or remote considerations of policy, utility, or justice." And democratic governments are not immune from such drives. They too are "subject to the impulses of rage, resentment, jealousy, avarice, and other irregular and violent propensities."

Senator Alan Simpson likes to tell a story of Senator Robert Dole's June 1990 trip to Iraq. Dole, who had been wounded in World War II, told the Iraqi dictator Saddam Hussein:

> "I've never spoken personally like this, but do you see this arm?" and he gestured with his withered right arm. "I have this daily reminder of the futility of war," he said. "That's why we're here." Even the Iraqi leader sat in stunned silence, Simpson said.[3]

Dole had expressed a profoundly untrue piety of contemporary politics. [At the time it was plausible to speculate that] Saddam's "stunned silence" reflected an awareness that Dole had, in fact, fought in the *least* futile war of the twentieth century. But [since then it became clear] that a victorious warlord who routinely (and on occasion, it is said, personally) executes political opponents would find it impossible to take seriously a senior statesman in the world's most powerful nation who thus dismissed the uses of force. And less than two months later, Saddam demonstrated his view of the utility of force (and opinion of American statesmanship) by one of the most blatant acts of aggression since the Munich crisis of 1938.

War, and potential war, will remain a feature of international politics. Its sources will be many and changing, from ethnic animosity to irredentism, from competition for power to religious fanaticism. Its stakes will include territory (including valuable off-shore properties), water rights, and control of populations. It will result from traditional kinds of animosities, but also from the second and third order consequences of developments that are intrinsically unforeseeable. Economic depression, for instance, need not breed violence directly, but it may, as in the 1930s, abet the development of new forms of tyranny, or increase the likelihood of the resort to violence by desperate countries.

The state system is undergoing its most dramatic changes since decolonization in the 1950s and 1960s. Entirely new states [have broken] off the hulk of the Soviet empire, creating the potential for a civil war as widespread and dis-

---

[3]"Dole Puts Bitterness of '88 Race Aside to Carry Out Bush Agenda," *Washington Post,* June 11, 1990, p. A8.

ruptive as any the world has known. In other parts of the world—even in Canada—there is more splitting, and Balkanization characterizes world politics as much as unification. No one can foresee the consequences of this kind of fragmentation, but it is hard to believe that it will necessarily be peaceful. Just the reverse, in fact: border disputes, the flight of ethnic refugees, and desperate efforts to build or maintain large political aggregations do not look to have entirely peaceful consequences. Neither, for that matter, do such structural problems as massive demographic pressures in North Africa, or competition for water in the Middle East. . . .

4

THE OBSOLESCENCE
OF MAJOR WAR

John Mueller

Observing the virtual absence of war between the great powers since World War II (alongside its continuation in the same period among the powerful and the weak in the Third World), John Mueller explores the various reasons why the probability of another major or general world war appears to have receded, and the consequences of the demise of the Cold War for this "imperfect" but prolonged postwar peace. Mueller is professor of political science at the University of Rochester, where he serves as director of the Watson Center for the Study of International Peace and Cooperation. He is author of *Policy and Opinion toward the Gulf War* (1994).

In discussing the causes of international war, commentators have often found it useful to group theories into what they term levels of analysis. In his classic work, *Man, the State and War,* Kenneth N. Waltz organizes the theories according to whether the cause of war is found in the nature of man, in the nature of the state, or in the nature of the international state system. More recently Jack Levy, partly setting the issue of human nature to one side, organizes the theories

Used by permission of John Mueller and Sage Publications Ltd. From the *Bulletin of Peace Proposals,* Vol. 21, No. 3 (1990). Some footnotes have been deleted, and others have been renumbered to appear in consecutive order.

according to whether they stress the systemic level, the nature of state and society, or the decisionmaking process.[1]

In various ways, these level-of-analysis approaches direct attention away from war itself and toward concerns which may influence the incidence of war. However, war should not be visualized as a sort of recurring outcome that is determined by other conditions, but rather as a phenomenon that has its own qualities and appeals. And over time these appeals can change. In this view, war is merely an idea, an institution, like dueling or slavery, that has been grafted onto human existence. Unlike breathing, eating, or sex, war is not something that is somehow required by the human condition, by the structure of international affairs, or by the forces of history.

Accordingly, war can shrivel up and disappear; and this may come about without any notable change or improvement on any of the level-of-analysis categories. Specifically, war can die out without changing human nature, without modifying the nature of the state or the nation-state, without changing the international system, without creating an effective world government or system of international law, and without improving the competence or moral capacity of political leaders. It can also go away without expanding international trade, interdependence, or communication; without fabricating an effective moral or practical equivalent; without enveloping the earth in democracy or prosperity; without devising ingenious agreements to restrict arms or the arms industry; without reducing the world's considerable store of hate, selfishness, nationalism, and racism; without increasing the amount of love, justice, harmony, cooperation, good will, or inner peace in the world; without establishing security communities; and without doing anything whatever about nuclear weapons.

Not only *can* such a development take place: it *has* been taking place for a century or more, at least within the developed world, once a cauldron of international and civil war. Conflicts of interest are inevitable and continue to persist within the developed world. But the notion that war should be used to resolve them has increasingly been discredited and abandoned there. War is apparently becoming obsolete, at least in the developed world: in an area where war was once often casually seen as beneficial, noble, and glorious, or at least as neces-

---

[1]Kenneth N. Waltz, *Man, the State and War* (New York: Columbia University Press, 1959); Jack S. Levy, "The Causes of War: A Review of Theories and Evidence," in Philip E. Tetlock, Jo L. Husbands, Robert Jervis, Paul C. Stern, and Charles Tilly, eds., *Behavior, Society, and Nuclear War,* Vol. 1 (New York: Oxford University Press, 1989), pp. 209–333. See also J. David Singer, "The Levels of Analysis Problem in International Relations," in Klaus Knorr and Sydney Verba, eds., *The International System* (Princeton, NJ: Princeton University Press, 1961), pp. 77–92; and James N. Rosenau, "Pretheories and Theories of Foreign Policy," in R. B. Farrell, ed., *Approaches to Comparative and International Politics* (Evanston, IL: Northwestern University Press, 1966), pp. 27–92.

sary or inevitable, the conviction has now become widespread that war would be intolerably costly, unwise, futile, and debased.[2]

Some of this may be suggested by the remarkable developments in the Cold War in the late 1980s. The dangers of a major war in the developed world clearly declined remarkably: yet this can hardly be attributed to an improvement in human nature, to the demise of the nation-state, to the rise of a world government, or to a notable improvement in the competence of political leaders.

TWO ANALOGIES: DUELING AND SLAVERY

It may not be obvious that an accepted, time-honored institution which serves an urgent social purpose can become obsolescent and then die out because many people come to find it obnoxious. But the argument here is that something like that has indeed been happening to war in the developed world. To illustrate the dynamic, [consider] two analogies: the processes by which the once-perennial institutions of dueling and slavery have all but vanished from the face of the earth.

Dueling

In some important respects, war in the developed world may be following the example of another violent method for settling disputes, dueling. Up until a century ago dueling was common practice in Europe and the USA among a certain class of young and youngish men who liked to classify themselves as gentlemen.[3] Men of the social set that once dueled still exist, they still get insulted, and they are still concerned about their self-respect and their standing among their peers. But they no longer duel. However, they do not avoid dueling today because they evaluate the option and reject it on cost-benefit grounds. Rather, the option never percolates into their consciousness as something that is available. That is, a form of violence famed and fabled for centuries has now sunk from thought as a viable, conscious possibility.

The Prussian strategist, Carl von Clausewitz, opens his famous 1832 book, *On War,* by observing that "War is nothing but a duel on a larger scale." If war, like dueling, comes to be viewed as a thoroughly undesirable, even ridiculous, policy, and if it can no longer promise gains, or if potential combatants come no longer to value the things it can gain for them, then war can fade away as a

---

[2]For a further development of these arguments, see John Mueller, *Retreat from Doomsday: The Obsolescence of Major War* (New York: Basic Books, 1989).

[3]For other observations of the analogy between war and dueling, see Bernard Brodie, *War and Politics* (New York: Macmillan, 1973), p. 275; Norman Angell, *The Great Illusion* (London: Heinemann, 1914), pp. 202–203; G. P. Gooch, *History of Our Time, 1885–1911* (London: Williams & Norgate, 1911), p. 249; J. E. Cairnes, "International Law," *Fortnightly Review,* Vol. 2, 1 November 1865, p. 650 n.

coherent possibility even if a truly viable substitute or "moral equivalent" for it were never formulated. Like dueling, it could become unfashionable and then obsolete.

Slavery

From the dawn of prehistory until about 1788 slavery, like war, could be found just about everywhere in one form or another, and it flourished in every age. Around 1788, however, the anti-slavery forces began to argue that the institution was repulsive, immoral, and uncivilized: and this sentiment gradually picked up adherents. . . .

. . . The abolitionists were up against an institution that was viable, profitable, and expanding, and moreover one that had been uncritically accepted for thousands—perhaps millions—of years as a natural and inevitable part of human existence. To counter this powerful and time-honored institution, the abolitionists' principal weapon was a novel argument: it had recently occurred to them, they said, that slavery was no longer the way people ought to do things.

As it happened, this was an idea whose time had come. The abolition of slavery required legislative battles, international pressures, economic travail, and, in the United States, a cataclysmic war (but it did *not* require the fabrication of a functional equivalent or the formation of an effective supranational authority). Within a century slavery, and most similar institutions like serfdom, had been all but eradicated from the face of the globe. Slavery became controversial and then obsolete.

War

Dueling and slavery no longer exist as effective institutions; they have largely faded from human experience except as something we read about in books. While their re-establishment is not impossible, they show after a century of neglect no signs of revival. Other once-popular, even once-admirable, institutions in the developed world have been, or are being, eliminated because at some point they began to seem repulsive, immoral, and uncivilized: bearbaiting, bareknuckle fighting, freak shows, casual torture, wanton cruelty to animals, burning heretics, flogging, vendetta, deforming corsetting, laughing at the insane, the death penalty for minor crimes, eunuchism, public cigarette smoking.

War may well be in the process of joining this list of recently-discovered sins and vices. War is not, of course, the same as dueling or slavery. Like war, dueling is an institution for settling disputes; but it was something of a social affectation and it usually involved only matters of "honor," not ones of physical gain. Like war, slavery was nearly universal and an apparently inevitable part of human existence, but it could be eliminated area by area: a country that abolished slavery did not have to worry about what other countries were doing, while a country that would like to abolish war must continue to be concerned about those that have kept it in their repertory.

On the other hand, war has against it not only substantial psychic costs, but also obvious and widespread physical ones. Dueling brought death and destruction but, at least in the first instance, only to a few people who had specifically volunteered to participate. And while slavery may have brought moral destruction, it generally was a considerable economic success.

In some respects then, the fact that war has outlived dueling and slavery is curious. But there are signs that, at least in the developed world, it too has begun to succumb to obsolescence.

TRENDS AGAINST WAR BEFORE 1914

There were a number of trends away from war in the developed world before World War I. Two of these deserve special emphasis.

The Hollandization Phenomenon

As early as 1800 a few once-warlike countries in Europe, like Holland, Switzerland, and Sweden, quietly began to drop out of the war system. While war was still generally accepted as a natural and inevitable phenomenon, these countries found solace (and prosperity) in policies that stressed peace. People who argue that war is inherent in nature and those who see war as a recurring, cyclic phenomenon need to supply an explanation for these countries. Switzerland, for example, has avoided all international war for nearly 200 years. If war is inherent in human nature or if war is some sort of cyclic inevitability, surely the Swiss ought to be roaring for a fight by now.

The Rise of an Organized Peace Movement

While there have been individual war opponents throughout history, the existence of organized groups devoted to abolishing war from the human condition is quite new. The institution of war came under truly organized and concentrated attack only after 1815, and this peace movement did not develop real momentum until the end of the century. . . .

Peace advocates were a noisy gadfly minority by 1900, and they had established a sense of momentum. Their arguments were inescapable, but, for the most part they were rejected and derided by the majority which still held to the traditional view that war was noble, natural, thrilling, progressive, manly, redemptive, and beneficial. Up until 1914, as Michael Howard has observed, war "was almost universally considered an acceptable, perhaps an inevitable and for many people a desirable way of settling international differences."

THE IMPACT OF WORLD WAR I

The holocaust of World War I turned peace advocates into a pronounced majority in the developed world and destroyed war romanticism. As Arnold Toynbee points out, this war marked the end of a "span of five thousand years during which war had been one of mankind's master institutions." Or, as Evan Luard observes, "the First World War transformed traditional attitudes toward war. For the first time there was an almost universal sense that the deliberate launching of a war could now no longer be justified."

World War I was, of course, horrible. But horror was not invented in 1914. History had already had its Carthages, its Jerichos, its wars of 30 years, of 100 years. Seen in historic context, in fact, World War I does not seem to have been all that unusual in its duration, destructiveness, grimness, political pointlessness, economic consequences, breadth, or intensity. However, it does seem to be unique in that it was the first major war to be preceded by substantial, organized anti-war agitation, and in that, for Europeans, it followed an unprecedentedly peaceful century during which Europeans had begun, perhaps unknowingly, to appreciate the virtues of peace.[4]

Obviously, this change of attitude was not enough to prevent the wars that have taken place since 1918. But the notion that the institution of war, particularly war in the developed world, was repulsive, uncivilized, immoral, and futile—voiced only by minorities before 1914—was an idea whose time had come. It is one that has permeated most of the developed world ever since.

WORLD WAR II

It is possible that enough war spirit still lingered, particularly in Germany, for another war in Europe to be necessary to extinguish it there. But analysis of opinion in the interwar period suggests that war was viewed with about as much horror in Germany as any place on the continent. To a remarkable degree, major war returned to Europe only because of the astoundingly successful machinations of Adolf Hitler, virtually the last European who was willing to risk major war. As Gerhard Weinberg has put it: "Whether any other German leader would indeed have taken the plunge is surely doubtful, and the very warnings Hitler received from some of his generals can only have reinforced his belief in his personal role as the one man able, willing, and even eager to lead Germany and drag the world into war." That is, after World War I a war in Europe could only be brought about through the maniacally dedicated manipulations of an exceptionally lucky and spectacularly skilled entrepreneur; before World War I, any dimwit—e.g. Kaiser Wilhelm—could get into one.

---

[4]For a further development of this argument, see John Mueller, "Changing Attitudes Toward War: The Impact of World War I," *British Journal of Political Science,* Vol. 21 (January 1991), pp. 1–28.

The war in Asia was, of course, developed out of the expansionary policies of distant Japan, a country which neither participated substantially in World War I nor learned its lessons. In World War II, Japan got the message most Europeans had received from World War I.

THE COLD WAR, THE LONG PEACE, AND NUCLEAR WEAPONS

Since 1945 major war [was] most likely to develop from the Cold War that . . . dominated postwar international history. The hostility of the era mostly [derived] from the Soviet Union's ideological—even romantic—affection for revolution and for revolutionary war. While this ideology [was] expansionistic in some respects, it . . . never visualized major war in the Hitler mode as a remotely sensible tactic.

East and West [were] never . . . close to major war, and it seems unlikely that nuclear weapons [were] important determinants of this—insofar as a military deterrent [was] necessary, the fear of escalation to a war like World War I or II [supplied] it. Even allowing considerably for stupidity, ineptness, miscalculation, and self-deception, a large war, nuclear or otherwise, has never been remotely in the interest of the essentially-contented, risk-averse, escalation-anticipating countries that have dominated world affairs since 1945. This is not to deny that nuclear war is appalling to contemplate and mind-concentratingly dramatic, particularly in the speed with which it could bring about massive destruction. Nor is it to deny that decisionmakers, both in times of crisis and in times of non-crisis, are well aware of how cataclysmic a nuclear war could be. It is simply to stress that the horror of repeating World War II is not all that much less impressive or dramatic, and that leaders essentially content with the status quo will strive to avoid anything that they feel could lead to either calamity. A jump from a fiftieth-floor window is probably quite a bit more horrible to contemplate than a jump from a fifth-floor one, but anyone who finds life even minimally satisfying is extremely unlikely to do either.[5]

In general the wars that have involved developed countries since World War II have been of two kinds, both of them declining in frequency and relevance. One of these concerns lingering colonial responsibilities and readjustments. Thus the Dutch got involved in (but did not start) a war in Indonesia, the French in Indochina and Algeria, the British in Malaya and the Falklands.

The other kind [related] to the Cold War contest between East and West. The communists . . . generally sought to avoid major war, not so much because

---

[5]For a further development of this argument, see John Mueller, "The Essential Irrelevance of Nuclear Weapons: Stability in the Postwar World," *International Security,* Vol. 13 (No. 2, Fall 1988), pp. 55–79.

they necessarily [found] such wars to be immoral, repulsive, or uncivilized, but because they [found] them futile—dangerous, potentially counter-productive, wildly and absurdly adventurous. However, for decades after 1945 they retained a dutiful affection for what they came to call wars of national liberation— smaller wars around the world designed to further the progressive cause of world revolution. The West [saw] this threat as visceral and as one that [had to] be countered even at the cost of war if necessary. Wars fought in this context, such as those in Korea and Vietnam, [were] essentially . . . seen [as] preventive—if communism [was] countered there, it [would] not have to be countered later, on more vital, closer turf.

The lesson learned (perhaps overlearned) from the Hitler experience is that aggressive threats must be dealt with by those who abhor war when the threats are still comparatively small and distant; to allow the aggressive force to succeed only brings nearer the day when a larger war must be fought. Thus some countries which abhor war have felt it necessary to wage them in order to prevent wider wars.

CONSEQUENCES OF THE DEMISE OF THE COLD WAR

Because of economic crisis and persistent ideological failure, . . . the Cold War . . . ended as the Soviet Union, following the lead of its former ideological soulmate, China, [has abandoned] its quest for ideological expansion, questing instead after prosperity and a quiet, normal international situation. Unless some new form of conflict emerges, war participation by developed countries is likely to continue its decline.

As tensions lapse between the two sides in what used to be known as the Cold War, there is a natural tendency for the arms that backed that tension, and in a sense measured it, to atrophy. Both sides have begun what might be called a negative arms race. . . .

The demise of the Cold War should also facilitate further expansion of international trade and interdependence. Trade and interdependence may not lead inexorably to peace, but peace does seem to lead to trade, interdependence, and economic growth—or, at any rate, it facilitates them. That is, peace ought to be seen not as a dependent but rather as an independent variable in such considerations. The 1992 economic unity of Europe and the building of a long-envisioned Channel tunnel are the consequences of peace, not its cause.

Left alone, enterprising business people will naturally explore the possibilities of investing in other countries or selling their products there. Averse to disastrous surprises, they are more likely to invest if they are confident that peace will prevail. But for trade to flourish, governments must stay out of the way not only by eschewing war, but also by eschewing measures which unnaturally inhibit trade.

Furthermore, if nations no longer find it sensible to use force or the threat of force in their dealings with one another, it may be neither necessary nor particularly desirable to create an entrenched international government or police force (as opposed to ad hoc arrangements and devices designed to meet specific problems). Indeed, an effective international government could be detrimental to economic growth since, like domestic governments, it could be manipulated to reward the inefficient, coddle the incompetent, and plague the innovative.

WAR IN THE THIRD WORLD

War has not, of course, become fully obsolete. While major war—war among developed countries—seems to be going out of style, war obviously continues to flourish elsewhere. The demise of the Cold War suggests that the United States and [Russia], in particular, are likely to involve themselves less in these wars. Moreover, it is possible that the catastrophic Iran–Iraq war [has sobered] people in the Third World about that kind of war. And it does seem that much of the romance has gone out of the concept of violent revolution as Third World countries increasingly turn to the drab, difficult, and unromantic task of economic development.

Thus it is possible that the developed world's aversion to war may eventually infect the rest of the world as well (international war, in fact, has been quite rare in Latin America for a century). But this development is not certain, nor is its pace predictable. As slavery continued to persist in Brazil even after it had been abolished elsewhere, the existence of war in some parts of the world does not refute the observation that it is vanishing, or has vanished, in other parts.

IMPERFECT PEACE

War, even war within the developed world, has not become impossible—nor could it ever do so. When it has seemed necessary, even countries like the United States and Britain, which were among the first to become thoroughly disillusioned with war, have been able to fight wars and to use military force-often with high morale and substantial public support, at least at first. The ability to make war and the knowledge about how to do so can never be fully expunged—nor, for that matter, can the ability or knowledge to institute slavery, eunuchism, crucifixion, or human sacrifice. War is declining as an institution not because it has ceased to be possible or fascinating, but because peoples and leaders in the developed world—where war was once endemic—have increasingly found war to be disgusting, ridiculous, and unwise.

The view presented in this [chapter] is based upon the premise that, in some important respects, war is often taken too seriously. War, it seems, is merely an idea. It is not a trick of fate, a thunderbolt from hell, a natural calamity, or a desperate plot contrivance dreamed up by some sadistic puppeteer on high. If war begins in the minds of men, as the UNESCO charter insists, it can end there as well. Over the centuries, war opponents have been trying to bring this about by discrediting war as an idea; the argument here is that they have been substantially successful at doing so. The long peace since World War II is less a product of recent weaponry than the culmination of a substantial historical process. For the last two or three centuries, major war has gradually moved toward terminal disrepute because of its perceived repulsiveness and futility.

It could also be argued that, to a considerable degree, people have tended to take *peace* too seriously as well. Peace is merely what emerges when the institution of war is neglected. It does not mean that the world suddenly becomes immersed in those qualities with which the word "peace" is constantly being associated: love, justice, harmony, cooperation, brotherhood, good will. People still remain contentious and there still remain substantial conflicts of interest. The difference is only that they no longer resort to force to resolve their conflicts, any more than young men today resort to formal dueling to resolve their quarrels. A world at peace would not be perfect, but it would be notably better than the alternative.

5

NUCLEAR MYTHS AND POLITICAL REALITIES

Kenneth N. Waltz

In this essay, Kenneth N. Waltz theorizes about the role that nuclear weapons and the deterrence strategies and doctrines governing their use have played in preventing great-power conflicts from escalating to war. Contrasting the logic of conventional and nuclear weaponry and tracing the history of the doctrines the superpowers have constructed to govern their use, Waltz evaluates why the age of nuclear "overkill" may provide a better foundation for the prevention of war than that afforded by reliance on conventional weapons. Waltz is professor of political science at the University of California, Berkeley, and has served as president of the American Political Science Association. He is the author of *Theory of International Politics* (1979).

Nuclear weapons have been given a bad name. . . . Uneasiness over nuclear weapons and the search for alternative means of security stem in large measure from widespread failure to understand the nature and requirements of deterrence. Not unexpectedly, the language of strategic discourse has deteriorated over the decades. This happens whenever discussion enters the political arena, where words take on meanings and colorations reflecting the preferences of their users. Early in the nuclear era *deterrence* carried its dictionary definition,

From *The American Political Science Review* (September 1990); originally presented as the presidential address at the annual meeting of the American Political Science Association in Washington, D.C., 1988. Used by permission of Kenneth N. Waltz and the American Political Science Association.

dissuading someone from an action by frightening that person with the consequences of the action. To deter an adversary from attacking one need have only a force that can survive a first strike and strike back hard enough to outweigh any gain the aggressor had hoped to realize. Deterrence in its pure form entails no ability to defend; a deterrent strategy promises not to fend off an aggressor but to damage or destroy things the aggressor holds dear. Both defense and deterrence are strategies that a status quo country may follow, hoping to dissuade a state from attacking. They are different strategies designed to accomplish a common end in different ways, using different weapons differently deployed. Wars can be prevented, as they can be caused, in various ways.

Deterrence antedates nuclear weapons, but in a conventional world deterrent threats are problematic. . . . Nuclear weapons purify deterrent strategies by removing elements of defense and war-fighting. Nuclear warheads eliminate the necessity of fighting and remove the possibility of defending, because only a small number of warheads need to reach their targets.

Ironically, as multiplication of missiles increased the ease with which destructive blows can be delivered, the distinction between deterrence and defense began to blur. Early in President Kennedy's administration, Secretary McNamara began to promote a strategy of Flexible Response, which was half-heartedly adopted by NATO in 1967. Flexible Response calls for the ability to meet threats at all levels from irregular warfare to conventional warfare to nuclear warfare. In the 1970s and 1980s more and more emphasis was placed on the need to fight and defend at all levels in order to "deter." The melding of defense, war-fighting, and deterrence overlooks a simple truth about nuclear weapons proclaimed in the title of a book edited by Bernard Brodie in 1946: Nuclear weapons are absolute. Nuclear weapons can carry out their deterrent task no matter what other countries do. If one nuclear power were able to destroy almost all of another's strategic warheads with practical certainty or defend against all but a few strategic warheads coming in, nuclear weapons would not be absolute. But because so much explosive power comes in such small packages, the invulnerability of a sufficient number of warheads is easy to achieve and the delivery of fairly large numbers of warheads impossible to thwart, both now and as far into the future as anyone can see. The absolute quality of nuclear weapons sharply sets a nuclear world off from a conventional one.

WHAT DETERS?

Most discussions of deterrence are based on the belief that deterrence is difficult to achieve. In the Eisenhower years "massive retaliation" was the phrase popularly used to describe the response we would supposedly make to a Soviet Union attack. Deterrence must be difficult if the threat of massive retaliation is required to achieve it. As the Soviet Union's arsenal grew, MAD (mutual assured destruction) became the acronym of choice, thus preserving the notion that deterrence depends on being willing and able to destroy much, if not most, of a country.

That one must be able to destroy a country in order to deter it is an odd notion, though of distinguished lineage. During the 1950s emphasis was put on the *massive* in *massive retaliation*. Beginning in the 1960s the emphasis was put on the *assured destruction* in the doctrine of MAD. Thus viewed, deterrence becomes a monstrous policy, as innumerable critics have charged. One quotation can stand for many others. In a warning to NATO defense ministers that became famous, Henry Kissinger counseled the European allies not to keep "asking us to multiply strategic assurances that we cannot possibly mean or if we do mean, we should not want to execute because if we execute, we risk the destruction of civilization." . . . The notion that the failure of deterrence would lead to national suicide or to mutual annihilation betrays a misunderstanding of both political behavior and nuclear realities.

Introducing the Eisenhower administration's New Look policy in January of 1954, John Foster Dulles gave the impression that aggression anywhere would elicit heavy nuclear retaliation. Just three months later, he sensibly amended the policy. Nuclear deterrence, Dulles and many others quickly came to realize, works not against minor aggression at the periphery, but only against major aggression at the center of international politics. Moreover, to deter major aggression, Dulles now said, "the probable hurt" need only "outbalance the probable gain." . . . Like Brodie before him, Dulles based deterrence on the principle of proportionality: "Let the punishment fit the crime."

What would we expect the United States to do if . . . a major conventional attack [were launched] against vital U.S. interests—say, in Western Europe? Military actions have to be related to an objective. Because of the awesome power of nuclear weapons, the pressure to use them in ways that achieve the objective at hand while doing and suffering a minimum of destruction would be immense. It is preposterous to think that if [an] attack [had broken] through NATO's defenses, the United States would strike thousands of [the aggressor's] military targets or hundreds of [its] cities. Doing so would serve no purpose. Who would want to make a bad situation worse by launching wantonly destructive attacks on a country that can strike back with comparable force, or, for that matter, on a country that could not do so? In the event, we might strike a target or two—military or industrial—chosen to keep casualties low. If the [aggressor] had run the preposterous risk of attacking the center of Europe believing it could escape retaliation, we would thus show them that they were wrong while conveying the idea that more would follow if they persisted. Among countries with abundant nuclear weapons, none can gain an advantage by striking first. The purpose of demonstration shots is simply to remind everyone—should anyone forget—that catastrophe threatens. Some people purport to believe that if a few warheads go off, many will follow. This would seem to be the least likely of all the unlikely possibilities. That no country gains by destroying another's cities and then seeing a comparable number of its own destroyed in return is obvious to everyone.

Despite widespread beliefs to the contrary, deterrence does not depend on destroying cities. Deterrence depends on what one *can* do, not on what one *will* do. What deters is the fact that we can do as much damage to them as we choose, and they to us. The country suffering the retaliatory attack cannot limit the damage done to it; only the retaliator can do that.

With nuclear weapons, countries need threaten to use only a small amount of force. This is so because once the willingness to use a little force is shown, the adversary knows how easily more can be added. This is not true with conventional weapons. Therefore, it is often useful for a country to threaten to use great force if conflict should lead to war. The stance may be intended as a deterrent one, but the ability to carry the threat through is problematic. With conventional weapons, countries tend to emphasize the first phase of war. Striking hard to achieve a quick victory may decrease the cost of war. With nuclear weapons, political leaders worry not about what may happen in the first phase of fighting but about what may happen in the end. As Clausewitz wrote, if war should ever approach the absolute, it would become "imperative . . . not to take the first step without considering what may be the last. . . ."

Since war now approaches the absolute, it is hardly surprising that President Kennedy echoed Clausewitz's words during the Cuban Missile Crisis of 1962. "It isn't the first step that concerns me," he said, "but both sides escalating to the fourth and fifth step—and we don't go to the sixth because there is no one around to do so. . . ." In conventional crises, leaders may sensibly seek one advantage or another. They may bluff by threatening escalatory steps they are in fact unwilling to take. They may try one stratagem or another and run considerable risks. Since none of the parties to the struggle can predict what the outcome will be, they may have good reason to prolong crises, even crises entailing the risk of war. A conventional country enjoying military superiority is tempted to use it before other countries right the military balance. A nuclear country enjoying superiority is reluctant to use it because no one can promise the full success of a disarming first strike. As Henry Kissinger retrospectively said of the Cuban Missile Crisis, the Soviet Union had only "60–70 truly strategic weapons while we had something like 2,000 in missiles and bombs." But, he added, "with some proportion of Soviet delivery vehicles surviving, the Soviet Union could do horrendous damage to the United States." . . . In other words, we could not be sure that our two thousand weapons would destroy almost all of their sixty or seventy. Even with numbers immensely disproportionate, a small force strongly inhibits the use of a large one.

The catastrophe promised by nuclear war contrasts sharply with the extreme difficulty of predicting outcomes among conventional competitors. This makes one wonder about the claimed dependence of deterrence on perceptions and the alleged problem of credibility. In conventional competitions, the comparative qualities of troops, weaponry, strategies, and leaders are difficult to gauge. So complex is the fighting of wars with conventional weapons that their outcomes have been extremely difficult to predict. Wars start more easily because the uncertainties of their outcomes make it easier for the leaders of states to entertain illusions of victory at supportable cost. In contrast, contemplating war when the use of nuclear weapons is possible focuses one's attention not on the probability of victory but on the possibility of annihilation. Because catastrophic outcomes of nuclear exchanges are easy to imagine, leaders of states will shrink in horror from initiating them. With nuclear weapons, stability and peace rest on easy calculations of what one country can do to another. Anyone—political leader or man in the street—can see that catastrophe lurks if events spiral out of control and nuclear warheads begin to fly. The problem of the credibility of deterrence, a big worry in a conventional world, disappears in a nuclear one. . . .

WHY NUCLEAR WEAPONS DOMINATE STRATEGY

Deterrence is easier to contrive than most strategists have believed. With conventional weapons, a number of strategies are available, strategies combining and deploying forces in different ways. Strategies may do more than weapons to determine the outcomes of wars. Nuclear weapons are different; they dominate strategies. As [Bernard Brodie] clearly saw, the effects of nuclear weapons derive not from any particular design for their employment in war but simply from their presence. . . . Indeed, in an important sense, nuclear weapons eliminate strategy. If one thinks of strategies as being designed for defending national objectives or for gaining them by military force and as implying a choice about how major wars will be fought, nuclear weapons make strategy obsolete. Nevertheless, the conviction that the only reliable deterrent force is one able to win a war or at least end up in a better position than the [adversary] is widespread. . . .

NATO policy well [illustrated] the futility of trying to transcend deterrence by fashioning war-fighting strategies. The supposed difficulties of extending deterrence to cover major allies . . . led some to argue [during the Cold War] that we require nuclear superiority, that we need nuclear war-fighting capabilities, and that we must build up our conventional forces. Once the Soviet Union achieved nuclear parity, confidence in our extended deterrent declined in the West. One wonders whether it did in the East. Denis Healey once said that one chance in a hundred that a country will retaliate is enough to deter an adversary, although not enough to reassure an ally. Many have repeated his statement; but none, I believe, has added that reassuring allies is unnecessary militarily and unwise politically. Politically, allies who are unsure of one another's support have reason to work harder for the sake of their own security. Militarily, deterrence requires only that conventional forces be able to defend long enough to determine that an attack is a major one and not merely a foray. For this, a trip wire force as envisioned in the 1950s, with perhaps fifty thousand U.S. troops in

Europe, would be sufficient. Beyond that, deterrence requires only that forces be invulnerable and that the area protected be of manifestly vital interest. West European countries can be counted on to maintain forces of trip wire capability.

Nuclear weapons strip conventional forces of most of their functions. Bernard Brodie pointed out that in "a total war" the army "might have no function at all." . . . Herman Kahn cited "the claim that in a thermonuclear war it is important to keep the sea lanes open" as an example of the "quaint ideas" still held by the military. . . . Conventional forces have only a narrow role in any confrontation between nuclear states over vital interests, since fighting beyond the trip wire level serves no useful purpose. Enlarging conventional capabilities does nothing to strengthen deterrence. Strategic stalemate does shift military competition to the tactical level. But one must add what is usually omitted: nuclear stalemate limits the use of conventional forces and reduces the extent of the gains one can seek without risking devastation. For decades U.S. policy . . . nevertheless aimed at raising the nuclear threshold in Europe. Stronger conventional forces would presumably have enabled NATO to sustain a longer war in Europe at higher levels of violence. At some moment in a major war, however, one side or the other— or perhaps both—would believe itself to be losing. The temptation to introduce nuclear weapons might then prove irresistable, and they would be fired in the chaos of defeat with little chance of limited and discriminant use. Early use would promise surer control and closer limitation of damage. In a nuclear world a conventional war-fighting strategy would appear to be the worst possible one, more dangerous than a strategy of relying on deterrence.

Attempts to gain escalation dominance, like efforts to raise the nuclear threshold, betray a failure to appreciate the strategic implications of nuclear weapons. Escalation dominance, so it is said, requires a "seamless web of capabilities" up and down "the escalation ladder." Earlier, it had been thought that the credibility of deterrence would be greater if some rungs of the escalation ladder were missing. The inability to fight at some levels would make the threat to use higher levels of force easy to credit. But again, since credibility is not a problem, this scarcely matters militarily. Filling in the missing rungs neither helps nor hurts. Escalation dominance is useful for countries contending with conventional weapons only. Dominance, however, is difficult to achieve in the absence of a decisive weapon. Among nuclear adversaries the question of dominance is pointless because one second-strike force cannot dominate another. Since strategic nuclear weapons will always prevail, the game of escalation dominance cannot be played. Everyone knows that anyone can quickly move to the top rung of the ladder. Because anyone can do so, all of the parties in a serious crisis have an overriding incentive to ask themselves one question: How can we get out of this mess without nuclear warheads exploding? Deescalation, not escalation, becomes the problem that the presence of nuclear weapons forces them to solve.

To gain escalation dominance, if that were imaginable, would require the ability to fight nuclear wars. War-fighting strategies imply that nuclear weapons are not absolute but relative, so that the country with more and better nuclear weapons could in some unspecified way prevail. No one, however, has shown how such a war could be fought. Indeed, Desmond Ball [in 1981] . . . argued that a nuclear war could not be sustained beyond the exchange of strategic warheads numbered not in the hundreds but in the tens. . . . After a small number of exchanges no one would know what was going on or be able to maintain control. Yet nuclear weapons save us from our folly: fanciful strategies are irrelevant because no one will run the appalling risk of testing them.

Deterrence has been faulted for its lack of credibility, its dependence on perceptions, its destructive implications, and its inability to cover interests abroad. The trouble with deterrence, however, lies elsewhere: The trouble with deterrence is that it can be implemented cheaply. The claim that we need a seamless web of capabilities in order to deter does serve one purpose: It keeps military budgets wondrously high. Efforts to fashion a defensive and war-fighting strategy . . . are pointless because deterrence prevails and futile because strategy cannot transcend the military conditions that nuclear weapons create.

NUCLEAR ARMS AND DISARMAMENT

The probability of major war among states having nuclear weapons approaches zero. But the "real war" may, as William James claimed, lie in the preparation for waging it. The logic of deterrence, if followed, circumscribes the causes of "real wars." . . . Nuclear weapons make it possible for a state to limit the size of its strategic forces as long as other states are unable to achieve disarming first-strike capabilities by improving their forces. . . .

Many who urge us to build ever more strategic weapons in effect admit the military irrelevance of additional forces when, as so often, they give political rather than military reasons for doing so: spending less, it is said, would signal weakness of will. Yet militarily, only one perception counts, namely, the perception that a country has second-strike forces. Nuclear weapons make it possible for states to escape the dynamics of arms racing; yet [during the Cold War] the United States and the Soviet Union . . . multiplied their weaponry far beyond the requirements of deterrence. Each . . . obsessively measured its strategic forces against the other's. The arms competition between them [arose] from failure to appreciate the implications of nuclear weapons for military strategy and, no doubt, from internal military and political pressures in both countries.

Many of the obstacles to arms reduction among conventional powers disappear or dwindle among nuclear nations. For the former, the careful comparison of the quantities and qualities of forces is important. Because this is not so with nuclear weapons, the problem of verifying agreements largely disappears. Provisions for verification may be necessary in order to persuade [a legislature] to ratify an agreement, but the possibility of noncompliance is not very worrisome. Agreements that reduce one category of conventional weapons may shift competition to other types of weapons and lead to increases in their numbers and capabilities. Because with nuclear weapons sufficiency is easily defined, there is no military reason for reductions in some weapons to result in increases in others. Conventionally, multiparty agreements are hard to arrive at because each party has to consider how shifting alignments may alter the balance of forces if agreements are reached to reduce them. In a world of second-strike nuclear forces, alliances have little effect on the strategic balance. The Soviet Union's failure to insist that British, French, and Chinese forces be counted in strategic arms negotiations may [have reflected] its appreciation of this point. Finally, conventional powers have to compare weapons of uncertain effectiveness. Arms agreements are difficult to reach because their provisions may bear directly on the prospects for victory or defeat. Because in a nuclear world, peace is maintained by the presence of deterrent forces, strategic arms agreements do not have military, but economic and political, significance. They can benefit countries economically and help to improve their relations.

A minority of U.S. military analysts have understood the folly of maintaining more nuclear weapons than deterrence requires. In the [former] Soviet Union, Mikhail Gorbachev and some others . . . put forth the notion of "reasonable sufficiency," defined as having a strategic force roughly equal to ours and able to inflict unacceptable damage in retaliation. [In 1989] Edward Warner [pointed] out that some civilian analysts have gone further, "suggesting that as long as the USSR had a secure second-strike capability that could inflict unacceptable damage, it would not have [had] to be concerned about maintaining approximate numerical parity with U.S. strategic nuclear forces." . . . If leaders in both countries [came] to accept the minority view—and [had they] also [realized] that a deterrent force [would have] greatly [reduced] conventional requirements on central fronts—both countries [could have enjoyed] security at much lower cost.

STRATEGIC DEFENSE

Strategic defenses would radically change the propositions advanced here. The Strategic Defense Initiative, in Reagan's vision, was to provide an area defense that would protect the entire population of the United States. Strategic defenses were to pose an absolute defense against what have been absolute weapons, thus rendering them obsolete. The consequences that would follow from mounting such a defense boggle the mind. That a perfect defense against nuclear weapons could be deployed and sustained is inconceivable.

First, nuclear weapons are small and light; they are easy to move, easy to hide, and easy to deliver in a variety of ways. Even an unimaginably perfect defense against ballistic missiles would fail to negate nuclear weapons. Such a defense would instead put a premium on the other side's ability to deliver nuclear weapons in different ways: firing missiles on depressed trajectories, carrying bombs in suitcases, placing nuclear warheads on freighters to be anchored in American harbors. Indeed, someone has suggested that [a nuclear adversary of the United States] can always hide warheads in bales of marijuana, knowing we cannot keep them from crossing our borders. To have even modestly effective defenses we would, among other things, have to become a police state. We would have to go to extraordinary lengths to police our borders and exercise control within them. Presumably, [a totalitarian state] does these things better than we do. It is impossible to imagine that an area defense can be a success because there are so many ways to thwart it. In no way can we prevent [another nuclear power] from exploding nuclear warheads on or in the United States if it is determined to do so.

Second, let us imagine for a moment that an airtight defense, however defined, is about to be deployed by one country or the other. The closer one country came to deploying such a defense, the harder the other would work to overcome it. When he was secretary of defense, Robert McNamara argued that the appropriate response to a Soviet defensive deployment would be to expand our deterrent force. More recently, Caspar Weinberger and Mikhail Gorbachev . . . made similar statements. Any country deploying a defense effective for a moment cannot expect it to remain so. The ease of delivering nuclear warheads and the destructiveness of small numbers of them make the durability of defenses highly suspect.

The logic of strategic defense is the logic of conventional weaponry. Conventional strategies pit weapons against weapons. That is exactly what a strategic defense would do, thereby recreating the temptations and instabilities that have plagued countries armed only with conventional weapons. If [two enemies] deploy defensive systems, each will worry—no doubt excessively— about the balance of offensive and defensive capabilities. Each will fear that the other may score an offensive or defensive breakthrough. If one side should do so, it might be tempted to strike in order to exploit its temporary advantage. The dreaded specter of the hair trigger would reappear. Under such circumstances a defensive system would serve as the shield that makes the sword useful. An offensive-defensive race would introduce many uncertainties. A country enjoying a momentary defensive advantage would be tempted to strike in the forlorn hope that its defenses would be able to handle a ragged and reduced response to its first strike. [Great-power rivals] would prepare to launch on warning while obsessively weighing the balance between offensive and defensive forces. . . . Strategic considerations should dominate technical ones. In a nuclear world defensive systems are predictably destabilizing. It would be folly to move from a condition of stable deterrence to one of unstable defense.

CONCLUSION

Nuclear weapons dissuade states from going to war more surely than conventional weapons do. In a conventional world, states going to war can at once believe that they may win and that, should they lose, the price of defeat will be bearable. World Wars I and II called the latter belief into question before atomic bombs were ever dropped. If the United States and the [Russian Federation] were now armed only with conventional weapons, the lesson of those wars would be strongly remembered—especially by Russia, since she has suffered more in war than [the United States has]. If the atom had never been split, the United States and [the other great powers] would still have much to fear from each other. The stark opposition of countries of continental size armed with ever-more-destructive conventional weapons would strongly constrain them. Yet in a conventional world even forceful and tragic lessons have proved to be exceedingly difficult for states to learn. Recurrently in modern history one great power or another has looked as though it might become dangerously strong: Louis XIV's and Napolean's France, Wilhelm II's and Hitler's Germany. Each time, an opposing coalition formed, if belatedly, and turned the expansive state back. The lesson would seem to be clear: in international politics, success leads to failure. The excessive accumulation of power by one state or coalition of states elicits the opposition of others. . . .

How can we perpetuate peace without solving the problem of war? This is the question that states with nuclear weapons must constantly answer. Nuclear states continue to compete militarily. With each state tending to its security interests as best it can, war is constantly possible. Although the possibility of war remains, nuclear weapons have drastically reduced the probability of its being fought by the states that have them. Wars that might bring nuclear weapons into play have become extraordinarily hard to start. Over the centuries great powers have fought more wars, and lesser states have fought fewer: the frequency of war has correlated less closely with the attributes of states than with the international standing. Yet because of a profound change in military technology, waging war has more and more become the privilege of poor and weak states. Nuclear weapons have reversed the fates of strong and weak states. Never since the Treaty of Westphalia in 1648, which conventionally marks the beginning of modern history, have great powers enjoyed a longer period of peace than we have known since the Second World War. One can scarcely believe that the presence of nuclear weapons does not greatly help to explain this happy condition.

6

WAR IN THE POST-COLD WAR ERA: STRUCTURAL PERSPECTIVES ON THE CAUSES OF WAR

Jack S. Levy

In this essay Jack S. Levy examines several theories that trace the roots of war to underlying structural forces in the international system. His analysis highlights the differing theoretical perspectives regarding the most important systemic causes of war. Levy is professor of political science at Rutgers University and author of *War in the Modern Great Power System, 1495–1975* (1983).

Although tribes, empires, and states have been fighting wars for millennia, it has become increasingly fashionable to suggest that the end of international warfare is in sight. Many had thought that the development of nuclear weapons and intercontinental delivery systems made war so destructive as to be obsolete as an instrument of national policy, at least for the nuclear powers.[1] Yet the frequency of international war was if anything greater in the period after the devel-

---

[1] Klaus Knorr, *On the Uses of Military Power in the Nuclear Age* (Princeton, N.J.: Princeton University Press, 1966). This is not the first time, however, that leading scholars and intellectuals had forecast the end of war. The belief was widespread before World War I that the economic costs of warfare had become so great that war was no longer a rational instrument of state policy. See Norman Angell, *The Great Illusion* (London: Heinemann, 1914). When World War I had to be fought, it was, at least for Woodrow Wilson and many other Americans, the "war to end all wars." Note also that current forecasts of the end of war do not all give primacy to the development of nuclear weapons. Some observers suggest that conventional weapons systems have themselves become so destructive that the world would be moving toward the obsolescence of great-power warfare even in the absence of the nuclear revolution. See John Mueller, *Retreat from Doomsday: The Obsolescence of War* (New York: Basic Books, 1989).

This essay was written especially for this book.

opment of nuclear weapons than before.[2] There may have been a "long peace" after World War II,[3] but this peace was confined to the great powers while much of the Third World was engulfed in warfare. Even the dangers of nuclear war did not prevent the superpowers from engaging in a costly arms race, intensely competitive behavior at all levels, and occasional international crises which carried considerable risks of escalation to a nuclear catastrophe.[4] Moreover, many argued that the U.S.-Soviet Cold War rivalry directly contributed to higher levels of warfare in the Third World and that many smaller wars were essentially proxy wars to advance the interests of the superpowers.

These and other considerations led many to expect that the end of the Cold War would reduce the frequency of international warfare around the world. Although these hopes were shattered by Iraq's invasion of Kuwait and the ensuing Persian Gulf War, the decisive defeat of Iraq led many to forecast the beginning of a new world order and a generation of peace. This new world order has done little to prevent ethnic cleansing in Bosnia or war among the former Soviet republics, however, and in fact the end of the Cold War has witnessed an increase rather than a decrease in the frequency of international war. Now there are hopes that the dramatic breakthrough in the peace process in the Middle East might end the cycle of violence in at least one critical area of the world. We can all hope that the optimists are right this time, but we should not forget that history has not been kind to forecasts of the end of international warfare.

The areas of the world in which war is most likely to be fought and the types of states which are most likely to fight these wars may have changed, but there is little evidence to suggest that war itself will soon cease to exist as a regular pattern of behavior in world politics. Nor can we dismiss the potential seriousness of these wars, in light of the increasingly sophisticated weapons systems available to many states throughout the world and the real possibility of the proliferation of chemical, biological, and nuclear weapons systems.

Most of us would like to eliminate war or at least to control its destructive consequences, but that requires that we first understand its causes.

Although philosophers, historians, social theorists, and others have been trying to understand why wars occur ever since Thucydides' account of the Peloponnesian War between Athens and Sparta nearly twenty-five centuries ago, no consensus has emerged regarding the answer to this vital question.[5]

---

[2]J. David Singer, "Peace in the Global System: Displacement, Interregnum, or Transformation?" in Charles W. Kegley, Jr., ed., *The Long Postwar Peace* (New York: HarperCollins, 1991), pp. 56–84.

[3]John Gaddis, *The Long Peace* (Oxford: Oxford University Press, 1987); Kegley, *The Long Postwar Peace.*

[4]President Kennedy apparently believed that during the Cuban missile crisis (1962) the chances of a U.S.-Soviet war were about one in three. Graham Allison, *Essence of Decision: Explaining the Cuban Missile Crisis* (Boston: Little, Brown, 1971).

[5]Thucydides, *History of the Peloponnesian War,* trans. by Rex Warner (New York: Penguin, 1954).

Some scholars argue that the underlying causes of war can be found in the structure of power and alliances in the international system or in the way that structure changes over time.[6] Others trace the roots of war to political, economic, social, and psychological factors internal to the nation-state. Immanuel Kant and many liberal theorists argue that liberal democratic regimes are inherently peaceful whereas authoritarian regimes are more warlike.[7] Marxist-Leninists argue that war results primarily from the tendencies of capitalist states to expand in search of external markets, investment opportunities, and raw materials.[8] War has also been traced to attempts by political leaders to solve their internal political problems through the adoption of hostile foreign policies, on the assumption that external conflict will promote internal harmony.[9] Some theorists argue that war results from misperception, the effects of stress on crisis decision making, bureaucratic rigidities, and other flaws in the decision-making process which prevent the selection of those policies that are most likely to advance the national interest.[10] Others insist that decisions for war are based on very careful cost-benefit calculations incorporating interests, constraints, and uncertainties.[11]

Scholars disagree on other things besides the identity of the most important causes of war. Some argue that a single theory (usually their own) explains all wars. Others argue that each war is unique and has a unique set of causes, or that there are several different causal sequences leading to war and that these arise under different and often unpredictable circumstances. Some theorists say that because of the enormous changes from one historical era to the next in military technology and forms of social and political organization, the causes of war have changed over time. Others argue that patterns of international behavior in general and of war in particular have demonstrated a profound continuity over time, and that the causes of war in the nuclear era are no different from the causes of war in the age of Thucydides. These disagreements apply not only to the question of the causes of war in general but also to the question of the causes of particular wars. Historians are nearly as divided regarding the origins of individual wars as political scientists are regarding an explanation for the general phenomenon of war.

---

[6]The leading proponents of a "structural" theory of international politics include Hans Morgenthau, *Politics Among Nations,* 4th ed. (New York: Knopf, 1967) and Kenneth N. Waltz, *Theory of International Politics* (Reading, Mass.: Addison-Wesley, 1979).

[7]Immanuel Kant, "Eternal Peace," in C. J. Friedrich, ed., *The Philosophy of Kant* (New York: Modern Library, 1949).

[8]V. I. Lenin, *Imperialism: The Highest Stage of Capitalism* (New York: International Publishers, 1939).

[9]Jack S. Levy, "The Diversionary Theory of War: A Critique." In Manus I. Midlarsky, ed., *Handbook of War Studies* (London: Unwin-Hyman, 1989), pp. 259–288.

[10]Robert Jervis, *Perception and Misperception in International Politics* (Princeton, N.J.: Princeton University Press, 1976); Richard Ned Lebow, *Between Peace and War* (Baltimore: Johns Hopkins, 1981), chaps. 5–7; Robert Jervis, Richard Ned Lebow, and Janis Gross Stein, *Psychology and Deterrence* (Baltimore: Johns Hopkins, 1985); Jack S. Levy, "Organizational Routines and the Causes of War," *International Studies Quarterly* 30 (June 1986): 193–222.

[11]Bruce Bueno de Mesquita, *The War Trap* (New Haven, Conn.: Yale University Press, 1981).

It will not be possible to examine all of the theories of the causes of war in this essay or to reach a definitive conclusion as to which is most consistent with the historical record.[12] Instead, we will restrict our attention to a few of the more important theories which focus on the underlying structural forces in the international system. These "systemic-level" theories assume that political leaders select those policies which best enable them to achieve their national interests, and that the primary determinants of war are the external constraints and opportunities affecting those foreign policy choices. This essay begins by examining international anarchy, or the absence of a centralized political authority in the world system, which is the most general structural characteristic of that system. It next turns to balance-of-power theory, one of the oldest theories of international relations, and then to power-transition theory, which posits a different set of relationships between the international distribution of power and the behavior of states.

ANARCHY AND THE SECURITY DILEMMA

Whereas in domestic political systems there exists a government with the legitimate authority and the power to regulate the disputes between individual citizens within the state, there is no such institution to regulate disputes between individual states in the international system. In the absence of a higher authority, sovereign states are forced to rely on themselves to provide for their security and other interests, so that each state is the ultimate judge and ultimate protector of its own interests. Force is the final arbiter of disputes, and in this sense wars occur because of the absence of anything to prevent them. States might usually prefer to settle their disputes peacefully; but since it is possible that any state might use force, all others must be prepared to use force or be willing to suffer the consequences of weakness. In such a high-threat environment, the maintenance of a minimal level of security tends to become the primary goal of states, one that must be satisfied before attention can be directed to other goals. The main means by which states provide for their security is the accumulation of military power and economic strength and the formation of alliances. The problem is that power and security tend to be relative rather than absolute. As Jean-Jacques Rousseau once argued,

> The state . . . always feels itself weak if there is another that is stronger. Its security and preservation demand that it make itself more powerful than its neighbors. It can increase, nourish and exercise its power only at their expense. . . . Because the grandeur of the state is purely relative it is forced to compare itself to that of the oth-

---

[12]For more thorough discussions of the causes of war see Geoffrey Blainey, *The Causes of War* (New York: Free Press, 1973); Jack S. Levy, "The Causes of War: A Review of Theories and Evidence," in Philip E. Tetlock, Jo L. Husbands, Robert Jervis, Paul C. Stern, and Charles Tilly, eds., *Behavior, Society, and Nuclear War,* vol. 1 (New York: Oxford University Press, 1989), pp. 209–333; John A. Vasquez, *The War Puzzle* (Cambridge: Cambridge University Press, 1993).

ers. . . . It becomes small or great, weak or strong, according to whether its neighbor expands or contracts, becomes stronger or declines.[13]

Thus there is no natural limit to the pursuit of power and security, and therefore states, and particularly the leading states in the system, engage in a continuous effort to increase or at least maintain their power and influence relative to their rivals. This contributes to the processes leading to war by generating conflicting and sometimes mutually incompatible interests between states. Because a purely fortress defense is not viable, states attempt to maintain an extended defense through the control of territory, resources, strategic areas, and vital sea lanes beyond their own borders. The external defense requirements of two or more states may be in direct conflict, however, and this is particularly likely for contiguous states. The conflict is especially serious if the political authorities of one state believe that their external security requirements include the control over part of the territory within another state, as illustrated by the current Israeli occupation of the Syrian Golan Heights. A related problem is that states often try, if they can, to minimize threats to their security by attempting to influence or even control the internal political processes of other states, especially those on their borders. This often takes the form of attempting to assure the ideological compatibility of adjacent states, as illustrated by the Soviet Union in Eastern Europe during much of the post–World War II era. Intervention in the internal affairs of other states is a major source of conflict between great powers and secondary states, and since the latter have an incentive to secure protection through an alliance with another great power, these conflicts sometimes escalate to great power confrontations. Great powers' perceptions of their security interests tend to expand even further, however, to include the maintenance of a balance of power, which prevents any rival from achieving such a dominant position that it is able to interfere with one's own ability to maintain an extended defense beyond one's borders. These conflicts between the concrete strategic interests of rival states trying to provide for their own security in an anarchic state system have undoubtedly been one of the most important causes of war.

The relativity of security and the continuous pursuit of power would be mitigated if it were possible for statesmen to distinguish between the aggressive and defensive intentions of others and between offensive and defensive weapons systems. But most weapons can serve offensive as well as defensive functions, and most actions of other states are inherently ambiguous. Even if the political leadership of the adversary were fully trusted, there is no guarantee how long they would be in power or that they would necessarily be succeeded by others with equally benign intentions. Given this uncertainty, political leaders prefer to err on the side of safety and to engage in worst-case analysis. They recognize

---

[13]Quoted in Robert Gilpin, *U.S. Power and the Multinational Corporation* (New York: Basic Books, 1975), pp. 34–35.

that false pessimism regarding the adversary's intentions might lead unnecessarily to a further escalation of tensions, but they fear that the consequences of a false optimism would be even worse. Thus even actions that are purely defensive in intent are often perceived as threatening by another state and lead it to take defensive countermeasures, which in turn are perceived as threatening by the first state, and so on. This action-reaction cycle or conflict spiral that often results from sincere attempts to increase one's security without threatening others may in fact decrease the security of oneself as well as one's adversaries. This classic "security dilemma" is extremely important, because it explains how states with primarily defensive motivations can be induced by the structure of the system to take actions that leave all states worse off than before.[14] Under certain conditions, the security dilemma can lead directly to war. If the nature of military technology is such as to give a major advantage to the state that strikes first in a crisis, states can be induced to initiate a preemptive attack even though both states would prefer to avoid war. The origins of World War I, for example, are often traced to the offensive war plans and rapid mobilization schedules that created strong incentives for both Germany and Russia to act preemptively.[15] Similarly, Israel was led by worst-case logic to act preemptively against Egypt in the 1967 war. Thus, while limited political objectives may decrease the likelihood of war, they do not guarantee that war will be avoided.

Although international anarchy and the security dilemma help explain the generally high level of conflict in the international system, they cannot explain the many extended periods of peace. More specific theories are needed to specify the conditions under which the continuous struggle for power and security is most likely to trigger an irreconcilable conflict of vital interests or a conflict spiral, and the conditions under which these escalate to war. Let us now turn to two of these theories.

BALANCE-OF-POWER THEORY

For a variety of reasons, this is not a well-articulated theory but, instead, a weakly integrated collection of propositions regarding the behavior of the leading states in an anarchic international system and the conditions for stability in such a system. Although the key concepts are ambiguous and some of the propositions inconsistent, the "theory" has had a tremendous impact on the study of international relations for the past century. In spite of their disagreements on a number of specific issues, most balance-of-power theorists share a common set of general assumptions: that states define their interests primarily in

---

[14]Robert Jervis, "Cooperation under the Security Dilemma," *World Politics* 30 (January 1978): 167–214.

[15]Steven E. Miller, Sean M. Lynn-Jones, and Stephen Van Evera, eds., *Military Strategy and the Origins of the First World War,* rev. ed. (Princeton, N.J.: Princeton University Press, 1991).

terms of security, that they attempt to maximize their power, and that power is defined mainly in terms of military strength. The primary means by which states increase their power is through the formation of alliances, internal increases in their military capabilities and the economic foundations of military potential, and, if necessary, territorial compensations and the threat or use of military force for intervention or war. The balance-of-power system is said to function effectively or to be "stable" if no single state achieves a dominant position, if the independence of the great powers is assured, and if major wars are avoided, though there is some disagreement regarding the relative importance of these different criteria.[16]

One key proposition on which all balance-of-power theorists agree is that if any single state threatens to achieve a position of "hegemony" from which it could dominate over the other states in the system, a military coalition of nearly all the other great powers will form to block it and a general or "hegemonic war" is likely to follow in order to restore equilibrium to the system. There are several historical cases that appear to fit this hypothesis, including the wars against Philip II of Spain in the late sixteenth century, wars involving Louis XIV of France in the late seventeenth century, the French Revolution and the Napoleonic wars a century later, and the two world wars with Germany in this century. Blocking coalitions are also likely to emerge if one state threatens to establish dominance over a regional system, as illustrated by the response to Saddam Hussein of Iraq in 1990.

This hypothesis regarding anti-hegemonic coalitions is an extension of the common balance-of-power hypothesis that a relatively equal distribution of military capabilities among the great powers is conducive to the avoidance of a major war, whereas the concentration of capabilities tends to be destabilizing. An alternative to this "parity hypothesis" is the "power preponderance" hypothesis, which asserts that parity only tempts aggressors whereas preponderance reinforces deterrence and stability, as illustrated by the periods of peace enforced by ancient Rome and by nineteenth-century Britain. Whereas preponderance theorists argue that war is too risky for weaker states and unnecessary for the dominant state, balance-of-power theorists are more skeptical of the peaceful intentions of dominant states. They believe in the corrupting effects of power and in the tendency for a state's expansionist ambitions to increase along with its strength; therefore they fear the consequences of the absence of countervailing power.

The parity/preponderance question is related to the debate over whether multipolar systems, characterized by several leading great powers, are more stable than bipolar systems, characterized by only two leading powers. In the context of the end of the Cold War, these conflicting hypotheses have generated an

---

[16]Inis L. Claude, Jr., *Power and International Relations* (New York: Random House, 1962); Edward Vose Gulick, *Europe's Classical Balance of Power* (New York: Norton, 1955).

interesting debate about whether the current transformation of the international system from bipolarity to multipolarity will lead to an increase in the instability of the system.[17]

Balance-of-power theorists also emphasize the role of alliances, though they generally make a distinction between relatively permanent peacetime alliances and "ad hoc" alliances. Ad hoc alliances, which form in response to specific threats of aggression or to dangerous shifts in the distribution of power in the system, are necessary to maintain an equilibrium in the system and are considered to be stabilizing. Permanent alliances, on the other hand, are said to be destabilizing because they limit the "flexibility" of the system to respond to threats of aggression by reducing the number of coalitions that might form against a potential aggressor (since some states are already committed). Permanent alliances are particularly destabilizing if they become polarized, creating two rival alliance blocs. These tend to increase tensions, reduce possibilities for compromise because states must defend their allies' interests as well as their own, and increase both the probability of war and of its expansion into a general conflict involving all of the major states. World War I is considered a classic case of the destabilizing effects of a polarized alliance system.[18]

POWER-TRANSITION THEORY

One critic of balance-of-power theory is A. F. K. Organski, who argues that the theory's focus on territory, armaments, and allies as the basis of power and security is too narrow. It ignores the importance of internal development in general and industrialization in particular as a source of the changing military power and potential of states. Organski's power-transition theory emphasizes that industrialization leads to uneven rates of economic growth and therefore to changing distributions of power in the international system, and that these changing power differentials between states have been the primary cause of war between the great powers for the past two centuries. Organski conceives of the international system as consisting of one dominant state at the top of the power hierarchy, a handful of rival great powers directly below, and a number of weaker states. As some great powers begin to grow in strength as a result of industrialization, they become increasingly dissatisfied with the existing international system and their own role in it and wish a share of the benefits and influ-

[17]On the greater stability of multipolar systems, see Morgenthau, chap. 21; Claude, chaps. 2–3. On the stability of bipolarity, particularly when combined with nuclear weapons, see Waltz, chap. 8; Gaddis, *The Long Peace,* chap. 8; John J. Mearsheimer, "Back to the Future: Instability in Europe After the Cold War," *International Security* 15 (Summer 1990): 5–56. See also Charles W. Kegley, Jr., and Gregory A. Raymond, *A Multipolar Peace? Great-Power Politics in the Twenty-first Century* (New York: St. Martin's Press, 1994).

[18]Balance-of-power theorists also suggest other conditions affecting international stability and peace, but those involving the distribution of power in the system and the pattern of alliances are the most important.

ence in the system commensurate with their newly acquired power. They also become an increasing military threat to the dominant state in the system. Organski argues that the likelihood of a major war is highest when the military power of a rising great power begins to approach that of the leading state in the system. The rising but still weaker challenger has an incentive to initiate a war in order to accelerate the power transition and secure the benefits to which it feels entitled by virtue of its military power. The underlying cause of World War I, in this view, was the rise of Germany and its challenge to the dominant position of Britain. It should be noted that in power-transition theory, in contrast to balance-of-power theory, alliances play very little role either as a factor affecting the distribution of power in the system or as a factor in the dynamic processes leading to major war.[19]

One curious element in power-transition theory is the fact that the rising challenger initiates a war against the dominant state while it is still militarily inferior, rather than waiting until the underlying trends in economic and military power thrust it into a stronger position. This has led some scholars to argue that the more likely mechanism by which power transitions lead to war is the initiation of a "preventive war" by the dominant state in a desperate attempt to block or retard the rise of the challenger before it is surpassed in strength. The declining leader has an incentive to fight a war now rather than risk a war under worsening circumstances later. Robert Gilpin suggests that preventive war is often perceived as the best option by a leading state in decline, and numerous historical cases have been interpreted as preventive wars. Many have argued that World War I was an attempt by Germany to secure its position before an increasingly powerful Russia had achieved a position of equality with Germany (which the latter expected to happen by 1917).[20]

Regardless of who initiates the war, differential rates of growth and the power transition are important phenomena in international relations. It is not necessary, however, to restrict the scope of the theory to the modern industrial era, as Organski does. In fact, Thucydides argued with respect to the Peloponnesian War that "What made war inevitable was the growth of Athenian power and the fear which this caused in Sparta," suggesting that differential rates of growth, power transitions, and preventive war were important long before the industrial revolution. Several scholars have elaborated on the power-transition model and integrated it into more general theories of world politics. Gilpin has analyzed the general economic, social, and political dynamics contributing to

[19]A. F. K. Organski, *World Politics,* 2nd ed. (New York: Knopf, 1968), chaps. 11–12; A. F. K. Organski and Jacek Kugler, *The War Ledger* (Chicago: University of Chicago Press, 1980), chap 1.

[20]Robert Gilpin, *War and Change in World Politics* (Cambridge, Eng.: Cambridge University Press, 1981), p. 191; Jack S. Levy, "Declining Power and the Preventive Motivation for War," *World Politics* 40 (October 1987): 82–107. On the preventive motivation in World War I, see Jack S. Levy, "Preferences, Constraints, and Choices in July 1914," *International Security* 15 (Winter 1990–91): 151–86.

hegemonic wars and transitions in any historical era, and Paul Kennedy has provided a detailed historical analysis of the rise and fall of great powers since 1500. Modelski and Thompson have developed a theory of long cycles of global leadership, global war, and leadership succession in world politics over the last five hundred years, based on naval power (combined with air power in the twentieth century) and the economic strength that supports it.[21]

IMPLICATIONS FOR THE FUTURE OF WAR

This essay has focused on a particular type of causes of war: the structure of power at the level of the international system, how that power is distributed among the various states in the system, and how that distribution changes over time. Although these structural theories were originally developed to explain the behavior of the great powers in international politics, we should not underestimate their applicability to other states as well. Theories of balance of power and power transition apply not only at the level of the international system but also at the level of regional systems which operate within the larger international system. Thucydides' comment about Sparta's fear of the rising power of Athens applies equally well to Israel's decision to launch a preventive strike against Iraq's nuclear reactor in 1981 in order to block the rising power of Iraq. It applies also to the United States in the Persian Gulf War, in that American concerns about Iraq's development of a biological and nuclear capability and its consequences for the regional balance of power and the security of world oil supplies contributed significantly to its decision to go to war to expel Iraq from Kuwait and in the process destroy much of Iraq's growing military capability.

Balance-of-power calculations also played a central role in the foreign policy decisions of Arab states. Many of these states aligned (diplomatically and economically) with Iraq in the Iran-Iraq War of 1980–88 because they perceived the primary threat to their interests as deriving from Iran and from Iranian efforts to spread its revolutionary doctrines throughout the Persian Gulf region (much like the European great powers formed a military coalition against revolutionary France in 1792). With the end of that war and the growth of Iraqi power, however, all the major Arab states except Jordan (and the PLO) shifted their alignments and joined a military coalition against Iraq in order to contain the growing Iraqi threat, even if it meant that they had implicitly aligned with their hated Israeli enemy.

[21]Thucydides, p. 49; Gilpin (1981); Paul Kennedy, *The Rise and Fall of the Great Powers* (New York: Random House, 1987); George Modelski, "The Long Cycle of Global Politics and the Nation-State." *Comparative Studies in Society and History* 20 (April 1978): 214–35; William R. Thompson, *On Global War* (Columbia: University of South Carolina Press, 1988). For a summary and critique of various theories of hegemonic transitions and hegemonic wars, see Jack S. Levy, "Long Cycles, Hegemonic Transitions, and the Long Peace," in Kegley, *The Long Postwar Peace,* pp. 147–76.

The politics of regional systems can also be directly affected by shifts in military power at the global level. The end of the Cold War has had a profound impact on the Middle East, for example. If Iraq had invaded Kuwait several years earlier, at a time when Soviet power rivaled that of the United States and when both superpowers competed for influence in the Middle East, it is extremely unlikely that the United States would have intervened with military force to expel Iraq from Kuwait, for fear of a provoking a direct military confrontation with the Soviet Union.[22]

The end of the Cold War and the diplomatic realignment in the Middle East in the aftermath of the Persian Gulf War also contributed significantly to the breakthrough in the peace process involving Israel and the PLO and other Arab states. These developments deprived the PLO of its major sources of economic support, and a weakened PLO needed a dramatic action in order to restore its diminishing influence in Middle Eastern and Palestinian politics. Similarly, Arab states such as Syria could no longer threaten war against Israel in the absence of a superpower backer whose protection might limit their losses in worst-case war scenarios by deterring Israeli escalation.

One cannot deny that there have been fundamental changes in international politics as a result of the enormous technological, social, economic, and political changes in the world in the past half century in general and the past half decade in particular. At the same time, however, it is clear that the changing structures of power in international and regional systems that have influenced decisions for war or peace so often in the past will continue to play a central role in such decisions in the future.

---

[22]Admittedly, it is less likely that Iraq would have invaded Kuwait under such conditions. A more powerful Soviet Union would have helped ease the desperate economic conditions which largely drove Saddam's aggressive policies, and Soviet fears of a confrontation with the United States would have led it to put pressures on Saddam for military restraint. In addition, a viable Soviet balancer against what Saddam perceived as the unmitigated and unconstrained hostility of the United States would have further reduced Saddam's sense of desperation about the future. See Lawrence Freedman and Efraim Karsh, *The Gulf Conflict, 1990–91* (Princeton, N.J.: Princeton University Press, 1993).

7

WHAT SHOULD BE DONE WITH NUCLEAR ARSENALS? DISARMAMENT AND WEAPONS PROLIFERATION

Michael Renner

Surveying recent progress in negotiated disarmament agreements, Michael Renner summarizes the reasons why further reductions in nuclear arsenals are in the security interests of the international community. He also considers the steps needed to sustain the disarmament process. Renner is a senior researcher at the WorldWatch Institute. He is the author of *Jobs in a Sustainable Economy* (1991).

In late 1981, Secretary of State Alexander Haig declared in Congressional hearings that the U.S. government was considering, if need be, the firing of nuclear "demonstration" shots to deter Soviet aggression against Western Europe. Amid unmistakable signs that East-West antagonism was rising to a new fever pitch, the statement helped trigger massive peace demonstrations in cities across North America and Western Europe.

Since then, the nuclear issue has receded remarkably, and demonstrators' energies have turned to other concerns. A nuclear holocaust is as unlikely today as it seemed imminent a decade ago. The Cold War rivalry has been buried. Instead of adding missiles and warheads, the U.S. and the remnants of the former Soviet Union are withdrawing large numbers of them. The conventional wisdom is that, with this historic reversal, people can begin to relax a little; the world has become a far safer place.

Reprinted from *USA Today* magazine, January 1994, copyright 1994 by the Society for the Advancement of Education.

Yet, the laying down of arms is a tricky process, and too much relaxing of scrutiny at this unprecedented juncture could be a mistake. As the demand for disarmament finds its way from banners and leaflets to government documents, the manner in which it is to be accomplished is crucial. Missiles are being scrapped, submarines decommissioned, and bombers mothballed, but the fate of the dangerous materials contained in nuclear warheads—plutonium and highly enriched uranium—remains to be decided. That fate is critical to the success of nuclear disarmament because such materials can not simply be destroyed. They can be recycled into new warheads, used as fuel for nuclear power plants, diverted into the hands of rogue nations, or stored and guarded, but whatever is done with them entails costs and risks. Yet, none of the treaties between the U.S. and the former Soviet Union even address these details. The other nuclear powers, both declared and undeclared, are not even in on the discussion.

To minimize any risk of current disarmament measures being reversed or abused, the nuclear powers will need to devise ways to implement a number of difficult, risky, and politically charged steps beyond merely deciding to scale down their arsenals. As these steps are taken, much of their effectiveness may be affected by public attitudes toward a longer-range question: Once arsenals are much smaller, can the nuclear powers plan to go to zero? A commitment by the nuclear "haves" to work toward the eventual elimination of *all* nuclear weapons would provide them with a legitimacy they now lack in confronting ominous proliferation trends.

The magnitude of the change now under way—and of the perils and opportunities that it entails—is impossible to appreciate without recognizing the incredible virulence with which the Cold War rivalries drove policies and built arsenals for 40 years. From the start of the nuclear age, the number of warheads grew rapidly, virtually unconstrained by arms control treaties. At its peak in 1988, the global stockpile included almost 25,000 strategic warheads and 35,000 tactical warheads, with the U.S. and the U.S.S.R. controlling more than 95%. The explosive power amassed was roughly 1,000 times the firepower used in all wars since the introduction of gunpowder six centuries ago, according to Ruth Sivard, author of the annual *World Military and Social Expenditures.*

The seemingly endless growth of the nuclear stockpile sputtered to a sudden halt when the Cold War ended—coinciding with rising budgetary constraints and the revelation of pervasive health and safety problems in the superpowers' weapons-production complexes. The 1987 Intermediate-Range Nuclear Force Treaty, eliminating U.S. and Soviet intermediate-range missiles, resulted in the first small, but real, reductions in the deployed arsenals. The 1991 Strategic Arms Reductions Talks (START) Treaty then aimed to reduce the number of strategic warheads (those with intercontinental range) by several thousand.

Fears that the disintegration of the Soviet Union might set off a wave of nuclear proliferation led to much deeper cutbacks undertaken outside the framework of formal arms negotiations. In late 1991 and early 1992, Presidents

George Bush, Mikhail Gorbachev, and Boris Yeltsin each announced unilateral cuts in existing weapons and proposed additional measures to be implemented if reciprocated by the other side.

As a result, the combined stockpiles of the U.S. and Russia (principal heir to the Soviet arsenal) will decline from 57,000 nuclear warheads in 1988 to an estimated 12,000 over the next decade or so, indicates Robert Norris, a senior scientist with the Natural Resources Defense Council. The U.S. and the Commonwealth of Independent States already have reduced the total number of nuclear weapons they deploy by about half. Great Britain, France, and China still are building theirs, but have offered some token measures of restraint; their combined total is projected to grow from about 1,500 warheads to 2,000 within the next few years.

The global stockpile thus is set for a dramatic drop, but there's a rub—the remaining weapons still contain more than enough firepower to annihilate all life on Earth. Although none of the nuclear powers is contemplating the eventual abolition of nuclear weapons, there are strong reasons to consider just such a goal. As long as even small numbers of super-weapons remain in the hands of a few countries, it may be impossible to dissuade other nations from coveting them.

A PROGRAM FOR NIXING NUKES

To proceed with even the planned levels of nuclear disarmament, governments need assurances that no cheating will take place. As long as former enemies deploy tens of thousands of warheads, it matters relatively little if some of them remain concealed. As arsenals shrink, though, it becomes more and more important to have some way of inspecting and verifying each other's activity. If the current round of reductions is accompanied by international safeguards, the world community may gain some of the confidence necessary to go even further—to zero.

Yet, nuclear disarmament isn't simply a matter of dismantling bombs. It will require shutting down test sites; closing the still-numerous facilities making weapons-grade material, warheads, and delivery systems; converting weapons design labs to civilian use; dismantling existing warheads; placing fissionable materials under international safeguards; and devising solutions for their long-term disposal. For all of these steps, it is essential to establish effective inspection and verification measures to monitor compliance.

The clearest signal that the nuclear arms race really is over would be a comprehensive test ban. As long as testing proceeds, numerical limits on weapons may be offset by qualitative advances. Some headway has been made. From as many as 58 in 1984, the number of test explosions declined considerably—to 14 in 1991 and an estimated seven or eight in 1992.

Shortly before its dissolution, the Soviet Union was forced by a strong grassroots movement to close its major test ground near Semipalatinsk, Kazakhstan.

Russia, which has a test site on the Arctic island of Novaya Zemlya, is observing a unilateral testing moratorium. France, too, has suspended its testing. However, both countries have warned that they will resume if the U.S. continues to reject a test ban. While President Bush had wanted to continue testing indefinitely, Congress forced him to accept new limits and an eventual ban.

Ending the nuclear era requires a ban not only on testing bombs, but on manufacturing warheads and weapons-grade materials. Here, too, there has been some progress. In the late 1980s, the U.S. government had the capacity to produce or modify some 3,500-4,000 warheads per year. Since July, 1990, though, no nuclear warheads have been manufactured and none are scheduled. Awash in stockpiled fissionable materials in the 1960s and overwhelmed by safety and environmental problems at its production complex in recent years, the U.S. stopped producing highly enriched uranium (HEU) in 1964 and plutonium in 1988.

The Soviet Union stopped making HEU in 1990. Plutonium production, currently continuing at three Russian reactors, is being phased out. Kazakhstan and Ukraine have inherited nuclear-armed missiles from the Soviet Union, but have no production facilities for fissionable materials. A formalized U.S.-Russian cutoff likely would increase the pressure on Britain, France, and China—and the nuclear "threshold" countries of Israel, India, Pakistan, and South Africa—to join in. Yeltsin has endorsed the idea, but the U.S. has continued to oppose a permanent production ban.

Even if not one gram of plutonium ever is produced again, the staggering amounts of fissionable materials still existing will need close scrutiny. Between them, the U.S. and the former Soviet Union possess more than 200 tons of weapons-grade plutonium and over 1,000 tons of HEU, either assembled in warheads or held in storage. (By comparison, there are 120 tons of separated plutonium in the civilian nuclear industry worldwide.)

Existing arms treaties say nothing about what to do—or what not to do—with the withdrawn warheads and the fissionable materials contained in them. Both the U.S. and Russia apparently have decided to dismantle most of them, rather than leave them intact and simply store them. To complete the job over the next decade, the U.S. government will be taking apart 2,000 warheads a year at its Pantex facility in Texas. Russia reportedly has the capacity to dismantle up to 6,000 warheads per year.

Still, the two governments do not appear to be equally willing to conduct the dismantling operations in a verifiable and irreversible manner. Russia had agreed not to recycle fissionable materials recovered from dismantled warheads into new weapons. Yet, *Disposition of Separated Plutonium,* a report by Princeton University's Center for Energy and Environmental Studies, explains that Washington refuses "to discuss bilateral safeguards . . . because it is unwilling to permit reciprocal inspections at U.S. sites."

With tens of thousands of warheads destined for withdrawal, the need for a stringent system to account for weapons-grade materials—to prevent their clandestine diversion or theft—is self-evident. With such a system, the U.S. and Russia—as the leading nuclear weapon states and the ones now committed to slashing their arsenals—could begin to build a framework for true nuclear disarmament. Once their stockpiles are closer in size to those of the other "haves," France, Britain, China, and Kazakhstan can be invited to join the former superpowers in cutting back still further. Finally, all of the threshold countries—those possessing undeclared nuclear weapons or technically capable of acquiring them—need to be brought into the process.

If a verification system is to be effective, it first must establish a detailed inventory of the types, quantities, and specific locations of all weapons-grade materials, whether deployed or in storage. The list also should include all production reactors, reprocessing and uranium enrichment plants, and other nuclear fuel-cycle facilities. (The exact number of the warheads and amounts of fissionable materials held by the nuclear powers remain tightly guarded secrets.) This can be done by an exchange of relevant data, to be verified by thorough on-site and remote inspections. To generate confidence among all participants that nuclear disarmament will enhance, not imperil, their security, all relevant material needs to be accounted for. Verification methods are likely to be highly intrusive.

Because the arsenals are so enormous, the actual dismantling of weapons will take many years. However, technicians could render the warheads inoperable much faster—for instance, by removing the batteries and other energy sources required for the weapons to function. Once disabled, warheads could be tagged electronically and sealed in tamper-proof containers to await disassembly. The disabling and dismantling operations, plus the subsequent removal of plutonium and HEU from military control, would take place under international safeguards. Through continuous on-site monitoring of declared facilities, augmented by challenge inspections at any suspect sites, inspectors would assure that the making of weapons does not start up again.

Inspections ideally would be conducted by an international agency. The International Atomic Energy Agency could play that role if its budget and staff were sufficiently enlarged. However, because the IAEA has a potential conflict of interest in its role as drumbeater for the civilian nuclear industry, the inspection tasks better might be entrusted to a separate, yet-to-be created, agency.

Verification usually depends on such means as satellite surveillance or inspection by teams of highly trained individuals. It would be useful to supplement these measures with "citizen inspection"—encouraging those who might have relevant knowledge to report any attempted violation of bans on nuclear weapons activities to the international inspection agency. This encouragement also would require providing international protection for such whistleblowers.

Despite the heavily guarded and secretive nature of modern weapons systems, a whistleblower provision could be effective. Seymour Melman, professor emeritus of industrial engineering at Columbia University, has pointed out that to produce such systems clandestinely requires the collaboration of many thousands of people. Even repressive governments can not take for granted that, with secrets spread so widely, word won't be leaked—as happened in Iraq, when several defectors helped UN inspectors unearth secret nuclear weapons facilities.

WHITHER PLUTONIUM?

Once nuclear weapons are dismantled, crucial questions remain: What should be done with the huge stocks of plutonium and highly enriched uranium? How should these extremely dangerous, yet virtually indestructible, substances be disposed of?

To be at all effective, the chosen method of disposal will have to be one that makes it difficult or impossible to steal or divert the fissionable materials back into new weapons. It also will have to meet at least minimum safety and environmental standards, as well as be affordable and verifiable.

In the short run, the simplest approach is to put the condemned materials into monitored storage, most likely at former production facilities. Storage is highly verifiable and relatively cheap. It does not, however, erect much of a barrier to military re-use if the government owning the materials so decides. In the long term, a different solution will be needed.

Weapons-grade uranium can be stored short term either in highly enriched or diluted form. Plutonium can be converted from metallic form into a more stable oxide substance. There are some environmental risks associated with this conversion process, but the advantage is that plutonium oxide is unsuitable for weapons use. Russia, though, has the capacity to oxidize only about one-quarter of the plutonium likely to be recovered annually from dismantled warheads. Currently, both the U.S. and Russia plan to store their plutonium in metal form.

The question of longer-term disposal of nuclear weapons is more troubling— and complicated. The most feasible of the proposed solutions include recycling HEU as nuclear reactor fuel and locking up plutonium glass blocks.

A 1990 study prepared by the Pacific Northwest Laboratory for the Department of Energy endorsed blending HEU with depleted or natural uranium, in effect diluting it from weapons-grade enrichments of 90 to 95% to below five percent, thus making it usable as commercial nuclear reactor fuel. Princeton University's Center for Energy and Environmental Studies estimates that existing stocks of HEU would be sufficient to fuel the world's nuclear power reactors for about two years. However, while the uranium no longer would be directly available for military purposes, burning it in reactors would generate another form of long-lived radioactive waste. Furthermore, it still is possible to extract plutonium from the spent reactor fuel.

The Russian government, desperate to earn hard currency, is exploring ways to export diluted HEU. Two U.S. companies have shown interest in purchasing 11 tons of HEU per year, enough to run about 10 commercial nuclear reactors. President Bush announced in September, 1992, that the U.S. would negotiate a contract to buy additional quantities—some 500 tons over the next 20 years.

For those who are concerned about the dangers of nuclear power, this announcement raises worries that demilitarizing the atom might come at the price of giving the civilian nuclear power industry a shot in the arm. While it is true that cheap sales of Russian uranium may provide Western utilities with a windfall, the prospect has set off alarm bells in the U.S. uranium and enrichment industries, which fear their market could be flooded and prices further depressed. Over all, the military uranium seems too small a factor to make or break the industry. Furthermore, a decision *not* to utilize diluted HEU only would result in the mining and processing of additional civilian uranium—entailing greater environmental damage than the use of HEU.

For plutonium, none of the options being discussed appear to offer an entirely satisfactory solution. For technical, environmental, financial, or political reasons, getting rid of the plutonium by such methods as exploding it underground, blasting it into the sun or solar orbit, burying it below the seabed, using it to feed breeder reactors, or transmuting it in accelerators either are unacceptable or unrealistic. Two other options are being given serious consideration.

First, plutonium oxide could be mixed with uranium and used to fuel commercial nuclear reactors. Existing capacities to fabricate so-called mixed oxide (MOX) fuel are limited, though. Even more formidable are the obstacles to using MOX fuel in reactors. Given high economic, regulatory, and political hurdles, utilities in the U.S. (and increasingly in Western Europe and Japan) are reluctant to use plutonium fuel. Russia's Ministry of Atomic Power and Industry has expressed interest in utilizing plutonium either in breeder reactors or conventional power reactors, but appears to be ill-equipped technically and economically to move ahead. MOX fuel fabrication also is controversial on safety and environmental grounds since its use in nuclear reactors generates some long-lived fission products. It also is possible, by reprocessing the spent fuel, to extract the plutonium yet again, making it potentially available for future weapons purposes.

The second—and perhaps best—option for plutonium may be to "glassify" it by mixing the plutonium oxide with liquid high-level radioactive waste and then solidifying the blend into ceramic or glass blocks for burial deep underground. Alternatively, the plutonium can be glassified without the waste.

That may not be a final answer, since neither this nor any other known solution is completely safe from sabotage and other disturbances. Still, glassification makes plutonium retrieval for weapons use nearly impossible—and also means the material is less likely to leach. U.S. facilities to vitrify military high-level wastes are sizable enough to accommodate all U.S. weapons plutonium.

TO ABOLISH OR NOT?

. . . Many strategists embrace the concept of minimal deterrence, which posits that, as nuclear arsenals are cut back, enough warheads will be retained so that any enemy still will be deterred from launching an attack. Depending on the analysts' assumptions, minimal deterrence could be achieved by retaining anywhere from a few dozen to a few thousand warheads.

It is understandable that governments and publics reared on the notion that nuclear weapons have kept the peace are reluctant to forsake their possession—to turn "nuclear-naked," as a *New York Times* editorial put it a few years ago. The countries now controlling nuclear arms obviously are not yet ready to renounce their ownership. The notion of nuclear abolition still seems utopian, but arguments for retaining nuclear arms indefinitely are not very convincing. It is difficult, for instance, to assume that Russia needs to be deterred when its leaders are suing for peace and pleading for Western economic assistance. However, what about governments that remain hostile and aggressive?

In the wake of Desert Storm, UN inspection teams brought to light a clandestine Iraqi nuclear weapons development program of surprising magnitude. The revelations might have seemed to underscore the need for a residual nuclear arsenal to deter Saddam Hussein and other dictators. Yet, in retrospect, the possession of atomic arms by the U.S. and other powers did nothing to deter Saddam from trying to acquire his own nuclear weapons; in fact, it may have spurred the Iraqi effort. Without doubt, Iraq was motivated to catch up with its arch-adversary, Israel—which widely is believed to possess a number of nuclear warheads.

Likewise, in other regions of the world, nations locked in intense rivalries with their neighbors—such as India and Pakistan or the two Koreas—seek to cross the nuclear threshold in the belief that weapons of mass destruction provide insurance against defeat in a conventional battle. Yet, should anyone welcome the spread of nuclear capabilities in the forlorn hope that a generalized balance of terror might snuff out conventional warfare? There is, of course, no guarantee that a nuclear standoff between any set of nations would not turn violent; one only needs to recall how perilously close the U.S. and the Soviet Union came to the nuclear abyss during the 1962 Cuban missile crisis.

The continued possession of nuclear weapons by a few countries—even small numbers—perpetuates the idea that they constitute a legitimate instrument for national defense. In doing so, it lends legitimacy to other countries' efforts to acquire them. As long as possession of a nuclear arsenal is perceived to have political or military value, conferring special status and diplomatic leverage, it is inevitable that other governments will continue their attempts to join the club.

Indeed, the future of the Nuclear Non-Proliferation Treaty (NPT) looks clouded. In this global covenant, the "have-nots" agreed to forgo possession of nuclear arms in return for a commitment from the "haves" to move seriously toward disarmament. As dramatic as the cuts pledged would seem, they still only would return strategic warhead numbers to the level they were at when the NPT was signed in 1968. The "have-nots" showed some resentment when the superpowers quadrupled their arsenals in two decades *after* the signing, and that resentment persists. An international conference is to decide in 1995 whether and under what conditions to extend the Non-Proliferation Treaty.

Those who are skeptical about the prospects for abolition sometimes recite the adage that the nuclear genie, once out of the bottle, can't be put back—or that "nuclear weapons can not be uninvented." Nevertheless, such arsenals don't have to be uninvented to be repudiated as a legitimate instrument in the conduct of human affairs. Societies are quite capable of electing *not* to acquire weapons they are technically capable of producing. That already is evident in the strides made toward banishing chemical and biological weapons.

As the world backs away from the nuclear threat that has loomed over all human affairs for the past half-century, the reduction of arsenals now under way has epochal importance. However, it will be the *next* step—from very small arsenals to complete elimination—that is the most critical.

To accomplish that final step may require a transitional strategy. A residual stockpile of warheads or weapons-grade materials may have to be retained, under international safeguards, yet still under physical control of the nation that owns the weapons. It would be possible to reverse this step if warranted—by the discovery, for instance, that another country has retained or built a clandestine arsenal. This possibility of reversal could make the prospect of complete disarmament a little less daunting, allowing the world community to become comfortable with the process of disarmament. As confidence grows and people find they need not depend on the availability of doomsday weapons to feel secure, governments can move toward rendering the sequestered warheads unusable for military purposes.

While the rationale for the doomsday arsenals largely has evaporated, the mindset that created them continues to resist fundamental change. Seeing itself as the winner of the Cold War confrontation, Washington does not want to be encumbered by international agreements converting the *de facto* halt in nuclear weapons development into formal and binding constraints. U.S. officials have rejected a comprehensive test ban treaty, refused to dismantle warheads in a verifiable manner, and insisted on retaining the right to "recycle" fissionable materials from dismantled warheads.

These policies, rationalized in the name of national security, well may backfire. In the absence of international treaties curtailing or banning nuclear weapons activities, the U.S. preserves its freedom of action—but so do other governments. The threat of proliferation hardly has been put to rest. In the future, Russia easily could become less cooperative and accommodating. A window of opportunity has opened unexpectedly, but it may close again just as rapidly.

The issues at hand may seem to be of a nature best left up to the experts, but nuclear weapons policy is too grave a matter to delegate to a national security priesthood. Just as public pressure was instrumental in getting governments back to the negotiating table during the Cold War, such pressure is crucial to keeping up the momentum of the first, tentative movements toward nuclear sanity. If the public's complacency about nuclear issues in the post-Cold War era persists, the real purposes behind dismantling thousands of warheads never may be realized.

8

CONTROLLING THE GLOBAL TRADE IN ARMS

Michael T. Klare

International arms transfers affect considerably the distribution of military power and the prospects for regional and global security. In this essay Michael T. Klare reviews recent trends in the global arms trade and its consequences. Noting that the trade continues to accelerate in the aftermath of the Cold War, Klare outlines the policies and programs available to bring this problem under control. Klare is professor of peace and world security studies at Hampshire College. He is co-editor (with Daniel C. Thomas) of *World Security: Challenges for a New Century* (1994).

The Persian Gulf conflict of 1991 and the many subsequent revelations regarding Iraq's clandestine weapons programs have focused an unprecedented degree of world attention on the problem of arms proliferation. Most of this attention has been focused on issues arising from the proliferation of *unconventional* weapons—nuclear, chemical, and biological munitions—and the missiles used to deliver them. But the Gulf war also called attention to problems arising from the proliferation of *conventional* weapons—the tanks, guns, planes, bombs, and missiles that constitute the basic instruments of warfare. Long neglected by policy makers and arms control experts, the trade in conventional arms has emerged as a major security concern in the troubled environment of the post-Cold War era. Because the ethnic and regional conflicts now plaguing many

This essay was written especially for this book.

parts of the world are fueled largely by conventional weapons, it is apparent that any long-term progress toward regional peace and stability will require curbs on the global trade in arms.[1]

Controlling the conventional arms trade is essential for several key reasons. First, the military might of likely regional aggressors is composed largely of modern conventional weapons acquired through international sales channels. Of course, the possession of ballistic missiles and weapons of mass destruction by these states also poses a significant risk to regional and international security, and must therefore be a matter of concern. But Iraq did not use its missiles to seize and occupy Kuwait—such aggressive moves can only be conducted by conventional forces. Thus, if we are to diminish the threat of regional conflict and aggression, we must seek to limit and shrink the conventional arsenals of potential belligerents.

Second, there is a close relationship between conventional arms transfers and the risk of nuclear and chemical escalation in regional conflicts. It is precisely because so many Third World countries have acquired large quantities of modern conventional weapons that some among them have *also* acquired unconventional weapons, as a hedge and a deterrent. Should any of these rising powers face catastrophic defeat in some future *conventional* conflict with their rivals, they are certain to consider the actual use of their unconventional munitions; indeed, this is the *most* likely way in which a regional nuclear war might erupt in the post-Cold War era.

Third, the diffusion of conventional arms-making technology is proceeding even more rapidly than the spread of nuclear, chemical, and missile technology. Approximately forty Third World countries now manufacture small arms and light artillery, while fifteen or so produce modern tanks, aircraft, ships, and missiles. The roster of Third World arms producers is likely to grow substantially in the years ahead, and those nations with existing arms facilities are likely to increase the quantity and sophistication of their output. Many of these countries, moreover, have entered the arms trade as suppliers, thus further contributing to the global glut of conventional weapons.[2]

Fourth, the growth in conventional arms sales to the states of the Third World is being accompanied by—and contributes to—a growing black-market trade with insurgents, terrorists, separatist groups, and other non-state entities. No matter how rigorous U.S. export controls and those of its allies, it is virtually inevitable that a certain percentage of state-to-state military transfers leak into the black-market arms trade; with the growing privatization of weapons produc-

---

[1]The author first developed this analysis in a number of earlier essays, including: "Who's Arming Who? The Arms Trade in the 1990s," *Technology Review,* May–June 1990, pp. 42–50; and "Controlling the Trade in Conventional Weapons," *Transnational Law and Contemporary Problems,* Vol. 2, no. 2 (Fall 1992), pp. 493–515.

[2]For discussion, see U.S. Congress, Office of Technology Assessment (OTA), *Global Arms Trade* (Washington, D.C.: OTA, 1991), esp. chaps. 2, 7–11.

tion in both East and West and with the breakdown in central control over arms exports in the former Soviet Union, this leakage appears to be growing larger all the time.[3]

For all these reasons, it should be apparent that uncontrolled arms sales represent a very significant threat to international stability. If there was any question about this before 1990, the Iraqi invasion of Kuwait and the subsequent crisis in the Persian Gulf should have dispelled any doubts about the matter.

THE IRAQI ARMS BUILDUP AND ITS AFTERMATH

Between 1980 and 1990, Iraq conducted one of the most ambitious buildups of conventional weapons ever undertaken by a Third World country. Between 1983 and 1990 alone, Iraq ordered $30.5 billion worth of imported weaponry from the major suppliers,[4] much of it consisting of advanced aircraft, missiles, tanks, and artillery systems.[5] By the summer of 1990, the Iraqis possessed one of the largest and most advanced military arsenals in the world, and this undoubtedly helps account for the sheer brazenness with which Saddam Hussein ordered the attack on Kuwait. In addition, the evident ease with which Hussein was able to acquire sophisticated arms and military technology from the major suppliers—all of which, except for the United States, sold arms to Baghdad in the 1980s—must have persuaded him that the major powers had no real objection to his barely concealed hegemonic aspirations.[6]

In the wake of this conflict, President George Bush and his senior advisers acknowledged the threat posed by unconstrained arms sales and affirmed the need for new arms trade controls. "The time has come," Secretary of State James Baker told the House Foreign Affairs Committee on February 6, 1991, "to try to change the destructive pattern of military competition and proliferation in [the Middle East] and to reduce the arms flow into an area that is already over-militarized."[7] Similar remarks were made by the leaders of other arms-supplying states, including presidents François Mitterrand of France and Mikhail Gorbachev of the Soviet Union.

---

[3]For background on the black-market arms trade, see Klare, "The Thriving Black Market for Weapons," *Bulletin of the Atomic Scientists,* April 1988, pp. 16–24; Edward J. Laurence, "The New Gunrunning," *Orbis,* Spring 1989, pp. 225–237.

[4]Richard F. Grimmett, *Conventional Arms Transfers to the Third World, 1983–1990* (Washington, D.C.: Congressional Research Service, U.S. Library of Congress, 1991), p. 54. (Hereinafter cited as Grimmett, *Arms Transfers 83–90.*)

[5]For data on specific Iraqi arms acquisitions, see Stockholm International Peace Research Institute (SIPRI), *SIPRI Yearbook 1990: World Armaments and Disarmament* (Oxford: Oxford University Press, 1991), pp. 280–282. (Hereinafter cited as SIPRI, *SIPRI Yearbook 1990.*)

[6]For discussion of Iraq's arms purchases and the role of Western governments in satisfying Baghdad's military needs, see Kenneth R. Timmerman, *The Death Lobby: How the West Armed Iraq* (Boston: Houghton Mifflin, 1991).

[7]Opening Statement by Secretary of State James Baker before the House Foreign Affairs Committee, Washington, D.C., February 6, 1991 (mimeo).

Sensing an opportunity to make progress on this issue, Bush called for meetings of the five permanent members (P-5) of the UN Security Council—the United States, Russia, Britain, France, and China—to consider the adoption of mutual guidelines for the control of conventional arms transfers. Bush's proposal was accepted by the other governments involved, and, on July 8–9, 1991, representatives of the P-5 states met in Paris to discuss proposals for conventional arms transfer restraint. In a communique issued at the conclusion of the meeting, the five states acknowledged that "indiscriminate transfers of military weapons and technology contribute to regional instability," and, in consequence, declared that "they are fully conscious of the special responsibilities that are incumbent upon them [as major suppliers] to ensure that such risks be avoided."[8]

In accordance with the July 9 communique, representatives of the P-5 states continued to meet over the summer and early fall and, at a meeting held in London on October 17–18, 1991, adopted a set of draft guidelines for the control of conventional arms transfers. In adopting the London document, the P-5 nations promised to consult with one another regarding the flow of arms to particular regions and to "observe rules of restraint" when deciding on major arms export transactions. They further pledged to avoid arms transfers that would be likely to (a) prolong or aggravate an existing armed conflict; (b) increase tension in a region or contribute to regional instability; and (c) introduce destabilizing military capabilities in a region.[9]

The adoption of these draft guidelines suggested a strong commitment by the United States and the other major arms suppliers to the principle of conventional arms transfer restraint. However, in subsequent negotiations, the P-5 states were unable to agree on specific, concrete measures to implement these guidelines. Several meetings were held in the winter and spring of 1992 to bridge the differences between the various parties, but all to no avail; the meetings were suspended in the fall of 1992 and have not been resumed since.

While these negotiations were proceeding, the major arms suppliers continued to seek customers for their weapons in major Third World markets—especially the Middle East and East Asia, where the demand for modern arms has remained strong. Since 1991, the United States has sold large quantities of arms to Egypt, Israel, Kuwait, Morocco, Saudi Arabia, South Korea, Taiwan, and Turkey; Russia has concluded major sales to China and Iran; Britain to Malaysia and Saudi Arabia; France to Taiwan and the United Arab Emirates; and China to Burma and Iran.[10] All told, these five suppliers sold $45.7 billion worth of arms to Third World countries in 1991–92, with the United States alone accounting for $27.2 billion of this amount.[11]

---

[8]For text of communique, see SIPRI, *SIPRI Yearbook 1992*, pp. 303–304.
[9]For full text of guidelines, see SIPRI, *SIPRI Yearbook 1992*, pp. 304–305.
[10]See SIPRI, *SIPRI Yearbook 1993*, pp. 498–518.
[11]Grimmett, *Arms Transfers 83–90*, p. 49.

The major suppliers' reluctance to interpret the London guidelines as a call for significant arms transfer restraint is undoubtedly a product of their continuing belief in the efficacy of arms transfers as a tool of foreign and military policy. This view of arms exports first arose during the early Cold War era, when both superpowers and their allies began to use such transfers as a device for winning and retaining the loyalty of Third World countries, especially in the Middle East.[12] Today, many U.S. policy makers continue to cling to these beliefs even though Moscow is no longer engaged in such competition and even though many Third World states are now ensconced in regional power struggles on their own.[13]

The major suppliers' ambivalent stance on arms transfer control also reflects growing political and economic pressures in these countries for increased foreign military sales. These pressures stem from the fact that the Cold War's end has produced a sharp decline in domestic military spending, thus jeopardizing the survival of many military production lines and arousing fears of increased unemployment in communities already hard-hit by economic recession. In order to soften the impact of domestic military cuts, many arms producers—along with leaders of the communities where their plants are located—have petitioned their national governments to permit increased sales of their products abroad. In response to these pressures and to the growing overseas demand for high-technology weapons, the leaders of these countries have approved major sales of high-tech arms to cash-paying customers in the Middle East and Asia.

For all these reasons, the major arms suppliers have failed to carry through on their promises to exercise restraint in their military sales activities and to implement the guidelines adopted in London in October 1991. The predictable result of this failure has been a stepped-up arms race in the Middle East and East Asia, along with increased belligerency on the part of some regional powers.[14] Furthermore, the increase in *overt, legitimate* arms transfers to areas of tension has contributed to an increase in *covert, illegitimate* transfers to guerrillas, insurgent groups, and sectarian armies of the sort operating in Bosnia and Somalia. Thus, as we move closer to the year 2000, we are seeing a significant increase in regional and ethnic conflict.

Clearly, if we are to slow the outbreak of regional and ethnic violence and promote peace negotiations in areas of conflict, we must—as suggested by Secretary of State Baker in 1991—seek to reduce the arms flow into areas that are

---

[12]For discussion, see Michael T. Klare, *American Arms Supermarket* (Austin: University of Texas Press, 1984), chaps. 3, 6, 7; Edward J. Laurance, *The International Arms Trade* (New York: Lexington/Macmillan, 1992), chap. 5; Andrew Pierre, *The Global Politics of Arms Sales* (Princeton: Princeton University Press, 1982), pp. 136–209; and Stephen M. Walt, *The Origins of Alliances* (Ithaca, N.Y.: Cornell University Press, 1987).

[13]For discussion, see William D. Hartung, "Curbing the Arms Trade: From Rhetoric to Reality," *World Policy Journal,* Spring 1992, pp. 219–247.

[14]For discussion of current arms race dynamics in the Asia-Pacific region, see Michael T. Klare, "The Next Great Arms Race," *Foreign Affairs,* Summer 1993, pp. 136–152.

already over-militarized. This will require the adoption of controls of the sort considered by the P-5 states in 1991–1992 and the development of other arms transfer control mechanisms. In addition, it will require the adoption of regional peace and security pacts in areas of tension (so as to reduce the *demand* for arms) and industrial conversion efforts in the major arms-producing countries (so as to reduce the pressures to *supply* weapons).

BUILDING AN ARMS TRANSFER CONTROL REGIME

In developing such mechanisms, advocates of conventional arms control can draw on several earlier attempts at arms export restraint. The earliest of these is the voluntary register of arms transfers maintained by the League of Nations during the interwar period.[15] Although not notably successful in restraining military sales during this period, the League effort does provide a model for more recent proposals concerning "transparency" in the arms trade. A second example is the Declaration of Ayacucho of 1974, under which eight South American nations pledged to restrain their purchases of offensively oriented weapons. This initiative also failed to slow the spread of weapons, but it, too, contains features that are being incorporated into more recent proposals.[16]

Finally, there is the "arms restraint" policy of then-President Jimmy Carter. Announced on May 19, 1977, the Carter plan included an annual ceiling on U.S. sales to most non-NATO nations and a ban on new-technology arms deliveries to Third World areas where such weapons did not then exist. The Carter policy also called upon the United States to meet with other major suppliers, particularly the Soviet Union, to negotiate multilateral controls on the arms trade. While the resulting Conventional Arms Transfer Talks (CATT) of 1977–1978 failed to result in any concrete agreements, they did produce a model for multilateral arms export controls and established a negotiating history that can be drawn upon in future talks of this sort.[17]

To supplement these few examples, conventional arms control proponents are also looking at a number of other treaties and agreements as possible models for action in the arms trade area. While not directly applicable to conventional arms transfers, these prototypes often incorporate specific features that can be woven into a conventional arms transfer control regime. These models include the Nuclear Non-Proliferation Treaty (NPT), the Missile Technology Control

---

[15]For discussion of the League's efforts in this area, see Naoum Sloutsky, *The League of Nations and the Control of Trade in Arms,* Report C/74-8 (Cambridge, Mass.: Center for International Studies, Massachusetts Institute of Technology, 1974).

[16]For discussion of the Ayacucho plan and its legacy, see Pierre, *The Global Politics of Arms Sales,* pp. 281–285.

[17]For text of the Carter statement of May 19, 1976, announcing the "arms restraint" policy, see U.S. Congress, House, Committee on Foreign Affairs, *Changing Perspectives on U.S. Arms Transfer Policy* (Washington, D.C.: U.S. Government Printing Office, 1981), pp. 122–123. For analysis of the Carter policy and the CATT talks, see Pierre, *The Global Politics of Arms Sales,* pp. 52–62.

Regime (MTCR), and the Conventional Forces in Europe (CFE) disarmament agreement of 1990.

By building on these prior initiatives, it is possible to conceive a comprehensive arms transfer control regime (CATCR) that would enable the world community to curb the flow of arms to areas of tension and conflict. Such a regime should consist of the following components.[18]

Transparency

The first step in imposing greater international control over the arms trade, in the view of many experts, is to promote greater "transparency" in the reporting of arms imports and exports. Proponents of transparency argue that greater openness in the arms trade will counteract the tendency of nations to over-arm in response to cloudy or incomplete data regarding their rivals' arms purchases (a tendency fed by the common inclination to assume the worst about an enemy's military capabilities) and will also provide an "early warning system" that can be used to detect major military buildups by potential belligerents.[19] In line with these views, the UN General Assembly voted 150 to 0 (with 2 abstentions) on December 9, 1991, to establish an international "register of conventional arms transfers." The register, when fully functioning, will collect and publish data on arms imports and exports by all member nations.[20]

Critics of transparency as a route to arms control charge that it will be impossible to gain support for such measures from many key countries and that even if such support does materialize, it would be impossible to prevent cheating by those with something to conceal. In response, proponents argue that transparency is not an all-or-nothing proposition but rather an evolutionary process that can develop over time into a comprehensive, mandatory system as the world gains confidence with such procedures. Proponents also suggest that it is possible and desirable to develop new systems of verification—including a UN monitoring agency—to support more advanced forms of transparency.[21]

Supply-Side Restraints

Although the technology to produce arms has been widely diffused, a handful of nations continue to dominate the trade in high-technology armaments. It is possi-

---

[18]The author first proposed a multi-tiered control system of this sort in "Gaining Control: Building a Comprehensive Arms Restraint System," *Arms Control Today,* June 1991, pp. 9–13.

[19]See United Nations, *Study on Ways and Means of Promoting Transparency in International Transfers of Conventional Arms,* U.N. Report A/46/301 (New York: United Nations, 1991), pp. 36–40.

[20]See SIPRI, *SIPRI Yearbook 1992,* pp. 299–301, 305–307.

[21]See Michael Brzoska, "Third World Arms Control: The Problems of Verification," *Bulletin of Peace Proposals,* Vol. 14, No. 2 (1983), pp. 165–173.

ble, therefore, to establish supply-side restraints or "supplier cartels" to control the spread of arms to particular regions. Such measures have been tested by the major Western powers in the past (notably through the 1950 Tripartite Declaration on the Middle East) but have generally proved to be of limited effectiveness because of the non-participation of the Soviet Union and China; with the successful UN embargo on arms to Iraq, however, it is now possible to conceive of supplier agreements that include all major suppliers, including Russia and China. This, indeed, is the basis for the P-5 talks initiated in Paris on July 7, 1991.

Assuming that the P-5 talks can be reconvened, what sort of measures should the major suppliers adopt? The goal of such restraints should not be to cut off the flow of arms entirely (as that will only boost the black-market traffic in arms); rather, the goals should be to *constrict* significantly the arms flow to areas of tension and to preclude deliveries of weapons that would have a destabilizing effect. To accomplish the former, the P-5 states could set an annual ceiling (of, say, $250 million) on total sales by any single supplier to any individual recipient; to accomplish the latter, the P-5 states could set maximum allowable force levels for each major weapons system in the arsenals of regional protagonists and ban the sale of any equipment that would exceed these levels.[22]

It is likely, of course, that supplier restraints of this sort will spur recipient countries to seek out other suppliers of such hardware or to develop (or expand) their own arms-production capabilities. Therefore, supply-side restraints should be accompanied by regional arms control agreements as described in "Regional Arms Control Agreements (by Recipients)" below. The P-5 talks should, moreover, be expanded at some later date to include other arms suppliers, such as Italy, Spain, Israel, and Brazil.

Regional Arms Control Agreements (by Recipients)

Ultimately, it will be impossible to halt the flow of arms into an area unless the nations of that region agree among themselves to exercise restraint in the acquisition of arms. Supplier restraints of the sort described above can never halt the delivery of all weapons to an area because the technology to produce conventional arms is now so widespread; moreover, such cartels are widely resented by many Third World leaders because of their association with imperial systems of control. Thus, any system for arms control within a region should rely as much on *recipient restraint* as on supplier restraint—with the latter used as a stimulus for the former or as a substitute when recipient restraint does not appear forthcoming.[23]

Previous attempts at regional self-restraint—notably the Ayacucho Declaration of 1974—have not been particularly successful. With the signing of the CFE treaty in 1990, however, arms control proponents can point to a new and

---

[22]For further discussion of supplier restraints and the obstacles to successful implementation of such measures, see Janne E. Nolan, "The Global Arms Market after the Gulf War: Prospects for Control," *The Washington Quarterly,* Spring 1991, pp. 126–131.

[23]For further discussion see Nolan, pp. 131–132.

highly successful model of regional arms control. Arms control analysts are now suggesting the establishment of similar negotiations in other areas. These proposals envisage a similar approach to that adopted in the Conference on Security and Cooperation in Europe (CSCE) process, involving consultations, cooperation in non-military matters, increased transparency, confidence-building measures, and other steps leading over time to specific arms control agreements.[24]

Technology Control Regimes

With the establishment of the Missile Technology Control Regime (MTCR) in 1987, the major Western powers created a prototype for multilateral controls on military technology that can usefully be applied to the proliferation of other military systems. Although limited in its applicability and lacking effective provisions for inspection and enforcement, the MTCR has been credited with a significant slowdown in the spread of missile technology; moreover, the regime has gained international legitimacy through the decisions by such nations as China, Israel, and Russia to join the regime or to abide by its provisions.[25]

The adoption of MTCR-type controls on other military systems is not likely to prove effective in curbing the spread of basic combat systems that are produced in many lands and whose technology is widely dispersed. It would also be unwise to view such controls as a substitute for all-inclusive constraints on arms transfers. However, this approach can and should be used to slow the proliferation of particular weapons systems whose introduction into conflict-prone areas would have a destabilizing effect. Using these criteria, the best candidates for further MTCR-like controls are submarines, cruise missiles, and deep-penetration bombers.

Fiscal Rewards and Disincentives

Except for a very few of the wealthier Third World nations, arms imports can reasonably be described as "luxury" items, in that they contribute little or nothing to development and consume scarce hard currencies and/or overseas borrowing authority. For this reason, excessive military spending by debt-burdened Third World countries has produced great concern among officials of the international lending agencies, notably the World Bank and the International Monetary Fund. The linkage between military spending and international lending was first raised by World Bank President Barber B. Conable in 1989. "It is important

---

[24]For discussion, see Geoffrey Kemp, *The Control of the Middle East Arms Race* (Washington: Carnegie Endowment for International Peace, 1992), pp. 124–128.

[25]For discussion of the MTCR's limitations and accomplishments, see Janne Nolan, *Trappings of Power: Ballistic Missiles in the Third World* (Washington, D.C.: Brookings Institution, 1991), pp. 145–155.

to place military spending decisions on the same footing as other fiscal decisions, and to explore ways to bring military spending into better balance with development priorities," he noted.[26]

On the basis of such remarks, it is possible to imagine an arms transfer restraint regime based on the use of economic rewards and disincentives—the award of extra loans and grants to states that reduce their arms spending and the denial of such aid to states that devote more than a certain percentage of their national income to military purposes. Such a regime would rely both on international measures, notably those adopted by the World Bank, and on cooperation by major donor nations.

At the same time, economic incentives—in the form of grants, loans, and technical assistance—should be provided to weapons firms in the major supplying countries that agree to convert their production to non-military commodities. Because many military contractors (and the communities in which they are located) are dependent on foreign sales to make up for any decline in domestic demand, there is an ever-present lobby for the relaxation or rejection of arms-export restraints. If these anti-restraint pressures are to be neutralized, it is essential that proposals for arms transfer control include assistance to firms and communities that undertake major conversion efforts.

Each of these mechanisms, operating independently, would provide government leaders with an effective instrument for controlling and constraining the conventional arms trade. None of them, however, can effectively address *all* the major concerns identified earlier in this essay. As in the nuclear field, a number of mechanisms—each addressing one or more fundamental problems—must be brought together into a comprehensive arms transfer control regime.

The task, then, is to begin construction of a multi-layered CATCR by inserting as many of these individual mechanisms as possible, recognizing that at any given time and in any given place it will be easier to make progress on some than on others. Progress in this field will thus require a multifaceted, evolutionary effort in which various national, regional, and international bodies work at developing and testing particular controls in the areas and fields under their jurisdiction—with the hope and expectation that these individual efforts will be extended to larger and larger geographic units until ultimately brought together in an integrated international system.

---

[26]Quoted in *The Washington Post*, November 27, 1989.

9

DISORDER IN THE NEW WORLD ORDER? THE FUTURE OF TERRORISM

Edward F. Mickolus

In this essay, Edward F. Mickolus explores the likely role that terrorism will play in world affairs in the wake of the Cold War. Noting recent reductions in the frequency of terrorist acts, the author inventories the old and new causes of this lethal activity and projects its likely continuation despite terrorism's inability to determine the course of world events. Mickolus is president of Vinyard Software, Inc., and the author of *Terrorism, 1988–1991: A Chronology of Events and a Selectively Annotated Bibliography* **(1993).**

The collapse of the Communist world and the rush of liberal democracies and market-based economies to fill the void have ushered in extensive speculation about the shape of the world to come. Many have suggested that a new world order will take the place of the old, led by a United Nations poised at last to stop brushfire wars, and economic competition taking the place of the balance of terror. The changes in the old regime came so quickly that few policymakers have had time to answer the questions, "How will we know when we have won the Cold War, and what do we want to take its place?"

The answers to such speculating and questioning, however, are perceived by many terrorist groups as simply irrelevant to their raisons d'être. Their causes are influenced only tangentially by these changes, and their clash with their

Reprinted from *National Forum: The Phi Kappa Phi Journal,* Volume LXXII, Number 4, Fall, 1992. Copyright © by Edward F. Mickolus. By permission of the publishers.

respective governments, or with the System in general, continues. For others, the transition period that we are now in may be their only chance to have an impact on what the new world order will mean in their regions. For still others, the specter of the Pax Americana (under whatever guise), which they had dreaded all of their careers, may spur them on to even greater acts of desperation.

DECLINE, BUT NOT ELIMINATION, OF TERRORISM

Charting the numbers of terrorist attacks since, say, the fall of the Berlin Wall shows a dramatic decline in the overall level of terrorist activities worldwide. In 1988, the U.S. Department of State logged 856 international terrorist incidents. (This figure does not count actions that did not involve more than one nationality or that did not cross borders.) For 1991, the figure was down to 557. Moreover, half of those incidents were attributed to protests against Operation Desert Storm. Casualties follow a similar pattern, dropping from 200 in 1990 to only 81 [in 1991]. The big story in terrorism in 1991 was the freeing of nine Western hostages in Lebanon, not some major attack.

This decline, however, should not be misinterpreted as an end of terrorism following on the heels of the end of history. Terrorists . . . continued their activities into 1992 . . . [and 1993. According to the U.S. Department of State, 361 attacks occurred in the former year and 427 occurred in the latter.—Eds.]

STATE SPONSORSHIP

Many observers of terrorism in the 1970s and 1980s believed that the Soviet Union and other members of the Warsaw Pact were providing assistance—including arms, training, safe haven, false documents, and intelligence—to terrorists around the world. Although one may argue that direct state support—by the Soviets, maverick Arab regimes, or anyone else—was relevant in only a small percentage of incidents, Marxist terrorists now face a new problem. Given their small numbers and necessarily clandestine existence, terrorist groups cannot survive for long without appreciable external aid, usually from sympathetic governments. Leftist terrorists, in addition to having lost their real-world models of what Marxist societies could be like, now find that they are also being pursued by their erstwhile patrons. The pages of *Pravda* now hail cooperation between the security organs of Russia and the West against international terrorists.

Third-World radical states have been slow in filling this support vacuum. The State Department currently lists only six nations—Cuba, Iran, Iraq, Libya, North Korea, and Syria—as sponsors of terrorism, but focuses on Iraq, Libya, and Iran as the most active. Such Islamic fundamentalist regimes as Iran have aided like-minded groups but seem to have little incentive for financially supporting the Marxists.

Radical Islamic groups, however, may find their stock going up as a counter-weight to the dominant parties in the new world order. Fundamentalists are already exploring how they can penetrate the new Islamic states in Central Eurasia, and they have continued to assist Palestinians in their goals. The massive car bombing of the Israeli Embassy in Buenos Aires [in 1992] has been attributed to radical Palestinians, assisted by Middle Eastern governments. Radicals may decide that the operational—if not public-relations—success of the Argentine attack could be replicated.

COOPERATION

The Desert Storm experience has led many to believe that the United Nations can at long last serve the peacekeeping purposes for which it was founded nearly a half-century ago. Increasingly intrusive inspections by the International Atomic Energy Agency of suspected nuclear-weapons programs have been a welcome consequence of the UN's successes in Desert Storm.

Supplementing such multilateral cooperation has been unprecedented bilateral success against terrorists. Although there were more than 200 terrorist attacks worldwide during the Gulf War, only a tiny handful involved loss of life or extensive property damage. The vast majority of the attacks were low-level bombings and arsons, perpetrated by temporarily radicalized students who were not full-time terrorists but were merely letting off excess political steam. Once this dramatic event had receded into the history books, so too did the reason for their actions, and terrorism levels have dwindled to their lowest levels in years.

That "professional" terrorists, aided by their Iraqi paymasters, were unable to make any inroads overseas during the Gulf crisis is attributable to the remarkable cooperation between security organizations throughout the world. Iraqi diplomats suspected of assisting terrorist operations were quickly expelled back to Baghdad. Warnings of planned attacks led to arrests of at-large terrorists. Although widely predicted in the pre-war media, terrorist spectaculars—hijackings, armed attacks, barricade-and-hostage takeovers, assassinations, suicide bombings, and the like—were halted by suffocating security precautions.

Such cooperation was not limited to the Gulf War. Terrorist exploitation of the Winter Olympics was feared, but nations again banded together to stop attacks. Although terrorist attacks on international conferences and sporting activities have been the grist for novels, we have not seen such attacks since the 1970s. Governments—singly and in tandem—have simply made it too tough for the terrorists to operate against such targets. Japan's planned plutonium shipments have been pinpointed by pundits as the next Holy Grail for terrorists seeking publicity (and a very eye-catching weapon), but again it is likely that governments will ensure that terrorists will be deterred from attacking.

Whatever the broad outlines of the new world order might be, it would appear that governments are increasingly aware of the importance of banding together to battle what is now perceived as a threat to all. Although some may benefit more than others from a new world order, governments appear to have accepted the idea that the order is preferable to unpredictable violence by terrorists. Such cooperation, then, is likely to continue and even to spill over into other areas of common concern, such as combating trafficking in narcotics and the proliferation of weapons of mass destruction. In addition to intelligence-sharing, governments around the world can so far point to an excellent record of adhering to UN-imposed sanctions against Iraq (an effort to prevent reinstitution of programs to develop weapons of mass destruction, some of which could be shared with terrorists) and Libya (the demand to extradite for trial in the West individuals suspected of involvement with airline bombings that led to mass casualties).

OLD AND NEW CAUSES

One cannot speak of any single cause, or even group of causes, of terrorism. Individuals engage in terrorism for numerous political, economic, social, and even personal reasons. A single-minded focus on dealing with these perceived causes can lead to the creation of new disaffected parties whose interests are harmed by the repair to the system that heeds the demands of the now-satisfied terrorists.

The new world order, in the view of radical Palestinians, for example, has little bearing on their cause and minimal effect on their operations. The drying up of their support from their erstwhile Soviet sponsors will mean increased reliance on maverick Arab regimes but will not change their goals.

The same can be said for ethnic separatist groups, such as the Irish Republican Army (IRA) or the Basque Fatherland and Liberty (ETA). Their decades-long feuds with their governments will not be solved by changes in the overall international political system.

The lifting of totalitarian repression of political expression in Central Eurasia, however, has perversely led to the possibility of the growth of terrorist movements within the new democracies. The republics of the new Commonwealth of Independent States and the carcass of Yugoslavia have seen the rise of revanchist ethnic movements intent upon settling old scores, this time unfettered by the state's monopoly on power. In addition to battles between governments and opposition forces, there have already been hijackings, kidnappings, and symbolic bombings. Other potential terrorists are waiting in the wings, watching to see how these dramas play out before they, too, venture forth.

Although as of this writing these groups are battling it out in the streets of the new capitals, eventually, some stability will come to the countries concerned. (One key indicator of such a truce will appear when the Rand McNally cartographers stop drawing their maps in pencil!) As we have seen in countless other cases, however, many hotheads will not be pleased with the new setup and will literally keep the home fires burning by going underground and pursuing the terrorist option. Some groups will seek to heighten international awareness of—and, in their dreams, international support for—their demands by taking their causes on the road and involving innocent third parties.

THE BOTTOM LINE

Terrorism will not fundamentally change the direction of the new world order. As has always been the case, terrorism serves as a sideshow to highlight specific demands but cannot ultimately influence political sea changes. Terrorism will continue to be an issue, but not a determinant, in the politics of nations and the conduct of world affairs.

10

SANCTIONS: A LOOK AT THE RECORD

Kimberly Ann Elliott

This essay examines the checkered record of efforts to use economic and other types of sanctions for purposes of exercising influence since World War II. Kimberly Ann Elliott determines that sanctions sometimes succeed as instruments of coercive diplomacy, namely, when they are imposed by a major power against a much weaker, unstable, and economically dependent foe with no allies among rival powers. She predicts that the conditions necessary for the effective application of unilateral economic sanctions are likely to narrow in the late 1990s. Elliott is a research associate at the Institute for International Economics. She is co-author (with Gary Clyde Hufbauer and Jeffrey J. Schott) of *Economic Sanctions Reconsidered* (1990).

The United States has been the principal user of economic sanctions since 1945, wielding them for a variety of reasons, including support of human rights and discouragement of nuclear weapons proliferation. In the Cold War, the United States also used sanctions in an attempt to weaken or coerce the Soviet Union and its allies. The United States was a key player in two-thirds of the 104 sanctions episodes from World War II until the U.N. embargo of Iraq. In 80 percent of U.S.-imposed sanctions, the policy was pursued with no more than minor cooperation from its allies or international organizations.

But from 1990 through early 1993, the United States imposed new unilateral sanctions in only one case (against Russia and India over a sale of missile technology) and expanded sanctions in another (Cuba). If this trend continues, it will mark a sharp reversal in the use of economic sanctions for foreign policy goals in the post–World War II period.

WHAT WORKS

Just how effective are economic sanctions? And what enhances or dulls their utility as a foreign policy tool? In 1990 Gary Clyde Hufbauer, Jeffrey J. Schott, and I conducted a study—*Economic Sanctions Reconsidered*—that suggests some answers.

The study defined economic sanctions as the deliberate, government-inspired withdrawal—or threat of withdrawal—of customary trade or financial relations. The "sender" refers to the country or groups imposing sanctions, while the "target" is the country against whom the measures are levied.

The success of an economic sanctions episode—as perceived by the sender country—has two parts: the extent to which a desired change was achieved, and the contribution made by sanctions (as opposed to other factors, such as military action). Our methodology ranked each of these elements on a scale from 1 (failed outcome, zero or negative sanctions contribution) to 4 (successful outcome, significant sanctions contribution). The two numbers were then multiplied to produce a "success score" ranging from 1 to 16. In our study, a score of 9, 12, or 16 was judged a successful outcome.

Information on six political and five economic variables was compiled for 115 episodes of foreign policy sanctions beginning with World War I and continuing through 1989 (the U.N. embargo of Iraq is not included in the database because it was ongoing when the book went to press). Analysis of the cases indicated that sanctions are most effective when:

• The goal is relatively modest, thus lessening the importance of multilateral cooperation—which often is difficult to obtain—and reducing the chances that a rival power will step in with "offsetting assistance" (compensating aid or trade meant to make up for the effects of sanctions on the target country).

• The target is politically unstable, much smaller than the country imposing sanctions, and economically weak (the average sender's economy was 187 times larger than that of the average target).

• The sender and target are friendly toward one another and conduct substantial trade (the sender accounted for 28 percent of the average target's trade in successful cases but only 19 percent in failures).

• The sanctions are imposed quickly and decisively to maximize impact (the average cost to the target as a percentage of GNP was 2.4 percent in successful cases and 1 percent in failures). This allows the target no time to adjust and enhances the political credibility of the sender, signaling its commitment to the sanctions.

• The sender avoids high costs to itself.

Although sanctions were successful by our definition in 34 percent of the 115 cases studied (the overall U.S. success rate was 32 percent), success has become increasingly elusive in recent years, especially for the United States. By splitting the sanctions episodes led by the United States into groups before and after 1973, a striking difference emerges: 51 percent of the sanctions episodes in the pre-1973 period ended successfully, whereas the success rate among cases begun after 1973 was a little less than 26 percent. Even more striking is the decline in the effectiveness of sanctions imposed in pursuit of modest goals— mostly sought by the United States—which plummeted from 75 percent to 21 percent.

FOREIGN POLICY AT A DISCOUNT

As an economic hegemon and political superpower, the United States in the decades following World War II attempted to impose its will on a wider variety of targets and sought a broader array of objectives than did any other country— including the Soviet Union, which generally confined its use of sanctions to keeping rebellious allies in line. The United States relied less on international cooperation and, on average, had more distant relations and weaker trade links with its targets than other users of sanctions.

In the early 1970s, the United States sharply increased its use of sanctions in pursuing relatively modest goals. Détente with the Soviet Union briefly allowed the United States to turn its attention to other matters, such as human rights violations and nuclear proliferation. Because the targets of these policies were more likely to be developing countries, they tended to be economically weaker and less stable than the average target in earlier years. Furthermore, détente combined with economic problems at home made the Soviet Union less and less willing to play the black knight and provide offsetting assistance to target countries.

All of these factors should have boded well for U.S. sanctions in the 1970s. All too often, however, resorting to economic sanctions appears to have been part of an effort to conduct foreign policy "on the cheap." After the withdrawal of American troops from Vietnam, U.S. presidents faced strong congressional and public opposition to military intervention, as well as economic problems including stagflation, fiscal constraints, and increasing trade deficits. Economic sanctions do not put a country's own citizens' lives directly at risk and—nearly as important—they are typically off-budget. But effective economic sanctions do not often come cheaply. Repeated failure, moreover, erodes the credibility of the sanctioning country or institution, an effect that may have been compounded by the decreased credibility of the U.S. military threat after Vietnam.

The global economy had changed dramatically, too. Although U.S. goals were relatively more modest and the targets usually smaller and weaker than before, the United States found that it had less leverage. In the early years after World War II, the U.S. economy was the reservoir for rebuilding war-devastated countries. It was also the major—if not sole—supplier of many goods and services. Well into the 1960s, the United States remained the primary source of economic assistance for developing countries.

Since the 1960s, however, trade and financial patterns have grown far more diversified. New technology has spread quickly, and the U.S. foreign aid budget has virtually dried up for all but a few countries. Recovery in Europe and the emergence of Japan have created new, competitive economic superpowers, and economic development has reduced the pool of potentially vulnerable targets. These trends are starkly illustrated by the declining average trade linkage between the United States and its targets (from 24 percent of the target's total imports and exports before 1973 to just 17 percent since), the lower average costs imposed on targets (1.7 percent of GNP versus 0.9 percent of GNP), and the fading utility of manipulating aid flows. For example, the success rate for financial sanctions used alone (usually by reducing aid to developing countries) declined from nearly 80 percent before 1973 to less than 20 percent since then.

The Soviet invasion of Afghanistan and the election of Ronald Reagan intensified the Cold War and restored an East-West flavor to sanctions campaigns. This change in emphasis manifested itself in several differences between sanctions in the 1980s and those in the preceding decade. Only about half of the 1980s cases involved modest goals, down from three-quarters in the 1970s; the incidence of companion policies nearly tripled (although from a low level given the predominance of modest goals in the 1970s); and the average cost imposed on the target doubled.

Perhaps in recognition of its declining leverage, the United States also tried to harness more international cooperation. Still, the costs imposed on targets remained below pre-1970 levels, the average trade linkage remained low, the average cost borne by the U.S. economy—though still small—increased, and the overall effectiveness of sanctions continued to decline.

The type of financial sanction used most frequently also changed. Economic aid was the dominant choice in the earlier period, whereas military assistance was prominent later, especially in human rights cases, where military governments were often the target. In some cases alternative sources of arms and financial assistance were available. Even more important, however, these governments perceived internal dissent to be a greater threat to their longevity than U.S. enmity and sanctions.

IN THE WAKE OF THE COLD WAR

The inevitable decline of American post-war economic hegemony has substantially reduced the usefulness of unilateral U.S. economic sanctions. The collapse of the Soviet Union, however, provides a geopolitical benefit that partially makes up for the negative economic trends that have made unilateral sanctions less potent. With the end of the Cold War, then, can the utility of unilateral U.S. sanctions be restored?

Cases involving offsetting assistance to a sanctions target most often were embroiled in Cold War politics, with one of the superpowers aiding its rival's target. Perhaps the best example is Fidel Castro's Cuba. The Soviet Union's subsidies to Cuba over the 30 years of the U.S. embargo are typically estimated in billions of dollars. In 1990, Soviet officials said that Soviet assistance to Cuba in recent years may have been as much as $2–3 billion annually. Sensing that Castro might be vulnerable after the collapse of the Soviet Union and the suspension of Soviet subsidies, Congress moved to tighten the embargo, but Castro remains in control.

The decline in superpower rivalry, combined with severe economic problems at home, means that Russia is unlikely to play black knight to countries seeking to ease the impact of U.S. sanctions. Although Libya and occasionally sympathetic neighbors (South Africa for Rhodesia and Saudi Arabia for Pakistan) have played this role, the resources and commitment of potential new black knights pale beside those of the Soviet Union at the height of the Cold War.

While offsetting assistance, if generous enough, can cause sanctions to fail, its absence does not guarantee success. Other factors, especially the difficulty of the goal and the political as well as economic vulnerability of the target, usually will be decisive.

Even if black knights are fewer in the 1990s, changes in the international economy in recent decades have reduced the number of targets likely to succumb to unilateral economic coercion. Many potential targets have developed strong and diversified economies that will never again be as vulnerable as they once were. And even relatively weak economies are more secure today as a result of the growth in world trade and the rapid dispersion of technology, which means that most U.S. exports can be replaced at little cost, and alternatives even to the large U.S. import market can usually be found.

Thus, one byproduct of the world economy's evolution since World War II has been a narrowing of the circumstances in which unilateral economic leverage may be effectively applied. A more interdependent global economy means that the effectiveness of unilateral sanctions depends increasingly on the subtlety, skill, and creativity with which they are imposed. . . .

11

THE CHANGING NATURE
OF WORLD POWER

Joseph S. Nye, Jr.

In this essay, Joseph S. Nye, Jr., draws fundamental distinctions among three
concepts—power, balance of power, and hegemony—and evaluates how the
revolutionary changes that have swept world politics since 1990 have changed their
meaning. Nye is Clarence Dillon Professor of International Affairs at Harvard
University and holds a position in the U.S. Department of Defense in the Clinton
administration. He has recently written *Understanding International Conflict*
(1992).

THE CHANGING SOURCES OF POWER

. . . Some observers have argued that the sources of power are, in general,
moving away from the emphasis on military force and conquest that marked
earlier eras. In assessing international power today, factors such as technology,
education, and economic growth are becoming more important, whereas geography, population, and raw materials are becoming less important. Kenneth
Waltz argues that a 5-percent rate of economic growth in the United States for
three years would add more to American strength than does our alliance with
Britain.[1] Richard Rosecrance argues that since 1945, the world has been poised

---

[1]Kenneth N. Waltz, *Theory of International Politics* (Reading, Mass.: Addison-Wesley, 1979), 172.

This article draws on material from Joseph S. Nye, Jr., *Bound to Lead: The Changing Nature of
American Power* (New York: Basic Books, 1990). Some footnotes have been deleted and others
have been renumbered to appear in consecutive order. Reprinted with permission from *Political Science Quarterly* 105 (Summer 1990): 177–182.

between a territorial system composed of states that view power in terms of land mass, and a trading system "based in states which recognize that self-sufficiency is an illusion." In the past, says Rosecrance, "it was cheaper to seize another state's territory by force than to develop the sophisticated economic and trading apparatus needed to derive benefit from commercial exchange with it."[2]

If so, perhaps we are in a "Japanese period" in world politics. Japan has certainly done far better with its strategy as a trading state after 1945 than it did with its military strategy to create a Greater East Asian Co-Prosperity sphere in the 1930s. But Japan's security vis-à-vis its large military neighbors—China and [Russia]—depends heavily on U.S. protection. In short, even if we can define power clearly, it still has become more difficult to be clear about the relationship of particular resources to it. Thus, we cannot leap too quickly to the conclusion that all trends favor economic power or countries like Japan.

Like other forms of power, economic power cannot be measured simply in terms of tangible resources. Intangible aspects also matter. For example, outcomes generally depend on bargaining, and bargaining depends on relative costs in particular situations and skill in converting potential power into effects. Relative costs are determined not only by the total amount of measurable economic resources of a country but also by the degree of its interdependence in a relationship. If, for example, the United States and Japan depend on each other but one is less dependent than the other, that asymmetry is a source of power. The United States may be less vulnerable than Japan if the relationship breaks down, and it may use that threat as a source of power.[3] Thus, an assessment of Japanese and American power must look not only at shares of resources but also at the relative vulnerabilities of both countries.

Another consideration is that most large countries today find military force more costly to apply than in previous centuries. This has resulted from the dangers of nuclear escalation, the difficulty of ruling nationalistically awakened populations in otherwise weak states, the danger of rupturing profitable relations on other issues, and the public opposition in Western democracies to prolonged and expensive military conflicts. Even so, the increased cost of military force does not mean that it will be ruled out. To the contrary, in an anarchic system of states where there is no higher government to settle conflicts and where the ultimate recourse is self-help, this could never happen. In some cases, the stakes may justify a costly use of force. And, as recent episodes in Grenada and Libya have shown, not all uses of force by great powers involve high costs.

Even if the direct use of force were banned among a group of countries, military force would still play an important political role. For example, the American military role in deterring threats to allies, or of assuring access to a crucial resource such as oil in the Persian Gulf, means that the provision of protective

[2]Richard N. Rosecrance, *The Rise of the Trading State* (New York: Basic Books, 1986), 16, 160.
[3]Robert O. Keohane and Joseph S. Nye, Jr., *Power and Interdependence* (Boston: Little, Brown, 1977), chap. 1. . . .

force can be used in bargaining situations. Sometimes the linkage may be direct; more often it is a factor not mentioned openly but present in the back of statesmen's minds.

In addition, there is the consideration that is sometimes called "the second face of power."[4] Getting other states to change might be called the directive or commanding method of exercising power. Command power can rest on inducements ("carrots") or threats ("sticks"). But there is also an indirect way to exercise power. A country may achieve the outcomes it prefers in world politics because other countries want to follow it or have agreed to a system that produces such effects. In this sense, it is just as important to set the agenda and structure the situations in world politics as it is to get others to change in particular situations. This aspect of power—that is, getting others to want what you want—might be called indirect or co-optive power behavior. It is in contrast to the active command power behavior of getting others to do what you want,[5] Co-optive power can rest on the attraction of one's ideas or on the ability to set the political agenda in a way that shapes the preferences that others express. Parents of teenagers know that if they have structured their children's beliefs and preferences, their power will be greater and will last longer than if they had relied only on active control. Similarly, political leaders and philosophers have long understood the power that comes from setting the agenda and determining the framework of a debate. The ability to establish preferences tends to be associated with intangible power resources such as culture, ideology, and institutions. This dimension can be thought of as soft power, in contrast to the hard command power usually associated with tangible resources like military and economic strength.[6]

[4]Peter Bachrach and Morton S. Baratz, "Decisions and Nondecisions: An Analytical Framework," *American Political Science Review* 57 (September 1963): 632–42. See also Richard Mansbach and John Vasquez, *In Search of Theory: A New Paradigm for Global Politics* (New York: Columbia University Press, 1981).

[5]Susan Strange uses the term *structural power,* which she defines as "power to shape and determine the structures of the global political economy" in *States and Markets* (New York: Basil Blackwell, 1988), 24. My term, *co-optive power,* is similar in its focus on preferences but is somewhat broader, encompassing all elements of international politics. The term *structural power,* in contrast, tends to be associated with the neo-realist theories of Kenneth Waltz.

[6]The distinction between hard and soft power resources is one of degree, both in the nature of the behavior and in the tangibility of the resources. Both types are aspects of the ability to achieve one's purposes by controlling the behavior of others. Command power—the ability to change what others *do*—can rest on coercion or inducement. Co-optive power—the ability to shape what others *want*—can rest on the attractiveness of one's culture and ideology or the ability to manipulate the agenda of political choices in a manner that makes actors fail to express some preferences because they seem to be too unrealistic. The forms of behavior between command and co-optive power range along this continuum:

Command	coercion	inducement	agenda-setting	attraction	Co-optive
power					power

Further, soft power resources tend to be associated with co-optive power behavior, whereas hard power resources are usually associated with command behavior. But the relationship is imperfect. For example, countries may be attracted to others with command power by myths of invincibility, and command power may sometimes be used to establish institutions that later become regarded as legitimate. But the general association is strong enough to allow the useful shorthand reference to hard and soft power resources.

Robert Cox argues that the nineteenth-century *Pax Britannica* and the twentieth-century *Pax Americana* were effective because they created liberal international economic orders, in which certain types of economic relations were privileged over others and liberal international rules and institutions were broadly accepted. Following the insights of the Italian thinker Antonio Gramsci, Cox argues that the most critical feature for a dominant country is the ability to obtain a broad measure of consent on general principles—principles that ensure the supremacy of the leading state and dominant social classes—and at the same time to offer some prospect of satisfaction to the less powerful. Cox identifies Britain from 1845 to 1875 and the United States from 1945 to 1967 as such countries.[7] Although we may not agree with his terminology or dates, Cox has touched a major point: soft co-optive power is just as important as hard command power. If a state can make its power legitimate in the eyes of others, it will encounter less resistance to its wishes. If its culture and ideology are attractive, others will more willingly follow. If it can establish international norms that are consistent with its society, it will be less likely to have to change. If it can help support institutions that encourage other states to channel or limit their activities in ways the dominant state prefers, it may not need as many costly exercises of coercive or hard power in bargaining situations. In short, the universalism of a country's culture and its ability to establish a set of favorable rules and institutions that govern areas of international activity are critical sources of power.[8] These soft sources of power are becoming more important in world politics today.

Such considerations question the conclusion that the world is about to enter a Japanese era in world politics. The nature of power is changing and some of the changes will favor Japan, but some of them may favor the United States even more. In command power, Japan's economic strength is increasing, but it remains vulnerable in terms of raw materials and relatively weak in terms of military force. And in co-optive power, Japan's culture is highly insular and it has yet to develop a major voice in international institutions. The United States, on the other hand, has a universalistic popular culture and a major role in international institutions. Although such factors may change in the future, they raise an important question about the present situation: What resources are the most important sources of power today? A look at the five-century-old modern state system shows that different power resources played critical roles in different periods. (See Table 11-1.) The sources of power are never static and they continue to change in today's world.

In an age of information-based economies and transnational interdependence, power is becoming less transferable, less tangible, and less coercive.

[7]Robert W. Cox, *Production, Power, and World Order* (New York: Columbia University Press, 1987), chaps. 6, 7.

[8]Stephen D. Krasner, *International Regimes* (Ithaca, N.Y.: Cornell University Press, 1983).

TABLE 11-1
LEADING STATES AND MAJOR POWER RESOURCES, 1500s–1900s

PERIOD	LEADING STATE	MAJOR RESOURCES
Sixteenth century	Spain	Gold bullion, colonial trade, mercenary armies, dynastic ties
Seventeenth century	Netherlands	Trade, capital markets, navy
Eighteenth century	France	Population, rural industry, public administration, army
Nineteenth century	Britain	Industry, political cohesion, finance and credit, navy, liberal norms, island location (easy to defend)
Twentieth century	United States	Economic scale, scientific and technical leadership, universalistic culture, military forces and alliances, liberal international regimes, hub of transnational communication

However, the transformation of power is incomplete. The twenty-first century will certainly see a greater role for informational and institutional power, but military force will remain an important factor. Economic scale, both in markets and in natural resources, will also remain important. As the service sector grows within modern economies, the distinction between services and manufacturing will continue to blur. Information will become more plentiful, and the critical resource will be the organizational capacity for rapid and flexible response. Political cohesion will remain important, as will a universalistic popular culture. On some of these dimensions of power, the United States is well endowed; on others, questions arise. But even larger questions arise for the other major contenders—Europe, Japan, [Russia], and China. But first we need to look at the patterns in the distribution of power—balances and hegemonies, and how they have changed over history, . . .

BALANCE OF POWER

International relations is far from a precise science. Conditions in various periods always differ in significant details, and human behavior reflects personal choices. Moreover, theorists often suffer from writing in the midst of events, rather than viewing them from a distance. Thus, powerful theories—those that are both simple and accurate—are rare. Yet political leaders (and those who seek to explain behavior) must generalize in order to chart a path through the apparent chaos of changing events. One of the longest-standing and most frequently used concepts is balance of power, which eighteenth-century philosopher David Hume called "a constant rule of prudent politics." For centuries, balance of power has been the starting point for realistic discussions of international politics.

To an extent, balance of power is a useful predictor of how states will behave; that is, states will align in a manner that will prevent any one state from developing a preponderance of power. This is based on two assumptions: that states exist in an anarchic system with no higher government and that political leaders will act first to reduce risks to the independence of their states. The policy of balancing power helps to explain why in modern times a large state cannot grow forever into a world empire. States seek to increase their powers through internal growth and external alliances. Balance of power predicts that if one state appears to grow too strong, others will ally against it so as to avoid threats to their own independence. This behavior, then, will preserve the structure of the system of states.

However, not all balance-of-power predictions are so obvious. For example, this theory implies that professions of ideological faith will be poor predictors of behavior. But despite Britain's criticism of the notorious Stalin-Hitler pact of 1939, it was quick to make an alliance with Stalin's Soviet Union in 1941. As Winston Churchill explained at the time, "If I learned that Hitler had invaded Hell, I would manage to say something good about the Devil in the House of Commons." Further, balance of power does not mean that political leaders must maximize the power of their own states in the short run. Bandwagoning—that is, joining the stronger rather than the weaker side—might produce more immediate spoils. As Mussolini discovered in his ill-fated pact with Hitler, the danger in bandwagoning is that independence may be threatened by the stronger ally in the long term. Thus, to say that states will act to balance power is a strong generalization in international relations, but it is far from being a perfect predictor.

Proximity and perceptions of threat also affect the way in which balancing of power is played out. A small state like Finland, for instance, [could not] afford to try to balance Soviet power. Instead, it [sought] to preserve its independence through neutrality. Balance of power and the proposition that "the enemy of my enemy is my friend" help to explain the larger contours of current world politics, but only when proximity and perceptions are considered. The United States was by far the strongest power after 1945. A mechanical application of power balance might seem to predict an alliance against the United States. In fact, Europe and Japan allied with the United States because the Soviet Union, while weaker in overall power, posed a proximate threat to its neighbors. Geography and psychology are both important factors in geopolitics.

The term *balance of power* is sometimes used not as a prediction of policy but as a description of how power is distributed. In the latter case, it is more accurate to refer to the distribution of power. In other instances, though, the term is used to refer to an evenly balanced distribution of power, like a pair of hanging scales. The problem with this usage is that the ambiguities of measuring power make it difficult to determine when an equal balance exists. In fact, the major concerns in world politics tend to arise from inequalities of power, and particularly from major changes in the unequal distribution of power.

HEGEMONY IN MODERN HISTORY

No matter how power is measured, an equal distribution of power among major states is relatively rare. More often the processes of uneven growth, which realists consider a basic law of international politics, mean that some states will be rising and others declining. These transitions in the distribution of power stimulate statesmen to form alliances, to build armies, and to take risks that balance or check rising powers. But the balancing of power does not always prevent the emergence of a dominant state. Theories of hegemony and power transition try to explain why some states that become preponderant later lose that preponderance.

As far back as ancient Greece, observers attempting to explain the causes of major world wars have cited the uncertainties associated with the transition of power. Shifts in the international distribution of power create the conditions likely to lead to the most important wars. However, while power transitions provide useful warning about periods of heightened risk, there is no iron law of hegemonic war. If there were, Britain and the United States would have gone to war at the beginning of this century, when the Americans surpassed the British in economic and naval power in the Western Hemisphere. Instead, when the United States backed Venezuela in its boundary dispute with British Guyana in 1895, British leaders appeased the rising American power instead of going to war with it.

When power is distributed unevenly, political leaders and theorists use terms such as *empire* and *hegemony*. Although there have been many empires in history, those in the modern world have not encompassed all major countries. Even the British Empire at the beginning of this century encompassed only a quarter of the world's population and Britain was just one of a half-dozen major powers in the global balance of power. The term *hegemony* is applied to a variety of situations in which one state appears to have considerably more power than others. For example, for years China accused the Soviet Union of seeking hegemony in Asia. When Soviet leader Mikhail Gorbachev and Chinese leader Deng Xiaoping met in 1989, they pledged that "neither side will seek hegemony in any form anywhere in the world."

Although the word comes from the ancient Greek and refers to the dominance of one state over others in the system, it is used in diverse and confused ways. Part of the problem is that unequal distribution of power is a matter of degree, and there is no general agreement on how much inequality and what types of power constitute hegemony. All too often, hegemony is used to refer to different behaviors and degrees of control, which obscures rather than clarifies that analysis. For example, Charles Doran cites aggressive military power, while Robert Keohane looks at preponderance in economic resources. Robert Gilpin sometimes uses the terms *imperial* and *hegemonic* interchangeably to refer to a situation in which "a single powerful state controls or dominates the lesser states in the system."[9] British hegemony in the nineteenth century is commonly cited even though Britain ranked third behind the United States and Russia in GNP and third behind Russia and France in military expenditures at the peak of its relative power around 1870. Britain was first in the more limited domains of manufacturing, trade, finance, and naval power.[10] Yet theorists often contend that "full hegemony requires productive, commercial, and financial as well as political and military power."[11]

Joshua Goldstein usefully defines hegemony as "being able to dictate, or at least dominate, the rules and arrangements by which international relations, political and economic, are conducted. . . . Economic hegemony implies the ability to center the world economy around itself. Political hegemony means being able to dominate the world militarily."[12] However, there are still two important questions to be answered with regard to how the term *hegemony* is used. First, what is the scope of the hegemon's control? In the modern world, a situation in which one country can dictate political and economic arrangements has been extremely rare. Most examples have been regional, such as Soviet power in Eastern Europe [during the Cold War], American influence in the Caribbean, and India's control over its small neighbors—Sikkim, Bhutan, and Nepal. In addition, one can find instances in which one country was able to set the rules and arrangements governing specific issues in world politics, such as the American role in money or trade in the early postwar years. But there has been no global, system-wide hegemon during the past two centuries. Contrary to the myths about *Pax Britannica* and *Pax Americana*, British and American hegemonies have been regional and issue-specific rather than general.

Second, we must ask what types of power resources are necessary to produce a hegemonic degree of control. Is military power necessary? Or is it enough to have preponderance in economic resources? How do the two types of power relate to each other? Obviously, the answers to such questions can tell us a great deal about the future world, in which Japan may be an economic giant and a

---

[9]Charles F. Doran, *The Politics of Assimilation: Hegemony and Its Aftermath* (Baltimore: Johns Hopkins University Press, 1971), 70; Robert O. Keohane, *After Hegemony* (Princeton, N.J.: Princeton University Press, 1984), 32; Robert Gilpin, *War and Change in World Politics* (New York: Cambridge University Press, 1981), 29.

[10]Bruce M. Russett, "The Mysterious Case of Vanishing Hegemony; or, Is Mark Twain Really Dead?" *International Organization* 39 (Spring 1985): 212.

[11]Robert C. North and Julie Strickland, "Power Transition and Hegemonic Succession" (Paper delivered at the meetings of the International Studies Association, Anaheim, Calif., March–April 1986), 5.

[12]Joshua S. Goldstein, *Long Cycles: Prosperity and War in the Modern Age* (New Haven, Conn.: Yale University Press, 1988), 281.

military dwarf while the [Russian Federation] may fall into the opposite situation. A careful look at the interplay of military and economic power raises doubt about the degree of American hegemony in the postwar period.

Theories of Hegemonic Transition and Stability

General hegemony is the concern of theories and analogies about the instability and dangers supposedly caused by hegemonic transitions. Classical concerns about hegemony among leaders and philosophers focus on military power and "conflicts precipitated by the military effort of one dominant actor to expand well beyond the arbitrary security confines set by tradition, historical accident, or coercive pressures."[13] In this approach, hegemonic preponderance arises out of military expansion, such as the efforts of Louis XIV, Napoleon, or Hitler to dominate world politics. The important point is that, except for brief periods, none of the attempted military hegemonies in modern times has succeeded. (See Table 11-2.) No modern state has been able to develop sufficient military power to transform the balance of power into a long-lived hegemony in which one state could dominate the world militarily.

More recently, many political scientists have focused on economic power as a source of hegemonic control. Some define hegemonic economic power in terms of resources—that is, preponderance in control over raw materials, sources of capital, markets, and production of goods. Others use the behavioral definition in which a hegemon is a state able to set the rules and arrangements for the global economy. Robert Gilpin, a leading theorist of hegemonic transition, sees Britain and America, having created and enforced the rules of a liberal economic order, as the successive hegemons since the Industrial Revolution.[14] Some political economists argue that world economic stability requires a single

[13]Doran, *Politics of Assimilation,* 15.
[14]Keohane, *After Hegemony,* 32; Gilpin, *War and Change,* 144.

TABLE 11-2
MODERN EFFORTS AT MILITARY HEGEMONY

STATE ATTEMPTING HEGEMONY	ENSUING HEGEMONIC WAR	NEW ORDER AFTER WAR
Hapsburg Spain	Thirty Years' War, 1618–1648	Peace of Westphalia, 1648
Louis XIV's France	Wars of Louis XIV	Treaty of Utrecht, 1713
Napoleon's France	1792–1815	Congress of Vienna, 1815
Germany (and Japan)	1914–1945	United Nations, 1945

Source: Charles F. Doran, *The Politics of Assimilation: Hegemony and Its Aftermath* (Baltimore: Johns Hopkins University Press, 1971), 19–20.

stabilizer and that periods of such stability have coincided with periods of hegemony. In this view, *Pax Britannica* and *Pax Americana* were the periods when Britain and the United States were strong enough to create and enforce the rules for a liberal international economic order in the nineteenth and twentieth centuries. For example, it is often argued that economic stability "historically has occurred when there has been a sole hegemonic power: Britain from 1815 to World War I and the United States from 1945 to around 1970. . . . With a sole hegemonic power, the rules of the game can be established and enforced. Lesser countries have little choice but to go along. Without a hegemonic power, conflict is the order of the day."[15] Such theories of hegemonic stability and decline are often used to predict that the United States will follow the experience of Great Britain, and that instability will ensue. Goldstein, for example, argues that "we are moving toward the 'weak hegemony' end of the spectrum and . . . this seems to increase the danger of hegemonic war."[16]

I argue, however, that the theory of hegemonic stability and transition will not tell us as much about the future of the United States. Theorists of hegemonic stability generally fail to spell out the causal connections between military and economic power and hegemony. As already noted, nineteenth-century Britain was not militarily dominant nor was it the world's largest economy, and yet Britain is portrayed by Gilpin and others as hegemonic. Did Britain's military weakness at that time allow the United States and Russia, the two larger economies, to remain mostly outside the liberal system of free trade? Or, to take a twentieth-century puzzle, did a liberal international economy depend on postwar American military strength or only its economic power? Are both conditions necessary today, or have modern nations learned to cooperate through international institutions?

One radical school of political economists, the neo-Marxists, has attempted to answer similar questions about the relationship between economic and military hegemony, but their theories are unconvincing. For example, Immanuel Wallerstein defines hegemony as a situation in which power is so unbalanced that

> one power can largely impose its rules and its wishes (at the very least by effective veto power) in the economic, political, military, diplomatic, and even cultural arenas. The material base of such power lies in the ability of enterprises domiciled in that power to operate more efficiently in all three major economic arenas—agro-industrial production, commerce, and finance.[17]

According to Wallerstein, hegemony is rare and "refers to that short interval in which there is simultaneously advantage in all three economic domains." At

---

[15]Michael Moffitt, "Shocks, Deadlocks and Scorched Earth: Reaganomics and the Decline of U.S. Hegemony," *World Policy Journal* 4 (Fall 1987): 576.

[16]Goldstein, *Long Cycles,* 357.

[17]Immanuel M. Wallerstein, *The Politics of the World-Economy: The States, the Movements, and the Civilizations: Essays* (New York: Cambridge University Press, 1984), 38, 41.

TABLE 11-3
A NEO-MARXIST VIEW OF HEGEMONY

HEGEMONY	WORLD WAR SECURING HEGEMONY	PERIOD OF DOMINANCE	DECLINE
Dutch	Thirty Years' War, 1618–1648	1620–1650	1650–1672
British	Napoleonic Wars, 1792–1815	1815–1873	1873–1896
American	World Wars I and II, 1914–1945	1945–1967	1967–

Source: Immanuel Wallerstein, *The Politics of the World Economy* (New York: Cambridge University Press, 1984), 41–42.

such times, the other major powers become "*de facto* client states." Wallerstein claims there have been only three modern instances of hegemony—in the Netherlands, 1620–1650; in Britain, 1815–1873; and in the United States, 1945–1967. (See Table 11-3.) He argues that "in each case, the hegemony was secured by a thirty-year-long world war," after which a new order followed— the Peace of Westphalia after 1648; the Concert of Europe after 1815; and the United Nations–Bretton Woods system after 1945.[18] According to this theory, the United States will follow the Dutch and the British path to decline.

The neo-Marxist view of hegemony is unconvincing and a poor predictor of future events because it superficially links military and economic hegemony and has many loose ends. For example, contrary to Wallerstein's theory, the Thirty Years' War *coincided* with Dutch hegemony, and Dutch decline began with the Peace of Westphalia. The Dutch were not militarily strong enough to stand up to the British on the sea and could barely defend themselves against the French on land, "despite their trade-derived wealth."[19] Further, although Wallerstein argues that British hegemony began after the Napoleonic Wars, he is not clear about how the new order in the balance of power—that is, the nineteenth-century Concert of Europe—related to Britain's supposed ability to impose a global free-trade system. For example, Louis XIV's France, which many historians view as the dominant military power in the second half of the seventeenth century, is excluded from Wallerstein's schema altogether. Thus, the neo-Marxist historical analogies seem forced into a Procrustean ideological bed, while other cases are left out of bed altogether.

Others have attempted to organize past periods of hegemony into century-long cycles. In 1919, British geopolitician Sir Halford Mackinder argued that unequal growth among nations tends to produce a hegemonic world war about every hundred years. More recently, political scientist George Modelski pro-

[18]Ibid.
[19]Goldstein, *Long Cycles,* 317.

TABLE 11-4
LONG CYCLES OF WORLD LEADERSHIP

CYCLE	GLOBAL WAR	PREPONDERANCE	DECLINE
1495–1580	1494–1516	Portugal, 1516–1540	1540–1580
1580–1688	1580–1609	Netherlands, 1609–1640	1640–1688
1688–1792	1688–1713	Britain, 1714–1740	1740–1792
1792–1914	1792–1815	Britain, 1815–1850	1850–1914
1914–	1914–1945	United States, 1945–1973	1973–

Source: George Modelski, *Long Cycles in World Politics* (Seattle: University of Washington Press, 1987), 40, 42, 44, 102, 131, 147.

posed a hundred-year cyclical view of changes in world leadership. (See Table 11-4.) In this view, a long cycle begins with a major global war. A single state then emerges as the new world power and legitimizes its preponderance with postwar peace treaties. (Preponderance is defined as having at least half the resources available for global order-keeping.) The new leader supplies security and order for the international system. In time, though, the leader loses legitimacy, and deconcentration of power leads to another global war. The new leader that emerges from that war may not be the state that challenged the old leader but one of the more innovative allies in the winning coalition (as, not Germany, but the United States replaced Britain). According to Modelski's theory, the United States began its decline in 1973.[20] If his assumptions are correct, it may be Japan and not the [Russian Federation] that will most effectively challenge the United States in the future.

Modelski and his followers suggest that the processes of decline are associated with long waves in the global economy. They associate a period of rising prices and resource scarcities with loss of power, and concentration of power with falling prices, resource abundance, and economic innovation.[21] However, in linking economic and political cycles, these theorists become enmeshed in the controversy surrounding long cycle theory. Many economists are skeptical about the empirical evidence for alleged long economic waves and about dating historical waves by those who use the concept.[22]. . .

[20]George Modelski, "The Long Cycle of Global Politics and the Nation-State," *Comparative Studies in Society and History* 20 (April 1978): 214–35; George Modelski, *Long Cycles in World Politics* (Seattle: University of Washington Press, 1987).

[21]William R. Thompson, *On Global War: Historical Structural Approaches to World Politics* (Columbia: University of South Carolina Press, 1988), chaps. 3, 8.

[22]Richard N. Rosecrance, "Long Cycle Theory and International Relations," *International Organization* 41 (Spring 1987): 291–95. An interesting but ultimately unconvincing discussion can be found in Goldstein, *Long Cycles.*

Vague definitions and arbitrary schematizations alert us to the inadequacies of such grand theories of hegemony and decline. Most theorists of hegemonic transition tend to shape history to their own theories by focusing on particular power resources and ignoring others. Examples include the poorly explained relationship between military and political power and the unclear link between decline and major war. Since there have been wars among the great powers during 60 percent of the years from 1500 to the present, there are plenty of candidates to associate with any given scheme.[23] Even if we consider only the nine general wars that have involved nearly all the great powers and produced high levels of casualties, some of them, such as the Seven Years' War (1755–1763), are not considered hegemonic in any of the schemes. As sociologist Pitirim Sorokin concludes, "no regular periodicity is noticeable."[24] At best, the various schematizations of hegemony and war are only suggestive. They do not provide a reliable basis for predicting the future of American power or for evaluating the risk of world war as we enter the twenty-first century. Loose historical analogies about decline and falsely deterministic political theories are not merely academic: they may lead to inappropriate policies. The real problems of a post-cold-war world will not be new challenges for hegemony, but the new challenges of transnational interdependence.

---

[23]Jack S. Levy, "Declining Power and the Preventive Motivation for War," *World Politics* 40 (October 1987): 82–107. See also Jack S. Levy, *War in the Modern Great Power System, 1495–1975* (Lexington: University of Kentucky Press, 1983), 97.

[24]Pitirim Aleksandrovich Sorokin, *Social and Cultural Dynamics: A Study of Change in Major Systems of Art, Truth, Ethics, Law and Social Relationships* (1957; reprint, Boston: Porter Sargent, 1970), 561.

DISCORD AND COLLABORATION

States necessarily direct their attention and resources toward the quest for security, as the threat of war is an ever-present danger in an anarchical society. Issues relating to arms and influence therefore occupy a prominent place on the foreign policy agendas of nation-states. Indeed, the pursuit of national security often constitutes the very essence of international politics. Hence the issues treated in Part I of *The Global Agenda* appropriately command central importance.

Compelling as this realist perspective is, it is at best a caricature of international politics, as it fails to acknowledge the broad range of issues and objectives that motivate states' behavior, even in their quest for security. The *high politics* of peace and security entails issues and strategies that lie beyond arms and war, deterrence, and the raw exercise of influence. It also includes activities of states that often have little or nothing to do with armaments or the threat of war, and it includes many motivated by the desire to collaborate with others so as to derive mutual benefits.

Indeed, contrary to the Hobbesian perspective, international politics is not exclusively a "war of all against all." States are not normally straining at the leash to attack one another. Nor do they devote the bulk of their day-to-day activities to planning the use of force against their perceived adversaries. The texture of world politics is shaped by more varied national interests and activities.

Part II of *The Global Agenda* directs attention to other ways that states seek to promote their national interests. Under normal conditions, of course, relations among states are often marked by conflict. Conflict is endemic to politics and hence is unavoidable. Nonetheless, we can assume that how states usually respond to conflict does not routinely involve preparations for war and the threat or use of force.

Part II begins with the assumption that states respond to a perceived need not only for power but also for order. States value a stable international environment. They therefore seek and support not just a strong defense but also common institutions and rules that contribute to the creation of a more orderly world. In short, world politics involves both discord as well as collaboration.

What factors influence whether amity or enmity will dominate the pattern of interaction among states? Clearly, there are many. Underlying all of them, it may be argued, are states' perceptions of reality. Reality is partially subjective—what states perceive it to be, not just what it is. Thus states' behavior is influenced strongly by policy makers' images of reality as well as by objective facts. Whether states see the world as fearful and hostile or as peaceful and cooperative will influence the postures they assume toward global issues and their reactions to the challenges and options those issues present.

Social scientists have developed models that describe and explain various properties of international relations and how images of international reality often shape our interpretations of it. Ole R. Holsti, in "Models of International Relations: Realist and Neoliberal Perspectives on Conflict and Cooperation," describes and summarizes two models fashioned by scholars to organize research and theorizing on world politics: the classical and modern versions of "realism" and the neoliberal challengers to it that emphasize the interdependent nature of global realities and the prospects for cooperation and change. He explicates the assumptions and conclusions about world politics suggested by the alternative theoretical orientations. In doing so, he provides a basis for understanding the diverse ways discord and collaboration manifest themselves in world affairs and why the potential for enduring conflict coexists with the potential for cooperation.

Models and theories provide a lens through which international realities are interpreted. Their usefulness depends in large part on the accuracy of the assumptions about international realities upon which they rest. Hence, the accuracy of observers' perceptions will matter greatly in determining the ways in which scholars and policy makers respond to the changes unfolding in the twilight of the twentieth century. In "Cold War, Chill Peace: Prospects for World Order and Disorder," Michael Howard casts his eye back in history in order to look at the future. Observing that "after every great war, whether hot or cold, there has been a chill peace," Howard finds the wake of the Cold War to be no exception. Indeed, the disruption and problems confronting the world today resemble in many ways the kinds of turmoil and instabilities that followed the Napoleonic Wars in 1815 and World Wars I and II. By looking to the past, we gain perspective on the discord and uncertainty that now prevails on the global landscape. Providing a philosophical interpretation of the trajectories of history now unfolding, Howard summarizes the global problems and assesses what they portend for "a new world order." From his survey we obtain a picture of the adjustments that will be required to those international circumstances that make for "an entirely new situation" arising "from long-term secular trends that we cannot control." Hence, Howard projects a mixture of order and disorder in a "chilly" new international climate—less frigid, to be sure, than the Cold War but less warm than most observers anticipated when that superpower contest ended. By placing these discrepant scenarios into perspective, Howard thus broadens our vision of the myriad issues that will occupy the crowded global agenda of the future.

Prospects for global collaboration may hinge on how the relationships between the great powers evolve. The probable character of their relationships is the subject of considerable controversy, because the intentions and external behavior of each emerging great power eludes precise definition. As Howard explains, for more than four decades the expectation of superpower discord remained high and the possibilities for lasting cooperation appeared remote, in large measure because of the distrust, ideological rivalry, and misperceptions that fueled the superpowers' animosity during the Cold War. But this antagonism has abruptly come to an end. As we look to the future, the likely shape of the great powers' relations with one another inspires hope that accommodation will prevail.

In "Great-Power Relations: Paths to Peace in the Twenty-First Century," Charles W. Kegley, Jr., and Gregory A. Raymond evaluate the diverse ways an embryonic set of relationships might develop to cement the great powers' future collaboration. They also explain the potential for a new wave of rivalry that may suspend the newly found (if fragile) harmony that has recently surfaced.

The assessment that Kegley and Raymond offer takes as its point of departure the probability that the international system is undergoing a historic transformation. The authors aver that military and economic capabilities are becoming increasingly diffused. As China, Japan, and Germany become rivals to the United States and Russia, the structure of the international system is gradually moving toward multipolarity.

Systems composed of several great powers roughly equal in capability are common historically. Some of these systems have been relatively stable. The more typical feature is an evolution toward rigid, antagonistic blocs—followed by the outbreak of a destructive global war. Accordingly, to cope with the welter of transnational security threats the world community will face in the future, it is imperative that the great powers do not once again become polarized into rival war-prone coalitions.

Three avenues are available to cope with the emerging security threats: the great powers can act alone; they can develop bilateral partnerships; or they can engage in multilateral cooperation. To Kegley and Raymond, neither unilateralism nor bilateralism bode well for the stability of a future multipolar system. Multilateralism, in the form of a two-tiered system of collective security, offers far better prospects for building on great powers' common interests and for diffusing the potentially bitter competition among them. Reviewing the contribution that might be made by the United Nations, the Conference on Security and Cooperation in Europe (CSCE), the geographically expanding North Atlantic Treaty Organization (NATO), and the Group of Seven (G-7), Kegley and Raymond conclude that any new multilateral security architecture can most constructively be built through a combination of ad hoc regional bodies tied together by the interlocking membership of the great powers. Without it, great-power rivalry may increase. Then war cannot be discounted.

How the world's wealthy countries interact with those who are poor is also pivotal to a stable future. Shahram Chubin examines the future of rich-poor relations from the vantage point of the former in "Southern Perspectives on World Order." Surveying the "attitudes of leaders in states of the South concerning the emerging international agenda," Chubin provides a searching overview of "the problems of security and development faced by these countries and the changing international context in which leaders of these states make choices." Emphasizing that the end of the Cold War has had "cataclysmic" consequences for the developing countries, Chubin worries that the North could now treat the Third World not as allies or equals but as objects of antipathy to be manipulated. That conclusion stems from his review of the key issues on the North-South agenda, "namely proliferation, arms control, and collective security." Chubin warns that "the South is under siege—from an international community impatient to meddle in its affairs." By framing the Third World's predicament, problems, and probable policy postures, Chubin shows why the divisive issues between the North and South can only be dealt with productively if they are defined, not as North-South security issues, but as "global security issues requiring dialogue, compromise, and grand bargains."

The distinction between North and South frequently turns on questions of material well-being. Cultural variables often also exert considerable weight, especially when cultures collide.

Throughout the world's history, when distinct cultures have come into contact, the collisions have ignited a combination of communication, cooperation, and conflict. At times, such cultural contact has produced a healthy respect for diversity, as the members of the interacting cultural traditions learned from each other. On many other occasions, however, familiarity has bred contempt. When followers have embraced the ethnocentric view that their own group's values are inherently superior, feuds and face-offs have prevailed.

Today, as the ideological contest between communism and capitalism has disappeared, ancient cultural cleavages and hatreds have resurfaced. Tribalism, religious fanaticism, and hypernational ethnicity are again rampant. Hypernationalism rationalizes large-scale violence and the subjugation of others. "Ethnic cleansing" accompanies ethno-cultural conflict. Its intent is to destroy unprotected subgroups rather than pursue accommodation and assimilation. Even genocide has resurfaced.

In "The Coming Clash of Civilizations Or, the West against the Rest," Samuel P. Huntington argues that world politics is entering a new era, where cultural conflict will be the fundamental problem. Because cultural conflict derives from cultural divisions, it will be neither primarily ideological nor economic. But it will "dominate global politics," according to Huntington, because cultural hostility between civilizations is deeply entrenched. As "the world is becoming smaller," increased global interactions have intensified "civilization consciousness" and the psychological identities that give much of the world meaning. In particular, because "the West is at a peak of its power" and engaged in an effort to promote worldwide its values of liberalism and democracy, Huntington predicts that the hostile resistance of others will grow increasingly intense. Huntington foresees the cultural conflict "along the fault line between Western and Islamic civilizations" as the most likely source of discord in the next millennium. The challenge, he maintains, is learning how to transcend this centuries-old antagonism.

A corollary dimension to inter-cultural conflict over core values concerns the influence of liberal democracy in global politics. Since the dawn of history, reformers have searched for the path by which peaceful coexistence between contentious actors might be achieved. Until recently, few students of international conflict paid serious attention to the contribution that democracy might make to the peaceful management of international disputes. This has changed, as a wave of democratization took root in 1989 at precisely the moment in history when the Cold War conflict began to thaw. For the first time in history, a majority of countries in the world were democratically ruled.

In response to this sea change, researchers and policy makers alike began to explore the proposition advanced by classic liberal theory that democracy serves as an antidote to warfare. Much evidence supports the belief that democracies are very unlikely to fight wars with each other. Whereas historically autocracies have been more expansionist and, in turn, more war-prone, democracies have been relatively pacific in their relationships with one another. In addition, democratic states are not only constrained in their warfare but also are prone to form overwhelming counter-coalitions against expansionist autocracies. Because democracies frequently police territorial expansionism through concerted cooperation to maintain the status quo, it follows that democracies are more likely to win wars against aggressive tyrannies. This augers well for neoliberal theorists' hope that a world of many democratic states will become a peaceful world.

Despite this optimism, conflict remains pervasive, even in a post-Cold War era populated by many fledgling new democratic states. Conflict has been especially recurrent and troublesome in the Middle East. In "Islam and Liberal Democracy: Muslim Perceptions and Western Reactions," Bernard Lewis provides a focused interpretation of the propositions advanced by Huntington and by the contribution that democratization arguably can make to the maintenance of peace.

The Middle East does not enjoy the same level of democratization as much of the rest of the world, and historically has frequently exploded into intense struggles between Islamic and Western norms. For fourteen centuries a series of attacks and reprisals, jihads and crusades, conquests and reconquests has erupted. Today, as in the past, fundamentalists in the Islamic world are driven by an intensely violent resentment of the West and its institutions, of its imperialism, and of its preferred representative form of governance. Lewis' purpose is to explore the question, "Can liberal democracy work in a society inspired by Islamic beliefs and principles and shaped by Islamic experience and tradition?" His explication goes far in enabling us to understand why Muslim religious precepts and memories of a glorious Muslim past now lost, exacerbated by recollections of humiliation at the hands of the industrialized West, have embittered the Muslim world and made it an inhospitable home for liberal democracy.

Although Islam has traditions that are not incompatible with representative government, in large measure Muslim resentment of the West's liberalism is deeply rooted, as Lewis explains. Because these differences are strongly felt, they are likely to cast their spell over future relations between the Middle East and the West. Especially worrisome, Lewis submits, is the danger that Western governments will succumb to the twin temptations either to "accept, and even to embrace, the most odious of dictatorships" or "to press Muslim regimes for concessions on human rights . . . and premature democratization." These reactions can be avoided, however, for Lewis believes that "now that the Cold War has ended and the Middle East is no longer a battlefield for rival power blocs, the peoples of the Middle East will have the chance—if they can take it—to make their own decisions and find their own solutions."

The specter of ethnic warfare and aggressive nationalism figures prominently in efforts to offset global discord with collaboration. The nasty trend of violent assaults on immigrants and the rise of racial violence cast an ugly shadow across the world. The problems afflicting the powerless in repressive societies are especially pronounced. While the threat of an all-out global war between the most powerful states has receded, Harvard political scientist Stanley Hoffmann in the *Harvard International Review* (Fall 1993) observes that many states

> are still pursuing the age-old game of power, threatening their neighbors and trying to satisfy old grievances or dreams of regional hegemony through the accumulation and eventual use of force. On the other hand, many of the central state actors in international politics are experiencing enormous internal turbulence, ranging from famine or revolt to disintegration, for a multitude of reasons: economic poverty or mismanage-

ment, ethnic or religious conflicts, ideological or power rivalries, oppressive measures by a tyrannical regime, and the list goes on.

The next two reading selections put these issues into perspective. In the first, "Human Rights in the New World Order," Jack Donnelly reviews the post-World War II development of human rights law and the impact of the Cold War's end on the protection of human rights. Donnelly shows why subsequent "international progress in human rights remains substantially constrained by deep structural forces" in international society.

To help us better understand why the international struggle for human rights "has just begun," Donnelly identifies the various barriers to the creation of rules to protect human rights. This leads him to conclude that human rights are unlikely to be any better protected in the emerging post-Cold War "world order" than previously. The pervasive optimism embraced by some "is unjustified," he argues, as "new threats to human rights are emerging, most notably increased ethnic violence" despite the demise of superpower support for repressive regimes. International human rights policy will thus likely remain a salient global issue in the post-Cold War world.

In "Out of the Cold: Humanitarian Intervention in the 1990s," Stanley Hoffmann extends the analysis by exploring what can be done to contain the prevalent abuse of human rights. In particular, he examines how the traditional legal prohibition of external military intervention in a state's internal affairs is increasingly being challenged as a result of the ethnic, economic, ideological, and tyrannical institutional problems identified above. Growing numbers of states have begun to recognize the immorality of ignoring terrible injustice in remote places beyond their borders. They therefore have begun to contemplate active use of intervention—not to subjugate foreigners but instead to police repressive governments' policies toward their own populations.

Humanitarian intervention by outsiders in others' domestic affairs is not without its critics, however. (Bernard Lewis's critique of Western interference in Muslim states is one example.) As a consequence of the controversial nature of this complex issue, defining the conditions under which moral and political criteria can justify intervention to "relieve the suffering of victims of internal conflicts and disasters" promises to be a critical issue throughout the remainder of the twentieth century. For, as Hoffmann concludes, "collective security is another word for war—it is internationally sanctioned war—and any war, even for a good cause, raises . . . fundamental moral issues of what constitutes a just and peaceful domestic order."

In "Wandering in the Void: Charting the UN's New Strategic Role," John Gerard Ruggie examines the contribution that the United Nations might make to peacekeeping. Collective security requires the creation of effective institutions to cope with threats to global stability. Since its birth at the end of World War II, the United Nations has to many symbolized perhaps the greatest hope (and most bitter disappointment) for preserving peace and containing violence.

Renewed respect for the United Nations was given impetus by the world organization's successes at resolving a number of international conflicts in the early post-Cold War era. As that epic struggle was dying, the UN was credited with brokering an end to the eight-year Iran-Iraq war and the withdrawal of Soviet troops from Afghanistan. The UN also supervised Nicaragua's first free elections as well as those in Namibia. Then, in the wake of Iraq's brutal invasion of Kuwait, it was through the UN Security Council that the world community organized a trade embargo against the renegade Iraqi dictator Saddam Hussein and later authorized the use of force against Iraq. This achievement was realized because the superpowers acted in concert rather than, as had been their custom throughout the Cold War, using their prerogatives to veto any action that might benefit their adversary. As collective security, which had been the original purpose of the United Nations, was revived, the organization was freed from paralysis and began to emerge as an important force for peace.

The recent achievements of the United Nations suggest that it might have begun finally to fulfill its original ambitious promise. But, as Ruggie notes, even in the post-Cold War atmosphere of great-power collaboration many long-standing disputes continue to resist conciliation. Moreover, in the new, relatively hopeful international climate which finds the Security Council often acting in concert, the United Nations finds itself strained materially and institutionally, as its overly ambitious efforts have brought the world organization "to the point of outright strategic failure." The problem, Ruggie argues, is that today "there is no clear-cut aggressor" to confront with the UN's military strategy of seeking "to deter, dissuade and deny (D^3)." Ruggie recommends that to fulfill its objectives, the international community should define precisely the domain between peacekeeping and UN-sanctioned military enforcement, and confine its efforts to operations that fall within these delineated boundaries.

How states respond to the challenge of managing global discord and promoting collaboration is exhibited also by the nature of the international legal system. In "The Reality and Relevance of International Law in the Post-Cold War Era," Christopher C. Joyner examines a wide spectrum of viewpoints regarding the functions of international law in world affairs. He concludes that despite its limitations (many of which are exaggerated by those uninformed about its principles and procedures), international law succeeds in doing what states ask of it. Not the least of its functions is maintaining the order, stability, and predictability that states prize. Joyner also predicts that international law's contribution to world order will grow and that its impact will continue to expand.

As we look to the future, will states approach the issues they face on the global agenda in a collaborative manner? Or will the tendency toward conflict command more attention? It is to this question that Robert Axelrod and Robert O. Keohane bring insight in the concluding selection of Part II of *The Global Agenda*. Using the primary structural feature of the international system as their point of reference—namely, that world politics takes place in anarchy, without

supranational regulation—Axlerod and Keohane show in "Achieving Cooperation under Anarchy: Strategies and Institutions" how cooperation occurs even
under conditions where it might appear most unlikely. Cooperation in world
politics is explained, they argue, by three factors: the interaction of mutual interests, "the shadow of the future" coloring states' images of subsequent behavior
by those with whom they interact, and the number of parties to transnational
cooperative ventures.

In helping us understand the success of attempts at cooperation in both
military-security relations and political-economic relations, Axelrod and Keohane highlight the ways in which new institutions and norms can contribute
to the development and maintenance of cooperation, as well as the strategies
and background conditions that foster them. Whether discord or collaboration
will be greater or lesser ingredients in the future of world politics will be
influenced considerably, they suggest, by the ways states reciprocate the
cooperative acts of others. Despite the reality of anarchy and discord, Axelrod and Keohane conclude that beneficial forms of international cooperation
can be promoted, particularly in the low-politics realm of material and non-
material well-being but also in the high-politics realm where security is at
stake.

12

MODELS OF INTERNATIONAL RELATIONS: REALIST AND NEOLIBERAL PERSPECTIVES ON CONFLICT AND COOPERATION

Ole R. Holsti

Two models that have been developed to describe and explain different properties of discordant and accommodative relations in world politics are described by Ole R. Holsti: classical and modern "realism" and the so-called neoliberal elaboration of traditional liberal theories. Holsti is George V. Allen Professor of International Affairs at Duke University and is a former president of the International Studies Association. He is the author with James N. Rosenau of *American Leadership in World Affairs: Vietnam and the Breakdown of Consensus* (1984).

The question of how best to understand international relations has been debated since the advent of the international system. This debate between proponents of alternative theories has customarily grown especially intense in times of profound turmoil and change.

In the twentieth century, the cataclysm of World War I resurfaced and intensified the dialogue between liberals, such as Woodrow Wilson, who sought to

Adapted for this edition of this book by Ole R. Holsti, from "Models of International Relations and Foreign Policy," *Diplomatic History* 13, 1 (Winter, 1989). Many footnotes were deleted and renumbered to appear in consecutive order. Alexander L. George, Joseph Grieco, Michael J. Hogan, Timothy Lomperis, Roy Melbourne, James N. Rosenau, and Andrew M. Scott kindly provided very helpful comments and suggestions on early drafts of that essay. For an alternate, extended theoretical analysis that also discusses Marxist and decision-making approaches, see also Ole R. Holsti, "Theories of International Relations and Foreign Policy: Realism and Its Challengers," pp. 35–65 in Charles W. Kegley, ed., *Controversies in International Relations Theory: Realism and the Neoliberal Challenge* (New York: St. Martin's Press, 1995). Reprinted by permission of the author.

create a new world order anchored in the League of Nations and realists, exemplified by Georges Clemenceau, who sought to use more traditional means to ensure their countries' security. World War II renewed that debate, but the events leading up to that conflict and the Cold War that emerged almost immediately after the guns had stopped firing in 1945 seemed to provide ample evidence to tip the balance strongly in favor of the realist vision of international relations. In the meantime, the growth of Soviet power, combined with the disintegration of the great colonial empires that gave rise to the emergence of some one hundred newly independent countries, gave prominence to still another perspective on world affairs, most variants of which drew to some extent upon the writing of Marx and Lenin.

More recent events, including the disintegration of the Soviet Union, the end of the Cold War, the re-emergence of inter- and intranational ethnic conflicts that had been suppressed during the Cold War, the Persian Gulf War, the continuing economic integration of Europe, and the declining international economic position of the United States have stimulated new debates about the theories of the international relations that can best contribute to understanding the emerging issues on the global agenda of the late twentieth century. This essay describes two prominent schools of thought on which contemporary theoretical inquiry presently centers. Although different, they speak to each other and place primary explanatory emphasis on features of the international system. These are the variants of realism and the newly revived liberal theories that challenge one or more of the core premises of both classical and modern realism.

Because "classical realism" is the most venerable and persisting model of international relations, it provides a good starting point and baseline for comparison with competing models. Following a discussion of classical realism, an examination of "modern realism" and "neorealism" identifies the continuities and differences between the two approaches. The essay then turns to an examination of the premises underlying neoliberal theories.

REALISM: CLASSICAL, MODERN, AND ITS NEOREALIST EXTENSION

Robert Gilpin (1981) may have been engaging in hyperbole when he questioned whether our understanding of international relations has advanced significantly since Thucydides, but one must acknowledge that the latter's analysis of the Peloponnesian War includes concepts that are not foreign to contemporary students of balance-of-power politics. There have always been Americans such as Alexander Hamilton who viewed international relations from a realist perspective, but its contemporary intellectual roots are largely European. Three important figures probably had the greatest impact on American scholarship: the historian E. H. Carr (1939), the geographer Nicholas Spykman (1942), and the political theorist Hans J. Morgenthau (1973). Other Europeans who have contributed significantly to realist thought include John Herz (1959), Raymond Aron (1966), Hedley Bull (1977), and Martin Wight (1973), while notable Americans of this school include scholars Arnold Wolfers (1962) and Norman Graebner (1984), as well as diplomat George F. Kennan (1951), journalist Walter Lippmann (1943), and theologian Reinhold Niebuhr (1945).

Classical Realism

Although realists do not constitute a homogeneous school—any more than do any of the others discussed in this essay—most of them share at least five core premises about international relations. To begin with, they consider the central questions to be the causes of war and the conditions of peace. They also regard the structure of the system as a necessary if not always sufficient explanation for many aspects of international relations. According to classical realists, "structural anarchy," or the absence of a central authority to settle disputes, is the essential feature of the contemporary system, and it gives rise to the "security dilemma": in a self-help system one nation's search for security often leaves its current and potential adversaries insecure, any nation that strives for absolute security leaves all others in the system absolutely insecure, and it can provide a powerful incentive for arms races and other types of hostile interactions. Consequently, the question of relative capabilities is a crucial factor. Efforts to deal with this central element of the international system constitute the driving force behind the relations of units within the system; those that fail to cope will not survive. Thus, unlike "idealists" or "liberals," classical realists view conflict as a natural state of affairs rather than a consequence that can be attributed to historical circumstances, evil leaders, flawed sociopolitical systems, or inadequate international understanding and education.

A third premise that unites classical realists is their focus on geographically based groups as the central actors in the international system. During other periods the primary entities may have been city-states or empires, but at least since the Treaties of Westphalia (1648) nation-states have been the dominant units. Classical realists also agree that state behavior is rational. The assumption behind this fourth premise is that states are guided by the logic of the "national interest," usually defined in terms of survival, security, power, and relative capabilities. To Morgenthau (1973: 3, 5), for example, "rational foreign policy minimizes risks and maximizes benefits." Although the national interest may vary according to specific circumstances, the similarity of motives among nations permits the analyst to reconstruct the logic of policy makers in their pursuit of national interests—what Morgenthau called the "rational hypothesis"—and to avoid the fallacies of "concern with motives and concern with ideological preferences."

Finally, the nation-state can also be conceptualized as a *unitary* actor. Because the central problems for states are starkly defined by the nature of the international system, their actions are primarily a response to external rather than domestic political forces. At best, the latter provide very weak explanations for external policy. According to Stephen Krasner (1978:33), for example, the state "can be treated as an autonomous actor pursuing goals associated with power and the general interest of the society." However, classical realists sometimes use domestic politics to explain deviations from rational policies.

Realism has been the dominant model of international relations during recent decades, perhaps in part because it seemed to provide a useful framework for understanding World War II and the Cold War. Nevertheless, the classical versions articulated by Morgenthau and others have received a good deal of critical scrutiny. The critics have included scholars who accept the basic premises of realism but who found that in at least four important respects these theories lacked sufficient precision and rigor.

Classical realism has usually been grounded in a pessimistic theory of human nature, either a theological version (e.g., St. Augustine and Reinhold Niebuhr) or a secular one (e.g., Machiavelli, Hobbes, and Morgenthau). Egoism and self-interested behavior are not limited to a few evil or misguided leaders, as the idealists would have it, but are basic to *homo politicus* and thus are at the core of a realist theory. But because human nature, if it means anything, is a constant rather than a variable, it is an unsatisfactory explanation for the full range of international relations. If human nature explains war and conflict, what accounts for peace and cooperation? In order to avoid this problem, most modern realists have turned their attention from human nature to the structure of the international system to explain state behavior.

In addition, critics have noted a lack of precision and even contradictions in the way classical realists use such concepts as "power," "national interest," and "balance of power." They also see possible contradictions between the central descriptive and prescriptive elements of classical realism. On the one hand, as Hans Morgenthau (1973:5) put it, nations and their leaders "think and act in terms of interests defined as power," but on the other, diplomats are urged to exercise prudence and self-restraint, as well as to recognize the legitimate national interests of other nations. Obviously, then, power plays a central role in classical realism. But the correlation between the relative power balance and political outcomes is often less than compelling, suggesting the need to enrich analyses with other variables. Moreover, the distinction between "power as capabilities" and "usable options" is especially important in the nuclear age.

Modern Realism

While classical realists have typically looked to history, philosophy, and political science for insights and evidence, the search for greater precision has led many modern realists to look elsewhere for appropriate models, analogies, metaphors, and insights. The discipline of choice is often economics, from which modern realists have borrowed such tools and concepts as rational choice, expected utility, theories of firms and markets, bargaining theory, and game theory. Contrary to the assertion of some critics, however, modern realists *share* rather than reject the core premises of their classical predecessors.

The quest for precision has yielded a rich harvest of theories and models, and a somewhat less bountiful crop of supporting empirical applications. Drawing in part on game theory, Morton Kaplan described several types of international systems—for example, balance of power, loose bipolar, tight bipolar, universal, hierarchical, and a unit-veto system in which any action requires the unanimous approval of all its members. He then outlined the essential rules that constitute these systems. For example, the rules for a balance-of-power system are "(1) increase capabilities, but negotiate rather than fight; (2) fight rather than fail to increase capabilities; (3) stop fighting rather than eliminate an essential actor; (4) oppose any coalition or single actor that tends to assume a position of predominance within the system; (5) constrain actors who subscribe to supranational organizational principles; and (6) permit defeated or constrained essential actors to re-enter the system" (Kaplan, 1957: 23).

Neorealism

Kenneth Waltz's *Theory of International Politics* (1979), the most prominent effort to develop a rigorous and parsimonious model of "neorealist" or "structural" realism, has tended to define the terms of recent theoretical debates. It follows and builds upon another enormously influential book in which Waltz (1959) developed the Rousseauian position that a theory of war must include the system level (the "third image") and not just first (theories of human nature) or second (state attributes) images. Why war? Because there is nothing in the system to prevent it.

Theory of International Relations is grounded in analogies from microeconomics: international politics and foreign policy are analogous to markets and firms. Oligopoly theory is used to illuminate the dynamics of interdependent choice in a self-help anarchical system. Waltz explicitly limits his attention to a structural theory of international systems, eschewing the task of linking it to a theory of foreign policy. Indeed, he doubts that the two can be joined in a single theory and is highly critical of many system-level analysts, including Morton Kaplan, Stanley Hoffmann, Richard Rosecrance, Karl Deutsch, and J. David Singer, and others, charging them with various errors, including "reductionism," that is, defining the system in terms of the attributes or interactions of the units.

In order to avoid reductionism and to gain rigor and parsimony, Waltz erects his theory on the foundations of three core propositions that define the structure of the international system. The first concentrates on the principles by which the system is ordered. The contemporary system is anarchic and decentralized rather than hierarchial; although they differ in many respects, each unit (state) is formally equal. Because Waltz strives for a universal theory that is not limited to any era, he uses the term "unit" to refer to the constituent members of the system; in the contemporary system these are states, but in order to reflect Waltz's intent more faithfully, the term "unit" is used here. A second defining proposition is the character of the units. An anarchic system is composed of similar sovereign units, and therefore the functions that they perform are also similar rather than different; for example, all have the task of providing for their own security. In contrast, a hierarchical system would be characterized by some type of division of labor, as is the case in domestic politics. Finally, there is the distribution of capabilities among units in the system. Although capabilities are a unit-level attribute, the distribution of capabilities is a system-level concept.

A change in any of these elements constitutes a change in system structure. The first element of structure as defined by Waltz is a quasi-constant because the ordering principle rarely changes, and the second element drops out of the analysis because the functions of units are similar as long as the system remains anarchic. Thus, the last of the three attributes, the distribution of capabilities, plays the central role in Waltz's model.

Waltz uses his theory to deduce the central characteristics of international relations. These include some non-obvious propositions about the contemporary international system. For example, with respect to system stability (defined as maintenance of its anarchic character and no consequential variation in the number of major actors), he concludes that because the Cold War's bipolar system reduced uncertainty, it was more stable than alternative structures. Furthermore, he contends that because interdependence has declined rather than increased during the twentieth century, this trend has actually contributed to stability; and he argues that the proliferation of nuclear weapons may contribute to rather than erode system stability (Waltz, 1970, 1981).

Unlike some system-level models, Waltz's effort to bring rigor and parsimony to realism has stimulated a good deal of further research, but it has not escaped controversy and criticism (see especially Grieco, 1984; Keohane, 1986; Baldwin, 1993; Kegley, 1995). Leaving aside highly charged polemics—for example, that Waltz and his supporters are guilty of engaging in a "totalitarian project of global proportions" (Ashley, 1984:228)—most of the vigorous debate has centered on four alleged deficiencies relating to interests and preferences, system change, misallocation of variables between the system and unit levels, and an inability to explain outcomes.

Specifically, a sparse structural approach suffers from an inability to identify adequately the nature and sources of interests and preferences because these are unlikely to derive solely from the structure of the system. Ideology or domestic considerations may often be at least as important. Consequently, the model is also unable to specify how interests and preferences may change. The three defining characteristics of system structure are too general, moreover, and thus they are not sufficiently sensitive to specify the sources and dynamics of system change. The critics buttress their claim that the model is too static by pointing to

Waltz's assertion that there has only been a single structural change in the international system during the past three centuries.

Another drawback is the restrictive definition of system properties, which leads Waltz to misplace, and therefore neglect, elements of international relations that properly belong at the system level. Critics have focused on his treatment of the destructiveness of nuclear weapons and interdependence. Waltz labels these as unit-level properties, whereas some of his critics assert that they are in fact attributes of the system.

Finally, the distribution of capabilities explains outcomes in international affairs only in the most general way, falling short of answering the questions that are of central interest to many analysts. For example, the distribution of power at the end of World War II would have enabled one to predict the rivalry that emerged between the United States and the Soviet Union (as de Tocqueville did more than a century earlier), but it would have been inadequate for explaining the pattern of relations between these two countries—the Cold War rather than withdrawal into isolationism by either or both, a division of the world into spheres of influence, or World War III. In order to do so, it is necessary to explore political processes *within* states—at minimum within the United States and the USSR—as well as *between* them.

Robert Gilpin shares with Waltz the core assumptions of modern realism, but his study of *War and Change in World Politics* also attempts to cope with some of the criticism leveled at Waltz's theory by focusing on the dynamics of system change. Drawing upon both economic and sociological theory, his model is based on five core propositions (Gilpin, 1981:10–11). The first is that the international system is stable—in a state of equilibrium—if no state believes that it is profitable to attempt to change it. Second, a state will attempt to change the status quo of the international system if the expected benefits outweigh the costs; that is, if there is an expected net gain for the revisionist state. Related to this is the proposition that a state will seek change through territorial, political, and economic expansion until the marginal costs of further change equal or exceed the marginal benefits. Moreover, when an equilibrium between the costs and benefits of further change and expansion is reached, the economic costs of maintaining the status quo (expenditures for military forces, support for allies, etc.) tend to rise faster than the resources needed to do so. An equilibrium exists when no powerful state believes that a change in the system would yield additional net benefits. Finally, if the resulting disequilibrium between the existing governance of the international system and the redistribution of power is not resolved, the system will be changed and a new equilibrium reflecting the distribution of relative capabilities will be established.

Unlike Waltz, Gilpin includes state-level processes in order to explain change. Differential economic growth rates among nations—a structural-systemic-level variable—play a vital role in his explanation for the rise and

TABLE 12-1
TWO MODELS OF THE INTERNATIONAL SYSTEM

	REALISM	NEOLIBERALISM
Type of model	Classical: descriptive and normative Modern: deductive	Descriptive and normative
Central problems	Causes of war Conditions of peace	Broad agenda of social, economic, and environmental issues arising from gap between demands and resources
Conception of current international system	Structural anarchy	Global society Complex interdependence (structure varies by issue-area)
Key actors	Geographically based units (tribes, city-states, nation-state, etc.)	Highly permeable nation-states *plus* a broad range of nonstate actors, including IOs, IGOs, NGOs, and individuals
Central motivations	National interest Security Power	Human needs and wants
Loyalties	To geographically based groups (from tribes to nation-states)	Loyalties to nation-state declining To emerging global values and institutions that transcend those of the nation-state and/or to subnational groups
Central processes	Search for security and survival	Aggregate effects of decisions by national and nonnational actors How units (not limited to nation-states) cope with a growing agenda of threats and opportunities arising from human wants
Likelihood of system transformation	Low (basic structural elements of system have revealed an ability to persist despite many other kinds of changes)	High in the direction of the model (owing to the rapid pace of technological change, etc.)
Sources of theory, insights, and evidence	Politics History Economics (especially "modern" realists)	Broad range of social sciences Natural and technological sciences

decline of great powers, but his model also includes propositions about the law of diminishing returns on investments, the impact of affluence on martial spirits and on the ratio of consumption to investment, and structural change in the economy. Table 12-1 summarizes some key elements of realism. It also contrasts them to a rival system-level model of international relations—the neoliberal model, to which we now turn our attention.

NEOLIBERALISM

Just as there are variants of realism, there are several neoliberal theories, but this discussion focuses on two common denominators; they all challenge the first and third core propositions of realism identified earlier, asserting that inordinate attention to the war/peace issue and the nation-state renders it an increasingly anachronistic model of global relations (Keohane and Nye, 1977; Morse, 1976; Rosenau, 1980, 1990; Mansbach and Vasquez, 1981; and Scott, 1982).

The agenda of critical problems confronting states has been vastly expanded during the twentieth century. Attention to the issues of war and peace is by no means misdirected according to proponents of a liberal perspective, but concerns for welfare, modernization, the environment, and the like are today no less potent sources of motivation and action. Indeed, many liberals define security in terms that are broader than the geopolitical-military spheres, and they emphasize the potential for cooperative relations among nations. Institution building to reduce uncertainty and fears of perfidy; improved international education and communication to ameliorate fears and antagonisms based on misinformation and misperceptions; and the positive-sum possibilities of such activities as trade are but a few of the ways, according to liberals, by which nations may jointly gain and thus mitigate, if not eliminate, the harshest features of international relations emphasized by the realists. Finally, the diffusion of knowledge and technology, combined with the globalization of communications, has vastly increased popular expectations. The resulting demands have outstripped resources and the ability of existing institutions—notably the nation-state—to cope effectively with them. Interdependence arises from an inability of even the most powerful states to cope, or to do so unilaterally or at acceptable levels of cost and risk, with issues ranging from trade to AIDS, and immigration to environmental threats.

Paralleling the widening agenda of critical issues is the expansion of actors whose behavior can have a significant impact beyond national boundaries; indeed, the cumulative effects of their actions can have profound consequences for the international system. Thus, although nation-states continue to be important international actors, they possess a declining ability to control their own destinies. The aggregate effect of actions by multitudes of non-state actors can have potent effects that transcend political boundaries. These may include such powerful or highly visible non-state institutions as Exxon, the Organization of

Petroleum Exporting Countries, or the Palestine Liberation Organization. On the other hand, the cumulative effects of decisions by less powerful or less visible actors may also have profound international consequences. For example, decisions by thousands of individuals, mutual funds, banks, pension funds, and other financial institutions to sell securities on 19 October 1987 not only resulted in an unprecedented "crash" on Wall Street but within hours its consequences were also felt throughout the entire global financial system. Governments might take such actions as loosening credit or even closing exchanges, but they were largely unable to contain the effects of the panic.

The widening agenda of critical issues, most of which lack a purely national solution, has also led to creation of new actors that transcend political boundaries, for example, international organizations, transnational organizations, nongovernmental organizations, multinational corporations, and the like. Thus, not only does an exclusive focus on the war/peace issue fail to capture the complexities of contemporary international life but it also blinds the analyst to the institutions, processes, and norms that permit cooperation and significantly mitigate some features of an anarchic system. In short, according to emerging new liberal perspectives, an adequate understanding of the proliferating issues in the evolving global system must recognize that no single model is likely to be sufficient for all issues, and that if it restricts attention to the manner in which states deal with traditional security concerns, it is more likely to obfuscate than clarify the realities of contemporary world affairs.

The liberal models have several important virtues. They recognize that international behavior and outcomes arise from a multiplicity of motives, not merely security, at least if security is defined solely in military or strategic terms. They also alert us to the fact that important international processes and conditions originate not only in the actions of nation-states but also in the aggregated behavior of other actors. These models not only enable the analyst to deal with a broader agenda of critical issues but, more importantly, they force one to contemplate a much richer menu of demands, processes, and outcomes than would be derived from power-centered realist models. Stated differently, liberal theories are more sensitive to the possibility that the politics of trade, currency, immigration, health, the environment, and the like may significantly and systematically differ from those typically associated with security issues.

On the other hand, some liberal analysts underestimate the potency of nationalism and the durability of the nation-state. Two decades ago one of them wrote that "the nation is declining in its importance as a political unit to which allegiances are attached" (Rosenau, 1968:39; see also Rosecrance, 1986; Herz, 1957, 1968). Objectively, nationalism may be an anachronism, but for better or worse, powerful loyalties are still attached to nation-states. The suggestion that because even some well-established countries have experienced independence movements among ethnic, cultural, or religious minorities, the sovereign territorial state may be in decline is not wholly persuasive. Indeed, that evidence perhaps points to precisely the opposite conclusion: in virtually every region of the world there are groups which seek to create or restore geographically based entities in which its members may enjoy the status and privileges associated with sovereign territorial statehood. Evidence from Poland to Palestine, Serbia to Sri Lanka, Estonia to Eritrea, Armenia to Afghanistan, and elsewhere seems to indicate that obituaries for nationalism may be somewhat premature.

The notion that such powerful non-national actors as major multinational corporations (MNCs) will soon transcend the nation-state seems equally premature. International drug rings do appear capable of dominating such states as Colombia and Panama. However, the pattern of outcomes in confrontations between MNCs and states, including cases involving major expropriations of corporate properties, indicate that even relatively weak nations are not always the hapless pawns of the MNCs. Case studies by Joseph Grieco (1984) and Gary Gereffi (1983), among others, indicate that MNC-state relations yield a wide variety of outcomes.

Underlying the liberal critique of realist models is that the latter are too wedded to the past and are thus incapable of dealing adequately with change. For the present, however, even if global dynamics arise from multiple sources (including non-state actors), the actions of nation-states and their agents would appear to remain the major sources of change in the international system.

THE REALIST-LIBERAL DIALOGUE AND THE FUTURE

A renowned diplomatic historian has asserted that most theories of international relations flunked a critical test by failing to forecast the end of the Cold War (Gaddis, 1992–93). This conclusion speculates on the related question of how well the theories discussed above might help us understand conflict and cooperation in the post-Cold War world. Dramatic events since the late 1980s would appear to have posed serious challenges for several theories, but one should be wary about writing premature obituaries for any of them. The importance of recent developments notwithstanding, one should avoid "naive (single case) falsification" of major theories. Further, in 1994, five short years after the Berlin Wall came down and only three years after dissolution of the Soviet Union, some caution about declaring that major events and trends are irreversible seems warranted.

Liberal theories have recently regained popularity, especially in efforts to explain relations among the industrial democracies. Progress toward economic unification of Europe, although not without detours and setbacks, would appear to provide significant support for the liberal view that, even in an anarchic world, major powers may find ways of cooperating and overcoming the constraint of the "relative gains" problem. Moreover, Woodrow Wilson's thesis that a world of democratic nations will be more peaceful has stood the test of time rather well, at least in the sense that democratic nations have not gone to war with each other (Doyle, 1983, 1986). His diagnosis that self-determination also supports peace may be correct in the abstract, but universal application of that principle is neither possible nor desirable, if only because it would result in immense bloodshed; the peaceful divorces of Norway and Sweden in 1905 and of the Czech Republic and Slovakia in 1992 are unfortunately not the norm. Although it appears that economic interests have come to dominate nationalist, ethnic, or religious passions among the industrial democracies, the evidence is far less assuring in other areas, including parts of the former Soviet Union, Central Europe, the Middle East, South Asia, Africa, and elsewhere.

Recent events appear to have created an especially acute challenge to structural realism. Although structural realism provides a parsimonious and elegant theory, its deficiencies are likely to become more rather than less apparent in the post-Cold War world. Its weaknesses in dealing with questions of system change and in specifying policy preferences other than survival and security are likely to be magnified. Moreover, whereas classical realism espouses a number of attractive prescriptive features (caution, humility, warnings against mistaking one's preferences for the moral laws of the universe), neorealism is an especially weak source of policy-relevant theory (George, 1993). Indeed, some of the prescriptions put forward by neorealists seem reckless, such as the suggestion to let Germany join the nuclear club (Mearsheimer, 1990). In addition to European economic cooperation, specific events that seem inexplicable by structural realism include Soviet acquiescence in the collapse of its empire and peaceful transformation of the system structure. These developments are especially telling because structural realism is explicitly touted as a theory of major powers (Waltz, 1979). Consequently, even as distinguished a realist as Robert Tucker (1992–93:36) has characterized the structural version of realism as "more questionable than ever."

More importantly, even though the international system remains anarchic, the possibility of war among major powers cannot wholly be dismissed, and proliferation may place nuclear weapons in the hands of leaders with little stake in maintaining the status quo, as the constraints imposed by systemic imperatives on foreign policy choices are clearly eroding. National interests and even national security have increasingly come to be defined in ways that transcend the military/strategic concerns that are at the core of realist theory. Well before the disintegration of the Soviet Union, an Americans Talk Security survey in 1988 revealed that the perceived threat to national security from "Soviet aggression around the world" ranked in a seventh place tie with the "greenhouse effect" and well behind a number of post-Cold War, non-military threats. Trade, drug trafficking, immigration, the environment, and AIDS are among the non-military issues that regularly appear on lists of top national security threats as perceived by both mass publics and elites.

The expanded agenda of national interests, combined with the trend toward greater democracy in many parts of the world, suggests that we are entering an era in which the balance between the relative potency of systemic and domestic forces in shaping and constraining foreign policies is moving toward the latter. Such issues as trade, immigration, and others can be expected to enhance the impact of domestic actors—including public opinion and ethnic, religious, economic, and perhaps even regional pressure groups—while reducing the ability of executives to dominate policy processes on the grounds, so frequently invoked during the Cold War, that the adept pursuit of national security requires secrecy, flexibility, and the ability to act with speed. In short, we are likely to see the increasing democratization of foreign policy in the post-Cold War era. And that brings us back to the point at which we started, for the relationship between democracy and foreign policy is another of the issues on which realists and liberals are in sharp disagreement. Realists such as de Tocqueville, Morgenthau, Lippmann, Kennan, and many others share a profound skepticism about the impact of democratic political processes, and especially of public opinion, on the quality and continuity of foreign policy. In contrast, liberals in the Kant-Wilson tradition maintain that more democratic foreign policy processes contribute to peace and stability in international politics. Thus, if domestic politics do in fact come to play an increasingly important role in shaping post-Cold War era foreign policies, that development will ensure continuation of the venerable debate between realists and liberals.

References

Aron, Raymond. (1966) *Peace and War.* Garden City, N.Y.: Doubleday.

Ashley, Richard K. (1984) "The Poverty of Neo-Realism," *International Organization* **38**:225–286.

Baldwin, David A., ed. (1993) *Neorealism and Neoliberalism: The Contemporary Debate.* New York: Columbia University Press.

Bull, Hedley. (1977) *The Anarchical Society: A Study of Order in World Politics.* London: Macmillan.

Carr, E. H. (1939) *Twenty Year Crisis.* London: Macmillan.

Doyle, Michael. (1983) "Kant, Liberal Legacies, and Foreign Affairs," *Philosophy and Public Affairs* **12**:205–235.

———. (1986) "Liberalism and World Politics," *American Political Science Review* **80**:1151–1170.

Gaddis, John Lewis. (1992–93) "International Relations Theory and the End of the Cold War," *International Security* **17**:5–58.

George, Alexander L. (1993) *Bridging the Gap: Theory and Practice in Foreign Policy.* Washington: U.S. Institute of Peace.

Gereffi, Gary. (1983) *The Pharmaceutical Industry and Dependency in the Third World.* Princeton, N.J.: Princeton University Press.

Gilpin, Robert. (1981) *War and Change in World Politics.* Cambridge: Cambridge University Press.

Graebner, Norman A. (1984) *America as a World Power: A Realist Appraisal from Wilson to Reagan.* Wilmington, Del.: Scholarly Resources.

Grieco, Joseph. (1984) *Between Dependence and Autonomy.* Berkeley: University of California Press.

Herz, John. (1959) *International Politics in the Atomic Age.* New York: Columbia University Press.

———. (1957) "The Rise and Demise of the Territorial State," *World Politics* **9**:473–493.

———. (1968) "The Territorial State Revisited: Reflections on the Future of the Nation-State," *Polity* **1**:12–34.

Kaplan, Morton. (1957) *System and Process in International Politics.* New York: Wiley.

Kegley, Charles W., Jr., ed. (1995) *Controversies in International Relations Theory: Realism and the Neoliberal Challenge.* New York: St. Martin's Press.

Kennan, George F. (1951) *American Diplomacy, 1900–1950.* Chicago: University of Chicago Press.

Keohane, Robert, ed. (1986) *Neorealism and Its Critics.* New York: Columbia University Press.

Keohane, Robert, and Joseph S. Nye, Jr. (1977) *Power and Interdependence.* Boston: Little, Brown.

Krasner, Stephen. (1978) *Defending the National Interest.* Princeton, N.J.: Princeton University Press.

Lippmann, Walter. (1943) *U.S. Foreign Policy: Shield of the Republic.* Boston: Little, Brown.

Mansbach, Richard, and John Vasquez. (1981) *In Search of Theory: A New Paradigm for Global Politics.* New York: Columbia University Press.

Mearsheimer, John. (1990) "Back to the Future: Instability in Europe after the Cold War," *International Security* **15**:5–56.

Morgenthau, Hans J. (1973) *Politics Among Nations,* 5th ed. New York: Knopf.

Morse, Edward. (1976) *Modernization and the Transformation of International Relations.* New York: Free Press.

Niebuhr, Reinhold. (1945) *The Children of Light and the Children of Darkness.* New York: Scribner.

Rosecrance, Richard. (1986) *The Rise of the Trading State.* New York: Basic Books.

Rosenau, James N. (1968) "National Interest," *International Encyclopedia of the Social Sciences,* **11**:34–40. New York: Macmillan.

———. (1980) *The Study of Global Interdependence.* London: F. Pinter.

———. (1990) *Turbulence in World Politics.* Princeton, N.J.: Princeton University Press.

Scott, Andrew M. (1982) *The Dynamics of Interdependence.* Chapel Hill: University of North Carolina Press.

Spykman, Nicholas. (1942) *America's Strategy in World Politics.* New York: Harcourt, Brace.

Tucker, Robert W. (1992–93) "Realism and the New Consensus." *National Interest* **30**:33–36.

Waltz, Kenneth W. (1959) *Man, the State, and War.* New York: Columbia University Press.

————. (1970) "The Myth of National Interdependence," in Charles P. Kindleberger, ed., *The International Corporation.* Cambridge: M.I.T. Press.

————. (1981) "The Spread of Nuclear Weapons: More May Be Better," *Adelphi Papers,* No. 171.

————. (1979) *Theory of International Relations.* Reading, Mass.: Addison Wesley.

Wight, Martin. (1973) "The Balance of Power and International Order," in Alan James, ed., *The Bases of International Order.* London: Oxford University Press.

Wolfers, Arnold. (1962) *Discord and Collaboration.* Baltimore: Johns Hopkins University Press.

13

COLD WAR, CHILL PEACE: PROSPECTS FOR ORDER AND DISORDER

Michael Howard

The historical foundations of the emerging post-Cold War era are described and analyzed in this essay by Michael Howard. Noting that "after every great war, whether hot or cold, there has been a chill peace," the essay summarizes the major dislocations and problems to which the world will have to adjust in the wake of the Cold War. Howard is Lovett Professor of Military and Naval History at Yale University and previously was Regius Professor of Modern History at Oxford University. His many books include *Lessons of History* (1991).

As the Berlin Wall crumbled and the Cold War came so miraculously to an end, I was rash enough to conclude an essay with the words: "As one whose conscious political experience now extends over fifty years I can say that I would rather be living in 1989 than in 1939—or indeed any date between the two."[1]

Should I now regret or retract that statement? Do I still feel so confident about the world today as I, and I think most of us, did then?

Well, [four years later], and speaking purely personally, I am not inclined either to regret or to retract it. It was a view that would probably have been shared at the time by the overwhelming majority of Europeans, East and West. During the previous half century we had, most of us, been under dire physical

[1] *Lessons of History* (Oxford University Press, 1991), p. 5.
This essay originally appeared in *World Policy Journal,* Vol. X, No. 4 (Winter 1993–1994).

threat. For much of the time during the Second World War it seemed that a lot of very clever and highly motivated people were trying very hard to kill me, and I did not relish the experience. Then, after a very brief interval, came the long era of "nuclear deterrence," when it was impossible for any reasonably well-informed observer to contemplate the risks inherent in the situation without a spasm of visceral terror. These were years in which we worked out our salvation almost literally "in fear and trembling." Nobody in his right mind could wish to live through them again.

It would be legitimate, indeed, to extend that troubled period backward for a generation, to 1914, for the two world wars had a basic continuity; so far as Europe was concerned, they can be regarded almost as a single Thirty Years' War. The years between 1914 and 1989 may come to be seen as ones of continuous armed confrontation and conflict, broken by periods of uneasy truce, not unlike the wars of the French Revolution and Napoleonic conquest between 1793 and 1815, except that in our own time we had to endure, not one, but two prolonged conflicts with two different major adversaries, and those conflicts shaped the minds, not of one generation, but of three.

Now, like the statesmen gathered at Vienna at the conclusion of the Napoleonic wars, we have to adjust ourselves to an entirely new situation. An era dominated by major military confrontations has ended. The huge armed forces made necessary by that confrontation are being disbanded, with all the consequent economic disruption and social stress. The political attitudes and social structures shaped by nearly a century of warfare no longer appear to be relevant. The problems we now face arise, not from the threat of foreign conquest or hegemony, but from social dislocation on a vast, indeed on a global scale—dislocation arising in part from the social and economic results of the wars themselves, but mainly from long-term secular trends that we cannot control and to which we can only adjust as best we can.

If we take the Napoleonic analogy seriously, the good news is that after 1815 nearly half a century was to pass before Europe saw another international war, and a century before there was a conflict on anything like so considerable a scale. The bad news is that during those years developments were under way that made the European system increasingly unstable: unstable internally, as industrialization transformed the economies of western Europe, bringing in its wake growing class conflict and fear of revolution, and externally, as the growth of railways (in particular) created a new major political and economic power in the center of Europe which was to shatter the international system with a series of wars—wars that began with the Prussian challenge to the Austrian Empire in 1866 and did not really conclude until the defeat and destruction of Nazi Germany in 1945. It would be an extraordinarily rash person who asserted today that similar economic and technological changes will not sooner or later transform the underlying power structure of the world in a way that may have to be tested—as it had always been tested in the past—by military conflict. This is, alas, a long-term possibility that cannot be lost to sight. But there are shorter-term probabilities that must quite rightly receive our prior attention.

WHO'S TO BE MASTER?

Before looking at those shorter-term problems, let me consider for a moment the huge conflicts, fought or unfought, that have wracked the world for most of our troubled century. What were they really about? What were the causes for which millions of young men were required to die and even more civilians had to suffer? The simple answer might be that given to Alice by Humpty-Dumpty: "Who's to be Master; that's all." For some—perhaps for most—of the belligerents, the two World Wars were fought simply to prevent Germany from achieving a hegemony over Europe, as earlier wars had been fought for the same purpose against France and Spain. Similarly, the Cold War was "fought" to contain Soviet power, not just in Europe but throughout the world. For many of those who fought, or were prepared to fight, that was probably reason enough, especially during the First World War: soldiers fought loyally for their countries, and civilians unquestioningly supported them. For that perhaps rather naive generation, "King and Country" was in itself a quite sufficient cause for which to fight and, if need be, to die.

We may now look back and condemn, or pity, the frenetic nationalism of the First World War, which saw in the enemy the embodiment of absolute evil and claimed for its own side a monopoly of virtue; but even then the national cause was equated, rightly or wrongly, with a higher morality and could command the loyalty of rational as well as honorable men and women. The young men who then fought and died "for England" embodied certain ideals of liberty and justice and individual freedom, ideals threatened, so they thought, by the jackboot of "Prussian militarism."

For the Americans, of course, the war was ideological from the very beginning: the United States entered the war, after long hesitation, to make the world "safe for democracy," believing that only if there was universal democracy could there be universal peace. The Germans for their part believed that a combination of Western materialism and Eastern barbarism threatened their unique culture, a culture rooted in deep historic instincts and finding expression in a state whose leadership demanded from its people complete individual subordination and heroic self-sacrifice: "heroes" were fighting "tradesmen." It was only after defeat and humiliation in a war that most of them regarded as entirely defensive and "just" that the Germans came to acquiesce in a regime whose philosophy was an evil caricature of their traditional patriotism, one that denied all individual rights against a state that claimed to embody the general will, whose power was its own justification, and which claimed a mandate to cleanse its own society of those groups it regarded as alien and to subordinate others it stigmatized as inferior.

It is worth taking a moment to consider the creed of National Socialism, or as it is more generically known, fascism, for it is beginning to have uncomfortable resonances for our own times. It was a philosophy that quite consciously rejected the whole tradition of the liberal Enlightenment that had been developing in the West over the past two centuries and for which the liberal democracies of the West continued, however inadequately, to stand. For the rights of the individual, fascism substituted the authority of the group and of the leader who embodied it. For the brotherhood of man, it substituted the right of the strong to enslave the weak. For the rule of reason, it substituted the primacy of visceral prejudice. And for the vision of peace among nations, it substituted that of perpetual war.

This was not a purely German phenomenon. It was a creed that, appealing as it did to primitive emotions of the nastiest kind, struck a chord in all societies, developed or undeveloped. Unfortunately, it still does. There are, and I am afraid always will be, those who are born Fascists. Perhaps most of us are, and have to be educated out of it. But there are those—and the Germans were an example—who have had fascism thrust upon them through the catastrophic failure of liberal political and economic ideals derived from the Enlightenment to solve the basic social problems they brought in their train. Reason might decree that all men should be free to work out their own political and economic salvation, emancipated from traditional religious or hierarchical authority. But what happens when such freedom results, as it did in postwar Germany, in six million unemployed?

Communism might, as we shall see, appeal to the proletariat for whom it was designed, but society consists of many more groups than the proletariat. For self-employed businessmen, petit-bourgeois employees, small farmers, dispossessed or threatened members of the old ruling classes—for all these people, a creed that seemed to defend traditional values in an age of chaotic change, that provided employment and restored their self-respect, that promised the young a life of adventure and excitement, and that clearly identified alien groups, internal or external, as the cause of all their miseries, such a creed had much to recommend it. The price was abdication of independent judgment to an authority that understood their prejudices and skillfully played on them to maintain itself in power. That was fascism and it still is. It is a creed that always appeals to misfits; and when a large proportion of the people within a particular society feel themselves to be misfits, it becomes very dangerous.

But there was another and parallel reaction against the philosophy of freedom. Representative democracy was only one child of the Enlightenment. It had a sibling that, appearing first in the latter days of the French Revolution, was to grow to maturity, after a hefty dose of Hegelian dialectic, as Marxism, and ultimately to achieve power in the Soviet Union and elsewhere as Marxist-Leninism. If Reason enabled man to understand and ultimately to control the process of Nature, so the argument went, it should no less enable him to understand and control the development of his own society. A combination of historical understanding and scientific analysis showed that the capitalistic system was only a harsh, if necessary, stage on mankind's road to a communist resolution of all social and political conflicts, and one to be traversed as quickly as possible. Those truly enlightened spirits whose superior insight enabled them to understand the inward meaning of History had not only the right but the duty to take charge of society, and to transform it in accordance with the intrinsic laws of social development, which they alone understood. For those who suffered most from the misery and alienation brought about by the early years of industrialization—not just the unemployed but the far larger number of those employed on starvation wages—the promise of communism looked seductive, not so much because it promised Utopia, but because it offered to industrial workers a measure of security that they could never enjoy in a world ruled by market forces. Further—and perhaps even more important—it offered to intellectuals the promise of a world they believed they would be able to control.

Thus, the Second World War was a war, not simply of nations, but of ideologies, and the victor would shape the world in its own image. The two branches of the Enlightenment family temporarily sank their differences and united to destroy a creed that threatened them both. Then, as Hitler had always hoped, they turned against one another, and the Cold War began. Because both creeds were international, or rather supranational, each had its adherents in the other's camp. If the Soviets had played their cards more skillfully, they might have had many more.

In the immediate aftermath of the Second World War, communism offered to many in the West an attractive alternative to the failures of prewar capitalism— and to many in the rest of the world an even more attractive alternative to prewar colonialism. As it was, confronted by a regime that had more in common with the worst kind of tsarist oppression than with the Brave New World depicted in Marxist propaganda, the Old Believers in the West (those hopeful but hapless professors at the Sorbonne and Oxbridge dons of the 1930s) died out and, thank God, were not replaced. The new countries of the Third World eventually came to recognize that the Soviet Union was a great power like any other, to be exploited for what it was worth but unable to provide help on a scale even remotely approaching that of the West. And, eventually, the Old Believers in the Soviet Union itself lost confidence in a regime so patently incapable of living up to the promises of its founders and justifying the terrible sacrifices it had imposed on its peoples by effective results.

So fascism had failed: it had lived by the sword and had perished by the sword. Marxist-Leninism had equally failed: it had appealed to historical processes that history, in due course, had discredited. Western democracy emerged apparently triumphant, and at least one American publicist claimed that history had now come to an end.

ANOTHER CHANCE FOR LIBERAL DEMOCRACY

Fortunately perhaps for historians, but unfortunately for everyone else, this obituary was premature. The Gibbonian chronicle of the crimes, follies, and wickedness of mankind is continuing uninterrupted, and those who believed that with the defeat of communism these would disappear and that we would see the dawn of yet another new world order are sadly disillusioned. The failure of rival creeds does not mean that our own is bound to succeed, only that it has been given another chance. Both fascism and communism emerged in Europe because liberal democracy failed to live up to its expectations. If we fail again, we may expect new and similar challenges, both in our own continent and throughout the world.

Such challenges will recur, if only because the process of change that brought our own Western societies into existence will continue unendingly to operate, creating new problems to which we may prove fatally slow to adapt. The fundamental cause of both the triumphs and failures of liberal democracy was the continuing impact of the Enlightenment itself. It was this that set in motion the whole process of modernization and industrialization two centuries ago, which continues with unslackening momentum. The Enlightenment taught us that we are free agents, endowed by reason with the capacity to understand the world around us and with the right to shape it in accordance with that understanding. Over the past two centuries, political and ecclesiastical authorities, social structures, and economic practices that had endured for a thousand years have been called into question, and, as often as not, overthrown, sometimes by violence, more often through a gradual erosion of their credibility. Their place was taken by free societies that, beginning in Europe and North America in the nineteenth century and spreading throughout the globe in the twentieth, have transformed the world. They have spanned it with railways and steamships and, ultimately, aircraft. They have created world systems of instant aural and visual communication that have led to a single global economy. They have conquered most of the diseases that since the beginning of recorded history have ravaged mankind, and vastly increased the world population as a result. They have crested huge cities, providing markets whose demand transformed traditional methods of agriculture, destroying entire rural communities in the process and sending their inhabitants further to swell the populations of the cities. Mankind has struck its tents, in Jan Christian Smuts's wonderful phrase, and is on the march. We have not yet found a resting place.

It is true that in the twentieth century Western societies have overcome many of the problems they created for themselves in the nineteenth, and the dire prophecies of Karl Marx and his followers have not come true. Indeed, it may well be that, in spite of what I have written at the beginning of this [essay], posterity will look back on the half-century between 1939 and 1989 as the golden age of capitalism. The Second World War solved the problem of unemployment, and the need to maintain social solidarity during that war nurtured a welfare system that underwrote security from the cradle to the grave. Called into being in order to defeat fascism, the same solidarity had to be maintained to repel communism. Underwritten by the huge wealth and defended by the military power of the United States, the pluralistic democracies of Western Europe and the Pacific Rim were able to provide their entire populations with a standard of living beyond the wildest imaginings of the most optimistic prophets of the nineteenth century, a model with which the Soviet Union could not begin to compete and which was the envy—and, increasingly, the despair—of the rest of the world.

Apart from the ever-present danger of nuclear war—and not very many people thought about this for very much of the time—it was easy to believe that we "had it made." Politics was simply concerned with the creation and distribution of an unending abundance of goods, both internally within our own societies and globally between North and South. All that seemed necessary for the achievement of global peace and prosperity was the maintenance of full production and the elimination of a communist threat that, as time went on, seemed increasingly threadbare. When that happened, surely history was bound to come to an end as the benefits of liberal democracy were extended throughout the world.

But only those who lacked any sense of historical perspective could believe this. The Enlightenment had, from the very beginning, brought not peace, but a whole armory of swords. It has always been Western capitalist societies that have been the motors of revolutionary change. Communist regimes, whatever their revolutionary professions, have in fact always tried to restrain the process of change, excluding disruptive Western influence, destroying entrepreneurial talent within their own borders, and imposing an artificial stability through totalitarian rule. The process of "modernization" unleashed and encouraged by the West, on the other hand, is unending and ineluctible. We have seen how in continental Europe it destroyed traditional structures—the dominance of an authoritarian Roman Catholic church, the rule of imperial dynasties and a privileged feudal aristocracy—beyond hope of recall and brought into being a new mass, egalitarian society that is still far from stable. Now the process is continuing elsewhere. Throughout the rest of the world, traditional societies are being destroyed. Modernization is certainly improving living standards for many, but this is often being achieved at much the same cost in disruption, misery, and alienation that characterized our own experiences in Europe a century and a half ago.

These problems are complicated, in what one must still call for lack of any better term the "Third World," by the difficulty of applying Western-generated political and economic models to non-Western societies. The fact that the communist model has failed is no guarantee that that of the West will necessarily succeed any better, that free-market economies can produce full employment, or that "human rights" as defined by Western jurists will be compatible with the cohesion developed in other cultures through generations of tribal or familial loyalties. In Asia and Africa today, as in Europe a century ago, improvements in science, medicine, and hygiene have produced an increase in population far larger than modern methods of agricultural production can absorb, or the land itself can sustain. The surplus flock to cities whose industries do not want them. But whereas their European counterparts of a hundred years ago could find in the United States an effective safety valve, these new unfortunate "huddled masses" cannot. Like their European counterparts, they are vulnerable to dreams of revolutionary utopianism, but they are even more vulnerable to the kind of xenophobic nationalism or religious fundamentalism whose leaders identify—and not without reason—the source of their discontents in the secular Western ideas that destroyed the old order, and who in consequence assert traditional values in novel and extreme forms.

Nor do our own societies show any greater degree of stability. I am not an economist or a sociologist, but a very naïve historian; nonetheless, it seems to me that we face, in Europe and the United States, a two-fold problem. First, there are the technological advances that enable us to produce an ever greater quantity of goods with ever less manpower, with such manpower as is needed requiring pretty high technical qualifications. The Marxist prophecy has been almost reversed: far from development in means of production having enabled the proletariat to eliminate the bourgeoisie, it has enabled the bourgeoisie very effectively to eliminate the proletariat. As a result, we see in most Western societies a large measure of systematic and apparently irreducible unemployment. This unemployment is exacerbated by a global mobility of capital and expertise that can leave whole regions desolate almost overnight, causing social dislocation and misery almost as devastating as that which resulted from the transition from agrarian to industrial production in the early nineteenth century. Today, thanks to the acceptance by the state of an ethic of social responsibility then confined to the private sector, unemployment no longer means the kind of penury and desperation that it did in the 1840s, but its social and psychological consequences hardly need to be spelled out. The resulting situation still bears a disquieting resemblance to the Two Nations depicted by Disraeli. There is an increasingly alienated underclass, unemployed and perhaps increasingly unemployable, uninterested in contributing and indeed unable to contribute to the society that supports it, and kept quiet only by a diet of mass-produced sport and entertainment, if not indeed by much more dangerous drugs.

I have already briefly referred to the second set of problems. They are those resulting from the erosion of traditional values and social norms, values that may have been developed under different and now anachronistic social conditions but which did provide a measure of social cohesion and which show no sign of being replaced by new ones more appropriate to the conditions of our own times. This sense of anomie may be more intense in Britain than elsewhere, because traditional values and standards have survived for longer there than elsewhere, and the British are now having to make adjustments that the Germans made 50, the French and the Americans 200 years ago. But the impact of the sexual revolution consequent on the development of reliable means of birth control is universal and is one of the most fundamental changes that has occurred in the history of mankind. The entire relationship between men and women has to be rethought. New generations are left to work out their own sexual morality, with little, if any, guidance from the past. The result may be liberating, but it is also bewildering, and can occasionally be disastrous. It is not surprising if visitors from the Third World, however enamored they may be of our technology, see in the society it has produced, not a model to be imitated, but one to be shunned.

These problems, the domestic and the international, are interconnected. The impact of Western science and technology has loosened the cohesion of non-Western societies where it has not destroyed it altogether, and the same technology has made it possible for their peoples to come in large numbers to our own shores. Their presence is seen as an additional threat by those in our own societies who already feel insecure. The introduction of their cultures has sometimes had a salutary effect, inducing in our own people a spirit of wider comprehension and tolerance; but often, as all of us know, it has had the opposite effect, producing intolerance and reactive dogmatism of the nastiest kind. If the social dislocation created by modernization has led to a fundamentalist backlash in developing societies, it has also evoked in Western societies the kind of xenophobic racism that Hitler and his imitators found so easy to exploit a couple of generations ago.

As if that were not enough, we face a third category of problems—those caused by the disintegration of former communist societies. We can now see how effectively the communist regime destroyed the basis of civil society in the regions that it dominated, and how shallow and artificial was the social order it imposed in its place. Our instinct, that we should do all that we can to draw our neighbors in the East into our own political and economic system, must be right. But we can do no more than provide the facilities to enable them to solve those problems themselves, whether those facilities are technical, economic, or political.

As for the anarchy in the Balkans, a region on the fringes of Europe (not in "the heart of Europe," as suggested by certain distinguished public figures whose compassion is stronger than their geography), this perplexes us as much as it did our great-grandfathers. Television brings it closer to us but provides us with no new means to resolve it. A "new order" in that region can only emerge from within, however long it may take. As in all cases of civil conflict, outsiders, however powerful and well-intentioned, can only limit the damage and do what they can to bind up the wounds. But the region provides a terrible example of the fragility of civil society, of its continuing vulnerability to ethnic prejudice, irrational hatreds, and not least the attraction of violence for its own sake—again, always one of the basic appeals of fascism.

THE CHILL PEACE

What then is to be done? Out of this unpromising material, what hope is there of a new world order? My survey has been pretty depressing, but after all, we have been here before. After every great war, whether hot or cold, there has been a chill peace. There was a decade of disruption and social misery after 1815, when Europe was kept in order only by the police powers of the Habsburg and Russian empires, and the specter of communism was stalking the continent a good 20 years after that. There was a similar period of wretchedness and confusion in Europe after 1918, interrupted only by the false dawn of the Locarno era. As for the aftermath of the Second World War, many of us . . . will remember the sense almost of despair with which we contemplated the ruins of Europe and wondered how, if ever, the continent could be restored to anything like a peaceful and democratic order. War, even cold war, concentrates the mind wonderfully: too wonderfully. Too many problems have to be put on the back burner, too many debts are incurred that eventually have to be paid. Enjoy the war, we used to say to one another in the 1940s, the peace will be terrible. For many, it was. But somehow we survived both the war and the peace.

We shall survive this peace, if we do not set our sights too high and try to do too much too fast. We cannot solve the problems of the world, even if CNN brings them every night into our sitting rooms. Nor, I believe, should we try to impose our own standards on the world; different cultures have to solve the problems of modernization in their own way. For the foreseeable future, a global order must inevitably be multicultural, and its enforcement minimalist. We should therefore approach world problems, not with the universalism of the lawyer, but with the pragmatic triage of the surgeon on the battlefield, who divides his patients into those who do not need help, those he cannot help, and those he can and must help. But the limits of our capacity to help anyone will be set by our ability to solve, or at least to control, the problems of our own no longer very rich, and no longer uniformly white, world.

If I may end as I began, by quoting myself, I concluded my final lecture at Oxford [in 1989] with a reference to Kant, who observed that "Nature does not seem to have been concerned with seeing that man should live agreeably, but that he should work his way onward to make himself by his own conduct worthy of life and well-being."[2] The way that Nature seems to have chosen to do this is to ensure that the solution of every problem she has set us poses new and ever more complex difficulties for us to solve, and to this process there is no end whatever. The road does indeed wind upward to the very end.

[2]Ibid., p. 200.

14

GREAT-POWER RELATIONS: PATHS TO PEACE IN THE TWENTY-FIRST CENTURY

Charles W. Kegley, Jr., and Gregory A. Raymond

Global power is shifting toward a new distribution in which three, four, or five major states will share roughly equal capabilities. Whether their relationships will be cooperative or competitive depends on the security institutions the great powers create. Exploring the contribution that the United Nations, the CSCE, NATO, and the Group of Seven can make to peace, this chapter argues that a two-tiered, concert-based collective security system provides the best mechanism for preserving global security. Kegley is Pearce Professor of International Relations at the University of South Carolina. Raymond is professor of political science at Boise State University. They have co-authored *A Multipolar Peace? Great-Power Politics in the Twenty-first Century* **(1994).**

Despite the end of the Cold War, the great powers have yet to forge a clear, coherent strategy for promoting global security. Instead, confusion and conflicting impulses abound. From efforts to deal with the civil war in what was once Yugoslavia to coping with domestic turmoil in Rwanda, their policies have been characterized by hesitation and false starts. Failure to prevent aggression stemming from long-suppressed ethnic hatreds has heightened apprehensions about whether the great powers will be able to maintain world order in the immediate future.

To some extent, their shortcomings are understandable. Creating a global security policy for a chaotic, complex, and confusing post-Cold War world is a

This essay was especially written for this book.

formidable challenge. The simple bipolar system of the recent past is giving way to a more complex configuration of power. The shifting weights of the great powers and a general uncertainty about their intentions combine to make crafting a new security strategy difficult.

Nonetheless, one of the properties of the emerging global distribution of power can be foreseen—military and economic might will be increasingly diffused among the great powers. In contrast to bipolarity, where two superpowers held a preponderance of strength compared to all other countries, the multipolar state system of the future appears destined to contain as many as five roughly equal great powers: the United States, China, Russia, Japan, and either Germany or a European Union with a common defense policy. A "power transition" (see Jack Levy's reading selection in this book) is well underway, and the changes promise to be fundamental. The military and economic capabilities of the great powers are rapidly changing, with the result that the global distribution of power is moving in the direction of approximate parity. Such a reordering of the pecking order raises several important questions. Which great powers might align with one another? Will these alignments be seen as a threat by others and therein stimulate the formation of counteralliances? Can a security regime be built to prevent the rise of rival great-power alliances who are primed for war?

THE CHARACTER OF A NEW MULTIPOLAR SYSTEM

The diffusion of strength among the world's leading states demands our attention because some forms of multipolarity have been more war-prone than others. For example, the multipolar system of antagonistic blocs that developed on the eve of World War I proved particularly dangerous. When a world of many great powers splits into rival camps, there is little chance that competitors in one policy arena will emerge as partners somewhere else, so as to mitigate the competition. Rather, the gains made by one side will be seen as losses by the other, ultimately causing minor disagreements to grow into larger face-offs from which neither coalition is willing to retreat.

Since the international system of the early twenty-first century will probably include three or more extremely powerful states whose security interests are global, it is important that they do not become segregated into rival blocs.

Aside from the danger of armed conflict among the great powers, the security threats of the future will also include such challenges as inter-bloc trade wars, environmental degradation, resource depletion, the rising tide of refugees, and a welter of health concerns ranging from AIDS to multidrug-resistant strains of tuberculosis. None of these global problems can be met without substantial great-power cooperation; they are truly transnational problems that necessitate not national but global solutions.

Whereas the impact of these non-traditional threats to global welfare promises to be potent, they do not necessarily mean geo-economics or ecopolitics will replace geo-politics. Conflict over political and territorial issues remains much in evidence. While we can rejoice in the end of Cold War hostility, differences in the interests of the great powers have not disappeared. As former U.S. Secretary of State Lawrence S. Eagleburger has pointed out, we are "returning to a more traditional and complicated time of multipolarity, with a growing number of countries increasingly able to affect the course of events." The primary issues are how well the United States and Russia can adjust to their unequal decline from overwhelming preponderance and how well China, Japan, and the European Union will adapt to their new-found importance. "The change will not be easy for any of the players, as such shifts in power relationships have never been easy."[1] The challenge to be confronted is ensuring that great-power cooperation, not conflict, becomes institutionalized. At issue is whether the traditional and non-traditional security threats that collectively face the world will be managed through concerted great-power action.

GREAT-POWER OPTIONS IN A MULTIPOLAR FUTURE

As power in the international system becomes more diffused, what can be done to prevent the re-emergence of an unstable form of multipolarity? How can the great powers avoid becoming polarized into antagonistic blocs? Three general courses of action exist: they can act unilaterally; they can develop specialized bilateral alliances with another state; or they can engage in some form of broad collaboration with many countries.

Of course, each option has many possible variations, and the foreign policies of most great powers contain a mix of acting single-handedly, joining with a partner, and cooperating globally. What matters for the stability of multipolar systems is the relative emphasis placed on "going it alone" versus "going it with others" and whether joint action is defined in inclusive or exclusive terms.

Unilateral policies, though attractive because they symbolize the nostalgic pursuit of national autonomy, are unlikely to be viable in a multipolar future. The end of the Cold War has reduced public anxieties about foreign dangers and, in some countries, led to calls for a reduction in the scale of foreign commitments. But a retreat from world affairs would imperil efforts to deal with the many transnational threats to global security mentioned above that require global activity and engagement.

On the other hand, a surge of unilateral activism by any of the great powers would be equally harmful. None of them holds unquestioned hegemonic status with enough power to override all others. Although the United States is unrivaled in military might, its offensive capability and unsurpassed military tech-

---

[1]Lawrence S. Eagleburger, "The 21st Century: American Foreign Policy Challenges," pp. 244–245 in E. K. Hamilton, ed., *America's Global Interests: A New Agenda* (New York: W. W. Norton, 1989).

nology are not paralleled by unrivaled financial clout. Like others, the U.S. economy faces problems that constrain and inhibit the projection of American power on a global scale. Given the prohibitive costs of shouldering the financial burden of acting alone and given the probability that other great powers would be unlikely to accept subordinate positions or assertive U.S. interventionism, unilateralism will be problematic in a multipolar future. Countries like Japan, Russia, and Germany "will have to relearn their old great-power roles, and the United States will have to learn a role it has never played before; namely, to coexist and interact with other great powers."[2]

An alternative to acting unilaterally is joining with selected states in a series of special alliance relationships. On the surface, this option also appears attractive. Yet in a world lacking the stark simplicities of bipolarity, differentiating friend from foe is exceedingly difficult, particularly when allies in the realm of military security are the most likely to be trade competitors in a cutthroat global marketplace. Instead of adding predictability to international affairs, a network of special bilateral relationships would foster a fear of encirclement among those who perceive themselves as the targets of these combinations.

Whether they entail informal understandings or formal treaties of alliance, all bilateral partnerships have a common drawback: they promote a politics of exclusion that can lead to dangerously polarized forms of multipolarity, in which the competitors align by forming countercoalitions. For example, the formation of a Russo-American alliance would concern many Western European leaders; similarly, construction of a U.S.–Russian–European Union axis stretching from the Atlantic to the Urals would alarm both China and Japan. The problem with shifting alliances is that they inevitably shun those standing outside the charmed circle. Resentment, revenge, and revanchist efforts to overturn the status quo are the predictable consequence. The freewheeling dance of balance-of-power politics typically produces much switching of partners, with some cast aside and thus willing to break up the whole dance. As a careful student of world politics concludes, balance-of-power alliances can

> hardly be classed as stabilizing manoeuvres or equilibrating processes, and one cannot take seriously any claim of maintaining international stability that does not entail the prevention of such disasters as the Napoleonic wars or World War I. . . . It is not easy to justify the contention that a system for the management of international relations that failed to prevent the events of 1914–1918 deserves high marks as a guardian of stability, or order, or peace. If the balance of power system does not aim at the prevention of world war, then it aims too low; if it offers no hope of maintaining the general peace, then the quest for a better system is fully warranted.[3]

[2]Kenneth N. Waltz, "The Emerging Structure of International Politics," *International Security* 18 (no. 2, 1993), p. 72.

[3]Inis L. Claude, Jr., "The Balance of Power Revisited," *Review of International Studies* 15 (January 1989), p. 78. For an alternate critique of the balance of power as a tinderbox for warfare, see Richard Rosecrance, "A New Concert of Powers," *Foreign Affairs* 71 (Spring 1992), pp. 64–82.

Beyond forming special bilateral alliances, great powers have the option of establishing broad, multilateral associations. Two common variants of this option are concerts and collective security organizations. The former involves regularized consultation among those at the top of the global hierarchy; the latter, full participation by all states. A concert offers the benefit of helping control the great-power rivalries that often spawn polarized blocs, though at the cost of ignoring the interests of those not belonging to the group. Alternatively, the all-inclusive nature of collective security allows every voice to be heard but makes difficult providing a timely response to threatening situations. Consensus-building is both difficult and delayed, especially in identifying the culpable party, in choosing an appropriate response, and in implementing the selected course of action. Since a decision-making body can become unwieldy as its size expands, what may be needed to make multilateralism a viable option for the multipolar future looming on the political horizon is a hybrid that combines elements of a great-power concert with elements of collective security.

A CONCERT-BASED COLLECTIVE SECURITY SYSTEM: RATIONALE AND REQUIREMENTS

Finding a mechanism to preserve peace in a multipolar world will be a serious challenge on the global agenda in the next century. Unilateral and bilateral approaches do not offer promising paths to lasting great-power peace. Multilateral approaches provide a better solution for checking great-power competition, should a truly multipolar system take shape. If no single state is more powerful than the combination of all other states in a collective security organization, the collectivity could jointly deter—and, if necessary, defeat—an aggressor, provided that the members (1) share a common commitment to maintain peace, (2) agree on who is a potential or actual threat to peace, and (3) apply prompt and powerful sanctions against that threat.

Unfortunately, whenever such an organization has existed, some members have sought to maximize their relative gains rather than to minimize their mutual losses. Thinking that they could rely on joint action to resist aggression, they either reduced their own military preparedness so as to free-ride on the defense efforts of their companions or mobilized at the first hint of trouble and thus expanded what might have remained small, local conflicts into larger wars. As political scientist Richard Betts notes, the history of collective security reveals twin deficiencies—it may "not work when needed, or that it would work when it should not."[4]

---

[4]Richard K. Betts, "Systems for Peace or Causes of War? Collective Security, Arms Control, and the New Europe," p. 214 in S. M. Lynn-Jones and S. E. Miller, eds., *America's Strategy in a Changing World* (Cambridge: The MIT Press, 1992).

Even if the post-Cold War environment is more hospitable to collective security than in the past, implementing it will be difficult. A solution to this problem is to create a modified version of collective security, one that is grounded in a *two-tiered, modular design* and that rests on a shared commitment to cooperation and common security. Under such a scheme, countries at the center of policy deliberations would shift as different kinds of problems arise. The system would be concert-based, with some great powers taking a leadership role on certain security issues, while others would do so on a different set of issues. At the same time, this great-power concert would be anchored in a larger collective security framework, where small and medium powers would have a voice in pending matters if their interests were affected or if they possessed expertise in dealing with the issue in question.

What conditions are necessary for such a mechanism to function adequately? For many theorists, common threats are the glue that holds security regimes together.[5] Previous concerts were formed after wars with potential hegemons or after a single, massively armed enemy appeared on the scene to threaten the existence of others. The passage of time or the demise of a threat always loosened these bonds. A shared sense of common threat, either from an aggressor bent on world domination or from a non-military challenge (such as global warming) that cannot be managed unilaterally, must arise to preserve the commitment to collective action. Without a threat common to and recognized by all, the chances that great powers will show self-restraint or forgo unilateral advantages predictably declines.

A second correlate of success is said to lie in including defeated or declining powers in the security regime. A dissatisfied great power lacking a voice in security matters will reject the legitimacy of the prevailing order, strive to destroy the status quo, and undermine the organization's capacity to act. Treating a defeated or declining power as an equal and respected member avoids this problem. (In this context, to include Russia, which appears condemned to prolonged economic difficulties and political instability, is crucial to the long-term success of any new security structure.)

The third potential contributor to the longevity of a security mechanism of this sort is a rough military balance among its members. The presence of a state that is significantly stronger than all the other great powers reduces the effectiveness of both concerts and collective security systems, since the preponderant state would be able to withstand any pressures that the others might initiate.

---

[5]For examples of recent thinking on the prerequisites for success, see Andrew Bennett and Joseph Lepgold, "Reinventing Collective Security after the Cold War and the Gulf Conflict," *Political Science Quarterly* 108 (No. 2, 1993), pp. 213–237; see also Inis L. Claude, "Collective Security after the Cold War," pp. 7–28 in I. L. Claude, S. Simon, and D. Stuart, eds., *Collective Security in Europe and Asia* (Carlisle Barracks: U.S. Army War College, Strategic Studies Institute, 1992).

A fourth factor affecting the viability of concert-based security systems is a sense of common duty coupled with diplomatic respect for the status of others. During the nineteenth century, when the Concert of Europe was at its zenith, a "just" equilibrium among the contending great powers meant more than an equal distribution of capabilities; it included recognition of the importance of extending honor, national rights, and dignity on all. In contrast, when a great power has been isolated, the wounded sense of national pride has served as the catalyst to its subsequent imperial impulses.

Finally, many theorists stress flexibility as a hallmark of effective security regimes. Just as a concert's small, uncomplicated structure makes it more supple and resilient than highly institutionalized collective security organizations, its informal processes of mutual consultation provide an opportunity to tailor solutions to the special requirements of the situation at hand.

Given the advantages of a concert-based collective security system in preventing the emergence of the most unstable types of multipolarity and given the conditions needed to make it effective, the question remains as to whether any existing multilateral organizations offer a potential home for such a security mechanism.

THE ARCHITECTURE FOR CONCERT-BASED COLLECTIVE SECURITY

Throughout history different types of multipolar systems have existed. Some of these systems of diffused power were unstable because they contained antagonistic blocs poised on the brink of war. We contend that the key to the stability of any future multipolar system lies in the inclusiveness of multilateralism. It is not a panacea for all the world's security problems, but it offers humanity a chance to avoid the kinds of polarized alignment patterns that have proved so destructive in the past.

At the minimum, building a concert-based collective security structure will require an institutional foundation that:

- Enlarges the circle of participation to include all the emergent great powers in collective decision making;
- Fosters movement away from reliance on strictly national defense and combines elements of collective defense against a particular potential aggressor with elements of collective security against all threats of aggression;
- Encourages greater security communication and cooperation among the states likely to acquire the most armed strength;
- Copes imaginatively with the security vacuum that has followed the implosion of the Warsaw Pact and the disintegration of the Soviet Union;
- Binds Germany and Japan to the pursuit of multilateral security, providing them with non-national nuclear deterrents;

• Incorporates representation from the Muslim world, in order to include a potential new Islamic power in a web of interdependence with the other great powers;
• Pursues the continuation of long-term efforts to further reduce existing nuclear inventories and prevents further proliferation of strategic weapons to regional powers;
• Establishes confidence-building measures among the great powers in East Asia and the Pacific; and
• Constructs rules for crisis management, supplemented by conflict-resolution mechanisms with enforcement capabilities.

Creating a new security architecture has seldom proven easy. When seen from the perspective of the mid-1990s, all the existing institutions upon which a concert-based collective security system might be constructed have limitations. Consider, for instance, the case of the United Nations. After the Persian Gulf War, many people assumed that the UN would at long last be able "to take effective collective measures for the prevention and removal of threats to the peace" as originally proclaimed in its Charter (Article 1, paragraph 1). Whether this becomes a reality depends on the political dynamics in the Security Council. According to the UN Charter, the Security Council has "primary responsibility for the maintenance of international peace and security" (Article 24, paragraph 1). Of its fifteen members, five hold permanent seats and possess the right to veto council actions—the United States, Russia, Britain, France, and China. The harmonious veneer we have witnessed for the past few years could fade. Moreover, if the Security Council's permanent membership is expanded to include Germany, Japan, and such regional powers as Brazil, India, or Nigeria, reaching agreement for collective action will become even more challenging.

To complicate matters further, there is a pervasive fear among UN members that the organization has become a captive of its strongest member at the moment, the United States. Although American influence is resented by many states, they still recognize the need for U.S. leadership if the United Nations is to play the peacekeeping and peacemaking role that many expect of it. This creates a dilemma: "Without U.S. leadership and power, the United Nations lacks muscle. With it, the United Nations loses its independent identity."[6]

Thus an invigorated, independent United Nations would need more resources to carry out its mandate for peacekeeping—a dim prospect since its members owe billions of dollars in back dues and the organization continues to suffer from severe criticism for financial mismanagement. Attempting to reform the United Nations while simultaneously coping with the exploding demand for UN peacekeepers has been described by Secretary-General Boutros Boutros-Ghali

---

[6]Leslie H. Gelb, "Tailoring a U.S. Role at the U.N.," *International Herald Tribune,* Jan. 2–3, 1993, p. 4.

as "trying to repair a car while you are driving at a speed of 120 miles per hour."[7] Undaunted by the difficulty of the task, he lobbied in 1993 for the creation of peace enforcement units that would allow the United Nations to deploy troops quickly to enforce ceasefires by taking coercive actions against violators. As with UN peacekeeping forces employed during the Cold War, the secretary-general recommended that these rapid deployment units be established by the voluntary contribution of member states, act when authorized by the Security Council, and serve under the command of the secretary-general. In contrast to traditional peacekeeping operations, however, their use could be ordered without the express consent of the disputants, and they would be trained and equipped to use force if necessary.

Despite Boutros-Ghali's energetic quest, the creation of a large, easily mobilized, multilateral contingency force positioned to manage disputes seems unlikely. The Clinton administration, perhaps fearing a possible loss of control, vetoed contributing U.S. military units to a permanent UN standby force in its Presidential Decision Directive 13 of 1994. Without active enthusiasm in Washington, the other great powers now appear unlikely to release command authority of their military units to the United Nations.

The Conference on Security and Cooperation in Europe (CSCE) offers a second option for a new concert-based security architecture. Although the Helsinki process has established principles supportive of a two-tier formula which gives the great powers incentives to share costs and responsibilities for security without reducing the lesser powers to second-class citizens, the CSCE has not yet proved itself up to the challenge of providing the foundation for a concert-based collective security mechanism. To begin with, consideration must be given to transforming this regional security organization into a body that includes Japan, China, and other affected states. Furthermore, it must devise a decision-making formula grounded in majority rule rather than in the unanimous consent of such a large, diverse membership.

The North Atlantic Treaty Organization (NATO) represents a third possible mooring for international security. For some people, however, NATO is more an anachronism than an anchor. The utility of any alliance tends to diminish when the common external threat that brought it together disappears. Without a Soviet or Russian threat, NATO must broaden its membership and the geographical definition of its responsibilities if it is to play a major security role in the twenty-first century.

Yet for all the symbolism surrounding the broadened, reconfigured NATO, fractures continue to traverse its membership. Until very recently, there was little evidence that NATO was prepared to take a bold step away from its original mission. With the creation of the North Atlantic Cooperation Council and acceptance of the Clinton administration's "Partnership for Peace" proposal, the

---

[7]*Wall Street Journal,* Dec. 17, 1992, p. A1.

security concerns of neutrals and former members of the Communist bloc have received greater attention. Still, NATO's Reinforcement Concept expresses satisfaction with backing the conflict-prevention efforts initiated by other multilateral institutions; and its new Strategic Concept eschews leadership in favor of shared risks and roles. Unless NATO reconstitutes itself to deal seriously with out-of-area operations, it will likely go out of existence.

To survive, NATO must redefine its mission to serve as the organizational home for a concert-based collective security mechanism that can deal with the kinds of ethno-nationalist clashes that pose grave threats throughout the globe. Even more critically in the long run, it must alleviate the fears of ostracism and encirclement by the other powers outside NATO's traditional zone of influence and operation. U.S. President Clinton recognized this principle when at the January 1994 Brussels summit he declared that his aim was ultimately "a security based not on Europe's division but on the potential of its integration." By extending and enlarging the Partnership for Peace, the possibility that ultra-nationalist forces in Russia would seek to reassert their nation's imperial sway over its lost empire was reduced.

Still, an excluded China and Japan are unlikely to look favorably to an enlarged NATO that defines its purpose as their containment. Exclusion is the match that historically has ignited revanchist fires. Restricting security protection to only the sixteen full-fledged members of NATO effectively denies it to the others and thus does nothing to prevent the organization from remaining a symbol of division. The "associate" status granted to some East European states, Russia, and Soviet successor states does not go far enough; it leaves them without a guarantee of help if attacked.

NATO's enlargement is the best antidote to a return to the days of a world divided in separate blocs, each seeking to contain the expansion of the other. The "separable but not separate" alternative invites the very kind of polarization into competing alliances that it seeks to avoid and could revive the division that followed Yalta—to no one's benefit. All twenty-one of NATO's "associate" partners need to be granted full membership, and the rest of the globe must be taken into account as well.

Finally, some people have suggested that the Group of Seven (G-7) should become the focal point for collective peacekeeping activities in the post-Cold War world. Two reasons typically underpin such arguments. First, G-7 members are democracies, and disputes between democracies rarely escalate to war because each side shares a common set of procedural norms, respects the other's legitimacy, and expects it to rely on peaceful means of conflict resolution. Second, as countries connected by a web of economic linkages, there are material incentives for the G-7 to avoid policies that will rupture profitable business transactions.

These reasons notwithstanding, the drawback of the G-7 as a security mechanism is that it functions like an exclusive club whose formal membership does not include Russia or China. While shared democratic values may lay the groundwork for cooperation among members of the club, economic friction can limit the scope of the club's activities. Trading relationships involve both costs and benefits. The rewarding aspects of commerce may be offset by fierce competition and unequal returns, resulting in envy, disputes, and hostility. In view of the differential growth rates among the great powers and their anxiety about trade competitiveness in an interdependent global marketplace, the major battles of the future may be clashes on the economic front rather than armed combat among soldiers. And even in the event that political solidarity overrides economic rivalry, the G-7 is ill-equipped to orchestrate peacekeeping missions. Its business is managing business, not warfare.

In sum, the United Nations, NATO, CSCE, and the G-7 all have limitations. Nevertheless, they will play prominent roles in the coming years if only because they are structures that already exist. Indeed, it is highly probable that any concert-based collective security architecture that emerges in the near future will consist of a combination of ad hoc regional bodies tied together by the interlocking membership of great powers. For example, the Eurasian landmass might have NATO or the CSCE anchoring its western flank, some kind of a Conference on Security and Cooperation in the Pacific devised for the eastern flank, and with relevant great powers holding memberships in both organizations and meeting regularly under the auspices of the UN Security Council. A full-fledged, comprehensive global collective security system, dedicated to containing aggression anywhere at any time, may be too ambitious and doomed to failure. But a restricted, concert-based collective security mechanism could bring a modicum of order in a fragile and disorderly new multipolar system.

SECURITY STRATEGIES FOR THE FUTURE

The impending structural shift to multipolarity rivets our attention on the historical preoccupation of contending great powers with relative gains. They appear to be natural competitors, relentlessly striving for position with one another in the global hierarchy. Whereas few powers seek to rule the world, all are averse to subservient status—as no great power wants equality with their inferiors, only with their superiors.

The diffusion of military and economic capabilities among states which invariably have divergent interests raises serious obstacles for maintaining order and solving transnational problems. Multilateralism, with its emphasis on consultative, shared decision making, provides an opportunity for the great powers to recognize common security threats and avoid the potentially bitter confrontations that otherwise would engender hostile, inflexible blocs. Not all international conflict is amenable to multilateral resolution, but by promoting mutual responsibility and multiple advocacy, multilateralism creates a legitimacy for policy initiatives that is lacking in unilateralism and special bilateral partner-ships.

Whether the actions taken by any concert-based collective security organiza-tion retain their legitimacy hinges on how such a body is perceived. Will it be seen as an agent of peaceful change or as a bulwark of the status quo? Great-power consensus on the rules of a security regime can reduce the probability that disputes will escalate to war, but it is no guarantee of international justice. Unless concert-based collective security is regarded as a mechanism for ensur-ing that desirable change can occur without coercive means, its long-term prospects will be disappointing. As political scientist E. H. Carr reminds us, establishing a mechanism for peaceful change in a ruthlessly competitive state system is "the fundamental problem" of international politics.[8]

[8]E. H. Carr, *The Twenty Years' Crisis, 1919–1939,* 2nd ed. (London: Macmillan, 1946), p. 222.

15

SOUTHERN PERSPECTIVES ON WORLD ORDER

Shahram Chubin

Shahram Chubin traces the key issues that now divide the developing nations of the South from the wealthy nations of the North. Arguing that "there are still good reasons to pay attention to the South," he warns that "the end of the Cold War has freed the North to indulge its basic antipathy toward the South, to dictate to it without delicacy or dialogue." To avert a new era of North-South hostility, Chubin argues that North and South must recognize the benefits of communication and compromise. Chubin is a specialist in Middle East politics and security studies. His books include _Germany and the Middle East: Patterns and Prospects_ (1992).

The international system of the last 50 years, one dominated and framed by the bipolar superpower rivalry, has been replaced by something more regionally fragmented and multifaceted, more plural and varied. Within this new system, the perspectives, interests, and security needs of the states of the South play an increasingly significant role. For lack of a better term, the "South" is used here to describe that diverse collection of countries in varying degrees developing, nonaligned, and heretofore peripheral to the centers of world politics. Whether they will contribute toward the emergence of a new order, or reinforce the drift

Reprinted from _The Washington Quarterly_, 16:4, Shahram Chubin, "The South and the New World Order," by permission of the MIT Press, Cambridge, Massachusetts. Copyright © 1993 by The Center for Strategic and International Studies and the Massachusetts Institute of Technology. Footnotes have been deleted.

toward anarchy, remains to be seen. The developed world is ill-prepared for this fact, both conceptually and as a matter of policy.

This [essay] surveys the perspectives and attitudes of leaders in states of the South concerning the emerging international agenda. It is an explication, not a defense, and a partial one at best. There is no such thing as a coherent world-view of the South. But the failure to understand the South and to translate such understanding into effective diplomatic, economic, political, and military strategies will have profound consequences. Partnership between North and South remains a possibility, although arguably an improbable one. Antipathy and confrontation are also possible, and made more likely by Northern complacency.

The [essay] begins with a review of the state of the South in the 1990s, evaluating the problems of security and development faced by these countries and the changing international context in which leaders of these states make choices. The analysis then turns to the key issues of world order on the North–South agenda, namely proliferation, arms control, and collective security. . . .

THE STATE OF THE SOUTH

Most scholars in the North appreciate that the South faces large challenges of economic development. But this is hardly enough. . . . The South faces, in fact, a daunting set of interconnected problems in the economic, political, social, and security domains. Many Southern countries are also corrupt, unrepresentative, and repressive. Because these problems coexist with rapidly rising expectations, these countries cannot develop at the more leisurely pace enjoyed by the now developed world, where progress toward the current level of development is measured in centuries, not decades. Thus, in some fundamental sense, the circumstances of the South are without precedent. Moreover, the South is under siege—from an international community impatient to meddle in its affairs. States of the South are losing their sovereignty, which in many cases was only recently or tentatively acquired.

The problems of development confronting the South do not require recitation here. The large gap in living standards between South and North is well known. Less well known is the fact that in many parts of the South population pressures, chronic misgovernment, political insecurity, and conceptual poverty combine to drive countries backward, not forward—so the gap widens. The revolution of expectations, both political and economic, is putting governments under new stresses to perform and to direct the myriad processes of change.

Northerners are now engaged in a debate about whether the essence of power is military or political, but for most Southern states this debate is immaterial—they are unable to achieve either. The rentier states of the Persian Gulf after two decades of respectable oil revenues have been unable to achieve sustained development, transform their economies to guarantee results without oil, cooperate meaningfully on regional security, or move toward democracy, which some of them deny to be compatible with their traditions. As for military power, the accumulation of arms has been an empty and futile policy gesture except as a means of buying into Western security by recycling oil money to the West—a modern form of subvention. . . .

In an era of growing global interdependence states of the South remain more vulnerable than their counterparts in the North and more sensitive to forces beyond their borders. Consider the sliding commodity prices over the past decade, or even the much weakened position of oil producers, a relatively privileged group. Consider, too, the issue of the environment, where Southern states are being asked to meet standards and to consider the question cooperatively and in terms of interdependence. Yet as Maurice Strong, former director general of the United Nations (UN) Environment Program, has said: "The absorptive capacity of the eco-system is being preempted by the North," which should accept the responsibility of "making space" for the others.

Furthermore, in much of the South, states and frontiers are relatively artificial, and the forces keeping them intact have weakened. The end of the Cold War and bipolarity undermined a framework that had favored the territorial status quo and made international intervention difficult. The end of the Communist empire has set off fissiparous tendencies long latent in the multinational composite bloc and simultaneously sapped and delegitimized authoritarianism everywhere.

Moreover, the developing states are undergoing change at a time of maximum exposure to political pressures. . . . It is no comfort to these countries that sovereignty has been, or is being, redefined in the home of the nation-state, with a turn toward smaller communities and intermediate institutions between government (the market) and the individual. . . .

The North's weakening commitment to the sovereignty of states of the South is evident in the increased concern about human rights as an international rather than strictly domestic concern, and the concomitant increased willingness to intervene in a state's internal affairs in defense of ostensibly international standards. This has made leaders of states of the South fearful. Their fear grows even more sharp when well-meaning analysts argue that as an antidote to the excesses and disintegrative tendencies of self-determination, minority (communitarian) or individual human rights should be stressed. . . .

To be sure, . . . criteria have been defined whereby intervention will occur only if human rights violations constitute a threat to international security. Nonetheless, it is easy to see that a right to intervention is an implicit challenge to states if not a direct threat, especially if broadened as an excuse for intervention to unravel and make over states. What the Islamic Republic of Iran disarmingly calls "international arrogance" can be precisely that. On these issues its views are not far from those of India, the [People's Republic of China], and many other states of the South. Few are sufficiently homogenous or confident of their policies toward their minorities to be unaffected by the cultivation of the right or duty to intervene that has been promulgated in recent years.

Advocates of the right of intervention would do well to note that despite all the global forces promoting cultural convergence or standardization, homogenization has not (yet) been achieved. Regrettably or not, nations remain different and determined to pursue their own ideas about politics, the role of the state, religion, independence, equality, and cultural liberation. . . .

In a multicultural world, life may be richer but disputes harder to resolve. Combined with inequalities and political resentments, cultural differences and incomprehension can exacerbate North–South relations in a profoundly negative way.

During the Cold War, the states of the South were able to partially compensate for their weaknesses by banding together under the rubric of nonalignment. But this political device is now lost to them. Nonalignment died with the Cold War. More than that, the way the East–West rivalry ended, with the values and systems of the West vindicated and triumphant, undermined the very basis of the nonaligned movement, which had adopted as its foundation a moral neutrality between the two blocs.

For the erstwhile nonaligned, the end of the Cold War has had cataclysmic results. The old uncertainties of the cold war structure, which tended to nurture the status quo and play to the strengths of authoritarian regimes, have given way to a more fluid world in which the assets of the South, whether individually or collectively, are transformed. No longer proxies, clients, and strategic bases, these states are judged by their adherence to standards, values, and procedures that are now generally and unabashedly seen as full international responsibilities. These states now face strong pressures to adhere to various norms (human rights and democratic procedures) and policies (adherence to nonproliferation of nuclear and other mass destruction weapons and limitations on military spending), which some may find difficult or undesirable.

On the other hand, the end of the Cold War has freed the North to indulge its basic antipathy toward the poorer South, to dictate to it without delicacy or dialogue, and to dispense with the appearance of soliciting its views or the pretense of equality. Given today's domestic preoccupations of the North, it may be difficult to generate sympathy for a South that seems mired in problems attributable to bad governance, corrupt elites, and docile and work-shy populaces more eager to resort to rhetoric, excuses, and feuds than to build the foundations for a better future. Indeed it is not clear that the South or the developing countries generally merit sympathy. They exploited the Cold War, used it as an excuse, pampered bloated armed forces, and in some cases acted as clandestine proliferators and shameless regional predators.

However much the postindustrial world may wish it, insulation from this other, more populous and turbulent, world is simply not possible. These worlds intersect most obviously in the former USSR, where the fate of Russia and its neighbors could weigh heavily in the balance between North and South. In other respects, too, the fate of the South inexorably impinges on that of the North. Due to the globalization of economies and the growth of interdependence (including the rise of transnational issues) areas cannot simply be insulated from the rest of the world. This is most evident with respect to political instabilities, in the presence of which uncertainty, repression, or persecution can give rise to large-scale migration into adjacent areas, perhaps disturbing the ethnic or national balance in the host country. It is even more clear when "domestic" issues like ethnic balance or policy toward minorities may give rise to civil wars spilling over into neighboring states and increasing the risks of "interstate war" and "outside" power intervention. (The very categories appear archaic and forced.) In the most obvious case, interstate conflicts spur migration and damage the economic prospects of belligerent states.

There are still other reasons to pay attention to the South. At the most obvious level, population pressures compel attention. Moreover, many of the new security issues such as environment and migration directly concern the South, and its fate and policies in this respect will inevitably affect those of the North. In much of the South the wave of democratization, however dimly sensed or remote from traditional culture, is welcomed by the populace and provides hope for their future. Furthermore, any world order, whether it is underpinned by balance of power, collective security, or unilateral or ad hoc interventions, must, if it is to become durable, eventually be seen to be legitimate. For this it must solicit the support of the widest number of states possible.

The United States will be a principal determinant of the character of North–South relations on these issues in the new international system. This fact alone has generated concern in the South. . . . The United States has translated its episodic interest in the external world and in the South into new pressure on those states to adhere not just to existing standards of international politics but to higher ones. It has enshrined human rights as a centerpiece of its global engagement, and in postwar Iraq it has used military force to partially dismember a state that failed to meet the new norm.

It has also enshrined nonproliferation. States of the South are now expected to exercise restraint in arms expenditures, to imitate the North (Europe and the superpowers) in arms control and disarmament, cultivate transparency, and practice "cooperative security." Whether or not they feel their security has been enhanced by the end of Cold War, they are being told to get into step with the North or else risk a cutback in development assistance. In emphasizing weapons proliferation as a new priority the United States appears to be targeting an issue that it feels can generate domestic concern and consensus; but it is arguably a false or exaggerated issue, and a crusading policy style that tends to unilateralism is the exact reverse of what is called for if the aim is to establish meaningful restraints rather than temporary obstacles to the spread of these weapons.

Thus, the South struggles not only with its own problems of political and economic development, domestic stability, and regional antagonisms, but also with a changing international system that promises it little in the way of assistance or relief. On the contrary, the South faces many international pressures well beyond its control, not least the actions of some leading actors in the international system to define and enforce new standards of behavior for which a common basis of international understanding does not exist. Unless North and South are able to arrive jointly at ordering concepts for the new international system, the possibility of conflict between them grows more likely. This is a shame, because it is avoidable and unnecessary.

WORLD ORDER: A VIEW FROM THE SOUTH

Whatever else the new world order portends, it does not mean the end of international hierarchies or a new age of equality. Nor is it clear, whatever its shape, how—or whether—it will incorporate the needs and demands of the South into its priorities or agenda. What is the new order? From the South, it looks like a new form of Western dominance, only more explicit and interventionist than in the past. In some Western states a shrillness is detectable when the South is discussed, as if the enemy has shifted there. Consider the following:

- New rationales for intervention appear to be minted daily—human rights, democracy, drugs, environment, and weapons proliferation. . . ;
- Armed forces structures and sizes are being configured and geared to contingencies in the South;
- The North Atlantic Treaty Organization (NATO) has designated a rapid-reaction force for "out-of-area" contingencies;
- An antitactical ballistic missile (ATBM) system against limited strikes—GPALS, or Global Protection Against Limited Strikes—has an explicitly Southern orientation and it is on these terms that it has been offered to and considered by Russia;
- Even nuclear targeting is being reassessed, justified, and recalibrated for contingencies involving Southern states;
- The Coordinating Committee for Multilateral Export Controls (COCOM) is being reconfigured for use and application against the South;
- A host of regimes to control and restrain suppliers are in place or soon will be, all designed to deny certain technologies to Southern states (the London Club or Nuclear Suppliers Group, the Australia Group in chemicals, the Permanent Five [P-5] of the UN Security Council on conventional arms transfer registers, the Missile Technology Control Regime [MTCR] on missile technology); and
- Arms-control initiatives, whether nuclear, chemical, biological or conventional, strategic or tactical/theater, are now planned and assessed for their

impact on the South. Consideration of a total nuclear test ban (CTB), verification mechanisms, reduced reliance on nuclear weapons, elimination of missiles of a certain range, and possible missile test bans, are now all considered in terms of their impact on the South. The Strategic Arms Reduction Treaty (START) is now presented as an important nonproliferation tool.

The North makes no apologies about being more demanding and is not timid about asserting its values since their vindication by the outcome of the Cold War. Illustrative is the North's increasing tendency to insist that there is a definite positive connection between democracy and economic development and democracy and international stability.

Economic assistance is being tied to reduced expenditure on arms. Barber Conable (president of the World Bank 1986–1991) argues that when military expenditures are above 5 percent or in excess of health and education combined "it is hard to see the good sense of lending to such countries." Robert McNamara argues that the West should link economic aid to the former Soviet republics with progress in shifting priorities from military to economic development. The recipient states (the G-24) have been reluctant to accept conditions imposed by the International Monetary Fund and World Bank that would establish a certain ceiling for military expenditures above which no aid would be forthcoming.

Such proposals appear to the South as earnest cant. Money is of course fungible. It is also arguable whether defense is the business of the Bretton Woods institutions. Military spending is simply another excuse, after human rights and the environment, not to transfer resources to poorer countries, to avoid a candid admission that the poorer countries are no longer of strategic interest.

Military spending in the South appears especially wasteful to Americans and Europeans now destroying, transferring, or converting arms. The costliness and futility of the past arms race appears to them all too apparent. Yet it is significant that there is no consensus on the role of arms and especially nuclear weapons in the Cold War: Did they deter a Soviet conventional attack? Were they instrumental in keeping the peace on the Continent? Would deterrence have been as effective at much lower levels of nuclear weapons? Were nuclear weapons essential? Without serious evaluation of the past role of nuclear weapons in the North it seems premature to deride their utility elsewhere. Also it may be noted by the states of the South that even in this phase of enthusiasm for arms control in the North, although some suggest a minimum deterrent posture, scarcely anyone suggests complete nuclear disarmament. Even nuclear weapons still retain a role in the security of the North, however residual. Why, it may be asked, can they not play a similar role in the South?

The fluidity of the current period has not made predictions any easier, yet it is evident that the hierarchy of power has been blurred as other forms of power have become more relevant. Although this blurring may have led to the "obsolescence of major war" in the North, as some suggest, this is less evidently the case elsewhere. Even in an interdependent world competition and rivalry will drive an interest in relative as opposed to absolute standing. States will still be concerned about their relative power positions. Traditionally war has been the means by which power and status have been defined and change has occurred. Choices about war and peace will depend on the alternatives and these choices are not always the same in the South as in the North. The South lacks a security community as a nucleus for order that is present in the North. The mechanisms for peaceful change in the South are not yet designed or constructed.

WEAPONS TRANSFERS AND PROLIFERATION

. . . As the risks of proliferation of new arms have become more apparent, Northern states have begun to consider ways of limiting arms and technology transfers to the South. As the developing countries now account for some 75 percent of arms traded, their military expenditures have grown at three times the pace of that of the North and now account for between two to three times their expenditures on health, education, and welfare. Apart from the distortion to their societies, such spending constitutes a potential threat to neighbors as well as the more distant North.

This Northern concern is, however, selective. Where states are poor and unable to pay for arms, Northern states advocate reduced military spending. Where there is a large market for arms, Northern suppliers compete to get orders for their shrinking defense industries (as in the Persian Gulf and East Asia). Little systematic consideration has been given to the types of arms that are particularly destructive, whether stabilizing or destabilizing; often this distinction corresponds to what you are selling as opposed to what your competitor is selling. The issue is difficult enough without commercial competition and hypocrisy, because all too often such definitions depend as much on the recipient's military doctrine as on the intrinsic characteristics of the weapon systems.

Equally little thought has been given to the relationships among various categories of arms and the reasons for proliferation. Focusing on particular weapon systems like missiles makes little sense out of context. In terms of destructive power and practical military effectiveness missiles do not (yet?) compare to advanced strike aircraft. Nor does an attempt to ban missiles treat the question of motivation in its context. Iran's quest for missiles, for example, came as a result of an inability to acquire parts for its air force (due to the embargo) and its need to counter the much larger and more varied stock of missiles of its adversary (Iraq). For Syria and others, missiles are a psychological comfort or equalizer, guaranteeing some penetration against a foe with a much superior air force.

Nonetheless, in the fight against weapons proliferation the United States in particular has singled out missiles and weapons of mass destruction. Concern about them seems to focus on the following: Under certain conditions they could increase incentives for preemption. Given their relative inaccuracy, population centers may be targeted; moreover, low accuracy may lead to a preference for mass destruction weapons over conventional ones. Some categories of unconventional weapon systems, like chemical weapons, that may be intended to deter an opponent's nuclear arms may complicate deterrence and blur thresholds. Missiles also to some extent decouple a capacity to damage or destroy an opponent from underlying industrial and societal sources of military power.

These concerns are too simplistic. Mating unconventional warheads to ballistic missiles is not easy. The effects of biological warheads are difficult to predict. [The Chemical Weapons Convention] banning chemical weapons should make the deployment and use of these particular weapons more difficult. In any case, the effort to ban only missiles with specified range and weight (300 km and 500 kilograms) tends to obscure the problem of improving accuracies. Even missiles with ranges shorter than 300 km, if forward-deployed and capable of delivering a strike against an opponent's military arsenal, increase the incentive to strike preemptively. As accuracies increase, more missiles may be used for counterforce strikes, and as ranges increase, they could pull into conflict a wider circle of states.

The direct military threat of these and other weapons to the North is as yet remote. But the potential threat is significant as delivery ranges increase. By one [1992] report, by the end of this decade, eight states of the South will have the ability to produce nuclear weapons, while six will have an intercontinental ballistic missile (ICBM) capability, presumably capable of reaching the United States. A larger number of countries will have the ability to build or acquire chemical and biological weapons and other missiles—perhaps as many as 50 states. Of course, the North faces a more immediate although more remote threat in terms of its access to certain regions or the possibility that regional conflicts will erupt under the nuclear umbrella it extends to a few allies in the South.

In a world where distances are shrinking while the capacity to wreak devastation is dispersing, it is not surprising that the Northern states should be inclined to do something. This impulse has translated into energetic efforts to restrict the trade and transfer of technologies that might increase these military capabilities. But this approach runs counter to much of the liberal and open exchange of information and the spread of technology that is part of the modern world. It also risks seeking to restrict dual-use technology for which Southern states may have legitimate commercial or developmental needs. . . .

NUCLEAR PROLIFERATION

After the end of the Cold War no issue appears to threaten global stability more or evokes as immediate a response as the prospect of nuclear proliferation. It conjures up images of direct attacks on the homeland of states of the North as well as a kind of global anarchy. Nuclear nonproliferation has been rediscovered with an intensity and vigor that suggest either blind neglect in the past or frenzied displacement of energy at present, for it cannot be justified by any evidence that more states are energetically looking toward nuclear weapons. It is also an issue around which the inchoate fears of the threat from the South can coalesce. . . .

Although there are many good reasons to suspect that more nuclear weapon states would contribute to global insecurity, these and other arguments do not fully satisfy skeptics, largely in the South. The recently revived crusade against proliferation suggests to some not a new threat, but a new need to focus on a threat—any threat—preferably one in the guise of an Islamic foe. In general, the poorer states find it difficult to stomach the patronizing, rueful air surrounding the subject of nuclear weapons. Despite McGeorge Bundy's conclusion that "in the long run, possessing nuclear weapons is hard work and in the absence of a threat, these weapons have little or no day-to-day value," the original nuclear powers are fated, it seems, to keep theirs because "they can't be disinvented." So the nuclear states of the North modernize their nuclear forces, even as the threats for which they were constructed have disappeared, while also pressing the South on the nuclear nonproliferation agenda.

The Southern skeptic asks why the argument of France and Britain that nuclear weapons are important for the "seat at the table" they ensure is not equally valid and just for nuclear-capable states of the developing world. They also ask why the North pursues a policy of "selective" proliferation rather than nonproliferation. Some Southerners find it difficult to understand why their major security threats cannot be met by nuclear weapons when they have little capacity to provide for a sophisticated conventional defense or deterrent.

Skeptics also take issue with the argument that stable deterrence cannot emerge outside of the "civilized" North. . . .

Concern about possible nuclear weapons use in the South is also difficult to understand for those who have endured many years of war on their territory. If conventional deterrence is less effective than nuclear deterrence, and the threat of nuclear war can deter conventional attacks, then, it is argued, perhaps nuclear deterrence might rid the South of repeated wars. As for irresponsibility, it is difficult to imagine a more dangerous policy than the "extended deterrence" that was the cornerstone of the Western alliance; prudent states would be reluctant to seek to widen the utility of nuclear weapons in this fashion.

None of this means that countries of the South are queuing up for nuclear weapons, or that the benefits of nuclear status are uppermost in their minds. Wars, conflict, and instability regrettably have been the lot of many of these states. Many have not had the means to assure their security unilaterally or through access to arms or alliances. Nor have they been able to fashion a diplomatic compromise.

Moreover, their security has not automatically been improved by the passing of the Cold War. Regional concerns persist. Yet these states are usually only noticed, or taken seriously, if they look as if they are interested in nuclear weapons. Otherwise they are ignored or marginalized. . . .

Nuclear weapons will continue to hold a fascination for states in an insecure and fluid world. Whether as shortcuts, equalizers, status symbols, or simply as "options" to be kept against the possibility of need at a future date, they will be sought by states anxious about their security and/or keen to play a role in international affairs. States poor in resources or technical manpower will find it hard to acquire nuclear weapons and may not even consider them. Those states in a security environment that does not dictate their consideration, such as Latin America, may pass them by. Still others may find the original motivation for them reduced (e.g., South Africa). This will leave a number of states of some wealth, incentive, or capability that, whether from ambition, security, status incentives, or considerations of prudence, will want either to develop nuclear weapons or maintain the option of developing them quickly later.

If arms-control responses are to be found to this strategic reality, they must strive for universal, equal obligations. The extension of positive security guarantees for those states renouncing nuclear weapons that might come under nuclear threat should be considered. . . . Political incentives for nuclear weapons seem to be given shorter shrift these days when the focus is on denial of technology.

Technology- and weapons-denial strategies are not only morally unsustainable—they can scarcely be counted upon as a long-term solution. The nature of the world—technologically, scientifically, and economically—is such as to make diffusion inevitable. The real question is whether the time bought by such measures is well used to erect more effective barriers against the use of weapons of concern. . . . Technology-denial regimes such as the MTCR are one-way arrangements in which the South has to like it or lump it. This is hardly the stuff of a consensual world order.

The case of North Korea is illustrative. Here is a state with few resources, no allies, and a dim future. Neither the threat of sanctions nor a military strike is an adequate or plausible response. It may be too late for technology denial as well. A policy that combines engagement, dialogue, and positive inducements stands a greater chance of success. . . .

COLLECTIVE SECURITY

If one primary element of the new world order agenda relates to the proliferation of advanced military capability, another relates to the rules and norms governing the use of force in international affairs. The term collective security has been used over most of the last half century to encompass the state of thinking about these matters that emerged at the end of World War II. Today, much hope is being placed by the North in a reinvigorated UN system, released from the fetters of the Cold War, to achieve the benefits of concerted international responses to aggression.

Unfortunately, the renovation of the UN system and of collective security is taking place in a haphazard and ill-defined way. Improvisation has perforce been the dominant motif. The risks of mistakes, incompetence, overload, and disappointment are real. Little effort has been made to clarify the criteria for UN intervention, whether to make, keep, or enforce the peace. This issue is especially salient for the states of the South—the likely target, after all, of such intervention. On the face of it, such matters are by definition under the jurisdiction of the Security Council, where the South has little or no say. . . .

Ambiguity is the stuff of international politics, and it is far from clear how ambiguous circumstances in the South will be evaluated by the great powers of the North. Within the South, there is considerable skepticism that its interests will be taken into account. An obvious example is the fate of Bosnia's Muslims. In the former Yugoslavia, the complexities of peacekeeping are great, the parallels with Kuwait few, and the potential for spillover of conflict into Western Europe quite real, but it is nonetheless striking how many Islamic states have felt it necessary to suggest that UN reluctance to act stems from a double standard concerning the fate of Muslims. . . .

A related concern of states of the South is that the Security Council today disproportionately reflects U.S. power. One need not agree with Mu'ammar Qadhafi that the UN Security Council risks becoming an extension of NATO to note that, with Russia in its present condition, the United States and its allies dominate the Security Council to an extraordinary degree. Moreover, talk among these countries of reforming the membership of the Council tends to focus on adding membership for Germany or Japan, and not any Southern state, except as a bogey or argument against reform. . . .

Talk of revitalizing the UN Security Council assumes a degree of consensus about the role of the United States that may not be present in today's still culturally diverse world. Collective security will continue to be defined selectively and unequally, reflecting limited resources among the great powers, different priorities among nations generally, and uneven commitment to underlying international norms. . . .

CONCLUSION

The issues dividing North from South today are numerous, ranging from the proliferation of nuclear, chemical, and biological weapons and missiles, to technology transfer, population growth, developmental inequality, migration, and environmental issues. None of them will be dealt with productively if conceived of, and treated as, North–South security issues. They are more accurately global security issues, requiring dialogue, compromise, and grand bargains.

The system of global order centered on the UN Security Council was based on the premise of great power collaboration. It languished for 45 years and now is being revived. That revival must go very far indeed—well beyond what the existing great powers now envisage—if it is to have a meaningful impact on the security agenda of the future.

As [political scientist] Hedley Bull observed, no international order sustained by the great powers can provide equal justice for all states, but much can be done to alleviate this perhaps necessary and inevitable inequality. To provide "central direction in international affairs," the major powers need to "explain, prepare, negotiate, coordinate and create a consensus with other states . . . to involve [them] directly in the defense of the existing distribution of power." Bull argued that the fact that great power management of the international order may not "afford equal justice" to all did not necessarily make it intolerable, because the great powers might have a greater stake in that international order of which they became guardians. But these same powers "do, however, have a permanent problem of securing and preserving the consent of other states to the special role they play in the system."

This managerial role, Bull believed, is only possible "if these functions are accepted clearly enough by a large enough proportion of the society of states to command legitimacy." Inter alia, great powers should "seek to satisfy some of the demands for just change being expressed in the world," which include economic justice and nuclear justice among others. Where the demand cannot be met, great powers need to go through the motions of considering them: "A great power hoping to be accepted as a legitimate managerial power cannot ignore these demands or adopt a contrary position."

The states of the North, with only one-fifth of the world's population and a dynamic two-thirds of the global economy, have a long-term interest in framing a new order that is acceptable to the majority of the world's populace. A world of diffuse discontent surely cannot be an orderly one. In a world where nuclear proliferation cannot be frozen permanently and where science and technology spread quickly, it is important to involve all states in elaborating norms and to give them a stake in the more plural world order that is at once desirable and inevitable.

16

THE COMING CLASH OF CIVILIZATIONS OR, THE WEST AGAINST THE REST

Samuel P. Huntington

Viewing the post-Cold War landscape and its prospects, Samuel P. Huntington predicts that in the future global conflict will be primarily cultural—a clash of civilizations—along the borders where different cultures come into contact. He explains why hypernationalism is on the rise and why the impending clash of cultures will pit Western civilization against the other major world civilizations. Huntington is professor of government and director of the Olin Institute for Strategic Studies at Harvard University. His books include *Political Development and Political Decay* (1993).

World politics is entering a new phase in which the fundamental source of conflict will be neither ideological or economic. The great divisions among mankind and the dominating source of conflict will be cultural. The principal conflicts of global politics will occur between nations, and groups of different civilizations. The clash of civilizations will dominate global politics.

During the cold war, the world was divided into the first, second and third worlds. Those divisions are no longer relevant. It is far more meaningful to group countries not in terms of their political or economic systems or their level of economic development but in terms of their culture and civilization.

A civilization is the highest cultural grouping of people and the broadest level of cultural identity people have short of that which distinguishes humans from other species.

Civilizations obviously blend and overlap and may include sub-civilizations. Western civilization has two major variants, European and North American, and Islam has its Arab, Turkic and Malay subdivisions. But while the lines between them are seldom sharp, civilizations are real. They rise and fall; they divide and merge. And as any student of history knows, civilizations disappear.

Westerners tend to think of nation-states as the principal actors in global affairs. They have been that for only a few centuries. The broader reaches of history have been the history of civilizations. It is to this pattern that the world returns.

Civilization identity will be increasingly important and the world will be shaped in large measure by the interactions among seven or eight major civilizations. These include the Western, Confucian, Japanese, Islamic, Hindu, Slavic-Orthodox, Latin American and possibly African civilizations. The most important and bloody conflicts will occur along the borders separating these cultures. The fault lines between civilizations will be the battle lines of the future.

Why? First, differences among civilizations are basic, involving history, language, culture, tradition and, most importantly, religion. Different civilizations have different views on the relations between God and man, the citizen and the state, parents and children, liberty and authority, equality and hierarchy. These differences are the product of centuries. They will not soon disappear.

Second, the world is becoming smaller. The interactions between peoples of different civilizations are increasing. These interactions intensify civilization consciousness: awareness of differences between civilizations and commonalities within civilizations. For example, Americans react far more negatively to Japanese investment than to larger investments from Canada and European countries.

Third, economic and social changes are separating people from long-standing local identities. In much of the world, religion has moved in to fill this gap, often in the form of movements labeled fundamentalist. Such movements are found in Western Christianity, Judaism, Buddhism, Hinduism and Islam. The "unsecularization of the world," the social [philosopher] George Weigel has remarked, "is one of the dominant social facts of life in the late 20th century."

Fourth, the growth of civilization consciousness is enhanced by the fact that at the moment that the West is at the peak of its power a return-to-the-roots phenomenon is occurring among non-Western civilizations—the "Asianization" in Japan, the end of the Nehru legacy and the "Hinduization" of India, the failure of Western ideas of socialism and nationalism and, hence, the "re-Islamization" of the Middle East, and now a debate over Westernization versus Russianization in Boris Yeltsin's country.

More importantly, the efforts of the West to promote its values of democracy and liberalism as universal values, to maintain its military predominance and to advance its economic interests engender countering responses from other civilizations.

The central axis of world politics is likely to be the conflict between "the West and the rest" and the responses of non-Western civilizations to Western power and values. The most prominent example of anti-Western cooperation is the connection between Confucian and Islamic states that are challenging Western values and power.

Fifth, cultural characteristics and differences are less mutable and hence less easily compromised and resolved than political and economic ones. In the former Soviet Union, Communists can become democrats, the rich can become poor and the poor rich, but Russians cannot become Estonians. A person can be half-French and half-Arab and even a citizen of two countries. It is more difficult to be half Catholic and half Muslim.

Finally, economic regionalism is increasing. Successful economic regionalism will reinforce civilization consciousness. On the other hand, economic regionalism may succeed only when it is rooted in a common civilization. The European [Union] rests on the shared foundation of European culture and Western Christianity. Japan, in contrast, faces difficulties in creating a comparable economic entity in East Asia because it is a society and civilization unique to itself.

As the ideological division of Europe has disappeared, the cultural division of Europe between Western Christianity and Orthodox Christianity and Islam has re-emerged. Conflict along the fault line between Western and Islamic civilizations has been going on for 1,300 years. This centuries-old military interaction is unlikely to decline. Historically, the other great antagonistic interaction of Arab Islamic civilization has been with the pagan, animist and now, increasingly, Christian black peoples to the south. On the northern border of Islam, conflict has increasingly erupted between Orthodox and Muslim peoples, including the carnage of Bosnia and Sarajevo, the simmering violence between Serbs and Albanians, the tenuous relations between Bulgarians and their Turkish minority, the violence between Ossetians and Ingush, the unremitting slaughter of each other by Armenians and Azeris and the tense relations between Russians and Muslims in Central Asia.

The historic clash between Muslims and Hindus in the Subcontinent manifests itself not only in the rivalry between Pakistan and India but also in intensifying religious strife in India between increasingly militant Hindu groups and the substantial Muslim minority.

Groups or states belonging to one civilization that become involved in war with people from a different civilization naturally try to rally support from other members of their own civilization. Decreasingly able to mobilize support and form coalitions on the basis of ideology, governments and groups will increasingly attempt to mobilize support by appealing to common religion and civilization identity. As the conflicts in the Persian Gulf, the Caucasus and Bosnia continued, the positions of nations and the cleavages between them increasingly were along civilizational lines. Populist politicians, religious leaders and the media have found it a potent means of arousing mass support and of pressuring hesitant governments. In the coming years, the local conflicts most likely to escalate into major wars will be those, as in Bosnia and the Caucasus, along the fault lines between civilizations. The next world war, if there is one, will be a war between civilizations.

If these hypotheses are plausible, it is necessary to consider their implications for Western policy. These implications should be divided between short-term advantage and long-term accommodation. In the short term, it is clearly in the interest of the West to promote greater cooperation and unity in its own civilization, particularly between its European and North American components; to incorporate into the West those societies in Eastern Europe and Latin America whose cultures are close to those of the West; to maintain close relations with Russia and Japan; to support in other civilizations groups sympathetic to Western values and interests; and to strengthen international institutions that reflect and legitimate Western interests and values. The West must also limit the expansion of the military strength of potentially hostile civilizations, principally Confucian and Islamic civilizations, and exploit differences and conflicts among Confucian and Islamic states. This will require a moderation in the reduction of Western military capabilities, and, in particular, the maintenance of American military superiority in East and Southwest Asia.

In the longer term, other measures would be called for. Western civilization is modern. Non-Western civilizations have attempted to become modern without becoming Western. To date, only Japan has fully succeeded in this quest. Non-Western civilizations will continue to attempt to acquire the wealth, technology, skills, machines and weapons that are part of being modern. They will attempt to reconcile this modernity with their traditional culture and values. Their economic and military strength relative to the West will increase.

Hence, the West will increasingly have to accommodate to these non-Western modern civilizations, whose power approaches that of the West but whose values and interests differ significantly from those of the West. This will require the West to develop a much more profound understanding of the basic religious and philosophical assumptions underlying other civilizations and the ways in which people in those civilizations see their interests. It will require an effort to identify elements of commonality among Western and other civilizations. For the relevant future, there will be no universal civilization but instead a world of different civilizations, each of which will have to learn to co-exist with others.

17

ISLAM AND LIBERAL DEMOCRACY: MUSLIM PERCEPTIONS AND WESTERN REACTIONS

Bernard Lewis

Many observers fear that the Muslim world is braced for conflict with the West. The reasons why the Islamic countries harbor deep resentments toward the West and, in particular, its liberal values and democratic institutions are explored by Bernard Lewis, who warns that Western attempts to pressure Muslim governments for human rights and democratic reforms could intensify Islamic rage and escalate into a new epoch of bitter conflict. Lewis is professor emeritus of Near Eastern studies at Princeton University and author of *Islam and the West* (1993).

There has been much discussion of late, both inside and outside the Islamic world, about those elements in the Islamic past and those factors in the Muslim present that are favorable and unfavorable to the development of liberal democracy. From a historical perspective it would seem that of all the non-Western civilizations in the world, Islam offers the best prospects for Western-style democracy. Historically, culturally, religiously, it is the closest to the West, sharing much—though by no means all—of the Judeo-Christian and Greco-Roman heritage that helped to form our modern civilization. From a political perspective, however, Islam seems to offer the worst prospects for liberal democracy. Of the fifty-one sovereign states that make up the international Islamic Confer-

Abridged from the article "Islam and Liberal Democracy" published in *The Atlantic,* Vol. 272, February 1, 1993, pp. 89–98. *The Atlantic* article was drawn from a longer paper prepared for a colloquium on "The Expansion of Liberal Society," sponsored by the Institute for Human Sciences in Vienna. The resulting volume has been published in German, but not yet in English.

ence, only one, the Turkish Republic, can be described as a democracy in Western terms, and even there the path to freedom has been beset by obstacles. Of the remainder, some have never tried democracy; others have tried it and failed; a few, more recently, have experimented with the idea of sharing, though not of relinquishing, power.

Can liberal democracy work in a society inspired by Islamic beliefs and principles and shaped by Islamic experience and tradition? It is of course for Muslims, primarily and perhaps exclusively, to interpret and reinterpret the pristine original message of their faith, and to decide how much to retain, and in what form, of the rich accumulated heritage of fourteen centuries of Islamic history and culture. Not all Muslims give the same answers to the question posed above, but much will depend on the answer that prevails. . . .

FUNDAMENTALISTS AND DEMOCRATS

There are many who see no need for any . . . change and would prefer to retain the existing systems, whether radical dictatorships or traditional autocracies, with perhaps some improvement in the latter. This preference for things as they are is obviously shared by those who rule under the present system and those who otherwise benefit, including foreign powers who are willing to accept and even support existing regimes as long as their own interests are safeguarded. But there are others who feel that the present systems are both evil and doomed and that new institutions must be devised and installed.

Proponents of radical change fall into two main groups—the Islamic fundamentalists and the democrats. Each group includes a wide range of sometimes contending ideologies.

The term "fundamentalism" derives from a series of Protestant tracts, *The Fundamentals,* published in the United States around 1910, and was used first in America and then in other predominantly Protestant countries to designate certain groups that diverge from the mainstream churches in their rejection of liberal theology and biblical criticism and their insistence on the literal divinity and inerrancy of the biblical text. The use of the term to designate Muslim movements is therefore at best a loose analogy and can be very misleading. Reformist theology has at times in the past been an issue among Muslims; it is not now, and it is very far from the primary concerns of those who are called Muslim fundamentalists.

Those concerns are less with scripture and theology than with society, law, and government. As the Muslim fundamentalists see it, the community of Islam has been led into error by foreign infidels and Muslim apostates, the latter being the more dangerous and destructive. Under their guidance or constraint Muslims abandoned the laws and principles of their faith and instead adopted secular— that is to say, pagan—laws and values. All the foreign ideologies—liberalism, socialism, even nationalism—that set Muslim against Muslim are evil, and the

Muslim world is now suffering the inevitable consequences of forsaking the God-given law and way of life that were vouchsafed to it. The answer is the old Muslim obligation of jihad: to wage holy war first at home, against the pseudo-Muslim apostates who rule, and then, having ousted them and re-Islamized society, to resume the greater role of Islam in the world. The return to roots, to authenticity, will always be attractive. It will be doubly appealing to those who daily suffer the consequences of the failed foreign innovations that were foisted on them.

For Islamic fundamentalists, democracy is obviously an irrelevance, and unlike the communist totalitarians, they rarely use or even misuse the word. They are, however, willing to demand and exploit the opportunities that a self-proclaimed democratic system by its own logic is bound to offer them. At the same time, they make no secret of their contempt for democratic political procedures and their intention to govern by Islamic rules if they gain power. . . .

Those who plead or fight for democratic reform in the Arab and other Islamic lands claim to represent a more effective, more authentic democracy than that of their failed predecessors, not restricted or distorted by some intrusive adjective, not nullified by *a priori* religious or ideological imperatives, not misappropriated by regional or sectarian or other sectional interests. In part their movement is an extension to the Middle East of the wave of democratic change that has already transformed the governments of many countries in Southern Europe and Latin America; in part it is a response to the collapse of the Soviet Union and the new affirmation of democratic superiority through victory in the Cold War. To no small extent it is also a consequence of the growing impact of the U.S. democracy and of American popular culture in the Islamic lands. . . .

It is precisely the catholicity, the assimilative power and attraction, of American culture that make it an object of fear and hatred among the self-proclaimed custodians of pristine, authentic Islam. For such as they, it is a far more deadly threat than any of its predecessors to the old values that they hold dear and to the power and influence those values give them. In the last chapter of the Koran, which ranks with the first among the best known and most frequently cited, the believer is urged to seek refuge with God "from the mischief of the insidious Whisperer who whispers in people's hearts. . . ." Satan in the Koran is the adversary, the deceiver, above all the inciter and tempter who seeks to entice mankind away from the true faith. It is surely in this sense that the Ayatollah Khomeini called America the great Satan: Satan as enemy, but—more especially and certainly more plausibly for his people—also as source of enticement and temptation.

In these times of discontent and disappointment, of anger and frustration, the older appeals of nationalism and socialism and national socialism—the gifts of nineteenth- and twentieth-century Europe—have lost much of their power. Today only the democrats and the Islamic fundamentalists appeal to something more than personal or sectional loyalties. Both have achieved some limited success, partly by infiltrating the existing regimes, more often by frightening them into making some preemptive concessions. Successes have in the main been limited to the more traditional authoritarian regimes, which have made some symbolic gestures toward the democrats or the fundamentalists or both. Even the radical dictatorships, while admitting no compromise with liberal democracy, have in times of stress tried to appease and even to use Islamic sentiment.

There is an agonizing question at the heart of the present debate about democracy in the Islamic world: Is liberal democracy basically compatible with Islam, or is some measure of respect for law, some tolerance of criticism, the most that can be expected from autocratic governments? The democratic world contains many different forms of government—republics and monarchies, presidential and parliamentary regimes, secular states and established churches, and a wide range of electoral systems—but all of them share certain basic assumptions and practices that mark the distinction between democratic and undemocratic governments. Is it possible for the Islamic peoples to evolve a form of government that will be compatible with their own historical, cultural, and religious traditions and yet will bring individual freedom and human rights to the governed as these terms are understood in the free societies of the West? . . .

The question . . . is not whether liberal democracy is compatible with Islamic fundamentalism—clearly it is not—but whether it is compatible with Islam itself. Liberal democracy, however far it may have traveled, however much it may have been transformed, is in its origins a product of the West—shaped by a thousand years of European history, and beyond that by Europe's double heritage: Judeo-Christian religion and ethics; Greco-Roman statecraft and law. No such system has originated in any other cultural tradition; it remains to be seen whether such a system, transplanted and adapted in another culture, can long survive. . . .

Traditional obstacles to democracy have in many ways been reinforced by the processes of modernization, and by recent developments in the region. . . . [The] power of the state to dominate and terrorize the people has been vastly increased by modern methods. The philosophy of authoritarian rule has been sharpened and strengthened by imported totalitarian ideologies, which have served a double purpose—to sanctify rulers and leaders and to fanaticize their subjects and followers. The so-called Islamic fundamentalists are no exception in this respect.

Self-criticism in the West—a procedure until recently rarely practiced and little understood in the Middle East—provided useful ammunition. This use of the West against itself is particularly striking among the fundamentalists. Western democracy for them is part of the hated West, and that hatred is central to the ideas by which they define themselves, as in the past the free world defined itself first against Nazism and then against communism.

The changes wrought by modernization are by no means entirely negative. Some, indeed, are extremely positive. One such improvement is the emancipation of women. Though this still has a long way to go before it reaches Western levels, irreversible changes have already taken place. These changes are indispensable: a society can hardly aspire realistically to create and operate free institutions as long as it keeps half its members in a state of permanent subordination and the other half see themselves as domestic autocrats. Economic and social development has also brought new economic and social elements of profound importance—a literate middle class, commercial, managerial, and professional, that is very different from the military, bureaucratic, and religious elites that between them dominated the old order. These new groups are creating their own associations and organizations, and modifying the law to accommodate them. They are an indispensable component of civil society—previously lacking, yet essential to any kind of democratic polity.

There are also older elements in the Islamic tradition, older factors in Middle Eastern history, that are not hostile to democracy and that, in favorable circumstances, could even help in its development. Of special importance among these is the classical Islamic concept of supreme sovereignty—elective, contractual, in a sense even consensual and revocable. The Islamic caliphate, as prescribed and regulated by the holy law, may be an autocracy; it is in no sense a despotism. According to Sunni doctrine, the Caliph was to be elected by those qualified to make a choice. The electorate was never defined, nor was any procedure of election ever devised or operated, but the elective principle remains central to Sunni religious jurisprudence, and that is not unimportant. . . .

This doctrine marks one of the essential differences between Islamic and other autocracies. An Islamic ruler is not above the law. He is subject to it, no less than the humblest of his servants. If he commands something that is contrary to the law, the duty of obedience lapses, and is replaced not by the right but by the duty of disobedience.

Muslim spokesmen, particularly those who sought to find Islamic roots for Western practices, made much of the Islamic principle of consultation, according to which a ruler should not make arbitrary decisions by himself but should act only after consulting with suitably qualified advisers. This principle rests on two somewhat enigmatic passages in the Koran and on a number of treatises, mainly by ulama and statesmen, urging consultation with ulama or with statesmen. This principle has never been institutionalized, nor even formulated in the treatises of the holy law, though naturally rulers have from time to time consulted with their senior officials, more particularly in Ottoman times.

Of far greater importance was the acceptance of pluralism in Islamic law and practice. Almost from the beginning the Islamic world has shown an astonishing diversity. Extending over three continents, it embraced a wide variety of races, creeds, and cultures, which lived side by side in reasonable if intermittent harmony. Sectarian strife and religious persecution are not unknown in Islamic history, but they are rare and atypical, and never reached the level of intensity of the great religious wars and persecutions in Christendom.

Traditional Islam has no doctrine of human rights, the very notion of which might seem an impiety. Only God has rights—human beings have duties. But in practice the duty owed by one human being to another—more specifically, by a ruler to his subjects—may amount to what Westerners would call a right, particularly when the discharge of this duty is a requirement of holy law.

TWO TEMPTATIONS

It may be—and has been—argued that these legal and religious principles have scant effect. The doctrine of elective and contractual sovereignty has been tacitly ignored since the days of the early caliphate. The supremacy of the law has been flouted. Tolerance of pluralism and diversity has dwindled or disappeared in an age of heightened religious, ethnic, and social tensions. Consultation, as far as it ever existed, is restricted to the ruler and his inner circle, while personal dignity has been degraded by tyrants who feel that they must torture and humiliate, not just kill, their opponents.

And yet, despite all these difficulties and obstacles, the democratic ideal is steadily gaining force in the region, and increasing numbers of Arabs have come to the conclusion that it is the best, perhaps the only, hope for the solution of their economic, social, and political problems.

What can we in the democratic world do to encourage the development of democracy in the Islamic Middle East—and what should we do to avoid impeding or subverting it? There are two temptations to which Western governments have all too often succumbed, with damaging results. They might be called the temptation of the right and the temptation of the left. The temptation of the right is to accept, and even to embrace, the most odious of dictatorships as long as they are acquiescent in our own requirements, and as long as their policies seem to accord with the protection of our own national interests. The spectacle of the great democracies of the West in comfortable association with tyrants and dictators can only discourage and demoralize the democratic opposition in these countries.

The more insidious temptation, that of the left, is to press Muslim regimes for concessions on human rights and related matters. Since ruthless dictatorships are impervious to such pressures, and are indeed rarely subjected to them, the brunt of such well-intentioned intervention falls on the more moderate autocracies, which are often in the process of reforming themselves in a manner and at a pace determined by their own conditions and needs. The pressure for premature democratization can fatally weaken such regimes and lead to their overthrow, not by democratic opposition but by other forces that then proceed to establish a more ferocious and determined dictatorship.

All in all, considering the difficulties that Middle Eastern countries have inherited and the problems that they confront, the prospects for Middle Eastern democracy are not good. But they are better than they have ever been before. Most of these countries face grave economic problems. If they fail to cope with these problems, then the existing regimes, both dictatorial and authoritarian, are likely to be overthrown and replaced, probably by one variety or another of Islamic fundamentalists. It has been remarked in more than one country that the fundamentalists are popular because they are out of power and cannot be held responsible for the present troubles. If they acquired power, and with it responsibility, they would soon lose that popularity. But this would not matter to them, since once in power they would not need popularity to stay there, and would continue to govern—some with and some without oil revenues to mitigate the economic consequences of their methods. In time even the fundamentalist regimes, despite their ruthless hold on power, would be either transformed or overthrown, but by then they would have done immense, perhaps irreversible, damage to the cause of freedom.

But their victory is by no means inevitable. There is always the possibility that democrats may form governments, or governments learn democracy. The increasing desire for freedom, and the better understanding of what it means, are hopeful signs. Now that the Cold War has ended and the Middle East is no longer a battlefield for rival power blocs, the peoples of the Middle East will have the chance—if they can take it—to make their own decisions and find their own solutions. No one else will have the ability or even the desire to do it for them. Today—for the first time in centuries—the choice is their own.

18

HUMAN RIGHTS IN THE NEW WORLD ORDER

Jack Donnelly

This chapter examines the prospects for stronger international rules to protect human rights in the post-Cold War era. Jack Donnelly explains why optimism is not warranted, given the substantial structural barriers that interfere with progress on this issue. Donnelly is professor of political science in the Graduate School of International Studies at the University of Denver. His publications include *International Human Rights* (1993).

A climate of optimism pervades discussions of human rights today. The end of the Cold War, the wave of democratizations and liberalizations in the Third World, and the collapse of rights-abusive regimes in Europe and the Soviet Union have contributed to a sense that human rights will be better protected in the new (and still emerging) world order than in the old.

Much of this optimism, however well-intentioned, is unjustified. The demise of old rights-abusive regimes will not necessarily lead to the creation of new rights-protective policies and regimes. Although some countries, such as Argentina and Czechoslovakia [now separate Czech and Slovak republics—eds.], are likely to make successful transitions to democracy, many will fall back into dictatorship, as demonstrated by the recent coups in Haiti, Togo, and Algeria.

This essay originally appeared in a slightly different form in *World Policy Journal,* Volume XI, No. 2 (Spring 1992). The author would like to thank Lea Brilmayer, Dave Forsythe, Marie Gottschalk, Rhoda Howard, and Ian Shapiro for their comments on and helpful criticism of earlier drafts.

Many other countries, such as Guatemala and the Philippines, today enjoy governments that are generally less oppressive than their predecessors, but still far short of consistently protecting the full range of internationally recognized human rights. In addition, new threats to human rights are emerging, most notably increased ethnic violence and the suffering caused by economic liberalization.

The end of the Cold War has removed the principal U.S. rationale for supporting repressive regimes, and the demise of the Soviet Union has eliminated the other major postwar pillar of support for such regimes. Here too, though, we should be wary of excessive optimism. An international atmosphere that is less hospitable to repressive regimes does not mean that these regimes will come tumbling down in fast order, let alone that new policies that are more protective and respectful of human rights will take hold. . . .

THE COLD WAR BASELINE

The Cold War era was a paradox with respect to human rights.[1] Although a time of pervasive anti-humanitarian interventions by both superpowers, it was also the period in which human rights first became an established subject of international relations.[2]

Before World War II, human rights were not considered a legitimate subject for international action. How states treated their own nationals in their own territory was considered a prerogative of national sovereignty and thus the business of no one else. Human rights were not even mentioned in the Covenant of the League of Nations, and in the interwar period human rights practices of states were officially discussed only in a few international forums, such as the International Labor Organization.

Postwar reflection on the horrors of the Holocaust and the shameful lack of an international response led to significant changes. The Nuremberg War Crimes Trials prosecuted individuals on the unprecedented charge of crimes against humanity. The United Nations Charter explicitly listed human rights as a principal concern of the new organization. In 1946, the U.N. Commission on Human Rights was established, and in 1948, the U.N. General Assembly

---

[1]Human rights are ordinarily understood as the rights that one has simply because one is a human being. In contemporary international relations, human rights have a special reference to the ways in which states treat their own citizens in their own territory. It is therefore conventional to distinguish, for example, international terrorism, war crimes, muggings, gangland violence, and drought-caused famine from "human rights" issues, even though they also lead to denials of life and security. I will adopt this relatively narrow focus here, both because it corresponds to standard usage and because it focuses our attention on a central problem of national and international politics.

[2]By antihumanitarian intervention I mean intervention that supports or establishes governments engaging in gross and systematic violations of internationally recognized human rights. In other words, it is the opposite of the familiar notion of "humanitarian intervention," that is, intervention, typically including the use of military force, to rescue people from imminent danger, usually as a result of gross and systematic human rights violations.

adopted the Universal Declaration of Human Rights. The International Human Rights Covenants, which further developed and sought to give binding legal force to the rights enumerated in the Universal Declaration, were completed in 1966 and entered into force in 1976.

The Universal Declaration of Human Rights treats civil and political rights and economic, social, and cultural rights in a single document without categorical distinctions. The "interdependence and indivisibility" of all human rights was, and remains, a much repeated theme in international discussions. Nonetheless, the Cold War both revealed and helped to create profound fissures in this verbal consensus. The United States criticized violations of civil and political rights in Soviet-bloc countries while condoning, or even encouraging, violations of the same rights in "friendly" countries. The Soviet Union emphasized the denial of economic, social, and cultural rights in the West, but systematically denigrated the importance of civil and political rights at home.

The universality of internationally recognized human rights was also challenged by the argument that there were "three worlds," or three distinctive and valid conceptions of international human rights norms. The First World conception, it was argued, stressed civil and political rights and the right to property. The Second World conception treated economic, social, and cultural rights as an overriding priority and a prerequisite to the enjoyment of civil and political rights. The Third World conception also emphasized economic, social, and cultural rights, along with the right to self-determination and the overriding importance of the struggle for development.

Nonetheless, most states continued to insist that all human rights were "interdependent and indivisible" and valid across cultural and political divisions. A broad, although shallow, international normative consensus thus developed on the full list of rights in the Universal Declaration. The Universal Declaration came to be recognized, in theory if not in practice, as providing a single comprehensive system of guarantees, rather than a list of rights from which states might choose as they saw fit. In the 1950s and 1960s, this verbal consensus had little or no discernible impact on policy. Altering the terms of debate, though, marked a first step toward altering practice.

In 1970, the U.N. Commission on Human Rights was authorized to conduct confidential investigations of systematic human rights violations. Nearly 40 countries have been subjected to such reviews in the ensuing two decades. The commission also developed largely depoliticized monitoring programs on disappearances, torture, and arbitrary and summary executions. In addition, over the past 30 years a number of human rights treaties have been adopted that require parties to submit periodic reports to independent monitoring committees.

The strongest "enforcement" power available to any of these bodies, however, was (and remains) adopting a critical public resolution or report. Most of the treaty-based committees do not even have this much power; they are largely limited to receiving and asking questions concerning the reports submitted by states. These are monitoring—not enforcement—procedures, which aim to bring informed international public opinion to bear. Human rights norms have been internationalized. Their implementation and enforcement, however, remain largely national.

The regional record is more varied. The regional enforcement regime covering the 23 (primarily West European) members of the Council of Europe stands at one end of the spectrum. The European Commission of Human Rights investigates complaints from individuals and states, and the European Court of Human Rights can, and does, issue binding legal judgments, with which states almost invariably comply. At the other end of the spectrum, there are still no intergovernmental regional human rights organizations in Asia and the Middle East. The Americas and Africa lie between these extremes.

The Inter-American Commission of Human Rights, an organ of the Organization of American States (OAS), has significant investigatory powers and its reports receive considerable regional and international publicity. For example, its reports on Chile and Argentina in the 1970s were major sources of information for international efforts against the military regimes in these countries. The Inter-American Commission, however, has no real enforcement powers. The Inter-American Court of Human Rights may issue legally binding judgments, but to date it has handed down decisions on only two cases (one dealing with a disappearance in Honduras, the other with military violence against two journalists in Peru).

The African regional regime is significantly weaker. The African Commission on Human and Peoples' Rights has very modest investigatory powers and no enforcement powers of any sort. In fact, it even lacks the resources to disseminate its reports. In addition, there is no regional human rights court.

In 1973, the "Helsinki process" of the Conference on Security and Cooperation in Europe (CSCE) was launched with the initial participation of 35 North American and European countries. It has since become a significant quasiregional human rights regime that operates among [54] European and North American countries. Its importance is attested to by the strong desires of many of the new governments of Central and Eastern Europe to deepen what is now called the human dimension of the CSCE. New investigation and conciliation procedures were established at the 1989 Vienna review meeting and important new statements of norms were issued in Copenhagan and Paris in 1990. Nonetheless, the Helsinki human rights process still lacks enforcement powers.

In addition to the creation of various multilateral human rights bodies, the last two decades of the Cold War era also saw the elevation of the significance of human rights in bilateral foreign policy. In 1973, the U.S. Congress called for, and in 1975 legislatively mandated, a link between human rights and foreign aid. In 1979, the Netherlands explicitly incorporated human rights into its foreign policy, and in the 1980s many other countries followed suit. One can point to few cases in which any state, large or small, has been willing to bear a significant foreign policy cost in pursuit of human rights objectives. Nonetheless, tougher talk on human rights, backed by an occasional halt in foreign aid, was a major change.

Another important development during the Cold War was the rise to prominence of human rights nongovernmental organizations (NGOs). Amnesty International, which was founded in 1961 and received the Nobel Peace Prize in 1977, is the best known such organization. In the United States, Human Rights Watch and the Lawyers Committee for International Human Rights have been especially active lobbyists for international human rights. These two organizations regularly document and publicize human rights violations, testify before congressional committees, lobby legislators and staff members working on human rights issues, do extensive work with the media, and issue an annual critique of the State Department's country reports on human rights. Other human rights NGOs engage in similar efforts to influence policy by acquiring and disseminating information and organizing public pressure. Again, though, their activities are limited to international monitoring, not implementation or enforcement, of human rights.

In summary, we can say that during the Cold War states lost their traditional immunity from public international scrutiny of their human rights practices. A fairly extensive system of formal and informal international human rights monitoring—by international and regional organizations, NGOs, and other states—was established. International action, however, was modest in scope and impact. Except in Europe, no procedures were established to provide real international enforcement of internationally recognized human rights.

Much of the new world order rhetoric suggests that the 1990s will see substantial strengthening of international human rights guarantees. It is very likely, however, that the end of the Cold War will have fewer positive consequences for international human rights policies than many people suspect, and that the depth and permanence of recent "democratizations" have often been seriously exaggerated.

THE IMPACT OF THE END OF THE COLD WAR

Both bipolarity and ideological struggle, defining features of the Cold War international order, have largely disappeared. While this has indeed helped to create an improved climate for the protection of human rights, significant limits to further progress remain.

We need only say "Guatemala, 1954" or "Czechoslovakia, 1968" to recall the major role of the superpowers in reversing progress toward the establishment of rights-protective regimes in their Cold War spheres of influence. Marcos in the Philippines, Duvalier in Haiti, Park in South Korea, the Shah in Iran, Pinochet in Chile, Stroessner in Paraguay, and Mobutu in Zaire are only some of the more prominent dictators who benefited from U.S. support. The Soviet record was comparably appalling. In addition to forcibly imposing repressive communist regimes in Central and Eastern Europe, the Soviets were the principal backers of the Mengistu regime in Ethiopia, one of the most barbaric Third World regimes of the past two decades, as well as Afghanistan's vicious Karmal and Najibullah governments.

Economic decline and internal political upheavals have largely eliminated Soviet (now Russian) incentives and capabilities for such behavior. The United States still retains an unrivaled capability to project immense conventional power at a great distance, as the Gulf War vividly illustrated. The end of the Cold War, however, has eliminated a central U.S. justification for supporting repressive regimes.

Whatever the root causes of U.S. foreign policy, most U.S. anti-humanitarian interventions during the Cold War were fueled by a substantial element of anti-communism, and few could have been sold to Congress or the public without it. During the Cold War, most unsavory dictators could acquire, or at least maintain, American support by playing on anticommunism. This is simply no longer the case. The post–Cold War international environment for human rights thus should be significantly improved. . . .

A similar picture of limited progress is apparent if we turn from the demise of Cold War ideological rivalry to recent shifts in the international balance of power. It is difficult today to characterize the current distribution of international political power. As a result, international political processes and outcomes vary dramatically from issue to issue. Although the end of U.S. and Soviet superpower rivalry may create new opportunities for progressive international action, it also means that we cannot automatically generalize from one issue area to another. In particular, we must avoid jumping to the conclusion that the significant changes of late in international economic relations portend comparable changes in international human rights policies.

Some developed states are indeed increasingly willing to relinquish significant elements of economic sovereignty. We see this not only in the increasing globalization of production, but also in the heightened interest in formal multilateral organizations (most notably in the European [Union]) as well as in less formal modes of international cooperation, such as the annual economic summits of the Group of Seven (G-7) industrialized countries. In addition, Third World states are increasingly surrendering economic sovereignty through IMF-imposed structural adjustment packages (although often out of dire necessity, rather than genuine desire).

More complex and less state-centric patterns of order and cooperation, based on relatively deep conceptions of international interdependence, are also emerging in some noneconomic issue areas. Consider, for example, the surprisingly rapid success in regulating ozone-depleting emissions through the 1985 Vienna Convention and the 1987 Montreal Protocol. In security relations, however, perceived interdependence has not penetrated very far, especially in U.S. policy. In fact, sovereignty [remained] at the core of [U.S. President George] Bush's vision of the new world order, which, he [in 1991 was] at pains to note, "[did] not mean surrendering our national sovereignty."

A state-centric, sovereignty-based conception of international order also remains the norm for international human rights. Most states still jealously guard their sovereign prerogatives with respect to human rights. Even in Europe, the relatively strong regional human rights system pales in comparison to the restrictions on state sovereignty achieved through regional economic institutions.

There has been much talk recently of an enhanced role for the United Nations in international peace and security, symbolized by the Security Council summit at the end of January [1992]. U.N. mediation efforts in Central America suggest that there may be the possibility for significant positive spillovers into human rights. Recent interest in multilateral monitoring of elections may signify a possible enhanced U.N. role in the final stages of phasing out repressive regimes. Nonetheless, in the core areas of monitoring and implementation, recent events at the United Nations suggest that simply maintaining the current (very modest) levels of activity in the area of human rights may be the best that can be hoped for.

For example, in 1990 the U.N. Commission on Human Rights failed to adopt an embarrassingly mild draft resolution on human rights in China that did not even explicitly condemn the 1989 massacre in Beijing. Japan was the only Asian country, Swaziland the only African country, and Panama the only Latin American country to vote for the resolution. Furthermore, the Third World's Group of 77 tried to further weaken and politicize the commission's already modest human rights monitoring efforts. It also tried to impose restrictions on the activities of human rights NGOs because of their independence from political control. Although these efforts ultimately failed, they suggest that new regimes can be as reluctant to allow strong international monitoring of national human rights practices as their authoritarian predecessors. . . .

The inherent sensitivity of human rights issues helps to explain the weakness of international human rights procedures and the persistently strong commitment to sovereignty. For example, the United States refuses to ratify the International Human Rights Covenants and almost all other international human rights treaties, although in most particulars American law and practice already conform to their requirements. But political sensitivity does not provide the full explanation.

International human rights policies rest largely on a perceived moral interdependence. By contrast, material interdependence underlies most (noncoercive) economic, environmental, or even security cooperation. These differing bases for cooperation are likely to lead to significantly different international political processes.

Moral interdependence is largely intangible. The international harm caused by a foreign state violating the human rights of its own nationals is a moral harm. Disgust, discomfort, or outrage is the result, rather than a loss of income, a deterioration in one's quality of life, or a reduction in perceived security. Most states, though, are unwilling to pay very much to act on or assuage their moral sensibilities. This does not mean that they do not see themselves as morally interdependent, any more than the refusal of many individuals to pay a large price to fulfill their moral responsibilities toward strangers (the homeless, for instance) means that private morality does not exist. It does, however, help to explain the low status that human rights have on the foreign policy agendas of most states.

But even if states did choose to give higher priority to international human rights, there are unusually high hurdles to clear in implementing international human rights policies. Retaliatory enforcement of international norms is inherently problematic. Moral suasion, which responds directly to the nature of the international offense, is notoriously weak. Any other type of retaliation, however, must be imported from another issue area, such as the economy, increasing both the cost of responding and the risk of escalating the dispute. Furthermore, because the means are not clearly and directly tied to the violation, their legitimacy may appear questionable.

The fact that it is easier for outside actors to undermine than to enhance human rights further increases the difficulty of international action. Although massive outside military force may ultimately fail to maintain repressive rule, foreign states may still have enormous power in the short and medium run to tip the political balance of power in favor of the forces of repression. Yet foreign intervention has rarely been central in establishing a strong and stable rights-protective regime. Even Japan and West Germany, in some ways exceptions, confirm the rule: change came only after total defeat in a devastating war that completely discredited the prior regime. Rights-protective regimes are almost always established by domestic, not international, political forces.

Taken together, these observations on the character of power and interdependence in the post-Cold War world suggest that international progress in human rights remains substantially constrained by deep structural forces. The impediments to establishing effective international human rights policies rooted in an international system of sovereign states remain essentially unchanged in the post–Cold War world.

The fate of human rights therefore will rest largely on national, not international, politics. Foreign policy initiatives must focus on responding constructively to national political processes, and our attention needs to shift now to some of the more prominent trends [at that level of analysis]. . . .

NATIONALISM AND HUMAN RIGHTS

The revival of nationalism in the wake of the collapse of the old order poses yet another threat to the establishment of rights-protective regimes. Internationally recognized human rights rest on the premise that all individuals, simply because they are human beings, have certain basic rights that they are entitled to enjoy equally. Aggressive, exclusive nationalism often challenges this central principle of political equality.

Although asserting national identity has often been an important element in struggles against outside domination, self-determination hardly guarantees that internationally recognized human rights will be protected. Nonetheless, because of its role in the overthrow of old forms of repression, nationalism has often been seen not only as a force with which to oppose oppressive ethnic domination, but as a guarantee of liberty and respect for human rights. This is another example of the gulf between ending old forms of abuse and establishing rights-protective regimes.

Throughout the former communist world, the demise of the old regimes has released long pent-up national animosities, most dramatically in Croatia. Some previously dominant groups, such as Serbs in Yugoslavia, have responded by becoming even more aggressive and overbearing. Others, such as Russians residing outside of Russia, now fear nationalist retribution. Some previously subordinate groups, such as Slovaks in [the Czech Republic], seem as concerned with addressing old ethnic grievances as with establishing a new democratic order. Many other ethnic groups remain subordinated, with their interests still ignored (e.g., ethnic Hungarians in [the Czech Republic]) or actively under attack (e.g., ethnic Turks in Bulgaria). Still other minorities have simply seen new ethnic oppressors replace the old. And the human rights problems posed by rising nationalism are likely to be at least as severe in sub-Saharan Africa, where many countries have ethnically diverse populations with a strong sense of group identity and loyalty.

Especially in conditions of economic scarcity, where an expanding supply of goods and services cannot be used to help defuse intergroup rivalries, there is a relatively high probability that communal competition will lead to ethnic conflict, and in some cases violence. Rapid economic growth allows some grievances to be addressed by directing a greater share of new resources to disadvantaged groups. In times of scarcity, however, especially in poor countries, politics tends to turn into a zero-sum contest for shares of an inadequate pie.

Separatism has been a solution of sorts in parts of the former Soviet Union and Yugoslavia. Balkanization, though, can create or exacerbate economic, political, and human rights problems. There were good (although perhaps not sufficient) reasons for creating a multiethnic Yugoslavia after World War I. . . . And the likely costs of fragmentation are even greater in much of Africa, where the problems of political transition and economic development are severe enough already without opening up the possibility of years, even decades, of nationalistic tumult and the creation of new, and even more feeble, states.

Nonetheless, separatist demands for self-determination must be taken seriously not only in cases where dominant nationalities are oppressive, but even in some instances where they are not. Both internally and internationally, we face a genuine dilemma. The next several years are likely to see a succession of crises, many of which will be resolved, after great financial, political, and human cost, to the satisfaction of no one. . . .

All international human rights issues are inherently problematic in a world structured around sovereign states. Questions of self-determination are perhaps the most problematic of all, because they are about defining the very units that are entitled to participate in international relations. Claims of self-determination also raise the question of defining the community within which human rights are to be pursued and protected. It is unclear whether foreign actors have a right to do anything at all beyond encouraging the peaceful resolution of disputes and attempting to moderate the severity of conflicts that led to violence. And even if they do have a right to become involved, foreign actors are in a particularly weak position to deal with this major threat to human rights. . . .

INTERNATIONAL HUMAN RIGHTS POLICY IN A POST–COLD WAR WORLD

What could be done if there was the political will? On what basis should we fashion an international human rights policy for the post–Cold War world? We must begin by recognizing the considerable national and international constraints on even well-intentioned and well-designed international human rights policies. This deserves special emphasis today because the heady days of the fall of entrenched dictators are largely over. . . . The struggle has shifted to the often slow and laborious, and certainly far less exhilarating, work of building new institutions and expectations that will provide entrenched, long-run protections for internationally recognized human rights. In some countries, just being able to maintain the current level of respect for human rights will have to be counted as a great success.

The often repeated claim that "we won" the Cold War, expressed in a particularly tasteless fashion in [U.S. President George] Bush's 1992 State of the Union Address, suggests that the international struggle for human rights is largely over. In fact, it has just begun. A continued, even redoubled, commitment to human rights is required by the often fragile new governments in Latin America, Africa, Europe, and elsewhere. . . .

19

OUT OF THE COLD: HUMANITARIAN INTERVENTION IN THE 1990s

Stanley Hoffmann

With the rise of ethnic conflict and governments' abuse of their own people's human rights as a global phenomenon, new attention has been given to humanitarian intervention to relieve the suffering of the victims. Stanley Hoffmann frames the principles that might justify this kind of external interference in sovereign states' domestic affairs and explains why revision of the classic legal prohibition against intervention has assumed importance as an issue on the global agenda. Hoffmann is Douglas Dillon Professor of the Civilization of France and director of the Minda de Gunzburg Center for European Studies at Harvard University. He has published (with Robert O. Keohane) *The New European Community: Decision Making and Institutional Change* (1991).

The post–Cold War world is no longer dominated by a single conflict capable of bursting into an all-out global war between nuclear superpowers and their allies. But it is still a troubled and dangerous world in which two kinds of issues intersect. On the one hand, many states are still pursuing the age-old game of power, threatening their neighbors and trying to satisfy old grievances or dreams of regional hegemony through the accumulation and eventual use of force. On the other hand, many of the central state actors in international politics are experiencing enormous internal turbulence, ranging from famine or revolt to disintegration, for a multitude of reasons: economic poverty or mismanagement, eth-

Reprinted by permission from *Harvard International Review,* Vol. 16, No. 1 (Fall 1993).

nic or religious conflicts, ideological or power rivalries, oppressive measures by a tyrannical regime, and the list goes on.

Suddenly, it seems that foreign policy has become obsessed with the question of intervention in domestic affairs—that is, with the erosion and decline of the legal norm of state sovereignty. For domestic affairs are at stake not only in the second group of issues I have mentioned, but also insofar as preventing a potential aggressive state from becoming a troublemaker may require outside measures aimed at keeping it from acquiring or producing weapons of mass destruction.

A number of recent crises spotlighted by the media have drawn attention to one particular kind of intervention, humanitarian intervention, whose purpose is to relieve the suffering of victims of internal conflicts or disasters. Famine in a number of African countries such as Sudan and Somalia, the plight of minority groups forced to choose between fleeing or being massacred by a repressive government—as in the cases of the Kurds and Shiites in Saddam Hussein's Iraq—and the tragedy of civilians murdered, starved and displaced by policies of ethnic cleansing—as in the former Yugoslavia—have put strong pressure on governments, regional organizations and the UN to act even if their moves meet with opposition from guilty or ineffective governments and amount to an infringement of sovereignty.

Chaos or the hostility of the government in place makes it necessary to send forces whose mission is to protect relief efforts from deliberate attack or swirling turmoil. Where private organizations such as the Red Cross go unarmed, public efforts combine the food kitchen and the armed guard, the hospice and the barracks.

For many years, private humanitarian organizations, such as the French group *Médecins sans Frontières,* have been pleading for a "right of interference" *(droit d'ingérence)* in humanitarian crises. In the Kurdish tragedy that followed the end of the Gulf War, the UN Security Council ordered Iraq to put an end to repression of the Kurds and helped organize their protection. In Somalia, humanitarian intervention by the UN occurred first at the request of a fast-collapsing Somalian administration and continued in the absence of any Somali government. In the Yugoslav case, UN operations for peacekeeping between Croatia and Serbia and for humanitarian aid for the victims in Bosnia have run into formidable difficulties, exposing the limits of collective action in the midst of a conflict that is both inter- and intra-state.

APPROACHING THE INTERVENTION ISSUE

Two kinds of questions need to be examined. First, is it possible to define clearly what constitutes a humanitarian intervention? Second, what can be done about the cases that seem to require collective intervention?

At first, humanitarian crises seem almost self-evident; the world is full of victims either deliberately harmed by evil governments, forced to flee from their homes and go into exile or suffering from natural or man-made disasters with which their governments are incapable of coping. Humanitarian intervention is the action of outside powers who come to the aid of these victims. International lawyers have debated whether the UN Charter's assertion of the principle of non-interference and ban on the use of force (except in a limited number of cases) tolerates humanitarian intervention when the targeted government does not consent. In practice, the Security Council has finessed the problem by stating that a given case (such as, say, the mistreatment of the Kurds) constitutes a threat to international peace and security, even though its nature is "internal." Thus, Chapter VII of the Charter, which empowers the Security Council to deal with threats to peace and security, comes into effect.

Nevertheless, two important conceptual headaches remain. First, is it possible, in order to justify collective intervention, to smuggle *all* humanitarian crises in under the tent of "threats to international peace and security?" When the UN first resorted to that description in order to get around the Charter ban on interference in domestic affairs, it was to condemn and take measures against apartheid in South Africa, an issue whose potential for regional and international violence justified such an interpretation. The attacks on the Kurds in the spring of 1991 resulted in a massive exodus of refugees from Iraq into Turkey.

On the one hand, is the invocation of international peace and security in the case of Somalia equally credible? Was it not more in the nature of a ritual formula allowing the UN to try to relieve the victims of a total domestic breakdown that had caught the attention of the media, even though its external effects were hard to identify? And on the other hand, when the combination of media inattention and lack of external repercussions makes such an invocation utterly unlikely, does it mean that no humanitarian intervention can take place legally, even if there are, in fact, thousands of victims—of floods, famines, nuclear reactor explosions, or government brutality?

There are many places in the world where massive violations of basic human rights can occur without any visible threat to international peace and security—unless one takes the moral stance that any such violations concern all of us and constitute *ipso facto* such a threat. But this is not a stance that the UN has endorsed, so far, as the case of Indonesia's mistreatment of East Timor has shown. As of today, a humanitarian crisis is a "threat to peace and security" only when the Security Council says so, and this raises a serious issue of consistency. (In the matter of famines: why Somalia and not Sudan? In that of assaulted minorities: why Iraq's Kurds but not Iraq's Shiites or Turkey's Kurds?)

The second headache is even greater. If the humanitarian crisis is not a kind of one-shot affair—a famine that overloads the capacity of the local government to cope with it, or, as happened often before 1914, a threat to foreigners caught in the middle of a civil war or a revolution—but if it is, in fact, "structural," provoked either by the disintegration of a state or by the deliberate evil policies of a government, it becomes extremely difficult for the interveners to remedy the humanitarian disaster without addressing the causes that produced it. If they do not consider the causes, in order to stick to a narrow humanitarian mandate—helping victims—they may well be doomed to playing Sisyphus. Humanitarian crises, especially those that really do threaten regional or international peace and security, often result from serious political flaws and troubles. If the political causes are not removed, victims will remain in danger and the intervention will risk, at best, being no more than a band-aid, and at worst, becoming part of the problem.

The fuzziness of the UN mandate in Somalia concerning the disarmament of gangs and the troubles of the humanitarian efforts to help Moslem Bosnians in the absence of a cease-fire and of a settlement illustrate the limits of humanitarianism. However, if in order to make sure that there shall be no more victims that will desperately need rescue, the UN or regional organizations went into the business of removing tyrannical regimes (such as Saddam Hussein's) or of mounting military operations against such mass producers of civilian casualties as the Serbs (and occasionally the Croats), what would happen to the sacrosanct notion of sovereignty and domestic jurisdiction? Would not, as in Somalia, the effort to go to the root of the problem risk adding to violence and creating victims of its own? Dealing with the humanitarian tip of the iceberg may be frustratingly too little; but dealing with the whole iceberg may be far too much, especially if one wants to move from rescue to prevention.

One could argue that the best way to avoid having to help millions of victims of nuclear or chemical warfare, or hundreds of thousands of victims of state brutality (*à la* Pol Pot) or of civil wars (as in Angola, Cambodia, El Salvador, Azerbaijan, Georgia, etc.) is to help install or restore democratic regimes that will respect minority and other human rights, allow inspections of their weapon programs, and so on. Despite the apparent success of the Organization of American States and American pressure in Haiti, and of the UN in Cambodia, the so-called world community is not ready for a crusade of such dimension.

HOW VIABLE AN OPTION?

Thus, organizing collective humanitarian intervention will remain a somewhat haphazard affair, with inconsistencies in the selection of cases and confusions in the definition of missions. Many . . . problems of enforcement . . . are likely to plague such operations. . . . Here, only three questions will be raised in connection with UN interventions.

First, each intervention will have to be put together by a concerned coalition of states. Just as collective security against aggression cannot be an automatic application of a moral reflex, but only the result of a combination of moral concerns and political calculations that varies from case to case, humanitarian interventions will or will not occur depending on the constellation of pressures, indignation and political considerations created by each case. This is another reason for inconsistencies. Moreover, the effectiveness of the intervention is likely to depend a great deal on the determination of key states to pilot the collective action and to see it through. The Bosnian affair is a lamentable example of what happens when there is no such driving force.

Second, insofar as humanitarian interventions require complex civilian and often military operations, the tendency of Security Council members to delegate a great deal of leeway to the Secretary-General may add a layer of political confusion. There could be a contest for control of the operations between the Secretary-General and the states that sponsor and provide the forces for the intervention, and there could also be tensions between him and his representatives on the scene.

Third, the UN and other organizations lack many of the capabilities that could help make humanitarian interventions more effective. Bureaucratic delays, ill-defined lines of command, frequent breakdowns between civilian delegates and military commanders, financial limitations and insufficient, often ill-prepared forces have plagued many operations. There have been a series of improvisations, and it is perhaps remarkable that there have not been more of the kinds of snafus that . . . marked the Somali expedition. "Reinventing" the UN is even more important than "reinventing" government in the US!

This brief essay has not addressed . . . moral issues. . . . But in conclusion, a few points must be made about them. First, there *is* an overwhelming moral case to be made on behalf of the victims of unspeakable crimes committed by their governments, or resulting from a civil war, and on behalf of the victims of disasters to which their governments are indifferent, or which these governments are incapable of eliminating. If, as Judith Shklar argued in *The Faces of Injustice,* injustice is not only a set of acts, but a series of omissions—not only cruelty and deliberate unfairness, but also indifference and neglect—then refusing to intervene because such interventions violate the sovereignty of states is morally indefensible, for the rights of states are not holy and depend in the final analysis upon the state's ability and will to uphold the rights of its people. The moral case for sovereignty, which is often strong—that sovereignty protects the people from alien domination and intrusion—breaks down in the instances in which humanitarian tragedies and abominations occur.

Second, critics of humanitarian intervention nevertheless deserve to be heard, insofar as they introduce a note of caution and cool common sense against crusading excesses. There may come a time when the intervener, well-intentioned but partly blind—dropped, so to speak, on alien soil—becomes part of the problem; . . . or when the presence of a humanitarian intervener becomes an alibi for political supineness and military passivity, as in Bosnia.

The critics remind us of all that is under the tip of the iceberg. Just as collective security is another word for war—it is internationally sanctioned war—and any war, even for a good cause, raises moral issues, humanitarian intervention, spurred by overriding moral concerns, raises the fundamental moral issue of what constitutes a just and peaceful domestic order. It also brings to light the vexing moral and political issue of what can be done, from the outside, to help establish such an order rather than to raise, involuntarily, the level of disorder even higher.

20

WANDERING IN THE VOID: CHARTING THE UN'S NEW STRATEGIC ROLE

John Gerard Ruggie

Hopes that the United Nations might play a decisive global role in international peacekeeping and peacemaking in the wake of the Cold War have been followed by disappointments about the organization's capacity to contain threats to security worldwide. In this essay John Gerard Ruggie outlines the problems and defines the boundaries within which the United Nations might successfully pursue strategies to deter, dissuade, and deny aggressors. Ruggie is dean of Columbia University's School of International and Public Affairs. He is author of *Multilateralism Matters: The Theory and Praxis of an Institutional Forum* (1993).

The United Nations has entered a domain of military activity—a vaguely defined no-man's-land lying somewhere between traditional peacekeeping and enforcement—for which it lacks any guiding operational concept. It has merely ratcheted up the traditional peacekeeping mechanism in an attempt to respond to wholly new security challenges. The result is that the majority of the nearly 70,000 blue-helmeted peacekeepers now out in the field serve in contexts for which peacekeeping was not intended. Even as the demand for these U.N. troops increases almost daily, they continue to function under rules of engagement and with equipment frequently inadequate to their missions. Moreover, they depend for their effectiveness and sometimes their very survival on a U.N. infrastructure that is increasingly not up to the task.

Reprinted by permission of *Foreign Affairs*, November/December 1993. Copyright 1993 by the Council on Foreign Relations, Inc.

This growing misuse of peacekeeping does more than strain the United Nations materially and institutionally. It has brought the world body to the point of outright strategic failure. Indeed, in Bosnia that line has been crossed already. The U.N. peacekeeping forces there have performed a valuable humanitarian role, to be sure. Nonetheless, having been deployed in a security environment for which the peacekeeping mechanism was not designed, they have ended up deterring, not ethnic cleansing, nor the dismemberment of an internationally recognized state, but the international community itself from undertaking more forceful action to arrest these acts. The Europeans thus opposed President Clinton's proposed air strikes against Serbian artillery positions because they have peacekeeping troops on the ground that are highly vulnerable to retaliation. Yet those troops—because of their small numbers, limited military capability and quasi-peacekeeping rules of engagement—were neither intended nor able to produce the military stalemate from which a political settlement could have emerged.

Governments must move quickly to assess the constraints and opportunities facing U.N.-sanctioned forces. If the United Nations continues on its present course, its newly constructed house of cards will collapse and take traditional peacekeeping as well as humanitarian intervention down with it. Recent developments in U.S. policy, culminating in the Clinton administration's Policy Review Document 13, indicate a greater willingness in [the United States] than at any time past to explore what the U.S. Permanent Representative to the United Nations, Ambassador Madeleine K. Albright, has dubbed "assertive multilateralism." To date, however, the notion lacks any corresponding expression in military doctrine and operational concepts. And President Clinton, in his September 25 [1993] speech to the United Nations, struck a decidedly cautious stance.

The international community must define the new domain of collective military activity that lies between peacekeeping and enforcement and figure out if and how its military requirements can be meshed with the national military capabilities and doctrines of those states that are able and willing to make a meaningful contribution to it.

FAMILIAR TERRAIN

Over the years the United Nations has evolved a well-articulated and widely recognized operational concept for peacekeeping. Brian Urquhart, who was present at its creation and presided over the activity for many years, has described peacekeeping as follows:

the use by the United Nations of military personnel and formations not in a fighting or enforcement role but interposed as a mechanism to bring an end to hostilities and as a buffer between hostile forces. In effect, it serves as an internationally constituted pretext for the parties to a conflict to stop fighting and as a mechanism to maintain a cease fire.[1]

Toward that end, U.N. troops observe and report. They carry only light arms and shoot only in self-defense. And because they lack any constitutional basis in the U.N. Charter, peacekeeping forces are sent only with the consent of the country or countries in which they are stationed. Unlike combat units, peacekeeping forces are not designed to create the conditions for their own success on the ground; those conditions must preexist for them to be able to perform their role. In short, theirs is essentially a nonmilitary mission, carried out by military personnel. Accordingly, the combat effectiveness of such units and the adequacy of U.N. headquarters operations that support them have not had to be a major issue of concern in the past.

Enforcement is primarily a legal, not a military, term. It refers to actions authorized under Chapter VII of the United Nations Charter. An aggressor is collectively identified and punished by an escalating ladder of means until its aggression is reversed. Ultimately, enforcement involves flat-out war-fighting—for example, the "all necessary means" of Resolution 678, authorizing what became Operation Desert Storm. War-fighting of that sort is everything that peacekeeping is not—doctrinally, in terms of on-the-ground assets, as well as in its command and control requirements. As defined by the U.S. Joint Chiefs of Staff, the doctrines and rules governing U.S. troops in Desert Storm and similar campaigns are antithetical to standard U.N. peacekeeping practice: the decisive, comprehensive, and synchronized application of preponderant military force to shock, disrupt, demoralize and defeat opponents.[2]

The United Nations does not have an institutionalized military enforcement capability, and it is exceedingly difficult to imagine how it could come to acquire one. Proposals for a U.N. standby force or an international volunteer force are likely to generate more debate than funding, facilities or troops. Large-scale U.N. military enforcement, therefore, will in the future remain episodic and, when it occurs at all, consist of U.N. authorization and general political oversight together with execution by ad hoc coalitions of states.

A NEUTRALIZING FORCE

It is in the gray area between peacekeeping and all-out war-fighting that the United Nations has gotten itself into serious trouble. The trouble stems from the

---

[1]Brian Urquhart, "International Peace and Security: Thoughts on the Twentieth Anniversary of Dag Hammarskjöld's Death," *Foreign Affairs,* Fall 1981, p. 6.

[2]*A Doctrinal Statement of Selected Joint Operational Concepts,* Washington: Office of the Joint Chiefs of Staff, U.S. Department of Defense, Nov. 23, 1992.

...... that the United Nations has misapplied perfectly good tools to inappropriate circumstances.

The ill-fated U.N. peacekeeping mission sent to Somalia prior to Operation Restore Hope (UNOSOM I) is a case in point. Gen. Mohammed Farah Aidid, so-called Interim President Ali Mahdi Mohammed and the other warlords did not create domestic anarchy in Somalia absentmindedly. The insecurity of the Somali population was their very objective, the basis of their power and revenues. Those hapless 400 Pakistani Blue Berets confined to Mogadishu airport were the only lightly armed contingent in the country. When international humanitarian assistance personnel wanted to move about they had to hire armed thugs to protect them, thereby reinforcing the very system that had created the human tragedy that brought them to Somalia in the first place.

The same is true in the former Yugoslavia. From the start, as Aleksa Djilas . . . [wrote in *Foreign Affairs* Summer, 1993], "Milošević counted on war, the ultimate condition of fear, to unite Serbs around him." There was no peace to be kept in Bosnia. And the displacement of Muslims in Bosnia is not an incidental by-product of the war, but the Serbs' very objective. Therefore, deploying a U.N. humanitarian mission to Bosnia by definition meant that its personnel would not be considered impartial and that they would, therefore, become potential pawns in the conflict. Seeking to protect them with peacekeepers only added to the number of potential international hostages on the ground.

Alas, the domain between peacekeeping and enforcement is a doctrinal void. Its core strategic logic can nonetheless be grasped by comparison to the traditional U.N. functions. Peacekeeping essentially attempts to overcome a coordination problem between two adversaries: the peacekeeper seeks to ensure that both parties to a conflict understand the agreed-upon rules of the game and that compliance with or deviation from these rules is made transparent. Enforcement, on the other hand, is akin to a game of chicken: the international community, through escalating measures that ultimately threaten war-making and military defeat, attempts to force an aggressor off its track.

Strategically, the United Nations' new domain resembles a suasion game: because there is no clear-cut aggressor, U.N. forces, by presenting a credible military threat, seek to convince all conflictual parties that violence will not succeed. International force is brought to bear not to defeat but to neutralize the local forces. The political objective is to prevent local force from becoming the successful arbiter of disputes and to persuade combatants that they have no viable alternative but to reach a negotiated settlement. The military objective of the strategy, then, is to deter, dissuade and deny (D^3).

Ideally, the timely show of sufficient international force would deter the local use of force altogether; a flotilla of warships off the coast of Dubrovnik, firing warning shots when the Serbs first shelled the city, might have gone a long way toward arresting armed conflict in the former Yugoslavia. If the time for deterrence has passed, or should deterrence fail, international force would be deployed in the attempt to dissuade local forces from continuing their military activities; Operation Restore Hope was an attempt—if not entirely successful— to accomplish that end. As a last step, international force would seek to deny military victory to any side in the dispute, thereby creating the military stalemate on which negotiated settlements often depend; President Clinton's "lift and strike" proposal for Bosnia would have been an instance had it been adopted.

To achieve any of these objectives, international forces above all must be militarily credible. Neither their size nor their technological and operational capabilities can be defined generically, but will depend foremost on the nature of their missions. At the high end of the spectrum, such a force might be indistinguishable from war-fighting units in all respects except its rules of engagement and its military as well as political objectives. The air-strike component of President Clinton's Bosnian "lift and strike" proposal would have exemplified that feature. But even at the lower end, as . . . illustrated by the . . . U.N. operation in Somalia, such forces require more extensive training than traditional peacekeepers, as well as heavier equipment, greater operational flexibility and mobility, access to more sophisticated communication and intelligence systems, and tactical direction by a viable field command.

Even if the proposed D^3 strategy were satisfactorily refined and adopted as policy by governments, however, a number of practical problems would have to be resolved before it could be successfully instituted.

TOWARD COLLECTIVE SECURITY

First, any move in this new direction would increase the international military presence of the major powers of the United Nations. Relatively few countries have the military capabilities to implement the strategy in any but minor conflicts. And those countries that do can hardly be expected simply to turn over their forces to the international body. Greater military involvement by the major powers would go a long way toward closing the U.N. military infrastructure gaps. But it would also increase the constant tension between the competing desires for U.N. versus national control over field operations and extend that struggle to headquarters operations. A mutually acceptable relationship would have to be devised.

Second, neither the capabilities nor the willingness would exist under the new arrangement any more than under the old to right all wrongs, even the relatively small number of wrongs that are deemed to warrant international action. Hence any such collective security system is bound to lack universal coverage. But that need not necessarily be a fatal flaw. The chief defining attribute of multilateralism, including collective security arrangements, should be construed not as universality but as nondiscrimination. Great care would have to be taken, therefore, to minimize geographical, ideological or any other bias. For any such bias would undo this mode of collective security, politically by reducing its legitimacy and militarily by reducing its deterrent effect.

Third, a doctrinal clash would have to be overcome between the U.S. military, in particular, and the United Nations. For the U.S. military, the D^3 strategy at first blush is likely to conjure up concepts of gradual escalation and limited war, discredited by and discarded after Vietnam. True, under the new strategy the political and military objectives of the deployment of international force would be limited. But there is no reason why those objectives could not be coupled with maximum military strength geared to the situation at hand. The United Nations, however, as both a collection of governments and an institution in its own right, is averse to the deployment of force and, once it is deployed, instinctively favors gradual escalation. The United Nations, therefore, would have to appreciate the classic distinction between the utility of force and its actual use.

Finally, the relationship between this new mode of collective security and traditional peacekeeping and humanitarian assistance would have to be worked out. On paper, the transition from Operation Restore Hope to UNOSOM II looked good. In practice, it [was] not smooth or entirely effective, largely because the military mission of the former was underspecified and inadequately executed.

Despite these problems, the United Nations must move in this new direction: U.N. peacekeeping has already been pushed too far, and U.N.-sanctioned military enforcement will continue to be a rarity. The domain of a potentially enhanced U.N. military role occupies the space between those two. The major challenge for the international community is to define that domain, and to mesh it effectively with national military capabilities and doctrines. Only then will the international community be able effectively to persuade local combatants that the use of force to resolve disputes will not succeed.

21

THE REALITY AND RELEVANCE OF INTERNATIONAL LAW IN THE POST-COLD WAR ERA

Christopher C. Joyner

International law reflects the need for order, predictability, and stability in international relations. The functions and impact of international law are analyzed by Christopher C. Joyner, who emphasizes both the strengths and limitations of legal norms as instruments for managing conflicts and promoting collaboration in world politics. Joyner is professor of political science at Georgetown University. He is the author of *Antarctica and the Law of the Sea* (1992) and co-editor (with Oscar Schachter) of *United Nations Legal Order* (1994).

The end of the Cold War reinvigorated the relevance and reality of modern international law. The disintegration of the Soviet Union; ethnic strife in the former Yugoslavia; resort to military force by an international coalition to oust Iraq from Kuwait; humanitarian intervention by the United Nations in Somalia; convening the Rio "Earth Summit" on global environment and development issues; the bombing of the World Trade Center in New York City; successful completion of the Uruguay Round of the General Agreement on Tariffs and Trade; the peace pact between Israel and the Palestinian Liberation Organization—these recent events among many others are clearly anchored by international legal implications. Yet, students of international relations rightly continue to ask certain fundamental questions about the nature and purpose of international law. Is international law really "law"? Or is it nothing more than "positive morality"?

This essay was written especially for this book.

How can international law work in a modern state system dictated by considerations of national interests and power politics? Is international law more of a restraint on national policy, or is it merely a policy instrument wielded by governments to further their own ad hoc purposes to gain legitimacy? In short, what is the reality and relevance of international law to contemporary world politics? This essay seeks to address these inquiries and in the process to explore the role of international law in contemporary international affairs.

THE CONCEPTUAL FOUNDATIONS OF INTERNATIONAL LAW

International law, often described as public international law or the law of nations, refers to the system of law that governs relations between states. States traditionally were the only subjects with rights and duties under international law. In the modern era, however, the ambit of international law has been greatly expanded to where it now encompasses many actors other than states, among them international organizations, multinational corporations, and even individual persons. Nevertheless, states remain the primary concern and focus of international law in world politics.[1]

It is important at the outset to note that the initial reaction of many students and laypeople alike to the notion of international law is one of skepticism. A prevalent view holds that national governments have scant respect for international law, and therefore they have little or no incentive to obey it, given the absence of a supranational system armed with sanctions capable of being enforced against a lawbreaker. In short, a popular belief is that international law is not really law.

However, the reality as demonstrated through their behavior is that states do accept international law as law and, even more significant, in the vast majority of instances they usually obey it. Though it is certainly true that international law is sometimes disobeyed with impunity, the same observation is equally true of any domestic legal system. For example, do local laws prevent traffic violations from occurring? Do municipal (i.e., domestic) laws against murder, rape, burglary, or assault and battery prevent those crimes from being committed? Put simply, does the presence of "enforced" law ipso facto insure compliance or even apprehension and prosecution? Clearly, in the real world, the answer is no. Richard Falk put it well when he observed,

> The success of domestic law does not rest in its capacity to solicit the respect of its subjects; the incidence of homicide and civil violence, and even of rebellion, is high. International law is a weak legal system not because it is often or easily flouted by

[1]See generally Alan James, *Sovereign Statehood: The Basis of International Society* (London: Allen and Unwin, 1986); Louis Henkin, *How Nations Behave: Law and Foreign Policy,* 2nd ed. (New York: Columbia University Press, 1979); and Jonathan I. Charney, "Universal International Law," *American Journal of International Law,* vol. 87 (October 1993), pp. 529–551.

powerful states, but because certain violations, however infrequent, are highly destructive and far-reaching in their implications.[2]

International law is not violated more often, or to a higher degree, than the law of other legal systems. Yet why does the contrary misconception persist? Two general reasons may offer much of the explanation. First, there is sensationalism; people tend to hear only about international law when blatant violations make the news. When states attack each other (or, for that matter, when a person is murdered), it becomes a newsworthy event. If the law is obeyed, and international relations between states proceed uninterrupted by violence, those affairs usually go unreported. The second reason for the misimpression that international law is frequently violated is the tendency of many people to presume that the mere existence of a transnational dispute automatically signifies that some law has been breached. This, of course, is not true; the fact that a dispute between states has arisen ought not to be taken to mean that a breach of international law has occurred, just as a civil dispute involving two individuals is not necessarily indicative of a breach in municipal law. Disputes between states may arise over many concerns, none of which may involve violations of law. For example, there may exist a genuine uncertainty about the facts of a case or uncertainty about the law itself; there may be need for new law to meet changing international conditions; or there may even occur the resort to unfriendly but legal acts (called retorsion) by one state against another. While these situations may be unfortunate and perhaps in some instances regrettable, they do not perforce constitute violations of the law.

Most criticism about international law can be generally categorized. First, there are those who view the law of nations as something that can never work and is therefore ignored by states, groups, or individuals. Law, in effect, becomes an "orphan" within the international community. On the other hand, there is the group that sees international law as an instrument of purpose, a "harlot" as it were, to be used, abused, or discounted in accord with one's own moment of convenience, interest, or capability. Still other critics perceive the law as not having any "teeth" or power of enforcement. The absence of an executive authority or international policeman thereby renders all values, norms, and rules subject to mere voluntary accession. International law in this instance becomes a "jailer." Perhaps more cynical is the view which asserts that international law does not exist and that it cannot exist until either all states agree to cooperate and coordinate the creation of mutually acceptable legal codes or this condition is imposed upon them. In this scenario, international law must assume the role of a "magician." Prevalent in the hard-line realist school of international politics, this perception suggests that international law provides nothing more

---

[2]Richard A. Falk, *The Status of Law in International Society* (Princeton, N.J.: Princeton University Press, 1970), p. 29.

than a utopian dream. That is, governments that place heavy emphasis upon inserting morality in foreign policy considerations live in a world of idealism, naively hoping for the mythical attainment in international affairs where law will govern supremely and people will be saved from a system of international anarchy. For these critics, proponents of international law thus represent a "never-never land" school of thought.[3]

The reality of international law does not fit either neatly or aptly into any of these perceptions. John Austin, who dominated jurisprudential thinking in Great Britain during the nineteenth century, contributed much in the way of theory suggesting the frailties of international law. Austin reasoned that for a legal system to exist in fact, three indispensable elements were essential: (1) There had to exist a clearly identifiable superior, or sovereign, who was capable of issuing (2) orders or commands for managing society, and (3) there had to be punitive sanctions capable of enforcing those commands. For Austin, law thus was defined as the general command emanating from a sovereign, supported by the threat of real sanctions. Since international law had neither a sovereign nor the requisite enforcement authority, Austin concluded that it was not really "law"; international law, he believed, ought to be considered merely as "positive morality."[4] The Austinian concept involves the relatively uncomplicated contention that genuine law has its rules laid down by a superior power (the executive), and that they are enforced by another superior power (the police). At first blush, this line of thinking may seem logically attractive. However, in the real world, it becomes intellectually simplistic to assume that law exists only when and where formal structures exist; moreover, it is likewise faulty to confuse characteristics of a legal system as being those prerequisites necessary to define law's existence. The remainder of this essay addresses these contentions.

THE NATURE OF INTERNATIONAL LAW

Generally speaking, the function of law is to preserve order. That is, law embodies a system of sanctioned regularity, a certain order in itself, which conveys the notion of expectations. Law provides for the regularity of activities that can be discerned, forecast, and anticipated in a society. Through law, the attempt is made to regulate behavior in order to insure harmony and maintain a society's values and institutions.[5]

In this connection, a system of law should have three basic characteristics. First, a statement of a prescribed pattern of behavior must be evident. Second, an

---

[3]These schools critical of international law are proposed in John H. E. Fried, "International Law—Neither Orphan Nor Harlot, Neither Jailer Nor Never-Never Land," in Karl Deutsch and Stanley Hoffmann, eds., *The Relevance of International Law* (New York: Doubleday, 1971), pp. 124–176.

[4]John Austin, *The Province of Jurisprudence Determined and the Uses of the Study of Jurisprudence* (London: Weidenfeld and Nicolson, 1954), pp. 121–126, 137–144.

[5]See Myres S. McDougal and Florentino P. Feliciano, *Law and Minimum World Order* (New Haven: Yale University Press, 1961).

obligational basis approved by the society must be present. And third, some process for punishing unlawful conduct in the society must be available. As essential facets, the measure of how well these elements interact will in large part determine the effectiveness of the legal system as a whole as well as the extent of its actual existence and performance.

Given these general observations, what significance can be attached to the nature of international law? Expressed in an Austinian sense, can a bona fide legal system that fulfills these objectives exist in the absence of a formal government structure, i.e., without a centralized system of law creation, law application, and law enforcement? The answer clearly is yes. International law does qualify as a legal system, albeit a somewhat primitive and imperfect one. International law consists of a set of norms that prescribe international behavior, although those patterns may at times seem vaguely defined. International law furnishes a principled foundation for policy decisions, albeit adherence to principle often becomes justifiable if it can be shown to be practical. Relatedly, reasons do exist for states to obey international law; i.e., an obligatory basis does in fact exist to support international law's operation in world affairs. Finally, a system of sanctions is available in international law, and it contributes to coercive enforcement of the law. To appreciate these observations more fully, it is worthwhile to examine the evolutionary nature and sources of international law, the obligational basis for its operation, and the enforcement process available for punishing illegal behavior in the international community.

THE SOURCES OF INTERNATIONAL LAW

No legal system flashes into existence fully panoplied. All orders of law, from the most primitive to the most sophisticated, have their roots in the society they govern. International law is no different. The modern law of nations has undergone a process of evolution as old as the nation-state system itself, owing its direct origins to the Treaty of Westphalia in 1648. Importantly in this regard, over the past three centuries, specific sources for the creation of new international law have become widely acknowledged in and accepted by the international community.[6]

Foremost among the sources of international law are international conventions and treaties.[7] When ratified by a substantial number of states, some multilateral conventions may be deemed tantamount to an international legal statute

---

[6]See generally Clive Parry, *The Sources and Evidences of International Law* (Dobbs Ferry, N.Y.: Oceana, 1965). The following enumeration of sources is based upon the priority set out in Article 38 of the Statute of the International Court of Justice, appended to the Charter of the United Nations.

[7]T. O. Elias, *The Modern Law of Treaties* (Leiden: Sijhoff, 1974); I. M. Sinclair, *The Vienna Convention on the Law of Treaties,* 2nd ed. (Dobbs Ferry, N.Y.: Oceana, 1984); Shabati Rosenne, *The Law of Treaties: A Guide to the Legislative History of the Vienna Convention* (Dobbs Ferry, N.Y.: Oceana, 1971); and Paul Reuter, *Introduction to the Law of Treaties* (New York: Columbia University Press, 1989).

and are aptly labeled "lawmaking" treaties. Examples of these types of treaties include the four 1949 Geneva Conventions on the Law of War, the four 1958 Geneva Conventions on the Law of the Sea, the 1969 Vienna Convention on the Law of Treaties, and the 1967 Outer Space Treaty. Also, general multilateral treaties can create the organizational machinery through which new international law can be developed. For example, specialized agencies of the United Nations, such as the World Health Organization, International Civil Aviation Organization, Universal Postal Union, and International Telecommunication Union—all of which were created by specific international treaties—have themselves become sources of rules and regulations throughout the international community. Thus international organizations that were created by international law contribute to the growth of additional law through the purpose of their functional operation.[8]

The second major source of international law is custom. In the eighteenth and nineteenth centuries, when interaction among states was relatively sporadic and less complex than today, certain habitual patterns of behavior often emerged to form obligatory rules. That is, through widespread adherence and repeated use, certain customary practices by governments became accepted as law, with normatively binding constraints.[9] Prominent among laws evolving from customary state practice were those pertaining to the law of the sea, in particular those regulations establishing the 3-mile territorial limit, the definition of piracy, and proper division of the spoils of war. Today, however, due to the increasing interdependence and complexity of modern international relations coupled with the spread of the traditional Eurocentric legal system beyond the borders of the Western world, custom as a body of unwritten though clearly recognized norms seems to be diminishing as a source of international law. Much of customary international law developed in the era of nineteenth century colonialism. Largely for this reason, it is now viewed with suspicion or held in disrepute by many of the newly independent states in the Third World. Another critical weakness of custom as a contemporary source of law is couched in the traditional requirement that customary law must grow into acceptance slowly, through a gradual, evolutionary process over many decades, perhaps even hundreds of years. This requisite for gradual evolution and slow acceptance of an

---

[8]See generally Oscar Schachter and Christopher C. Joyner, eds., *United Nations Legal Order* (Cambridge: Cambridge University Press, 1994) and Rosalyn Higgins, *The Development of International Law through the Political Organs of the United Nations* (London: Oxford University Press, 1963). Significantly, however, resolutions adopted by the United Nations General Assembly are deemed only to be recommendations and are not lawfully binding upon the membership. See Christopher C. Joyner, "The U.N. General Assembly Resolutions and International Law: Rethinking the Contemporary Dynamics of Norm-Creation," *California Western International Law Journal*, Vol. 11, No. 3 (Summer 1981), pp. 445–478.

[9]See Anthony A. D'Amato, *The Concept of Custom in International Law* (Ithaca, N.Y.: Cornell University Press, 1971); and H. W. A. Thirlway, *International Customary Law and Codification* (Leiden: Sijhoff, 1972).

emergent customary norm leaves that rule vulnerable to become archaic or anachronistic even before it can become accepted as law. This likelihood undoubtedly is at work today as rapid advances in technology play havoc with traditional legal parameters and jurisdictional designs—a reality that makes imperative the constant need for international law to keep pace with technological developments.

The third primary source of international law is the general principles of law recognized by civilized nations.[10] Often general principles are associated with the Roman notion of *jus gentium,* the law of peoples. These principles of law, derived largely from municipal experience, hold relevant legal connotations for the international realm; consequently, they have been assimilated into the corpus of international law. General principles of law—which include notions such as "equity" (justice by right), "comity" (voluntary courtesy), and *pacta sunt servanda* ("pacts made in good faith are binding," the underpinning precept for treaty agreement)—serve as sources by analogy for the creation and perfection of international legal norms. Yet general principles of international law are encumbered by the difficulty of being framed as sources of law in terms of morality and justice. "Morality" and "justice" remain highly subjective concepts, susceptible to disparate interpretations; thus, in their application, general principles may be vulnerable to vagaries perceived in the situation or the particular context in which they are set.

The final source of modern international law is twofold and deemed to be secondary and indirect as compared to treaties, custom, and general principles. This source, first, encompasses judicial decisions of courts—both national and international—and, second, teachings and writings of the most qualified jurists and publicists. Two important points merit mention here. The first is that for international law, court decisions are principally employed as guidelines; they cannot set precedents. There is no *stare decisis* in the law of nations; accordingly, a decision by any court or tribunal, inclusive of the International Court of Justice, cannot be held as binding authority for subsequent judicial decisions. The second point is that while writings by scholars and jurists supply a rich seedbed for opinions on the law, they too carry no binding legal authority. Text writers by themselves cannot create or codify international law; however, their importance as sources of the law may become amplified to the extent that governments may adopt suggestions and interpretations in the application of international law to foreign policy.[11]

---

[10]See generally Wolfgang Friedmann, "The Uses of 'General Principles' in the Development of International Law," *American Journal of International Law,* Vol. 57 (April 1963), pp. 279–299; Arnold McNair, "The General Principles of Law Recognized by Civilized Nations," *British Yearbook of International Law,* Vol. 33 (1957), pp. 1–19; and Georg Schwarzenberger, *The Dynamics of International Law* (South Hackensack, N.J.: Rothman, 1976).

[11]See, e.g., *Restatement (Third) of the Foreign Relations Law of the United States* (St. Paul, Minn.: American Law Institute Publications, 1987).

International law is broad in scope and far-reaching in content; for convenience, it may be divided into laws of peace and laws of war. Under the realm of peace, international law provides norms for stipulating its subjects and sets out the process of recognition for states and governments: the rights and duties of states, how title to territory is acquired, how national boundaries are determined, and various regulations for use of ocean, air, and outer space. Also in this respect is the international law pertinent to individuals. It not only encompasses rules affecting nationality, diplomatic agents, resident aliens, and extradition but also more recent norms pertaining to international criminal law, refugees, and the protection of human rights. Within the ambit of laws relating to war, much ground is likewise covered. Included here are those laws and procedures promoting peaceful settlement of disputes; techniques available for self-help short of war; the legal nature of and requirements for belligerency; the laws of armed conflict on land, on sea, and in the air; conditions for neutrality; and the treatment and definition of war crimes.[12] Important to remember here is that these international legal considerations have been integrated into states' national laws, usually by treaty but also through specific legislation, judicial decisions, or executive fiat. This realization, however, should not imply that international law is thus rendered subservient to domestic laws. It is not, either in theory or in factual application.[13]

Though made up of a wide-ranging body of norms, international law has no specific codes or statutes. The closest approximations to municipal legal codes are called digests in international law. These digests, each of which usually entails a series of several volumes, are compendia containing selections from court decisions, international treaties, foreign policy statements, government memoranda, juridical opinions, scholarly publications, and other like materials that furnish detailed views on international legal matters. While held as important comments on the law, digests are not regarded in and of themselves to be definitively authoritative or legally binding in their contents.[14]

---

[12]The texts available on international law are manifold. For representative samples, see William W. Bishop, ed., *International Law: Cases and Materials,* 3rd ed. (Boston: Little Brown, 1971); Michael Akehurst, *A Modern Introduction to International Law,* 6th ed. (London; Allen & Unwin, 1987); Mark W. Janis, *An Introduction to International Law,* 2nd ed. (Boston: Little, Brown & Co., 1993); Gerhard von Glahn, *Law Among Nations: An Introduction to Public International Law,* 6th ed. (New York: Macmillan, 1992); and Werner Levi, *Contemporary International Law: A Concise Introduction,* 2nd ed. (Boulder, Colo.: Westview, 1991). The classic modern treatise on international law is L. F. L. Oppenheim, *International Law: A Treatise:* Vol. 1, *Peace,* 8th ed., edited by Hersch Lauterpacht (New York: Longmans Green, 1955) and Vol. 2, *Disputes, War and Neutrality,* 7th ed., edited by Hersch Lauterpacht (New York: Longmans Green, 1952).

[13]At least one prominent scholar of international law has cogently argued to the contrary, namely that the law of nations in fact represents a higher order than domestic or national law. See Hans Kelsen, *Principles of International Law,* 2nd ed. (New York: Holt, Rinehart & Winston, 1966).

[14]For examples, see the following: Green H. Hackworth, *Digest of International Law,* 8 vols. (Washington, D.C.: U.S. Government Printing Office, 1940–1944); John Bassett Moore, *A Digest of International Law,* 8 vols. (Washington, D.C.: U.S. Government Printing Office, 1906); and Marjorie M. Whiteman, *Digest of International Law,* 15 vols. (Washington, D.C.: U.S. Government Printing Office, 1963–1973).

Notwithstanding doubts and skepticism, then, the unmistakable fact remains that international law has definite sources and exists as a body, a reality that mirrors the fundamental conviction by states that such law is necessary. The law of nations has evolved over nearly four centuries into a body of treaty-based and customary rules, undergirded by general principles of law and explicated through judicial decisions as well as in the writings of prominent jurists and publicists. Intimately connected to this are the attendant realizations that an obligatory basis exists for international law and that, in substantial measure, the law is obeyed.

BASIS OF OBLIGATION IN INTERNATIONAL LAW

Perhaps the archfiction of international law is the notion of absolute sovereignty. Such sovereignty embodies the idea of totality and completeness; as a legal creation, sovereignty consequently becomes a paradox, if not an impossibility, when placed into the interdependent complexities of the modern state system. More significantly, unlimited sovereignty has become unacceptable today as the preeminent attribute of states, a fact which national governments have increasingly recognized as more and more of their sovereignty has been relinquished to international commitments. For example, traditionally in international law, absolute, unfettered sovereignty allowed for states to exercise free national will in deciding whether or not to resort to war. Given the incredible power of military capability today, the costs of this license could literally lead to destruction of the entire international community; as a consequence, through international legal instruments promoting arms control and national restraint, such sovereignty has been diminished by states themselves for the sake of international security. Recent examples clearly demonstrating this trend include the 1990 Conventional Forces in Europe Treaty (CFE), the 1991/1992 Strategic Arms Reduction Talks Treaty (START I), the 1993 START II Treaty between the United States and former Soviet republics, and the 1993 International Chemical Weapons Convention.

The above observations prompt the obvious question concerning why states should obey international law. That is, what is the obligatory basis upon which the rule of law is founded in contemporary world affairs? The answer is plain and undeniable: It is in the states' fundamental interest to do so. States are the lawgivers in the international community. Agreement upon a legal norm and the effectiveness of its application clearly rest in how it affects each state's own national interests. Consent therefore remains the keystone to international law's efficacy because it appeases the desire of states to maintain their relative freedom of action in the name of national sovereignty. In short, states obey international law because they agree to do so. But why should they? Several plausible reasons may be proffered: National governments recognize the utility of the law; they prefer some degree of order and expectation over unpredictable anarchy; obedience is less costly than disobedience; a certain sense of justice may motivate their willingness to obey; or, habit and customary practice in international dealings over many years have operated to promote obedience.

More significant than any of these explanations, however, is the recognition that reciprocity contributes to the efficacy of international law and, correspondingly, to more regularized patterns of behavior in the international system. Put simply, states accept and obey international law because governments find it in their national interest to do so. It serves a state's national interest to accept international legal norms if other states also accept these norms, and this reciprocal process can give rise to predictive patterns of interstate conduct in international relations. States, like individual persons, have discovered that consent to be bound by and obligated to certain rules can serve to facilitate, promote, and enhance their welfare and opportunities in the society. Contemporary international law consequently has come to embody a consensus of common interests—a consensus which plainly indicates that international law works efficiently and most often when it is in the national interest of states to make it work.[15]

ENFORCEMENT OF INTERNATIONAL LAW

The third critical consideration in determining the effectiveness of international law—the quality of its enforcement—is still left hanging: What happens when states fail to obey the law, when they violate the agreed-upon norms? How is the law to be enforced or, put differently, how are violators of international law to be punished? International law does supply means for both sanction and enforcement, although, to be sure, these means are primitive in comparison to municipal procedures. Despite development over the past seventy years of relatively sophisticated, universalistic, sanctions-equipped international organizations—namely, the League of Nations[16] and the United Nations[17]—the world community still relies primarily upon the principle of self-help to enforce international legal sanctions.

---

[15]See generally Thomas M. Franck, *The Power of Legitimacy Among Nations* (Oxford: Oxford University Press, 1991); Oscar Schachter, *International Law in Theory and Practice* (Amsterdam: Martinus Nijhoff, 1991); and Louis Henkin, "International Law: Politics, Values and Functions," *Recueil des Cours d'Academie de Droit International,* Vol. 216 [Part IV] (1989), pp. 9–130.

[16]The League of Nations Covenant, which was incorporated as Part I of the Treaty of Versailles (1919), contained in Article 16 sanction provisions that would subject a member "who committed an act of war" against another member to "the severance of all trade or financial relations, the prohibition of all intercourse between their nationals and the nationals of the Covenant-breaking State, and the prevention of all financial, commercial or personal intercourse between the nationals of the Covenant-breaking State and the nationals of any other State, whether members of the League or not."

[17]After determining "the existence of any threat to the peace, breach of the peace or act of aggression" as authorized in Article 39 of the United Nations Charter, the Security Council is empowered under Article 42 to "take such action by air, sea, or land forces as may be necessary to maintain or restore international peace and security. Such action may include demonstrations, blockade, and other operations by air, sea, or land forces of Members of the United Nations."

The principle of self-help permits sanctions to be applied by one party in reaction to perceived illegal conduct committed by another party. Self-help has emerged as the major means for effecting sanctions in the international community.[18] Not only must states perceive when their rights have been violated; they must also confront the state that allegedly has committed that illegal act and must compel the state to make restitution for its wrongdoing. Techniques for applying self-help range from diplomatic protest to economic boycott to embargo to war. Consequently, in international law, states literally *must* take the law into their own hands to protect their legal rights and to get the law enforced. It is not surprising, then, that international law is often characterized as being primitive.

In assessing the sanctions process in international law, it is fair to conclude that as international disputes become more serious and are viewed by governments as placing national prestige or survival increasingly at risk, the principle of limited self-help as a sanctioning process is likely to make the legal system correspondingly less effective. Absent a centralized agency for approving and supervising the sanctioning action, self-help may be rendered subject to prevalent conditions in the environment. In sum, self-help's prominent role in international law places a major limitation upon that legal system's effectiveness. As revealed in the international legal order, resort to self-help for law enforcement represents a necessary but limiting compromise between a sanctioning process required by international law and the desires by states to retain their independence, i.e., their sovereignty. Self-help thus highlights the observation that international law is a relatively weak, decentralized, and primitive legal system. The fact remains, however, that international law still enjoys the status of being a legal system—one that works effectively nearly all the time and for nearly all situations when its participant member states want it to do so.

On balance, the performance of international law is hampered by disabilities within those very elements that generally contribute to the effectiveness of legal systems. First, there is a lack of international institutions for clarifying and communicating legal norms; that is, modern international law is still characterized by an imperfect process of norm creation. Second, there is no central, generally recognized belief system to serve as an obligatory authority for international law. The obligatory basis for international law lies with the states themselves. Third, and perhaps most debilitating, international law is without an efficient, corporate process for perceiving and punishing illegal behavior in the world community. Resort by states to self-help remains the principal means for sanctioning international wrongdoing.

---

[18]Even so, specific legal limitations have been set on the use of force, i.e., the degree and kind of "self-help" exercised. See, e.g., Anthony C. Arend and Robert J. Beck, *International Law and the Use of Force* (New York: Routledge, 1993); Benjamin Ferencz, *Defining International Aggression: The Search for World Peace,* 2 vols. (Dobbs Ferry, N.Y.: Oceana, (1975); and Sydney D. Bailey, *Prohibitions and Restraints in War* (London: Oxford University Press, 1972).

Yet, what appears really faulty with international law does not stem from these weaknesses in the international legal process. Rather, it derives from the decentralized international community which that law is attempting to regulate. In short, that the operation of contemporary international law may be less than wholly effective can be attributed mainly to the condition that there does not presently exist sufficient international consensus among states to demand that the law be made more effective in its application.

All this should not be inferred to mean that international law is either surrealistic or irrelevant in the post-Cold War world. It certainly is neither. To rush to the conclusion that international law's frailties leave it with little real function in international relations today would be not only superficial but also shortsighted. It would overlook the hundreds of decisions made by national and international tribunals aimed at settling claims and setting arbitration awards. It ignores the thousands of international law cases affecting contractual relations between corporations and governments. It fails to account for the constant, pervasive process of international intercourse that goes on involving states, organizations, and individual persons. In a modern age of satellite telecommunications, worldwide transportation, and interdependent global commerce, international law has become indispensable. Setting frequencies for telecommunication broadcasts, flight routes for aircraft, conditions for international postage and media communication, monetary exchange rates, navigation transit by ocean vessels carrying goods in trade—all these activities and myriad others are made possible only through the channels afforded by international legal agreement, i.e., through international law. International law codifies ongoing solutions for persistent international problems. The law of nations has become in effect the lubricant that permits transnational commerce, communication, transportation, and travel to operate smoothly and on course in the global community.[19]

CONCLUSION

Law prescribes the conduct of a society's members and makes coexistence and the survival of that society possible. Not surprisingly, then, the law of nations is pervasive and fundamental. It not only seeks to regulate or lessen possibilities for conflict but also works to promote international exchange and cooperation on a broad, multifaceted scale. International law is man-made; governments of states in the international society can in large part determine the nature of that society and formulate laws to meet those ends. Hence, the ingredients of international law are neither preordained nor immutable.

International law is law. It is not some form of diplomatic maneuvering or rhetorical camouflage. International law has form and substance: there exists a

[19]For a thoughtful treatment of this situation, see Marvin S. Soroos, *Beyond Sovereignty: The Challenge of Global Policy* (Columbia: University of South Carolina Press, 1986).

clearly identifiable corpus of rules and regulations which have been generally accepted by states in their dealings with one another. International law has specific sources from which legal norms can be derived, and self-imposed sanctions are available to states to punish illegal behavior. Yet international law should not be construed as being pure law; in other words, it is not apolitical, nor is it wholly comprised of normativism or legalism. International law cannot be so because the very components of that legal system—states—are highly politicized actors in their own right.[20]

International law is crafted not accidentally or capriciously but carefully and intentionally by the states themselves. The law of nations is a product of the times and of the national governments that operate in the international milieu. It can change, adapt, and evolve. International law is not static; it is a dynamic and evolutionary process that is shaped by events and influences events. Contemporary international law reflects the nature of the changing world because it must be responsive to that evolving reality. Flexibility therefore remains one of international law's chief strengths. Even so, ironically, it is sometimes blamed for fostering one of the law's greatest weaknesses: namely, the lack of a centralized, formal structure for codifying international norms, an omission that invites distortions in legal interpretation as well as self-serving policy positions.

International law must not be regarded as a panacea for prohibiting unlawful international conduct nor as a brake on incorrigible governments. It does, however, provide internationally acceptable ways and means of dealing with these situations. Modern international law may not satisfy all national governments all of the time, nor can it supply every answer for all the international community's ills. Nevertheless, it remains far preferable to the alternative of no law at all and, similarly, it is far wiser for national governments to appreciate the existence and function of this international legal system than to overlook the mutual advantages it affords. International law remains the best touchstone and only consistent guide for state conduct in a complex, multicultural world.[21]

With the passing of the Cold War and East-West ideological rivalry, grave global problems have emerged as foci for serious international concern in the 1990s. The Third World debt crisis, international armed conflict, transnational terrorism, overpopulation, deforestation, global warming, AIDS, deterioration of the ozone layer, drug trafficking, and proliferation of nuclear weapons—none of these issues are amenable to domestic or unilateral resolution. If politically viable solutions are to be reached, international cooperation is essential. The

---

[20]On this theme, see Francis Anthony Boyle, *World Politics and International Law* (Durham: Duke University Press, 1985) and Anne-Marie Slaughter Burley, "International Law and International Relations Theory: A Dual Agenda," *American Journal of International Law*, Vol. 87 (April 1993), pp. 205–239.

[21]For discussion on this point, see Christopher C. Joyner and John C. Dettling, "Bridging the Cultural Chasm: Cultural Relativism and the Future of International Law," *California Western International Law Journal*, Vol. 20, No. 2 (1989–1990), pp. 275–314.

law of nations supplies proven ways and means to facilitate these collaborative international efforts. Indeed, in the search for global solutions to global problems, international law supplies the best opportunities for accommodating national interests with international priorities.

In the final analysis, international law does not fail in contemporary world society. Instead, it is the states themselves that fail the law whenever they choose not to adhere to its basic norms. Thus the need to surmount this fundamental obstacle of self-serving, sovereign-state interests must remain as the preeminent challenge on international law's global agenda in the next century. To be sure, given the profound lessons of state conduct in the past, it will not be an easy task.

22

ACHIEVING COOPERATION UNDER ANARCHY: STRATEGIES AND INSTITUTIONS

Robert Axelrod and Robert O. Keohane

In this essay Robert Axelrod and Robert O. Keohane weave together the various strands of thinking about the means by which international cooperation occurs under conditions of anarchy. Arguing that collaboration sometimes develops even in circumstances that discourage it and instead encourage competition, the authors analyze the structural properties of the international system that make collaboration less improbable than might be otherwise imagined, identify the preconditions necessary for achieving interstate cooperation, and discuss how new institutions and norms might facilitate significant levels of cooperation in the international system. Axelrod is professor of political science and public policy at the University of Michigan; his books include *The Evolution of Cooperation* (1984). Keohane is professor of government at Harvard University and author of *After the Cold War: International Institutions and State Power* (1993).

Achieving cooperation is difficult in world politics. There is no common government to enforce rules, and by the standards of domestic society, international institutions are weak. Cheating and deception are endemic. Yet, . . . cooperation is sometimes attained. World politics is not a homogeneous state of war: cooperation varies among issues and over time.

. . . Cooperation is not equivalent to harmony. Harmony requires complete identity of interests, but cooperation can only take place in situations that con-

Reprinted from *World Politics* 38: 226–254 (1985) by permission of The Johns Hopkins University Press. Footnotes have been deleted.

tain a mixture of conflicting and complementary interests. In such situations, cooperation occurs when actors adjust their behavior to the actual or anticipated preferences of others. Cooperation, thus defined, is not necessarily good from a moral point of view.

Anarchy also needs to be defined clearly. As used here, the term refers to a lack of common government in world politics, not to a denial that an international society—albeit a fragmented one—exists. Clearly, many international relationships continue over time, and engender stable expectations about behavior. To say that world politics is anarchic does not imply that it entirely lacks organization. Relationships among actors may be carefully structured in some issue-areas, even though they remain loose in others. Likewise, some issues may be closely linked through the operation of institutions while the boundaries of other issues, as well as the norms and principles to be followed, are subject to dispute. Anarchy, defined as lack of common government, remains a constant: but the degree to which interactions are structured, and the means by which they are structured, vary.

It has often been noted that military-security issues display more of the characteristics associated with anarchy than do political-economic ones. . . . This does not mean, however, that analysis of these two sets of issues requires two separate analytical frameworks. . . .

[Two] dimensions . . .—the shadow of the future, and the number of players—help us to understand the success and failure of attempts at cooperation in both military-security and political-economic relations. . . .

THE SHADOW OF THE FUTURE

. . . Concern about the future helps to promote cooperation. . . . Specific factors that help to make the shadow of the future an effective promoter of cooperation . . . include:

1 long time horizons;
2 regularity of stakes;
3 reliability of information about the others' actions;
4 quick feedback about changes in the others' actions.

The dimension of the shadow of the future seems to differentiate military from economic issues more sharply than does the dimension of payoffs. Indeed, its four components can be used to analyze some of the reasons why issues of international political economy may be settled more cooperatively than issues of international security, even when the underlying payoff matrices are similar. . . . Most important is a combination of the first two factors: long time horizons and regularity of stakes. In economic relations, actors have to expect that their relationships will continue over an indefinite period of time; that is, the games they play with each other will be iterated. Typically, neither side in an economic interaction can eliminate the other, or change the nature of the game decisively in a single move. In security affairs, by contrast, the possibility of a successful preemptive war can sometimes be a tempting occasion for the rational timing of surprise. Another way to put this is that, in the international political economy, retaliation for [nonreciprocated cooperation] will almost always be possible. . . . In security affairs, it may be [difficult] to limit or destroy the opponent's capacity for effective retaliation. . . .

The length of the shadow of the future . . . is not necessarily dictated by the objective attributes of a situation. On the contrary, . . . expectations are important. International institutions may therefore be significant, since institutions embody, and affect, actors' expectations. Thus institutions can alter the extent to which governments expect their present actions to affect the behavior of others on future issues. The principles and rules of international regimes make governments concerned about precedents, increasing the likelihood that they will attempt to punish defectors. In this way, international regimes help to link the future with the present. That is as true of arms control agreements, in which willingness to make future agreements depends on others' compliance with previous arrangements, as it is in the General Agreement on Tariffs and Trade, which embodies norms and rules against which the behavior of members can be judged. By sanctioning retaliation for those who violate rules, regimes create expectations that a given violation will be treated not as an isolated case but as one in a series of interrelated actions.

NUMBER OF ACTORS: SANCTIONING PROBLEMS

The ability of governments to cooperate . . . is affected . . . also by the number of players [in an interactive relationship] and by how their relationships are structured . . . Reciprocity can be an effective strategy to induce cooperation among self-interested players. . . . However, . . . when there are many actors, . . . it may be impossible to identify, much less to punish, [non-cooperation]; even if it is possible, none of the cooperators may have an incentive to play the role of policeman. Each cooperator may seek to be a free-rider on the willingness of others to enforce the rules.

We may call the difficulty of preventing defection through decentralized retaliation the "sanctioning problem." [This can occur as an result of] the inability to identify defectors, . . . [or] when [states] are unable to focus retaliation on [non-cooperaters, or] when some members of a group lack incentives to punish [such actors]. This obstacle to cooperation often arises where there are many actors, some of which fail to cooperate in the common effort to achieve some collective good. . . . When sanctioning problems are severe, cooperation is in danger of collapsing. One way to bolster it is to restructure the situation so that sanctioning becomes more feasible.

THE CONTEXT OF INTERACTION

Whether cooperation can take place without central guidance depends . . . also on the context within which interaction takes place. Context may, of course, mean many different things. Any interaction takes place within the context of norms that are shared, often implicitly, by the participants. [Political scientist] John Ruggie has written of the "deep structure" of sovereignty in world politics, and also of the way in which shifting values and norms of state intervention in society—the emergence and legitimation of the welfare state—affected the world political economy between 1914 and 1945. . . .

Interactions also take place within the context of institutions. . . . Institutions alter the payoff structures facing actors, they may lengthen the shadow of the future, and they may enable [conflicts] to be broken down into [conflicts] with smaller numbers of actors. . . .

GROPING TOWARD NEW INSTITUTIONS AND NORMS

[We] began with a set of hypotheses about how specific features of an international setting would affect the chances for the development of cooperation. Factors included were . . . the shadow of the future and the number of actors. These hypotheses [are] supported by a broad set of cases that . . . [cover] trade disputes, monetary policy, and debt rescheduling as well as arms races, the outbreak of war, and diplomatic concerts. [These two] factors [can be shown to] help to account for both cooperation and conflict.

We [discover from a reading of history] that . . . the actors [are] not satisfied with simply selecting strategies based upon the situation in which they [find] themselves. In many cases we [can observe] deliberate efforts to change the very structure of the situation by changing the context in which each of them would be acting. Decision makers themselves [perceive] (more or less consciously) that some aspects of the situations they [face tend] to make cooperation difficult. So they worked to alter these background conditions. Among the problems they [encounter are] the following:

1 how to provide incentives for cooperation so that cooperation would be rewarded over the long run, and defection punished;

2 how to monitor behavior so that cooperators and defectors could be identified;

3 how to focus rewards on cooperators and retaliation on defectors;

4 how to link issues with one another in productive rather than self-defeating ways and, more generally, how to play multilevel games without tripping over their own strategies.

A fundamental strategic concept in attaining these objectives is that of reciprocity. Cooperation in world politics seems to be attained best not by providing benefits unilaterally to others, but by conditional cooperation. Yet reciprocity encounters many problems in practice. . . . Reciprocity requires the ability to recognize and retaliate against a defection. And retaliation can spread acrimoniously.

Actors in world politics seek to deal with problems of reciprocity in part through the exercise of power. Powerful actors structure relationships so that countries committed to a given order can deal effectively with those that have lower levels of commitment. This is done by establishing hierarchies. . . .

Another way to facilitate cooperation is to establish international regimes. Regimes can be defined as "sets of implicit or explicit principles, norms, rules, and decision-making procedures around which actors' expectations converge in a given area of international relations." International regimes have been extensive in the post-1945 international political economy, as illustrated by the international trade regime (centered on the GATT [General Agreement on Tariffs and Trade]) and the international monetary regime (including the [International Monetary Fund] as well as other organizations and networks). Since the use of power can facilitate the construction of regimes, this approach should be seen as complementary to, rather than in contradiction with, an emphasis on hierarchical authority. Regimes do not enforce rules in a hierarchical sense, but they do change patterns of transaction costs and provide information to participants, so that uncertainty is reduced. . . .

International regimes do not substitute for reciprocity; rather, they reinforce and institutionalize it. Regimes incorporating the norm of reciprocity delegitimize defection [from cooperative ventures] and thereby make it more costly. Insofar as they specify precisely what reciprocity means in the relevant issue-area, they make it easier to establish a reputation for practicing reciprocity consistently. Such reputations may become important assets, precisely because others will be more willing to make agreements with governments that can be expected to respond to cooperation with cooperation. Of course, compliance is difficult to assure; and international regimes almost never have the power to enforce rules. Nevertheless, since governments with good reputations can more easily make agreements than governments with bad ones, international regimes can help to facilitate cooperation by making it both easier and more desirable to acquire a good reputation.

International regimes may also help to develop new norms. . . . Major banks today are trying mightily to strengthen norms of repayment (for debtors) and of relending (for banks), but it is not at all clear that this will be successful. Better examples of creating norms may be provided by the evolution of thinking on chemical and biological warfare, and by the development, under [the World Trade Organization] of norms of nondiscrimination. Evidently, it is difficult to develop new norms, and they often decay in reaction to conspicuous violations.

Establishing hierarchies, setting up international regimes, and attempting to gain acceptance for new norms are all attempts to change the context within which actors operate by changing the very structure of their interaction. It is important to notice that these efforts have usually not been examples of for-ward-looking rationality. Rather, they have been experimental, trial-and-error efforts to improve the current situation based upon recent experience. Like other forms of trial-and-error experimentation, they have not always worked. . . .

Eventually, any institution is likely to become obsolete. The question is under what conditions international institutions—broadly defined as "recog-nized patterns of practice around which expectations converge"—facilitate sig-nificant amounts of cooperation for a period of time. Clearly, such institutions can change the incentives for countries affected by them, and can in turn affect the strategic choices governments make in their own self-interest. . . .

The experimental groping by policy makers does not necessarily lead to stronger and ever more complex ways of achieving cooperation. The process proceeds by fits and starts. The success of each step is uncertain, and there is always danger that prior achievements will come unstuck. New experiments are often tried only under obvious pressure of events (as in debt rescheduling). And they are often dependent upon the active leadership of a few individuals or states who feel a serious need for change and who have the greatest resources. . . .

But . . . states are often dissatisfied with the structure of their own environ-ment. . . . Governments have often tried to transform the structures within which they operate so as to make it possible for the countries involved to work together productively. Some of these experiments have been successful, others have been stillborn, and still others have collapsed before fully realizing the dreams of their founders. We understand the functions performed by interna-tional regimes, and how they affect strategies pursued by governments, better than we did a number of years ago . . . Even within a world of independent states that are jealously guarding their sovereignty and protecting their power, room exists for new and better arrangements to achieve mutually satisfactory outcomes, in terms both of economic welfare and military security.

This does not mean that all endeavors to promote international cooperation will yield good results. Cooperation can be designed to help a few at the expense of the rest; and it can accentuate as well as alleviate injustice in an imperfect world. Yet the consequences of failure to co-operate—from warfare to the intensification of depressions—make us believe that more cooperation is often better than less. If governments are prepared to grope their way toward a better-coordinated future, scholars should be prepared to study the process. And, in a world where states have often been dissatisfied with international anarchy, scholars should be prepared to advance the learning process—so that despite the reality of anarchy, beneficial forms of international cooperation can be promoted.

PART THREE

POLITICS AND MARKETS

Increasingly the global agenda embraces issues related to international trade protectionism, balance-of-payments adjustments, and international monetary instability. These have been matched by comparable issues on the domestic agendas of many nations as they have struggled with inflation, unemployment, budget deficits, external debts, and economic stagnation. The two sets of issues are not unrelated. Under conditions of global interdependence—defined as a condition of *mutual sensitivity* and *mutual vulnerability*—decisions made in one nation often have important implications and consequences for other nations. Efforts to control inflation in one country, for example, can affect the value of others' currencies and hence influence the direction of their international trade and capital flows. This in turn may affect still other nations' trade and payments balances, which chart their imports, exports, and other financial transactions with the rest of the world. Changes in nations' economic fortunes often also affect their imperviousness or vulnerability to external political influences. Thus politics—the exercise of power and influence—and economics—the distribution of material wealth—are often tightly interconnected.

The term *political economy* highlights the intersection of politics and economics, whose importance in world politics enjoys a long heritage. A combination of political and economic considerations gave rise to the nation-state more than three centuries ago and has helped to shape patterns of dominance and dependence ever since. Today the term highlights the extensive interdependent relationships between states that knit national and global welfare into a single tapestry. Political economy thus comprises an analytical perspective that accommodates the complex realities of the contemporary global system.

By blurring the distinctions between foreign and domestic policy and between political power and economic well-being, the political economy of interdependence raises important questions about the problems that have long dominated world politics. Traditionally, issues relating to economics and other welfare matters were regarded as matters of *low politics*. While the *high politics* of peace and security issues engaged the attention of nations' policy-making elites, the low politics of more routinized international economic affairs could be left to the devices of lower-level bureaucrats.

The distinction between high and low politics has always been overdrawn, perhaps, but the complexity and urgency of political economy issues are now more apparent than ever. Today, as controversies over the distribution of wealth and the processes and institutions that govern it affect everyone, transnational economic issues—fueled by the expansion of world trade since World War II and the globalization of production and finance—are among the most important political issues on the global agenda and often command the utmost attention of policy-making elites. Indeed, with the end of the Cold War it has become commonplace to argue that geo-economics will replace geo-politics as the motive force behind states' struggle for preeminence in the new world order. Competition for market share, not political-military allies, will animate relations among nations. And commercial advantage, not military might, will determine who exercises influence over whom and who feels threatened and who secure.

As this brief overview suggests, insights from political economy are necessary to answer the classic question of politics: Who gets what, when, and how? Robert Gilpin points us in the direction of important answers in the first essay in Part III. He summarizes and critically analyzes "Three Ideologies of Political Economy": the liberal, nationalist (sometimes called mercantilist), and Marxist paradigms. The three are regarded as ideologies, as they purport "to provide scientific descriptions of how the world *does* work while they also constitute normative positions regarding how the world *should* work." Their importance derives from their impact on both scholarship and national and international affairs for centuries.

The differences among the three ideologies turn on "their conceptions of the relationships among society, state, and market." Liberalism focuses on "the market and the price mechanism as the most efficacious means for organizing domestic and international economic relations." Thus economics and politics should be completely separated into distinct spheres. This viewpoint has dominated policy thinking in many nations in the industrial world. It was the guiding principle underlying the international economic system created after World War II under U.S. leadership (hegemony), whose interests liberalism served.

Unlike liberalism, the central idea in the nationalist (mercantilist) ideology "is that economic activities are and should be subordinate to the goal of state building and the interests of the state. All nationalists ascribe to the primacy of the state, of national security, and of military power in the organization and functioning of the international system." Because they see interdependence as a source of conflict and insecurity, economic nationalists are concerned not only with *absolute gains* in their material well-being but also with how they fare in comparison with others, their *relative gains*. Thus economic nationalism as an ideology of political economy bears a striking resemblance to the doctrine of political realism as applied to international politics.

The end of the Cold War has witnessed a surge of privatization and other efforts to unleash market forces throughout the world. Moreover, the liberal principle of nondiscrimination and free trade continues to dominate thinking internationally. Still, economic nationalism is a potent force in the world. It underlies much of the protectionist sentiment toward trade issues rife throughout the developed and developing worlds. It also rationalizes the growing appeal of strategic trade theory, a form of industrial policy that seeks to create comparative advantages by targeting government subsidies toward particular industries. Gilpin notes that whatever its shortcomings, "economic nationalism is likely to be a significant influence in international relations as long as the state system exists."

The appeal of Marxism, on the other hand, is much diminished. Marxism-Leninism has been repudiated in the former Soviet Union and throughout eastern Europe and is on the wane in Cuba and Vietnam. Although Marxism-Leninism (communism) remains the official ideology in China, even here the forces of liberalism are evident in the Chinese acceptance of private markets. Nonetheless, in the history of ideas that have animated world politics during the past two centuries Marxism and Marxism-Leninism still command attention.

Like economic nationalism, Marxism places economic issues at the center of political life. But whereas nationalists are concerned primarily with the international distribution of wealth, Marxism focuses on both the domestic and international forces that affect the distribution of wealth. The ideology also focuses on international political change. "Whereas neither liberalism nor nationalism has a comprehensive theory of social change, Marxism emphasizes the role of economic and technological developments in explaining the dynamics of the international system."

Lenin's reformulation of Marxist doctrine in his famous treatise on *Imperialism* focuses particular attention on the role that differential rates of growth in power play in promoting international conflict and political change. For Marx, class struggle over the distribution of wealth was the central force of political change. For Lenin, international political relations among capitalist states was more important. He argued that "intensification of economic and political competition between declining and rising capitalist powers leads to economic conflict, imperial rivalries, and eventually war. He asserted that this had been the fate of the British-centered liberal world economy of the nineteenth century."

Gilpin conjectures that "today he would undoubtedly argue that, as the U.S. economy declines, a similar fate threatens the twentieth-century liberal world economy, centered on the United States."

Gilpin assesses the strengths and limitations of the three political economy perspectives. Because of the ideological character of each it is impossible to determine which one is "right." Nonetheless, all continue to make important contributions to political economy theory and practice. Liberalism and nationalism/mercantilism in particular compete for the attention of policy makers and analysts today, as the remaining essays in Part III of *The Global Agenda* amply demonstrate.

As noted, the liberal vision guided policy makers during and after World War II as they sought to create trade and monetary systems that would avoid repetition of the economic collapse of the 1930s, to which aggressive economic nationalism was believed to have contributed measurably. The tremendous growth in international trade since the 1940s, which has fueled an unprecedented expansion of global welfare, is a measure of the success of liberalism. Now, however, the continued integration of the world political economy through trade and transnational investment is threatening the political autonomy and decision-making authority of the world's preeminent capitalist centers, the United States, Japan, and the European Union (as the European Community was recently renamed). Ironically, therefore, liberalism is now encouraging mercantilism.

The tension between liberalism and mercantilism is the focus of Erik R. Peterson's chapter, "Looming Collision of Capitalisms?" Peterson argues that "accelerating global economic competition is bringing national economic policies into sharper competition." As manifest in the temptation to pursue "defensive strategies by supporting national 'strategic' industries," he worries that the major capitalist centers will increasingly "succumb to the . . . tendency to 'pursue relative gains at the expense of mutual gains [and] political power at the expense of economic welfare.'"

The continuing growth of world trade and capital flows is among the forces leading to the acceleration of global economic integration. As Peterson notes, there are many others: "Advances in communication and information technologies, the pursuit by multinational enterprises (MNEs) of complex cross-border strategies, the formation and development of regional trading blocs, the GATT [General Agreement on Tariffs and Trade] process, economic liberalization undertaken in a host of developing economies, and ongoing efforts at marketization in former command economies are metamorphosing the international economic and financial system." The description is nothing less than a menu of the forces propelling a dramatic restructuring of the world political economy. Given these developments, states increasingly find that existing international institutions are insufficiently able to cope with the challenges they now face, as the "integration of politics is lagging behind [the] integration of markets." In response, the principal economic powers in particular are "more and more . . .

finding the answer in drawing lines beyond which they will resort to defense strategies grounded in parochial interests. The result is the development of political conditions that encourage the outbreak of economic nationalism."

Peter F. Drucker also surveys recent developments in the world political economy in "Trade Lessons from the World Economy," with particular attention to developments relating to international trade and the lessons they suggest. He argues that an increasing proportion of international trade occurs not in traditional items of merchandise—washing machines, shoes, and the like—but in services—stocks and insurance, for example. Furthermore, multinational business practices such as "transfer pricing" and the use of "alliances" ("joint ventures, partnerships, knowledge agreements and out-sourcing arrangements") are becoming more ubiquitous. In both cases there is little difference between foreign and domestic partners.

The erosion of the distinction between the international economy and national economies described by Drucker carries with it important policy implications. Drucker finds little in the historical record to suggest that policy makers are able to steer their economies effectively through the boom and bust of typical business cycles. He is also critical of the kinds of managed (strategic) trade strategies that Peterson sees increasingly likely in the years ahead. Instead—and in the tradition of economic liberalism as well as on the basis of some nations' experience—Drucker urges policy makers to give priority to the international over the domestic economy: "Managed trade is a delusion of grandeur. Outright protectionism can only do harm. . . . What is needed is a deliberate and active—indeed, aggressive—policy that gives the demands, opportunities and dynamics of the external environment priority over domestic policy demands and priorities."

Drucker's prescriptions are firmly wedded to the ideology of economic liberalism. In contrast, Robin Broad and John Cavanagh embrace the *economic nationalism* model in their essay, "No More NICs." Their views are also colored with a strong tint of *dependencia,* a contemporary variant on Marxism that draws attention to the often unequal exchanges between the industrial nations of the North and the developing nations of the South.

The newly industrializing countries (NICs)—most notably Hong Kong, Singapore, South Korea, and Taiwan—have enjoyed an unusual degree of economic growth in recent decades by pursuing an export-led path to economic development. The strategy itself is a reflection of the neo-mercantilist policies toward economic matters now practiced by many states. Neo-mercantilism in the contemporary context refers to the use of state power to maintain domestic production and employment by reducing imports, stimulating domestic production, and promoting exports.

Broad and Cavanagh argue that while the neo-mercantilist strategy may have worked for some developing nations and while the World Bank and others have promoted its widespread use, for a variety of reasons it cannot work for others.

Principal among the reasons is the changing nature of the world political economy and the role of developing nations in the emerging international division of labor. "The changing world economy has created a desperate need to rethink the kinds of adjustments that will produce growth and development," they argue. "At the very least, the adjustment strategies must be built on realistic assumptions. The NICs were the product of a radically different world economy. That they cannot be replicated . . . is an indication of how much the world economy has changed."

A principal change in the world economy to which many analysts allude is its growing regionalization. Today the three "economic superpowers"—the United States, Japan, and the European Union—are the principal nodes around which global economic activities revolve. Some (most?) analysts regard this development with alarm, seeing it as threat to global liberalism, a possible precursor to geo-economic conflict, and, perhaps, to geo-political conflict. The next four selections in *The Global Agenda* address various aspects of the debate about and concern for regionalization.

Robert D. Hormats makes the (admittedly unusual) case *for* regionalism in "The Regional Way to Global Order." He argues that regionalism offers a particularly attractive venue for integrating developing economies into the world political economy. His premise is based on a survey of many of the same transnational forces Peterson and Drucker consider, but now the focus is on the "two broad tracks" along which the post-Cold War economic order is likely to evolve. "One track will emphasize regional negotiations between newly market-oriented economies as well as between them and industrialized market economies." The other "will consist of efforts . . . to strengthen international rules and organizations so that sub-global arrangements will be consistent with the non-discriminatory and accountability prerequisites of open world markets."

Against this background, Hormats assesses the advantages and disadvantages of regionalism, lacing his analysis with reference to many specific developments around the world that point toward a breakdown of the long-standing division between the rich nations of the North and the poorer nations of the South. Among his conclusions is that "Asia's future attitude toward regional integration could influence the world economy more profoundly than that of any other region."

Europe also figures prominently in any assessment of regionalism. In 1985 the then European Community (EC) adopted the Single European Act which sought boldly to jump-start momentum for the integration of the twelve western European countries comprising the EC. The target date for realization of a single, continent-wide European common market was 1992. In December 1991, political leaders of the community of twelve signed the Maastricht treaty, a maneuver clearly designed to build on the "Europe 1992" initiative in nudging Europe toward tighter political as well as economic union. Europe would now speak with one voice in trade and monetary affairs and with a growing unity on political and military matters. Thus Maastricht would not only facilitate the regionalization of the world political economy by augmenting Europe's position as an economic superpower but also propel the emergence of *Europe* as a major actor on the world political stage, as the treaty envisioned a unified European political and military role in world affairs. The change in the EC's name to the *European Union* called for in the treaty encapsulated the vision.

What the Maastricht visionaries did not foresee is that many ordinary Europeans did not share their view of Europe's future. Stiff national opposition to the treaty was eventually overcome but not before inflicting damage on its original intentions. Moreover, the European monetary system on which hopes for eventual economic union rested suffered terrible pounding in a 1992 currency crisis, undermining and perhaps postponing hopes for a single European currency by the end of the century.

Michael J. Brenner, in "EC/EU: Confidence Lost," examines the reasons underlying the stall in Europe's march toward a federal political structure. He suggests that a principal reason for the failure of the Maastricht vision is found in the changing nature of *sovereignty* in the European context. Sovereignty is, of course, the principal concept underlying the contemporary international system of independent nation-states. It implies that states alone are responsible for what happens within their borders, and they, too, alone are responsible for their own security. The integration process in Europe over the past several decades suggests that individual European nations have given measurable amounts of their sovereign prerogatives to the central institutions of the European Union, but the union in turn has failed to act as a sovereign power. "The European Union's members could take the supranational route without concern for how well suited its institutions were for taking on the traditional core responsibilities of sovereign states: foreign policy and security," writes Brenner. Yet the "institutions in Brussels continue to lack independent sources of authority to draw on when the tough decisions arise." Thus the integration process has stalled because of "the contradiction between the attitudes that at least until now have made economic integration possible, on the one hand, and those needed to forge a legitimate political union, on the other." The March 1994 vote by the European Union to admit Austria, Finland, Norway, and Sweden into the EU by January 1995 did not alleviate these contradictions; in fact, it might, as the EU expands, compound the problem of reaching agreement on economic policies.

The shortcomings of Europe's institutions were nowhere more evident than in the inability of the EU to act decisively to bring about a resolution to the civil conflict in the (now former) Yugoslavia. That failure "will seriously hamper the Community in coping with Europe's next security crisis." Similarly, a Europe "absorbed with the rearrangement of its own internal affairs" is less likely to be either a model or a source of assistance for the fledgling democracies in eastern Europe.

On the other side of the Atlantic, the United States, Canada, and Mexico took an important step in developing a regional economic system in the Western Hemisphere when they signed the North American Free Trade Agreement (NAFTA). Put into place on January 1, 1994, the agreement creates the largest free trade area in the world.

The NAFTA accord proved to be unusually controversial in the United States, and its approval by Congress was by no means assured. Labor groups feared the loss of jobs to lower-paid Mexican workers, and environmentalists worried that companies would move to Mexico to take advantage of Mexico's comparatively lax environmental laws and its lax enforcement of those laws. As a result, large numbers of Americans mobilized against the agreement.

In "After NAFTA: Global Village or Global Pillage?" Jeremy Brecher examines the challenges to "the place of working people in the New World Economy" that NAFTA symbolized and assesses the way several private groups responded to them. He begins by summarizing what he sees as the "'seven danger signals' of cancerous, out-of-control globalization." Following this are "seven prescriptions" that draw on the lessons of the struggle against NAFTA by a series of newly emergent transnational networks of groups and individuals seeking "to counter the effects of global economic restructuring." Noteworthy is that these networks are not proposing exclusionary objectives—which is what trade protectionism implies, for example—but instead embrace constructive proposals to cope with challenges posed by the "New World Economy [which] is not going to vanish from the political agenda."

The fourth in the series of essays on the nature and implications of the regionalization of the world political economy is "Mercantilism and Global Security," by Michael Borrus, Steve Weber, and John Zysman, with Joseph Willihnganz. As the title suggests, the authors are concerned with the security implications of regionalism and the kinds of international security systems that are likely to be associated with alternative configurations of economic power.

Borrus, Weber, Zysman, and Willihnganz begin with the premise that the decline of American power sets the stage for new patterns of political economy. "For the moment, the U.S. still leads," they argue, "but more by default than from strength. . . . Its technological and economic position is declining relative to the other industrialized nations. As a result, the government's ability to exact compliance or exercise leverage in the international system is diminished." Thus the United States, despite being the world's "sole remaining superpower," will not be able to shape the post-Cold War world political economy in the same way that it shaped the post-World War II world.

The authors outline several visions of how a triangular world political economy "will set the parameters within which security issues are resolved." They conclude that "bitter economic rivalry" is a likely outcome because of fear that "there can be *enduring* national winners and losers from trade competition"—which is the logic underlying strategic trade theory. Strategic trade practices combined with the way technology develops and the changing relationship between civilian and military research and development will tempt states to " 'grab' key technologies and markets before others can: doing so would guarantee domestic availability of the industrial resources needed to field state-of-the-art military forces and eliminate the need to make unacceptable concessions." The result would be mercantile rivalry among the world's principal trading blocs in which "fear of one another" may be the only force binding them together.

What are the security implications of such a system? "If regions come to view trade as a zero-sum game in which one region's gain is another's loss," Borrus, Weber, Zysman, and Willihnganz conclude, "they could start to regard each other as rivals competing not just for one-time gains in wealth, but for long-term growth and welfare. . . . Existing international institutions would be hard pressed to cope with the instability that would result."

For more than two decades access to oil has shaped the states' security concerns, particularly those of the industrial world whose economies depend critically on this vital resource. We conclude Part III with an essay by Joseph Stanislaw and Daniel Yergin entitled "Oil: Reopening the Door," in which the authors examine recent changes in the political economy of oil against the backdrop of past lessons.

"Today," the authors write, "economics is taking precedence over politics." This is radically different from the energy environment the world faced two decades ago, when Middle Eastern oil-producing countries in particular sought to use their "commodity power" to political advantage. Oil producers now recognize that they depend on oil consumers in the same way that consumers depend on producers. Their interdependence permits a "mutuality of interests" between producers and consumers that forms the basis for a new form of energy security. The sense of security will be reinforced by the "interweaving of investment, trade and finance" that will be necessary to ensure adequate supplies of energy into the twenty-first century. The end of communism ensures that the former Soviet empire will be among the doors opened to the global oil industry.

Stanislaw and Yergin observe that "the Persian Gulf War illustrates both the critical position of oil in the global balance of power and the importance of interdependence between producers and industrial consumers." They also note that an "increasingly important question [is] how to reconcile energy use and environmental imperatives." This and related environmental issues are addressed in Part IV of *The Global Agenda*.

23

THREE IDEOLOGIES OF POLITICAL ECONOMY

Robert Gilpin

Robert Gilpin summarizes and critically analyzes three "ideologies" of political economy: liberalism, nationalism (mercantilism), and Marxism. Each ideology alleges "to provide scientific descriptions of how the world *does* work, while they also constitute normative positions regarding how the world *should* work." Together the three ideologies have had a profound impact on world affairs. Gilpin is Dwight D. Eisenhower Professor of International Affairs at Princeton University. His books include *War and Change in World Politics* (1981).

Over the past century and a half, the ideologies of liberalism, nationalism, and Marxism have divided humanity. . . . The conflict among these three moral and intellectual positions has revolved around the role and significance of the market in the organization of society and economic affairs. . . .

These three ideologies are fundamentally different in their conceptions of the relationships among society, state, and market, and it may not be an exaggeration to say that every controversy in the field of international political economy is ultimately reducible to differing conceptions of these relationships. . . .

It is important to understand the nature and content of these contrasting "ideologies" of political economy. The term "ideology" is used rather than "theory" because each position entails a total belief system concerning the nature of human beings and society. . . . These commitments or ideologies allege to provide scientific descriptions of how the world *does* work while they also constitute normative positions regarding how the world *should* work.

Although scholars have produced a number of "theories" to explain the relationship of economics and politics, these three stand out and have had a profound influence on scholarship and political affairs. In highly oversimplified terms, economic nationalism (or, as it was originally called, mercantilism), which developed from the practice of statesmen in the early modern period, assumes and advocates the primacy of politics over economics. It is essentially a doctrine of statebuilding and asserts that the market should be subordinate to the pursuit of state interests. It argues that political factors do, or at least should, determine economic relations. Liberalism, which emerged from the Enlightenment in the writings of Adam Smith and others, was a reaction to mercantilism and has become embodied in orthodox economics. It assumes that politics and economics exist, at least ideally, in separate spheres; it argues that markets—in the interest of efficiency, growth, and consumer choice—should be free from political interference. Marxism, which appeared in the mid-nineteenth century as a reaction against liberalism and classical economics, holds that economics drives politics. Political conflict arises from struggle among classes over the distribution of wealth. Hence, political conflict will cease with the elimination of the market and of a society of classes. . . . Both nationalism and Marxism in the modern era . . . developed largely in reaction to the tenets of liberal economics. . . .

THE LIBERAL PERSPECTIVE

Some scholars assert that there is no such thing as a liberal theory of political economy because liberalism separates economics and politics from one another and assumes that each sphere operates according to particular rules and a logic of its own.[1] This view is itself, however, an ideological position and liberal theorists do in fact concern themselves with both political and economic affairs. Whether it is made explicit in their writings or is merely implicit, one can speak of a liberal theory of political economy.

There is a set of values from which liberal theories of economics and of politics arise; in the modern world these political and economic values have tended to appear together. . . . Liberal economic theory is committed to free markets and minimal state intervention, although . . . the relative emphasis on one or the other may differ. Liberal political theory is committed to individual equality and liberty, although again the emphasis may differ. . . .

---

[1]The term "liberal" is used . . . in its European connotation, that is, a commitment to individualism, free market, and private property. This is the dominant perspective of most American economists and of economics as taught in American universities. . . .

The liberal perspective on political economy is embodied in the discipline of economics as it has developed in Great Britain, the United States, and Western Europe. From Adam Smith to its contemporary proponents, liberal thinkers . . . are committed to the market and the price mechanism as the most efficacious means for organizing domestic and international economic relations. Liberalism may, in fact, be defined as a doctrine and set of principles for organizing and managing a market economy in order to achieve maximum efficiency, economic growth, and individual welfare.

Economic liberalism assumes that a market arises spontaneously in order to satisfy human needs and that, once it is in operation, it functions in accordance with its own internal logic. Human beings are by nature economic animals, and therefore markets evolve naturally without central direction. As Adam Smith put it, it is inherent in mankind to "truck, barter and exchange." To facilitate exchange and improve their well-being, people create markets, money, and economic institutions. . . .

The rationale for a market system is that it increases economic efficiency, maximizes economic growth, and thereby improves human welfare. Although liberals believe that economic activity also enhances the power and security of the state, they argue that the primary objective of economic activity is to benefit individual consumers. Their ultimate defense of free trade and open markets is that they increase the range of goods and services available to the consumer.

The fundamental premise of liberalism is that the individual consumer, firm, or household is the basis of society. Individuals behave rationally and attempt to maximize or satisfy certain values at the lowest possible cost to themselves. Rationality applies only to endeavor, not to outcome. Thus, failure to achieve an objective due to ignorance or some other cause does not, according to liberals, invalidate their premise that individuals act on the basis of a cost/benefit or means/ends calculus. Finally, liberalism argues that an individual will seek to acquire an objective until a market equilibrium is reached, that is, until the costs associated with achieving the objective are equal to the benefits. Liberal economists attempt to explain economic and, in some cases, all human behavior on the basis of these individualistic and rationalistic assumptions. . . .

Liberalism also assumes that a market exists in which individuals have complete information and are thus enabled to select the most beneficial course of action. Individual producers and consumers will be highly responsive to price signals, and this will create a flexible economy in which any change in relative prices will elicit a corresponding change in patterns of production, consumption, and economic institutions; the latter are conceived ultimately to be the product rather than the cause of economic behavior. . . . . Further, in a truly competitive market, the terms of exchange are determined solely by considerations of supply and demand rather than by the exercise of power and coercion. If exchange is voluntary, both parties benefit. In colloquial terms, a "free exchange is no robbery."

Economics, or rather the economics taught in most American universities (what Marxists call orthodox or bourgeois economics), is assumed to be an empirical science of maximizing behavior. Behavior is believed to be governed by a set of economic "laws" that are impersonal and politically neutral; therefore, economics and politics should and can be separated into distinct spheres. Governments should not intervene in the market except where a "market failure" exists . . . or in order to provide a so-called public or collective good. . . .

A market economy is governed principally by the law of demand. . . . This "law" (or, if one prefers, assumption) holds that people will buy more of a good if the relative price falls and less if it rises; people will also tend to buy more of a good as their relative income rises and less as it falls. Any development that changes the relative price of a good or the relative income of an actor will create an incentive or disincentive to acquire (or produce) more or less of the good; this law in turn has profound ramifications throughout the society. Although certain exceptions to this simple concept exist, it is fundamental to the operation and success of a market system of economic exchange.

On the supply side of the economy, liberal economics assumes that individuals pursue their interests in a world of scarcity and resource constraints. This is a fundamental and inescapable condition of human existence. Every decision involves an opportunity cost, a tradeoff among alternative uses of available resources. . . . The basic lesson of liberal economics is that "there is no such thing as a free lunch"; to get something one must be willing to give up something else.

Liberalism also assumes that a market economy exhibits a powerful tendency toward equilibrium and inherent stability, at least over the long term. This "concept of a self-operating and self-correcting equilibrium achieved by a balance of forces in a rational universe" is a crucial one for the economists' belief in the operation of markets and the laws that are believed to govern them (Condliffe, 1950, p. 112). If a market is thrown into a state of disequilibrium due to some external (exogenous) factor such as a change in consumer tastes or productive technology, the operation of the price mechanism will eventually return it to a new state of equilibrium. . . .

An additional liberal assumption is that a basic long-term harmony of interests underlies the market competition of producers and consumers, a harmony that will supercede any temporary conflict of interest. Individual pursuit of self-interest in the market increases social well-being because it leads to the maximization of efficiency, and the resulting economic growth eventually benefits all. Consequently, everyone will gain in accordance with his or her contribution to the whole, but, it should be added, not everyone will gain equally because individual productivities differ. Under free exchange, society as a whole will be more wealthy, but individuals will be rewarded in terms of their marginal productivity and relative contribution to the overall social product.

Finally, most present-day liberal economists believe in progress, defined most frequently as an increase in wealth per capita. They assert that the growth of a properly functioning economy is linear, gradual, and continuous. . . . Although political or other events—wars, revolution, or natural disasters—can dramatically disrupt this growth path, the economy will return eventually to a stable pattern of growth that is determined principally by increases in population, resources, and productivity. Moreover, liberals see no necessary connection between the process of economic growth and political developments such as war and imperialism; these political evils affect and may be affected by economic activities, but they are essentially caused by political and not by economic factors. For example, liberals do not believe that any causal relationship existed between the advance of capitalism in the late nineteenth century and the upheavals of imperialism after 1870 and the outbreak of the First World War. Liberals believe economics is progressive and politics is retrogressive. Thus they conceive of progress as divorced from politics and based on the evolution of the market.

. . . Today, the conditions necessary for the operation of a market economy exist, and the normative commitment to the market has spread from its birthplace in Western civilization to embrace an increasingly large portion of the globe. Despite setbacks, the modern world has moved in the direction of the market economy and of increasing global economic interdependence precisely because markets *are* more efficient than other forms of economic organization. . . .

In essence, liberals believe that trade and economic intercourse are a source of peaceful relations among nations because the mutual benefits of trade and expanding interdependence among national economies will tend to foster cooperative relations. Whereas politics tends to divide, economics tends to unite peoples. A liberal international economy will have a moderating influence on international politics as it creates bonds of mutual interests and a commitment to the status quo. However, it is important to emphasize again that although everyone will, or at least can, be better off in "absolute" terms under free exchange, the "relative" gains will differ. It is precisely this issue of relative gains and the distribution of the wealth generated by the market system that has given rise to economic nationalism and Marxism as rival doctrines.

THE NATIONALIST PERSPECTIVE

Economic nationalism, like economic liberalism, has undergone several metamorphoses over the past several centuries. Its labels have also changed: mercantilism, statism, protectionism, the German Historical School, and, recently, New Protectionism. Throughout all these manifestations, however, runs a set of themes or attitudes rather than a coherent and systematic body of economic or political theory. Its central idea is that economic activities are and should be subordinate to the goal of state building and the interests of the state. All nationalists ascribe to the primacy of the state, of national security, and of military power in the organization and functioning of the international system. . . .

Although economic nationalism should be viewed as a general commitment to state building, the precise objectives pursued and the policies advocated have differed in different times and in different places. Yet, as Jacob Viner has cogently argued in an often-quoted passage, economic nationalist (or what he calls mercantilist) writers share convictions concerning the relationship of wealth and power:

> I believe that practically all mercantilists, whatever the period, country, or status of the particular individual, would have subscribed to all of the following propositions: (1) wealth is an absolutely essential means to power, whether for security or for aggression; (2) power is essential or valuable as a means to the acquisition or retention of wealth; (3) wealth and power are each proper ultimate ends of national policy; (4) there is long-run harmony between these ends, although in particular circumstances it may be necessary for a time to make economic sacrifices in the interest of military security and therefore also of long-run prosperity (Viner, 1958, p. 286).

Whereas liberal writers generally view the pursuit of power and wealth, that is, the choice between "guns and butter," as involving a tradeoff, nationalists tend to regard the two goals as being complementary. . . .

Economic nationalists stress the role of economic factors in international relations and view the struggle among states—capitalist, socialist, or whatever—for economic resources as pervasive and indeed inherent in the nature of the international system itself. As one writer has put it, since economic resources are necessary for national power, every conflict is at once both economic and political (Hawtrey, 1952). States, at least over the long run, simultaneously pursue wealth and national power.

As it evolved in the early modern era, economic nationalism responded to and reflected the political, economic, and military developments of the sixteenth, seventeenth, and eighteenth centuries: the emergence of strong national states in constant competition, the rise of a middle class devoted at first to commerce and increasingly to manufacturing, and the quickening pace of economic activities due to changes within Europe and the discovery of the New World and its resources. The evolution of a monetarized market economy and the wide range of changes in the nature of warfare that have been characterized as the "Military Revolution" were also critically important (Roberts, 1956). Nationalists (or "mercantilists," as they were then called) had good cause to identify a favorable balance of trade with national security.

For several reasons, the foremost objective of nationalists is industrialization. . . . In the first place, nationalists believe that industry has spillover effects (externalities) throughout the economy and leads to its overall development. Second, they associate the possession of industry with economic self-sufficiency and political autonomy. Third, and most important, industry is prized because it is the basis of military power and central to national security in the modern world. In almost every society, including liberal ones, governments pursue policies favorable to industrial development. As the mercantilist theorist of American economic development, Alexander Hamilton, wrote: "not only the wealth but the independence and security of a country appear to be materially connected to the prosperity of manufactures"; . . . no contemporary dependency theorist has put it better. This nationalist objective of industrialization . . . is itself a major source of economic conflict.

Economic nationalism, both in the early modern era and today, arises in part from the tendency of markets to concentrate wealth and to establish dependency or power relations between the strong and the weak economies. . . .

In a world of competing states, the nationalist considers relative gain to be more important than mutual gain. Thus nations continually try to change the rules or regimes governing international economic relations in order to benefit themselves disproportionately with respect to other economic powers. As Adam Smith shrewdly pointed out, everyone wants to be a monopolist and will attempt to be one unless prevented by competitors. Therefore, a liberal international economy cannot develop unless it is supported by the dominant economic states whose own interests are consistent with its preservation.

Whereas liberals stress the mutual benefits of international commerce, nationalists as well as Marxists regard these relations as basically conflictual. Although this does not rule out international economic cooperation and the pursuit of liberal policies, economic interdependence is never symmetrical; indeed, it constitutes a source of continuous conflict and insecurity. Nationalist writers from Alexander Hamilton to contemporary dependency theorists thus emphasize national self-sufficiency rather than economic interdependence. The desire for power and independence have been the overriding concern of economic nationalists.

Whatever its relative strengths and weaknesses as an ideology or theory of international political economy, the nationalist emphasis on the geographic location and the distribution of economic activities provide it with powerful appeal. Throughout modern history, states have pursued policies promoting the development of industry, advanced technology, and those economic activities with the highest profitability and generation of employment within their own borders. As far as they can, states try to create an international division of labor favorable to their political and economic interests. Indeed, economic nationalism is likely to be a significant influence in international relations as long as the state system exists.

THE MARXIST PERSPECTIVE

Like liberalism and nationalism, Marxism has evolved in significant ways since its basic ideas were set forth by Karl Marx and Friedrich Engels in the middle of the nineteenth century. Marx's own thinking changed during his lifetime, and his theories have always been subject to conflicting interpretations. Although Marx viewed capitalism as a global economy, he did not develop a systematic set of ideas on international relations; this responsibility fell upon the succeeding generation of Marxist writers. The Soviet Union and China, furthermore, having adopted Marxism as their official ideology, . . . reshaped it when necessary to serve their own national interests. . . .

Marxism characterizes capitalism as the private ownership of the means of production and the existence of wage labor. It believes that capitalism is driven by capitalists striving for profits and capital accumulation in a competitive market economy. Labor has been dispossessed and has become a commodity that is subject to the price mechanism. In Marx's view these two key characteristics of capitalism are responsible for its dynamic nature and make it the most productive economic mechanism yet. Although its historic mission is to develop and unify the globe, the very success of capitalism will hasten its passing. The origin, evolution, and eventual demise of the capitalist mode of production are, according to Marx, governed by three inevitable economic laws.

The first law, the law of disproportionality, entails a denial of Say's law, which (in oversimplified terms) holds that supply creates its own demand so that supply and demand will always be, except for brief moments, in balance. . . . Say's law maintains that an equilibrating process makes overproduction impossible in a capitalist or market economy. Marx, like John Maynard Keynes, denied that this tendency toward equilibrium existed and argued that capitalist economies tend to overproduce particular types of goods. There is, Marx argued, an inherent contradiction in capitalism between its capacity to produce goods and the capacity of consumers (wage earners) to purchase those goods, so that the constantly recurring disproportionality between production and consumption due to the "anarchy" of the market causes periodic depressions and economic fluctuations. He predicted that these recurring economic crises would become increasingly severe and in time would impel the suffering proletariat to rebel against the system.

The second law propelling the development of a capitalist system, according to Marxism, is the law of the concentration (or accumulation) of capital. The motive force of capitalism is the drive for profits and the consequent necessity for the individual capitalist to accumulate and invest. Competition forces the capitalists to increase their efficiency and capital investment or risk extinction. As a result, the evolution of capitalism is toward increasing concentrations of wealth in the hands of the efficient few and the growing impoverishment of the many. With the petite bourgeoisie being pushed down into the swelling ranks of the impoverished proletariat, the reserve army of the unemployed increases, labor's wages decline, and the capitalist society becomes ripe for social revolution.

The third law of capitalism is that of the falling rate of profit. As capital accumulates and becomes more abundant, the rate of return declines, thereby decreasing the incentive to invest. Although classical liberal economists had recognized this possibility, they believed that a solution could be found through such countervailing devices as the export of capital and manufactured goods and the import of cheap food. . . . Marx, on the other hand, believed that the tendency for profits to decline was inescapable. As the pressure of competition forces capitalists to increase efficiency and productivity through investment in new labor-saving and more productive technology, the level of unemployment will increase and the rate of profit or surplus value will decrease. Capitalists will thereby lose their incentive to invest in productive ventures and to create employment. This will result in economic stagnation, increasing unemployment, and the "immiserization" of the proletariat. In time, the ever-increasing intensity and depth of the business cycle will cause the workers to rebel and destroy the capitalist economic system.

The core of the Marxist critique of capitalism is that although the individual capitalist is rational (as liberals assume), the capitalist system itself is irrational. The competitive market necessitates that the individual capitalist must save, invest, and accumulate. If the desire for profits is the fuel of capitalism, then investment is the motor and accumulation is the result. In the aggregate, however, this accumulating capital of individual capitalists leads to the periodic overproduction of goods, surplus capital, and the disappearance of investment incentives. In time, the increasing severity of the downturns in the business cycle and the long-term trend toward economic stagnation will cause the proletariat to overthrow the system through revolutionary violence. Thus, the inherent contradiction of capitalism is that, with capital accumulation, capitalism sows the seeds of its own destruction and is replaced by the socialist economic system.

Marx believed that in the mid-nineteenth century, the maturing of capitalism in Europe and the drawing of the global periphery into the market economy had set the stage for the proletarian revolution and the end of the capitalist economy. When this did not happen, Marx's followers, such as Rudolf Hilferding and Rosa Luxemburg, became concerned over the continuing vitality of capitalism and its refusal to disappear. The strength of nationalism, the economic successes of capitalism, and the advent of imperialism led to a metamorphosis of Marxist thought that culminated in Lenin's *Imperialism* (1939), first published in 1917. Written against the backdrop of the First World War and drawing heavily upon the writings of other Marxists, *Imperialism* was both a polemic against his ideological enemies and a synthesis of Marxist critiques of a capitalist world economy. In staking out his own position, Lenin in effect converted Marxism from essentially a theory of domestic economy to a theory of international political relations among capitalist states. . . .

In the years between Marx and Lenin, capitalism had experienced a profound transformation. Marx had written about a capitalism largely confined to western Europe, a closed economy in which the growth impulse would one day cease as it collided with various constraints. Between 1870 and 1914, however, capitalism had become a vibrant, technological, and increasingly global and open system. In Marx's day, the primary nexus of the slowly developing world economy was trade. After 1870, however, the massive export of capital by Great Britain and subsequently by other developed economies had significantly changed the world economy; foreign investment and international finance had profoundly altered the economic and political relations among societies. Furthermore, Marx's capitalism had been composed mainly of small, competitive, industrial firms. By the time of Lenin, however, capitalist economies were dominated by immense industrial combines that in turn, according to Lenin, were controlled by the great banking houses *(haut finance)*. For Lenin, the control of capital by capital, that is, of industrial capital by financial capital, represented the pristine and highest stage of capitalist development.

Capitalism, he argued, had escaped its three laws of motion through overseas imperialism. The acquisition of colonies had enabled the capitalist economies to dispose of their unconsumed goods, to acquire cheap resources, and to vent their surplus capital. The exploitation of these colonies further provided an economic surplus with which the capitalists could buy off the leadership ("labor aristocracy") of their own proletariat. Colonial imperialism, he argued, had become a necessary feature of advanced capitalism. As its productive forces developed and matured, a capitalist economy had to expand abroad, capture colonies, or else suffer economic stagnation and internal revolution. Lenin identified this necessary expansion as the cause of the eventual destruction of the international capitalist system.

The essence of Lenin's argument is that a capitalist international economy does develop the world, but does not develop it evenly. Individual capitalist economies grow at different rates and this differential growth of national power is ultimately responsible for imperialism, war, and international political change. Responding to Kautsky's argument that capitalists were too rational to fight over colonies and would ally themselves in the joint exploitation of colonial peoples (the doctrine of "ultra-imperialism"), Lenin stated that this was impossible because of what has become known as the "law of uneven development." . . .

In effect, . . . Lenin added a fourth law to the original three Marxist laws of capitalism. The law is that, as capitalist economies mature, as capital accumulates, and as profit rates fall, the capitalist economies are compelled to seize colonies and create dependencies to serve as markets, investment outlets, and sources of food and raw materials. In competition with one another, they divide up the colonial world in accordance with their relative strengths. Thus, the most advanced capitalist economy, namely Great Britain, had appropriated the largest share of colonies. As other capitalist economies advanced, however, they sought a redivision of colonies. This imperialist conflict inevitably led to armed conflict among the rising and declining imperial powers. The First World War, according to this analysis, was a war of territorial redivision between a declining Great Britain and other rising capitalist powers. Such wars of colonial division and redivision would continue, he argued, until the industrializing colonies and the proletariat of the capitalist countries revolted against the system.

In more general terms, Lenin reasoned that because capitalist economies grow and accumulate capital at differential rates, a capitalist international system can never be stable for longer than very short periods of time. In opposition to Kautsky's doctrine of ultra-imperialism, Lenin argued that all capitalist alliances were temporary and reflected momentary balances of power among the capitalist states that would inevitably be undermined by the process of uneven development. As this occurred, it would lead to intracapitalist conflicts over colonial territories. . . .

Lenin's internationalization of Marxist theory represented a subtle but significant reformulation. In Marx's critique of capitalism, the causes of its downfall were economic; capitalism would fail for economic reasons as the proletariat revolted against its impoverishment. Furthermore, Marx had defined the actors in this drama as social classes. Lenin, however, substituted a political critique of capitalism in which the principal actors in effect became competing mercantilistic nation-states driven by economic necessity. Although international capitalism was economically successful, Lenin argued that it was politically unstable and constituted a war-system. The workers or the labor aristocracy in the developed capitalist countries temporarily shared in the exploitation of colonial peoples but ultimately would pay for these economic gains on the battlefield. Lenin believed that the inherent contradiction of capitalism resided in the consequent struggle of nations rather than in the class struggle. Capitalism would end due to a revolt against its inherent bellicosity and political consequences.

In summary, Lenin argued that the inherent contradiction of capitalism is that it develops the world and plants the political seeds of its own destruction as it diffuses technology, industry, and military power. It creates foreign competitors with lower wages and standards of living who can outcompete the previously dominant economy on the battlefield of world markets. Intensification of economic and political competition between declining and rising capitalist powers leads to economic conflicts, imperial rivalries, and eventually war. He asserted that this had been the fate of the British-centered liberal world economy of the nineteenth century. Today he would undoubtedly argue that, as the U.S. economy declines, a similar fate threatens the twentieth-century liberal world economy, centered in the United States. . . .

A CRITIQUE OF THE PERSPECTIVES

As we have seen, liberalism, nationalism, and Marxism make different assumptions and reach conflicting conclusions regarding the nature and consequences of a world market economy or (as Marxists prefer) a world capitalist economy.

. . . Each of the three perspectives has strengths and weaknesses, to be further explored below. Although no perspective provides a complete and satisfactory understanding of the nature and dynamism of the international political economy, together they provide useful insights. . . .

Critique of Economic Liberalism

Liberalism embodies a set of analytical tools and policy prescriptions that enable a society to maximize its return from scarce resources; its commitment to efficiency and the maximization of total wealth provides much of its strength. The market constitutes the most effective means for organizing economic relations, and the price mechanism operates to ensure that mutual gain and hence aggregate social benefit tend to result from economic exchange. In effect, liberal economics says to a society, whether domestic or international, "if you wish to be wealthy, this is what you must do." . . .

. . . Liberal economics can be criticized in several important respects. As a means to understand society and especially its dynamics, economics is limited; it cannot serve as a comprehensive approach to political economy. Yet liberal economists have tended to forget this inherent limitation, to regard economics as the master social science, and to permit economics to become imperialistic. When this occurs, the nature and basic assumptions of the discipline can lead the economist astray and limit its utility as a theory of political economy.

The first of these limitations is that economics artificially separates the economy from other aspects of society and accepts the existing sociopolitical framework as a given, including the distribution of power and property rights; the resource and other endowments of individuals, groups, and national societies; and the framework of social, political, and cultural institutions. The liberal world is viewed as one of homogeneous, rational, and equal individuals living in a world free from political boundaries and social constraints. Its "laws" prescribe a set of maximizing rules for economic actors regardless of where and with what they start; yet in real life, one's starting point most frequently determines where one finishes. . . .

Another limitation of liberal economics as a theory is a tendency to disregard the justice or equity of the outcome of economic activities. Despite heroic efforts to fashion an "objective" welfare economics, the distribution of wealth within and among societies lies outside the primary concern of liberal economics. . . .

Liberalism is also limited by its assumption that exchange is always free and occurs in a competitive market between equals who possess full information and are thus enabled to gain mutually if they choose to exchange one value for another. Unfortunately, as Charles Lindblom has argued, exchange is seldom free and equal (Lindblom, 1977, pp. 40–50). Instead, the terms of an exchange can be profoundly affected by coercion, differences in bargaining power (monopoly or monopsony), and other essentially political factors. In effect, because it neglects both the effects of noneconomic factors on exchange and the effects of exchange on politics, liberalism lacks a true "political economy."

A further limitation of liberal economics is that its analysis tends to be static. At least in the short run, the array of consumer demands, the institutional framework, and the technological environment are accepted as constants. They are regarded as a set of constraints and opportunities within which economic decisions and tradeoffs are made. . . . Liberal economists are incrementalists who believe that social structures tend to change slowly in response to price signals. Although liberal economists have attempted to develop theories of economic and technological change, the crucial social, political, and technological variables affecting change are considered to be exogenous and beyond the realm of economic analysis. As Marxists charge, liberalism lacks a theory of the dynamics of international political economy and tends to assume the stability and the virtues of the economic status quo.

Liberal economics, with its laws for maximizing behavior, is based on a set of highly restrictive assumptions. No society has ever or could ever be composed of the true "economic man" of liberal theory. A functioning society requires affective ties and the subordination of individual self-interest to larger social values; if this were not the case the society would fly apart. . . . Yet Western society has gone far in harnessing for social and economic betterment a basic tendency in human beings toward self-aggrandizement. . . . Through release of the market mechanism from social and political constraints, Western civilization has reached a level of unprecedented affluence and has set an example that other civilizations wish to emulate. It has done so, however, at the cost of other values. As liberal economics teaches, nothing is ever achieved without a cost.

Critique of Economic Nationalism

The foremost strength of economic nationalism is its focus on the state as the predominant actor in international relations and as an instrument of economic development. Although many have argued that modern economic and technological developments have made the nation-state an anachronism, at the end of the twentieth century the system of nation-states is actually expanding; societies throughout the world are seeking to create strong states capable of organizing and managing national economies, and the number of states in the world is increasing. Even in older states, the spirit of nationalist sentiments can easily be inflamed. . . . Although other actors such as transnational and international organizations do exist and do influence international relations, the economic and military efficiency of the state makes it preeminent over all these other actors.

The second strength of nationalism is its stress on the importance of security and political interests in the organization and conduct of international economic relations. One need not accept the nationalist emphasis on the primacy of security considerations to appreciate that the security of the state is a necessary precondition for its economic and political well-being in an anarchic and competitive state system. A state that fails to provide for its own security ceases to be independent. . . .

The third strength of nationalism is its emphasis on the political framework of economic activities, its recognition that markets must function in a world of competitive groups and states. The political relations among these political actors affect the operation of markets just as markets affect the political relations. In fact, the international political system constitutes one of the most important constraints on and determinant of markets. Since states seek to influence markets to their own individual advantage, the role of power is crucial in the creation and sustaining of market relations; even Ricardo's classic example of the exchange of British woolens for Portuguese wine was not free from the exercise of state power. . . . Indeed, as Carr has argued, every economic system must rest on a secure political base (Carr, 1951 [1939]).

One weakness of nationalism is its tendency to believe that international economic relations constitute solely and at all times a zero-sum game, that is, that one state's gain must of necessity be another's loss. Trade, investment, and all other economic relations are viewed by the nationalist primarily in conflictual and distributive terms. Yet, if cooperation occurs, markets *can* bring mutual (albeit not necessarily equal) gain, as the liberal insists. The possibility of benefit for all is the basis of the international market economy. Another weakness of nationalism is due to the fact that the pursuit of power and the pursuit of wealth usually do conflict, at least in the short run. The amassing and exercising of military and other forms of power entail costs to the society, costs that can undercut its economic efficiency. Thus, as Adam Smith argued, the mercantilist policies of eighteenth-century states that identified money with wealth were detrimental to the growth of the real wealth created by productivity increases; he demonstrated that the wealth of nations would have been better served by policies of free trade. Similarly, the tendency today to identify industry with power can weaken the economy of a state. Development of industries without regard to market considerations or comparative advantage can weaken a society economically. Although states in a situation of conflict must on occasion pursue mercantilistic goals and policies, over the long term, pursuit of these policies can be self-defeating.

In addition, nationalism lacks a satisfactory theory of domestic society, the state, and foreign policy. It tends to assume that society and state form a unitary entity and that foreign policy is determined by an objective national interest. Yet, as liberals correctly stress, society is pluralistic and consists of individuals and groups (coalitions of individuals) that try to capture the apparatus of the state and make it serve their own political and economic interests. Although states possess varying degrees of social autonomy and independence in the making of policy, foreign policy (including foreign economic policy) is in large measure the outcome of the conflicts among dominant groups within each society. Trade protectionism and most other nationalist policies result from attempts by one factor of production or another (capital, labor, or land) to acquire a monopoly position and thereby to increase its share of the economic rents. Nationalist policies are most frequently designed to redistribute income from consumers and society as a whole to producer interests.

Nationalism can thus be interpreted as either a theory of state building or a cloak for the interests of particular producer groups that are in a position to influence national policy. In their failure to appreciate fully or distinguish between the two possible meanings of economic nationalism, nationalists can be faulted for not applying, both to the domestic level and to the determination of foreign policy, their assumption that the political framework influences economic outcomes. They fail to take sufficient account of the fact that domestic political groups frequently use a nationalist rationale, especially that of national security, to promote their own interests. . . .

The validity of nationalists' emphasis on protectionism and industrialization is more difficult to ascertain. It is true that all great industrial powers have had strong states that protected and promoted their industries in the early stages of industrialization and that without such protectionism, the "infant" industries of developing economies probably would not have survived the competition of powerful firms in more advanced economies. Yet it is also the case that high levels of protectionism in many countries have led to the establishment of inefficient industries and even retarded economic development. . . . In the final quarter of the twentieth century, economies like those of Taiwan and South Korea, which have limited protectionism while favoring competitive export industries, have performed better than those less developed countries that have attempted to industrialize behind high tariff walls while pursuing a strategy of import substitution.

The nationalist's bias toward industry over agriculture also must get a mixed review. It is true that industry can have certain advantages over agriculture and that the introduction of industrial technology into a society has spillover effects that tend to transform and modernize all aspects of the economy as it upgrades the quality of the labor force and increases the profitability of capital. Yet one must remember that few societies have developed without a prior agricultural revolution and a high level of agricultural productivity. . . . In fact, certain of the most prosperous economies of the world, for example, Denmark, the American farm belt, and western Canada, are based on efficient agriculture. . . . In all these societies, moreover, the state has promoted agricultural development.

One may conclude that the nationalists are essentially correct in their belief that the state must play an important role in economic development. A strong state is required to promote and, in some cases, to protect industry as well as to foster an efficient agriculture. Yet this active role of the state, though a necessary condition, is not a sufficient condition. A strong and interventionist state does not guarantee economic development; indeed, it might retard it. The sufficient condition for economic development is an efficient economic organization of agriculture and industry, and in most cases this is achieved through the operation of the market. Both of these political and economic conditions have characterized the developed economies and the rapidly industrializing countries of the contemporary international system.

It is important to realize that, whatever its relative merits or deficiencies, economic nationalism has a persistent appeal. Throughout modern history, the international location of economic activities has been a leading concern of states. From the seventeenth century on states have pursued conscious policies of industrial and technological development. Both to achieve stable military power and in the belief that industry provides a higher "value added" . . . than agriculture, the modern nation-state has had as one of its major objectives the establishment and protection of industrial power. As long as a conflictual international system exists, economic nationalism will retain its strong attraction.

Critique of Marxist Theory

Marxism correctly places the economic problem—the production and distribution of material wealth—where it belongs, at or near the center of political life. Whereas liberals tend to ignore the issue of distribution and nationalists are concerned primarily with the *international* distribution of wealth, Marxists focus on both the domestic and the international effects of a market economy on the distribution of wealth. They call attention to the ways in which the rules or regimes governing trade, investment, and other international economic relations affect the distribution of wealth among groups and states. . . .

Another contribution of Marxism is its emphasis on the nature and structure of the division of labor at both the domestic and international levels. As Marx and Engels correctly pointed out in *The German Ideology,* every division of labor implies dependence and therefore a political relationship. . . . In a market economy the economic nexus among groups and states becomes of critical importance in determining their welfare and their political relations. The Marxist analysis, however, is too limited, because economic interdependence is not the only or even the most important set of interstate relations. The political and strategic relations among political actors are of equal or greater significance and cannot be reduced to merely economic considerations, at least not as Marxists define economics.

The Marxist theory of international political economy is also valuable in its focus on international political change. Whereas neither liberalism nor nationalism has a comprehensive theory of social change, Marxism emphasizes the role of economic and technological developments in explaining the dynamics of the international system. As embodied in Lenin's law of uneven development, the differential growth of power among states constitutes an underlying cause of international political change. Lenin was at least partially correct in attributing the First World War to the uneven economic growth of power among industrial states and to conflict over the division of territory. There can be little doubt that the uneven growth of the several European powers and the consequent effects on the balance of power contributed to their collective insecurity. Competition for markets and empires did aggravate interstate relations. Furthermore, the average person's growing awareness of the effects on personal welfare and security of the vicissitudes of the world market and the economic behavior of other states also became a significant element in the arousal of nationalistic antagonisms. For nations and citizens alike, the growth of economic interdependence brought with it a new sense of insecurity, vulnerability, and resentment against foreign political and economic rivals.

Marxists are no doubt also correct in attributing to capitalist economies, at least as we have known them historically, a powerful impulse to expand through trade and especially through the export of capital. . . . Capitalists desire access to foreign economies for export of goods and capital; exports have a Keynesian demand effect in stimulating economic activity in capitalist economies, and capital exports serve to raise the overall rate of profit. Closure of foreign markets and capital outlets would be detrimental to capitalism, and a closed capitalist economy would probably result in a dramatic decline in economic growth. There is reason to believe that the capitalist system (certainly as we have known it) could not survive in the absence of an open world economy. The essential character of capitalism, as Marx pointed out, is cosmopolitan; the capitalist's ideology is international. Capitalism in just one state would undoubtedly be an impossibility.

In the nineteenth and twentieth centuries the dominant capitalist states, Great Britain and the United States, employed their power to promote and maintain an open world economy. They used their influence to remove the barriers to the free flow of goods and capital. Where necessary, in the words of Simon Kuznets, "the greater power of the developed nations imposed upon the reluctant partners the opportunities of international trade and division of labor" (Kuznets, 1966, p. 335). In pursuit of their own interests, they created international law to protect the property rights of private traders and investors. . . . And when the great trading nations became unable or unwilling to enforce the rules of free trade, the liberal system began its steady retreat. Up to this point, therefore, the Marxists are correct in their identification of capitalism and modern imperialism.

The principal weakness of Marxism as a theory of international political economy results from its failure to appreciate the role of political and strategic factors in international relations. . . . Although competition for markets and for capital outlets can certainly be a cause of tension and one factor causing imperialism and war, this does not provide an adequate explanation for the foreign policy behavior of capitalist states.

The historical evidence, for example, does not support Lenin's attribution of the First World War to the logic of capitalism and the market system. The most important territorial disputes among the European powers, which precipitated the war, were not those about overseas colonies, as Lenin argued, but lay within

Europe itself. The principal conflict leading to the war involved redistribution of the Balkan territories of the decaying Ottoman Empire. And insofar as the source of this conflict was economic, it lay in the desire of the Russian state for access to the Mediterranean. . . . Marxism cannot explain the fact that the three major imperial rivals—Great Britain, France, and Russia—were in fact on the same side in the ensuing conflict and that they fought against a Germany that had few foreign policy interests outside Europe itself.

In addition, Lenin was wrong in tracing the basic motive force of imperialism to the internal workings of the capitalist system. As Benjamin J. Cohen has pointed out in his analysis of the Marxist theory of imperialism, the political and strategic conflicts of the European powers were more important; it was at least in part the stalemate on the Continent among the Great Powers that forced their interstate competition into the colonial world (Cohen, 1973). Every one of these colonial conflicts (if one excludes the Boer War) was in fact settled through diplomatic means. And, finally, the overseas colonies of the European powers were simply of little economic consequence. As Lenin's own data show, almost all European overseas investment was directed to the "lands of recent settlement" (the United States, Canada, Australia, South Africa, Argentina, etc.) rather than to the dependent colonies in what today we call the Third World (Lenin, 1939 [1917], p. 64). In fact, contrary to Lenin's view that politics follows investment, international finance during this period was largely a servant of foreign policy, as was also the case with French loans to Czarist Russia. Thus, despite its proper focus on political change, Marxism is seriously flawed as a theory of political economy.

References

Carr, Edward Hallett. 1951 [1939]. *The Twenty Years' Crisis, 1919–1939.* 2d ed. London: Macmillan.

Cohen, Benjamin J. 1973. *The Question of Imperialism: The Political Economy of Dominance and Dependence.* New York: Basic Books.

Condliffe, J. B. 1950. *The Commerce of Nations.* New York: W. W. Norton.

Hawtrey, Ralph G. 1952. *Economic Aspects of Sovereignty.* London: Longmans.

Kuznets, Simon. 1966. *Modern Economic Growth: Rate, Structure, and Spread.* New Haven: Yale University Press.

Lenin, V. I. 1939 [1917]. *Imperialism: The Highest Stage of Capitalism.* New York: International Publishers.

Lindblom, Charles E. 1977. *Politics and Markets: The World's Political-Economic Systems.* New York: Basic Books.

Roberts, Michael. 1956. *The Military Revolution, 1560–1660.* Belfast: Boyd.

Viner, Jacob. 1958. *The Long View and the Short: Studies in Economic Theory and Policy.* New York: Free Press.

24

LOOMING COLLISION
OF CAPITALISMS?

Erik R. Peterson

Global economic integration is accelerating at a rapid economic pace, but, argues Erik R. Peterson, the "integration of policies is lagging behind integration of markets." Rapid globalization thus threatens to bring the major centers of capitalism into conflict with one another as they pursue "defensive strategies grounded in parochial interests . . . that encourage the outbreak of economic nationalism." Peterson is director of studies at the Center for Strategic and International Studies in Washington, D.C.

Accelerating global economic integration is bringing national economic policies into sharper competition, especially among the advanced capitalist economies. How these competing domestic policies are managed through the turn of the century and beyond will have profound implications not only for the international economy but also for broader international security and political relations. The risk is that increasingly nationalist economic policies, fanned by deteriorating economic conditions and social pressures, will propel the preeminent economic powers—and the rest of the world with them—into an era of *"realeconomik"* in which parochial economic interests drive governments to pursue marginal advantage in an international system marked by growing interdependencies.

Reprinted from *The Washington Quarterly,* 17:2, Erik R. Peterson, "Looming Collision of Capitalisms?" by permission of The MIT Press, Cambridge, Massachusetts. Copyright © 1994 by The Center for Strategic and International Studies and the Massachusetts Institute of Technology. Some footnotes have been deleted.

The conclusion in December 1993 of the General Agreement on Tariffs and Trade (GATT) Uruguay Round, the culmination of seven years of tortuous negotiation by governments to strip away more of their own policy prerogatives, refuted the proposition that the major economic powers—the United States, the European Union (EU), and Japan—were leading the collective effort to break down traditional trade barriers and trade-distorting domestic policies globally. Although it culminated in agreement, the process revealed the extent to which those powers were disinclined to do the "heavy lifting" in liberalizing their policies that many of the less prominent economies had already done to advance the round. In effect, the protracted negotiations highlighted the thresholds of national tolerance among the predominant economies beyond which the political costs for the respective governments were unacceptably high.

There is little doubt that the current economic troubles confronting Washington, Brussels, and Tokyo were a major factor in limiting the scope of the final GATT agreement. Those troubles have also elevated the levels of economic nationalism and unilateralism, both of which can be expected to intensify further as longer-term structural problems in all three economies generate additional political and economic dislocations in the years ahead.

Because of the increasingly binding constraints placed on national economic policy making by the process of global economic integration, the temptation for the major economies to engage in defensive strategies by supporting national "strategic" industries—especially high-technology industries—could bring the major capitalisms into collision. The operative question is whether the governments concerned will succumb to the growing tendency to "pursue relative gains at the expense of mutual gains [and] political power at the expense of economic welfare,"[1] or whether they will be able to devise a system of rules and an appropriate institutional vehicle to defuse the potential for escalating economic clashes between respective "national champions."

ACCELERATING ECONOMIC GLOBALIZATION

It has long been recognized that the traditional line of demarcation between domestic and international economic policy making is fading. Economic shocks ranging from the oil embargo by the Organization of Petroleum Exporting Countries to the "Black Monday" international stock market crash in October 1987 have underlined the susceptibility of national markets to developments abroad. For governments worldwide, the internationalization of the world economy has also meant the progressive deterioration of their capacity to manage their economies. Macroeconomic policies have been increasingly undermined by the offsetting effects of international responses; an increase in interest rates

---

[1]Theodore H. Moran, "An Economics Agenda for Neorealists," *International Security* 18 (Fall 1993), p. 211.

to decelerate economic growth, for example, is more likely than ever before to be countered by an increase in interest-sensitive capital flows from abroad.

But international trade and investment linkages have expanded to such an extent that sensitivities of economies to decision making in other economies are now substantially more pronounced. Advances in communication and information technologies, the pursuit by multinational enterprises (MNEs) of complex cross-border strategies, the formation and development of regional trading blocs, the GATT process, economic liberalization undertaken in a host of developing economies, and ongoing efforts at marketization in former command economies are metamorphosing the international economic and financial system. As these elements bring about higher levels of global integration, constraints on national economic policy making will continue to grow—and with them the potential for wider conflict over national policies.

The real-time capabilities offered by new communication and information technologies have already had a tremendous impact on international capital flows. Daily global capital movements have increased to well over $1 trillion in 1992. The implications of these movements for national macroeconomic policy making are profound. Alan Greenspan, chairman of the Federal Reserve, noted in August 1993 that the internationalization of finance and the reduction in constraints on international capital flows "expose national economies to shocks from new and unexpected sources, with little if any lag." As a result, he stressed the importance central banks should attach to developing new ways of assessing and limiting risk. But those ways remain to be identified.

Nowhere has the impact on policy making of these cross-border capital flows been more obvious recently than in the EU, where international speculative pressures played a significant role in the partial collapse in the European Monetary System in 1992. Those forces contributed to the circumstances that led London and Rome to withdraw from the semifixed exchange rates under the Exchange Rate Mechanism (ERM); since the British and Italian withdrawal, they have also forced the Spanish to devalue the peseta and brought the Belgian franc under extreme stress. As the *Economist* noted in October 1993, "[t]he financial markets have discovered, in a way they are unlikely to forget for years, their power to crack the system."[2] In short, we have entered a new stage in the development of international finance in which financial markets—and even some individuals—can dramatically influence the outcome of policy decisions by states.

MNEs are another major driver of global economic integration. By virtue of increasingly complex strategies involving multitier networks of firms that are geographically dispersed and through strategic alliances with other firms, MNEs are establishing unprecedented linkages among economies worldwide. According to the United Nations Conference on Trade and Development (UNCTAD),

---

[2]"Europe's Monetary Future: From here to EMU," *Economist,* October 23, 1993, p. 25.

the strategies of MNEs have generally moved beyond a "simple integration" approach involving strengthened links with their foreign affiliates and with independent firms serving as subcontractors or licensees; the new strategy, which UNCTAD characterizes as "complex integration," provides for heightened geographical distribution of the value-added chain.[3] That MNEs account for a staggering one-third of world private productive assets suggests how important the ramifications of such a shift of strategy are.

According to UNCTAD, sales by MNEs outside their countries of origin were $5.5 trillion in 1992—as opposed to total world exports for the same year of about $4.0 trillion; furthermore, the stock of foreign direct investment (FDI) worldwide reached $2 trillion in 1992, as opposed to one-half that amount in 1987.[4] These data reflect the substantial role that MNEs are playing in integrating the world economy and suggest the extent to which private-sector forces have become a factor in national economic decision making. As discussed in greater detail below, a number of countries with policies that were previously anathema to MNEs have refashioned their approaches so that attraction of foreign investment is a key component of their economic development strategies.

The development of regional trading blocs has also generated higher levels of economic interdependence and by definition represents the voluntary acceptance by the respective member states of constraints on national policy prerogatives. Because the EU, the North American Free Trade Agreement (NAFTA), and the emerging trading framework in Asia are based on political as well as economic considerations, the trend toward regionalism transcends the surrender of policy prerogatives for purely economic reasons. Nevertheless, the impact is to advance economic integration between member states. In the case of the EU, where the impact of German monetary policy clearly transcends the national economic challenges inherent in reunification, the linkages may be more pronounced than some member states would want.

The GATT process, of course, has also steadily broken down barriers between international and domestic policy making. The GATT is no longer the vehicle through which only tariff barriers are broken down; the non-tariff barriers that were the focus of the Tokyo Round and the issues at the fore of the Uruguay Round—trade in services, trade-related investment measures, intellectual property protection, price supports and subsidies, countervailing duties, dumping, and dispute settlement—have exposed the nerves of national economic interests as never before. The demonstrations from Brussels to Tokyo attested to the degree to which GATT negotiations have become (and should be) a major domestic political issue. By definition, the GATT process and the

---

[3]UNCTAD, *World Investment Report 1993: Transnational Corporations and Integrated International Production* (New York, N.Y.: United Nations, 1993), pp. 4–5, 115–133.
    [4]*Ibid.,* pp. 13–14.

Uruguay Round . . . represent "another stake in the heart of the idea that governments can direct economies."[5]

Economic and financial liberalization in developing economies represents another stimulus to growing integration. A select number of developing countries with liberalized investment environments are now primary targets of portfolio and foreign direct investment flows.[6] Over the past 10 years, international portfolio investment in developing countries has mushroomed. Market capitalization has grown by a factor of 11, from $67 billion in 1982 to $770 billion in 1992. As a percentage of world equity market capitalization, developing countries increased their share over this period from 2.5 to 7 percent. The trend can be expected to continue as secondary markets in developing countries widen and deepen. . . . The key reason for this rapid growth in developing-country capital markets is profitability. . . . Over the past eight years emerging markets as a group have significantly outperformed their counterparts in developed countries.

The pattern of FDI to developing countries has been no less extraordinary. According to UNCTAD, FDI flows to developing countries increased from $25 billion in 1991 to $40 billion in 1992; if high growth is sustained in Asia and Latin America, annual flows could double in real terms to $80 billion by the end of the century. What is behind this trend? Simply put, economic liberalization has replaced statism, trade liberalization has followed protectionism, and privatization has replaced nationalization. For these countries, the necessity of conforming their national economic decision making to the realities of the international system is now a matter of record. In many cases, those adjustments have extended beyond actions to attract FDI inflows to include fundamental policy shifts such as imposing discipline on fiscal deficits, developing clear legal and commercial systems, streamlining bureaucracies, simplifying taxation systems, and liberalizing trade policies.

Although they are not yet as fully integrated into the world economic system, the former command economies that are seeking to marketize their systems are another driver of international integration. For the first time since the beginning of the century, they are opening their economies to the world economic system and enacting national policies designed to encourage the development of market forces.

INTEGRATING MARKETS VERSUS INTEGRATING POLICIES

It should be stressed that there are fundamental differences among these forces driving international economic integration. Some can be referred to as "organic"

---

[5] "The World Wins One," *Wall Street Journal,* December 15, 1993, p. A-16.

[6] Argentina, Brazil, the People's Republic of China, Egypt, Hong Kong, Mexico, Nigeria, Singapore, Taiwan, and Thailand. See UNCTAD, *World Investment Report.*

integration—the private cross-border flows of capital, goods and services, technology, and information driven in large part by MNEs. Others promote "inorganic" integration—the formal and politically oriented trade agreements forged among countries to reduce tariff and non-tariff barriers and harmonize trade-relevant domestic economic policies.

Organic integration is the result of strategies enacted by international private-sector actors to maximize the efficiency of their operations in the light of increasing global competition. As noted above, to an ever greater extent MNEs are distributing their operations internationally regardless of political institutions and frameworks to seek innovation or to achieve cost savings at various stages in the value-added chain. Although the pattern of this distribution of economic activity may be (and often is) influenced by regional economic blocs such as the EU and the NAFTA, it will be influenced only to the extent that such frameworks can be incorporated into prevailing global strategies. Increasingly, however, that activity is falling outside the regional blocs and generating higher levels of more global economic integration in the process.

These kinds of private-sector-driven economic dependencies must be differentiated from the "inorganic" or formalized efforts at economic cooperation undertaken among and between states. Such arrangements are based by definition on perceived mutual gains from economic cooperation, but generally they also represent a mixture of economic and political concern. The EU is clearly grounded in political and security objectives advanced in the period immediately after World War II; for its part, the NAFTA also has a strong political character. As a result, the inorganic integration fostered by regional blocs may not necessarily reflect the market fundamentals that are driving the interdependence now created by the private sector. Furthermore, the political nature of regional blocs suggests the possibility that they might be tempted to engage in aggressive trade policies that could generate a protectionist equivalent of an arms race. They could ultimately become the means by which organic integration is resisted.

Together, these organic and inorganic forces driving economies into heightened interdependence . . . progressively limit the area in which national economic policy making is feasible. It follows that governments are likely to resist the restrictions this kind of global convergence places on their policy prerogatives, especially when they are facing acute short-term economic challenges or when the adjustments forced by growing integration entail profound economic or social change. In short, integration of policies is lagging behind integration of markets.

CAPITALISMS IN COLLISION?

The salient question is how governments can protect their national economic interests in an increasingly integrated global economic and financial framework.

More and more, the preeminent economic powers in particular are finding the answer in drawing lines beyond which they will resort to defensive strategies grounded in parochial interests. The result is the development of political conditions that encourage the outbreak of economic nationalism.

The current political and economic environments in the United States, Europe, and Japan do not augur well for the level of cooperation necessary to avoid the neomercantilist confrontation that could flow from competing national policies. The overarching security concerns generated by the common threat from the erstwhile Soviet Union are a thing of the past, and immediate economic concerns now overshadow residual security ties. It is a time of fundamental redefinition of security, political, and economic relations—but the process of redefinition is proceeding in the absence of the international leadership and corresponding institutions necessary to meet the challenges of escalating economic rivalry.

The trauma that Washington experienced in fall 1993 in deciding on whether to adopt a free-trade agreement with Mexico—an economy only 4 percent of the U.S. gross national product and with a $5.5 billion trade deficit—amounted to a highly visible demonstration of U.S. attitudes about trade. Although of course the NAFTA was adopted, the emotional and sometimes vacuous debate served to highlight the extent to which economic nationalism threatens the historic role of the United States as leader of the global economic system. But apart from the NAFTA debate, there are other symptoms of this uncertainty. Regular calls in the U.S. Congress and elsewhere for unilateralist approaches to trade and foreign investment issues suggest that the concepts of "fair" rather than "free" trade and "reciprocal treatment" rather than "national treatment" in international capital flows are steadily gaining ground.

These warning signs are the result of the growing perception in the United States that new approaches are necessary to ensure fair access for trade and investment by U.S. firms. The perception is grounded in the view that what was recently referred to as "unilateralist national treatment"[7]—namely, the position on international investment that Washington has maintained for decades—is not being reciprocated by many of its investment partners. Of course, the recent domestic economic difficulties have thrown fuel on the fire.

In Europe, where the economic problems at present are even more pronounced, where the partial collapse of the ERM has generated profound doubts about the outlook for a single European currency, and where the tenuous ratification process of the Maastricht agreement has left leaders searching for ways to advance the integration agenda, attention is predominantly inward. The seriousness of the challenge was underlined in October 1993 when the president of the European Commission, Jacques Delors, warned that the then European

---

[7]See Office for Technology Assessment, *Multinationals and the National Interest: Playing by Different Rules* (Washington, D.C.: OTA, 1993).

Community was drifting toward becoming a free-trade zone that could break up in as little as 15 years. The EU is clearly in a period of intense consolidation and restructuring.

Japan is also engaged in political and economic soul-searching. The Hosokawa coalition has embarked on a program of political reform with potentially important longer-term implications for Tokyo's position in the international economic system. The outcome, however, is by no means assured. To sustain the reform process that it initiated immediately prior to the November 1993 meeting of the members of APEC (the Asia-Pacific Economic Cooperation), the government must continue to pass through the political thicket of its own eight-party coalition before contesting with the opposition Liberal Democratic Party to push through its initiatives. It must also do so against the backdrop of stagnating or declining growth, severe volatility in the financial markets, less than promising longer-term growth projections, and a highly resistant bureaucracy. [Prime Minister Hasokawa and his successor, Tsutomu Hata, both resigned prematurely amid continuing domestic turmoil in Japan.—eds.]

When considered together, these developments in the United States, Europe, and Japan have led some analysts to revisit arguments advanced in the 1970s about the ungovernability of democracies.[8] But there is also reason to question whether relations between the capitalist countries themselves will be governable. It is no exaggeration to suggest that the political agendas in all three major economic powers are predominantly inward-looking and focus primarily on reviving national economic growth and employment. All three are engaged in economic triage. Evidence of economic parochialism in the pursuit of those objectives appears to be growing on a day-by-day basis. In short, they could be on a course that suggests the potential for the rise of neomercantilism.

"STRATEGIC" TRADE AT ISSUE

In particular, there is the possibility of an escalation of industrial policies that would bring "national champions" and "strategic" industries—especially those in high technology—into sharper conflict. The magnitude of the threat has been set out by the Organization for Economic Cooperation and Development (OECD):

> Government support for economically strategic industries could become a major source of international dispute in the 1990s. The move over the last decade towards subsidies and other forms of state assistance for important technologically advanced sectors is set to accelerate. The proliferation of such policies, which affect a relatively narrow band of often identical sectors, could well develop into a keenly competitive

---

[8]See, for example, the articles on ungovernability by Michel Crozier, Samuel P. Huntington, and Joji Watanuki in *American Enterprise* 4 (November/December 1993), pp. 28–41. The three authors originally addressed the issue in a research effort in the early 1970s sponsored by the Trilateral Commission, chaired by Zbigniew Brzezinski, which culminated in the book entitled *The Crisis of Democracy* (New York, N.Y.: New York University Press, 1975).

"subsidy race," with harmful and far-reaching implications for the international system of trade, investment and technology.[9]

Despite the predominately unfavorable—or, at best, mixed—experience with allocating government resources in support of strategic industries, the temptation for governments is to engage in "picking winners" because of the political benefits they engender and the rationale under "strategic trade" theory that "technology trajectories" have a clustering effect of positive externalities extending throughout a wider part of the economy.[10] Some advocates of this theory suggest that such interventionist national policies can be advanced without undermining the pursuit of an open, integrated world economy.[11] Others point to the impending competition for "national futures."[12] That this new genre of thought on competition theory is predicated on results with pronounced sensitivities to changes in assumptions has not prevented it from assuming rising political currency.[13] Nor have the new political advocates of strategic trade been deterred by steadily mounting empirical evidence suggesting that protection and subsidization of industries can actually weaken their competitive position.

Whatever the underlying explanations, from the standpoint of competing national policies the advancement of strategic trade objectives can be achieved through a wide array of policy measures—including but not limited to trade-related policies such as "orderly marketing agreements," industrial and technology policies that provide subsidy, research and development support and other "cover," discriminatory procurement practices, and exemption of relevant sectors from antitrust law.

Assuming such strategic trade policies are adopted more fully by all three major world economic powers, it follows that competition between the respective "beggar-thy-neighbor" approaches could mount quickly because they are based on zero-sum thinking. As Michael Porter has noted,

> [i]f the rate of innovation slows because an "us versus them" attitude leads to subsidy, protection, and consolidation that blunts incentives, the consequences for advanced and less advanced nations alike are severe.[14]

Government intervention in a host of sectors has been a long-established practice in the EU. From ESPRIT to EUREKA, from Concorde to Airbus, from the TGV rail initiative in France to aircraft production in the Netherlands,

[9]OECD, *Strategic Industries in a Global Economy: Policy Issues for the 1990s* (Paris: OECD Publications, 1991).

[10]See Wayne Sandholtz et al., *The Highest Stakes: The Economic Foundations of the Next Security System* (New York, N.Y.: Oxford University Press, 1992).

[11]See Peter F. Cowhey and Jonathan D. Aronson, *Managing the World Economy: The Consequences of Corporate Alliances* (New York, N.Y.: Council on Foreign Relations Press, 1993).

[12]Sandholtz, *Highest Stakes,* p. 182.

[13]Michael E. Porter, *The Competitive Advantage of Nations* (New York, N.Y.: The Free Press, 1990), p. 812, n. 46.

[14]Porter, *The Competitive Advantage,* p. 682.

industrial policy is already a part of the European economic topography. In Japan, where the connection between the government and the private sector is also well established, decision makers have a less visible but nevertheless significant role in promoting industries through a variety of policies. And in the United States, where sector support has been less prevalent, momentum is mounting for a shift to a higher profile for the government in selected strategic industries. The shift is in response to the perception that "our competitors close off their markets to American firms while looking for ways to tap into our rich market . . . and we let them."[15] A senior Clinton administration official recently put it this way: "If no one else wants to play the game [our way], we'd look pretty silly [doing nothing] while they clean our clock."[16]

These divergent positions on industrial policy serve to highlight the more general differences between the capitalisms of the United States, the EU, and Japan. At issue is the differing relationship between government and business in each of the major economic powers and how those relations translate into national policies that have international repercussions. At one end of the spectrum is the consumer-oriented system of capitalism in the United States, where linkages between government and business have been loose and sometimes at odds as a result of the tradition of limiting the extent to which market concentrations occur; at the other end is Japan, which by fostering a producers-oriented form of capitalism is marked by substantially closer ties between the public and private sectors; and in the middle is the EU, where government intervention— traditionally based on social welfare criteria—is more pronounced than in the United States.

A MULTILATERAL RESPONSE?

A common approach by the three preeminent economies to defining acceptable limits to industrial policy is necessary if spiraling competition for marginal advantage is to be averted. The prospect for the negotiation of multilateral rules governing industrial policy is, however, remote at best. No international framework is in sight that could represent a release valve for the emerging pressures associated with these competing policies. The Group of Seven (G-7) falls substantially short of representing a forum through which a detailed agreement could be reached. Despite its past attention to the issue, the OECD is not likely to become the forum for the United States, the EU, and Japan to seek to reconcile their differences because of the large membership involved, although the OECD could take an active role in defining more specifically how the highly industrialized economies might proceed more generally in fashioning an

---

[15]Scott Gibson and Saul Goldstein, "The Plane Truth: How European Deals Are Killing U.S. Jobs," *Washington Post,* October 10, 1993.

[16]Hobart Rowen, "A Little Boost from Washington," *Washington Post,* October 7, 1993, p. A-23. Rowen was quoting President Bill Clinton's science adviser, John H. Gibbons.

approach to the issue. The experience of the Uruguay Round suggests that the next stage of negotiations under the [World] Trade Organization will be equally if not more arduous as differences in competition and investment policies come to the fore.

Furthermore, no single economic power seems predisposed to spearhead an effort to defuse the potential of conflicting industrial policies. In the meantime, "competition between governments [is progressively replacing] competition between companies as industrial activities become more and more global."[17]

It is an irony that at this critical historical juncture—when many of the former command economies are embarking on transitions to market systems and a number of developing countries have substantially liberalized their economies after decades of failed statist policies—the highly industrialized powers are in economic distress and embroiled in efforts to reinvigorate their domestic economies. If, as expected, the macroeconomic difficulties in the United States, Europe, and Japan persist or intensify, the attempt at integration into the world economy by significant parts of the second and third worlds—a historically unprecedented development that for decades has been the lodestar of the highly industrialized states themselves—will have been unassisted by the major global economic players and in some ways impeded by their paralysis.

Another fundamental irony of the immediate post-cold war period is that with the decline of the threat from Moscow, the emphasis is shifting from the clash between capitalism and communism to the differences between the "capitalisms" of the highly industrialized economies. The threat is that traditional political and security linkages will be recast as subordinate features of a competition for industrial advantage—or supremacy.

In the face of rising domestic economic problems and accelerating global economic integration, the manner in which the major economic powers manage their relations through the turn of the century and beyond will have an enormous impact on the world economy. A descent into a period of *realeconomik,* pitting government against government in a global competition for markets, would have a deleterious effect on the capacity of those same governments to meet future national and international economic challenges. Such a descent would also threaten the integrity of political and security relations in a highly uncertain period. To avoid this outcome, policymakers need to heed the advice of Akio Morita, who in an open letter to the G-7 heads of state in June 1993 argued:

> You, as political leaders, have the power to take the steps necessary to make the increasing de facto globalization of business the most creative, positive, and beneficial force it can be, rather than the source of new international conflict.[18]

---

[17][Candice Stevens, "Industrial Internationalisation and Trade Friction," *OECD Observer,* no. 173 (December 1991–January 1992)], p. 30.

[18]Akio Morita, "Toward a New World Economic Order," *Atlantic Monthly,* June 1993, pp. 88–89.

25

TRADE LESSONS FROM THE WORLD ECONOMY

Peter F. Drucker

Peter F. Drucker argues that in recent years profound changes have occurred in the structure and processes of the world economy that have important if often ignored policy implications. "What is needed," he argues, "is a deliberate and active—indeed, aggressive—policy that gives the demands, opportunities and dynamics of the external economy priority over domestic policy demands and problems." Drucker is Clarke Professor of Social Science and Management at the Claremont Graduate School. *Post-Capitalist Society* (1993) is among his many books.

ALL ECONOMICS IS INTERNATIONAL

In recent years the economies of all developed nations have been stagnant, yet the world economy has still expanded at a good clip. And it has been growing faster for the past 40 years than at any time since modern economies and the discipline of economics emerged in the eighteenth century. From this seeming paradox there are lessons to be learned, and they are quite different from what practically everyone asserts, whether they be free traders, managed traders or protectionists. Too many economists, politicians and segments of the public treat the external economy as something separate and safely ignored when they make policy for the domestic economy. Contrary lessons emerge from a proper understanding of the profound changes in four areas—the structure of the world

Reprinted by permission of *Foreign Affairs,* January/February 1994. Copyright 1994 by the Council on Foreign Relations, Inc.

economy, the changed meaning of trade and investment, the relationship between world and domestic economies, and the difference between workable and unworkable trade policies. . . .

WHAT TRADE DEFICIT?

For practically everyone international trade means merchandise trade, the import and export of manufactured goods, farm products and raw materials. But international trade is increasingly services trade—little reported and largely unnoticed. The United States has the largest share of the trade in services among developed countries, followed by the United Kingdom. Japan is at the bottom of the list. The services trade of all developed countries are growing fast, and it may equal or overtake their merchandise trade within ten years. Knowledge is the basis of most service exports and imports. As a result, most service trade is based on long term commitments, which makes it—excluding tourism—impervious to foreign exchange fluctuations and changes in labor costs.

Even merchandise trade is no longer confined to the sale and purchase of individual goods. Increasingly it is a relationship in which a transaction is only a shipment and an accounting entry. More and more merchandise trade is becoming "structural" and thereby impervious to short-term (and even long-term) changes in the traditional economic factors. Automobile production is a good example. Plant location decisions by manufacturers and suppliers are made at the time of product design. Until the model is redesigned, say in ten years, the plants and the countries specified in the original design are locked in. There will be change only in the event of a catastrophe such as a war or fire that destroys a plant. Or take the case of a Swiss pharmaceutical company's Irish plant. Rather than sell a product, it ships chemical intermediates to the company's finished-product plants in 19 countries on both sides of the Atlantic. For this the company charges a "transfer" price, which is a pure accounting convention having as much to do with taxes as with production costs. The traditional factors of production are also largely irrelevant to what might be called "institutional" trade, in which businesses, whether manufacturers or large retailers, buy machinery, equipment and supplies for new plants or stores, wherever located, from the suppliers of their existing plants, that is, those in their home countries.

Markets and knowledge are important in these types of structural and institutional trade decisions; labor costs, capital costs and foreign exchange rates are restraints rather than determinants. More important, neither type of trade is foreign trade, except in a legal sense, even when it is trade across national boundaries. For the individual business—the automobile manufacturer, the Swiss pharmaceutical company, the retailer—these are transactions within its own system.

Accounting for these developments, U.S. trading activity is more or less in balance. The trade deficit bewailed in the media and by public and private officials is in merchandise trade, caused primarily by an appalling waste of petroleum and a steady decline in the volume and prices of farm exports. The services trade account has a large surplus. According to little-read official figures, published every three months, the services trade surplus amounts to two thirds of the merchandise trade deficit. Moreover, government statisticians acknowledge gross underreporting of service exports, perhaps by as much as 50 percent.

THE COMING OF ALLIANCES

Traditional direct investment abroad to start or acquire businesses continues to grow. Since the 1980s direct investment in the United States by Europeans, Japanese, Canadians and Mexicans has grown explosively. But the action is rapidly shifting to alliances such as joint ventures, partnerships, knowledge agreements and outsourcing arrangements. In alliances, investment is secondary, if there is any at all. A recent example is the dividing up of design and production of an advanced microchip between Intel, a U.S.-based microchip *designer,* and Sharp, the Japanese electronics *manufacturer.* Both will share the final product. There are alliances between scores of university research labs and businesses—pharmaceutical, electronic, engineering, food processing and computer firms. There are alliances in which organizations outsource support activities; a number of American hospitals, and some in the United Kingdom and Japan, let independent suppliers do their maintenance, housekeeping, billing and data processing, and increasingly let them run the labs and the physical therapy and diagnostic centers. Computer makers now outsource the data processing for their own businesses to contractors. . . . They are also entering alliances with small, independent software designers. Commercial banks are entering alliances with producers and managers of mutual funds. Small and medium-sized colleges are entering alliances with one another to do paperwork jointly.

Some of these alliances involve substantial capital investment, as in the joint ventures of the 1960s and 1970s between Japanese and U.S. companies to produce American-designed goods in Japan for the Japanese market. But even then the basis of the alliance was not capital but complementary knowledge—technical and manufacturing knowledge supplied by the Americans, marketing knowledge and management supplied by the Japanese. More and more, investment of whatever size is symbolic—a minority share in each other's business is regarded as "bonding" between partners. In many alliances there is no financial relationship between the partners. (There is apparently none between Intel and Sharp.)

Alliances, formal and informal, are becoming the dominant form of economic integration in the world economy. Some major companies, such as Toshiba, the Japanese electronics giant, and Corning Glass, the world's leading maker of high-engineered glass, may each have more than 100 alliances all over the world. Integration in the Common Market is proceeding far more through alliances than through mergers and acquisitions, especially among the middle-sized companies that dominate most European economies. As with structural and institutional trade, businesses make little distinction between domestic and foreign partners in their alliances. An alliance creates a relationship in which it does not matter whether one partner speaks Japanese, another English and a third German or Finnish. And while alliances increasingly generate both trade and investment, they are based on neither. They pool knowledge.

THE VITAL LINK

For developed economies, the distinction between the domestic and international economy has ceased to be a reality, however much political, cultural or psychological strength remains in the idea. An unambiguous lesson of the last 40 years is that increased participation in the world economy has become the key to domestic economic growth and prosperity. Since 1950 there has been a close correlation between a country's domestic economic performance and its participation in the world economy. The two major countries whose economies have grown the fastest in the world economy, Japan and South Korea, are also the two countries whose domestic economies have grown the fastest. The same correlation applies to the two European countries that have done best in the world economy in the last 40 years, West Germany and Sweden. The countries that have retreated from the world economy (most notably the United Kingdom) have consistently done worse domestically. In the two major countries that have maintained their participation rate in the world economy within a fairly narrow range—the United States and France—the domestic economy has put in an average performance, neither doing exceptionally well nor suffering persistent malaise and crisis like the United Kingdom.

The same correlation holds true for major segments within a developed economy. In the United States, for instance, services have tremendously increased their world economy participation in the last 15 years; finance, higher education and information are examples. American agriculture, which has consistently shrunk in terms of world economy participation, has been in continual depression and crisis, masked only by ever-growing subsidies.

Conversely, there is little correlation between economic performance and policies to stimulate the domestic economy. The record shows that a government can harm its domestic economy by driving up inflation. But there is not the slightest evidence that any government policy to stimulate the economy has an impact, whether it be Keynesian, monetarist, supply-side or neoclassical. . . . The evidence not only suggests that government policies to stimulate the economy in the short term are ineffectual but also something far more surprising: they are largely irrelevant. Government, the evidence shows clearly, cannot control the economic weather.

The evidence of the past four decades does show convincingly that participation in the world economy has become the controlling factor in the domestic economic performance of developed countries. For example, a sharp increase in manufacturing and service exports kept the U.S. economy from slipping into deep recession in 1992, and unemployment rates for adult men and women never reached the highs of earlier post-World War II recessions. Similarly, Japan's sharply increased exports have kept its current recession from producing unemployment figures at European levels of eight to ten percent.

WHAT WORKS, WHAT DOES NOT

The evidence is crystal clear that both advocates of managed trade and conventional free traders are wrong in their prescriptions for economic growth. Japan's industrial policy of attempting to select and support "winning" business sectors is by now a well-known failure. Practically all the industries the Japanese Ministry of International Trade and Industry (MITI) picked—such as supercomputers and pharmaceuticals—have been at best also-rans. The Japanese businesses that succeeded, like Sony and the automobile companies, were opposed or ignored by MITI. Trying to pick winners requires a fortune-teller, and the world economy has become far too complex to be outguessed. Japan's economy benefited from a competency—an extraordinary ability to miniaturize products—that was virtually unknown to MITI. Pivotal economic events often take place long before we notice their occurrence. The available data simply do not report important developments such as the growth of the service trade, of structural and institutional trade, of alliances.

Still, the outstanding overall performance of Japan and other Asian countries cannot be explained away as merely a triumph of conventional free trade. Two common economic policies emerge from a recent World Bank study of eight East Asian "superstars"—Japan, South Korea, Hong Kong, Taiwan, Singapore, Malaysia, Thailand and Indonesia. First, they do not try to manage short-term fluctuations in their domestic economies; they do not try to control the economic weather. Moreover, not one of the East Asian economies took off until it had given up attempts to manage domestic short-term fluctuations. All eight countries focus instead on creating the right economic climate. They keep inflation low. They invest heavily in education and training. They reward savings and investment and penalize consumption. The eight started modernizing their economies at very different times, but once they got going, all have shown similar growth in both their domestic and international economies. Together they now account for 21 percent of the world's manufactured goods exports, versus nine percent 30 years ago. Five percent of their populations live below the poverty line, compared with about 40 percent in 1960, and four of them—Japan, Hong Kong, Taiwan and Singapore—rank among the world's richest countries. Yet the eight are totally different in their culture, history, political systems and tax policies. They range from laissez-faire Hong Kong to interventionist Singapore to statist Indonesia.

The second major finding of the World Bank study is that these eight countries pursue policies to enhance the competitiveness of their industries in the world economy with only secondary attention to domestic effect. These countries then foster and promote their proven successes in the world economy. Though MITI neither anticipated nor much encouraged Japan's world market successes, the whole Japanese system is geared to running with them. Japan offers its exporters substantial tax benefits and credits, which remain scarce and expensive for domestic businesses, and it deliberately keeps prices and profits high in a protected domestic market in order to generate cash for overseas investment and market penetration.

The same lessons were being taught until recently by the two countries in the West that showed similar growth: West Germany and Sweden. These countries, too, have very different domestic policies. But both created and maintained an economic growth climate, and through the same measures: control of inflation, high investment in education and training, a high savings rate obtained by high taxes on consumption and fairly low taxes on savings and investment. Both also gave priority to the world economy in governmental and business decisions. The moment they forgot this—when the trade unions a few years back began to subordinate Germany's competitive standing to their wage demands, and the Swedes subordinated their industries' competitive standing to ever-larger welfare spending—their domestic economies went into stagnation.

An additional lesson of the world economy is that investment abroad creates jobs at home. In both the 1960s and the 1980s, expanded U.S. business investments overseas spurred rapid domestic job creation. The same correlation held for Japan and Sweden, both of which invested heavily in overseas plants to produce goods for their home markets. In manufacturing—and in many services, such as retailing—investment per worker in the machinery, tools and equipment of a new facility is three to five times annual production. Most of this productive equipment comes from institutional trade (that is, from the home country of the investor), and most of it is produced by high-wage labor. The initial employment generated to get the new facility into production is substantially larger than the annual output and employment during its first few years of operation.

The last 40 years also teach that protection does not protect. In fact, the evidence shows quite clearly that protection hastens decline. Less-protected U.S. farm products—soybeans, fruit, beef and poultry—have fared a good deal better on world markets than have the more subsidized traditional crops, such as corn, wheat and cotton. Equally persuasive evidence suggests that the American automobile industry's share of its domestic market went into a precipitous decline as soon as the U.S. government forced the Japanese into "voluntary" export restraints. That protection breeds complacency, inefficiency and cartels has been known since before Adam Smith. The counterargument has always been that it protects jobs, but the evidence of the last 40 years strongly suggests that it does not even do that.

FREE TRADE IS NOT ENOUGH

The world economy has become too important for a country not to have a world-economy policy. Managed trade is a delusion of grandeur. Outright protectionism can only do harm, but simply trying to thwart protectionism is not enough. What is needed is a deliberate and active—indeed, aggressive—policy that gives the demands, opportunities and dynamics of the external economy priority over domestic policy demands and problems. For the United States and a number of other countries, it means abandoning ways of thinking that have dominated American economics perhaps since 1933, and certainly since 1945. We still see the demands and opportunities of the world economy as externalities. We usually do not ask whether domestic decisions will hurt American competitiveness, participation and standing in the world economy. The reverse must become the rule: will a proposed domestic move advance American competitiveness and participation in the world economy? The answer to this question determines what are the right domestic economic policy and business decisions. The lessons of the last 40 years teach us that integration is the only basis for an international trade policy that can work, the only way to rapidly revive a domestic economy in turbulence and chronic recession.

26

NO MORE NICs

Robin Broad and John Cavanagh

For many years the export-led path to economic development pursued with great success by the newly industrializing countries (NICs) has been promoted as a model for other developing nations. Robin Broad and John Cavanagh argue the model is of doubtful relevance due to structural changes in the global political economy and the rise of protectionist sentiments in industrial countries. Broad is a professor at the School of International Service at The American University. John Cavanagh is a fellow at the Institute for Policy Studies and the Transnational Institute. Together they have published *Plundering Paradise: The Struggle for the Environment in the Philippines* (1993).

For more than a decade the most common policy advice to developing countries the world over has been a simple formula: Copy the export-oriented path of the newly industrializing countries, the celebrated NICs. These economies—Brazil, Hong Kong, Mexico, Singapore, South Korea, and Taiwan—burst onto world manufactures markets in the late 1960s and the 1970s. By 1978 these six economies plus India accounted for fully 70 per cent of the developing world's manufactured exports. Their growth rates for gross national product (GNP) and exports were unequaled.

From *Foreign Policy 72* (Fall 1988). Copyright 1988 by the Carnegie Endowment for International Peace. Used by permission of *Foreign Policy.* Footnotes have been deleted.

No wonder the call was sounded for others to follow. Dozens have tried. But with the possible exceptions of Malaysia and Thailand, no country has come close. Why not? The answer lies in far-reaching changes in the global economy—from synthetic substitutes for commodity exports to unsustainable levels of external debt—that have created a glut economy offering little room for new entrants.

Despite these shifts the foremost international development institutions, the World Bank and the International Monetary Fund (IMF), continue to promote the NIC path as the way for heavily indebted developing countries to escape the debt crisis. Yet in 1988, 8 years into a period of reduced growth in world markets, the bankruptcy of this approach should be all too apparent. By the end of the 1970s the World Bank had singled out the four Asian NICs as models to be studied by a second rung of developing countries. Having mastered the production of textiles, clothing, shoes, simple consumer electronics, and other light-manufactured wares, the four NICs were moving into more sophisticated products like automobiles and videocassette recorders. Therefore, the Bank argued, as the NICs' level of industrial development advanced, they would abandon the more basic industries to other countries. . . .

But the World Bank did more than offer the intellectual underpinnings for this development theory. In the late 1970s it positioned itself as a central actor in pushing the would-be NICs up the ladder to the NIC rung. In May 1979 then World Bank President Robert McNamara, in an address to a United Nations Conference on Trade and Development (UNCTAD) meeting in Manila, called for developing countries to "upgrade their export structure to take advantage of the export markets being vacated by more advanced developing countries." McNamara added that the Bank would move to the forefront of this new "program of action." To do so, however, the Bank needed to move beyond its more traditional microlevel project lending with a new instrument that would maximize its leverage with developing countries. Loans for hydroelectric dams, highways, and urban renewal, among other projects, had made the Bank the key international development player; but they did not confer on the Bank adequate leverage for the proposed global restructuring.

Consequently, the Bank turned to a new set of policy prescriptions, dubbed "structural adjustment," the key ingredient of which was structural adjustment loans (SALs). These large balance-of-payments loans—targeted toward broad sectors and heavily conditioned on a recipient's economic reforms—sought to hasten the new international division of labor whereby the would-be NICs would mimic the established NICs' light-manufactures export successes. The SALs were "the World Bank's best weapon yet," as a close aide of McNamara said in 1981.

SALs carried a broad set of policy prescriptions that focused on trade-related economic sectors; they were designed to enhance efficiency and export orientation. . . .

Who are these would-be NICs that the World Bank and the IMF hoped to push up the development ladder? According to various classification systems, including those of the World Bank, this group comprises up to 30 second-tier less developed countries (LDCs) across Africa, Asia, and Latin America.

These would-be NICs largely received the big loans and amplified attention from the Bank during the late 1970s and early 1980s. Of the 9 LDCs rewarded with a structural adjustment loan of more than $50 million as of mid-1982, 7 were would-be NICs and 1 was a NIC. Moreover, the IMF's attention largely complemented the Bank's. Of the 20 LDCs that by mid-1982 had received one of the IMF's extended fund facilities—highly conditioned loans with a 10-year repayment period—of more than $50 million, 12 fell into the would-be NICs grouping and 2 were NICs.

More insight into the Bank's role in the would-be NICs can be gained by looking at one illuminating case, the Philippines. By the end of Ferdinand Marcos's administration in February 1986, the Philippines had borrowed more than $4.5 billion from the World Bank in more than 100 project and program loans. The country was, in the words of Gregorio Licaros, one of Marcos's Central Bank governors, the "guinea pig" for structural adjustment. Indeed, one of the Bank's first SALs was a $200 million loan geared specifically toward restructuring the Philippine industrial sector. . . .

After a record Philippine balance-of-payments deficit of $570 million in 1979, the Bank put together the 1980 SAL package, which was attached not to a specific project but to a group of policies stipulating an export-oriented course for Philippine industry. Former high-ranking Philippine officials, including both proponents and opponents of the reforms, agree that the negotiations marked a critical juncture in the Philippine development path. Tariffs were slashed. Protective import restrictions were lifted. The exchange rate began a steady and steep devaluation, while export- and investment-promotion policies diverted resources from domestically oriented output. New free-trade tax havens, using generous incentives for transnational corporations (TNCs) to exploit low-cost Filipino labor, were established across the archipelago. Individual light-manufacturing industries, such as textiles, cement, food processing, furniture, and footwear, were slated for restructuring according to World Bank specifications.

During this period, similar policies were pushed in other would-be NICs. World Bank SALs to the Ivory Coast, Kenya, Pakistan, Senegal, and Turkey— like the Philippine SAL—all concentrated on improving export incentives and performance. In Thailand, where a Central Bank official vowed in mid-1979 that the World Bank's policies would "never be listened to or followed by top people here," the government implemented economic policy changes almost identical to those of the Philippines a few years and a SAL later. In other cases, notably Chile and Indonesia, would-be NICs followed the Bank's blueprint for development without a formal SAL.

NIC RIVALRY

In effect the World Bank was helping to create a group of countries that would compete against each other to become NICs. The result was two vicious battles—one to offer cheaper, more docile labor forces and more attractive financial incentives to lure TNC assembly lines away from the other countries, and the other to win scarce export markets.

This competition soon became clear to each would-be NIC. As a deputy governor to the Philippine Central Bank remarked in a 1980 interview: "We've got to always be careful now, always watching, on the lookout for other [developing] nations' next moves. . . . And then we've got to make sure we meet their offer and better it." Sri Lanka's advertisement in the October 16, 1981, issue of the *Far Eastern Economic Review* said it well: "Sri Lanka challenges you to match the advantages of its Free Trade Zone, against those being offered elsewhere. . . . Sri Lanka has the lowest labor rates in Asia." Variations on that appeal were issued by one would-be NIC after another, putting TNCs in a choice position from which to bargain the most lucrative investment or subcontracting deals.

The competition encouraged labor repression and exploitation. One Manila-based TNC executive explained in a 1981 interview: "We tell the [Philippine] government: you've got to clamp down [on labor]. . . . Or we threaten to move elsewhere. And we'll do just that. There's Sri Lanka [and] now China too."

Most of the Bank's public documents sought to play down the problems associated with rivalry among the would-be NICs. But the Bank was not unaware of the potential zero-sum game. In a January 1979 working paper assessing the LDCs' manufacturing export potential, two leading Bank economists, Hollis Chenery and Donald Keesing, forecast that "the increasing number of successful competitors may make it increasingly difficult for newcomers to get established" and that the success of a "few" could leave "too little" opportunity for the rest. . . .

Yet who had set in motion this chain of competition? An October 1979 World Bank report had counseled the Philippines to take advantage of the fact that its wages had "declined significantly relative to those in competing . . . countries," notably Hong Kong and South Korea. Almost simultaneously, as reported in the *Southeast Asia Chronicle* in December 1981, the Bank helped steer Indonesia onto a parallel course, advising that "incentives for firms to locate there rather than in some other Southeast Asian country . . . must be provided." Meanwhile, Sri Lanka received a $20 million World Bank loan to establish a new export platform for apparel subcontracting, and the Bank pushed the People's Republic of China (PRC), Thailand, and some of the Caribbean Basin countries into the light-manufactures arena as well.

The competition among would-be NICs was further exacerbated by the exporters of an earlier era, the Asian NICs of Hong Kong, Singapore, South Korea, and Taiwan. World Bank theory to the contrary, these countries were not abandoning textiles, apparel, and electronics assembly as they moved into higher stages of industrialization. Indeed, since the 1960s the Asian NICs had been spreading throughout the entire range of industry—from light to heavy, from unsophisticated to sophisticated—leaving little space for would-be NICs. . . .

Another factor also was inhibiting the would-be NICs' economic ascension—new technologies. The more than a decade that separated the NICs' debut from that of the would-be NICs witnessed technological advances in several sectors that changed the very definition of Third World industrialization.

By the late 1970s technological innovations, led by the microprocessor revolution, made the global fragmentation of production highly profitable and desirable. Whereas the original NICs had received complete industrial processes such as shipbuilding and machinery, the would-be NICs won marginal segments of scattered assembly lines for semiconductors and consumer electronics, textiles, and apparel. In Sri Lanka, for example, workers in export-processing zones used basic sewing machines to stitch together garments from imported fabric. In the Philippines, female workers in 1980 were performing only 1 of the 10 major operations of electronic production, attaching hairlike gold wires to silicon chips.

As a result, these new global assembly lines left gaping disparities between the gross value of the would-be NICs' industrial export earnings and the actual value added to the product in the developing country. Consider again the Philippine case. When proclaiming the nontraditional-export strategy's supposed triumphs, the Philippine government naturally focused on . . . the gross value of exports. Yet when stripped of import components' costs, the "value added" by the domestic side of production was but a fraction of the export earnings.

With the Philippines importing cartons for its banana exports, cans for some food exports, and a wide assortment of machinery and component parts for its limited apparel and electronic assembly lines, value added in most Philippine industries was quite low. . . . For every dollar of nontraditional-export earnings, only 25 cents stayed in the Philippines; the rest was siphoned off by import payments. Low value added was a fact of life in the Philippines' part in the new international division of labor.

According to one of the best analyses of electronics subcontracting, the longterm outlook for increasing the amount of value added in developing countries in the industry was bleak. As the December 1981 United Nations Industrial Development Organization report, *Restructuring World Industry in a Period of Crisis,* detailed, the per cent of value added attributable to new LDC microprocessor production lines rose until 1973. By 1977, however, value added in the newest LDC factories already had begun to fall. This downward turn came even as the gross value of semiconductors re-exported to the United States soared tenfold from 1970 to 1978. Of the seven LDCs studied, the Philippines was the last to start silicon chip assembly. Entering on the downswing of the curve, value added in its factories was the lowest of all.

Since 1977 a growing share of the value was being held in the electronics companies' home countries. The UN report emphasized that, "as the complexity of circuitry increases, more value added is produced in the early wafer-fabrication stage, i.e., in the United States, in Japan, or in some locations in Western Europe. Furthermore, the more complex circuits require much more complex, computerized final testing, which again is usually done in OECD [Organization for Economic Cooperation and Development] locations, particularly in the United States and Japan."

If the production side of the would-be NIC experience offered less than what was advertised, the marketing side was even grimmer. For light-manufactured exports to be the engine of growth for the would-be NICs, world trade—that is, global demand for these products—had to grow each year. There was no way to escape this logic in the aggregate.

But in the late 1970s and early 1980s, at precisely the time when would-be NICs were induced to embark on a nontraditional-export path, these necessary conditions were decidedly absent. Over the decade from 1963 to 1973 the volume of world exports rose at a rapid average annual rate of 8.5 per cent. Beginning in 1973, however, an economic deceleration slowed the average annual expansion to 4 per cent. By 1980 exports were crawling ahead at only 1 per cent per year, and in 1981 they showed no growth. Moreover, 1981 had the dubious distinction of being the first year since 1958 to experience an actual decrease in world trade in current dollar terms, a shrinkage of 1 per cent.

Behind these global trade statistics lurked the domestic stagnation of the industrialized economies. According to IMF figures, from 1976 to 1979 the real GNP of industrialized countries grew at a tolerable average yearly rate of 4 per cent. By 1980, OECD growth was limping ahead at only 1.25 per cent; the next year it increased again by only 1.25 per cent. These 2 years presaged a decade of vastly reduced growth. From 1981 to 1985 world output slowed to an average of 2.7 per cent per year and trade to 2.8 per cent. These aggregate statistics become even more dismal if Eastern Europe and the PRC are excluded: Output over the first half of the 1980s grew at an average annual rate of only 1.4 per cent in developing countries and 2.3 per cent in developed countries.

As more countries battled for the same tepid export markets, prices plunged. Between 1981 and 1985, world prices of food commodities fell at an average annual rate of 15 per cent; agricultural raw materials dropped at an average annual rate of 7 per cent; and minerals and metals fell 6 per cent. The year 1986 proved even dimmer, when a 30 per cent decline in the developing countries' terms of trade (the ratio of prices of developing-country exports to prices of their imports) translated into a staggering $94 billion to the developed world.

Another pitfall facing the LDCs' export-oriented industrialization was the panoply of quantitative restrictions that had spread to cover fully one-half of global trade. Despite official encomiums to "free trade," the OECD countries increasingly were barricading themselves behind what even President Ronald

Reagan's Council of Economic Advisers admitted were "neomercantile" policies.

These defensive machinations to moderate the recessionary bite at home were baptized the "new protectionism"—a proliferation of American, European Economic Community, and Japanese trade barriers, notably quotas on LDC-manufactured exports. "New" referred to the dazzling array of nontariff barriers not regulated by the General Agreement on Tariffs and Trade. Voluntary export restraints and orderly marketing arrangements flourished. As the World Bank and the IMF encouraged free-trade policies on LDCs, the major voting blocs within those institutions retreated from any semblance of free trade at home. The retreat of free trade became inextricably meshed with the recession: As OECD growth slackened, quotas were tightened. The more successful a particular LDC export category was, the more restrictive the quota became.

By the calculations of the World Bank's own economists in 1979, the most dangerous of the new protectionist barriers was centered in the apparel, textile, and footwear sectors. Yet it was precisely these sectors—along with furniture, wood products, electronics, and other light-manufactured exports—that the Bank had pinpointed as the engine of growth for the would-be NICs. The restrictive allotments of the Multi-Fiber Arrangement made textiles and apparel perhaps the most heavily controlled sectors in international trade. As a result, the LDCs' share of textile and apparel exports began to shrink in the early 1980s.

Did the Bank adequately address the impact of slow global economic growth and rising protectionism on its policy directives? As early as 1974 the Bank understood certain pitfalls that the 1970s and 1980s might hold for export-oriented industrialization. That year McNamara, in an address to the Board of Governors, noted: "The adverse effect on the developing countries of . . . a reduction in economic growth in their major markets would be great. There is a strong—almost one-to-one—relationship between changes in the growth of OECD countries and that of oil importing nations." . . . And in his May 1979 address to the UNCTAD conference in Manila, McNamara noted that the World Bank had perceived the onset of the new protectionism as early as 1976.

Yet in the late 1970s and early 1980s Bank officials who were planning Third World development strategies continually made assumptions that ignored slow growth and rising protectionism. Their model, grounded in theories of free trade and comparative advantage, posited the absence of such conditions. They opted instead for what was termed "one set of reasonable assumptions" without explaining their legitimacy. The set of "reasonable" assumptions about trade and protectionism that underpinned the Bank's structural adjustment reports and advice to would-be NICs was some permutation of the following: Industrial countries were to grow 4 per cent annually in the 1980s; "worldwide economic recovery" stood on the horizon; and "no major set-backs" would occur in major markets. . . .

The potential effects of this unsubstantiated optimism about the . . . would-be NICs were never seriously considered by Bank officials. The development prescriptions of Bank officials were transformed into a kind of dogma: "The more hostile the external environment, the more urgent" the need for restructuring, an August 1980 *Report and Recommendation* urged. In one instance, a Bank director took the floor at the executive board's final meeting on the Philippine SAL to question the management's scenario of Philippine "dynamic" export-led growth in light of "an adverse environment [including] lower than projected growth rates in industrial countries and increased protectionism." The board chairman's response epitomized the Bank's unquestioning attitude: "If the environment turned out to be more adverse than projected, then the ultimate benefits under the adjustment program would be reduced, but the nature of the adjustment needed would not be changed." But such a response was no more than conjecture. No hard evidence and no computer runs were offered to answer what should have been a basic question: If world trade did not grow, and if key markets became increasingly protected, would export-oriented industrialization be the optimal route to growth? . . .

It was becoming increasingly clear that the World Bank had no vision of development in a world economy of curtailed growth. To a large extent Bank officials had equated growth with development. To them, development did not primarily mean providing adequate food, clean water, clothing, and housing—in short, offering a standard of living consistent with human dignity. Those had become secondary concerns to be met through growth. In the Bank's view, no growth meant no development and therefore could not be considered seriously. . . .

In recent public Bank documents, slow growth in the world economy is still viewed as a short-term or cyclical aberration that does not undermine the basic soundness of the Bank's structural adjustment advice. Indeed, as late as its 1987 *World Development Report,* the Bank was still stressing that the world economy was continuing to "expand," albeit at a "modest and uneven" rate. That outlook enabled the Bank to continue unabashedly to counsel "the outward-oriented trade policies which have proved so successful for the NICs in recent years."

A NEW WORLD ECONOMY

World Bank forecasts notwithstanding, global stagnation is likely to prove harder to shake than most would like to believe. Aside from protectionism pressures, a series of corporate developments has stunted demand globally, leaving increasing numbers of people at the margins of market activity. Prominent among these developments are the commercial banks' handling of the Third World debt crisis, corporate substitution for Third World raw materials, and labor-saving technological innovations in the developed world.

The debt crisis arose inevitably from the export-oriented development strategies, which depended on heavy borrowing for infrastructure and in many countries fed corruption and capital flight. In the early 1980s, as oil prices and interest rates rose and primary commodity prices fell, country after country announced its inability to service debts owed to banks in the developed world. In rapid succession the creditor banks sent these countries through IMF austerity programs, which prescribed a kind of shock treatment to bring countries' balance of payments out of deficit. Wage freezes, currency devaluations, and government spending cuts reduced imports into the Third World; indeed, many countries wiped out trade and national budget deficits within a few years. But lowered wages and imports also dampened global economic growth.

Technological breakthroughs in substitutes for Third World raw materials also hurt growth performance in the developing world. A single anecdote typifies the impact of longer-term corporate development on commodity markets. Until 1981 the largest consumer of the world's sugar was Coca-Cola. That year, in a move rapidly emulated by other soft drink giants, Coca-Cola began to shift its sweetener from sugar to corn syrup. Western consumers might not have viewed the change as significant to them, but it displaced millions of Third World sugar workers for a product produced within industrial countries.

Advances in plastics, synthetic fibers, food chemistry, and biotechnology are bringing similar far-reaching changes to other raw material and commodity markets. Cumulatively these substitutions have pushed tens of millions of Third World workers into the margins of the marketplace, further curbing global demand.

Likewise, new corporate technologies are transforming developed-country economies. The computer revolution, the major technological breakthrough of the last two decades, is strikingly dissimilar from earlier technological breakthroughs. The advent of electricity and the automobile, for example, generated millions of jobs in related industries and sparked economic booms in the leading countries. The microprocessor revolution has also created millions of jobs. However, applications of microprocessors have spread through almost every manufacturing and service sector in uses that are labor saving. Bank tellers, supermarket check-out clerks, assembly-line workers, and others are all joining the ranks of the unemployed. This phenomenon is reflected in Western Europe, where for 17 straight years the unemployment rate has risen.

The result of these three changes is that all over the world industry is turning out more than consumers can buy. The new global glut economy coexists with billions of people with enormous needs and wants but with little ability to buy.

As world economic growth has slowed, so have the Third World activities of its central private institutions: TNCs and banks. Much of the growth of the 1960s and 1970s was based on a rapid expansion of production around the world by subsidiaries of such TNCs as Ford, John Deere, and Texas Instruments. Western banks followed to provide financing. Then, after 1973, they became major economic actors in the developing world in their own right as recyclers of billions of petrodollars.

This is no longer the case. Banks and corporations go where there is growth and hence profit. Since the early 1980s the Third World basically has stopped growing; many countries have even slipped backward. Consequently, U.S. banks have returned home for new short-term rewards—consumer credit, corporate mergers, and the get-rich-quick gimmicks of financial speculation.

Again, the statistics are stark. In 1983 international bank lending to developing countries, excluding offshore bank centers, totaled $35 billion. By 1985 a mere $3 billion in new lending had trickled in.

Unfortunately, the drop-off in bank and corporate involvement and the factors that spelled a longer-term slowdown did not seem to influence the policy advice of the World Bank and the IMF. . . .

By 1985, however, austerity had bred considerable resistance across the Third World. The United States responded in October 1985 with a plan proposed by Treasury Secretary James Baker. Although it seized the political initiative from the Latin American debtors, the Baker plan offered little that was new. . . .

Yet the changing world economy has created a desperate need to rethink the kinds of adjustments that will produce growth and development. At the very least, the adjustment strategies must be built on realistic assumptions. The NICs were the product of a radically different world economy. That they cannot be replicated . . . is an indication of how much that world economy has changed.

Rather than increasing their reliance on a hostile world environment, developing countries should try to reduce this dependence and to diversify trading partners and products. This approach implies a careful restructuring of trade and financial linkages to conform with a development logic that is driven by internal economic forces.

If economies can no longer be pulled along primarily by external growth, stronger internal buying power must be generated. The great challenge is to transform crushing social needs into effective demand and then to meet that demand by turning first to domestically produced goods and services, next to the region, and only after that to the wider world market. In most developing countries this development framework implies vast internal adjustment quite different from the World Bank's brand of structural adjustment. Most of the Third World's people cannot afford to purchase many goods and services. Wages are locked into rock-bottom subsistence rates; wealth and income are heavily skewed toward a relatively small, wealthy elite. As a result, spreading income more evenly requires, for a start, extensive land reform, progressive taxation policies, and guarantees of worker rights.

To offer more specifics on internal demand-driven development strategies is risky. Vastly different resource bases and social strata among countries suggest that a country-specific approach is essential. Indeed, the sin of universality in development strategies was perhaps the central weakness of IMF and World Bank adjustment programs. Further, the successful implementation of any development strategy depends on its acceptance by entrenched interests in that country. However desirable comprehensive agrarian reform may be in the Philippines, for example, a powerful landowning group has substantial influence in the government and is likely to block serious reform efforts.

These caveats noted, a few general principles for development in a hostile world economy can be sketched out. Most would-be NICs remain predominantly agricultural societies; hence the starting point of internal demand-led development must be in farming. Two undertakings are central to increasing buying power in the countryside: redistributing wealth and raising productivity.

Agrarian reform remains the major means of redistributing wealth and income and thereby increasing the effective purchasing power of the rural population. The people in Third World rural areas are largely either poor tenants or agricultural workers who earn only subsistence wages. They have meager resources to consume in the marketplace. Only through agrarian reform can this population begin to produce a surplus that can be translated into consumption. In economic terms, small farmers have a higher "marginal propensity" to consume than larger ones, and much of their consumption could be satisfied by locally produced products.

Raising productivity depends in large part on upgrading infrastructure—from irrigation and roads to credit institutions and marketing channels. . . .

From this starting point, industrialization based on maximizing industrial linkages with agriculture makes great sense. In particular, three strands of industry could be encouraged:

Agricultural inputs. An agricultural sector with rising productivity will need locally produced fertilizer, pesticides, water pumps, and a wide range of tools, from plows to tractors.

Processing farm products. From cocoa and coffee to sugar and cotton, increased domestic processing offers more foodstuffs for local consumption and increases the value added of exports.

Consumer goods. As purchasing power grows in the countryside, so does the market for locally produced textiles, clothing, shoes, bicycles, refrigerators, and other consumer goods. . . .

The cycle of agriculture-linked industrialization does not stop there. As industry grows, the increased buying power of industrial workers provides an expanding market for farm goods from rural areas. Agriculture and industry would grow in tandem. It is worth pointing out that, popular myths notwithstanding, South Korea pursued this basic strategy in its earliest phase of industrialization. . . .

In a highly interdependent world, such demand-centered development does not and cannot imply autarky. What cannot be produced locally is produced nationally. What cannot be produced nationally is purchased from regional part-ners—which suggests the importance of revitalizing regional integration institu-tions. Only for those products for which regional producers cannot satisfy demand is trade necessary with countries on the other side of the globe. Domes-tic needs should shape trade patterns rather than vice versa. . . .

Beyond domestic market policies in agriculture and industry, development strategies should seek to curtail the wasteful economic activities that are ram-pant in some countries. These range from large, unproductive landholdings and capital flight to production and export monopolies and cronyism. Rooting out these practices is a monumental political task, threatening as it does entrenched groups of speculators, moneylenders, and landlords and bloated militaries. Development strategies also must pay closer attention to the pressing need to maintain fragile natural resource bases around the world. The disappearance of rain forests, plant and animal species, clean rivers, and clean air has become the dominant trend in too many countries.

. . . Most observers continue to view the Asian NICs as role models. And they offer glowing imagery in support of their view: Asian NICs have "already taken off," and the rest of the noncommunist Southeast Asian countries are "on the runway revving" up to follow, as former Japanese Foreign Minister Saburo Okita has described it.

The would-be NICs have fallen for such prophecies for nearly a decade. Now is the time to demand not imagery but a realistic assessment of options. The debate on adjustment and development should be reopened; strategies that proclaim that the only option is greater dependence on an increasingly hostile and turbulent world economy need to be challenged. It is time to ask whether any more developing countries can really hope to become the South Korea . . . or the Hong Kong of the . . . 1990s.

27

THE REGIONAL WAY TO GLOBAL ORDER

Robert D. Hormats

Robert D. Hormats makes the (unusual) case that the emergence of a regionalized international trade system is a positive, not negative, development. Among other advantages, regionalism provides a means to incorporate many of the now developing nations into the global political economy, thus erasing the divide between North and South. Hormats is a vice chairman of Goldman Sachs International in New York. He served previously as an assistant secretary of state for Economic and Business Affairs in the U.S. Department of State and is author of *American Albatross: The Foreign Debt Dilemma* (1988).

COPING WITH NEW COMPETITORS

The answers to two great questions will soon set the direction of the world economy. One: Will the industrialized democracies cooperate to sustain an open, market-oriented world trade and financial order? To do so, they must rise above the different ways they practice capitalism and mounting domestic pressures for economic nationalism. Two: Can these countries integrate into such an order those countries that are turning from state controls toward market capitalism?

The second challenge, on which this article focuses, requires vision, will and a comprehensive strategy. Established powers normally have difficulty coping with new competitors: France with Britain in the early nineteenth century,

Reprinted with permission of *Foreign Affairs,* March/April 1994. Copyright 1994 by the Council on Foreign Relations, Inc.

Britain with America later, and most recently the United States with Japan. Now, as a group, the industrialized democracies must integrate into the world economy not one but many developing countries, some with enormous economic potential. This process is producing acute concerns among established powers. Will jobs be lost, wages lowered, investment capital diverted? Can workplace and environmental standards be maintained, much less improved?

Despite the frictions of getting from here to there, expanding the participation of these nations in the world economy will greatly enhance the economic growth of developed democracies. Such was the case for the United States in the decades after World War II when farsighted assistance helped revive and reintegrate Japan and West Germany into the world economy. In the next few decades, phasing into a global economic order the newly market-oriented countries of Asia, Latin America and formerly communist Europe would harness the enormous productive capacity and market potential of some three billion people. The result would be an unprecedented transformation and growth of the global economy and a powerful antidote to divisiveness and instability.

But unlike the post-World War II years, no encompassing system like Bretton Woods exists, and no dominating power like the United States was at the time can impose a new order on the world economy. Today's driving forces are private trade and investment flows. They are vital to growth, technological progress and job creation. These flows are creating inexorable momentum toward the further integration of economies within and across regions. How rapidly that integration proceeds, on what terms and in which parts of the world will shape the new global economic order. The challenge for governments is to reinforce these market trends to harvest long-term benefits while resisting pressures to protect against the short-term adjustments needed for future growth.

The arduously wrought compromises that proved necessary to complete GATT's Uruguay Round and the North American Free Trade Agreement (NAFTA) amply illustrate that resistance to freer trade has increased. Within developed countries, sentiment is growing that inherent unfairness results from trading with poorer countries where low labor costs are assumed to be the primary source of comparative advantage. And many Americans and Europeans share the apprehension that rising imports from Asia eliminate domestic jobs.

Thus political tolerance would be in short supply for another global trade negotiation soon after the seven-year Uruguay Round. Just fixing the terms for a new round would be time-consuming, and obtaining new fast-track legislation from the U.S. Congress would be problematic. A successor round of global negotiations involving GATT's more than 100 members will not likely occur until the next century, if ever. In the meantime, many of the issues the Uruguay Round left unresolved—environmental regulations, investment rules, intellectual property protection and access for suppliers of services—lend themselves better to bilateral and regional settlements, where direct reciprocity between countries is a more compelling motivator and lowest common denominator resolutions are more avoidable.

TWO TRACKS TO LIBERALIZATION

The choice need not be between a seamless free trade world, desirable as that may be in the long term, and antagonistic regional blocs. A greater dispersal of economic power will mark the post-Cold War order. Different layers and categories of trade relationships—multilateral, regional, subregional and bilateral—will coexist. This web of relationships can incorporate newly market-oriented countries into the global system in different ways and on different schedules. The new order is likely to evolve on two broad tracks.

One track will emphasize regional negotiations between newly market-oriented economies as well as between them and industrialized market economies. The greatest progress in opening foreign markets is likely to occur through these regional relationships before the turn of the century. Commercial opportunities will flow from initiatives and expansion of the European Union (EU), Asia-Pacific Economic Cooperation (APEC), the Association of South East Asian Nations (ASEAN), NAFTA and other western hemisphere free-trade arrangements. Additional opportunities will flow from the evolution of natural, subregional trading areas like those comprising China's coastal provinces and their offshore neighbors.

The other track will consist of efforts—short of a global negotiating round—to strengthen international rules and organizations so that sub-global arrangements will be consistent with the nondiscrimination and accountability required of open world markets. Countering centrifugal forces and assuring shared responsibility for the world economy will demand much from international organizations such as the new World Trade Organization (GATT's successor), the World Bank, the International Monetary Fund, the Group of Seven (G-7), and the Organization for Economic Cooperation and Development (OECD). Orchestrating the cooperation required to ensure consistency between global and regional trade expansion will demand strong American leadership, as the salvaging of the Uruguay Round demonstrated. The burden of such leadership should seem lighter given America's clear self-interest. As the world's largest exporting nation, the United States loses if regional blocs are allowed to become protectionist.

Regionalism, while more the focus of upcoming trade negotiations, is not a unified concept and cannot by itself be the organizing principle for a new global economic order. For example, the EU with its common agricultural policy and common external tariff is far more institutional than NAFTA, which has no common internal policies or common external tariff. Both contrast with East Asia, where the private sector has driven economic integration. Second, regionalism does not answer how trade should be conducted among regions, nor does it ultimately provide a basis for integrating large economies like China, India and Russia into the global economy. Third, many countries will not likely be part of a major regional group in the near future. Finally, geographic regions are not necessarily natural trading areas; witness the greater U.S. trade with Malaysia, Singapore and Thailand in 1992 than with all of South America.

THE REGIONAL ADVANTAGE

While not a paradigm for it, regional trade zones can contribute importantly to a new global economic order. Regional free trade agreements can improve resource allocation by enlarging markets, expanding investment flows, and creating economies of scale. In some cases such agreements reinforce already close private investment and trade links by further lowering barriers and improving cooperation on domestic policies. Public attention often focuses on tariff reductions in regional negotiations, but business finds equally important the protection of investment and intellectual property, and improvements in the security of market access. Without these provisions, conflicting national laws can undermine the ability of corporations to integrate production processes and support services efficiently.

Regional negotiations can serve as laboratories for experimenting with new rules. For example future multilateral negotiations could adopt as prototypes NAFTA's investment protection codes, dispute settlement arrangements and environmental provisions. The EU's harmonization of competition policy and product standards are also appropriate as models. Additionally, the emulation effect has encouraged progress toward regional free trade arrangements because an agreement among one group of countries makes others feel compelled to do likewise to improve their attractiveness to traders and investors.

Much of the impetus for regionalism results from a breakdown of the two major global divisions that artificially obstructed trade and investment among regional neighbors for decades. The first division was a philosophical one between the market-oriented industrialized world and the state control-oriented Third World. The second division was military and ideological, symbolized by the Iron Curtain in Europe. Removal of these barriers during the 1980s has allowed geography to play a greater role in determining trade and investment flows.

In Mexico and much of Latin America the debt crisis led to rejection of import substitution policies in favor of internal liberalization, privatization and unilateral tariff cuts. These policies opened the way for NAFTA and broader regional trade. Through market reforms China became a major regional trading partner, while East and Central Europe became open to opportunities for the West after the demise of communism and of the restrictive Council for Mutual Economic Assistance.

NAFTA and the EU-East European association agreements bear witness to the new incentives for industrialized and emerging economies to negotiate free trade agreements. Through NAFTA, Mexico linked up with its largest market and source of capital, while the United States realized more direct reciprocity in regional trade than it might have obtained from GATT negotiations. For similar reasons, the EU and Eastern Europe have concluded association agreements, which are steps toward full EU membership. In both cases, the industrialized partners recognized that more purchases from and investment in regional emerging economies would ultimately reduce the threat of destabilizing emigration. Yet another consideration is the framework that economic integration provides for alleviating environmental problems, which the public increasingly demands as a part of trade agreements.

For developing countries that are casting off state controls, free trade agreements with industrialized nations can provide critical stepping-stones into the world market. Developing countries can attract additional foreign investment and still phase in the exposure of their industries to competition, first at the regional and then the global level. Free trade agreements can also gird up domestic reforms. Mexico hopes that NAFTA obligations will lock in its new market-oriented laws, and the governments of Poland, Hungary and the Czech Republic look to EU membership to have the same reinforcing effect that it had for Spanish and Portuguese reforms in the 1970s.

Newly market-oriented countries see trade agreements among themselves as increasing economies of scale and luring capital that might otherwise go elsewhere. For example, the ASEAN countries hope to avoid diversion of investment capital to China and Vietnam by reducing intraregional trade barriers. South American countries, sensing the benefits of NAFTA for Mexico and eager to appeal to investors preoccupied with Asia, are creating free trade zones. In 1989 members of the once-protectionist Andean Pact agreed to establish a free trade area by 1995. In 1990 the moribund Central American Common Market was transformed into a free trade area. In 1991 Argentina, Brazil, Paraguay and Uruguay agreed to establish a common market by 1995. With different degrees of intensity Turkey and republics of Central Asia, South Africa and countries to its north, and Israel and its Arab neighbors are also contemplating free trade areas.

One result of economic internationalization is the development of subregional trade links across national borders, such as ties between the U.S. Pacific Northwest and British Columbia and, as previously mentioned, between coastal Chinese provinces and their offshore neighbors. China's enormous size has led to a transition that is integrating coastal provinces into the world market at a faster pace than inland provinces. Guandong province and the Shenzen Special Economic Zone have established bonds with Hong Kong, their primary source of capital and main channel to Western markets. Fujian province has close non-governmental trade and financial relations with Taiwan, to which it is tied by language, and northeastern provinces are building on cultural affinities to attract investment from and accelerate trade with South Korea and Japan.

Plans were begun in 1990 to establish a subregional growth triangle to combine Singapore's technology and financial power with the labor and resources of the Riau archipelago in Indonesia and Malaysia's southern state of Johore. Similar efforts to strengthen commercial ties are linking Bohemia in the Czech Republic, Saxony in Germany and Silesia in Poland. Other subregional ties are emerging between the Lombardy region of Italy and contiguous areas of France and Switzerland and among an increasingly autonomous Russian far east, Japan, northern China and South Korea. Closer to home the American Southwest and northern Mexico are establishing commercial bonds.

REGIONALISM'S OTHER FACE

Unless structured to complement the global thrust for open markets, regional free trade groupings could turn inward and erect protectionist barriers that would cripple the potential growth of the world economy. In itself, parochialism could be a source of major friction and conflict, hence the need for strong countervailing leadership during the hiatus between multilateral negotiating rounds. While the GATT's progressive lowering of world tariffs over 40 years has reduced the external barriers that can shield regional trading zones, nontariff barriers imposed by regions can have a similarly restrictive effect. High regulatory barriers can divert purchases away from competitive external producers. Product standards can be used to discriminate against outsiders. So can rules-of-origin requirements, which prevent goods produced with foreign materials in excess of a specified level in one member of a free trade area from qualifying for duty-free access to the market of another.

Business and labor often convince their governments to impose such restrictions as the price for granting their support. Under NAFTA, Mexican-made apparel will only qualify for the elimination of U.S. duties and quotas if produced from textiles and yarn made in North America. The EU has similar provisions. When competitive imports threaten a sensitive industry in a free trade area there is a tendency to protect the industry at the expense of outside imports. Foreign fears of losing regional markets often divert investment into those markets for defensive reasons. Free trade areas also can divert energies from the effort required to reduce barriers globally. The EU's internal preoccupations drew attention and political capital away from the Uruguay Round; for a time the Clinton administration's effort to secure congressional passage of NAFTA did likewise.

Regional free trade groupings are not much help to the poorest of nations. Such nations have weaker bargaining power in any type of negotiations with industrialized nations. And many of them, such as the small market states of Africa, are not likely to be grouped in free trade areas with major economic powers. Even developing countries several notches above the poorest must struggle, as Eastern European countries have with the EU, to obtain desired market access. They have had to acquiesce to restrictive safeguards by limiting exports into the EU if volumes increase rapidly. Mexico had to accept unilateral American demands for changes in NAFTA to secure passage by the U.S. Congress.

Recessions and structural uncompetitiveness can turn a trade region's vision inward. Both factors weighed heavily in the EU's resistance in the Uruguay Round to liberalization in key sectors. Looking ahead, high unemployment in the EU countries could stimulate more aggressive restrictions on imports. Europeans and Asians fear harm from NAFTA's rules-of-origin requirements, particularly if the agreement is extended to include other western hemisphere countries. Americans and Europeans are afraid that tighter intra-Asian trade and investment linkages will be disadvantageous to nations outside Asia. So far, increased trade and investment in Asia has been market-driven. More than any other part of the world Asia has practiced open regionalism. Given the size and vitality of its economic activity, Asia's future attitude toward regional integration could influence the world economy more profoundly than that of any other region.

THE NEED FOR GLOBAL NEGOTIATIONS

Friction among regions will result unless an overarching framework prevents the conduct of commerce within regions from discriminating against outsiders. Such a framework must assure expanded market and investment access to all regions and enforce international accountability for regional and national policies. In most instances, modifying existing institutions and procedures can accomplish this efficiently.

A crucial test will face the new World Trade Organization. It must fulfill its assignment of enforcing the implementation of Uruguay Round agreements and not allow a repeat of lax compliance as occurred with the subsidies agreement reached in the Tokyo Round in the 1980s. New multilateral trade rules will lose credibility unless deals made in the Uruguay Round are faithfully implemented and dispute resolution procedures work fairly and expeditiously. To assure itself a good start, the WTO should develop coalitions of the willing—it should mobilize small groups of countries to further liberalize market access among themselves in key areas such as services and telecommunications and invite other countries to sign on as they make appropriate commitments. A sparing use of the conditional most-favored-nation concept, which the United States introduced in financial services negotiations of the Uruguay Round, would potentially be useful. This concept, or variants of it, could achieve breakthroughs in areas in which the majority of WTO members are not yet prepared to liberalize. The tool addresses the "free rider" issue by discouraging countries from holding back on liberalization in the hope of increasing foreign market access without improving access to their own markets.

Modification also would increase the effectiveness of the OECD, a group of 23 industrialized democracies. Opening membership to Mexico, South Korea and Singapore, as well as to selected East European states, would bolster the OECD's relevance in the emerging economic order. A few of these countries have a greater impact on world trade and finance than some current OECD members. Several areas lend themselves to OECD leadership: liberalizing the treatment of foreign investment, harmonizing environmental practices, formulating guidelines to ensure that freer trade and improved environmental practices are not in conflict and resolving differences in competition policies to ensure against anticompetitive business practices impeding market access.

Annual meetings of top officials of the WTO, IMF and World Bank could coordinate policies and objectives concerning trade, investment, currency and development issues. Last September's meeting to promote the Uruguay Round was a prototype. Region-by-region reviews between top officials of these institutions and ministers representing major free trade areas could confirm that regional trade, investment and exchange rate policies were consistent with global rules and a well-functioning world economy. Reviews now take place for individual countries. The IMF's surveillance procedures evaluate national monetary and fiscal policies. The GATT conducts similar reviews under its trade policy review mechanism.

The Group of Seven (G-7) also needs to examine guidelines for ensuring that regional trade agreements not only open regional markets but also advance global trade liberalization. In recent years the G-7 appropriately focused on the Uruguay Round, but now it must chart the future evolution of multilateralism and how multilateralism interacts with regionalism and subregionalism. Little thought has been devoted to the implications of regionalism for world commerce or international political and security cooperation. Summit governments must forge a consensus on the type of international economic order they will support in the post-Cold War period and not drift into it through uncoordinated actions that could lead to conflict. Like the OCED, the G-7 can leaven its primarily European membership by inviting the leaders of key emerging states like China and regions like Eastern Europe to post-summit discussions on a new global order. And a meeting the day before summit deliberations with the heads of the IMF, World Bank and WTO would reinforce the roles of these institutions and focus attention on priority global issues.

THE CENTRALITY OF U.S. POLICY

The United States' centrality to the shaping of the post-Cold War economic order stems from its commanding worldwide economic and political status. American influence, although less dominant since the rise of other economies, particularly those of Asia, is still the driving force for expanding world trade. As in clinching completion of the Uruguay Round, the United States must continue its vigilant championing of global institutions and open international markets. A pluralistic global economy also will require more active multiregional economic diplomacy. Last fall the Clinton administration effectively utilized the "fear of exclusion" factor. Concerns that NAFTA would limit their access to the North American market induced a number of Asian countries to take a more forthcoming attitude toward APEC. In turn, the Seattle summit of APEC induced the EU to become more accommodating in the Uruguay Round to prevent closer American trade ties to Asia.

The United States can influence the dynamics of future negotiations by opportunistically pursuing bilateral and regional arrangements that promise to expand America's market access in key foreign sectors and areas. The United States and the EU can liberalize access to one another's financial services markets and invite Asian countries to sign on later if they did likewise. Similarly any U.S.-Asian agreements on mutual recognition of product standards and testing could be opened to the EU.

The United States will have to manage a wide spectrum of regional relationships. Already the president holds semiannual summits with leaders of EU countries, and he is scheduled to attend annual summits of APEC leaders over the next several years. These and ministerial-level meetings provide opportunities to propose changes in international institutions and rules.

Abroad, NAFTA will be closely watched. Whether the United States seeks to add new members to NAFTA, whether rules of origin regulations are implemented fairly and whether hemispheric trade relations are pursued at the expense of multilateral relations will affect policies of other regions. Pressures are growing on Japan, which is now emphasizing closer political and commercial ties with its Asian partners, to participate in an intra-Asian trade group. If Asia faces growing discrimination in this hemisphere or in Europe, calls for a more institutionalized form of regional economic cooperation will grow.

President Clinton's new trade agenda, which places priority on environmental protection, antitrust regulation and labor standards, will also be closely watched. The challenge will be to support higher workplace and environmental standards in emerging economies while simultaneously broadening global trade opportunities.

American leadership will be crucial in advancing a strategy that combines the proven benefits of open trade and investment with the new realities and advantages of regional and cross-regional trade arrangements. That requires adapting existing institutions to expand market access around the world and to align the policies of regions, subregions and nations with the goal of open markets. Inaction would leave the field open to the temptations of protectionism and thus would undermine the current, promising opportunities to craft a prosperous and secure order going into the 21st century.

28

EC/EU: CONFIDENCE LOST

Michael J. Brenner

The 1991 Maasricht Treaty on European Union was designed as the next step in the decades-old effort of the members of the European Community (now called the European Union, or EU) to use economic integration as the building bloc toward a broader European political union. Now, however, skepticism abounds. Among the reasons, argues Michael J. Brenner, is that the attitudes that made economic integration possible undermine Europe's ability to play a larger political role on the continent and elsewhere. Brenner is professor of international affairs at the University of Pittsburgh and author of *Nuclear Power and Non-proliferation: The Remaking of U.S. Policy* **(1981).**

When the Berlin Wall came down, a new day dawned in Central Europe. Two years later, the failed Moscow putsch followed by the collapse of the Soviet Union itself seemed to put all Europe on the path to democracy and peace. Then at Maastricht, in the Netherlands, where West Europeans pledged to build a political union, the European Community (EC) cast itself as the model and mentor for Europe's transformation. The United States, godfather to a reborn Europe, was for the moment content in the knowledge that past labors had borne fruit and that future labors would be lightened.

Today, bright promise has given way to apprehension. The main cause for the dramatic mood swing is the bitter, bloody civil war in the former

Reprinted with permission from *Foreign Policy* 91 (Summer 1993). Copyright 1993 by the Carnegie Endowment for International Peace.

Yugoslavia. It has revived visions of a Europe racked by discord and ancient rivalries. Atavistic nationalism is welling up elsewhere in the former communist lands, too, bringing with it old phobias and new fears. In Russia, xenophobes are joining hands with unrepentant Communists to challenge Boris Yeltsin's democratic reformers. Their cause is fueled by events in the Balkans. Most troubling, the [EU] has shown itself to be lacking the unity and will to act as custodian of continental security. Yugoslavia has sapped the [EU's] confidence and undermined its credibility, thereby contributing to the crumbling of popular support for the Maastricht Treaty on European Union, signed in December 1991. That pact completed its hazardous journey toward ratification. But it arrived damaged, its deficiencies as a blueprint for a competent federal Community exposed. Certainly, Western Europe no longer looks the sturdy partner ready to shoulder the principal responsibility for superintending the Continent's post–Cold War order. . . .

The EC's success in building supranational institutions depended on the special conditions that characterized postwar Europe. Most striking [was] the predominance of economic welfare concerns in the political life of the Western democracies. The support for outward-looking, enlightened policies was based on utilitarian calculations of material reward. The ever-rising prosperity that [was] the product of intense economic cooperation, in turn, has created a reservoir of good will for Community institutions, while taking the edge off national rivalries. Politics has become domesticated.

Ambitious nationalism and ideological militancy have faded. Political elites with an appetite for adventure or heroic enterprise are but a memory. Ambition is circumscribed. Exclusive integral nationalism is dead in the West; so is doctrinal faith. The result is the draining of passion from political life, along with the disappearance of commitment to grand causes. That attenuated scope to politics, with its focus on interest satisfaction, was a condition for and a reinforced effect of European integration. Prosaic economic issues of the technocratic state were also behind the latest move to expand Brussels institutions. The fear of losing out in a relentless international competition with the United States and Japan was the spur to the single European market, inaugurated on January 1, 1993.

Mounting popular skepticism about the Maastricht vision for the [EU] owes much to the current economic downturn. Today's hardships have combined with fears that remote authorities in Brussels will prove insensitive to local needs with the result that faith in the integration process itself has eroded. Many have backed their leaders on European construction with the tacit understanding that it was contingent on the process's delivering the goods: rising incomes and minimal dislocation. More economic decision-making power for Eurocrats along with new supranational organizations, such as the planned European central bank, may be seen by political elites as necessary steps toward their desired political union. The citizenry at large takes a narrower, self-interested view.

They are readily taking out their grievances over immediate economic hardships on ruling parties and leadership, able neither to reassure nor to inspire. The French legislative elections in March 1993 that devastated the governing Socialists are the most dramatic sign of a surly political mood, also evident in Germany, Great Britain, and Italy. That pervasive disillusionment shows how fragile are the foundations for Maastricht's architectonic design for a fully integrated West European economy.

The more ambitious project for building a federal Europe, one equipped with a common defense and able to conduct a common foreign policy, adds a purely political dimension to EC institution building. It came in reaction to the challenges posed by the end of the Cold War, the end of Europe's division, and—not least—by the growing strength (monetary and political) of a united Germany. Fusing the political and economic dimensions of Community construction was a gamble and a hope. The hope was that the methods of integration that worked for the harmonization of economies could be applied to political unification. The gamble was making Western Europe's huge stake in both its own solidarity and conciliation with the East hostage to that hope. That gamble now appears to be failing, if it is not yet lost. The reason is the contradiction between the attitudes that at least until now have made economic integration possible, on the one hand, and those needed to forge a legitimate political union, on the other.

Maastricht, the ultimate embodiment of benign technocratic management, is in one sense the endpoint of a logic that places material gain at the apex of social values. However, it may be a dead end as far as political union is concerned. Indeed, achieving the desired goal of full monetary union, too, may be beyond the capabilities of the [EU's] current modus operandi. Maastricht was an effort to extend the functionalist logic to constitute a rudimentary federal state. The strategy laid down at Maastricht was bold, even audacious, in its goal but deceptive and fearful in its methods for attaining that goal. Without serious public debate about either the aims of this historic exercise in constitution building on a semi-continental scale, or the basis for its legitimation, leaders of the 12 member states committed their peoples to a plan for relocating the sovereign authority that governs them.

THE SOVEREIGNTY GAP

Sovereignty is at the heart of the debate over Maastricht. Architects of a federal Europe have been operating on a limited, and therefore defective, notion of sovereignty. The term embraces two concepts: supreme power—the ultimate, final authority over public matters; and the class of public matters on which that power is authorized to act. In principle, sovereign leaders and institutions have exclusive authority over the most vital aspects of a society's collective existence, namely its physical security and constitutional integrity. The character of sovereign actions is distinctive: They can demand sacrifice—especially on questions of war and peace.

Those responsibilities that historically have defined the sovereign state have been eclipsed in much of Western Europe since World War II by an ever more intense concentration on economic performance and social welfare. Western Europe has been preoccupied with the practical methods for achieving those economic and social goals. The region's long peace, and its reliance on American protection, has also encouraged that focus. Thus, [EU] members could take the supranational route without concern for how well suited its institutions were for taking on the traditional core responsibilities of sovereign states: foreign policy and security. The [EU's] current crisis is accentuated by the large number of member governments that no longer seem able to employ the standard powers of state. They do not provide directly for their own security, and they have limited capacity to do things that could cause their citizens pain—be it economic or on a battlefield. Uniting by treaty states that in some instances do not now exercise the full prerogatives of sovereignty will not overcome that deficiency. Supranational institutions in Brussels continue to lack independent sources of authority to draw on when the tough decisions arise.

What does all that have to do with political order and continental stability in postcommunist Europe? There are two noteworthy connections. First, an [EU] preoccupied with fractious disputes over how to fulfill its collective economic needs is finding it difficult to meet its obligations to assist the fledgling democracies in the East to consolidate their liberal revolutions. The [EU] is hesitant to provide the necessary material assistance and markets or to offer associate membership in the future. The strains placed on the fabric of European cooperation by such contentious issues as the [Union's] agricultural support policies and the status of the Maastricht-envisaged European central bank reveal both the strengths of parochial interests and the weaknesses of governments unwilling or unable to invest the political capital to override them.

The effect is to hold any substantial help for the East hostage to interest politics in the West—a politics aggravated, rather than muted, by community construction. Maastricht has been sold to a skeptical citizenry with promises of greater reward and further rights and privileges as citizens of a federalizing Europe. A European [Union] so conceived cannot authoritatively resolve interest disputes above a certain level of intensity. That holds for farmers, fishermen, steelworkers, or any other organized group that sees its economic position menaced from new sources. It holds equally for a citizenry at large that shows little inclination to embrace wholeheartedly continental cousins liberated from communism—as best illustrated by the prevailing attitudes in Germany's western *länder.*

Consequently, the [EU] is in danger of becoming a less-relevant model and a less-respected tutor for the societies in Eastern Europe that are struggling to remake themselves. Western Europe's material abundance remains a powerful pole of attraction. But the [EU's] parochial, self-interested outlook also carries the message that enlightened cooperation has definite limits, especially for those not privileged to be members of the club. The need for self-reliance by Eastern countries is a related lesson, one that too easily can be turned into the political maxim that fortune favors the willful and single-minded. In an environment marked by economic dislocation and weak democratic traditions, that line of thinking favors the rise of nondemocratic forces—especially intolerant, assertive nationalism.

Second, a Europe—and a West—absorbed with the rearrangement of its own internal affairs is also less willing to provide the requisite attention and political will to deal with security threats when they do arise. That has been strikingly evident in Europe's handling of the Yugoslav situation. The [EU] intermediation in the Yugoslav crisis was widely touted as the [EU's] debut on the international stage. Its inability to prevent a destructive civil war raises serious questions about its readiness for taking custody of continental security. . . .

The [EU's] failure to act in timely and decisive fashion on the Balkan crisis has had a dismaying outcome. Its aspiration to act as a political entity on security matters was not matched by the authority and instruments a true sovereign power requires. . . . The [European Union's] principal deficiency was in the political will needed to overcome divisions on the hardest decisions—the most crucial concerning the possible concerted use of military means to check Serb advances or to enforce a settlement.

Many West Europeans defend the [European Union's] record by making the brave argument that they achieved the reachable, and not unimportant, objective of containing the conflict. What critics see as hesitancy and irresolution is taken to be political realism. To allow moral outrage to dictate intervention could have led to an even greater bloodbath with no assurance of a stable, or just, outcome. Whatever one makes of that defense, there is no gainsaying that the [EU's] performance—one that revealed a wide gap between stated intention and action—has lost credibility in Washington and especially in Eastern Europe. That will seriously hamper the [EU] in coping with Europe's next security crisis. . . .

29

AFTER NAFTA: GLOBAL VILLAGE OR GLOBAL PILLAGE?

Jeremy Brecher

The massive movement of capital in the world economy is a major contributing force in its rapid integration. Labor is not as mobile as capital, which leads to concerns about job security and loss of income. Both figured prominently in the debate about U.S. entry into the North American Free Trade Agreement (NAFTA). Jeremy Brecher recounts perceived dangers associated with globalization and the response to them NAFTA stimulated among private citizens and interest groups in the United States. Brecher is a historian and co-editor (with John Brown Childs and Jill Cutler) of *Global Visions: Beyond the New World Order* **(1993).**

For most of the world's people, the "New World Economy" is a disaster that has already happened. Those it hurts can't escape it. But neither can they afford to accept it. So many are now seeking ways to reshape it. . . .

. . . Elements of the struggle against NAFTA [North America Free Trade Agreement] prefigure a movement that could radically reshape the New World Economy. Out of their own experiences and observations, millions of Americans have constructed a new paradigm for understanding the global economy. Poor and working people in large numbers have recognized that NAFTA is not primarily about trade; it is about the ability of capital to move without regard to national borders. Capital mobility, not trade, is bringing about the "giant sucking sound" of jobs going south. . . .

THE NEW GLOBAL PILLAGE

NAFTA became a symbol for an accumulation of fears and angers regarding the place of working people in the New World Economy. The North American economic integration that NAFTA was intended to facilitate is only one aspect of the rapid and momentous historical transformation from a system of national economies toward an integrated global economy. New information, communication, transportation and manufacturing technologies, combined with tariff reductions, have made it possible to coordinate production, commerce and finance on a world scale. Since 1983, the rate of world foreign direct investment has grown four times as fast as world output.

This transformation has had devastating consequences. They may be summarized as the "seven danger signals" of cancerous, out-of-control globalization:

Race to the Bottom   The recent quantum leap in the ability of transnational corporations to relocate their facilities around the world in effect makes all workers, communities and countries competitors for these corporations' favor. The consequence is a "race to the bottom" in which wages and social and environmental conditions tend to fall to the level of the most desperate. This dynamic underlies U.S. deindustrialization, declining real wages, eradication of job security, and downward pressure on social spending and investment; it is also largely responsible for the migration of low-wage, environmentally destructive industries to poor countries like Mexico and China.

Global Stagnation   As each work force, community or country seeks to become more competitive by reducing its wages and its social and environmental overheads, the result is a general downward spiral in incomes and social and material infrastructures. Lower wages and reduced public spending mean less buying power, leading to stagnation, recession and unemployment. This dynamic is aggravated by the accumulation of debt; national economies in poor countries and even in the United States become geared to debt repayment at the expense of consumption, investment and development. The downward fall is reflected in the slowing of global GNP growth from almost 5 percent per year in the period 1948-1973 to only half that in the period 1974-89 and to a mere crawl since then.

Polarization of Haves and Have-Nots   As a result of globalization, the gap between rich and poor is increasing both within and between countries around the world. Poor U.S. communities boast world-class unemployment and infant mortality. Meanwhile, tens of billions of dollars a year flow from poor to rich regions of the world, in the form of debt repayment and capital flight.

Loss of Democratic Control   National governments have lost much of their power to direct their own economies. The ability of countries to apply socialist or even Keynesian techniques in pursuit of development, full employment or other national economic goals has been undermined by the power of capital to pick up and leave. Governmental economic power has been further weakened throughout the world by neoliberal political movements that have dismantled government institutions for regulating national economies. Globalization has reduced the power of individuals and communities to shape their destinies.

Walter Wriston, former chairman of Citicorp, recently boasted of how "200,000 monitors in trading rooms all over the world" now conduct "a kind of global plebiscite on the monetary and fiscal policies of the governments issuing currency. . . . There is no way for a nation to opt out." Wriston recalls the election of "ardent socialist" François Mitterrand as French President in 1981. "The market took one look at his policies and within six months the capital flight forced him to reverse course."

Unfettered Transnational Corporations Transnationals have become the world's most powerful economic actors, yet there are no international equivalents to national antitrust, consumer protection and other laws that provide a degree of corporate accountability.

Unaccountable Global Institutions The loss of national economic control has been accompanied by a growing concentration of unaccountable power in international institutions like the International Monetary Fund, the World Bank and the General Agreement on Tariffs and Trade (GATT). For poor countries, foreign control has been formalized in the World Bank's "structural adjustment plans," but I.M.F. decisions and GATT rules affect the economic growth rates of all countries. The decisions of these institutions also have an enormous impact on the global ecology.

Global Conflict Economic globalization is producing chaotic and destructive rivalries. In a swirl of self-contradictory strategies, major powers and transnationals use global institutions like GATT to impose open markets on their rivals; they pursue trade wars against one another; and they try to construct competing regional blocs like the European [Union] and NAFTA. In past eras, such rivalries have ultimately led to world war.

In sum, the result of unregulated globalization has been the pillage of the planet and its peoples.

TRANSNATIONAL ECONOMIC PROGRAMS

What are the alternatives to destructive globalization? The [political] right offers racism and nationalism. Conventional protectionism offers no solution. Globalization has also intellectually disarmed the [political] left and rendered national left programs counterproductive. Jimmy Carter's sharp turn to the right in 1978; François Mitterrand's rapid abandonment of his radical program; the acceptance of deregulation, privatization and trade liberalization by poor countries from India to Mexico; and even the decision of Eastern European elites to abandon Communism—all reflect in part the failure of national left policies.

But the beginnings of a new approach emerged from the anti-NAFTA movement itself. Rather than advocate protectionism—keeping foreign products out—many NAFTA opponents urged policies that would raise environmental, labor and social standards in Mexico, so that those standards would not drag down those in the United States and Canada. This approach implied that people in different countries have common interests in raising the conditions of those at the bottom.

Indeed, the struggle against NAFTA generated new transnational networks based on such common interests. A North American Worker-to-Worker Network links grass-roots labor activists in Mexico, the United States and Canada via conferences, tours, solidarity support and a newsletter. Mujer a Mujer similarly links women's groups. The Highlander Center, Southerners for Economic Justice, the Tennessee Industrial Renewal Network and a number of unions have organized meetings and tours to bring together Mexican and U.S. workers. There are similar networks in other parts of the world, such as People's Plan 21 in the Asian-Pacific and Central American regions and the Third World Network in Malaysia.

These new networks are developing transnational programs to counter the effects of global economic restructuring. Representatives from environmental, labor, religious, consumer and farm groups from Mexico, the United States and Canada have drawn up "A Just and Sustainable Trade and Development Initiative for North America." A parallel synthesis, "From Global Pillage to Global Village," has been endorsed by more than sixty grass-roots organizations. Related proposals by the Third World Network have . . . been published as "Towards a New North-South Economic Dialogue."

Differing in emphasis and details, these emerging alternative programs are important not only because of the solutions they propose but also because those solutions have emerged from a dialogue rooted in such a diversity of groups and experiences. Some require implementation by national policy; some by international agreement; some can be implemented by transnational citizen action. Taken together, they provide what might be described as "seven prescriptions" for the seven danger signals of the unregulated global economy:

International Rights and Standards   To prevent competition from resulting in a race to the bottom, several of these groups want to establish minimum human, labor and environmental rights and standards, as the European [Union's] "social charter" was designed to do. The International Metalworkers Federation recently proposed a ten-point "World Social Charter," which could be incorporated into GATT.

"A Just and Sustainable Trade and Development Initiative for North America" spells out in some detail an alternative to NAFTA that would protect human and worker rights, encourage workers' incomes to rise in step with productivity and establish continental environmental rights, such as the right to a toxics-free workplace and community. Enforcement agencies would be accessible to citizens and could levy fines against parties guilty of violations. The initiative especially emphasizes the rights of immigrants. Activists from nongovernmental organizations in all three countries have proposed a citizens' commission to monitor the human, labor and environmental effects of trade and investment.

Upward Spiral   In the past, government monetary and fiscal policy, combined with minimum wages, welfare state programs, collective bargaining and other means of raising the purchasing power of have-nots, did much to counter recession and stagnation within national economies. Similar measures are now required at international levels to counter the tendency toward a downward spiral of inadequate demand in the global economy. The Third World Network calls on the I.M.F. and World Bank to replace their ruinous structural adjustment plans with policies that "meet the broad goals of development . . . rather than the narrower goal of satisfying the needs of the creditors." It also demands a reduction of developing country debt. "A Just and Sustainable Trade and Development Initiative" proposes that the remaining debt service be paid in local currency into a democratically administered development fund. Reversing the downward spiral also ultimately requires a "global Keynesianism" in which international institutions support, rather than discourage, national full-employment policies.

An upward spiral also requires rising income for those at the bottom—something that can be encouraged by international labor solidarity. Experiments in cross-border organizing by U.S. unions like the Amalgamated Clothing and Textile Workers and the United Electrical Workers, in cooperation with independent unions in Mexico, aim to defeat transnationals' whipsawing by improving the wages and conditions of Mexican workers.

Redistribution from Haves to Have-Nots   "A Just and Sustainable Trade and Development Initiative" calls for "compensatory financing" to correct growing gaps between rich and poor. A model would be the European [Union] funds that promote development in its poorer members. The Third World Network calls for commodity agreements to correct the inequities in the South's terms of trade. It also stresses the need to continue preferential treatment for the South in GATT and in intellectual property protection rules.

Strengthened Democracy   NAFTA, GATT and similar agreements should not be used—as they now can be—to preempt the right of localities, states, provinces and countries to establish effective labor, health, safety and environmental standards that are higher than the guaranteed minimum in international agreements. Above all, democratization requires a new opportunity for people at the bottom to participate in shaping their destiny.

Codes of Conduct for Transnational Corporations   Several transnational grass-roots groups call for codes of conduct that would, for example, require corporations to report investment intentions; disclose the hazardous materials they import; ban employment of children; forbid discharge of pollutants; require advance notification and severance pay when operations are terminated; and prohibit company interference with union organizing. United Nations discussions of such a code, long stymied by U.S. hostility, should be revived.

While the ultimate goal is to have such codes implemented by agreements among governments, global public pressure and cross-border organizing can begin to enforce them. The Coalition for Justice in the Maquiladoras, for example, a group of religious, environmental, labor, Latino and women's organizations in Mexico and the United States, has issued a code of conduct for U.S. corporations in Mexico and has used "corporate campaign" techniques to pressure them to abide by its labor and environmental provisions.

Reform of International Institutions   Citizens should call on the U.N. to convene a second Earth Summit focusing on democratizing the I.M.F. and the World Bank, and consider formation of new institutions to promote equitable, sustainable and participatory development. International citizen campaigns, perhaps modeled on the Nestlé boycott and the campaign against World Bank-funded destruction of the Amazon, could spotlight these institutions.

Multiple-Level Regulation   In place of rivalry among countries and regions, such programs imply a system of democratically controlled public institutions at every level, from global to local.

AFTER NAFTA: GLOBALIZATION FROM BELOW

These proposals provide no short-term panacea; they are objectives to organize around. The New World Economy is not going to vanish from the political agenda. Neither will the passions and political forces aroused by the NAFTA debate. Many of the same issues will resurface in connection with the Asia-Pacific Economic Cooperation Forum and with GATT. As the fiftieth anniversaries of the I.M.F. and World Bank approach, calls for their reform are being sounded all over the world.

The struggle against NAFTA has shown that those harmed by the New World Economy need not be passive victims. So many politicians were so unprepared for the strength of the anti-NAFTA movement because it represented an eruption into the political arena of people who have long been demobilized. But to influence their economic destinies effectively, they need a movement that . . . must act on the understanding that the unregulated globalization of capital is really a worldwide attack of the haves on the have-nots. And it must bring that understanding to bear on every affected issue, from local layoffs to the world environment. "From Global Pillage to Global Village" suggests a vision to guide such a movement:

> The internationalization of capital, production and labor is now being followed by the internationalization of peoples' movements and organizations. Building peoples' international organizations and solidarity will be our revolution from within: a civil society without borders. This internationalism or "globalization from below" will be the foundation for turning the global pillage into a participatory and sustainable global village.

The organizations that have led the fight against NAFTA have a responsibility not to retreat to parochial concerns. They must regroup and begin addressing the broader impact of economic globalization on people and planet.

30

MERCANTILISM AND GLOBAL SECURITY

Michael Borrus, Steve Weber, and John Zysman, with Joseph Willihnganz

Michael Borrus, Steve Weber, John Zysman, and Joseph Willihnganz probe the security implications of the tripolar world political economy that is emerging in the wake of the decline of American economic power and prowess. They worry in particular about the "powerful intellectual, political, and technological forces that could push the world into . . . mercantile rivalry" and the likely inability of existing international institutions "to cope with the instability that would result." Borrus, Weber, and Zysman teach at the University of California, Berkeley. They are co-authors of *The Highest Stakes: The Economic Foundations of the Next Security System* (1992), a product of the Berkeley Roundtable on the International Economy (BRIE) co-directed by Borrus and Zysman. Willihnganz is an editor at BRIE.

For the third time this century the United States faces a new world. It looks in many ways like the world that America has for forty years struggled to create, a world it hardly dared hope for. But even so it poses new and difficult questions about the international system and America's place in it. American competitive troubles, Asian industrial might, and continuing European integration create the basis for a wholly new system of relations among the major powers that will substantially reduce American influence. For the moment, the U.S. still leads, but more by default than from strength.

Reprinted with permission © *The National Interest,* No. 29, Washington, D.C. Some footnotes have been deleted.

For over four decades the postwar security system presumed a Soviet enemy, a U.S. military umbrella over allies in Western Europe and Asia, and a system of free trade and stable finance dominated and coordinated by the United States. This system of trade and finance, established within GATT, Bretton Woods, and successor agreements, rested on American industrial and technological leadership. That foundation of power made it possible for the United States to support the rebuilding of Europe and Japan, establish for itself favorable terms of trade, and channel compliance with its security aims.

But now the United States is slipping. Its technological and economic position is declining relative to the other industrialized nations. As a result, the government's ability to exact compliance or exercise leverage in the international system is diminished. The United States has been painfully constrained in its ability to contribute development aid to the Baltics or to invest in reform in Central Europe. If the United States were to conclude that massive assistance to Russia was in fact advisable, it would have to raise the money hat-in-hand just as it did to finance the Gulf War. This change in capabilities is not just a result of temporary trends, and it will not be reversed by balanced-budget amendments, the end of the current [1990–1992] recession, or other tinkering at the margins. It is a fundamental change. Having lost its technological and industrial hegemony, the United States will be increasingly subject to the kinds of constraints that it used to impose on others.

America's economic position relative to its two strongest allies has shifted from almost 4 to 1 in 1970 to virtual parity in 1990.[1] For years, many argued that America's decline was mostly the result of industrial catch-up in Europe and Asia. Others blamed imperial overreach, arguing that extensive foreign policy commitments were exhausting the economy's resources. But it is now plain that Europe and Japan have done more than simply catch up in the same old game. The declining U.S. position is largely a reflection of American industry's inability to adjust competitively to changes in global markets, to play effectively in a new game. Many U.S. industries that ignored or simply missed out on production revolutions originating abroad must now buy critical materials and technologies from foreign competitors. Growing numbers of U.S. firms now retain their market position only through heavy doses of trade protection.

The U.S. has fallen in less than a decade from the world's largest creditor to the world's largest debtor. Moreover, overseas borrowing has gone disproportionately into consumption and interest payments on past debt, not into investment in new technology and industrial process. The boom in American exports

---

[1]This measure, comparative GDP, expresses two changes: America's declining position and the change of its principal allies. In 1970 Britain and France were America's principal allies. By 1992, Japan and Germany had regained full sovereignty and become the other principal powers.

in the latter half of the 1980s has come only at historically low real exchange rates between the dollar and other principal currencies. This can't hide what is a real change in competitive position, since lowering the exchange rate (reducing prices) amounts to lowering real wages: our firms can compete, but only on less attractive terms for the society. The devaluation has not re-established [the U.S.] position or stymied imports in consumer durables sectors such as autos and electronics. The surge in exports has been in lower value-added and a handful of high-technology sectors rather than in the broad middle ground of industries like capital equipment and consumer durables that American manufacturing used to dominate.

These shifts in America's industrial, financial, and technological position have been complemented by the rapid emergence of powerful new capabilities in Japan and Europe that go beyond mere catch-up. During the postwar years, while the United States held fast to the tried-and-true formula of mass production and consumption, other countries began to innovate more rapidly. [Its] most successful competitors, in particular Germany and Japan, undertook new approaches in two critical domains: policy and production.

In the policy realm, both states made smart use of the fact that their defense burden was relatively light and chose to emphasize investment over consumption, which created excellent macroeconomic conditions for rapid growth. Both governments also encouraged the rapid adoption and widespread diffusion of technology acquired abroad and helped provide for a well-trained work force ready to use it. In Japan, government went a step further by closing through formal and informal means its domestic market to foreign firms, reserving growth in domestic demand for Japanese producers. These kinds of policies helped build strong industries by sheltering them from foreign competition, guaranteeing domestic demand, and encouraging continuous rounds of reinvestment which in time led to real innovations in production. Government policy in effect "created" competitive advantage for domestic firms and "comparative" advantage for the nation in higher wage industries.

But it is innovation in production and production organization that has increasingly separated the United States and its competitors. New methods of manufacturing and technology development, emerging in countries as diverse as Japan, Italy, and Germany, are quickly giving leading firms a competitive edge in technology-intensive, high value-added industries. These new methods, which combine high-volume production, organizational innovations, and advances in microelectronics, amount to a wholly new approach to making and selling goods. The most powerful new model of production is labeled variously as flexible volume production, flexible automation, or lean production. It allows firms not only to produce a variety of products with costs, quality, and market responsiveness far superior to mass production, but also to adjust quickly to changes in consumer tastes by introducing a new product and then adjusting to consumer reaction by fine-tuning product configurations and vol-

umes to actual demand. Heavy investment and these new approaches to manufacturing and marketing establish a real advantage in component, materials,
and machinery technologies that have broad commercial and military application.

The U.S. economy retains the advantage of being the world's largest; its
technological and scientific resources are still broader and deeper than those of
its competitors. But rapidly expanding capabilities in Europe and Asia now permit a serious challenge to American economic leadership and create the potential for autonomy where there was once U.S.-imposed constraint. Indeed, it is
America's autonomy that is now threatened as it risks substantial dependence in
industry, finance, and critical segments of technology.

Such a realignment of economic capabilities will have political consequences. At a minimum, the balance of constraints and opportunities facing
states will shift dramatically. In 1956 the United States threatened a run on
the pound to constrain British, French, and Israeli foreign policy. Today
Japan and Germany have the financial leverage to influence the American
exchange rate and monetary policy. Again, consider what happened when the
United States wanted to punish Toshiba for having sold precision military
technology to the Soviet Union. The U.S. government sought to ban Toshiba
products from the U.S. market, but could not: too many major U.S. customers depend on Toshiba for critical components and technologies. Such
examples demonstrate that America's ability to exact compliance through its
position in trade and finance has been deeply eroded, leaving it without the
array of foreign policy levers it enjoyed in the past and with vulnerabilities it
has not had to cope with until now.

In sum, a radical re-alignment of economic capabilities, combined with the
end of the Cold War, creates the possibility of fundamentally new relationships
among great powers, and the regions that they dominate. The certainties of the
bipolar world are gone, and the bonds that were a part of that world are loosening.

THREE REGIONS

The security system that develops over the next decade will reflect a world that is
slowly dividing itself into three powerful trading groups: Asia, North America,
and Europe. Though the world may be "globalizing," its major components are
these three regions. Multinational corporations and financial institutions roam the
globe, but each has a home—a country that necessarily shapes its character, and
both constrains and directs its choices. And though the three major regions are
interconnected (in part by the activities of these firms), each also commands an
independent industrial and technological base, vast financial resources, and a
developed domestic market capable of sustaining steady growth. This provides
each with the economic foundations for independent action.

Consider first the Japan-centered Asian trade and investment region. Since 1985, trade within Asia has grown substantially faster than between Asia and other regions. The major source of imports for each Asian economy is usually another Asian economy, most often Japan. By almost any significant measure Japan, rather than the United States, is now the dominant economic player in Asia. Japan is the region's technology leader, its primary supplier of capital goods, its dominant exporter, and its largest foreign direct investor and foreign aid supplier. Financial ties further reinforce intra-Asian trends. From 1984 to 1989, for example, there was as much Japanese investment in Asia as in the previous thirty-three years, doubling the cumulative total. The result of such trade and investment is a network of producers across Asia, generally controlled by Japanese firms, that diffuses technology and production know-how to other firms in the Japanese periphery. As other Asian nations absorb production knowledge and emulate the Japanese model of success, innovations in policy and manufacturing spread throughout the region much more quickly and effectively than they do to either Europe or North America. The presence of such broad economic strength across Asia guarantees the region increasing autonomy.

Next, consider Europe. Trade within the European Community [now the European Union] has grown faster than trade between the region and the rest of the world since the establishment of the EC in 1958. Intra-[EU] trade is now the dominant proportion of each member-state's trade. Discounting intra-European trade, Europe's percentage of world exports and imports drops dramatically: exports from 44.6 percent to 13.8 percent, and imports from 42.6 percent to 11 percent. Trade within Europe will only increase further with the creation of a single market and possibly a single currency. And, as in Asia, financial ties reinforce trade ties. Like Japan and the rest of Asia, Europe appears to have both an industrial/technological base capable of providing for itself and an emerging political will to develop and maintain that capability, and to respond more effectively to external constraints. Though Europe (like Asia) is by no means a single political actor, European governments increasingly cooperate to create regional economic capabilities and policy. Today Europe is in a position to court autonomy.

The United States, with the largest economy in the world, sits at the center of the North American region, which is also strengthening internal trade and financial ties. Canada and the United States are already each other's largest trading partners. The North American Free Trade Agreement, if implemented successfully, will expand that trade further and bring Mexico—America's third largest trading partner—fully into the fold. The Free Trade Agreement may also spawn de facto trade barriers to goods and services coming from outside the region, thus insulating it from the two other groups and reinforcing the drive toward autonomy.

COMPETING VISIONS

Economic relations among these three trading regions will set the parameters within which security issues are resolved. There are several visions of what the emerging system could be like.

The most attractive vision is an extension of the present system of free trade. Though trade in the industrialized world is rarely wholly "free," the unrestricted flow of goods, services and capital among regions, as within them, would remain the overarching goal of such a system. Governments would continue to act on the belief that progressively freer trade benefits everyone in the end, even given the painful costs of domestic adjustments to competition. Governments would primarily negotiate the rules of trade, not trade outcomes, and they would continue to make use of the framework for these negotiations established in the postwar multilateral institutions like GATT. The system would be managed by a loose alliance of the three regions' principal powers. A consensus on shared goals for the world economy would replace a hegemonic distribution of power as the foundation for cooperation and stability. There might be relative shifts in position among the three centers of power. Some countries might get rich more quickly, but all would get richer over time, and the significance of those differences would be submerged in the shared goal of peaceful economic expansion. The security system that would emerge from such an order could be built around collaboration and cooperation among the advanced countries, something approximating a latter-day (but global) concert of Europe. We call this kind of world "true multilateral cooperation." In it, the United States would continue to be *primus inter pares.*

A less desirable vision begins with the economic regions fending off trade competition from one another as a way of avoiding most of the painful domestic adjustments. Each region would concentrate on its own internal development and would try to avoid the strains of direct competition by protecting markets. Round after round of "defensive protectionism" would disengage further the three economies and transform the world by steps into three nearly independent subeconomies. Trade would continue to become more concentrated within each group and perhaps decrease among them. Each group would work to limit its exposure to and dependence on the others, and whatever unavoidable links were left between them would be managed by agreement, rather than by markets. In this world of economic regions each group would command its own currency, industrial and technological base, and its own financial system—all insulated from those of the others. The result in economic terms would be three relatively autonomous trading groups with low levels of sensitivity to each other's choices and even lower levels of vulnerability to each other's actions. There might be some shift in relative position in this scenario as well, but all would be wealthy—though, having given up the benefits of global free trade, not as wealthy as they could be.

What kind of security system could we expect from such an economic arrangement? Three large, inwardly oriented groups could coexist comfortably—in principle—so long as there was mutual recognition that the drive for regional autonomy and political stability within each group was defensively motivated and posed no threat to similar arrangements outside. With internal growth and autonomy assured at home, disputes between regions could be marginal in this live-and-let-live world of regional coexistence.

Security arrangements in this relatively benign world could, however, look very different from what we have become accustomed to in the postwar world. In fact, this might not be a security "system" at all. Certainly, low levels of interdependence would make conflict among the regions unlikely. Would there be much cooperation? The optimistic view is that there would probably not be formal, institutionalized cooperation (as there was in NATO, where an attack on one was an attack on all), but that would not necessarily be a bad thing. As security threats in the new world will be more diffuse than in the past, regions, or countries, would cooperate on an ad hoc basis, with like-minded countries forming coalitions around specific challenges—a "Persian Gulf" coalition, or a "Sarajevo" coalition, for example. In a world without hegemony, "security cooperation á la carte" sounds practical, cheap (compared to supporting institutions like NATO) and fairly stable. In security debates this vision has become something approaching conventional wisdom as a "second-best" solution in the post-Cold War world.

What's wrong with this picture? Many would say the only real downside is that the gains from inter-regional free trade would be lost. While this loss would be unfortunate, it is maintained, the only real "threat" it poses is moderately lower income levels for all. The real trouble, however, is that this vision of regional coexistence rests on outdated arguments. Regional coexistence is not likely to be stable in the twenty-first century because of new patterns of technology development, and new ideas that have evolved to explain and interpret the competition that results. Powerful material and intellectual forces exist that could tilt this peaceful world into mercantile rivalry and unpredictable conflict.

THE CULT OF THE ECONOMIC OFFENSIVE

The principal force that could propel the regions into bitter economic rivalry is the possibility that there can be *enduring* national winners and losers from trade competition. This possibility is grounded in provocative new theories of trade and technology that undermine the basic intellectual premises of free trade and confirm recent experiences in high-technology competition.

Strategic trade theory, as it is often called, proposes that governments can by unilateral action permanently alter the competitive balance of trade in critical industries. By providing subsidies or protection, governments can give domestic firms—or entire industries—resources to build an improved global market position. If other countries do not similarly support their firms, the first country will have "created" advantage. If the industries selected for this special treatment serve as catalysts for the rest of the economy, their improved welfare benefits the entire economy. By promoting these key sectors governments can, in effect, secure permanent gains for the nation as a whole.

The trouble is that these gains come at the expense of other nations and possibly at their permanent expense. As one state's firms capture increasing market share, another state's firms suffer; and since the firms suffering are in the same critical catalyst position in their own economy, the whole economy suffers. Moreover, if the industries in question are natural oligopolies because of high investment or technological barriers to entry (as with the aircraft or semiconductor industries), the "created" advantage one firm enjoys might be enough to drive other firms permanently from the market. This generates serious consequences for other national economies, which find themselves suddenly dependent on critical components and technologies they can no longer produce at home. The promise of autonomy becomes, instead, a threat of dependence.

When we combine strategic trade arguments with an understanding of how technology develops, and how strongly that development affects the evolution of modern industrial economies, the implications become even sharper. The clearest way to think about how technology develops is to picture each nation moving along a technology "trajectory." Industrial technologies are not like pure science in that they do not come in a universal language with open and equal access to everyone. Production technologies accrue locally in networks of shared knowledge, learning, and experience—in firm-supplier links, skilled workers, and the like. This kind of knowledge is rarely traded among nations (except as partially embodied in products and technology licenses). This means that technological innovation tends to build up local assets within national borders and place states on distinct trajectories, or paths, that powerfully shape possibilities for future growth. If a nation's markets and firms are organized in such a way that these innovations spread easily, a few critical industries can strongly influence how an economy fares.

Together, strategic trade and technology theories open up the possibility that nations or regions could come to see themselves competing in a win-or-lose, zero-sum game for their economic futures. But can promotional policies really affect competition as profoundly as these theories suggest? Can governments really pick winners over losers? The answer is that it may not matter whether they can or not. It only matters whether nations *believe* they can. And if one government plays the strategic trade game, other governments will have trouble standing aside. In fact, nations, or regions, might feel provoked to develop strategic trade policies simply out of the fear that others might be doing the same.

Governments will find it difficult to deny themselves the tools of strategic trade. Strategic trade is based on the notion of a "first mover advantage." This advantage can prove decisive in capturing markets and particularly in generating a cycle of reinvestment and learning that creates enduring advantage in high-technology competition. For these reasons, it is not a viable policy to sit back and watch while others move ahead. In fact, it can be seen as potentially devastating if governments believe that markets and technologies critical to supporting further economic development at home will be lost to those who moved first.

The dynamic is reminiscent of "the cult of the offensive" among European military organizations prior to World War I. In that case, a group of states set up and trained their armies according to the idea that military offense was dominant over defense—which led to the conclusion that a tremendous advantage came to the side that struck first. They turned out to be wrong about the nature of war in 1914—in fact the defense turned out to have the advantage—but "the cult of the offensive," as wrong as it was, nevertheless changed the character of relationships among the European states. On the strength of the idea, states that prepared their armies for quick decisive strikes forced their neighbors to do the same rather than plan for defense. In a world where offense was believed dominant, even states that preferred the status quo had to protect themselves against the possibility that others would launch pre-emptive strikes—and the only way to do that seemed to be by preparing to do the same thing themselves. Readying armies to pre-empt became a prudent policy even if the advantages of doing so were uncertain, because what was clear was that it would certainly be much worse *not* to act while somebody else did. The logic of strategic trade coupled with the notion of technology trajectories has similar implications for economic competitors. Nations or regions may be provoked to develop strategic trade policies in an effort to seize a first mover advantage, or simply out of fear that others might be doing the same. In either case even the appearance or suspicion that other governments might be attempting to do this could be sufficient to tip benign regionalism into mercantile rivalry.

This tendency will be reinforced by a new dynamic developing between military and commercial technology. In the Cold War system technologies "spun-off" from military to commercial applications because military technologies were frequently more sophisticated than those available in the civilian sector. The classic example is integrated circuit technology which was developed first for military and aerospace application. Now, because of the new industrial capabilities mentioned earlier, the dynamic is frequently reversed—that is, advanced commercial technologies "spin-on" into military applications.

What does this portend for security cooperation? The advent of spin-on has already prompted governments to regard many commercial technologies as militarily sensitive and therefore warranting secrecy orders. But this is not the most significant implication. More important, spin-on implies that nations which cede commercial markets may also sacrifice the ability to develop critical military systems. Lacking the supply base of resident skills, knowledge, process, and subsystems know-how of related commercial industries, it may not be possible to maintain leading-edge military capability. This creates a whole new level of security vulnerability; for the control that trade rivals have over militarily relevant commercial technologies can be used to extract concessions or impose constraints in return for granting access to technology. Taken together, these dangers reinforce the temptation to "grab" key technologies and markets before others can: doing so would guarantee domestic availability of the industrial resources needed to field state-of-the-art military forces and eliminate the need to make unacceptable concessions.

The prospects for mercantile rivalry between three large economic regions, each with a market large enough to influence global competition and large enough to capture most scale economies, are real. If they are unconnected by intimate ties of trade and investment, free from any common threat, standing in relative autonomy, one must ask of these three regions: What will bind them together? The only answer may be this: Fear; fear of one another.

IDEAS MATTER

The next security system could be defined by true multilateral cooperation, by peaceful regional coexistence, or, most dangerously, by mercantilist regional rivalry. The risk is that if regions come to view trade as a zero-sum game in which one region's gain is another's loss, they could start to regard each other as rivals competing not just for one-time gains in wealth, but for long-term growth and welfare. There are powerful intellectual, political, and technological forces that could push the world into this kind of mercantile rivalry. Existing international institutions would be hard pressed to cope with the instability that would result. . . .

Relationships are based not only on the distribution of power but also on ideas and the institutions that are connected to them. The security system that emerges over the next decade will reflect the new realities of economic power but it will also be shaped by the visions brought to it by the major actors. This was true even within the demanding constraints of a bipolar world. At the end of World War II, the United States and the Soviet Union both moved to construct security systems to balance the power of the other, but they chose to do so in very different ways according to different sets of ideas. The Soviet Union put together a network of bilateral treaties that connected Moscow to each of the Eastern European states but kept those states separate from each other: the organizing principle was "divide and conquer" and its success lay in making each Warsaw Pact nation individually dependent on Stalin for security and economic intercourse. The United States could have done the same and there would have been concrete advantages to doing so. But Washington chose a different model, the model that became NATO, where the allies were bound together in a system of indivisible security and each was protected equally by an American military umbrella. Security in the West became what economists call a "nonexcludable good"—which was at the root of the burden-sharing or free-riding complaints that the United States frequently leveled at its allies. But it did so only because the United States chose to fashion its alliance relationships in that way.

The point is that this choice was not determined by the distribution of power, but was based on a distinctive set of American ideas about world order, ideas that were firmed up by American diagnoses of the failures of international arrangements during the interwar years. The United States sought to avoid the discriminatory bilateral trade deals with Eastern Europe that contributed to Nazi power and the "checkerboard" system of weak guarantees in Western Europe that gave way so easily to aggression. Americans also believed that pluralistic and democratic states that traded freely could live together peacefully and grow economically, without threatening each other's vital interests.

The two sets of ideas were brought together in the multilateral institutions of the postwar Western world. Peace, prosperity, and democracy might not have been shared equally within those institutions, but they were to be shared by all. What emerged from this design did not match perfectly the American conception, but it came remarkably close. Economic and military power certainly helped the United States induce or compel sometimes reluctant nations to join the fold and comply with the bargains. But the substance of the bargains was as much a product of American vision as it was a product of economic strength.

Today a new basis for security relationships is forming. Hegemonies are gone, economic power is dispersed, and new ideas—about trade, security, development, and order—are emerging from new centers of power. These ideas will help to shape the relationships which in turn will determine the quality of life in the international system for both the most powerful states and their smaller neighbors. There are more strong voices on the world stage today than fifty years ago, and each has different things to say. The United States will have to listen. It must also shape the script.

THE CHALLENGE

It is possible for the United States to be effective without being dominant, but this will require a clear presentation of the kind of world we want to live in ten years hence and a program for getting from here to there. Mercantilist rivalry is not a necessary consequence of the new distribution of power, but it could arrive by default. To avoid it, the United States must act from strength at home and with multilateral cooperation abroad.

The first priority is to re-establish American economic strength. Neither external agreements nor combative trade policy can compensate for what we fail to do for ourselves. Only [the United States] can provide the kind of macro-economic environment, human and physical infrastructure, and mechanisms for the domestic development and diffusion of technologies that make it possible to be one of the winners in the big leagues of global economic competition.

The trick will be to re-establish American economic strength while avoiding beggar-thy-neighbor trade and technology practices that could push the world into mercantilist rivalry. That is where multilateral cooperation comes in: America's own economic redevelopment agenda provides the opportunity to establish new multilateral agreements to contain mercantilist behavior.

Achieving such multilateral cooperation will require several new actions. The United States and its allies need to agree to a set of principles that endorses reciprocal access to regional markets, investment opportunities, and supply-base technologies. Reciprocity of access permits as much openness as each regional economy can tolerate politically, and forces compromises in domestic practices that impede access whenever domestic industries seek foreign market opportunities. Effective reciprocity will in turn depend upon some degree of consensus about what domestic and business practices are appropriate. Some code of behavior will be needed to eliminate the most extreme and disruptive practices. To make up for the inevitable gaps and loopholes in that code, states will have to negotiate specific bargains.

The complex arrangements needed to achieve these goals will be difficult to negotiate in large multilateral forums like GATT. . . . Indeed, most of what will be accomplished will be on a bilateral basis. Consequently, it is crucial that bilateral negotiations take place in a multilateral context with rules of procedure and sufficient transparency to ensure that those who are not direct participants can make their needs and interests felt. The agenda for cooperation is daunting, but no more daunting than the GATT agenda must have looked to statesmen at the end of the 1940s.

The stakes may be as high now as when the GATT was conceived. Now, as then, real wealth and power are at stake. Then it was concentrated in U.S. hands; now it is regionally dispersed. Then we expected the system would benefit U.S. interests; now the United States has no such confidence. Hegemony is long gone, and a new world beckons. Now America needs to act not from the belief that [it is] and can remain dominant, but from an understanding of how [it] can be effective in circumstances in which [it] no longer [is].

31

OIL: REOPENING
THE DOOR

Joseph Stanislaw and Daniel Yergin

**For more than two decades oil has played a critical role in calculations of political
and economic power in the world. Joseph Stanislaw and Daniel Yergin assess
changes in the political economy of oil today against the backdrop of past lessons.
The end of the Cold War and growing environmental concerns are among the
forces that will shape a new relationship between oil producers and consumers in
the years ahead. Stanislaw is managing director and Yergin is president of
Cambridge Energy Research Associates. Yergin won the 1992 Pulitzer Prize for his
book *The Prize: The Epic Quest for Oil, Money, and Power* (1991).**

GLOBAL AGAIN

Twenty years after it burst into international politics with the 1973 crisis, oil
remains a strategic commodity critical in the global balance of power. But,
looking toward the 21st century, the perspective has changed radically since
those days when it seemed that oil power would engulf world politics.

Today, economics is taking precedence over politics. Many exporting countries court the international oil companies that they once shunned. The door that
was slammed shut in the 1970s is being reopened. In fact, with the prospect of
the opening of the petroleum reserves in Russia and many other countries that

up to now have been politically inaccessible oil is truly a global business for the first time since the barricades went up with the Bolshevik Revolution.

In retrospect, the shocks of the 1970s can be seen as the high point of oil nationalism. It was the era when the world economy hung on the comments of oil ministers in the hallways of OPEC meetings and when the wrongs of colonialism were to be set right. It was to be the beginning of the "new international order," a zero-sum game that would see a wholesale redistribution of wealth from the North to the South and a diminution of the international stature of the United States and the other major industrial powers.

Much of that is now history. The oil exporters learned that they needed the importers as much as the importers needed them. The producers may have had oil to sell, but the consumers provided the markets. They could also provide, when needed, security. These developments lead to new questions about the very meaning of security, and what durable relationships are now possible between consumers and producers that will serve the longer-term interests of both. The Persian Gulf War illustrates both the critical position of oil in the global balance of power and the importance of interdependence between producers and industrial consumers. There is also the increasingly important question of how to reconcile energy use and environmental imperatives.

With the collapse of communism, the global security issues that were uppermost have receded. Regional security issues, however, remain. The world is now shifting back to oil dependence on the Middle East, where modernization and Islamic revivalism are in conflict. Moreover, oil's traditional relationship to other global issues continues. It is intertwined with Russia's transition to free markets and Asia's economic growth. The United States is back on the track of higher oil imports, which means that its foreign policy will remain acutely sensitive to developments in oil-exporting countries.

In the years ahead, the global oil industry will require much higher levels of investment than in the recent past to meet both energy needs and environmental requirements. Politics, which in the 1970s sundered economic links between producers and consumers, is now permitting the reconnection of those links, though on a different basis. Thus, a new dimension of security between exporting nations and oil companies will come from the interweaving of investment, trade and finance. This reconstruction will mobilize the investment necessary to develop supplies for the next century. As a result, producers will be able to tap into the capital, technology and skills of consuming countries while supplying their markets.

LESSONS OF THE OIL CRISES

In September 1973, Japan's prime minister went so far as to predict that an oil crisis would come within ten years. It came in more like ten days, with the surprise attack that launched the 1973 Yom Kippur War, quickly followed by the oil embargo. In fact, the crisis had been building over the previous three years as the world market tightened and oil exporters began pushing up prices and asserting control over the oil resources within their borders. The resulting oil crunch took on the political cast of a battle between South and North.

The 1973 crisis drove prices from $2.50 to $10 a barrel and sent the global economy into a downturn. Then, at the end of the 1970s, revolution disrupted supplies from Iran, creating a panic that drove prices from $13 to $33 a barrel, seeming to foretell a permanent shortage and continuing turmoil.

Within a few years, however, it became evident that the price increases and the specter of shortages were creating powerful counter reactions. Non-OPEC oil development proceeded at a rapid pace. Conservation proved far more powerful than generally expected. All over the world utilities switched from oil to other fuels. Confronted with such developments, the exporters found that they could maintain high prices only through laboriously negotiated production quotas.

OPEC was soon faced with declining oil demand and diminishing market shares. Its share of the world oil market (excluding the former Soviet Union) fell from 63 percent in 1972 to 38 percent by the end of 1985. In one memorable quarter, Saudi Arabia's oil production had slumped to less than that of the British sector of the North Sea. In 1986, in the exporters' quest to regain market share, oil prices collapsed, falling to $10 before recovering to about $18 a barrel.

In the meantime, the consuming countries established security measures that would help moderate future crises. These included the International Energy Agency, an international emergency sharing system, increased communications, and prepositioned stocks such as the U.S. strategic petroleum reserve.

In the same years, the oil market became more flexible and transparent, with the development of trading ("oil as just another commodity") and the rise of futures markets. Oil is now carried around the world not only in behemoth supertankers but also in a sea of electronic information that instantaneously sweeps through trading rooms on every continent. While it can take a decade or more to develop a major new oil field, today's markets can swiftly adjust to changes in current supply and demand. For example, oil prices rose dramatically at the beginning of the gulf crisis but began declining in response to adjustments after only two months, as other producers hastened to bring unused capacity back into production. By the eve of Desert Storm, oil prices were actually lower than they had been a half-year earlier, in the weeks before the Iraqi invasion of Kuwait.

WELCOMING BACK OLD ENEMIES

These changes have brought a dramatic shift in the perspectives of oil exporting countries. They are redefining their relationship with the market and with the international oil industry. For the exporting nations, the essential issue of sovereignty has been answered. They own their resources and determine what happens to them. That was their essential victory in the 1970s. Now undisputed, this fundamental political recognition provides the exporting countries with the flexibility to focus on their longer-term economic interests.

Part of this reflects a shift in the broad intellectual currents in the global economy. In the 1970s the trend was toward increased state control—whether nationalization in developing countries or price controls in the United States. Today, the trend is quite the opposite—toward privatization, deregulation and commercialization. "The God that Failed" is not only the intellectual's adherence to Marxism but the very socialist model embraced as the path to development throughout much of the Third World.

Many of these developing countries are also in an economic bind. Populations are growing rapidly. When combined with flat oil prices, that means declining real per capita income. The OPEC surpluses, which so worried central bankers in the 1970s, have long since disappeared. What is less recognized is the debt burden and the budget and balance-of-payments pressures many of these countries are under. Like many other governments around the world, they need to reduce government spending and deficits. Yet they face political difficulties in making such adjustments. In a world in which oil prices are not even keeping pace with inflation, oil earnings can be increased only through greater productivity and increased output. But that takes significant investment—money that many exporters do not have.

Thus economic imperatives and changing ideologies are moving current and would-be exporting countries to seek the international oil industry's capital, technology and management skills. . . .

Around the world, doors are being reopened. Venezuela, which nationalized foreign companies in 1976, is cautiously inviting them back to develop marginal fields. Argentina, which established the first state oil company in 1922, is now privatizing it, and at the same time is encouraging foreign companies to explore and produce within its borders. Algeria is actively inviting in companies to stem the threatened decline in its oil production and to bolster natural gas output. And Vietnam, no longer on a Soviet dole, has offered some of the most attractive terms to entice companies to explore there. It is already the site of a mini-oil boom and will become the site of a bigger boom once U.S. restrictions on American companies are lifted. China, worried about the adequacy of energy to sustain its economic growth, is opening new areas to Western companies as well.

RUSSIA'S NEW REVOLUTION

But of all the doors, the biggest and most uncertain opens into the former Soviet Union, where the successor states, particularly Russia, are engaged in what may be described as the most extreme privatization in the world—the privatization of the revolution.

Behind this transformation lies the failure of state enterprise, which is central to the overall collapse of the Soviet economy. Just [a few] years ago, the Soviet Union was the world's largest oil producer, having pushed its production to 12.5 million barrels per day. As an oil exporter the Soviets had been among the biggest beneficiaries of the price increases of the 1970s. The huge windfall in foreign earnings enabled the Soviet Union to postpone economic reform. . . . After the 1986 oil price collapse, the Soviet system paid a terminally heavy price for its failure to grapple with reform earlier.

In addition, its stellar production numbers obscured the grave weaknesses—overinvestment in terms of return, poor oil field practices and outdated technology. Most of the Soviet oil production was concentrated in Russia—11.5 million out of 12.5 million barrels per day in 1988. In the five years since 1988, however, production in Russia . . . collapsed to 7 million barrels per day. The astonishing drop is equal to 60 percent of total U.S. oil production and is greater than the output of any OPEC nation except Saudi Arabia.

The impact of this decline on the world market has been cushioned by the precipitous drop in Russia's economy, which has drastically reduced its domestic oil demand, and by the reduction in nonhard currency exports from Russia to the other former Soviet republics. Hard currency exports of oil and gas are essential to Russia's economic recovery, as they currently represent half of total hard currency earnings. . . .

Until the late 1980s, the Soviet oil industry was closed to the outside world. Even statistics on the size of reserves were a state secret. While its personnel had high-level skills, they worked with technology 30 or 40 years behind that of the West. Since the late 1980s, Western oil companies have been able to carry out geological research with advanced technologies. As a result, while output continues collapsing, the estimates of the potential have been growing. Reserves, now thought to be three or four times the unofficial number of the 1980s, are in the class of the big Middle East producers. They will, however, be more expensive and less convenient to find and produce than those in the Middle East. . . .

Foreign investment could make a major difference. It is estimated that investment on the order of $50 billion between now and the year 2000 will be needed to stabilize Russian oil production at its current levels. Otherwise output could fall to as low as 4 million barrels a day, which could be disastrous for Russia. . . . Foreign investment, by bringing in Western technologies, will also substantially improve environmental performance. The end of communism has revealed a devastating and deadly pattern of environmental abuse. No exception is the oil industry, which is estimated to leak annually the equivalent of 400 supertanker cargoes from pipelines into the soil.

But significant foreign investment will not occur until the legal, fiscal, financial and institutional foundations are in place, at least to some degree. In turn, that depends on the overall evolution of the Russian political system. The current situation is too volatile and unpredictable for international oil companies to make large commitments.

Another hindrance is the opposition of some Russians to foreign participation. They argue that they do not want to be "colonized" and that the Russian industry can modernize itself and generate its own surplus for investment. If there is Western participation, they say, it should be on Russian terms and Russian terms alone. . . .

That investment flows are available is illustrated by the shift of capital out of the United States. [Since 1988] oil companies have dramatically realigned their spending away from America to the rest of the world. Driving the shift is the quest for better opportunities, reinforced by increasing operating constraints and environmental barriers to exploration and production in the United States. . . .

It is hard to see how the Russian oil industry can be turned around without Western participation. . . . Facilitating the involvement of Western companies in Russian oil development in ways that Russians themselves will regard as beneficial and fair is a matter of the highest priority. Such cooperation will not only help support the overall stability of the world oil market. It is also of critical importance to Russia's ability to make the transition to democracy and free markets, which in turn will be one of the key factors in global security.

But the risks also have to be reasonable for the Western investors. That means creating a framework that will give investors confidence over the longer term. . . .

THE CHALLENGE OF ENVIRONMENTALISM

The opening of doors around the globe points to a competition between countries for investment and a surge in activity by private companies. Yet producers and consumers face a new potential for divisiveness—over environmental policies. In the 1970s the dominant fear was of running out of oil. In the 20 years since, proven world oil reserves have doubled to over one trillion barrels. Today the policies of industrial countries increasingly focus on the environmental effects of energy use, particularly of oil.

A host of industrial world policies has singled out oil as the product whose use is to be discouraged. To the exporting countries, these policies disadvantage the product central to their national incomes. "Petrophobia" is the label given to this trend by Saudi Arabian Petroleum Minister Hisham Nazer. "Oil," he has said, "has been made the culprit."[1]

The conflicting interests are embodied in the controversy over broad-based energy taxes, such as the come-and-gone BTU tax in the United States and the European [Union's] would-be carbon tax. For the industrial countries, such

---

[1]Hisham Nazer, "The Development of the Environment and the Environment for Development," speech, Houston, TX, February 1993.

taxes raise revenues that contribute to closing yawning budget deficits and meeting environmental goals. To the exporters, however, such taxes mean a reallocation of revenues, or economic "rent," between producers and consumers, thus damaging the exporting countries' main source of national income. . . .

The drive for increased energy taxes has two effects on oil exporters. First, it makes them question their pricing strategies. Second, and of longer-term significance, it makes exporters question the value of investing in capacity necessary to support a growing oil demand that the industrial countries are trying to discourage.

Yet vigorous environmentalism is a reality that all participants in the international petroleum industry must recognize. Oil has been a business of technological change since the first well was drilled in Pennsylvania in 1859. Increasingly, the technological effort will be applied to meet the environmental agenda. The investment and technology that will be required—whether in production or in refining cleaner products—provide a new dimension in which the interests of producers and consumers will coincide and cooperation will be essential.

THE NEW PRIZE

Oil demand, left stagnant or declining by the 1970s' oil crises, only began to grow again after the 1986 price collapse. By 1989, world consumption finally regained the previous record level of 1979, and is continuing to grow. Indeed, if Russia is excepted, world oil demand is currently increasing at 1.8 percent per year, even in the midst of a weak global economy.

But the pattern of growth has changed. Demand is rather flat in North America and Western Europe, reflecting, among other things, the growing use of more efficient automobiles. In these nations the oil industry is preoccupied with the costs of staying in business. . . .

Demand growth is elsewhere—reflecting economic advancement in the developing world. The new prize is Asia. Economic "miracles," sustained growth, and rising incomes require energy. Many of these countries are swiftly applying higher environmental standards. But they do not want to be impeded from striving for higher living standards. Over a decade, Asia will require in excess of a trillion dollars of energy investment to support economic growth. Oil demand will increase by five million barrels or more. By early in the next decade, Asia will be consuming more oil than North America. . . .

Despite continued conservation, global oil demand could be 15 to 20 percent higher a decade from now. The trend could, of course, be changed by the considerable research and development efforts to find alternatives to oil, particularly in transportation. Yet, as things are today, oil is more than economically competitive—something that would have seemed unlikely in the era of the oil crises.

The years ahead will see an economic and environmental competition among energy sources, a technological horse race in which tens of billions of dollars will be wagered. To date, oil is proving to be environmentally competitive, keeping up with or even running ahead of new standards, albeit with considerable investment.

Natural gas, once the unwanted by-product of oil production, is now oil's biggest competitor and becoming the premium fuel around the world. A great deal of the financial resources of the "oil and gas industry" will actually be going into natural gas. It is an environmentally attractive fuel; some even call it the "politically correct" energy source. A decade from now there is likely to be a vigorous and diversified international trade in natural gas. Natural gas is not a significant competitor in transportation, where oil reigns supreme. Rather, the battle for markets will be played out around the world in electric generation, where the emphasis will very much be on environmental attributes.

But there is a question mark over oil supplies. . . . The world oil market is operating at about 92 percent of production capacity, quite different from the 1980s, when it was down to 80 percent. Today's market is reminiscent of the balance in the 1970s on the eve of the first oil shock.

Although political considerations and producer-consumer relations are very different from the 1970s, a tight oil market is vulnerable to shocks in a way that an oversupplied market is not. Projecting into the next century, one sees no shortage of potential crises that could affect world oil supplies, with dangerous consequences. Future crises could arise from the Middle East, as in the past. . . . But future crises could also arise from events in other parts of the world, such as some kind of disruption in the former Soviet Union.

If a disruption occurred in a tight market a few years from now, perhaps at a time of economic growth around the world, the effects could be quite sharp, both as measured in inflation and recession and in terms of raising international tensions.

Such risks underline the continuing need to assure an adequate "security margin" that can absorb such shocks. Moreover, considerable new production capacity will have to be added to support a growing world economy, but the timing of those additions is uncertain. What happens to oil prices, with all that they signify for the world economy, depends very much on the relative timing of demand growth and investment in new production capacity.

Where will the additional supplies come from? Not from the United States, where oil production has fallen [dramatically] since 1986 and is continuing to decline. The domestic U.S. oil production industry is deeply depressed, and the U.S. oil services industry, which is the global leader, is also under heavy economic pressure. U.S. oil imports are likely to continue rising in the years ahead. Some of it will come from oil development that is being encouraged by more open investment policies around the world. As Russia struggles to stem its economic decline, at least two of the newly independent republics, Azerbaijan and Kazakhstan, will become important players in the world oil market.

Much of the new supplies will come from the Middle East, in particular from Saudi Arabia. . . . In light of the political and social forces in the region, and the potential for yet another surprise or two in the decade ahead, security of supply will be a continuing concern for importing countries, even as the exporters continue to worry about "security of demand."

There is no single answer to these two security questions. Rather, the best bet for stability in a changing world arises from a global pattern of investment and trade in which security is enhanced by the diversity and density of economic and political links and by the commonality of interests in an environmental age.

In the years ahead, relations between producers and consumers could become strained again if, for instance, economic and demographic pressures mount in the exporting countries, or if political instability becomes pervasive, or if ideology again shifts, or if changes take place in the balance of power of the kind for which Saddam Hussein bid. Or, for instance, if the exporting countries come to see the implementation of the environmental agenda in developed countries as an assault on their main source of national income.

Yet even as the Cold War division between East and West has lost its significance, so economic progress is also erasing the division between North and South that was once so intense. Today, producers and consumers have a common interest in the technological advances needed to keep oil environmentally as well as economically competitive. The global energy supply system itself has become much more flexible. Over the last two decades, both producers and consumers have learned powerful lessons that reinforce their mutuality of interests and recognition of interdependence. Those lessons in themselves are a form of security. They constitute a major element in a framework that can help buffer whatever surprises may lie ahead.

ECOLOGY AND POLITICS

Some years ago T. S. Eliot lamented poetically that the world would end not with a bang but with a whimper. For decades the nuclear sword of Damocles hung by the slenderest of threads, threatening a fiery and shattering apocalypse. The quest for security continues, and the nuclear threat, while diminished, remains. Still, the end of the Cold War signals a dramatic change. For a generation, the *Bulletin of the Atomic Scientists* has used the hands of a clock—with the hour hand pointed toward midnight and the minute hand moving seemingly inexorably toward it—to symbolize how close humankind stands to the nuclear precipice. In 1988, for the first time in sixteen years, the minute hand was moved away from the witching hour, not toward it—from three to six minutes to midnight. In April 1990 the clock was again reset, this time at ten minutes to midnight, as the editors reasoned that "the termination of the Cold War has lifted a grim weight from the human psyche. It has returned to humanity its hope for a future, and the chance to create one." And in December 1991, when the editors concluded that "the world has entered a new era," the hands were moved to seventeen minutes from twelve, the largest movement ever.

Even as the threat of a nuclear apocalypse recedes, numerous challenges broadly conceived as *ecological* threaten that the final cataclysm may still occur, though now more by accretion than by design or accident—but with results no less fatal. Whether the world's nations and others touched by environmental challenges will cope effectively is problematic.

Part IV of *The Global Agenda* examines the politics of the ecological agenda. *Ecology* in this context refers to the relationship between humans and their physical and biological environments. The importance of ecological issues in world politics derives from the combination of world population growth and unsustainable consumption patterns that has placed increasing strains on the earth's delicate life-support systems. Food and resource scarcities have plagued the ecopolitical landscape from time to time in recent years as world population continues to grow inexorably, but it is a series of other environmental challenges—including acid rain, depletion of the stratospheric ozone layer, destruction of tropical rainforests, and global warming—that has captured worldwide attention and, together with the demise of Cold War competition, pushed the ecological problematique toward the top of the global agenda.

Environmental stresses result from human efforts to expand the global carrying capacity and to stretch the ability of the global habitat to sustain ever higher living standards for ever larger numbers of people. Technological innovations that propel modern industrialization permit new and more efficient use of environmental resources. They also result in pollution and other forms of environmental degradation of waterways, landmasses, and the atmosphere that threaten the environment future generations will inherit. The global commons— resources such as the oceans, the seabed, the radio spectrum, and outer space— previously regarded as the common heritage of humankind, are now able to be exploited by the technologically sophisticated, who may seek to deny them to others.

Environmental issues sometimes bear directly on issues of war and peace, the central concerns of traditional international relations theory and practice. A global environment characterized by scarcities of renewable and nonrenewable resources may invite the classic kinds of interstate conflict that once characterized competition over territory. Even comparatively abundant but unevenly distributed resources may create global conflicts if they lead to a level of dependence on foreign suppliers perceived as a threat to national security. Fear that Iraq's Saddam Hussein might gain control over a significant portion of world oil supplies following his invasion of Kuwait was certainly a primary motivation underlying the 1991 Persian Gulf War. If population growth and resource scarcities also portend, as some have argued, that there are "limits to growth" and that the consumption patterns of the past necessary to support the standards of living to which at least the industrial world has become accustomed must be curtailed in the future, questions of equity and justice, already so prominent on the North-South axis of the global agenda, will become magnified. The future of all people and nations is thus affected by how these issues are addressed, and the world that our children and their children inherit will be profoundly affected by the choices made today.

Nation-states, acting alone, may be the appropriate vehicles for dealing with some environmental issues. For others, they are not. Acid rain and other transboundary pollutants know no limits. Nuclear contamination of the atmosphere threatens many nations. Climatological changes induced by fossil fuel consumption and destruction of the protective ozone layer caused by other abuses imperil all. Concerted international collaborative efforts are required to deal with these and the many other ecological issues on the global agenda.

As this brief menu suggests, the range of global political issues encompassed by the ecological agenda is broad and, like issues of peace and security and economic interactions, complex. Until recently, however, the critical importance of ecological issues has been less well recognized. For most people ecological issues are typically remote. Unless we are touched directly by an issue, such as the disposal of toxic chemical waste or spent nuclear fuel, or atmospheric contamination in the form of acid rain, or soil erosion due to strip mining or deforestation, or life-threatening drought caused by excessive heat, ecological issues seem so distant as to be of little immediate relevance or concern. Despite this, there is a growing awareness worldwide—supported by survey data throughout the developed and developing world—that environmental issues are critically important to the quality of life individuals now enjoy and that their children will inherit.

An important milestone in the development of public consciousness among governments and their citizens occurred with the Earth Summit, which took place in June 1992 in Rio de Janeiro, Brazil. Formally known as the United Nations Conference on Environment and Development (UNCED), the summit brought together more than 150 nations, 1400 nongovernmental organizations, and some 8000 journalists. UNCED Secretary-General Maurice F. Strong characterized the work of the summit as "a new beginning," the "first steps on a new pathway to our common future." The major documents signed at the Earth Summit are statements of principles relating to the environment and development and to the management of the earth's forests, conventions on climate change and biodiversity, and a program of action—*Agenda 21*—which embodies a political commitment to the realization of a broad range of environmental and development goals.

Prior to the Earth Summit the environment and development had been treated separately—and often regarded as in conflict with one another, as development frequently imperils and degrades the environment. Now the concept *sustainable development* was used to galvanize a simultaneous treatment of environmental and development issues.

Sustainable development was a central tenet of the Earth Summit and permeates all its documents. The concept was first articulated in *Our Common Future,* the 1987 report of the World Commission on Environment and Development, popularly known as the Brundtland Commission after the Norwegian Prime Minister who was its chair. The commission defined a sustainable society in timeless fashion: It is one that "meets the needs of the present without compromising the ability of future generations to meet their own needs."

Because "sustainability" means living off the Earth's interest without encroaching on its capital, it draws attention to problems of intra- and intergenerational equity. At issue is how current needs can be met without depriving future generations of the resources necessary for their own survival. Literally hundreds of books and articles have asked in one way or another how this ambitious goal might be achieved. A common thread throughout them is that the goal of sustainability cannot be achieved without dramatic changes in the social, economic, and political fabric of the world as we now know it.

Our first essay in Part IV of *The Global Agenda,* "The Ecological Perspective on International Politics" by Dennis Pirages, introduces a way of thinking about global issues that stresses the interrelatedness in international politics of political communities with one another and with their environment. A key element of the perspective focuses on the demands placed by human populations on the carrying capacity of the physical environment. A second concerns natural resource constraints. Much of the history of international politics, Pirages explains, can be understood in terms of the domestic pressures for expansion abroad generated by the maldistributuion of the supply and demand for natural resources worldwide.

Technology is the third key element. On the one hand, technology, as noted above, can increase the efficiency of natural resource utilization. On the other hand, it can also lead to "by-products that can destroy important links in life-sustaining ecosystems." Thus technology has enhanced the ability of nations to play the game of international politics, but it is also "altering dramatically the relations of human populations with each other as well as the ecosphere."

As nations prepared for the Earth Summit, they confronted—some for the first time—many of the complex interrelationships comprising the ecological perspective. The background to their preparations included a growing recognition of the environmental threat posed by continued population growth and the degradation already suffered by land, water, and air resources. Crispin Tickell touches on this background in our next selection, "The Earth Summit and Beyond." He also notes the often differing values that groups of states brought to the assessment of environmental concerns. The industrial countries "comforted themselves with the belief that environmental degradation was essentially a problem of the poor. . . . Few recognized the scale of the problem or their own direct involvement." The developing countries, on the other hand, "tended to view Rio as an ideal opportunity to extract more financial help from the rich." They neglected the critical point that "they are more vulnerable to change than anyone else and would stand to lose most if the environment were damaged in an irretrievable way." As a result of these differing values and perceptions, the Earth Summit often took on the trappings of another chapter in the continuing contention between the rich nations of the North and the poor nations of the South.

The Earth Summit documents reflect these divisions and, because of them, achieved less than was once hoped. Other issues were dealt with incompletely or ignored altogether, including issues related to "resource use and population trends." Tickell addresses the accomplishments and shortcomings of Rio and concludes that, in the final analysis, "we must rethink the way in which we run our societies. . . . The environment must be brought into virtually every aspect of the way we conduct our affairs."

The ambitious program of action contained in *Agenda 21* would, if implemented, impact on every aspect of human affairs. Its vision, as articulated in Daniel Sitarz's *"Agenda 21:* Toward a Strategy to Save Our Planet," is the creation of "an entirely new relationship between and among nations . . . , a global partnership based on common interests, mutual needs and common yet differentiated responsibilities." Realizing that vision will require addressing complex, interconnected problems loosely summarized in six central themes: the quality of life on earth; the efficient use of earth's natural resources; protection of the global commons; the management of human settlements; the management of chemicals and waste; and sustainable economic growth. Implementing the many specific recommendations contained in *Agenda 21*—which may cost hundreds of billions of dollars—is a seventh theme. It will require nothing less than "a monumental and sustained commitment."

Demographic changes taking place throughout the world in many ways reinforce the differing interests and inequalities evident in the world and the variant approaches that states adopt toward environmental perils and challenges. We live in a demographically divided world. Population growth in the industrial countries of the North has slowed, but it continues its rapid pace in the developing nations of the South, where in the next thirty to forty years 3 billion people will be added to the world's present population of more than 5.5 billion. Because of these differing rates of growth, demographic variables relate to sociopolitical phenomena in different ways, as the editors of *The Global Agenda,* Charles W. Kegley, Jr., and Eugene R. Wittkopf, explain in "Population Pressures and the Global Habitat." "Generally the impact of population growth on economic development is the most immediate and important question facing developing countries," they write. "In contrast the main issues for developed nations tend to focus more on the impact of affluence on world resources and the global commons." However, because the world is interdependent economically and environmentally, the demographically divided North and South will both experience the multiple consequences of demographic trends already in place.

Patterns of emigration and immigration, often propelled by adverse ecological conditions, are among the ways our demographically divided world is knit together. Doris Meissner examines these patterns in "Managing Migrations." She notes that while most migration occurs within states, migrations to developed countries in recent years "have led to fierce political debate and calls for dramatic policy changes." In part this is because immigrants often challenge the dominant social and cultural patterns in the receiving country. The concerns raised "are magnified when the immigrant groups are ethnically, racially, or religiously different from host societies, as is the pattern with much immigration today in the West." The collapse of the Soviet empire and the vestiges of Cold War rivalry in many parts of the developing world are among the forces that have stimulated intra- and international migration. Thus migration and related policy issues, including "the right to stay," have been thrust onto the post-Cold War global agenda.

Another demographic link between North and South is found in the pressures exerted by population growth and rising affluence on world food supplies. During the 1970s, when the phrase "limits to growth" was used to capture the widespread belief among policy makers and the informed public about the world's eco-political future, it was expected that the inability of national agricultural systems to meet rising demand for food would lead to widespread global food insecurity. A decade later, however, the phrase "a world awash in grain" was equally widespread, as both technological developments and shifts in the global marketplace undermined the neo-Malthusian gloom so evident only a short time earlier. By the early 1990s, however, a combination of environmental degradation, population growth, and rising prices in the face of reduced production again raised doubts about the prospects for ensuring global and national food security.

Realizing global food security is often described as the first priority of sustainable development. The challenge of sustainable agricultural development in turn is viewed as a necessary step in providing enough food for the world's growing population without destroying earth's life-support base. However, Nabil Megalli, in "Hunger versus the Environment: A Recipe for Global Suicide," paints an alarming picture of the devastation now occurring throughout the world. "Agriculture is devouring its own base in three continents that cover two-thirds of the world's area and house four-fifths of its population," he writes. "The world is galloping towards a situation where it will not be able to feed itself, no matter what it does."

The causes underlying this bleak assessment read like a catalog of the specific elements underlying each of the six central themes addressed in *Agenda 21*. They include overfishing, overgrazing, overcropping, overfertilization, overcrowding, deforestation, desertification, salinization, soil erosion, and pollution of water resources. "If humanity is to feed itself," Megalli concludes, "this environmental degradation has to stop—and stop soon."

Technology has caused many of these worrisome adverse changes in the earth's delicate life-support systems, but it has also made possible widespread improvements in the standard of living of people throughout the world. It has enabled farmers worldwide to increase agricultural productivity at a rate that has surpassed even the rapid rate of population growth since World War II. Orville L. Freeman worries, in "Agriculture and the Environment: Meeting Global Food Needs," that concern for preserving the environment may inhibit the application of new (if still uncertain) technology to meet the enormous expansion in food production that the growth of world population during the remainder of this decade and into the next will require. What is needed, he argues, is a delicate balancing act designed "to bring the goals of feeding the world's population and protecting the world's environment into harmony. . . . Yes, we must protect our fragile environment and use our resources wisely. But there is a very serious danger that the voice of the world's hungry will not be heard if the environmental and food-related agenda is written to meet only the needs of well-intentioned but well-fed interests."

Ensuring global food security depends on access to water, among other things. In many parts of the world, however, a combination of rising population and increasing demand is overtaxing nature's water bodies. In our next essay, "The Politics of Water," Sandra Postel argues that "water scarcity" threatens to become "a major source of economic and political instability."

Noting that "nearly 40 percent of the world's people depend on river systems shared by two or more countries," Postel directs attention to the politics of water as it relates to the three major river basins that serve the people and nations of the Middle East. She notes in particular how downstream countries may be disadvantaged by the decisions of nations farther upstream. This often creates zero-sum situations, in which one state's gain becomes another's loss. The politics of water also creates cooperative opportunities, in which mutual gain is the outcome, but the claim of some states to "absolute sovereignty" over water within their boundaries and without regard to their neighbors makes resolution of water conflicts difficult. More broadly, achieving mutual gain faces "a chicken-and-egg problem": "Cooperation can breed win-win solutions to water problems, which in turn can defuse tensions, but tensions have to be defused before nations will cooperate."

Environmental protection is now a widely shared international goal. So, too, is free international trade. Often, however, the two are deemed incompatible, as the realization of one comes at the expense of the other. As other essays in this section of *The Global Agenda* make clear, protecting the environment requires conservation of global resources, but expanding world trade often implies accelerating the rate of resource consumption.

In "The GATT: Environmental Menace or Ally?" Hilary F. French probes the tension between the goals of free trade and environmental protection. Central to that conflict is the determination of the General Agreement on Tariffs and Trade (GATT) to reduce barriers to trade and the often equal determination of environmentalists to use trade barriers to protect the environment. The belief that GATT's decision-making procedures are elitist and used to deny environmental victories that pro-trade forces are unable to win in domestic decision-making settings fuels the fire. French finds lessons in the negotiations leading to the North American Free Trade Agreement (NAFTA) linking the United States, Canada, and Mexico that may be applied globally, and she suggests several ideas for changes in GATT's rules that may "green" the trade organization. The objective is to "restore [GATT's] tarnished reputation" and to make it responsive to "today's environmental imperatives."

When resources are held in common, individual actors have an incentive to exploit them to their maximum, because the collectivity must bear the costs of exploitation but they alone realize the benefits. The metaphor of the tragedy of the commons, a stock concept in environmental politics, helps explain this typical national response to the global commons. Marvin S. Soroos examines the applicability of the metaphor in our next selection, "The Tragedy of the Commons in Global Perspective," and uses it as a springboard to probe several environmental issues and to explore strategies for avoiding environmental tragedies. Importantly, he relates these strategies to values (conservation, production, equity, and freedom), the realization of which necessarily often entails tough political choices as states seek to cope with ecological exigencies. Soroos concludes, surprisingly, perhaps, that at least in the area of atmospheric pollutants, states have undertaken a greater degree of unilateral, voluntary actions to cope with environmental degradation than the tragedy of the commons would have predicted. He also concludes that the basic international infrastructure for avoiding disaster has also been put into place.

William Ophuls and A. Stephen Boyan, Jr., pose a sharply different viewpoint in "The International State of Nature and the Politics of Scarcity." The authors are much less sanguine about the ability of humankind to manage its common problems given the anarchical "state of nature" of the international system. Despite increased global consciousness about environmental perils, Ophuls and Boyan find that the challenge of scarcity is more likely to precipitate conflict than cooperation. The absence in the international system of either higher law or higher authority and the persistence of the principle of sovereignty encourage struggle and pursuit of narrow self-interest , not collaboration. It may be a system crying out for recognition that under prevailing circumstances the future of each depends on the future of all, Ophuls and Boyan observe, but it is nonetheless a system that in the short run rewards those who "help themselves" at the expense of others. The danger, they warn, is that all will likely suffer.

The essays in Part IV of *The Global Agenda* direct attention to many sources of environmental degradation and to the way that international conflict may be stimulated by ecological contention. War itself, of course, often precipitates desecration of the environment. Rome sowed salt on a defeated Carthage to prevent its resurgence. The Dutch breached their own dikes to allow ocean saltwater to flood fertile farmlands in an effort to stop the advancing Germans during World War II. The United States used defoliants on the dense jungles in Vietnam in an effort to expose enemy guerrillas. And Iraq engaged in acts of "environmental terrorism" when it released millions of gallons of oil into the Persian Gulf during the war over Kuwait.

As military capabilities continue to increase, threats to the environment also multiply. In all the cases cited above, environmental damage was confined to a comparatively small locale or region. Should a nuclear exchange ever occur, the damage threatens an environmental calamity of global proportions. As explained by the theory of "nuclear winter," a nuclear exchange would spew so much dust, smoke, and poisonous gas into the atmosphere that it would transform the earth into a dark, frozen wasteland incapable of sustaining humankind's delicate life-support systems by precipitating a prolonged period of abnormal coldness, darkness, and ancillary atmospheric disturbances.

The end of the Cold War and the "disarmament race" between the United States and Russia and others reduces (but does not eliminate) the probability that a fateful nuclear exchange may occur. As nuclear and other threats linked to the Cold War recede, analysts have wondered about the future threats to national security nations are likely to face. Many have concluded that environmental threats now pose significant national security threats.

As noted, war itself often desecrates the environment. Whether resource scarcities and other environmental perils themselves also pose security threats is less clear. Although it has become fashionable in the post-Cold War world to equate ecological and security threats, Daniel Deudney, in "Environment and Security: Muddled Thinking," questions the wisdom of doing so. He critically examines ways environmental analysts anticipate that resource scarcity and environmental stress may lead to violent conflict. And he worries that efforts to wrap environmental concerns in the mantle of national security may be counterproductive: "Instead of linking national security to the environment, environmentalists should emphasize that global ecological problems call into question the nation-state and its privileged status in world politics. Ecological decay is not a threat to national security, but it challenges the utility of thinking in national terms." Thus the agenda of ecology and politics challenges all of us to think anew about the linkages between the politics of peace and security and the politics of material and non-material well-being. It is a fitting challenge with which to conclude *The Global Agenda*.

32

THE ECOLOGICAL
PERSPECTIVE ON
INTERNATIONAL POLITICS

Dennis Pirages

Dennis Pirages describes the way human populations, natural resources, and technology intertwine to form the building blocks of an ecological perspective on international relations. The perspective focuses on the interaction of human relationships with the global ecosystem, humankind's sustaining environment, and on the social and political issues such interaction stimulates. Pirages is a professor in the Department of Government and Politics at the University of Maryland. He is author of *Global Technopolitics: The International Politics of Technology and Resources* (1989).

In 1971 Harold and Margaret Sprout introduced an important new perspective into the study of international relations with publication of *Toward a Politics of the Planet Earth*. Building a bridge between their earlier work on man-milieu relationships and the growing field of ecology, the Sprouts advanced visionary ideas now recognized as offering a new unifying paradigm for twenty-first-century social science. They suggested an "ecological" approach to the study of international relations built around four related concepts: environment, environed populations, environmental relationships and interrelated complexes (or

Reprinted with permission of the author and Blackwell Publishers. From *International Studies Quarterly,* 27, pp. 243–255.

communities) that compose, in the aggregate, an ecosystem coterminous with the earth's surface (Sprout and Sprout, 1971: 30). . . .

The ecological approach pioneered by the Sprouts offers a potentially powerful organizing framework for two reasons. First, this approach is anchored in an evolutionary perspective which stresses changes in environment-society relationships over time. Although present global environmental pressures certainly call attention to this perspective, these man–environment relationships have been and will continue to be crucial factors in shaping relations among people and nations. . . . Second, the ecological perspective . . . gives theoretical priority to physical realities—man–environment relationships central in shaping social phenomena—and also recognizes tremendous variations in social responses to the same environmental pressures. The approach focuses on the interface between environmental ecosystems and human behavior. Human beings, social institutions and related value systems have shaped as well as been shaped by physical environments. But while the impact of changing natural environments on the physical evolution of human and other species has been carefully documented in the biological sciences, the related study of the environmental linkage to the evolution of social institutions, cultural values and relations among nations is still at the formative stage.

ELEMENTS OF AN ECOLOGICAL APPROACH

. . . An ecological perspective applied to international relations begins with the observation that human beings share an ecosystem with many other species of flora and fauna. Seen in this manner, humans are "a population of organisms and non-living matter (in) a biotic community, or ecosystem" (Sprout and Sprout, 1971: 27). An ecosystem is composed of the total array of plant and animal species in an environment as well as the matter which cycles through the system (Watt, 1973: 5). This perspective stresses the reciprocal functional relationships among organisms and between organisms and their physical environments (Ehrlich, 1977: 128). The international ecosystem is the entire interrelated set of smaller systems nourishing life on this planet and is referred to as the biosphere, ecosphere, or global ecosystem. *Homo sapiens,* in this perspective, is a species governed by basic ecological principles applicable to other occupants of the ecosphere. Theories that attempt to explain how human beings, individually or collectively, behave in relation to nature or other human beings can be usefully anchored in the study of the evolution of the ecosystem–society interface.

Inquiry within an ecological framework profits from an understanding of at least three important concepts. The first concept is human populations and their related growth dynamics. In the most general sense, the human population of the world [now exceeds] five billion persons. But human beings live within and identify with smaller populations, closely knit groups that interact mainly with other members. Biologists and ecologists define a population of any species as a "dynamic system of interacting individuals . . . that are potentially capable of interbreeding with each other" (Watt, 1973: 1). While human populations could be defined in the same manner, it is more useful to define them by the relative frequency of communication among them. With minor exceptions, the clusters of most frequent verbal and mediated human communications are coincident with the boundaries of interbreeding human populations. Human populations can then be defined by the "marked gaps in efficiency of communications," a social scientific definition that is nearly identical with the biological equivalent (Deutsch, 1964: 100). These communication gaps and inefficiencies both maintain and are maintained by differences in language, culture, values, beliefs, and levels of socioeconomic development.

Prior to the global spread of the industrial revolution, there were thousands of relatively isolated human groups that met either biological or communications tests as distinct populations. But the dynamics of modernization have pressed many of these disparate human groups into national populations. While the boundaries of states usually demarcate human populations, there are many subnational groups that have not been effectively integrated, thus complicating ecological analysis.

Human populations are subject to ecological and biological imperatives similar to those governing other species. These include a tendency to grow in numbers and demands until the limits of the carrying capacity of the relevant physical environment are reached, or even exceeded, in Malthusian dramas that have been repeated in all regions of the world throughout history. When food and other necessary resources have been abundant, human populations have expanded to utilize them, only to migrate or be trimmed back by pestilence and famine when factors such as weather or environmental despoilation have reduced the available resource base.

Natural resources are the second important concept in building a link between human populations and ecosystems. From an ecological perspective, a resource "is anything needed by an organism, population or ecosystem which, by its increasing availability up to an optimal or sufficient level, allows an increasing rate of energy conversion" (Watt, 1973: 20). Translating this into political terms, human populations, like populations of other species, have consumption potentials that are limited by the resource necessary for economic growth that is in shortest supply. Human populations have experienced tremendous increases in demand for added varieties and quantities of critical resources as a result of the industrial revolution, and most mature industrialized countries cannot now be sustained solely by the resources existing within national boundaries. The mix of available resources structures a population's potential for autonomous growth and development. However, the resources required for contemporary industrialization have not been distributed equally among states. In some cases countries have been generously endowed with resources, though decades of industrial activity have all but exhausted them. In other cases required resources have never been available. Whatever the reason, most highly industrialized countries . . . now depend on resource bases outside of their domestic jurisdiction.

As national populations historically have run up against natural resource constraints on growth, domestic pressures have built up for accessing new supplies. This "lateral pressure" has resulted in various types of expansionist activity that has had different impacts on external actors. As Choucri and North (1975: 16) have put it, "When demands are unmet and existing capabilities cannot be altered at a reasonable cost within national boundaries, they may be sought beyond."

The behavioral manifestations of lateral pressure and techniques used to channel it have assumed many different forms based upon the strength of perceived needs, types of domestic sociopolitical organization, culturally determined justifications, and the power of neighboring nations. Lateral pressure often resulted in initiatives that are harmful to those affected by them. In the historical development of many Western European countries a point was reached where external resources were perceived to be accessible and superior replacements for domestic supplies. Thus, it has been suggested that aggressive outward expansion of European influence in the fifteenth and sixteenth centuries resulted, at least in part, from twin domestic pressures of ecological scarcity and rising expectations (Wallerstein, 1974: 39–48). The Portuguese, Dutch, British, Germans and eventually other European powers acquired territories in distant parts of the world that provided food, minerals, and even human resources. At the beginning of World War I, 84 percent of the world's land was or had been controlled by colonial powers (Fieldhouse, 1973: 3).

From an ecological perspective these adventures by Western European nations could be seen as a response to enhanced technological capabilities combined with resource and growth dilemmas. From the perspectives of the inhabitants of conquered territories, they were experienced as exploitation and imperialism. In the colonizing nations, by contrast, such moves across borders were easily justified. The entrepreneurs responsible for colonization were supported by elaborate moral justifications for what, in retrospect, was the human variant of behavior typical of any species pushing against resource limits. In these cases, however, the human populations possessed technological capabilities to do something about the problem.

While colonialism and war represent malevolent aspects of lateral pressure, other solutions to resource limitations have had a somewhat more benevolent impact on global development. The creation of an integrated world economy and related division of labor based on comparative advantage is one such response. Benefits of these new economic arrangements, however, are not always perceived as being equitably shared by all populations involved, giving rise to charges that the old system of direct colonial resource exploitation has given way to a new one based upon economic inequities in market relationships (see Laszlo *et al.,* 1978: Chapter 2).

Technology is the third important concept in developing an ecological perspective. It is a force that has altered dramatically relationships of human populations with those of other species and with supporting ecosystems. Technological innovations have created both new demands for a wider variety of natural resources and increased efficiency of natural resource utilization. The bulk of technological innovation occurring during the industrial revolution took place under circumstances of relative resource abundance. The result was a series of innovations that met human needs largely by expanding the quantity of resources used. Over the last decade, however, in an environment characterized by perceived resource scarcity, technological innovation now focuses on qualitative improvements in resource utilization as well, more effectively using each consumed unit of natural resource. Technology is somewhat responsive to price signals and, in effect, "creates" additional resources through new efficiencies under situations of perceived scarcity (Hueckel, 1976). It remains to be seen, however, if technology can survive its current diminishing returns and sustain a protracted efficiency revolution (see Giarini and Loubergé, 1978).

Technology also modifies human relationships with the environment by creating by-products that can destroy important links in life-sustaining ecosystems. "With no exceptions, technological economic development has entailed increasing accumulations of residues, many of which cause damage to human and nonhuman populations, and continuing hazards of future damage" (Sprout and Sprout, 1978: 24–25). The price paid for industrial economic growth has been an increased human impact on, and transformation of, ecosystems within which human evolution occurs. While technological progress has expanded the growth potential of human populations, its by-products threaten future long-term damage to the ecosystems sustaining human life if technology is not properly managed. Thus, the impact of technological development on relations among nations has been significant. Technology has enhanced national capabilities and the present international hierarchy, with its pronounced differences in wealth, power, and consumption, is in large measure a creation of uneven technological development. On a global scale, however, the waste products of industrial growth, such as acid rain and increased build-up of carbon dioxide, are altering dramatically the relations of human populations with each other as well as the ecosphere.

In summary, an ecological perspective on social behavior and institutions calls attention to human dependence upon the sustaining environment (ecosystems) within which life has evolved, for continued growth and well-being. The same ecological imperatives governing other species also shape relations among human beings both within and among countries. The problem of maintaining access to resources required for growth in human numbers and living standards plays an important role in motivating human behavior, shaping institutions and determining relations among nations. Technology is a key element facilitating transformation of resources into the artifacts that enhance individual, group, and national capabilities. . . .

. . . If human institutions, behavior and values are, to a significant extent, environmentally determined, it is better to understand these relationships than to pretend that they do not exist. But more important, many scholars have written about an impending "post-industrial" revolution led by, among other things, a revolution in genetic engineering. . . . A post-industrial social scientific revolution could help avert an "overshoot" of the global resource base by designing institutions based upon prescriptions deduced from a better understanding of environment-social evolution relationships.

References

Choucri, N. and R. North. (1975) *Nations in Conflict.* San Francisco: W. H. Freeman.

Deutsch, K. (1964) *Nationalism and Social Communication.* Cambridge: MIT Press.

Ehrlich, P. (1977) *Ecoscience: Population, Resources, Environment.* San Francisco: W. H. Freeman.

Fieldhouse, D. (1973) *Economics and Empire, 1830–1914.* New York: Cornell University Press.

Giarini, O. and H. Loubergé. (1978) *The Diminishing Returns of Technology.* New York: Pergamon.

Hueckel, G. (1976) "A Historical Approach to Future Economic Growth," *Science,* March 14.

Laszlo, E., *et al.* (1978) *The Objectives of the New International Economic Order.* New York: Pergamon.

Sprout, H. and M. Sprout. (1971) *Toward a Politics of the Planet Earth.* New York: Van Nostrand Reinhold.

Sprout, H. and M. Sprout. (1978) *The Context of Environmental Politics: Unfinished Business for America's Third Century.* Lexington: University of Kentucky Press.

Wallerstein, I. (1974) *The Modern World System.* New York: Academic Press.

Watt, K. (1973) *Principles of Environmental Science.* New York: McGraw-Hill.

33

THE EARTH SUMMIT
AND BEYOND

Crispin Tickell

Crispin Tickell provides a brief but trenchant overview of the environmental problems facing the world as countries prepared for the Earth Summit—the 1992 United Nations Conference on Environment and Development (UNCED) held in Rio de Janeiro—the accomplishments and shortfalls of the summit, and the challenges that lay ahead. He describes the differing perceptions of the industrial nations of the North and the developing nations of the South on the issues addressed at the summit as a "clash of uncomprehending cultures within and between countries and peoples." Tickell is warden of Green College at Oxford University and served previously in the British Diplomatic Service. He is president of the Royal Geographical Society and chair of the Climate Institute in Washington, D.C.

. . . The Rio Summit brought together, or crystallized, a change in people's feelings about the environment that had been gathering pace over many years. History is always invidious, but let me single out some landmark events. The first UN Conference on the Environment took place at Stockholm in 1972. The same year, the Club of Rome published a highly influential book that challenged

Reprinted from *The Washington Quarterly*, Crispin Tickell, "The Earth Summit and Beyond," by permission of the MIT Press, Cambridge, Massachusetts. Copyright © 1993 by The Center for Strategic and International Studies and The Massachusetts Institute of Technology. Some footnotes have been deleted or renumbered.

conventional economics and was entitled *The Limits to Growth.*[1] These were the first in a series of events, books and the like, that has gathered in volume ever since. There followed the creation of the UN Environment Program (also in 1972); the First World Climate Conference (1979); the work in the United States that culminated in 1979 in the document *Global 2000;*[2] the critically important Brundtland Commission report on environment and development in 1987;[3] declarations on the environment in the series of summit meetings held in 1989 including that of the nonaligned countries in Belgrade; the Second World Climate Conference, held in 1990; . . . and finally the run-up to Rio itself.

The total effect of the rise in awareness caused by these events was that it made people think differently. Twenty-five years ago most people would have found all this attention to the environment bizarre. But environmental concerns radically challenge entrenched orthodoxies and prevailing assumptions. By now most ordinary people are aware that something has gone wrong with the way in which we manage our affairs. The environmental dimension is established in public life and has become permanent. The question is how to cope with it.

BACKGROUND TO RIO

Before we look at what was accomplished at Rio, certain historical perspectives should be borne in mind. We are perhaps the first generation to see the downside of the industrial revolution. But first remember the upside. This includes, for example, the revolutions in technology—the latest the devices of solid-state electronics. Fewer resources produce more and more. In industrial countries the rise in material living standards has been amazing. Economic wealth in a general sense rose at an almost incredible rate during most of this century. Global gross domestic product was on the order of U.S. $600 billion in 1900. It stood at $5 trillion in 1960, and at about $17 trillion in 1988. Such growth was highly uneven: of the $17 trillion, around $14.7 trillion came from the industrial countries (accounting for 23.2 percent of the world's population), and $2.5 trillion from the rest of the world (accounting for 76.6 percent of its population).

Population   But all this has been at a price. Uncertainties on the subject remain but population increase is undoubtedly one of the most alarming items on the account. At the end of the last ice age, when humans started to spread into the Americas, the population was roughly 10 million. In 1930, it was 2 billion. Unless a global catastrophe takes place, it will be 8.5 billion in 2025. At

---

[1]Donella H. Meadows, et al., *The Limits to Growth* (New York: Universe Books, 1972).

[2]Gerald O. Barney, ed., *The Global 2000 Report to the President: Entering the 21st Century.* A report prepared by the Council on Environmental Quality and the Department of State (Washington, D.C., 1980).

[3] . . . World Commission on Environment and Development, *Our Common Future* (New York: Oxford University Press, 1987). . . .

present there are nearly 100 million more people every year or, put differently, 8 more New Yorks every year. In Africa alone the population rose from 288 million in 1970 to 384 million in 1980 and to 505 million in 1990.

Damage to Land   A second worry is the deterioration of land, which is of course linked to the proliferation of the population. The World Resources Institute, among the most respected of environmental bodies, has recently produced a report that shows that approximately 10 percent of the vegetation-bearing surface of the earth is suffering from moderate to extreme degradation that has occurred because of human activity since 1945.[4] That is an area bigger than the United States. Industrial pollution has adversely affected 16 percent of the former Soviet Union.

Water Resources   Sea water is 97 percent of the earth's water supply: we have long regarded the sea as a sink into which we can pour pollutants. As a result virtually no part, no matter how remote, of the oceans is free of contamination. The situation is worst along coastlines and within the continental shelf; but such chemicals as PCBs or DDT can now be found in the tissue of Arctic creatures like penguins or seals that have never been anywhere near a human being. Meanwhile, demand for fresh water continually increases. It doubled between 1940 and 1980 and will double again by the end of the century. As an illustration, all states bordering the Nile plan—indeed need—to take out more water, but the river's total volume has diminished in recent years and there is no reason to believe it will be able to meet demand in the future.

Another illustration is the fate of the Colorado River. Many have seen it racing magnificently through the Grand Canyon and fertilizing areas downstream. Fewer have seen the sickly, salty stream that eventually reaches the Pacific. It has long been a prime cause of dissension between the United States and Mexico. This example represents a prototype of the dissension that will arise between many other states over the use of many other rivers in the future. Water, indeed, will be a more important issue than oil.

The Atmosphere   There are three aspects to the problems of the atmosphere. Acidification due to industrial wastes is local in character and can be cured if the will to do so is there. Ozone depletion is the indirect product of the manufacture and use of those useful molecules known as chlorofluorocarbons and is caused when they rise into the upper atmosphere. The ozone layer is a shield protecting us from certain wavelengths of ultraviolet light. Without it life itself would be put at risk. Even its depletion risks increasing the incidence of skin cancer and cataract in humans. It is profoundly encouraging that the perils

[4]World Resources Institute, *World Resources 1992–93: A Guide to the Global Environment* (New York: Oxford University Press, 1992), pp. 111–112.

of chlorofluorocarbons have been generally recognized and that international agreements are now in place to eliminate their manufacture. But the effects will be with us for a long time to come.

Global Warming   It is much less easy to cope with the likelihood of global warming. The climate varies all the time, and thousands of years from now the earth will probably return to an ice age. In the meantime we are artificially increasing the quantity of gases in the atmosphere—carbon dioxide, methane, nitrous oxide, and so on—that have the effect of trapping more of the earth's heat and increasing the temperature at the surface. The facts are not in doubt. The questions are of degree and extent. It is predicted that there will be a 2.5°C average temperature rise between 1990 and 2100. During this period the seas could rise by 48 centimeters. This rise may be increased or abated by natural variations, but one-third of the human race lives on the shores of bodies of water and would be strongly affected. One of the achievements of Rio was a Climate Convention that at least—and at last—recognized the hazards.

Threats to Biodiversity   . . . We are destroying [the] diversity [of life] on a scale comparable to the effect of the asteroid that wiped out the dinosaurs. There is substantial elimination of species—and an alarming ignorance of their value. Death is one thing, but the end to birth is another! Churches have much to answer for in the sense that they have led us to regard ourselves as apart from the rest of the animal and vegetable worlds. In fact we are all part of the same tissue of life. Without bacteria we could not digest our food, and without our food we could not live. No one can yet measure the complexities of interdependence or the impact of the destruction of other species, but we do know that the scale of the damage is immense, especially in moist, tropical rainforests, which contain over 50 percent of species on 7 percent of the land surface. Again, an achievement of Rio was the Convention on Biodiversity.

ATTITUDES TOWARD ENVIRONMENTAL CHANGE

These changes in the environment are driven by two main forces. On the one hand is unsustainable consumption of the earth's resources, principally by and in industrial countries. In other countries the problem is pressure on resources, which itself is exacerbated by population increase. We are a long way from measuring the consequences, which were seen very differently by the different participants at Rio. On one side the industrial countries comforted themselves with the belief that environmental degradation was essentially a problem of the poor. They were ready to give some help. But few recognized the scale of the problem or their own direct involvement. None was ready to give an example of restraint. Here the United States was particularly at fault. With about 5 percent of the world's population, it produces about 25 percent of the world's pollution. Of course it is not easy for a democratic government to adopt policies that could affect jobs, families, and the economy as a whole. But if we in the West cannot set an example, we cannot expect much from those in a much worse position than ourselves.

On the other hand, poor countries have equally besetting illusions. As might be expected, they tended to view Rio as an ideal opportunity to extract more financial help from the rich. They neglected a critical point: that they are more vulnerable to change than anyone else and would stand to lose most if the environment were damaged in an irretrievable way.

Nearly everyone agrees such problems exist: the difficulties arise over action. But the more global a problem, the more difficult it is to take action and to deal with its national or local manifestations. In any case, the issues are outside people's general experience and slippery to define. There is a clash of uncomprehending cultures within and between countries and people.

The attitudes of the industrial countries are less than honest or realistic. They believe that environmental problems are for others and that the question is how little is necessary to buy off the rest of the world. They show no enthusiasm for setting an example; yet the industrial countries produce around 70 percent of pollution. To take the case of the extra carbon dioxide that the activities of our species is putting into the atmosphere, the United States alone contributed some 23 percent in 1988.

The attitudes of others are scarcely more helpful. Many are stuck in the mental world of the 1970s with the Brandt Commission and the New World Economic Order. They have no realization of their own vulnerability and want only to imitate the industrial world.

DOCUMENTS GENERATED AT RIO

As a result much time was wasted at Rio, much useless argument took place, many expectations turned out to be illusions. The final documents are sufficient illustration. They are badly drafted, stuffed with jargon, politically correct according to the canons of UN-speak, shot through with ambiguities, and lacking measurable commitment.

The first document set out the broad principles of environmental responsibility.[5] . . . Principles can have real practical value. Two examples are the principles enshrined in the declaration on human rights of 1948, which transformed human attitudes the world over, even in those countries least inclined to respect human rights, and the principles in the Helsinki Declaration of 1975, following the Conference on Security and Cooperation in Europe, which greatly contributed to loosening the oppressive bonds of the Soviet empire.

[5]UN Conference on Environment and Development, Rio de Janeiro, June 3–14, 1992, *The Rio Declaration on Environment and Development*, A/CONF.151/5/Rev. 1, June 13, 1992.

Second, there are two legally binding conventions. These are the Convention on Climate Change and the Convention on Biodiversity. It is a matter of keen regret that President George Bush, under pressure from certain vested interests, watered down the first and refused to sign the second. [President Clinton signed the biodiversity treaty on behalf of the United States following his election.— Eds.] These conventions open the way to establishing new international arrangements for managing these fundamental problems. They were far from perfect, but we can build on them.

Then there are the so-called forestry principles, which are guidelines for the management of forests worldwide.[6] These were a cruel disappointment. Many had hoped for a lot more in the form of a legally binding convention. But the principles are better than nothing.

Finally, and potentially most important, there was Agenda 21 as a text for managing the environment in the 21st century.[7] It is an enormous ragbag in 4 chapters and 475 pages, which looks at social and economic dimensions, conservation and management of resources for development, strengthening the role of certain groups (from women and children to unions, businessmen, scientists, and farmers), and means of implementation. The contents have yet to be sorted and graded. Some are rhetorical. Some could be of crucial importance. It remains to be seen. . . .

AFTER RIO

The result of the conference is an interesting mixture of some success and much failure. There is a need for greater public and governmental awareness and realization, not least among the poor nations, of the value of their resources. But the foundations are laid for the future. We have the institutions: the conventions with their secretariats and subsidiary bodies; the Sustainable Development Commission, a new UN mechanism designed to monitor the agreements of Rio; and the revamped Global Environment Facility (GEF) of the World Bank to manage funding. And there are encouraging signs of greater cooperation among nations.

A little extra money is available but not nearly enough. Some $3 billion was promised to replenish the GEF but the secretariat of the conference estimated that $10 billion a year for 10 years was needed to make Agenda 21 work. This disproportion, allowing for exaggeration on both sides, was startling.

[6]UN Conference on Environment and Development, Rio de Janeiro, June 3–14, 1992, *Non-legally binding authoritative statement of principles for a global consensus on the management, conservation and sustainable development of all types of forests*, A/CONF.151/6/Rev. 1, June 13, 1992.

[7]UN Conference on Environment and Development (Rio de Janeiro, Brazil, 1992), *Agenda 21* (Conches, Switzerland: UNCED, 1992).

We had the coming together of the nongovernmental organizations, which worked reasonably well together. Unfortunately they sometimes get out of touch with their members and are already suffering a fall in interest and support.

But certain gross deficiencies remain. Rio generated almost nothing on such key issues as resource consumption in industrial countries, including use of energy, and on population issues worldwide. And now there is a loss of international impetus and a universal tendency for governments to revert to business as usual.

Where are we to go next? The conventions need to be ratified and steps taken to fulfil the obligations contained in them, especially as to how the industrial countries should help the others. . . .

Reform of the GEF is necessary but will be very difficult. The World Bank has not endeared itself to those interested in environmental problems or shown much new sensitivity to the environmental dimension. It has a long history of megaprojects, ranging from the doubtful to the disastrous. . . . An argument persists between those such as Britain and the United States, which want the GEF to focus on project lending, and such others as Germany and the Netherlands, which want capacity building.

The practical recommendations in Agenda 21 must be sorted out and given effect. International obligations must be converted into action at the national and local community level.

Work should be done on issues that were left incomplete or ignored at Rio, such as resource use and population trends. We do not want simply to leave things to nature: AIDS may reverse current population trends in some places; change in the character of employment in technically advanced societies may leave a vast oversupply of labor everywhere. This provides food for discussion at . . . the UN Conference on Population in 1994—the UN being the only and obvious place in which to deal with population problems. There is also a need to reverse the general reluctance to face the fact that environmental issues must be tackled together, not one by one. The solution of one can worsen another, for instance, when clearing pollution only leads to more ozone damage.

We must try to look again to the next crises. Human displacement will take its toll in land degradation. The new spread of old and new diseases must be anticipated and means to cope with them devised. Changing patterns of moisture and warmth could have devastating effects. For example, the tsetse fly is extending its range as areas hitherto protected from it by their cooler temperatures warm up. With greater warmth, algae carrying cholera bacilli undergo blooms, such as may have contributed to the Latin American cholera epidemic. And, of course, hazards are created by increasing bacterial resistance to drugs.

Finally we must rethink the way in which we run our societies. This in turn requires refashioning the means by which we think about these issues, a particular responsibility of economists but also of everyone. The environment must be brought into virtually every aspect of the way we conduct our affairs.

I end with a . . . quotation . . . from a new book by the authors of *The Limits to Growth*. This book, published on the 20th anniversary of its predecessor, is entitled *Beyond the Limits*. Building on their 1972 models, the authors show that the world economy tends to overshoot capacity because of expanding population and continuing economic growth. To sustain this growth, people draw down resources below certain thresholds at which the whole economy behaves differently. This is because of the step-like, nonlinear character of change: it proceeds by jumps, not curves. The authors wrote that:

> Any population-economy-environment system that has feedback delays and slow physical responses, that has thresholds and erosive mechanisms, is literally unmanageable. In most [of our computer] runs . . . the world system does not run out of land or food or resources or pollution absorption capability, it runs out of the ability to cope.[8]

Let us make sure we do not do so.

---

[8]Donella H. Meadows, et al., *Beyond the Limits: Global Collapse or a Sustainable Future* (London: Earthscan, 1992), p. 179.

34

AGENDA 21: TOWARD A STRATEGY TO SAVE OUR PLANET

Daniel Sitarz, editor

Approved by countries representing 98 percent of the world's population at the 1992 Earth Summit, the massive *Agenda 21* is the program of action to be implemented now and into the twenty-first century in a way that deals simultaneously with the need to manage and protect the global environment and to bring about a more prosperous future for all in a rapidly growing world. This is the essence of *sustainable development,* a central concept in *Agenda 21.* The selection here addresses the rationale underlying the program of action. Sitarz is an attorney active in environmental issues. He worked directly with United Nations Publications in preparing the edited version of *Agenda 21* on which this summary is based.

AGENDA 21 proposes an array of actions which are intended to be implemented by every person on Earth. The actions are specific and concrete proposals which are meant to address the sustainable and efficient use of our global natural resources, the effective management of pollution and the waste products of development and the achievement of a basic standard of living for all humanity. The bold goal of *AGENDA 21* is to halt and reverse the environmental damage to our planet and to promote environmentally sound and sustainable development in all countries on Earth. It is a blueprint for action in all areas relating to the sustainable development of our planet into the 21st century. It calls for specific changes in the activities of all people. It includes concrete measures and incentives to reduce the environmental impact of the industrialized nations, revitalize development in developing nations, eliminate poverty world-wide and stabilize the level of human population. . . . An entirely new relationship between and among nations is envisioned: a global partnership based on common interests, mutual needs and common yet differentiated responsibilities. The relationship proposed is one in which developing and industrialized countries will have both the incentive and the means to cooperate in protecting the global environment while meeting the needs and aspirations of its citizens for economic growth. . . .

The comprehensive approach of *AGENDA 21* provides a blueprint for action in all areas of human activity. Virtually every aspect of human civilization is addressed by some portion of *AGENDA 21*. Specifically, 40 separate sections of concern are addressed and 120 separate action programs are outlined. All of these areas and programs are inter-connected in a myriad of ways, reflecting the inter-related nature of the problems. In each of the action programs, specific activities are proposed for confronting the particular problem which is addressed. . . . The main program areas are grouped around seven central themes.

THE QUALITY OF LIFE ON EARTH

The first major theme of *AGENDA 21* relates to the quality of life on Earth. In many portions of the world, the day-to-day quality of life is deteriorating due to a combination of poverty, malnutrition, unemployment, population growth, lack of health care and pollution. At the same time, a minority of humanity continues to sustain a lifestyle which is based on highly wasteful consumption patterns and pollution-generating production processes. To confront these two problem areas, a dual approach is necessary.

People in the developing regions of the world must be encouraged and enabled to achieve sustaining livelihoods which do not destroy the environment or undermine the resource base upon which they rely. To do so, the inefficient consumption patterns in the industrialized countries which encourage resource waste must be drastically modified. This will entail fundamental and difficult changes in consumer preferences and practices. It will also require major shifts in the manufacturing base of the industrialized countries.

The overall levels and patterns of human consumption and production must be compatible with the finite capacities of the Earth. As the human population on Earth increases, there will be ever greater pressure for people throughout the world to attain a higher standard of living. If the model lifestyle for this increasing populace is based on the current excessive consumption levels and inefficient production methods of the industrialized countries, the thresholds of economic and environmental disaster will soon be reached. Sustainable patterns of consumption and efficient methods of production must be developed and encouraged in all societies.

One of the most important root causes of the intensifying human impact on our planet is the unprecedented growth in the sheer numbers of human beings in the last 50 years. The world's population is now growing by nearly 100 million people every year. Population pressures are placing increasing stress on the ecological systems of the planet. All countries must improve their ability to assess the environmental impact of their population growth rates and develop and implement appropriate policies to stabilize populations.

The general levels of health in many regions of the world have been deteriorating, in many cases due to environmental damage. Poverty is often a direct determinant of the health and disease levels in local populations. Achieving primary health care for all humanity requires sustainable social and economic development. Sustainable development and improved health are reciprocal. The general health of a particular population will be enhanced by developing reliable sources of food and energy; by encouraging safe and environmentally sound methods of resource use; and by implementing safe practices into the process of development.

The fundamental goal of . . . *AGENDA 21* is to achieve a sustainable living for all of the inhabitants of our planet for many generations to come. This lofty, but achievable, goal entails the eventual eradication of poverty world-wide, the availability of healthy and equitable livelihoods for all and the implementation of consumption patterns that drastically reduce damage to the environment. . . .

EFFICIENT USE OF THE EARTH'S NATURAL RESOURCES

The efficient use of the world's natural resources forms the basis for the second theme of *AGENDA 21*. The finite resource base of our world is being depleted and degraded at an increasingly rapid rate. Altering consumption patterns and containing population growth will reduce some of the demand for these resources. It is essential, however, that more efficient and environmentally sound methods of utilizing our precious resources be developed. Both the Earth's renewable and nonrenewable resources must be managed much more carefully in order to sustain their yield far into the future.

In the past, the Earth's seemingly unlimited supply of natural resources and its ability to assimilate waste were taken for granted. The enormous increase in human numbers and activities in this century has placed profound stress on these capacities. Fundamentally, it must be accepted that there are finite limits to both the Earth's resources and the Earth's capacity to handle the waste of human society. The carrying capacity of the Earth must be valued as an economic resource if it is to be assured of protection.

The actions in this area focus on the necessity to reverse the destruction of our renewable resources and implement strategies to conserve and provide for the sustainable use of our non-renewable resources. The protection of the global resources of land, fresh water, biological and genetic resources and energy must be paramount. Development of the Earth's resource base must be accomplished in a manner which raises productivity and meets rising global demands, while ensuring protection of the fragile ecosystems of our planet. The deserts, mountains and forests of the Earth must be afforded special protection as resource demand increases. Concern for environmental protection must be intimately incorporated into the process of resource development.

The challenge of sustainable agricultural development is to raise productivity and incomes without irreversibly depleting or degrading global soil and water resources. Without damaging the environment, there must be sufficient production, distribution and access to affordable and nutritious food supplies for all humanity. Again, in areas of the most fragile global ecosystems, special attention must be paid to providing access to ecologically sound farming techniques and alternative livelihoods.

Water is an essential ingredient to life on Earth. With the explosive growth in the world population and rapidly increasing economic activities, demand for water has already outstripped supply in many areas. This has led to critical water management problems and, in some areas, to potential sources of severe conflict. These global water supply problems have been intensified in many areas by increasing levels of water pollution. Coherent water resource policies must be developed as an integral part of sustainable development. These policies must be flexible enough to take into account local and regional constraints and demands, as well as anticipated needs and opportunities for future growth.

Energy use is at the heart of some of the principal environmental problems faced by humanity. The unprecedented economic growth that has occurred during this century in the industrialized countries has depended to a great extent on the easy availability of low-cost energy—principally fossil fuels. Although oil is a non-renewable resource which will eventually be depleted, it is still the dominant global energy source and will remain so for the foreseeable future. Coal is the most environmentally damaging of all the fossil fuels. It is also in abundant supply and is the most available source of new energy in many major developing countries. Special efforts must be made on a world-wide basis to find ways to reduce the environmental impact of the use of these two major fossil fuels.

Curbing the global appetite for fossil fuels is the single most important action that must be taken to reduce the adverse impacts of energy use on the atmosphere. This will necessitate a dramatic shift in consumer and industrial practices that are deeply entrenched. It will require rapid change toward a pattern of energy production and consumption that relies more heavily on efficiency and environmentally sound energy systems, particularly clean and renewable energy sources. This transition will be one of the most difficult to accomplish. Most of the industrial and transportation foundations of modern human society are based on the production and use of fossil fuels. To establish the basis for the transition to a new energy economy, efforts must be concentrated in those areas where economic and environmental considerations reinforce each other. The complete transition will require a major redeployment of research and development efforts towards new and renewable sources of energy.

The forests of the world play a number of critically important environmental and developmental roles. They are essential for the absorption and storage of carbon dioxide and as a primary source of biodiversity. Forests also play an important role in stabilizing watersheds and tempering local climates. Trees and forest lands also have significant economic development value. They are sources of habitat and livelihoods for millions of people, particularly traditional and indigenous communities. Many of these local populations have long understood the benefits of sustainable livelihoods obtained from forests. Only recently, however, have the developmental and environmental value of forests become apparent at the global level. The realization that forests significantly affect the lives of both local and global populations has helped place forest-related issues on the international agenda.

Each year large areas of the Earth are transformed into desert areas. Although desertification is a natural process, in recent years human activity has greatly accelerated the rate at which productive lands are being converted to deserts. Particularly in sub-Saharan Africa, desertification has lead to dramatic decreases in agricultural production causing widespread famine and human suffering. Slowing the process of desertification and coping with drought are problems of immediate concern in many regions of the world.

The biological diversity of plants and animals is one of the principal assets of the Earth. The vital environmental and developmental roles of this diversity are crucial to the future of humanity, yet it is presently accorded no value. The true social and economic values of biological resources are vastly underestimated and poorly appreciated. Too often, only their short-term commercial value is taken into account, leading to over-exploitation and destruction. The potential contributions of global biodiversity to human health and welfare are enormous. The benefits of deriving new and improved food crops, developing innovative pharmaceutical products and improving biotechnological processes can not be overstated. Urgent measures are required to halt the current trends of species loss and declining global biodiversity. To accomplish this, close international cooperation is essential. Most of the world's remaining biodiversity exists in the developing world, while the technological and financial capacity to develop and conserve these genetic resources exists in the industrialized world.

Biotechnology has wide applications of great economic relevance for both developing and industrialized countries. New biotechnological techniques can substantially increase the economic values available from the Earth's living resources. Sophisticated biotechnological tools and products are now being developed which offer an impressive array of possible applications for global development. These technologies should be made widely available to all countries to increase their food, animal feed and fiber production—and enhance their overall quality of life. These new techniques must be applied, however, in a manner that is both environmentally sound and in step with traditional methods of resource use. There is an immediate need for programs which use biotechnology for development, while providing mechanisms to insure that such use is safe for human health and the environment.

A wide array of actions is presented in . . . *AGENDA 21* to begin a global transition to a more efficient and environmentally sound use of the Earth's resources. These actions are intended for use by the farming, manufacturing and resource development industries (mining, forestry, oil production, etc.) as well as by local and national governments and individual citizens. As with all phases of *AGENDA 21,* private organizations and educational institutions must play a decisive role in promotion of the principles of *AGENDA 21.*

THE PROTECTION OF OUR GLOBAL COMMONS

Related to the efficient use of resources is the third central theme of *AGENDA 21:* the protection and management of our global commons—the atmosphere and the oceans. Global climate and weather and the physical processes which give rise to life on Earth are directly influenced by the atmosphere and oceans. Adverse human impact on these once-pristine domains has now reached perilous levels.

The Earth's capacity to sustain and nourish life depends primarily on the quality and composition of the atmosphere. Human activities have now reached the stage where the delicate balancing mechanisms of the atmosphere are being effected. The depletion of the ozone layer, climate change, acid rain, forest destruction, desertification and air pollution are some of the critical and complex atmospheric problems facing humanity. One of the principal difficulties in dealing with these complicated problems is that the time frames involved tend to separate the causes from the effects. Traditional economic and political decision-making is not accustomed to dealing with time spans that stretch beyond a human lifetime. New and innovative methods of dealing with these problems must be developed and put into action. The risks involved are of a critical, perhaps even decisive, nature to the future of humanity. Precaution must be the dominant principle applied in correcting these global problems.

The world's oceans play a dominant role in the life-sustaining processes of our planet. The oceans are also a vast source of food and mineral resources. Huge increases in marine catches in the last two decades have resulted from the introduction of new fishing technologies. Some of these new techniques, however, have caused the dramatic depletion of many fish, bird, reptile and mammal populations. Many seal and whale species have been overexploited, some to the verge of extinction. A fundamental cause of this exploitation is the status of marine life as common property—owned by no one—with no legal protection or appropriate global management plans. This common-property status encourages the over-exploitation of our marine resources by the use of such wasteful techniques as: habitat destruction, dynamite and chemical fishing, incidental capture and destruction of non-target species, unselective seining, wide-range driftnetting and indiscriminate trawling.

Marine pollution can be observed from the poles to the tropics and from the beaches to the abyssal depths. High-seas waste dumping and maritime activities each contribute around 10 percent to the total pollution load of the oceans. It is land based activities which add the bulk of the contaminants: 40 percent from river run-off, 30 percent via airborne pollution from land sources and an additional 10 percent from direct land-based dumping of wastes. The last few decades have seen a dramatic decline in catches of numerous marine fish species through both overfishing and marine pollution. The oceans are fast approaching their capacity to tolerate this environmental abuse.

The physical and ecological degradation of coastal areas is also accelerating. The root cause of the destruction of coastal marine habitat is the explosive growth of human numbers and activities. The rapid development of coastal settlements, an expansion of recreational areas and a concentration of industrial development along fragile coastal areas all have resulted in increasing coastal destruction.

Small island nations are at particular risk involving problems related to oceans and marine life. Their isolation, small size and dependence on the sea for sustenance place them in direct jeopardy whenever levels of marine life decline. Climatic changes which may cause increased tropical storms, hurricanes or sea-level rise threaten their very existence.

Regional and global agreements must be developed to ensure the fair and responsible use of global resources which are outside of national boundaries. Local and regional activities which cause environmental damage to these common areas must be understood and controlled. Immediate steps must be taken to reverse the perilous trends that have arisen in the past few decades. . . . *AGENDA 21* outlines actions in which all levels of society must participate. Specifically, industries involved in development, the fishing industry, chemical manufacturing concerns and all other industries which impact upon the common areas of the globe must become more deeply involved with both the protection and management of these shared areas.

THE MANAGEMENT OF HUMAN SETTLEMENTS

The fourth central theme addressed in *AGENDA 21* involves the management of human settlements. The quality of human life depends, in large part, on the physical, social and economic conditions of the settlements where people live— whether those communities are villages, towns or cities. Today, some 2.5 billion people live in urban settlements. This number is expected to increase rapidly in the years to come. Over 3 billion people are expected to inhabit urban areas by the year 2000 and over 5 billion by the year 2025. Thus, in the span of one generation, the urban population of the world is expected to double. The repercussions of this rapid and often uncontrolled urban expansion are profound. In many countries, the breakdown of urban services, the spread of slums and the accompanying social decline may well pose the most immediate threat to human well-being and the environment.

A fundamental challenge facing humanity is to develop coherent methods of managing human urban areas in order to reduce these risks. The quality of water supplies must be insured. Adequate shelter must be provided. The careful management of increasing quantities of solid waste and sewage must be established. Energy distribution and transportation systems must be expanded. Adequate health care, education and other essential services must be provided. All of these demands must be handled in a manner which reduces rather than increases the toll on the environment.

Most urban municipal systems in developing countries cannot meet this demand. Their fragile economies are often heavily burdened by external debt. They must deal with unfavorable trade terms, importation of most food and energy supplies and inadequate institutions with which to cope with explosive urban growth. The resulting environmental deterioration quickly translates into economic decline and human suffering.

The industrial activities, energy plants, transportation systems and municipal waste management of many of the world's urban areas were developed with little or no regard for environmental protection. While cities in industrialized countries have made great progress in upgrading their infrastructure to higher environmental standards, this is not generally the case in most developing countries. Urban pollution is at dangerous and increasing levels throughout the developing world. A priority must be to develop the capacities of urban settlements to deal with rapid growth while reducing the basic levels of pollution. A broad, preventive approach to environmental protection must be adopted and instituted for the management of both industrialized and developing urban areas. Pollution prevention at the source, waste minimization and cleaner technologies must be made available in urban areas on a broader basis.

. . . *AGENDA 21* offers plans for both the environmental and developmental management of urban areas throughout the world. These plans are designed to be put into effect by local, state and national officials and fostered by local and regional business, financial and educational communities.

CHEMICALS AND THE MANAGEMENT OF WASTE

The use of chemicals and the management of human and industrial waste is the focus of the fifth central theme of *AGENDA 21*. The use of resources and the process of production necessarily generates waste. If industrial production continues to increase world-wide and excessive consumption patterns remain in place, economic development may well be overwhelmed by the amount of waste and pollution that it produces. There has been a recent increase in the amount of residue waste products that are not or cannot be reintegrated into the world's ecosystems. These ultimate waste products are causing significant problems for human health and environmental quality. The volume and complexity of waste materials has also accelerated in recent years, overpowering efforts to effectively control and manage their disposal.

Inadequate waste disposal severely affects national wealth and productivity in many ways. The impact on human health is perhaps the most significant. Over 80 percent of all disease and over one-third of deaths in developing countries are caused by the ingestion of waste-contaminated food and water. As much as 10 percent of each person's productive time in developing countries is sacrificed to waste-related diseases. The economic burden and human suffering caused by this problem has substantial consequences for any attempts at progress in developing countries.

The use of chemicals has become essential to the development process and to the promotion of human well-being. Chemicals are extensively used in all societies, regardless of the stage of development. Their misuse, however, can have adverse effects on human health and cause extensive damage to the environment. It is extremely important that the properties of chemicals are sufficiently known and that adequate precautions are taken in their manufacture, handling, use and disposal.

The action programs adopted in . . . AGENDA 21 include plans to reduce waste generation, recycle waste materials into useful products, find safe methods of human and chemical waste disposal and eliminate the illegal trade in hazardous waste. . . .

SUSTAINABLE ECONOMIC GROWTH

The sixth theme is global economic growth based on sustainability. Most of the environmental problems in the world have their origins in the processes of industrialization and development. Much of the world has been affected in recent years with declining standards of living. Income levels are stagnant or falling. The infrastructures and levels of public services throughout the world are declining. Air and water pollution are increasing, bringing with them greater health hazards. People throughout the world are gradually losing the economic resilience necessary to combat these difficulties. This deterioration in the quality of life is of particular concern in the developing world where debilitating poverty severely affects over 1 billion people.

The goal of . . . AGENDA 21 is to accelerate the correction of these economic problems and yet do so on a basis which is sustainable well into the future. Sustainable development and environmental soundness must be integrated into all levels of political and economic decision-making. The system of incentives and penalties which motivates economic behavior must be re-oriented to support sustainability. Corporate and national accounting practices must be amended to reflect the true impact of development on the environment and the real value of natural resources. . . . By re-orienting the system of economic accounting to reflect the true costs of development and resource use, market forces can act as a powerful stimulant for the global transition to a sustainable society. By insuring that the environmental costs of projects and policies are considered, the protection of the environment can be given a proper place in the market economy of the world. This fundamental change in economic accounting has wide implications.

At present, the industrialized countries import products and resources from developing countries at costs which reflect neither the loss of the resource base in the developing country nor the environmental damage incurred. In recent years, many developing countries have encountered a substantial fall in the price of commodities which they export. The falling prices earned by commodity export has had three primary effects. First, it has severely affected the foreign exchange earnings of the exporting countries. Second, the lower purchase prices in the importing countries have fostered wasteful patterns of consumption of the commodities. Finally, it has encouraged the developing countries to export ever greater quantities of their natural resources in order to earn an equivalent income, often leading to over-exploitation of the resources and damage to the environment. International trade policy can ensure that the price of goods reflects the true value of the natural resources and the costs of necessary environmental protection measures.

AGENDA 21 provides a comprehensive plan of activities to coordinate this economic transition. . . . As with virtually all aspects of AGENDA 21, there will be a difficult and wrenching period of change incurred in implementing these plans. The support and backing of the international trade community is crucial to enable this transition to take place.

IMPLEMENTING *AGENDA 21*

The above six themes form the basis of the core of AGENDA 21: the action programs designed to foster the sustainable use of natural resources for human development while ensuring a basic and healthful standard of living for all humanity. . . .

A monumental and sustained commitment will be imperative to build the human and technological capacity to save our planet. World-wide, in all societies, there are deeply-entrenched patterns of behavior which collectively threaten life on Earth. These patterns must be changed. Development strategies since the Industrial Revolution have been based on an extravagant use of energy and resources that can no longer be sustained. Environmentally sound technologies must be developed and made available on a world-wide basis. In the wave of industrial development that has swept over the Earth in the past century, pollution has been seen as an inevitable by-product. This can no longer continue. Effective pollution abatement and recycling technologies must be developed. The Earth's natural systems cannot provide infinite natural resources nor an endless capacity to assimilate waste.

There is a critical global need for environmentally sound technology. Meeting this need will require much greater international scientific cooperation. The transfer of this technology to the developing countries of the world is crucial in order to prevent outmoded and environmentally destructive technologies from being put into place. The Earth, very simply, cannot support a global civilization which consumes and pollutes at the current levels of the industrialized world. The burgeoning populations of the developing countries of Earth are clamoring for a greater standard of living. These desires for an improved life must be met with technology that does not further destroy the environment. . . .

The legal and regulatory framework of the Earth, as it relates to environment and development, must be also restructured and streamlined in order to effectively promote sustainable development. Five guiding principles are identified which should be the basis for changes and progress in this area. The improvements should foster democracy, participation, openness of the decision-making process, cost-effectiveness and accountability. . . .

A substantial flow of new and additional financial resources to developing countries must be made to achieve global environmentally sound and sustainable development. The current cost estimates of international financing and aid from industrialized countries to implement all of the actions of *AGENDA 21* is an annual average level of $125 billion through the year 2000. This level of funding amounts to only 0.7 percent of the Gross National Product of the industrialized countries on Earth. In addition to this funding, the required national expenditures of the governments and industry in the developing and industrialized countries is estimated at approximately $400 billion annually through the year 2000. Thus, the total estimated expenses for implementing all of the comprehensive and dramatic action programs envisioned by *AGENDA 21* amounts to less than $100 per person per year on a global basis. . . .

The responsibility for our common future is in our own hands. The prospect of inevitable global environmental disaster or world-wide social upheaval must not be the legacy which we leave our children. Within the lifetime of a child born today, we have the opportunity to create a world in which concern for life is paramount—a world in which suffering is not taken for granted—a world in which nature is revered and not exploited—a world which is just, secure and prosperous—a world in which our children's children are assured of enjoying the bounty of nature and the splendor of life.

This particular point in history offers a unique opportunity for humanity to make the transition to a global community which provides a sustainable living for all. The end of the Cold War, the world-wide thrust for democracy and other recent political events have created an atmosphere of hope that positive and productive change can occur and occur very rapidly. The fundamental changes necessary to make the global transition to a sustainable global society are admittedly difficult, but they are possible. By postponing the difficult choices proposed in *AGENDA 21,* humanity will not manage to avoid such choices. It will only narrow the already limited options available. It will only magnify the extent of action needed to overcome the unavoidable problems which it faces. It will only increase the dangers of passing the irreversible thresholds of ecological and social catastrophe. More so than at any other time in history, the collective decisions that humanity makes in the next few years will irrevocably determine the future of life on Earth. . . .

35

POPULATION PRESSURES AND THE GLOBAL HABITAT

Charles W. Kegley, Jr., and Eugene R. Wittkopf

The world is divided demographically, as the industrial countries of the North approach zero population growth but the developing countries of the South continue to experience rapid increases in their numbers. Charles W. Kegley, Jr., and Eugene R. Wittkopf explore the domestic and transnational social, economic, environmental, and political problems that grow out of a demographically divided but economically and environmentally interdependent world. Kegley is Pearce Professor of International Relations at the University of South Carolina. Wittkopf is R. Downs Poindexter Professor of Political Science at Louisiana State University. Together they have published *World Politics: Trend and Transformation* (1995).

How many people can the earth support? What is its ultimate carrying capacity? No one knows for sure, in part because human ingenuity and rapidly advancing technology keep stretching the boundaries. Thus the growth projected for today's billions of inhabitants into the next century will doubtlessly be accommodated. But at what cost—to human freedom, human welfare, and ultimately to the environment necessary to sustain humankind?

TRENDS IN WORLD POPULATION GROWTH

Today's world population of more than 5.5 billion people constitutes a significant proportion of all the people who have ever lived, and it continues to grow. If

This essay was especially written for this book.

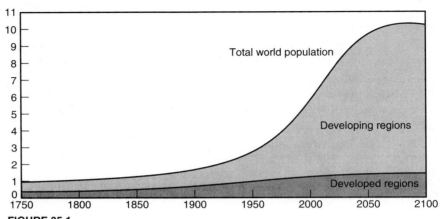

FIGURE 35.1
WORLD POPULATION GROWTH, GLOBAL REGIONAL TRENDS, 1750–2100
Source: Thomas W. Merrick, "World Population in Transition," *Population Bulletin,* vol. 41, no. 2 (Washington, D.C.: Population Reference Bureau, Inc., January 1988 reprint), p. 4.

present population trends are projected ahead eight centuries, ours will be a standing-room-only planet, with land surface of only one square foot per person. No one can seriously regard such a world as likely. Nor are the other images that have been conjured up to shock the public consciousness realistic portraits of the future. But what they do tell us is that the pressures of population growth pose a serious threat to the human condition, one unprecedented in scale.

The explosive proportions of today's population growth are illustrated in Figure 35.1, which indicates that it took from the beginning of time until the early 1800s for world population to reach 1 billion people. Because of substantial declines in death rates, the world population reached 2 billion about 130 years later, around 1930. Since then, additional billions have been added even more rapidly: 3 billion by 1960, 4 billion by 1975, and 5 billion by 1987. As present trends unfold, the world will reach the 6-billion figure before the turn of the twentieth century and ultimately stabilize at something over 11 billion sometime in the twenty-second century.

How rapidly the world adds billions to its number is predicted by its growth rate. Worldwide, the rate of population growth peaked at just over 2 percent in the late 1960s and then declined to 1.7 percent by the 1980s. Even this small slowing of the global rate of population growth is consequential, for it means that world population in the year 2000 will be 20 percent less than the 7.5 billion people that the birth and death rates of the 1950s would have produced had they continued uninterrupted.

Whatever the ultimate rate of growth, the trends are apparent and the consequences inevitable; it is not a question of whether the world will become more crowded but of how crowded it will become. In the early 1990s the world grew by more than 90 million people annually, an amount equivalent to adding the entire population of Austria to the world again each month or the Bahamas each day. Even more will be added each year in the future. In fact, as Figure 35.1 illustrates, more people will be added to the globe's population in the last fifth of the twentieth century than at any other time in history—even though the world's population growth rate has slowed markedly and will continue downward in the years ahead. We can better understand why this result is inevitable if we go beyond the simple arithmetic of population growth and explore its dynamics.

Factors Affecting National and Regional Variations in Population Growth

The rate of natural population increase in the United States in 1991 was 0.8 percent. This is an annual rate typical of developed nations today, where births and deaths have nearly stabilized. Hence, the difference between a typical industrial nation and the world population growth rate of 1.7 percent is largely attributable to a population surge in the Third World, where sharply lower death rates since World War II have resulted from advances in medical science, agricultural productivity, public sanitation, and technology. The paradox posed by reduced death rates is that this favorable development has contributed to an accelerating rate of population growth in precisely those nations least able to support a burgeoning number of people.

Variations in national and regional population growth virtually ensure that today's demographic division of the world will persist into the future. In fact, it will widen: The 3.7 billion people who inhabited the Third World in 1985 will have grown to 4.8 billion by the year 2000, whereas the comparable increase among the developed nations will be only from 1.2 to 1.3 billion.

The developing countries' high fertility rates (which measure the number of births by women in their prime reproductive years) derive from a variety of sources. Apart from the pleasures that children provide, religious norms often encourage parenting, prescribing the bearing of children (particularly male offspring in some cultures) as both a duty and a path to a rewarding afterlife. In addition, many societies' cultural traditions ascribe prestige and social status to women according to the number of children they bear. But most importantly perhaps, high fertility rates are affected by economic factors. Large families add more hands to a family's labor force today and may be a source of social security for parents in societies without public programs for the elderly. Under such conditions, parents usually try to have as many children as possible to increase their family income today and ensure they will be cared for in their old age. When the infant mortality rate is high, the incentives for many progeny are even greater: The larger the number of children that are born, the greater the chance that some will survive.

Population Momentum

Even more important to understanding the implications of today's population surge in the Third World (which is a result of high, but declining, birthrates and rapidly falling death rates) for tomorrow's world is the "momentum" factor. It helps explain why in the last quintile of the twentieth century more people will be added to the globe's population than at any other time in history.

Population momentum is especially great in societies with high proportions of young people. In these societies, families are formed and babies produced at a rate faster than older persons die. Even if these young people choose to have only two children, large numbers of young couples can still produce extremely large numbers of total births and hence a continuing momentum of growth. This process will continue until the age structures shift toward equal numbers of people in each age group.

Slowing expanding population implies that the Third World must move toward a replacement-level rate of fertility—that is, two children to replace two parents—as many industrial nations have already done. Even then, momentum will continue to fuel an expanding population. In general, population growth will continue for as many as fifty to seventy years after replacement-level fertility is achieved. This startling fact underscores the urgency of grappling with the population problem; for every decade of delay in achieving replacement-level fertility, the world's peak population will be some 15 percent greater.

The obvious question, then, is how to achieve replacement-level fertility. The demographic transition theory, which is the most widely accepted explanation of population changes over time, provides important answers.

The Demographic Transition Theory

The demographic transition theory seeks to explain the transition that Europe and, later, North America experienced between 1750 and 1930, when a condition of high birthrates combined with high death rates was replaced by a condition of low birthrates and low death rates. The transition started when death rates began to fall, presumably because of economic and social development and especially because of rising standards of living and improved control of disease. In such circumstances, the potential for substantial population growth was, of course, great. But then birthrates also began to decline, and during this phase population growth slowed. Such declines occur, according to the theory, because economic growth alters attitudes toward family size. In preindustrial societies, children are economic bonuses. As industrialization proceeds, children become economic burdens, as they inhibit social mobility and capital accumulation. The transition from large to small families, with the associated decline in fertility, is therefore usually assumed to arise in industrial and urban settings. This fourth stage in the demographic transition was achieved in Europe and North America when both the birth and death rates reached very low levels. With fertility levels near the replacement level, the result was a very low rate of population growth, if any at all.

In contrast, developing nations have not yet experienced the rapidly falling birthrates following the extraordinarily rapid increase in life expectancy that occurred after World War II. In fact, their precipitous decline in death rates has largely been the result of more effective "death-control" measures introduced by the outside world. The decline in the developing nations' death rates thus differs sharply from the long-term, slow declines that Europe and North America experienced. They have been the result of externally introduced and rapid environmental changes rather than the fundamental and evolutionary changes that affect a nation's policies, institutions, or ways of life. In particular, the developing nations have not experienced the more or less automatic decline in fertility rates that follows the decline in the rate of mortality normally accompanying economic development. A population "explosion" is the inevitable result.

Beyond the Demographic Transition Theory

Although developing countries have yet to move toward replacement-level fertility, demographers generally expect that this will happen. This is the assumption underlying the projections that the transition to low fertility and mortality will occur by the year 2025 and that fertility will decline to replacement level by 2040. Given the assumption, it is possible to foresee a stable global population of around 11 billion people early in the twenty-second century.

Projections so far into the future are inevitably subject to error. Uncertainty about death rates is one reason. A large-scale conventional war or a limited nuclear war that could induce a climatic catastrophe through "nuclear winter," for example, would abruptly destroy perhaps millions of people and make current population projections meaningless. A more populous world is also a more vulnerable one. Consider, for example, the difference in population density in Bangladesh and the state of Louisiana in the United States, two deltas of similar size. Four and a half million people lived in Louisiana in 1990; 115 million populated Bangladesh, giving it a population density of over 2000 people per square mile. A natural disaster in Bangladesh—where typhoons are commonplace—carries a proportionately greater threat to life.

Death due to malnutrition and starvation may also affect the long-term growth of the world population. Twice in recent years, in the 1970s and again in the 1980s, broad stretches of the Sahel area in Africa experienced life-threatening drought and famine. Africa as a continent is also (for the time being) more threatened than others by acquired immune deficiency syndrome (AIDS). The World Health Organization predicts that AIDS could triple the current death rate in Africa. The threat posed by that frightening and fatal disease knows no national boundaries and has in fact spread to virtually every quarter of the world, threatening to become the plague of the twenty-first century in much the same way the Black Death ravaged the Middle Ages.

Turning from deaths to births, the demographic transition theory, which is essentially based on the European experience prior to World War II, may be incomplete. It envisages four phases: (1) high birthrate, high death rate; (2) high birthrate, falling death rate; (3) declining birthrate, relatively low death rate; and (4) low birthrate, low death rate. The experience in Western Europe since the 1970s suggests a possible fifth phase: low death rate, declining birthrate. Some have called this Europe's "second" demographic transition (van de Kaa, 1987). As a result, a secular decline of Europe's population has been set in motion. It will take over a thousand years for Italy's population to double, and a German population less than three-quarters its current size is now foreseeable.

A second puzzle that the demographic transition theory does not solve applies to developing nations: Some seem to be stuck somewhere between the second and third stages of the transition. In such widely separated places as Costa Rica, Korea, Sri Lanka, and Tunisia, for example, death rates have fallen to very low levels, but fertility rates seem to have stabilized well above the replacement level (Merrick, 1986). Perhaps the reason lies in the absence of change in social attitudes toward family size of the sort Europe and North America have experienced.

Changes in cultural attitudes toward limitations on family size have been shown to be an important ingredient in environments where social and economic improvements are taking place. Research also shows that the education and status of women in society have an important influence on family size preferences.

> Women who have completed primary school have fewer children than those with no education. Having an education usually means that women delay marriage, seek wage-paying jobs, learn about and have more favorable attitudes toward family planning, and have better communication with their husbands when they marry. Educated women have fewer infant deaths; high infant mortality is associated with high fertility. Similarly, when women have wage-paying jobs, they tend to have fewer children (and conversely, women with few children find it easier to work). Unfortunately, as women in developing countries attempt to move into the paid labor force, they will be competing with men for scarce jobs. (Population Reference Bureau, 1981)

Although the demographic transition theory leaves some questions unanswered, it carries with it important policy implications. "Development is the best contraceptive" is one. Many Third World nations have eagerly seized on this prescription as a way to extract resources from the world's rich nations in an effort to realize broad development objectives. Interestingly, however, recent research suggests that "contraceptives are the best contraceptive" (Robey, Rutstein, and Morris, 1993). This view, based on surveys of more than 300,000 women conducted over nearly a decade, suggests that fertility rates in developing nations have fallen even when economic development has not occurred. The findings have "extraordinary implications for future efforts to slow population growth," as they suggest that family planning and access to newer forms of contraception may dramatically reduce the number of children born to women in their childbearing years (Robey, Rutstein, and Morris, 1993). With that, world population levels may stabilize below currently projected levels even in the absence of widespread economic development.

CORRELATES OF DEMOGRAPHIC CHANGES

The composition and distribution of societies' populations significantly affect how demographic variables relate to other sociopolitical phenomena. The high proportion of young people in developing countries places strains on certain social institutions, for example, whereas the higher proportion of older people in the developed countries creates other problems.

Generally the impact of population growth on economic development is the most immediate and important question facing developing countries. In contrast, the main issues for developed nations tend to focus more on the impact of affluence on world resources and the global commons. The growing imbalance of the world population between the have and the have-not nations as played out in global patterns of emigration and immigration bridges the two viewpoints.

Population Growth and Economic Development

Growth pessimists place considerable emphasis on the adverse effects of population growth on economic development. Clearly, population growth has contributed to the widening income gap between the world's rich nations and its poor. At the individual level, population growth also contributes to lower standards of living, as poor people tend to have more children to support than do those who are relatively better off. "Also, by depressing wages relative to rents and returns to capital, rapid population growth devalues what poor households have to sell—their labor. Property owners gain relative to wage earners when the labor force grows quickly" (Repetto, 1987).

It is also true, however, that "politics and economic policies influence the distribution of income within countries far more than population growth rates do" (Repetto, 1987). This fact lies close to what is emerging as the conventional view among demographers and development economists of the effects of population growth on economic development. Contrary to the view of growth pessimists, the emerging consensus casts population "not as the sole cause of underdevelopment, but an accomplice aggravating other existing problems" (*The New Population Debate*, 1985).

The Third World   Consider, for example, the relationship between the age structures of developing societies and other socioeconomic variables. In developing countries, dependent children (those younger than fifteen years old) typically comprise about 40 percent of the total population (compared with 25 percent in the developed world). This means there is only about one working-age adult for each child under fifteen in the Third World, compared with nearly three working-age adults in the developed countries. Such a large proportion of dependent children places a heavy burden on public services, particularly the educational system. It also encourages the immediate consumption of economic resources rather than their reinvestment to promote future economic growth.

As these same children reach working age, they also contribute to the enormous unemployment and underemployment problems that the developing nations typically face. Yet countries whose populations grow faster than their economies do cannot absorb increasingly large numbers of working-age people into the productive mainstream of their societies. Worldwide there is an unprecedented need to create new jobs. "The enormity of the task is captured by the following statistics. By 2010, about 730 million new workers will have entered the labor force in the developing world. During the period of the most robust job growth in the United States in the 1980s, the economy produced about 2 million new jobs" (Meissner, 1992: 81).

The search for jobs contributes to the rapid growth of already massive urban areas. In 1950 less than a third of the world's population lived in cities; by 1990 the proportion had grown to over 40 percent; and by the year 2020 as many as 60 percent will live in urban areas. Urbanization is a global phenomenon, but increasingly the world's largest cities will be in the Third World. London, New York, and Shanghai were the only cities with populations of 10 million or more in 1950. By the turn of the century some two dozen cities will be this large—all but six of them in the less developed nations of Africa, Asia, and Latin America, where a combination of natural population growth and a desire to escape poverty in the countryside will fuel the expansion of the megalopolises.

Wherever urbanization occurs, it taxes severely the capacity for effective governance. It places added pressures on the demand for expanded social services associated with rapid population growth, as urban development requires more investment in infrastructure than does rural development. It also increases the pressures on local agricultural systems, because there are fewer hands in the countryside to feed the growing number of mouths in the city. Urbanization thus adds to the need to import food from abroad, further straining already limited resources. And within the urban areas themselves, the often deplorable living conditions contain the seeds of social unrest and political turmoil. Already thousands upon thousands of urban dwellers live in cramped, shantytown hovels without adequate water, sanitation, health, education, and other social services. They also live in the constant shadow of pervasive crime and violence. Being outside the urban elite and middle class, they are "acutely aware of the great disparity in wealth and poverty about them," which "contributes to alienation and frustration on a massive scale" (U.S. Department of State, 1978). Consider the conditions on the West Bank and the Gaza Strip, where in 1993 some 2500 Palestinians were cramped per square mile ("Harper's Index," 1993: 15). Little wonder that crime and violence are ubiquitous.

Ironically, as present trends unfold, Third World countries will bear not only the greatest burden of a burgeoning population of young people but also, eventually, of older people as the enormous number of today's youth grow to maturity and old age fifty years hence. Although the Third World today contains three-quarters of the world's people, it contains only half of those over sixty. By 2025, the Third World will increase its share of the "gray generation" to three-quarters ("The Age of Aging," 1982: 82). As the experience of the more developed economies demonstrates, demands for social services, particularly expensive health care, will again multiply.

The First World   As noted earlier, the United States has recently moved toward zero population growth, but in many other parts of the industrial world below-replacement fertility is now the norm. Population *decline* is the inevitable result. As longevity increases, an aging population is also inevitable.

The aging of the First World is especially striking in Japan, where the demographic transition began later than elsewhere but was completed more rapidly. Today Japan is the most rapidly aging society in the world. The number of elderly (over sixty-five) Japanese is expected to increase from 12.5 million in 1985 to 31.5 million in 2025, by which time they will comprise nearly a quarter of the population (Martin, 1989: 7). Already the median age of Japanese workers is over forty (Merrick, 1989: 11). As it continues to rise, Japan will have to confront worrisome questions about its ability to continue the vigorous economic productivity and high domestic saving rates that have been key factors in the projection of its economic power abroad.

Beyond the particular case of Japan's export-oriented economy, some gerontologists argue that the move toward zero or negative population growth in advanced industrial societies will have untoward effects on growth in their aggregate demand, on which their economies depend. Others speculate that a gradually aging society will be a more conservative one politically. Evidence refutes both of these views (see Weller and Bouvier, 1981). Still, what is beyond dispute is that older people will increasingly pose a social and potential political force worldwide and escalate the demand for age-related social services.

Providing for the increasing number of dependent elderly people relative to the number of productive workers is already a political concern throughout the First World. "Child shock" is the Japanese term used to draw attention to the growing crisis forecast by the decline in workers and growth in pensioners. The Japanese government and private-sector groups have joined forces to promote pronatalist attitudes among the Japanese people, whose purpose is to raise fertility rates. However, unlike similar efforts undertaken during the 1930s (when war between Japan and the United States loomed on the horizon), other socio-economic forces in Japan have dampened efforts to stimulate birthrates.

In Europe the wisdom of pursuing pronatalist policies has been a matter of intense political debate. Much of the dialogue turns on questions of individual versus collective welfare. Proponents of pronatalist measures are concerned with the "continued vitality of national populations that do not replace themselves: no children, no future, is the key phrase" (van de Kaa, 1987). National pride, concern for the nation's place among the world powers, and sensitivity to the vitality of European culture in a world where non-European countries grow much faster are also at issue.

Opponents of pronatalist measures, on the other hand, "dismiss as exaggerated the specter of Europe as a decrepit society of ruminating octogenarians." They "attach no special value to their own cultures" and oppose stimulating population growth in a world where this is already a serious problem. They believe that "economic resources rather than military resources or population size determine a country's international standing" and that "economic integration is a much more effective way to maintain Europe's international position than stimulating the birth rate." Finally, they question whether it makes sense to stimulate births when Europe already suffers from high levels of unemployment. "With modern technology eliminating jobs, workers are encouraged to work shorter hours, part-time, or retire early and immigration is halted," the argument continues, "so why should we have more people?" (van de Kaa, 1987).

Pronatalist policies have not been at issue in the United States—although right-to-life issues have long dominated the national political scene. The aging of society is nonetheless pertinent to both domestic and international politics as the United States struggles to remain competitive in the world political economy. Educational skills must be enhanced as the economy shifts from manufacturing toward high technology and service industries, but the government will be pressured simultaneously to distribute a greater share of limited resources, drawn from a declining pool of productive workers, to care for the elderly. Immigrants from throughout the world will seek to enter the United States in search of political freedom and economic opportunity, as they have for more than two hundred years, but jobs will continue to be "exported" to youthful, labor-rich countries "offshore," where the costs of production are markedly lower. Thus the aging of the United States, like that of the rest of the industrial world, will prove to be profoundly important not only domestically but also internationally.

The Impact of Population Growth on the Global Commons

The untoward effects of population growth on economic development often play themselves out through excessive pressures on natural resources and the desecration of the delicate life-support systems on which humankind depends.

Worldwide, there is mounting evidence of rapid deforestation, desertification, and soil erosion. It is most acute where population growth and poverty are most apparent. In the case of the Sahel in Africa, growing populations of livestock as well as humans hastened the conversion of productive land into a desert that ultimately led to famine. Nowhere is the tragedy of the commons illustrated more graphically.

Lester Brown and his associates at the Washington-based WorldWatch Institute describe what happens to biological systems where population growth remains high:

> A three-stage "ecological transition" emerges that is almost the reverse of the demographic transition in that its end result is disastrous. In the first stage, expanding human demands are well within the sustainable yield of the biological support system. In the second, they are in excess of the sustainable yield but still expanding as the biological resource itself is being consumed. And in the final stage, human consumption is forcibly reduced as the biological system collapses. (Brown et al., 1987: 26–27)

The process of desertification demonstrates how overshoot of the carrying capacity of biological systems multiplies.

> Once the demand for fuelwood exceeds the sustainable yield of local forests, it not only reduces tree cover but also leads to soil erosion and land degradation. When grasslands deteriorate to where they can no longer support cattle, livestock herders often take to lopping foliage from trees, thus putting even more pressure on remaining tree cover. Both contribute to a loss of protective vegetation, without which both wind and water erosion of soil accelerate, leading to desertification—a sustained decline in the biological productivity of land.
>
> A decline in the diversity of plant and animal communities marks the onset of desertification. This in turn leads to a reduction of soil organic matter, a decline in soil structure, and a loss of water retention capacity. It also lowers soil fertility, reduced further by increasing wind and water erosion. Typically the end result is a desert: a skeletal shell of soil consisting almost entirely of sand and lacking in the fine particles and organic matter that make soil productive. (Brown et al., 1987: 26)

The Threat of Mass Consumption
to Environmental Preservation

Excessive population growth doubtlessly strains the environment and contributes to destruction of the global commons, but excessive consumption is even more damaging. In this respect it is not the disadvantaged four-fifths of humanity in the burgeoning South who place the greatest strains on the global habitat but the affluent one-fifth in the consumption-oriented North. Consider some evidence:

• A typical resident of the industrialized . . . world uses 15 times as much paper, 10 times as much steel, and 12 times as much fuel as a Third

World resident. The extreme case is . . . the United States, where the average person consumes most of his or her own weight in basic materials each day—18 kilograms of petroleum and coal, 13 kilograms of other minerals, 12 kilograms of agricultural products, and 9 kilograms of forest products. (Durning, 1991: 161)

• The average Japanese consumes nine times as much steel as the average Chinese, and Americans use more than four times as much steel and 23 times as much aluminum as their neighbors in Mexico. U.S. paper consumption per person is over a dozen times the average for Latin America, and Americans use about 25 times as much nickel apiece as someone who lives in India. (Young, 1991: 40)

A consuming society is also a throwaway society. "The Japanese use 30 million 'disposable' single-roll cameras each year, and the British dump 2.5 billion diapers. Americans toss away 180 million razors annually, enough paper and plastic plates and cups to feed the world a picnic six times a year, and enough aluminum cans to make 6,000 DC-10 airplanes" (Durning, 1991: 161). Each American threw away an average of 1460 pounds of garbage in 1988, and the amount is expected to grow to nearly 1800 pounds per person by 2010 (Young, 1991: 28). As the mountains of garbage grow, disposing it has become increasingly difficult. The growing volume of solid waste in the North mirrors the dramatic increase in consumption that has occurred in industrial societies since World War II.

Other issues related to the preservation of the global habitat that are linked to the energy-intensive, consumption oriented lifestyles of the industrial nations can be cited.

One is *deforestation*. In the South it is occurring as expanding populations search for fuelwood and clear rainforests for development purposes. In Germany and elsewhere in Europe it is occurring for reasons that remain uncertain, but most experts believe that chemical changes in the atmosphere are responsible for killing the forests (see Postel, 1986).

Acid rain is a common atmospheric consequence of burning fossil fuels. The burning of coal in particular produces sulphur and nitrogen oxides in the atmosphere which, after traveling long distances, return to the earth in rain or snow, thus contributing to the acidification of lakes, the corrosion of materials and structures, and the impairment of ecosystems. Acid rain has fallen in measurable amounts in the Scandinavian countries, the United States, and Canada. In recent years Canada has alleged that it suffers adversely from the failure of the United States to curb atmospheric pollution, which causes the acid rain that kills aquatic life and damages crops and forests in Canada.

The burning of fossil fuels also contributes to the *greenhouse effect*. Combustion releases carbon dioxide into the atmosphere. As the concentration of carbon dioxide increases, it could cause the average temperature of the earth's surface to rise by several degrees, with an even greater increase in the now-frigid polar regions. Eventually, shifts in the world's climatic patterns could have political, social, and economic consequences, as the world's traditional food-producing areas are affected, its rainfall patterns are altered, and its coastal waters rise. The industrial nations of the North account for a disproportionate share of the greenhouse gases released into the atmosphere. However, as the nations of the South develop economically, they will use ever larger amounts of energy, thus contributing to further increases in atmospheric pollution due to fossil-fuel combustion. Global climate change may thus be inevitable.

The advanced industrial countries have also contributed disproportionately to the destruction of the ozone layer that protects the earth from dangerous, cancer-producing ultraviolet rays from the sun. The damage occurs when artificial chemicals known as chlorofluorocarbons (CFCs) are released into the atmosphere, where they can remain active for more than a century. The chemicals are widely used in refrigerators and air conditioners as refrigerants, in styrofoam cups, in cleansers for computer components, and as aerosol propellants for such things as deodorants. Fortunately, international agreements are now in place that will restrict the use of CFCs and related compounds and eventually lead to their elimination.

Other examples of environmental stress associated with affluence can be added to this brief list. They include soil erosion caused by the expansion of energy-intensive, mechanized agriculture to marginal lands; water shortages caused by the massive requirements of modern agriculture, industry, and residential living; and depletion of ocean fisheries caused by technology-intensive overfishing and pollution of spawning beds. Together they reinforce a fundamental point: The belief that there are "too many people" ultimately has meaning only in relation to something else, such as the availability of food and renewable and nonrenewable resources and pressures on the global commons. Measured against any of these yardsticks, it is not the world's less developed nations of the South that exert the greatest demands and pressures on the global carrying capacity; it is the advanced industrial societies of the North.

LOOKING OUTWARD: PATTERNS OF INTRA-
AND INTERNATIONAL MIGRATION

Fertility and mortality are two of the key demographic variables that determine population dynamics. Migration is the third. It has long been important but promises to become even more so in defining the contours of our demographically divided world as it responds to the population dynamics of environmental stress and the end of the Cold War. Managing migration is the subject of the next selection of this book.

References

"The Age of Aging." (1982) *UN Chronicle* 19 (July): 82–84.

Brown, Lester R., Edward C. Wolf, Linda Starke, William U. Chandler, Christopher Flavin, Cynthia Pollock, Sandra Postel, and Jodi Jacobson. (1987) *State of the World 1987.* New York: Norton.

Durning, Alan Thein. (1991) "Asking How Much Is Enough," pp. 153–169 in Lester R. Brown, Christopher Flavin, Sandra Postel, Linda Starke, Alan Durning, Hilary F. French, Jodi Jacboson, Marcia D. Lowe, Michael Renner, Nicholas Lenssen, John C. Ryan, and John E. Young, *State of the World 1991.* New York: Norton.

Harper's. (1993) "Harpers Index," *Harper's* 209 (November): 15.

Martin, Linda G. (1989) "The Graying of Japan," *Population Bulletin* 44 (no. 2). Washington, D.C.: Population Reference Bureau.

Meissner, Doris. (1992) "Managing Migrations," *Foreign Policy* 86 (Spring): 66–83.

Merrick, Thomas W. (1986) "World Population in Transition," *Population Bulletin* 41 (no. 2). Washington, D.C.: Population Reference Bureau.

———. (1989) *America in the 21st Century: A Global Perspective.* Washington, D.C.: Population Reference Bureau.

The New Population Debate: Two Views on Population Growth and Economic Development. (1985) Washington, D.C.: Population Reference Bureau.

Population Reference Bureau. (1981) *World Population: Toward the Next Century.* Washington, D.C.: Population Reference Bureau.

Postel, Sandra. (1986) *Altering the World's Chemistry: Assessing the Risks.* Worldwatch Paper 71. Washington, D.C.: Worldwatch Institute.

Repetto, Robert. (1987) "Population, Resources, Environment: An Uncertain Future," *Population Bulletin* 42 (no. 2). Washington, D.C.: Population Reference Bureau.

Robey, Bryant, Shea O. Rutstein, and Leo Morris. (1993) "The Fertility Decline in Developing Countries," *Scientific American* 269 (December): 60–67.

U.S. Department of State. (1978) "World Population: The Silent Explosion—Part I," *Department of State Bulletin* 78 (October): 45–54.

van da Kaa, Dirk J. (1987) "Europe's Second Demographic Transition," *Population Bulletin* 42 (no. 1). Washington, D.C.: Population Reference Bureau.

Weller, Robert H., and Leon F. Bouvier. (1981) *Population: Demography and Policy.* New York: St. Martin's Press.

Young, John E. (1991) "Reducing Waste, Saving Materials," pp. 39–55 in Lester R. Brown, Christopher Flavin, Sandra Postel, Linda Starke, Alan Durning, Hilary F. French, Jodi Jacboson, Marcia D. Lowe, Michael Renner, Nicholas Lenssen, John C. Ryan, and John E. Young, *State of the World 1991.* New York: Norton.

36

MANAGING MIGRATIONS

Doris Meissner

International migration involving illegal aliens, asylum seekers, and refugees has become a pervasive element in our demographically divided world. Doris Meissner examines the social, economic, and political conditions in the advanced industrial societies, the former Soviet empire, and the Third World propelling intra- and international migration in the post-Cold War world and the changes it portends. Meissner is a senior associate at the Carnegie Endowment, where she directs its program on immigration and U.S. foreign policy, and is a former acting commissioner of the U.S. Immigration and Naturalization Service. She is author of *International Migration Challenges in a New Era: Policy Perspectives and Priorities for Europe, Japan, North America, and the International Community* (1993).

Migration has always been a force for change, and it will be especially powerful in the post–Cold War era. The Kurdish exodus from Iraq at the close of the Persian Gulf war illustrated how population dislocations can confound statecraft. Shiploads of Albanians bound for Italy dramatized the desperation afflicting the former communist states. The surge of Haitian boat people . . . increased the pressure to reverse that country's latest military coup. Most dramatic of all was the outward stampede of East Germans prompted by then Soviet leader Mikhail Gorbachev's renunciation of the Brezhnev Doctrine, freeing Eastern Europe. By

Reprinted with permission from *Foreign Policy,* 86 (Spring 1992). Copyright 1992 by the Carnegie Endowment for International Peace.

precipitating the unification of Germany, this migration transformed the political and security assumptions upon which the postwar Western alliance had been built.

Today's migrations are fundamentally economic phenomena: People move because of processes unleashed by the globalization of trade and markets, and by economic development patterns that generate rural-to-urban migrations sometimes stretching across national borders. But contemporary migrations are also increasingly generated by wars, mass human rights deprivations, and poverty. As a result, large numbers on the move can be the source of political instability and dangerous upheavals.

Whether motivated by economic or political reasons, or a mixture of both, the vast majority of migrants remain within their own countries. The next largest share move across national boundaries within the less-developed world, and a relatively small share cross borders to industrially advanced states. Though proportionately small, the migrations to developed countries are sizable and have led to fierce political debate and calls for dramatic policy changes, especially in Europe.

To the extent that countries have migration policies at all, most handle them as narrow, particularistic functions. Yet the causes of international migration are deeply embedded in the social, economic, and political conditions of our times. . . .

Migrants fall into five basic categories:

Legally admitted immigrants and non-immigrants. For traditional immigrant-receiving countries, the 1980s [were] a period of historically high immigration levels that promise to rise further through the 1990s. More than 8 million newcomers arrived in the United States, for example, second only to its highest immigration decade, the years 1901–1910. Numbers of non-immigrants have increased dramatically in all industrialized countries: Foreign students, technically trained personnel, multinational corporation executives and managers, scientists, and specialists in a wide variety of fields in global enterprises now constitute a growing international elite.

Contract labor migrants. Many countries rely on foreign workers. Contract labor arrangements exist between labor-surplus countries in parts of Asia and countries in other regions of the world, especially the Middle East. The instability inherent in these arrangements was vividly illustrated at the outbreak of the Gulf war when almost 2 million workers poured out of Iraq, Kuwait, and Saudi Arabia in an attempt to return home to countries unable to provide jobs and simultaneously hit by the loss of substantial remittances. Nonetheless, these arrangements are mutually beneficial and will remain prevalent.

Illegal immigrants. Virtually every industrialized country now houses populations of illegal immigrants. Some slip across borders. Others overstay the terms of authorized visas or travel documents. Illegals generally work in marginal or undesirable jobs. By and large, they do not directly displace native workers. However, illegal immigration undermines working conditions for native workers on the lower rungs of the economic ladder and forestalls automation and other efficiency measures over the longer term.

Asylum-seekers. Before the 1980s, political asylum was an exceptional event. Since then, caseloads in all industrialized countries except Japan have ballooned. Although some asylum applications are frivolous, most asylum-seekers come from countries where a mixture of economic failures and political chaos prevails. As a result, the more than 80 per cent of applicants who are rejected frequently are not expelled. They may not be bona fide refugees, but most countries are unwilling to return people to places like El Salvador, Somalia, and Sri Lanka.

Refugees. United Nations estimates set the global number of refugees at about 17 million. Probably an equal number are displaced within national borders. The victims of protracted wars and civil strife, most of today's refugees live in the less-developed world (the 20 countries hosting the highest proportion have average annual per capita incomes of $700). Less than 1 per cent will be resettled in the West. They generally live in camps administered by the U.N. and private agencies.

Although there are many important issues associated with the first two categories of migrants—legal immigrants and contract labor migrants—it is the latter three categories—illegal immigrants, asylum-seekers, and refugees—around which the current migration debate in the industrialized world revolves. Quite simply, this is because unregulated and emergency migrations bespeak a loss of control. They challenge the capacity of governments to uphold basic sovereignty, in this case the choice of who resides in one's own country. . . .

In practice, immigration can have a profound impact on the economy, the culture, and society as a whole. As economic actors, migrants enhance productivity in a number of ways. They accept temporary or marginal jobs, work hard, initially pay more in taxes than they take in services, and establish vibrant small business sectors. Writ large, immigration played a vital role, for example, in transforming the United States into a world power and rebuilding Europe after World War II. However, when growth lags and unemployment rises, immigrants provoke hostility and resentment. They are also among the most economically vulnerable, losing their jobs more quickly and having less of a cushion to fall back on. . . .

. . . Immigration invokes a broad panorama of concerns that are magnified when the immigrant groups are ethnically, racially, or religiously different from host societies, as is the pattern with much immigration today to the West.

The political potency of immigration is most vivid in Europe, where the issue has become one of the most incendiary on the domestic political agenda. In Germany, on the first anniversary of reunification, a spate of vicious attacks on foreigners electrified an already tense constitutional debate over whether to curtail the rights of foreigners to claim political asylum. Björn Engholm, the leader of Germany's Social Democrats, [said] he [could] envision the need for troops on the country's eastern border. France's prime minister, Edith Cresson, . . . proposed chartering planes to deport illegal immigrants.

Europeans are reacting as much to the changes immigration has already thrust upon their societies as they are to the prospect of additional newcomers. Europe has received substantial numbers of immigrants since it halted guestworker recruitment programs in the early 1970s. It experienced higher net immigration in 1990 than at any time since after World War II. France, with foreign-born residents making up 8 per cent of its population, and Germany, with 7.5 per cent, for example, have larger shares of foreign-born populations today than does the United States, with 6 per cent. . . .

From an economic standpoint, there is a good case for immigration. However, economic factors are but one part of the equation. Strong counterpressures pervade European thinking on social, political, and cultural grounds. . . . They raise a basic question about national identity—in effect, "Who are we?" . . .

For Europeans, membership in their societies is tied to shared ethnicity and nationality. People from northern Africa or Turkey, though they may have lived and worked in France or Germany for many years and may even be citizens, cannot share membership. This is very different from Australia, Canada, and the United States, where nation building through immigration led to ideas of membership based on civic participation and a generally shared commitment to democratic values. In asserting that they are non-immigrant nations, European states reject ethnic diversity as a positive societal value. Immigration, therefore, is seen as a fundamental threat to national unity and the common good.

To date, migration policymaking has been narrowly construed. Most developed countries have steadily decreased the percentage of approvals for burgeoning political asylum caseloads. . . . Traditional immigration countries are raising overall admissions levels by accepting greater numbers of skilled immigrants. They have implemented legalization measures, increased border and employer enforcement, and decreased the number of refugees admitted from former Soviet-bloc states.

These measures help reassure publics that their governments are taking action, and they discourage some potential migrants. But they are not sufficient. Migration pressures must be addressed with policies of far greater scope and ambition. Sadako Ogata, the United Nations High Commissioner for Refugees (UNHCR), urges that migration be treated not only "as a matter for humanitarian agencies of the U.N. but also as a political problem which must be placed in the mainstream of the international agenda as a potential threat to international peace and security."

This recognition is emerging with respect to the former Soviet empire. Western political and security interests now rest on the success of radical economic and political reforms there. Mass migrations or even large, unregulated flows would reflect crisis in the reform process and could cause states to take harsh countermeasures that would severely cramp or reverse reforms. The West is coming to recognize the important role that averting migration emergencies will play in preserving the stability of Eastern Europe and the former Soviet Union. Such a focus should help integrate migrations into the mainstream of post–Cold War global concerns. . . .

MOVEMENTS IN THE EAST

Of utmost urgency are the powerful economic and political forces unleashed by the collapse of the Soviet empire and the destruction of the union itself. Economically, the transition from centrally planned to market-oriented economies will cause high unemployment. In Poland, where the most aggressive reform program is underway, unemployment exceeds 10 per cent. Predictions for Eastern Europe overall put unemployment at 14 million, or 21 per cent. The economic crisis in the former Soviet Union is even more acute.

High unemployment and relatively low living standards do not automatically translate into migration. If people see things improving, and have hope, they will endure hardships. But if reform processes bog down, expectations can sour and an exit psychology can set in. This outcome is more likely when exile communities abroad are already established, as is the case for some ethnic groups in Eastern Europe and the former Soviet republics.

So far, migration within and from Eastern Europe has increased. This was to be expected after decades of harsh travel prohibitions. But the numbers have been in the hundreds of thousands, far less than the millions that some feared. A smattering of Bulgarians, Hungarian Gypsies, Poles, Romanians, and a range of ex-Soviet national groups are heading west in search of work and better lives. [The former] Czechoslovakia and Hungary now host refugee and illegal worker populations from Yugoslavia, Romania, Bulgaria, and the former Soviet Union; in Poland, a shadow economy of traders from the Baltic states, Russia, and Ukraine has emerged. Bringing home goods in short supply is valued almost as much as hard currency earnings. Most of those coming to Western Europe are either tourists, many of whom stay, or illegal workers, who will continue to arrive. Their numbers are likely to increase in the years ahead. At the same time, feared recurring migration crises, like that ignited in East Germany in 1989, have not materialized and are not likely unless there is war or wholesale social collapse.

Emigration to the West from the former Soviet republics has been organized and largely confined to specific groups: Armenians, ethnic Germans, Greeks, and Jews, for example. Receiving states and communities elsewhere have authorized and nurtured these movements. With the exception of intellectuals and the highly educated, members of other groups have generally not tried or had the opportunity to leave. The task, therefore, is a new form of containment: preventing a migration rationale and mentality from taking hold.

Politically, the ascendancy of nationalism is a harbinger of potentially dangerous emergency migrations. With the breakdown of communism, ethnic nationalism is providing an alternative vision of community. Democracy is viewed as the chance for separatism—to each his homeland—not as a crucible of pluralism. . . . [The civil war that splintered Yugoslavia] illustrates this tendency all too well.

The potential for such conflicts is most serious in the former USSR, where nationalities were purposely relocated, divided, and mixed during the Stalinist era. Historic hatreds inflamed by Joseph Stalin's legacy have already produced violence and refugees. The Armenian-Azerbaijani clashes in early 1988 were the most severe. . . . Similar outbreaks have occurred elsewhere, especially in the former Soviet Central Asian republics. Russian officials estimate that 700,000 people are now displaced, but the actual number may be as high as 2 million or more.

Of the 60–70 million people estimated to be living outside the regions of their ethnic identities, the largest group is the Russians—25 million—who live in the Baltic states, Kazakhstan, Ukraine, and elsewhere. The majority of people in these diasporas are well integrated. The Russians, in particular, tend to be the technical, educated elite wherever they live. . . .

Among non-Russians, there is far greater likelihood of serious problems. New states such as Azerbaijan, Georgia, and Uzbekistan harbor impulses toward dictatorships reminiscent of the old order, yet unabashedly nationalist. The number of internal refugees is growing as conflicts escalate, causing terrible hardship and social strain due to insufficient housing and employment. The absence in the former Soviet system of any tradition and mechanisms to accommodate intrastate population mobility, combined with dire economic conditions, only heighten the danger.

If minority and majority populations cannot establish workable relationships, violence and large refugee migrations could spread. Such migrations are not likely to spill into Western Europe. Instead, they would be primarily internal, threatening the staying power of the new Commonwealth of Independent States. Governments confronting migration crises will be perceived by their populations to have lost control and to be unable to deliver improved standards of living. Under some circumstances, such migrations could touch Eastern Europe, undermining fragile new democracies there. Refugee emergencies would also lead the West to act on its security fears. Instead of building a "common European home," the West would become disenchanted with the East and new divisions would arise.

Geographically a border state, and with almost 3 million ethnic kin in Eastern Europe and the former USSR, Germany has led the way in mounting a comprehensive response. In addition to sending massive food shipments, it has signed historic border and nonaggression pacts with Poland and the old Soviet Union that include guarantees of the rights and cultural integrity of German populations where they currently live. It has also made agreements with Poland stipulating types and levels of legal employment for Poles within Germany. By establishing clear and controlled avenues for migration, such measures normalize expected flows.

These actions point to themes that must be urgently pursued on bilateral and multilateral fronts. For economic reform programs to succeed without deleterious migration side effects, they will have to be accompanied by broad economic help from the West. . . . In addition, new political systems must embrace individual and minority rights, fostering tolerance as a fundamental requirement of democracy. . . .

Just as the Helsinki act's insistence on individual rights and democratic systems lit a beacon on the path to the revolutions of 1989, building the institutions and attitudes through which democracy works must constitute the next generation of human rights imperatives. A combination of substantial economic and human rights assistance by the West is paramount if ruinous migration pressures in the former East bloc are to be contained.

PROXY WAR LEGACIES

While the Cold War is definitely over in Europe, for many outside of Europe the Cold War's legacy of misery and ruin has endured. This is most true in those Third World countries that played host to the proxy wars of the superpowers. When the Soviet Union withdrew from Afghanistan, Vietnam left Cambodia, Namibia held its plebiscite, and Violeta Chamorro outpolled Daniel Ortega in Nicaragua, it truly seemed that peace was breaking out all over. But the possibility of peace brings with it the challenge of reconstruction, a challenge that consists in large part of repatriating millions of refugees.

Of the world's approximately 17 million refugees, the majority originally fled because of the disruption and danger of proxy wars. Most have been uprooted for more than a decade. A generation of children has been born in camps and knows only a life of boredom and dependency. About two-thirds would "retire" from the refugee rolls if they were able to return to home areas in Afghanistan, Central America, Indochina, and southern Africa.

But repatriation is just the beginning. Ninety per cent of the casualties in these proxy wars were civilians; the conflicts fractured lives and communities as never before. And the devastation continues: The most urgent task in countries like Cambodia and Namibia is removing land mines that litter countrysides, claiming lives and limbs every day. What little existed for these populations before has been destroyed. Homes, villages, roads, potable water, and livelihoods must be restored.

Moreover, the governments of these countries will be tentative, built upon tenuous political coalitions and beset by deep societal divisions that predate big-power involvement. In some places, armed insurrections will continue. New leaders will need sustained support and will find it difficult to impose austere economic regimes and survive.

Large sums will not be forthcoming from the international community, and these countries would in any event lack the capacity to use them effectively. . . . With the ideological war over, though, there is the real danger that the world will turn a blind eye to the former battlegrounds.

The repatriation of refugees and the reconstruction of their homes have been entrusted to the U.N. and other international bodies. However, success will require these organizations to effect major changes in their outlook, capabilities, and resource allocations. . . . A more streamlined U.N. structure, adequate financing, and the political support of governments are crucial ingredients that must be better mobilized if the U.N. is to bring the Cold War's legacy of long-term refugee burdens to a close and expand its capabilities to meet new emergencies. The alternative is that today's refugee camps will become tomorrow's Palestinian-style enclaves, or that unsuccessful repatriation will threaten stability for hard-won peace agreements and generate a whole host of new problems, complete with new refugees.

THE NORTH-SOUTH GAP

Be it Algerians in France, Tunisians in Italy, Turks in Germany, Pakistanis in Great Britain, Mexicans in the United States, Sikhs in Canada, or Filipinos in Australia, newcomers personifying South-North migration are the most volatile element of the international migration picture for industrialized countries. The disparities in income and living standards that underlie South-North flows are, over the longer term, the most daunting challenge on the migration agenda.

Flows from underdeveloped countries are not proliferating randomly. They track well-established connections rooted in colonialism, war and military occupation, labor recruitment, and economic penetration. Indians move to Britain and Canada, their commonwealth partners. Korean war brides led the way for today's heavy Korea–United States flows. Turkish *Gastarbeiter* (guestworkers) in Germany sent for family members rather than returning to them in Turkey. Cuban elites, who identified with capitalism and whose wealth derived from American investment on the island, fled to Miami after the 1959 communist revolution.

Once migration footholds are established, family members join successful migrants, remittances link communities across great distances, and established immigrant groups help the newly arrived find work and negotiate seemingly alien ways and places. Migration itself then becomes a new connection between countries, evolving into a social process that is increasingly sustained by internal factors largely beyond the realm of government action or the economic impulses that originally generated it. Colonialism and military occupation may be outdated forms, but analogous transnational links are being created as economic interdependence deepens. These links give rise to new forms and sources of migration.

Economic development is the obvious answer to the inequality among countries that produces South-North migration. But, . . . in the short to medium term, development stimulates, rather than slows, migration. This effect occurs because development is inherently disruptive, forcing workers out of subsistence jobs into new areas of economic activity. . . .

Although South-North migration may present unhappy policy choices, a realistic assessment of the long-term interests of developed societies requires far more aggressive steps to reverse economic trends in the less-developed world. Without outside economic intervention these trends can only become more desperate and dangerous. Even if receptivity to immigration in the West were to change dramatically, immigration opportunities there would remain inconsequential when viewed against the employment needs of the rest of the world. New immigration countries would replicate what traditional immigration countries are doing—using immigration to compensate for skill deficits in domestic work forces. Though a sensible strategy for the developed countries, it deepens the crisis for developing countries by robbing them of the people most likely to conduct commerce and modernize their societies. Simply stated, immigration cannot solve the problem of underdevelopment.

The enormity of the task is captured by the following statistics. By 2010, about 730 million new workers will have entered the labor force in the developing world. During the period of the most robust job growth in the United States in the 1980s, the economy produced about 2 million new jobs annually. The global need to generate jobs is unprecedented. . . .

The immigration dimensions of global economic trends are only in the earliest stages of being analyzed and understood. A former senior U.S. official who served in an economic development agency for 10 years recently observed that migration had never once entered their thinking about the objectives or impacts of development programs. With development and migration the two sides of a coin, that must change. Just as we are learning that development must become "user friendly" where environmental issues are concerned, the migration implications of particular development, investment, and trade strategies must also be treated as issues of critical importance.

In an ideal world, migration pressures would be managed in ways that prevent sudden mass movements and humanitarian emergencies; eliminate involuntary migrations due to life-threatening circumstances, both political and economic; and establish mechanisms to regulate and channel flows that are inevitable. To these ends, policymaking must be directed at several priority tasks: building viable economies and functioning democracies in the former

East bloc countries; repatriating refugees created by Cold War proxy conflicts and rebuilding their countries; and intensifying economic development efforts in the South.

However, even if the right to stay becomes a working principle, developed countries will face substantial immigration for the foreseeable future. States have an obligation to control entry into their societies. They should do so by establishing reasoned admissions policies for labor market, refugee, and family immigrant groups, along with firm, judicious enforcement regimes.

But as a practical matter, immigration control in democracies is highly imperfect because of the range of legitimate reasons for entering, the obligations embedded in due process-based legal systems, economic interests and political values that are inimical to expulsion, and migration pressures from and connections with other countries. International migration poses a range of difficult issues for the world community; successfully managing growing ethnic and racial diversity at home may be the biggest challenge of them all.

37

HUNGER VERSUS THE ENVIRONMENT: A RECIPE FOR GLOBAL SUICIDE

Nabil Megalli

Realizing global food security is often described as the first priority of sustainable development, yet "the more humans there are to feed, the more we gnaw away at the Earth's ability to feed us." This is the message of Nabil Megalli's fast-paced review of the impact of environmental stress on humankind's food-producing systems. "If humanity is to feed itself," he concludes, "this environmental degradation has to stop—and stop soon." Megalli is a journalist with the *Deutscher Presserat.*

Have you eaten enough today? One-fifth of the world population is not so lucky. Furthermore, the odds are that your children will suffer, one way or another, from the fall-out from the rabid race between global hunger, rampant environmental degradation, and population growth gone berserk.

The picture of hunger in the last decade of the 20th century is frightening. Already, one billion people do not have the minimum to eat, and there will be one billion more mouths to feed by the year 2000. Agriculture is devouring its own base in three continents that cover two-thirds of the world's area and house four-fifths of its population. The world is galloping towards a situation where it will not be able to feed itself, no matter what it does.

In the United States, farmers are suffering from droughts at a frequency unprecedented in modern history. Global warming has already led to three

By Nabil Megalli, reprinted with permission by *Our Planet,* copyright 1992.

severely drought-reduced harvests in the United States during the 1980s, even though droughts have, as a rule, occurred there once every 20 years.

There is evidence that a plateau has been reached in global efforts to increase the area under cultivation and enhance yields per hectare through agrochemicals. This desperate squeezing of the land for more food is accelerating environmental degradation, which turns millions of hectares each year into wasteland. According to UNEP's Global Assessment of Soil Degradation (GLASOD), there were 4700 million hectares of agricultural land in 1988, but 1230 million hectares—that is, about 25 percent—suffered from some degree of human-induced degradation. In this hunger- and debt-driven hunt for food or profits, or both in the case of many small-scale developing world farmers, the search for new agricultural land is an irresistible cause of deforestation, overgrazing, over-cropping and overfertilization. In turn, this causes desertification, salinization, pollution of water resources and erosion of valuable topsoil. It is often the cream of agricultural land which is lost, while the new land is inevitably less suitable and less productive, and so more rapidly degraded.

Current global topsoil losses are estimated to be 24 billion tonnes annually. In the US Corn Belt, studies show that each inch of topsoil lost reduces crops by 6 percent. In West Africa, topsoil loss has already reduced land productivity by 50 percent. Red Cross studies indicate that Ethiopia, which has only 6 percent of its forest cover left, is bleeding its topsoil into rivers at the rate of 2000 tonnes per square kilometre per year. Globally, per capita food production is retreating on another front, as population growth continues to defy all demographic predictions and birth control campaigns. The world population currently stands at 5.5 billion and current estimates indicate it is likely to reach between 10.4 and 14 billion before it levels off.

The world fish catch, estimated at 91 million tonnes in 1986, has probably already exceeded the maximum sustainable yield of 100 million tonnes. From that point on, the fish catch can only go on a downward spiral. The UN Food and Agriculture Organization (FAO) says that overfishing and pollution have severely reduced the catch by small-scale fishermen, which is the main source of protein for their families and small local communities in many parts of the world. A lower fish catch means lower livestock production, since up to 45 percent of the catch is used as animal feed.

Attempting to play down the effects of pollution and global warming is as futile as the belief that some regions can continue playing the role of global breadbaskets, at a high cost to themselves and to the rest of the world. It is estimated that the industrial giants in the 25-nation Organization for Economic Cooperation and Development (OECD) spend more than US$150 billion annually in direct and indirect agricultural subsidies to keep potentially low-cost farmers in the developing nations from entering the market. The result is agricultural ruin on both sides of the artificial North-South divide. Agricultural subsidies eat up to three-quarters of the European [Union's] budget, and the cost of storing and destroying surplus [EU] foods has been estimated at US$225 million per week. In the United States, the Comptroller General has reported that governmental water subsidies often surpass the value of crops produced in arid and semi-arid areas. In these regions, wasteful irrigation consumes up to 80 percent of valuable water resources.

According to UNEP's *The World Environment 1972–1992*, the estimated annual costs of combating desertification globally stand at between US$10 billion and US$22 billion, while economic losses due to desertification are about US$42 billion. The longer the delay in confronting this accelerating degradation, the more costly an exercise it becomes. In 1980, the estimated cost of a 20-year programme to combat desertification was US$90 billion. In 1990–91, the estimated cost of a 20-year programme had risen threefold to US$270 billion, because the area affected and the costs of land reclamation are increasing.

Desertification affects 3.6 billion hectares or 70 percent of the world's potentially productive drylands, that is, nearly 25 percent of the total land area of the world. These figures exclude naturally occurring hyper-arid deserts.

The implications are made worse by the industrialized countries' use of up to three-quarters of global agrochemical supply on their limited territory, in order to fuel their agricultural 'miracle'. Traces, albeit minute in some cases, of carcinogenic pesticides have turned up in all groundwater reservoirs tested in the United States. In Europe, which uses 50 times as much fertilizer as Africa, nitrate concentrations in some major rivers have been increasing at an annual rate of 0.15 milligrams per litre since 1960 and have in some cases already surpassed the World Health Organization's acceptable limit of 11.3 milligrams per litre. Thus, the agricultural earnings of the industrialized world are dished back in the form of mushrooming health care costs and a lower quality of life for every citizen.

Studies have shown that one-sixth of North America's inhabitants in the Great Lakes area are exposed to the highly toxic substance dioxin. Many water wells in the eastern United States have been abandoned because of toxicity levels. Excessive pumping of ground water for agriculture has caused subsidence. The ground in some areas of California's San Joaquin Valley is already 30 feet below its level 50 years ago. Such stratification is a factor not fully taken into consideration when assessing the flooding potential of global warming. This has particularly ominous implications for regions which rely almost exclusively on ground water supplies, such as some small island states and the coastal regions where, incidentally, 50 percent of the world's inhabitants live. The problem of sinking ground level is compounded by the extraction of other minerals, particularly petroleum deposits in coastal states. Meanwhile, water pollution is threatening expensive coastal water desalination and power plants in regions which have invested heavily in this field.

On the so-called Southern side of the planet, peasants, who form the majority of populations in many developing countries, have slipped from subsistence to near-starvation. Here, the status of the average farmer is the exact opposite of his counterpart in the North. Because of agricultural protection, farmers are effectively insulated from any beneficial price increases that may occur on the international agricultural bazaar. Governments keep prices artificially low to maintain 'social peace' in the overcrowded urban areas. The net result is a fall in returns to farmers, followed by a fall in food production, growing potential for civil strife and social decay in the countryside.

Some 47 percent of the world's population will be living in cities by the year 2000, in comparison with 10 percent in 1980 and 1 percent in 1940. There will be megacities of up to 20 million inhabitants . . . and social friction and crime of unprecedented dimensions. About 90 percent of the projected population increase will take place in developing countries, and two-thirds of that increase will be in cities.

Mounting foreign debt payments also drive governments into encouraging export cash crops based on monocultures, at the expense of the vast genetic diversity of natural environments. More forest has to be axed, while, all too often, soils are driven to exhaustion by incessant cropping and reduced fallow periods. The result is that hunger feeds on itself in a vicious cycle of environmental degradation and expanding famines.

Three-quarters of the inhabitants in Africa work in the agricultural sector, and the continent was a net exporter of food 20 years ago. Today, as Somalia's devastation all too clearly attests, Africa is the leading example of food insecurity in the world, not only because of warfare, but also because of massive deforestation. Around the growing number of refugee camps in Ethiopia, Somalia and Sudan, the deforestation is frighteningly clear, as the refugees cut the sparse vegetation for fuel.

By the year 2000, there are likely to be up to 130 million hungry people in the Sahel countries of Africa as a result of drought and desertification. Whereas Asia has the largest number of hungry people, Africa stands out in terms of the percentage of people affected—25 percent of the population. Africa has one-quarter of the international refugee community, even though it contains only one-tenth of world population. The World Bank warns that 'Africa's food situation is not only serious, it is deteriorating'.

Worldwide, per capita food production rose by one-third in the period 1950–1984, but it . . . declined by 7 percent in the 1984–1989 period and is expected to fall by another 7 percent by the year 2000. In Africa, per capita food production has plummeted 20 percent from its peak in 1967. Extrapolation of present trends by World Bank analysts yields a 'nightmare scenario' for the entire continent.

In Latin America, the same phenomenon has been in evidence since 1981. Brazil, which at the time had the ninth largest gross national product in the world, in 1987 approached the World Food Programme for emergency aid to feed 2.5 million peasants in its northeastern region. They had swollen the state capital of Ceará Mirim by nearly one million during the mid-1980s. This is attributable in part to unprecedented drought and changing rain patterns linked to the surface temperatures of the El Niño currents in the Pacific. But equal blame falls on rapid deforestation, a fall of up to 75 percent in food crops matched by similar increases in export crops, and the contraction of the role of small farmers, while less than 8 percent of the population are garnering 80 percent of the land.

The downward agricultural spiral in developing countries has reversed only in cases where the average peasant has been allowed to add his input to the land he had jealously nurtured for millenia as his one and only source of sustainable livelihood. Cooperatives and non-governmental organizations play an indispensable part in this process. Improving the status of women and recognizing their key role in agricultural communities has been an important factor where agricultural output has increased.

Without improving the human side of the agricultural equation, there is little hope for added productivity through technical input or putting more area under cultivation. Response to fertilizers is leveling off after a 3 percent annual increase between 1950 and 1984 which boosted output 2.6 times. Meanwhile, there is a steady loss of irrigated areas, which provide one-third of the world's crops from only 18 percent of its agricultural territory. Irrigated areas grew from 232 million acres in 1950 to 615 million acres in 1980, but these areas are now being lost, largely because of increased salinity and a steady fall in the water table. According to UNEP's *The World Environment 1972–1992*, 43 million hectares of irrigated land (30 percent of all irrigated dryland) show evidence of degradation, mainly waterlogging and its resultant salinization and/or alkalinization. In the United States, groundwater levels beneath much of the irrigated land are falling between 0.15 metres and 1.3 metres a year, and even greater drops have been recorded in China. Any further increases in agricultural lands will be in marginal and high-cost areas, or through deforestation, which will add further to the ruin.

If humanity is to feed itself, this environmental degradation has to stop—and stop soon.

38

AGRICULTURE AND THE ENVIRONMENT: MEETING GLOBAL FOOD NEEDS

Orville L. Freeman

Feeding the world's burgeoning population will require a massive increase in global food production. In this essay the author argues that a balance must be struck between concern for protecting the world's environment and the development and application of agricultural and food-related technology necessary to avoid mass starvation. Orville L. Freeman served as U.S. secretary of agriculture during the Kennedy and Johnson administrations and is president of the Agriculture Council of America.

Estimated population growth for the next quarter century is so enormous that warning bells should be sounding in every quadrant of the globe. Feeding this population may well be the greatest challenge we have ever faced—one that will test the world's productive and technological capabilities to their very limits. . . . [It] will take total mobilization of all global productive resources, including land, infrastructure, people skills, and technology, to prevent massive famine in the decade of the 1990s and beyond.

Even conservative projections call for a population increase of over one billion people—bringing the world's population to 6.2 billion by the year 2000. These same projections predict a population of nearly 11 billion by the year 2050. This increase will take place in a world where already over

Reproduced with permission from *The Futurist,* published by the World Future Society, 7910 Woodmont Avenue, Suite 450, Bethesda, Maryland 20814.

75% of the population can barely feed themselves, almost 500 million people are severely malnourished, and 15 million children worldwide die each year from starvation and related illnesses—that is over 41,000 every day. In this regard, I think that many people—particularly those in the relatively well-fed industrialized world—simply cannot relate to the concept of subsistence, where securing enough food to sustain life is the focal point of each day's activities.

In the United States, for all but a relatively small segment of the population, the task of securing food means no more than a trip to the nearby supermarket, where we choose from more than 8,000 items to meet our needs. In fact, one of our major food-related concerns is how to eat less! For that reason, I sometimes think we are ill-prepared to wrestle with the realities of what it will take to feed the rising number of people in the world. In fact, there is no precedent in our history that even comes close to approximating the population and food-supply pressures we will experience in the next 10–20 years.

To give some definition to the magnitude of the challenge this presents, let me cite one statistic that drives this point home more clearly than any other I have encountered: In the next two to four generations, world agriculture will be called on to produce as much food as has been produced in the entire 12,000-year history of agriculture. This is a very sobering prospect and a challenge of unprecedented magnitude. To meet this challenge, difficult and delicate choices will have to be made, none of which will likely emerge without heated debate.

A DIFFICULT BALANCING ACT

Choosing alternatives or making trade-offs is most difficult when each is desirable and the moral imperatives for each are both clear and compelling. Nowhere is this dilemma more apparent than in the current debate over protecting our planet's increasingly fragile environment and feeding its growing hungry population. Here we have goals that should be compatible. After all, the earth's resources were put in place to meet humanity's needs, the most basic of which is eating.

Unfortunately, the balancing act between producing food and preserving the environment appears cast in an increasingly hostile framework that in the end can only be counterproductive. We must exercise every caution to guard against the tyranny of a single issue dominating what must by definition be a very complex balancing act that frequently calls for difficult trade-offs.

In order of priority, then, the first challenge we must address is how to bring the goals of feeding the world's population and protecting the world's environment into harmony. They need not and must not be mutually exclusive. To maximize our productive capabilities and minimize the effect this production has on the environment, the vital connective tissue is technology. We must foster and harness the technological means through which both goals can be served—applying science to meet the objectives of both humanity and our environment.

Unfortunately, this does not seem to be the direction in which we are headed. From what I read and hear of late, technology is being cast in an increasingly dim light—a scapegoat for a host of environmental ills that humans have inflicted on their planet.

Application of technology, including agricultural application, has certainly not been without its missteps over the years. But fortunately, the industrial world is demonstrating a growing understanding that the price of environmental abuse is high and that the damage can be irreversible. We must strengthen this realization where agriculture is concerned.

At the same time, however, we must acknowledge that, without sophisticated food-production technology, we would not have the food supply we enjoy today and certainly could never meet the needs of the population realities nearly upon us.

POPULATION GROWS, FOOD PRODUCTION FALLS

In the three decades following the early 1950s, the world—led by Europe and the United States, followed by many Third World countries—witnessed unprecedented advances in the development and application of agricultural and food-related technology. The resulting increases in production and delivery of food—the so-called Green Revolution, in which world grain output multiplied 2.6 times—has been truly phenomenal. Since the early 1980s, however, a gradual tightening of the world food situation on the production side is taking place with little corresponding response on the population side of the equation.

India, for example, more than tripled its wheat harvest between 1965 and 1983. Since that time, India has not increased its grain production at all, and its population—with 500 million people at the subsistence level—continues to climb rapidly. China boosted its grain production by nearly half between 1976 and 1984, but it has not reached the 1984 level since that record year—and population continues to grow. In Africa and South America, the two continents with the fastest-growing populations, food production has fallen far behind population growth. Since 1980, Africa's population has grown at an explosive 3% rate annually. But in that time period, its food production has grown only 1.8% annually—barely half as much as the rate of population growth. In most African countries, food production continues to fall progressively behind population growth.

If we are to avoid mass starvation among the exploding populations in Third World countries, we need to examine what caused the Green Revolution, because that type of production surge is exactly what has to be repeated in the decades ahead. We also need to look at the factors that caused the slowdown in productivity to see what can be done to return to previous growth levels.

THE NEED FOR ANOTHER GREEN REVOLUTION

There seems to be general agreement on five major forces behind the Green Revolution:

1 The hybridization of corn.
2 The ninefold increase in fertilizer use between 1950 and 1984.
3 The near tripling of irrigated areas in that same period.
4 The rapid spread of new, high-yielding wheat and rice seeds in Third World countries.
5 The use of chemical insecticides, herbicides, rodenticides, and fungicides.

This latter category—crop-protection chemicals plus nitrogen fertilizer—currently is the popular whipping boy in the environmental debate. But we would do well to remember that these chemicals currently account for as much as 40%–50% of world agricultural production, particularly in light of the anticipated population–food pressures.

Regarding the causes of the slowdown in productivity growth, there is less solid agreement, but some of the problems we recognize are:

1 Shortage of land, with millions of acres withdrawn from production because of erosion.
2 Scarcity of water from drought and heavy irrigation, which has drawn down water tables rapidly in many places in the world.
3 The current absence of dramatic new technology that matches that which was so instrumental in stimulating productivity between 1960 and 1984, despite the predicted potential of future biotechnology.

Whatever the causes, it is clear that world grain carry-over has dropped to an alarmingly low level— . . . very close to the 1973–1974 situation, when the United States became so concerned about tight supplies that it embargoed soybeans.

In the face of the reduced number of acres planted worldwide and a rising global demand, this trend will likely continue unless returning the world to a high rate of food productivity commands a top priority as we look to the future. To do this, there is no question that technology must play a major role. Any effective blueprint for increasing agricultural productivity worldwide must incorporate development and application of crop and food-related technology. To suggest that agricultural technology is the enemy of humanity or the environment is to ignore the realities of food production and population trends. Of course, there are potential risks in agricultural and food-related technology that should keep us ever vigilant. We must constantly strive for smart use and avoid misuse.

REJECTING THE "GOOD OLD DAYS"

At the same time as we measure the impact of technology, we must take into account the effects of advances in scientific techniques that are taking place with breathtaking speed. . . . In seeking solutions to complex questions, we have to exercise an abundance of caution to avoid tossing out the baby with the bathwater. . . .

As attractive as some would make it sound, a return to the "good old days" and a pristine environment simply is not feasible. Many of us were around for some of those so-called "good old days." I, for one, am not interested in going back. I remember unpasteurized milk, no penicillin, wormy apples, and fresh fruit and vegetables only in the summer months. A return to that would represent a giant step backward and one that ignores the needs of our growing world population.

Technology that is intelligently conceived and carefully implemented, including the measured and careful application of fertilizer and crop-protection chemicals, represents the hope for the future and, as such, should be a cornerstone of food and agricultural policy for the coming decades. In this regard, the way must be paved for coming biotechnology and the fantastic possibilities this whole area of science opens up regarding both crop and livestock production and uses of agricultural products. Agricultural technology can be the tool that brings humanity and the environment into harmony and productive coexistence. For that reason, it should be embraced, not rejected, both in its conception and its application.

SERVING HUMANITY AND THE ENVIRONMENT

I think we make a potentially dangerous mistake when we frame the question in an adversarial light: to serve humanity or the environment. The needs are not mutually exclusive. In fact, they are totally interdependent. My caution is this: In our haste to atone for environmental "sins" of the past, we must not delude ourselves about the realities of the future. What we have to do is measure and manage carefully how we apply technology today and how we oversee the evolution from one type of technological solution to another. We must guide the world to technology that meets the needs of both humanity and the environment. . . .

There is no question that meeting the food needs of the coming decades will exert increasing pressure on an already strained environment. However, no matter how compelling the case for reducing these environmental pressures is, we simply cannot turn our backs on the needs of the hungry.

The realities of food production in much of the Third World, where the population increases will be the greatest, are vastly different from what is experienced in the bountiful agricultural lands of the United States. Developing countries are striving for subsistence, while U.S. production currently is approximately 40 percent over domestic needs—and that is with millions of acres idled. The United States must keep its productivity high in order to provide food assistance to starving people and also to sustain and stimulate emerging agriculture in the developing world. Third World countries need the technological means through which their infant agriculture can achieve productive levels capable of feeding their growing populations and at the same time strengthening growth and expansion of their entire economy.

These are real needs and real solutions that cannot be ignored. Yet, there is danger that they will be obscured while the affluent 10% of the world looks for a broad brush and quick fix to environmental problems that have been decades in the making. Here I urge caution. Yes, we must protect our fragile environment and use our resources wisely. But there is a very serious danger that the voice of the world's hungry will not be heard if the environmental and food-related agenda is written to meet only the needs of well-intentioned but well-fed interests.

39

THE POLITICS OF WATER

Sandra Postel

Water that traverses national boundaries is a renewable resource but also a finite one that promises to grow more scarce, thus threatening to become "a major source of economic and political instability" in world politics. Sandra Postel examines the prospects for both conflict and cooperation that water issues raise. She concludes on a cautiously optimistic note: "It may just be that the mutual gains possible from cooperation on water issues will move some longstanding rivals toward the larger goal of peace." Postel is vice president for research at the Worldwatch Institute and author of *Last Oasis: Facing Water Scarcity* (1992).

The threat of nations going to war over oil-rich territories is nothing new, but in the coming years it may be that *water* sparks more political flare-ups than "black gold." In some areas of the world, water scarcity may be to the 1990s what the oil price shocks were to the 1970s—a major source of economic and political instability.

Unique among strategic resources, water not only courses easily across political boundaries, it also gives upstream countries a distinct advantage over downstream neighbors. Tensions between countries that depend on the same water sources are already running high. In a 1989 address before the U.S. Congress, Boutros Boutros-Ghali, then Egypt's Minister of State for Foreign

Reprinted with the permission of Worldwatch Institute. Excerpted from *World Watch* (July/August 1993). Author: Sandra Postel.

Affairs, spoke frankly of the critical importance of water to his country, which falls last in the receiving line for the precious stuff of the Nile. "The national security of Egypt," he said, "is in the hands of the eight other African countries in the Nile basin."

Although water is a renewable resource, it is also a finite one. Nature makes only so much available in a given region each year—and supplies can drop considerably below average in times of drought. As human numbers climb, and more and more water is needed to supply farms, factories and households, nature's water bodies are becoming overtaxed. And as competition increases for ever more limited supplies, international frictions over water are worsening.

Nearly 40 percent of the world's people depend on river systems shared by two or more countries. India and Bangladesh haggle over the Ganges River, Mexico and the United States over the Colorado, and Czechoslovakia [now the Czech and Slovak republics] and Hungary over the Danube. An emerging hotspot is Central Asia, where five newly independent countries splintered off from the former Soviet Union now share two overused rivers, the Amu Darya and the Syr Darya. It is in the Middle East, however, that water disputes are shaping political landscapes and economic futures most definitively.

The specter of a "water crisis" in the Middle East has become almost legendary. With some of the highest population growth rates in the world and heavy reliance on irrigation for their agricultural productivity, Middle Eastern countries have much at stake when it comes to dividing up the region's supplies. Enough leaders have spoken of the potential for wars over water that new warnings have lost their bite. But these repeated admonitions may, in fact, presage some pivotal events in Middle East politics. Over the next decade, water issues in the region's three major river basins—the Jordan, the Nile, and the Tigris-Euphrates—will lead to either an unprecedented degree of cooperation or a combustible level of conflict.

NO LONGER "DEEP AND WIDE"

Water scarcity is most acute in the Jordan River basin, which is shared by Israel, Jordan, the occupied West Bank, and part of Syria (see map). Israel's annual water use already exceeds its renewable supply (the amount of water that nature makes available each year) by some 15 percent, meaning that in a typical year Israel has to overdraw its groundwater account to meet its needs. With an expected influx of up to a million immigrants from former Soviet states, Israel's yearly water deficit will only worsen.

The Jordanians use less than half as much water as the Israelis on a per capita basis. But their demands are also bumping up against supply limits, even as the country's population rises by 3.4 percent a year, one of the highest growth rates in the world. With the nation's water use projected to increase by 40 per-

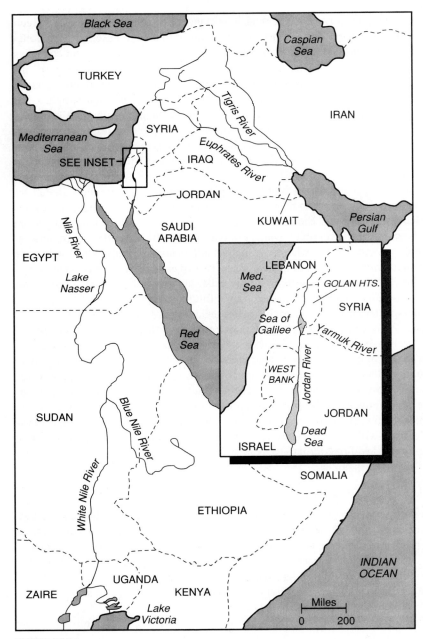

FIGURE 39.1
MIDDLE EAST RIVER BASINS

cent during this decade, competition grows keener each year. King Hussein declared in 1990 that water was the only issue that could take him to war with Israel.

As negotiators work to hammer out a peace agreement in the region, the issue of water rights looms large. Most proposals involve Israel returning some of the territory it has occupied since the 1967 Arab-Israeli war—which, since many of Israel's prime water sources are located in the disputed areas, could ultimately mean relinquishing control over substantial water supplies. Some 25 to 40 percent of Israel's sustainable water supply comes from the Yarqon-Taninim aquifer, which runs along the foothills of the West Bank and flows westward across the Green Line (the demarcation of pre-1967 Israeli territory) toward the Mediterranean Sea. Though Israel can tap water on either side of the Green Line, the aquifer's main recharge area lies on the West Bank. Israel has severely restricted the amount of water that West Bank Arabs can pump from this underground reserve, even as it continues overdrawing the aquifer for its own uses—an inequity that has greatly angered the Arab population.

Another portion of Israel's water supply originates in the Golan Heights, which Israel claimed from Syria after the 1967 war and then annexed in 1981. The Golan Heights forms part of the catchment for the Sea of Galilee, which is Israel's largest surface water reservoir and the source for the National Water Carrier, a huge canal and pipeline that transports water from the north to the drier south. Control of the Golan Heights also gives Israel some rights to the Yarmuk River, the last major undeveloped tributary in the basin. So far, Israel has blocked a joint plan by Jordan and Syria to construct a dam on the Yarmuk to increase their supplies, fearing that the dam could reduce flows into the Jordan River, and thus jeopardize its water security.

A third important water source for Israel is the coastal aquifer bordering the Mediterranean. It lies entirely within the pre-1967 territory, so the question of water rights does not arise. But decades of overpumping have caused seawater to invade this key freshwater source. . . .

Some 20 percent of the coastal aquifer is contaminated by salts or nitrates from urban and agricultural pollution, and water officials predict that a fifth of its wells may need to be closed over the next few years—increasing Israeli dependence on the West Bank Yarqon-Taninim reserve. "It is water, in the final analysis," says Thomas Naff, Middle East water analyst at the University of Pennsylvania, "that will determine the future of the Occupied Territories, and by extension, the issue of conflict or peace in the region."

ONE RIVER, NINE COUNTRIES

Across the Sinai Peninsula, political pressures over the waters of the famed Nile River basin may also be coming to a head.

Egypt epitomizes the dilemmas and insecurities faced by water-scarce countries with rapid population growth and very limited indigenous water sources. Fifty-six million people in Egypt depend almost entirely on the Nile's waters, but none of the Nile originates within the nation's boundaries. About 85 percent of the river is generated by rainfall in Ethiopia, flowing as the Blue Nile into Sudan before entering Egypt. The remainder comes from the White Nile system, which has headwaters at Lake Victoria in Tanzania, and joins the Blue Nile near Khartoum. The world's longest river, the Nile supplies nine countries in all—of which Egypt is last in line.

Under a 1959 agreement with Sudan, Egypt is entitled to 55.5 billion cubic meters (bcm) of Nile water each year; Sudan is allotted 18.5 bcm. To meet its needs, Egypt supplements Nile water with small amounts of groundwater, agricultural drainage water, and treated municipal wastewater. In all, Egypt had 63.5 bcm available in 1990. Unfortunately, even modest projections show Egypt's demand rising to 69.4 bcm by the end of the decade—about 9 percent more water than is available now.

Plans for meeting this demand depend on some questionable components—including the extraction of deep groundwater in the desert, a fivefold increase in treated sewage water, and increased availability of Nile water following completion of a canal project with Sudan. The Jonglei canal would channel water through the Sudd swamps, a vast wetland in southern Sudan that harbors millions of migratory birds each year. Although the project would disrupt portions of this critical habitat, Egyptian officials strongly favor the canal because it would reduce the amount of water lost to evaporation in the swamp and thereby increase the Nile's flow into Egypt. Civil war in Sudan brought construction to a halt in 1983, and, with the Sudanese People's Liberation Army opposed to the scheme, it seems unlikely that the project will be completed in the foreseeable future.

As if the problems of finding more water were not enough, Egypt could actually lose some of its existing supply when Ethiopia begins to develop the Nile's headwaters. Ethiopia recognizes no obligation to limit its use of Nile waters for the sake of Egypt and Sudan. Indeed, it was concern about Ethiopia's water development plans that led Egyptian President Anwar Sadat to observe, shortly after signing the historic peace accords with Israel, that "the only matter that could take Egypt to war again is water."

Fortunately for Egypt, Ethiopia's plans to dam upper Nile waters have yet to materialize. Lake Tana, the Blue Nile's source, is remote, complicating development efforts already hindered by political and economic turmoil. But it is just a matter of time before Ethiopia begins to tap these waters. Indeed, in early 1990, Egypt was reported to have temporarily blocked an African Development Bank loan to Ethiopia for a project that Cairo feared would reduce downstream supplies. As Egypt's water security becomes increasingly jeopardized by new projects in Ethiopia, tensions between the two countries are sure to build.

TUG-OF-WATER

The Tigris-Euphrates is the only Middle East river basin with the luxury of having a fair amount of water left after the region's current needs are met. Yet even with this relative abundance—which isn't likely to last—the region has experienced strained water politics. Here, too, the failure of the basin's three countries—Iraq, Syria, and Turkey—to reach water-sharing agreements has created a potentially dangerous atmosphere of mistrust.

The mountains of eastern Turkey give rise to both rivers, with the Euphrates flowing through Syria and Iraq before reaching the Persian Gulf and the Tigris running directly through Iraq to the Gulf. Poor in oil but rich in water and agricultural land, Turkey has undertaken a massive water development scheme, the Southeast Anatolia Project, that is designed to boost its hydropower capacity by some 7,500 megawatts and its irrigated area by half, as well as to promote economic development in the region. Referred to as the GAP, after the Turkish acronym, the Anatolia scheme includes construction of 25 irrigation systems, 22 dams, and 19 hydropower stations. . . .

Syria and Iraq fear that this huge endeavor could foil their own development plans and leave them short of water. The GAP could reduce the Euphrates' flow into Syria by 35 percent in normal years and substantially more in dry ones, besides polluting the river with irrigation drainage. Iraq, third in line, would see a drop as well. The Iraqi government also worries about *Syria's* plans to tap more of the Euphrates, both for irrigation and for meeting the domestic needs of a Syrian population that, at current growth rates, will double in 18 years. Damascus, Aleppo, and other Syrian cities have already experienced supply cutbacks in recent years, and all three Euphrates basin countries weathered water shortages in 1989, when drought cut the river's flow in half.

In January 1990, Turkey heightened the anxieties of its downstream neighbors by stopping for one month the flow of the Euphrates below the Ataturk Dam, the GAP's centerpiece. Although Turkey told Syria and Iraq the previous November of its plans to start filling the reservoir behind the dam—and offered to compensate them by increasing downstream flows from November until mid-January—they both protested Turkey's action.

Then-President Turgut Ozal (who died suddenly in April) tried to reassure the two countries that Turkey would never use its power over the river to "coerce or threaten them." The assurance rang a bit hollow, however, given his government's veiled threat in late 1989 to cut the Euphrates' flow because of Syria's support of Kurdish insurgents. And early in the 1991 Persian Gulf War, closed-door discussions reportedly were held at the United Nations about the possibility of using Turkey's dams to cut off a portion of Iraq's water supply as a response to the Iraqi invasion of Kuwait. Turkey apparently opposed the idea.

Turkey has underscored its role as water broker in the region by proposing to build what it calls "peace pipelines" to drier Middle East nations. A western pipeline would deliver drinking water to cities and towns in Jordan, Syria, and Saudi Arabia; another would follow a Gulf route and take supplies to Kuwait, Saudi Arabia, the United Arab Emirates, Qatar, Oman, and Bahrain.

The pipelines would cost an estimated $21 billion, however, and outside financing from international lenders such as the World Bank would depend on all parties reaching a broader water-sharing agreement. Moreover, at this point the downstream Arab nations do not want to place their water security in Turkey's hands, or to bank on a technological solution that would be vulnerable to attack in so many countries. So, for the time being at least, the "peace pipelines" are likely to remain a pipe dream.

A ZERO-SUM GAME?

Much of the strain surrounding water in the Middle East stems from the fact that one nation's gain is usually another's loss. If Ethiopia develops upper Nile waters, Egypt will lose out. If Syria and Jordan build a dam on the Yarmuk River, Israel will likely lose out—and so forth. As long as nations remain locked in tension and distrust, such a zero-sum game will persist. But with cooperation, a new realm of win-win propositions could open up, which could help solve common water problems and defuse mounting pressures.

Israel, for instance, has irrigation technology and expertise that could benefit the entire region. In the 1960s, the country's agricultural engineers pioneered the commercial development of "drip irrigation," which conserves supplies by piping only as much water as crops need and delivering it directly to their roots. This highly efficient method is now used on nearly half of Israel's irrigated cropland. Combined with other water-saving practices, it has helped reduce the average amount of water needed for each irrigated acre in Israel by a third—and boosted crop yields at the same time.

Joint efforts to increase the use of water-saving technologies could help solve the water problems of many regions. For instance, Israel and the largely Muslim Central Asian republics of the former Soviet Union have put religious differences aside in favor of the mutual benefits of trading irrigation technology. Projects in Kazakhstan and Uzbekistan reportedly have increased crop yields several-fold while cutting water consumption by up to two-thirds. Spreading Israeli know-how more broadly in the Jordan basin itself—with Israel perhaps getting a share of the water saved as partial payment for its technical assistance—might benefit all parties and lessen water pressures overall. Some Middle East analysts have also suggested storing winter flows from the Yarmuk River in Israel's Sea of Galilee for use in summer by Jordan and possibly the West Bank—a strategy that could eliminate the need for Syria and Jordan to build the expensive new storage dam on the Yarmuk. For its part, Israel would benefit from the sweetening of the slightly salty Galilee water, one of its primary drinking water sources.

Similar win-win solutions likely exist in each water-scarce river basin. For the

Nile system, storing more of the rivers' water in reservoirs in the Ethiopian highlands, where evaporation is much lower than at Egypt's Aswan Dam, could result in more water for all three Blue Nile basin countries—Ethiopia, the Sudan, and Egypt. Such a scheme would need careful study, since it would inevitably alter the ecology of the Ethiopian Highlands and likely curtail Egypt's hydropower production at the Aswan Dam. But the benefits could be substantial. . . .

Of course, a chicken-and-egg problem plagues all of this. Cooperation can breed win-win solutions to water problems, which in turn can defuse tensions, but tensions have to be defused before nations will cooperate. Recognizing that peace without water security can only be a tenuous truce at best, some nations have at least gone to the bargaining table. Unfortunately, they have yet to make much progress.

Efforts to reach a water-sharing agreement in the Jordan basin date back to the early 1950s. In 1953, a basin-wide plan to share the waters of the Jordan system was drafted by a U.S. engineering firm and brought to the Middle East via a special envoy of President Eisenhower. Four rounds of difficult and fractious negotiation over a two-year period eventually resulted in all sides agreeing to the technical details of the plan. But, as Middle East water analyst Miriam Lowi of Princeton University has written, the talks broke down for political reasons, mainly because of the Arab parties' unwillingness to enhance in any way the development prospects of the new state of Israel. The negotiations ceased in 1955. At various points since then, mediation efforts regarding specific issues, such as the proposed dam on the Yarmuk, have taken place, but no resolution of water disputes in the Jordan basin has been reached.

The Nile basin countries have had a forum for cooperation through a group called Undugu (Swahili for "fraternity"), in which all the Nile states have participated. Yet meaningful collaboration—particularly among Ethiopia, Egypt, and Sudan—does not appear likely in the near future. At the African Water Summit, a high-level meeting in Cairo in June 1990, Ethiopia was unwilling even to share basic hydrological data with its neighbors. For Ethiopia, cooperation is contingent on a decision to renegotiate the 1959 water-sharing agreement between Egypt and Sudan. Because that treaty allots so much of the Nile's water to these two downstream countries, which contribute very little to the river's flow, Ethiopia views the compact as unfair and unworkable.

A similar logjam exists over sharing the Euphrates. Turkey and Syria signed a protocol in 1987 that guarantees to Syria a minimum flow of 500 cubic meters per second, about half of the Euphrates' volume at the border. Syria wants its guaranteed share increased, a request that Turkey has so far denied. Just last year [1992], Turkish Prime Minister Suleyman Demirel reportedly remarked about Syrian requests for more Euphrates water, "We do not say we should share their oil resources. They cannot say they should share our water resources." . . .

ENTER THE LAWYERS

At the moment, international law offers little help in resolving water conflicts. Despite much effort, no water law acceptable to all nations has yet been devised. Upstream countries, given their natural advantage, have been reluctant to accept the notion that international waters should be managed cooperatively and shared equitably. Indeed, some still hold the view that nations have "absolute sovereignty" over water within their borders and have little obligation to their neighbors.

However, an international code of conduct for shared watercourses has been steadily evolving, primarily through the work of two organizations: the private International Law Association, which in 1966 laid down the "Helsinki Rules" (which have since been revised), and the United Nations International Law Commission, which in 1991 issued its draft recommendations. Both put forth a number of important principles, including four obligations: to inform and consult with water-sharing neighbors before taking actions that may affect them (such as Turkey shutting off the Euphrates' flow); to exchange hydrologic data regularly; to avoid causing substantial harm to other water users; and to allocate water from a shared river basin reasonably and equitably.

While they may be laudable ideals, these principles offer little practical guidance so far. What constitutes "reasonable and equitable" use—the crux of any water-sharing agreement—is open to widely differing interpretations. Population size, geography, climate, historical use, and availability of other water sources are among the many factors that could be taken into account in determining equitable allocations among countries, but a clear formula for doing so does not exist. In allocating the waters of the Nile, for instance, Egypt's priorities would undoubtedly be very different from Ethiopia's. . . .

In the absence of a formal body of clear and enforceable law, the resolution of international water disputes depends on the negotiation of treaties among neighboring countries. Among the most notable to date is the Indus Waters Treaty signed in 1960 by India and Pakistan, which still offers some relevant lessons.

Conflict over the Indus began when the subcontinent was partitioned in 1947. The international boundary delineating India and Pakistan cut right through the river and the world's largest contiguous irrigation network, which encompassed 37 million acres. The next year, the Indian province of East Punjab attempted to claim sovereign rights over the water within its territory by stopping the flow into two large canals that fed Pakistan's irrigated land. East Punjab's decision sparked a water dispute that nearly escalated into a war.

For the next eight years, the two countries went round and round in difficult negotiations. The World Bank played a key mediating role, helping to devise a water allocation strategy that both nations could agree to, and drumming up international funding needed to implement the water-sharing agreement. Bank mediators were not able to convince Pakistan and East Punjab to manage the basin jointly—and therefore optimally—but the agreement did divide water use equitably and establish a permanent commission to ensure its continued success.

As a result, the Indus agreement has endured as a testament to the benefits of international water-sharing arrangements: for more than three decades it has helped promote agricultural and economic development in the region by assuring relatively secure water supplies for both parties.

NO TIME TO WASTE

Water shortages are worsening rapidly in many regions, as population growth and rising water demands stretch supplies to their limits. Tensions over water scarcity could reach a feverish pitch this decade not only in the Middle East, but in Central Asia, where five countries newly independent from the former Soviet Union face an ecosystem and an economy suffering from lack of water. As Soviet republics, they had hoped Moscow would help by diverting some of Siberia's water wealth to their parched lands and shrinking Aral Sea. With that hope gone, and ethnic and political rivalries running strong, confrontations over control of water seem inevitable.

The immediate challenge for the international community is to recognize water scarcity as an increasingly powerful force of political and social instability, and, accordingly, to raise it to a higher place on the crowded policy agenda. The Middle East and Central Asia are obvious hotspots, but where else might the destabilizing influence of water scarcity rear its head? There is China, which is home to 22 percent of the world's people but only 8 percent of its fresh water—yet has a population growing by 15 million a year. And there are India and Bangladesh, both poor, agrarian countries that cannot agree on how to divide the waters of the Ganges River.

Once likely flashpoints are identified, it then becomes possible to encourage cooperation before conflicts break out. If countries can begin to share hydrologic and water use data, to undertake joint projects to conserve water and use it more efficiently, and to share technological and policy innovations, some new foundations of trust and collaboration can be built. Groups such as the United Nations Environment Programme, the World Bank, and independent non-governmental organizations can serve as impartial brokers and help devise win-win strategies.

No country can be economically or socially stable without an assured water supply. Even with an all-out effort to use their resources more efficiently, countries in water-scarce regions like the Middle East will ultimately need to fundamentally restructure their economies and greatly reduce population growth if they are to balance water demands with available supplies. Those difficult tasks will be easier to accomplish if water-sharing agreements are firmly in place.

History suggests that to the victors go the spoils. If so, wars over water might create some winners. But in today's interdependent world, any spoils of victory would soon be offset by the costs of regional instability. It may just be that the mutual gains possible from cooperation on water issues will move some long-standing rivals toward the larger goal of peace.

40

THE GATT:
ENVIRONMENTAL
MENACE OR ALLY?

Hilary F. French

The purpose of the General Agreements on Tariffs and Trade (GATT) is to reduce barriers to international trade. Protecting the environment, on the other hand, often requires restrictions on trade. Hilary F. French examines the tension between the goals of free trade and environmental protection and why environmentalists often regard GATT as a menace rather than an ally. She concludes with suggestions for "greening" GATT. French is a senior researcher at the Worldwatch Institute and co-author of *State of the World 1994.*

From Embassy Row to Capitol Hill in Washington, D.C., it suddenly seemed as though they were everywhere: in the fall of 1991, posters began popping up around the city showing a "GATTzilla" monster with a dolphin in one hand and a can of pesticides in the other, crushing the U.S. Capitol under its foot. The caption: "What you don't know *can* hurt you." The posters were soon followed by a series of full-page advertisements in major newspapers around the country signed by a coalition of environmental and consumer groups warning that the General Agreement on Tariffs and Trade (GATT), the international agreement that stipulates world trade rules and arbitrates disputes over its terms, posed little-known but grave environmental threats. The ads called for a grassroots campaign to turn back efforts to expand GATT's powers through the Uruguay

---

Reprinted with the permission of Worldwatch Institute. Excerpted from *World Watch* (September/October 1993). Author: Hilary F. French.

Round of negotiations, which had been underway since 1986 and was thought at the time to be nearing completion. [The Uruguay Round was finally concluded in late 1993.— Eds.]

How could an arcane international agreement to reduce trade barriers among more than 100 countries harm the environment? In a number of ways, according to the advertisements. Most fundamentally, the anti-GATT activists worried that environmental laws would be found to violate world trade rules—and would be overturned. The fear was aroused by a GATT dispute panel ruling that provisions of the U.S. Marine Mammal Protection Act violated the GATT, and it has been further excited by a rash of recent environmental trade disputes. For instance, Austria was recently forced to abandon plans to introduce a 70 percent tax on tropical timber, as well as a requirement that tropical timber be labeled as such, when the Association of Southeast Asian Nations (ASEAN) complained that the law violated GATT. In two ongoing disputes, the United States is charging that a levy imposed by the Canadian province of Ontario on non-refillable alcoholic beverage containers is a disguised trade barrier, and the European [Union] has formally challenged two U.S. automobile taxes intended to promote fuel efficiency—the Corporate Average Fuel Economy Law and the gas-guzzler tax.

The GATT-alarm ads painted a global conspiracy theory, according to which opponents of U.S. laws on environmental, health, and consumer safety legislation who had tried and failed to roll back decades of progress through the democratic process were now aiming to achieve their goals through the back door of the secretive, corporate-controlled GATT proceedings.

The international trade community was taken aback by this "demonization" of the GATT, which many viewed as a key to the relative prosperity enjoyed by nations in the post-[World War II] era—a triumph of efforts to protect the collective good over the selfish goals of "protectionist" special interests. Since its creation in 1947, the GATT has indeed been remarkably successful on its own terms. Over the course of seven different negotiating rounds, tariffs have been cut in industrial countries from an average of 40 percent in 1947 to 5 percent in 1990.

The characterization of GATT as an imposing monster bore a certain irony, since many countries look to the multilateral trading system embodied by GATT as a means of protecting their interests against efforts by economic power-houses, especially the United States, to unilaterally impose their will on the world. Developing countries viewed the environmental campaign against the GATT with particular alarm, both as part of what they saw as an unfortunate tendency on the part of Northern Greens to care more about whales and dolphins than about people, and as a cover for more sinister efforts to keep Third World goods out of northern markets.

In the intervening years, some progress has been made in merging these clashing views. Governments have committed themselves to making trade and the environment "mutually supportive," though they have a long way to go before determining exactly how. The GATT itself, however, remains very much a product of its times. When the original agreement was forged in 1947, protecting the environment was not yet on most national agendas, let alone a pressing international concern. The General Agreement on Tariffs and Trade urgently needs updating and clarification if it is to become an instrument for furthering, rather than undermining, the goal to which governments pledged themselves at the June 1992 Rio "Earth Summit." That goal, the environmentalists like to remind the GATT, is to find a path to development that does not deplete the resource base upon which future economic well-being depends.

THE TUNA-DOLPHIN CHALLENGE

What brought the issue to a head in late 1991 was the outrage over a GATT panel's ruling that Mexico had a valid case in arguing that it should be allowed to import tuna to the United States regardless of how it was caught. Mexican fishers use dolphins as markers for tuna swimming below, before setting out purse-seine nets which then ensnare the dolphins as well as the targeted tuna. Though this practice was once also prevalent among U.S. fishers, the 1972 Marine Mammal Protection Act effectively outlawed it by mandating tight dolphin mortality quotas for domestic and imported tuna alike. . . . The panel ruling sent shockwaves through the environmental community, as it called into question the GATT-compatibility of a gamut of trade measures used to achieve environmental ends.

Though there had been cases in the past in which health and safety laws had been challenged as trade barriers, the tuna-dolphin ruling provoked a far greater backlash. That Mexico had won its case meant that a U.S. law had been not only questioned but struck down—and that could have led to the law's repeal, as bucking GATT's authority would not stand the United States in good stead when its turn came to charge another country with being out of step with world trade rules. As it happened, the U.S. law remains in place because Mexico decided not to press the point, not wanting to antagonize the United States in the midst of negotiations over a North American Free Trade Agreement (NAFTA). Most fundamentally, however, the ruling provoked cries of alarm not because of any nationalistic pride on the part of environmentalists, but because of the reasoning employed by the GATT panelists. If similar logic were applied in future cases, provisions of a large number of national environmental laws and even international treaties could be overturned. The ruling thus focused attention on shortcomings in the existing GATT text, and provoked an international discussion on what—if anything—should be done to change it.

At the heart of the GATT ruling was the notion that countries should not be allowed to use trade tools to influence practices outside their borders for environmental ends. This, according to the panel, would amount to foisting a country's own environmental laws and values on the rest of the world, thereby riding roughshod over the once-inviolable principle of national sovereignty. More specifically, the panel decreed that the GATT rules, which generally allow countries to apply national laws governing *products* (such as car emissions standards or pesticide residue limitations) to imported goods at the border, did not cover this case because it was the *process* by which the tuna was produced (the setting of purse-seine nets on dolphins), rather than the tuna itself, that was being rejected by the United States—and this *process* took place outside U.S. jurisdiction.

The flaw in this logic, in the eyes of U.S. environmentalists, at least, is that it makes no distinction between environmental issues of purely national concern and those designed to protect the global commons—the oceans and the atmosphere. By applying the "domestic borders" criterion, the judges determined, in effect, that there is virtually no way short of an international agreement for nations to protect the Pacific dolphin, whose habitat is not contained in any country's borders. Actions to reduce the use of harmful drift nets in fishing, protect tropical forests, or stave off ozone depletion or global warming would also be severely circumscribed. Ominously, even provisions of *international* agreements designed to protect the global commons could be found to be GATT-illegal based on this reasoning.

It was thus particularly exasperating to environmentalists when the GATT judges further argued that the lack of an international agreement on dolphin protection practices in tuna fishing made the U.S. action suspect. Though international agreements are widely supported in principle, the process of reaching consensus can take years and even decades—time the world cannot often afford as global ecological decline continues its steady course. Indeed, nations had been trying for some time to reach an agreement on dolphin-friendly fishing practices, through the Inter-American Tropical Tuna Commission. In fact, it is most often a unilateral action by one country, sometimes backed by trade measures against others, that eventually spurs the international community to act collectively. Any challenges to the rights of countries to pursue these kinds of policies thus poses great threats to prospects for successfully heading off the deterioration of the biosphere.

THE IMPLICATIONS

Under the logic of the tuna-dolphin ruling, other laws—many of them highly effective at achieving their environmental goals—could well be found to violate GATT if they were challenged. For instance, under a law known as the Pelly Amendment, the United States can prohibit the import of products from countries undermining the effectiveness of international fishery or wildlife agreements. Though the sanctions have never been invoked, the threat that they might be has brought about some significant changes in national behavior. It helped secure the participation of Iceland and Norway in the 1982 international whaling ban and of Japan and Taiwan in the U.N.'s 1993 worldwide moratorium on destructive drift net fishing, and helped convince Japan to stop importing endangered sea turtles for use in jewelry and eyeglass frames.

Though the United States has been the staunchest defender of the right to use unilateral trade tools for environmental goals, it is not alone in the practice. Despite its criticism of unilateral actions by the United States, the European [Union] has imposed a ban to take effect after 1994 on imports of furs from countries where painful "leghold" traps are permitted.

According to the GATT, at least 17 international environmental treaties involve limitations on trade—and could be rendered toothless if the tuna-dolphin reasoning holds up. Yet, in agreements like the Basel Convention on hazardous waste export, or the CITES treaty on endangered species, restricting trade is the very *purpose* of the agreement. In other cases, such as the landmark Montreal Protocol on depletion of the ozone layer, restrictions are used to try to prevent countries that have not signed the treaty from undermining its effectiveness. In the future, they may be needed to enforce compliance by uncooperative signatories.

This presents the world's governments with a momentous legal problem. With GATT aimed at limiting most restrictions on trade, and most environmental treaties requiring them, two sets of international agreements are in head-on conflict. Which treaty should take precedence? International law is unclear on this question. If the treaties in conflict are on roughly the same subject matter, and both parties to the dispute are signatories to both agreements, the most recent treaty generally prevails—which would tend to protect most environmental treaties. But trade and environmental treaties might not be viewed as sufficiently similar for this formula to apply. Furthermore, problems could develop if a country not party to the environmental treaty were to argue that GATT should rule—though so far, no such cases have arisen. To thicken the plot still further, . . . conclusion [of] the Uruguay Round might mean that GATT [will] supplant the environmental treaties as the most recent agreement.

THE URUGUAY ROUND THREAT

It was not just the tuna-dolphin wake-up call that riveted environmentalists' attention on the GATT in late 1991, but the Uruguay Round, which raised some troubling new environmental questions above and beyond the vulnerabilities revealed by the tuna-dolphin ruling. . . .

. . . The Uruguay Round will expand GATT controls in a number of areas, including agriculture, services, and intellectual property, many of which promise to have wide-ranging environmental implications. Unfortunately, exactly how a given reform would affect the environment is often a complicated question that can cut many different ways—some positive and some negative.

And governments seem to be heading toward committing themselves to these changes with little study—or understanding—of their implications. . . .

Though the environmental implications of a vast agreement like the Uruguay Round are not well understood, a diverse array of interests has raised concerns about aspects of the agreement. Family farm groups worry that the reduction of agricultural subsidies envisioned under the pact will be about as helpful to them as a plague of locusts. They have enlisted some environmental support for their campaign, arguing that smaller farms are often more ecologically sustainable than large ones. (A good example of how these things can cut both ways, however, is that reductions in agricultural subsidies can also mean reductions in production, which means less use of inputs such as toxic pesticides and scarce water.) Another concern is that exports of unsustainably-produced commodities, including agricultural, timber, and mineral products, might be stepped up as a result of tariff reductions on these goods.

Developing countries fear that provisions sought by the North to strengthen intellectual property rights protection in developing countries might impede the transfer of environmentally advanced technologies such as solar photovoltaic cells and energy efficient furnaces. They also fear that this would make it easier for pharmaceutical and agribusiness interests to monopolize products made with biotechnology, while jeopardizing developing countries' rights to remuneration for biological resources extracted from their territories—the recognition of which was viewed by many as the linchpin of the treaty on biological diversity agreed to at the Earth Summit.

The greatest focus of concern, however, has been that with many quotas already eliminated and tariffs drastically reduced through previous negotiating rounds, the Uruguay Round . . . aimed at the reduction of so-called non-tariff barriers to trade. The problem is that what looks to one country like a non-tariff barrier to trade is often another's hard-won environmental law, as the recent string of environmental trade disputes makes clear. For instance, in the Ontario-U.S. "bottle battle," U.S. negotiators are convinced the tax on non-refillable bottles is really aimed at keeping out U.S. beer, which is mostly sold in cans, while Ontario environmentalists insist that the levy is critical to preserving the province's 99 percent rate of bottle refilling, one of the highest in the world.

The draft text of the Uruguay Round addresses two different categories of product "standards": those designed to protect food safety, such as pesticide residue limits ("phytosanitary standards"), and so-called "technical barriers to trade"—a broad class that could include just about any specification, including car emissions standards, environmental labeling programs, and recycled content requirements, among others. In both cases, the Uruguay Round promotes the "harmonization" of these laws as a way to prevent unnecessary trade barriers. Environmental and consumer advocates fear that the "harmonization" will be downward, creating a least common denominator effect that would jeopardize countless environmental protections at the national and local levels.

The text does allow for nations to exceed the agreed international norm under certain conditions—such as a demonstration of "scientific justification," or a proof that the "least trade-restrictive" approach possible was used to meet a given environmental goal. Some trade specialists argue that these conditions are necessary to ferret out cases in which countries are wrapping what is really protectionism in a green cloak. They point out with suspicion, for example, that the Ontario non-refillable tax applies only to alcoholic beverages, and not to soft drinks, which, unlike beer, Ontario companies sell in cans in abundance.

Though at first glance these tests seem innocuous enough, they may prove a major obstacle to environmental progress. For one thing, scientists hold widely divergent views on questions of major importance to environmental policymaking, and might thus disagree among themselves on the question of "justification." And the messy political fact of the matter is that laws are often passed because of unholy alliances among those who stand to gain. A requirement that a given measure be the "least trade-restrictive" could easily be enough to doom any action at all.

Environmentalists also charge that the "harmonized" standards are set through a secretive, undemocratic process dominated by industrial interests. And if a national law were challenged as a trade barrier, the case would be heard behind closed doors by a panel of professors and bureaucrats steeped in the intricacies of world trade law, but not in the exigencies of the planet. Judgment on whether or not a law was "scientifically justified" would be handed down by an appointed GATT panel, rather than by an elected legislature. To make matters worse, . . . the Uruguay Round would make it far more difficult for a country to block a panel report not to its liking. Under the current rules, *adopting* a panel report requires unanimous consent; under the new ones, unanimity would be required to *reject* a report.

The Uruguay Round also includes plans to create a new Multilateral Trade Organization (MTO) to give institutional form to the GATT, modeled on the International Trade Organization that was originally envisioned in the 1940s, but that was never created, in part due to concerns in the U.S. Congress over the potential invasion of sovereignty. It was a measure of the gulf between the trade and environment communities that just as public concern over possible conflicts between trade and environmental goals was reaching new heights, plans were moving ahead to create a sweeping new institution with little if any attention given to the environmental implications. [The final Uruguay Round agreement contains provisions for a new multilateral trade organization.—Eds.]

NO TIME LIKE THE PRESENT

. . . The U.S. government . . . was able to incorporate into the North American Free Trade Agreement some of the changes that the environmental and consumer activists are also urging for the GATT. . . . For instance, under the

NAFTA, the "scientific justification" test for standards deviating from international norms was loosened to require only the demonstration of a "scientific basis" for the law. In addition, the NAFTA suggests that harmonization should be in an upward direction. In the area of dispute resolution, NAFTA may again pave the way for needed changes. Unlike the GATT process, the NAFTA requires environmental expert advice to be provided if one party to the dispute requests it, and usually places the burden of proof on the country challenging, rather than the one defending, a domestic environmental law. . . .

There are a number of issues that governments . . . need to take up if the GATT is to be thoroughly greened. . . . Pressure is building for a more extensive environmental negotiation. . . . Indeed, governments are already laying the groundwork for such talks in negotiations at the Organization for Economic Cooperation and Development and in a working group of the GATT itself. Former GATT Director-General Arthur Dunkel has called for the next GATT round to be an explicitly "green" one. . . .

FIXING TUNA-DOLPHIN

The obvious first priority in such a negotiation would be to address the shortcomings of the current GATT agreement that were exposed by the tuna-dolphin ruling—the ominous ambiguity as to whether or not it is (or should be) consistent with GATT for countries to use trade tools to protect the environment outside their borders. . . .

Though the unilateral use of environmental trade measures has surprisingly few defenders beyond the United States, there is somewhat greater support for them when undertaken through international environmental agreements. The NAFTA addressed the problem by stipulating that where there are conflicts between the provisions of the NAFTA and those of three international environmental agreements (Montreal, Basel, and CITES), the international environmental agreement shall in most cases prevail. The provision is not as far-reaching as some environmentalists had hoped for (agreements other than these three are not protected), but the provision represents a considerable improvement over the GATT status quo, and could serve as a model. Unfortunately, recent indications are that many GATT members may wish to limit, rather than protect, the use of trade measures even in international agreements.

GREEN SUBSIDIES

The second priority in an extended "green" round is to address GATT's position on the relationship between subsidies and environmental protection. The GATT generally frowns on subsidies as trade distortions, and in some instances allows countries to impose "countervailing duties" on imports to compensate for them. These rules could threaten some environmentally helpful government programs, such as subsidies for the development of pollution control technology. On the other hand, GATT could also provide a powerful *green* weapon with which to attack environmentally damaging subsidies such as the $36 billion paid in energy subsidies by U.S. taxpayers, according to a recent report by the Washington, D.C.-based Alliance to Save Energy, or the implicit subsidy provided by granting logging companies cut-rate access to federal lands.

Under current GATT rules, the scope for challenging such subsidies is limited, though in one example of the potential, the European [Union has] listed subsidized water sales in California as an unfair trade practice. A "Green Round" could make a significant environmental contribution by overhauling its subsidy rules so that the harmful ones would be at least as vulnerable to challenge as the beneficial ones—if not more so.

Another idea gaining support is to define lax environmental protection or enforcement as an unfair subsidy, making it possible to levy countervailing duties or take other compensating action. Lower standards do add up to a sizable hidden subsidy, according to the World Commission on Environment and Development, which estimated that developing countries exporting to the OECD countries in 1980 would have incurred pollution control costs of at least $5.5 billion if they had been required to meet the requirements then prevailing in the United States. . . .

Such tariffs would ensure that a country is not penalized in international markets for internalizing environmental costs more than its trading partners do. Without such measures, there is a danger that industrial production might increasingly locate in so-called "pollution havens"—areas where regulation or enforcement is lax. Fears of losing out to foreign competition in the global marketplace might also deter countries from adopting strict domestic environmental laws—as in fact happened recently in the debate over energy taxes both in the United States and in the European [Union]. However, proposals for levying border tariffs for this purpose raise a number of difficulties, such as that of evaluating exactly how much trade advantage is being gained (how large the countervailing duty should be), and whether such duties might create an opening for hidden protectionism. . . .

Finally, there is the possibility of granting trade concessions such as preferential tariff treatment for environmentally sound goods, rather than simply penalizing the bad. Already, the United States makes tariff reductions on developing country imports under the Generalized System of Preferences program contingent on respect for internationally recognized worker rights. In one example of how this idea could be applied to environmental concerns, the government of Colombia has requested exemption from [E.U.] import duties for oils produced from certain organically grown plants such as lemon grass. The GATT could endorse this sort of initiative, and encourage its wider application.

THE GREENING OF GATT

A historian combing the record several centuries hence may find the tuna-dolphin episode to be a revealing symbol of the passing of an era when nations could provide for the needs of their citizens by acting alone.

With security increasingly defined in economic and environmental rather than military terms, governments are coming to recognize that protecting their citizens from threats as diverse as sea-level rise induced by global warming, and unemployment created by industries migrating in search of pollution havens, will require an unprecedented level of international coordination.

If governments can work together to devise minimum rules of environmental conduct, it will greatly reduce the potential for trade conflict to erupt over environmental matters. Just as the International Labor Organization has formulated hundreds of workplace rules covering matters like child labor and occupational exposure to toxic chemicals, so could a U.N. environment agency be given the mandate to begin enunciating minimal standards of environmental behavior and generating the funds required for poorer nations to meet them. This process is already well underway in the European [Union], and beginning to be developed under the NAFTA. Internationally, the more than 170 international environmental treaties that governments have agreed to constitute a decisive move in this direction.

In the meantime, if the GATT wishes to restore its tarnished reputation, it will need to be updated to reflect today's environmental imperatives. The buying power of consumers and nations is a powerful force that can be harnessed to encourage economic production that protects rather than ravages the earth's natural resource base. GATT should be a leader in this effort, rather than an obstacle to it.

41

THE TRAGEDY
OF THE COMMONS
IN GLOBAL PERSPECTIVE

Marvin S. Soroos

The "tragedy of the commons" is a key concept in ecological analysis. Marvin S. Soroos describes the metaphor, relates it to many of the specific issues on the global agenda of environmental issues, and suggests strategies for averting environmental tragedies. Noteworthy is his observation that "remarkable progress has been made in recent decades to lay the international infrastructure for an assault on the wide range of environmental problems that pose significant dangers for humankind." Soroos is professor of political science at North Carolina State University and is author of *Beyond Sovereignty: The Challenge of Global Policy* (1986).

THE ENVIRONMENT ON THE GLOBAL AGENDA

The convergence of 118 heads of state on Rio de Janeiro in June 1992 for the United Nations Conference on the Environment and Development, otherwise known as the Earth Summit, confirmed the rise of the deteriorating natural environment to a prominent position on international agendas. The environment is a relatively new issue, having received substantial attention from policy makers and the public for little more than a quarter century. While some specific ecological problems were addressed considerably earlier, they were not viewed as part of a much larger crisis in the relationship between a rapidly growing and industrializing world population and the natural order upon which it depends for its survival.

This essay was written especially for this book.

Two events took place in 1972 that were especially important in the emergence of the environment as a global issue. One was the publication of the Club of Rome's influential and controversial report entitled *The Limits to Growth* (Meadows et al., 1972). It warned of an uncontrollable collapse of modern civilization within a century if bold steps were not taken to control exponential growth trends in population and industrial production that would otherwise overshoot the availability of food, deplete the planet's one-time endowment of non-renewable reserves of fossil fuels and minerals, and seriously degrade the environment with pollutants. The other event was the convening of the United Nations Conference on the Human Environment in Stockholm, which focused world attention on a wide range of interrelated environmental problems and led to the creation of the United Nations Environment Programme (UNEP) that has done much to stimulate national and international efforts to preserve the natural environment.

Numerous problems appear on the global environmental agenda, each of which has serious consequences in its own right. On the land areas, tropical forests are being burned or logged at an alarming rate with little concern for the resulting extinction of untold numbers of species of plants and animals, many of which remain to be recorded. Deserts are expanding in many parts of Africa and Asia, in large part due to human activities—in particular the stripping of wood areas for firewood, the overgrazing of livestock, and improper irrigation. Overuse and misuse of land has reduced its fertility and led to substantial erosion of topsoil; aquifers are rapidly drawn down to irrigate expanding agricultural operations. A legacy of toxic waste dumps threatens the health of millions of people.

The marine environment has been badly contaminated by pollutants, especially in largely self-contained areas such as the Mediterranean Sea, the Baltic Sea, the Caribbean Sea, the Red Sea, and the Persian Gulf. The most spectacular sources of pollutants into the oceans have been accidents involving supertankers, the best known being the groundings of the *Torrey Canyon* in 1967, the *Amoco Cadiz* in 1978, and the *Exxon Valdez* in 1989. Larger quantities of pollutants enter oceans and seas from land-based sources, such as river systems laden with sewage, industrial effluents, and runoff from agricultural areas containing fertilizers and pesticides. The oceans have also been a repository for toxic substances ranging from chemical weapons and radioactive wastes to sludge from sewage treatment plants.

Atmospheric pollutants became the leading environmental concern during the 1980s. In the heavily industrialized regions of Europe and North America, the severe consequences of the transboundary flow of pollutants, in particular sulfur and nitrogen oxides responsible for acid precipitation, became all too apparent as aquatic life disappeared in numerous freshwater lakes and a phenomenon known as "forest death syndrome"—widely referred to by the German term *waldsterben*—spread rapidly and intensified in forested areas. The 1986 disaster at the Chernobyl nuclear power plant in the Soviet Union exposed hundreds of millions of Europeans to potentially health-damaging levels of radioactive iodine-131 and cesium-137.

Even more alarming are the warnings of the scientific community about the depletion of the stratospheric ozone layer and the apparent trend toward a general warming of the atmosphere. These two problems are central to what has become known during the past decade as the "global change" problematique, which refers to a number of complex and interrelated alterations of the natural environment resulting from the growing scale of human activities.

Concern over ozone depletion has been heightened in recent years by the discovery of a large "ozone hole" over Antarctica during the spring season and a general thinning elsewhere. Scientists have linked most of the destruction of stratospheric ozone to a family of synthetic chemical compounds known as CFCs, which have been widely used in aerosol sprays, refrigerants, foam packaging and insulation, and cleaning solutions, as well as to halons used primarily in fire extinguishers. A diminishing of the ozone layer, which shields the earth from the sun's intense ultraviolet radiation, would have significant consequences for human health, in particular the incidence of the deadly melanoma form of skin cancer. More importantly, increased exposure to ultraviolet radiation would likely disrupt aquatic and terrestrial ecosystems.

Forecasts of a general warming of the atmosphere take into account the increased concentrations of "greenhouse gases" such as carbon dioxide, methane, and CFCs. A 1.5 to 4.5°C increase in average temperatures is a distinct possibility by the mid-twenty-first century if current trends continue in the buildup of greenhouse gases. Many scientific questions remain to be answered on the consequences of a warming of this magnitude. Coastal cities and low lying agricultural areas may be inundated as ocean levels rise by an anticipated .5 meters, farming elsewhere may be disrupted by changing temperatures and rainfall patterns, and numerous ecosystems such as forests may be unable to adapt to rapidly migrating climatic zones.

The international community has been very active over the past twenty-five years in its efforts to address many of these environmental problems. The Stockholm conference of 1972 was the first of a series of major world conferences sponsored by the United Nations, sometimes referred to as "global town meetings," that keyed on specific global problems, several of which are environmentally related. Among these were world conferences on population (1974 and 1984), food (1974), human settlements (1976), water (1977), desertification (1977), new and renewable sources of energy (1981), and outer space (1982). The Third United Nations Law of the Sea Conference (UNCLOS III), which was convened twelve times between 1973 and 1982, took up several environmental problems, most notably the depletion of marine fisheries and pollution of the oceans. The World Meteorological Organization (WMO) co-sponsored with the Canadian government a conference on "The Changing Atmosphere" in

Toronto in 1988 in addition to World Climate Conferences in 1979 and 1990. Two major recent gatherings are the 1992 Earth Summit in Rio and the 1994 Conference on Population and Development in Cairo.

A more significant development, however, has been the establishment of a network of international institutions that address environmental issues. The United Nations Environment Programme (UNEP), which is headquartered in Nairobi, Kenya, plays a central role in stimulating and coordinating action on environmental problems both by other international agencies and by nations. The organization has taken a leading role in identifying and investigating ecological problems and in monitoring the state of many aspects of the environment through its Global Environmental Monitoring System (GEMS). Several specialized agencies affiliated with the United Nations have a longer history of concern with environmentally related problems, including the International Maritime Organization (IMO) on pollution from oceangoing vessels, the WMO on the effects of atmospheric pollutants on the weather, the World Health Organization (WHO) on the impact of pollutants on human health, the International Atomic Energy Agency (IAEA) on the dangers of radioactive substances, the Food and Agricultural Organization (FAO) on the condition of ocean fisheries and the world's forests and the effect of environmental degradation on food production, and the International Labor Organization (ILO) on environmental hazards in the work place. Environmental problems have also occupied a prominent place on the agendas of numerous regional organizations, most notably those of the European Union.

Non-governmental organizations (NGOs) have been active participants in efforts to address global environmental problems at both national and international levels. The Stockholm conference drew participation from 237 NGOs, and more than 6000 are registered with the Environmental Liaison Center in Nairobi. Upward of 7000 NGOs participated in the official meetings of the Earth Summit or the informal, and more boisterous, Environmental Forum that took place in the parks of downtown Rio. The International Union for the Conservation of Nature and Natural Resources (UCN) and the World Wildlife Fund (WWF) have been collaborating with UNEP on the World Conservation Strategy that was launched in 1980. The International Council of Scientific Unions (ICSU) has been called upon for much of the scientific information that has guided the formulation of international policies and regulations on environmental matters. In the mid-1980s, ICSU launched the International Geosphere-Biosphere Program, an international scientific project that will mobilize the world's scientists to conduct research on the relationships between atmospheric, marine, and terrestrial ecosystems and the impact of human activities on them. Public interest groups such as Greenpeace, Friends of the Earth, European Environmental Bureau, and the Sierra Club International publicize environmental problems and prod national governments and international bodies to take action on them.

Despite the relative newness of the environment as a global policy problem, remarkable progress has been made in establishing the international institutional infrastructure needed to preserve the natural environment. There is certainly reason to wonder, however, whether more than 180 sovereign states will achieve the level of international cooperation necessary to effectively address problems of the magnitude and complexity of climate change.

GLOBAL TRAGEDIES OF THE COMMONS

Garrett Hardin's (1968) well-known parable of the "tragedy of the commons" is a useful model for analyzing the human sources of many environmental problems and the strategies by which they might be addressed. The parable has applicability to all levels of political organization ranging from the smallest village to the global community of states. Let us first review Hardin's story and then consider how it applies to several of the global environmental problems mentioned in the previous section. Potential strategies for averting a "tragedy" are taken up in the next section.

We are asked to imagine an old English village that has a community pasture on which the resident herders are freely permitted to graze their individually owned cattle for their own profit. Such an arrangement, known as a "commons," works well as long as the number of cattle is small relative to the size of the pasture. But once the combined herd of the villagers reaches and exceeds the "carrying capacity" of the pasture, the grasses are gradually depleted and the undernourished cattle produce less milk for their owners. If more and more cattle are added to an already overcrowded pasture, the result is its total destruction as a resource and the villagers can no longer derive a profit from grazing cattle on it. Such an unfortunate eventuality is what Hardin refers to as the "tragedy."

Hardin contends that such a tragedy is virtually inevitable when there are no legal limits on the number of cattle the villagers may graze on the pasture. Each villager can be expected to calculate that the profits derived from adding a cow to the pasture will accrue to himself exclusively. Alternatively, whatever costs arise due to what this cow contributes to an overgrazing of the pasture will be divided among all the herders of the village. Therefore, the individual villager figures that there is more to gain personally from adding a cow to the pasture than to lose from the resulting damage from overgrazing. Moreover, the logic that leads the villager to add a single cow to an already overused pasture also holds for even further additions by him. And what is rational behavior for one villager is equally rational for others. Thus, if the villagers pursue their individual self-interest, the pasture will be destroyed by the ever-increasing herd.

Why do the village herders, upon seeing the early signs of the unfolding tragedy, fail to exercise restraint in adding cattle, realizing that they will all pay a heavy price if the pasture becomes badly overgrazed? The answer lies in the possibility that at least one among them will not act responsibly but rather will continue to add cattle to the pasture. This so-called "free rider" not only takes advantage of the restraint of the other villagers for his own financial benefit but may also bring about the very tragedy they were attempting to avert. Thus, unless the villagers are confident that all will limit their herds, they become resigned to the inevitability of a tragedy and continue adding cattle to the over-crowded pasture in order to maximize their personal share of what the pasture has to offer before it is rendered useless.

Global environmental problems are obviously much more complex than the story of destruction of the common pasture in the English village. Nevertheless, distinct parallels exist between the causes of some global problems and the reasons for the tragedy in Hardin's parable. The similarity is especially notable in the case of the living resources of the ocean. Coastal populations have harvested fish in the oceans for millennia, but until recently the catch was well below the carrying capacity of the fisheries. The situation has changed dramatically in recent decades, both because of a rapidly growing world population that is look-ing more to the oceans for a source of protein and because technological advancements have made it possible to greatly increase the catch. Schools of fish can now be located more efficiently using helicopters, radar, and sonar, while strong synthetic fibers and mechanical hauling devices allow for the use of larger nets that hold much greater quantities of fish. Drift nets up to 30 miles in length have been widely used with a devastating impact on marine life. Per-haps the biggest change in the modern fishing industry has been the use of gigantic stern-ramped trawlers and factory ships which have the capacity for on-board processing of the catch and which are often accompanied by numerous specialized support vessels. Such a "fishing armada" can stay away from its home port for many months while intensively harvesting fisheries in distant reaches of the oceans.

Traditionally, international law has treated the oceans as a commons, the only exception being a 3-mile zone of territorial waters that for centuries was recognized as being within the jurisdiction of coastal states. Fishing interests from all lands could help themselves to the ocean's bounty for their private gain because fish became their property upon being caught. Under these rules the total world catch has nearly quintupled since 1950 in reaching 99.6 million met-ric tons in 1989, which is perilously close to the Food and Agriculture Associa-tion's (FAO) estimate of a sustainable yield from the oceans of 100 million met-ric tons annually (World Resources Institute, 1992, pp. 178–179). A "tragedy" has already occurred in some regions for species such as cod, halibut, herring, anchovy, swordfish, haddock, and the California sardine, as evidenced by a dra-matic drop in catches because not enough fish were left to regenerate the stock for the future.

Depletion of these fisheries came about for essentially the same reasons that the herders added cattle to an already overgrazed pasture in Hardin's English village. Operators of fishing fleets receive all the profits from the sale of their catch while dividing the costs associated with overfishing with all others harvesting the same fishery. Furthermore, fugitives that they are, fish passed up by one fleet in the interests of conservation are likely to turn up in the nets of others, who as free riders continue to deplete the fishery.

Pollution of the oceans and atmosphere also fits the pattern of Hardin's tragedy of the commons. But rather than taking something out of an area that is beyond the jurisdictions of nations, pollution involves the disposal of unwanted substances. Few problems arose as long as the amount of pollution generated by human activities was small relative to the vastness of the mediums into which they were introduced. But as with other resources, there are limits to the amount of pollutants that can be absorbed and dispersed by the oceans and atmosphere before serious problems begin to emerge, as is now apparent in the case of the ozone-depleting and greenhouse pollutants. The task of determining harmful levels of pollution is complicated by the delay between the time that substances are introduced into the environment and the time at which the consequences become apparent.

As sinks for pollutants, the oceans and the atmosphere have also traditionally been treated as international commons. All countries have been free to make use of them for getting rid of wastes whose disposal would otherwise be expensive or inconvenient. Introducing pollution into these mediums can have considerable offsetting costs, but from the perspective of the polluters, these costs are shared very widely while the benefits of having a cheap way of discarding wastes accrue to them exclusively. Thus, strong financial incentives are present for continuing the polluting activity. Moreover, any restraint that is exercised out of concern for the quality of the environment is likely to be futile and self-defeating if other polluters, including one's competitors, do not exercise similar responsibility.

Population can also be looked upon as a tragedy of the commons type of problem, as Hardin does in his original essay and his later theory of "lifeboat ethics" (Hardin, 1974). In this formulation, food and other resources correspond to the pasture of the English village, births to the addition of cattle to the pasture, and parents of the new arrivals to the herders. Parents, it could be argued, derive significant private benefits from children, such as companionship and affection, a source of labor, and security in old age. The environmental costs associated with what their children contribute to the overpopulating of their country or the world as a whole are shared with the rest of the population. Couples may also calculate that any restraint they exercise in limiting the size of their families will have little or no beneficial impact, because others who are less ecologically responsible will continue to have large numbers of offspring. The parallel is strained by the fact that most people do not have free access to the food and resources they need for their children but must pay for them. Hardin's suggestion is that free access to necessities, as through welfare payments or international food assistance, in effect creates a commons and the subsequent behavior that brings about its destruction.

AVERTING ENVIRONMENTAL TRAGEDIES

Several strategies hold some promise for avoiding the tragedy that Hardin forecasts will occur if all villagers have open access to the community pasture. One is to encourage *voluntary restraint,* possibly through education about the ecological consequences of irresponsible actions and by bringing social pressures to bear on members of the community who have not moderated their actions. Hardin has little faith in voluntary restraints because of the prospect that free riders will take advantage of the situation. A second option is to adopt *regulations* that limit the number of cattle each villager can graze on the pasture. Such rules, which can take the form of limits, prohibitions, and standards, should be restrictive enough to keep the total use of a resource from exceeding its carrying capacity. For regulations to be effective, however, there must be sufficiently strong inducements for compliance, such as stiff penalties for violators.

The last two possibilities for averting a tragedy would discard the commons arrangement. The pasture could be *partitioned* into fenced-in plots, each of which would be assigned to an individual villager. Under this setup, each villager would not only receive all the profits from grazing cattle on his section but also absorb all the costs if he allows it to become overgrazed. Thus, a built-in incentive exists for him to conserve his plot, or what Hardin refers to as "intrinsic responsibility." *Community ownership* of the herd is the final alternative. Rather than allowing privately owned cattle to graze the pasture, as under the other arrangements, access would be limited to a publicly owned herd, with the profits being distributed among the villagers. Under such an arrangement, the community as a whole would not only receive all the profits but also absorb all the costs of overgrazing. Thus, the managers of the community herd would have little incentive for allowing the pasture to become overgrazed.

Examples of all four of these strategies can be observed in the efforts of the international community to address environmental problems. Because nations are reluctant to sacrifice any part of their sovereignty to a higher authority, it is sometimes impossible to do more than encourage them to act responsibly to minimize damage to the environment beyond their borders. In this regard, one of the most commonly cited articles of the Stockholm Declaration of 1972 sets forth the principle that "States have . . . the responsibility to ensure that activities within their jurisdiction or control do not cause damage to the environment of other States or of areas beyond the limits of national jurisdiction."

Appeals to states to act voluntarily in an ecologically responsible manner have generally not been auspicious successes. However, there has been an encouraging tendency in recent years for a number of European countries to act unilaterally in setting target years for ambitious reductions of emissions of air pollutants, such as sulphur and nitrogen oxides that are responsible for acid precipitation and CO_2 that contributes to global warming. This tendency has been especially pronounced in the case of SO_2 as eleven countries have declared goals of reducing emissions well below the 30 percent cutback (from 1980 levels) mandated by an international protocol adopted in 1985. Sweden set the ambitious goal of an 80 percent reduction by 2000, which it has already largely achieved. These unilateral commitments to deep reductions in air pollution are ostensibly a response to political pressures from the environmentally concerned public and an effort to set an example that other countries will hopefully follow.

More is accomplished to ameliorate environmental problems when specific obligations are written into regulations that are negotiated and adopted in international institutions. Approximately twenty international fishery commissions, the equivalents of the village government in Hardin's story, were created by fishing nations to conserve the fisheries that they harvest in common. Some of these commissions established rules that limited the annual catch below what is known as the "maximum sustainable yield" (MSY) of the fishery. One strategy was to limit fishing to a prescribed season, which was abruptly closed when the combined efforts of the fishing operators approached the MSY. Other commissions assigned a share of the MSY to countries based on their historical proportion of the catch from a fishery.

International restrictions have also been adopted to reduce pollution of the marine environment. The landmark Convention for the Prevention of Pollution by Oil was adopted in 1954 and amended several times in the International Maritime Organization (IMO). Among the provisions of the treaty is a prohibition on discharges of crude and heavy fuel oils in the seas within 50 miles of coastlines. In 1973, the IMO adopted another convention, known as MARPOL '73, that covered a broader range of pollutants and extended the prohibition to the discharge of oily substances to areas deemed especially vulnerable to damage from pollution. The disposal of toxic substances in the seas is the subject of other international treaties, the most important one being the London Dumping Convention of 1972. It establishes a "black list" of highly toxic chemicals such as mercury, DDT, PCBs, persistent plastics, high-level radioactive wastes, and agents of chemical or biological warfare that may not be disposed of in the oceans and a "gray list" of less harmful wastes that may be dumped under controlled conditions. In 1993 the parties to the London Convention adopted a permanent ban on the dumping of all radioactive wastes at sea.

Compared to the oceans, the atmosphere is still a relatively underdeveloped subject of international law. The Economic Commission for Europe (ECE), which includes eastern and western European countries in addition to the United States and Canada, adopted a protocol in 1985 that committed ratifiers to a 30 percent reduction in SO_2 emissions by 1993 (based on 1980 levels). A 1988 protocol freezes nitrous oxide emissions at 1987 levels by 1994, while a 1991 protocol limits the release of volatile organic compounds. Similarly, the 1987 Montreal protocol mandated a 30 percent reduction in the production of CFCs by 1993 and a 50 percent cutback by 1998. Alarming reports on the Antarctic ozone hole prompted ninety-three countries to agree in London in June 1990 to a complete phaseout of ozone-destroying chemicals by 2000, with the exception of less developed countries, who will have a ten-year grace period. At a meeting in Copenhagen two years later, the date for phasing out most of the controlled substances was moved up to either 1994 or 1996.

For international regulations to be effective, mechanisms may be needed both for detecting violations and for sanctioning the violators. Few international agencies are well equipped to perform these tasks. Certain international fishery commissions have had programs for monitoring compliance with their rules through on-board inspections of fishing vessels. Likewise, the ECE sponsors a network of stations that monitors the transboundary flow of air pollutants between its members. Sanctions are generally left to other states that have an interest in seeing to it that international rules are being followed. For example, a United States law provides that countries which violate international agreements on the protection of marine mammals will lose 50 percent of the quota of fish they would otherwise be permitted to harvest in the 200-mile coastal fishery zone of the United States.

The partitioning of resources used by numbers of states is a feasible strategy for avoiding some but not all environmental problems. Pollutants introduced into the atmosphere cannot be confined within the boundaries of states because air circulates with prevailing wind currents. Likewise, ocean currents widely disperse many of the pollutants introduced into the marine environment.

Ocean fisheries, most of which are located near coastlines, are more susceptible to partitioning. The Convention on the Law of the Sea, which was adopted in 1982 but still lacks the sixty ratifications needed to come into effect, would grant coastal states jurisdiction over the resources of the oceans and seabed out to a distance of 200 nautical miles off shorelines, in what is called an "exclusive economic zone" (EEZ). Coastal states are empowered to determine the maximum catch within their EEZs and to decide who will be allowed to harvest fish up to this limit. They may reserve the fisheries for their own nationals or allow foreign operators to take part of the catch, possibly for a negotiated fee.

Such an arrangement can be an effective way of conserving fisheries consisting of localized or sedentary species provided the coastal state is diligent in managing them and has the means of enforcing the limits that it has set. Unfortunately, the experience so far has been that most coastal states exercise too little restraint on their nationals, who have been quick to increase the intensity of their harvesting, thus provoking a tragedy on their own. Highly migratory species, such as the skipjack tuna and some species of whales, which move through the EEZs of two or more countries and the high seas as well, pose a more complicated problem because cooperation among several states is needed to prevent overharvesting. A similar problem occurs with anadromous species, most notably salmon, which live most of their life spans in the high seas, where they can be harvested legally by any country, but migrate to freshwater streams to spawn. Coastal states are reluctant to invest heavily to conserve spawning habitats if the stock is likely to be overfished by other countries on the high seas. Here again, cooperative arrangements among several states are necessary if the fishery is to be conserved.

Community ownership of the means of using a resource is rare at the international level. The primary stumbling block to an international consensus on the new Law of the Sea Treaty is the provision for a commercial arm of an International Seabed Authority, to be known as the Enterprise. This international public corporation would mine the mineral-rich nodules lying on the floor of the deep seas in competition with private seabed-mining firms. The private firms will be required to assist the Enterprise both by sharing the fruits of their prospecting efforts and by making mining technologies available at reasonable commercial rates. The objective behind the creation of the Enterprise would not, however, be to conserve the nodules, which are in bounteous supply. Rather it is designed to ensure that less technologically advanced countries will have an opportunity to participate in the development of a resource declared to be the "common heritage of mankind" by the UN General Assembly in 1970.

Of the four principal types of strategies that can be adopted to avert a tragedy, regulations appear to have the broadest applicability and the greatest potential for success. Appeals for voluntary restraint too often go unheeded, and some of the most critical natural resources cannot physically be divided into self-contained sections. Moreover, a community in which sovereign states are the predominant actors is simply not ready for international public enterprises to play a major role in exploitation of natural resources. The governments of most nations, however, recognize the need for rules to preserve those aspects of the global environment that are beyond the jurisdiction of any state. This is not to say, however, that they don't often balk at agreeing to specific regulations and complying with them.

RECONCILING ALTERNATIVE VALUES

Each of the four strategies outlined in the previous section for averting an environmental tragedy has certain advantages and disadvantages. Which is the most appropriate in a specific context depends in part on the relative priority that is given to values such as conservation, production, equity, and freedom.

Conservation implies that the resource is neither overused or misused, so that its future value is not substantially diminished. In the analogy of the English village, conservation means that the pasture is not overgrazed to the point that there is a noticeable decline in the grass cover, which reduces the number of cattle that can be sustained. In the case of ocean fisheries, conservation implies that enough of the stock of the fish remains after the harvest to allow for a regeneration of the fishery up to its optimal levels. In regard to pollution, conservation can be interpreted to mean not allowing pollutants to reach a level at which serious harm to the environment begins to take place. For example, acid-forming precipitants would not be allowed to reach the concentrations at which forests and freshwater aquatic life show signs of dying.

Maximizing production is often a strong competing priority. The villagers depended upon their cattle for a livelihood and, therefore, could not accept sharp cutbacks on their herds. Their interests would be best served by an arrangement that allows them to graze as many cattle as possible without bringing about an environmentally destructive overshoot. International fishery commissions have sought to calculate a maximum sustainable yield on the basis of the best available scientific evidence on the number of fish that can be caught annually without jeopardizing their regeneration. This figure is then used to set limits on the annual catch. Requiring costly equipment for preventing pollution can have a substantial effect on industrial production, especially if a total cleanup is the objective. It should be noted that the dictates of short-term production and profit may be at odds with the same values over the longer run. Short-term gain may be achieved by ravaging the resource until it is totally destroyed, while long-term profitability depends upon careful stewardship of the resource to preserve its future value.

Equity implies fairness in the strategy that is adopted. What is fair is subject to divergent interpretations. For example, in the village setting, does the principle of equity dictate that all the herders be allowed to graze the same number of cattle on the pasture regardless of size of family or the number of cattle they owned before limits were imposed? Likewise, if the pasture is partitioned, would it be necessary for all to have equally sized plots? If the pasture is to be used by a community-owned herd, should all households receive an equal share of the profits? Similar issues of equity have complicated the task faced by fishery commissions in dividing up the total allowable catch among member countries. To what extent should the national shares be based on factors such as geographical proximity, population size, investment in fishing fleets, and distribution of the catch historically? The fairness of the provisions for EEZs under the new ocean law has been criticized on grounds that most of the productive fisheries will come under the control of a few states.

In the case of measures to control pollution, the fairness question arises over whether the percentage reductions in emissions should be required of all countries. Less developed countries, which historically are responsible for a small share of the pollutants causing problems such as ozone depletion and global warming, may contend that it is their "turn to pollute" to achieve their aspirations for economic development and a higher standard of living for their populations.

From one perspective equity is a matter of all being equally free to exploit a resource even though some, by virtue of their capital and advanced technologies, may be better able to take advantage of available opportunities. From another perspective, equity is an outcome that is equally favorable to all members of the community, including the poorer, less advantaged ones. At UNCLOS

III a sharp dispute arose over rules for developing the seabed between a small group of advanced states that possessed technologies for mining the mineral-rich nodules and the large majority of countries that would be left out of the potential mineral bonanza unless they could participate in an international enterprise.

Freedom suggests flexibility in the types of activities that are permitted. Most actors—be they states, corporations, or individuals—value freedom and are reluctant to submit to limitations on their behavior. Freedom for states is embodied in the principle of sovereignty; for corporations, in the doctrine of free enterprise; and for individuals, in the principle of human rights, as expressed in documents such as the Universal Declaration of Rights of 1948. In a frontier situation, where population is sparse, a greater amount of freedom of action can be tolerated without the prospect of severe environmental degradation. As population becomes more dense and puts heavier demands on the environment, as it has done globally in recent decades, maintaining the quality of the environment becomes a more pressing problem.

Reliance on voluntary restraints is an attractive possibility from the standpoint of maintaining maximum freedom of action, but stronger measures are usually needed to preserve the environment. Thus, fishing fleets have had to accept limits on their catch or confine their efforts to prescribed seasons. Some have had to negotiate for the right to fish in waters that fall within the newly created EEZs of coastal states, whereas before they had open access under the "freedom of the seas" doctrine. Operators of supertankers must submit to many rules that pertain to the structure of their vessels, how they are equipped, and where they may dispose of oily substances. Chinese couples, because of their country's one-child policy, have lost the right to determine the size of their families.

No strategy can be expected to maximize all four of these values. While conservation is often compatible with the achievement of equity, it is likely that sacrifices will have to be made in production, at least for the short run, and especially in freedom of action. Conservation measures may, however, work in favor of maximizing the long-term production of renewable resources. In regard to freedom, it should be kept in mind that the freedom of one party to act often impinges on the freedom of others. For example, the freedom to use CFCs indiscriminately may negate the freedom of others to enjoy being in the sunshine without fear of excessive exposure to ultraviolet radiation.

CONCLUSIONS

Having taken note of the emergence of the environment as a major global issue and the initiation of an international response, this chapter demonstrates some ways the story of the overgrazing of the pasture of the English village parallels several of the most serious environmental problems appearing on the agendas of international institutions. Hardin's story is helpful for understanding the motivation behind a variety of environmentally destructive behaviors, even by those who are well aware of the consequences of their actions. It is also useful for identifying courses of action that have potential for averting an environmental tragedy and the problems inherent in reconciling the objective of conservation with other values, such as maximizing production, achieving equity, and allowing freedom of action.

The parable fits some situations much better than others. It is especially applicable to the exploitation of limited resources in international commons, such as the oceans, atmosphere, radio waves, and outer space. It is of less value in analyzing the exploitation of resources that lie entirely within the boundaries of states, notably fossil fuels, minerals, forests, and agricultural land, which have not been freely accessible to users from other countries. Proposals have been made, however, that some of these latter resources be considered parts of the "common heritage of mankind." For example, the millions of species of plants and animals that exist on the planet have been described as the "genetic heritage of mankind," even though the specimens of many are geographically concentrated within the borders of a single state (Myers, 1984). Likewise, unique human artifacts from ancient civilizations, such as temples, sculptures, and paintings, have been designated by UNESCO as the "cultural heritage of mankind." Identifying them as such confers a responsibility on the states in which they are located to preserve them for present and future generations of the world's population.

References

Hardin, Garrett. (1968) "The Tragedy of the Commons." *Science* 162: 1241–1248.

———. (1974) "Living on a Lifeboat," *Bioscience* 24: 561–568.

Meadows, Donnella H., Dennis L. Meadows, Jørgen Randers, and William H. Behrens. (1972) *The Limits to Growth* (New York: Signet).

Myers, Norman. (1984) *The Primary Resource: Tropical Forests and Our Future* (New York: Norton).

World Resources Institute. (1992) *World Resources 1992–93* (New York: Oxford University Press).

42

THE INTERNATIONAL
STATE OF NATURE
AND THE POLITICS
OF SCARCITY

William Ophuls and A. Stephen Boyan, Jr.

Is international conflict more or less probable in a world of scarcity? William Ophuls and A. Stephen Boyan, Jr.—in an update of Ophuls' critically acclaimed 1977 study—argue that conflict is more likely. The reason inheres in the principle of sovereignty, embraced by all countries. "Without some kind of international machinery with enough authority and coercive power over sovereign states to keep them within the bounds of the ecological common interest of all on the planet," they conclude, "the world must suffer the ever-greater environmental ills ordained by the global tragedy of the commons." Ophuls is a former United States foreign service officer. Boyan is a political scientist on the faculty of the University of Maryland, Baltimore County.

THE INTERNATIONAL MACROCOSM

If in the various national microcosms constituting the world political community the basic dynamics of ecological scarcity apply virtually across the board, in the macrocosm of international politics they operate even more strongly. Just as it does within each individual nation, the tragic logic of the commons brings about the over-exploitation of such common-pool resources as the oceans and the atmosphere. Also, the pressures toward inequality, oppression, and conflict are even more intense within the world political community, for it is a community in name only, and the already marked cleavage between rich and poor threatens to become even greater. Without even the semblance of a world government, the solutions of such problems depends on the good will and purely voluntary cooperation of over 170 sovereign states—a prospect that does not inspire optimism. . . .

THE GLOBAL TRAGEDY OF THE COMMONS

The tragic logic of the commons operates universally, and its effects are readily visible internationally—in the growing pollution of international rivers, of seas, and now of even the oceans; in the overfishing that has caused a marked decline in the fish catch in some areas, as well as the near extinction of the great whales; and in the impending scramble for seabed resources by maritime miners or other exploiters. There is no way to confine environmental insults or the effects of ecological degradation within national borders, because river basins, airsheds, and oceans are intrinsically international. Even seemingly local environmental disruption inevitably has some impact on the quality of regional and, eventually, global ecosystems. Just as it does within each nation, the aggregation of individual desires and actions overloads the international commons. But, like individuals, states tend to turn a blind eye to this, for they profit by the increased production while others bear most or all of the cost, or they lose by self-restraint while others receive most or all of the benefit. Thus Britain gets the factory output while Scandinavia suffers the ecological effects of "acid rain"; the French and Germans use the Rhine for waste disposal even though this leaves the river little more than a reeking sewer by the time when, downstream, it reaches fellow European [Union] member Holland.

Even though the problems are basically the same everywhere, the political implications of the tragedy of the commons are much more serious in the international arena. It has long been recognized that international politics is the epitome of the Hobbesian state of nature: Despite all the progress over the centuries toward the rule of international law, sovereign states, unlike the citizens within each state, acknowledge no law or authority higher than their own self-interests; they are therefore free to do as they please, subject only to gross prudential restraints, no matter what the cost to the world community. For example, despite strong pressures from the international community, including a 5-year moratorium on commercial whaling by the International Whaling Commission, Japan and Iceland continue to hunt whales. More than 13,000 whales have been killed since the international community banned whaling. The United States relentlessly spews huge amounts of carbon dioxide into the air commons, despite efforts among other industrialized nations to get an agreement to reduce greenhouse emissions.

In international relations, therefore, the dynamic of the tragedy of the commons is even stronger than within any given nation state, which, being a real political community, has at least the theoretical capacity to make binding, authoritative decisions on resource conservation and ecological protection. By contrast, international agreements are reached and enforced by the purely voluntary cooperation of sovereign nation states existing in a state of nature. . . . The likelihood of forestalling by such means the operation of the tragedy of the commons is extremely remote. Worse, just as any individual is nearly helpless to alter the outcome by his or her own actions (and even risks serious loss if he or she refuses to participate in the exploitation of the commons), so too, in the absence of international authority or enforceable agreement, nations have little choice but to contribute to the tragedy by their own actions. This would be true even if each individual state was striving to achieve a domestic steady-state economy, for unless one assumes agreement on a largely autarkic world, states would still compete with each other internationally to maximize the resources available to them. Ecological scarcity thus intensifies the fundamental problem of international politics—the achievement of world order—by adding further to the preexisting difficulties of a state of nature. Without some kind of international governmental machinery with enough authority and coercive power over sovereign states to keep them within the bounds of the ecological common interest of all on the planet, the world must suffer the ever-greater environmental ills ordained by the global tragedy of the commons.

THE STRUGGLE BETWEEN RICH AND POOR

Ecological scarcity also aggravates very seriously the already intense struggle between rich and poor. As is well known, the world today . . . is sharply polarized between the developed, industrialized "haves," all affluent in a greater or lesser degree and all getting more affluent all the time, and the underdeveloped or developing "have nots," all relatively and absolutely impoverished and (with few exceptions) tending to fall further and further behind despite their often feverish efforts to grow. The degree of the inequality is also well known: The United States, with only 6% of the world's population, consumes about 30% of the total energy production of the world and comparable amounts of other resources; it throws away enough paper and plastic plates and cups to set the table for a worldwide picnic six times a year. . . .

The rest of the "haves," though only about half as prodigal as the United States, still consume resources far out of proportion to their population. Conversely, per capita consumption of resources in the developing world ranges from one-tenth to one-hundredth that in the "have" countries. To make matters worse, the resources that the "haves" enjoy in inordinate amounts are largely and increasingly imported from the developing world. For example, developed nations consume two-thirds of the world's steel, aluminum, copper, lead, nickel, tin, zinc, and three-fourths of the world's energy. Thus economic inequality and what might be called ecological colonialism have become intertwined. In view of this extreme and long-standing inequality (which, moreover, has its roots in an imperialist past), it is hardly surprising that the developing world thirsts avidly for development or that it has become increasingly intolerant of those features of the current world order it perceives as obstacles to its becoming as rich and powerful as the developed world.

Alas, the emergence of ecological scarcity appears to have sounded the death knell for the aspirations of the [less developed countries]. Even assuming (contrary to fact) that there were sufficient mineral and energy resources to make it possible, universal industrialization would impose intolerable stress on world ecosystems. And humans, in particular, could not endure the pollution levels that would result. Already, the one-fifth of the world's population that lives in industrial countries generates most of the world's toxic wastes, two-thirds of the world's greenhouse emissions, three-fourths of the world's nitrogen oxides and sulfur emissions, and 90% of the gases that are already destroying the world's protective ozone layer.

In short, the current model of development, which assumes that all countries will eventually become heavily industrialized mass-consumption societies, is doomed to failure.[1] Naturally, this conclusion is totally unacceptable to the modernizing elites of the developing world; their political power is generally founded on the promise of development. Even more important, simply halting growth would freeze the current pattern of inequality, leaving the "have nots" as the peasants of the world community in perpetuity. Thus an end to growth and development would be acceptable to the developing world only in combination with a radical redistribution of the world's wealth and a total restructuring of the world's economy to guarantee the maintenance of economic justice. Yet it seems absolutely clear that the rich have not the slightest intention of relieving the plight of the poor if it entails the sacrifice of their own living standards. Ecological scarcity thus greatly increases the probability of naked confrontation between rich and poor.

---

[1]The ecologically viable alternative . . . is a locally self-sufficient, semi-developed, steady-state society based on renewable or "income" resources such as photosynthesis and solar energy. Only Bhutan seems self-consciously to be developing sustainably as a matter of principle. . . . Others find themselves unable to see such apparent frugality as a realistic option. All the pressures impel them toward "efficiency," standardization, centralization, and large scale. In addition, because sustainable development does not work when population pressure is extreme and most developing countries are heavily overpopulated, choosing restraint or frugality sometimes implies a willingness to use harsh measures—for example, compulsory abortions to stabilize populations or forced resettlement to save the rainforests. It is not surprising that most leaders prefer to continue in the illusory hope of achieving heavy industrialization. In addition, the lust for status and prestige, the desire for military power, and many other less than noble motives are also prevalent, and the frugal modesty of semi-developed self-sufficiency can do little to satisfy them.

WHO ARE NOW THE "HAVES" AND THE "HAVE NOTS"?

An important new element has been injected into this struggle. The great "resource hunger" of the developed world, and even of some parts of the developing world, has begun to transfer power and wealth to those who have resources to sell, especially critical resources such as petroleum. As a result, the geopolitics of the world is changing.

This process can be expected to continue. The power and wealth of the major oil producers are bound to increase over the next five decades, despite North Sea and Alaskan oil and regardless of whether or not the Organization of Petroleum Exporting Countries (OPEC) manages to act in a unified manner.

Some believe that oil is a special case and that the prospect of OPEC-type cartels for other resources is dim. . . . These assessments may be correct, but it seems inevitable that in the long run an era of "commodity power" must emerge. The hunger of the industrialized nations for resources is likely to increase, even if there is no substantial growth in output to generate increased demand for raw materials, because the domestic mineral and energy resources of the developed countries have begun to be exhausted. The United States, for example, already imports 100% of its platinum, mica, chromium, and strontium; over 90% of its manganese, aluminum, tantalum, and cobalt; and 50% or more of 12 additional key minerals. . . . However, the developed countries seem determined to keep growing, and assuming even modest further growth in industrial output, their dependence on developing world supplies is bound to increase markedly in the next few decades.[2] Thus, whatever the short-term prospects for the success of budding cartels in copper, phosphates, and other minerals, the clear overall long-term trend is toward a seller's market in basic resources and therefore toward "commodity power," even if this power grows more slowly and is manifested in a less extreme form than that of OPEC.

Thus the basic, long-standing division of the world into rich and poor in terms of GNP per capita will eventually be overlaid with another rich-poor polarization, in terms of resources, that will both moderate and intensify the basic split. Although there are many complex interdependencies in world trade—for example, U.S. food exports are just as critical to many countries as their mineral exports are to us—it is already clear that the resource-rich nations of the developing world stand to gain greater wealth and power at the expense of the "haves." . . . Unfortunately, the defense the industrial powers are most likely to use against unfriendly economic or political moves on the part of any

---

[2]Naturally, there will be short-term exceptions. Developed countries, for example, will remain somewhat independent of Middle Eastern oil supplies while North Sea oil production and Alaskan oil production remain at high levels and as long as other non-OPEC sources of oil exist. On the other hand, one of the reasons for the Persian Gulf war was undoubtedly the desire to keep Kuwaiti oil in friendly hands. The respites from the overall trend toward increasing dependence will be transitory and limited to particular commodities.

of these countries will be military, as it was in the Persian Gulf war, where the industrial nations have an overwhelming advantage.

This discussion leaves out the majority of poor countries—those without major resources of their own. As they are forced to pay higher prices to resource-rich countries, they will suffer—indeed, they already have suffered— major setbacks to their prospects for development. This is true not only of the hopelessly poor countries of Africa and Asia but also of countries whose development programs have already acquired some momentum.

In sum, world geopolitics and economics are in for a reordering. Western economic development has involved a net transfer of resources, wealth, and power from the current "have nots" to the "haves," creating the cleavage between the two that now divides the world. In recent years, developed nations have added the additional burden of debt repayment, increasing the wealth transferred to them from the "have nots." In the long term, this situation will change; wealth will also be transferred to those nations that have scarce resources. But only the relatively few "have nots" that possess significant amounts of resources will gain; the rest of the poor will become more abject than before. Thus the old polarization between rich and poor seems likely to be replaced by a threefold division into the rich, the hopelessly poor, and the newly enriched—and such a major change in the international order is bound to create tension.

CONFLICT OR COOPERATION?

How this tension will play out in the years ahead is hard to say. The danger is that to many of the declining "haves," ill-equipped to adapt to an era of "commodity power" and economic warfare, the grip of the newly enriched on essential resources will seem an intolerable stranglehold to be broken at all costs. At the same time the poor, having had their revolutionary hopes and rising aspirations crushed, will have little to lose but their chains. Thus the world may face turmoil and war on top of ecological scarcity—a horrible prospect, given the ecologically destructive character of modern warfare. . . .

Some, on the other hand, hope or believe that ecological scarcity will have just the opposite effect: Because the problems will become so overwhelming and so evidently insoluble without total international cooperation, nation states will discard their outmoded national sovereignty and place themselves under some form of planetary government that will regulate the global commons for the benefit of all humanity and begin the essential process of gradual economic redistribution. In effect, states will be driven by their own vital national interests (which they recognize as including ecological as well as traditional economic, political, and military factors) to embrace the ultimate interdependence needed to solve ecological problems. . . . According to this hypothesis, the very direness of the outcome if cooperation does not prevail may ensure that it will.

The pattern, so far, has fallen somewhere between these extremes. War for resources has broken out on occasion; as we have noted, one of the reasons for frequent United States military activity in the Middle East is to keep the control of oil fields and commerce in friendly hands. On the other hand, there has also been considerable talk about cooperative international action to deal with the problems of environmental degradation, and some momentum toward greater cooperation has developed. However, with the possible exception of agreements among the nations of the European [Union] which are in a common market, international environmental agreements have been piecemeal and unenforceable, or what they have required has been that which the most reluctant nation has been willing to concede—measures that are usually inadequate. The international environmental regulatory process thus resembles process politics in the American context, with this difference: The players—in this case the polluters—cannot be forced to come to the bargaining table; if they do come, they can't be forced to agree to anything; and if they do agree to something, the agreement cannot be enforced. . . .

AN UPSURGE IN CONFERENCE DIPLOMACY

A look at the record of international environmental agreements thus far concluded reveals only modest accomplishments. . . . The first international Law of the Sea Conference took place in 1973. Its supporters wanted to establish an all-encompassing treaty dealing with overfishing, seabed mining, and pollution controls, premised on the view that the oceans are the "common heritage of mankind." They failed. By the time a draft treaty was finally agreed to in 1982, it had carved the oceans into national zones of exploitation for 200 miles out from each nation's coasts; the nation controlling the Exclusive Economic Zone may control who, if anyone, may enter the zone for economic purposes. Only seabeds were declared a "common heritage of mankind," to be mined according to regulations established by an International Seabed Authority. However, even this was too much for the United States and many other industrial countries. The U.S. position is that seabeds should be mined on a first-come, first-served basis, without international regulation. Therefore, the United States has refused to sign or ratify the treaty. Behind these differences in legal position are differing national interests, not just differing views on the best way to protect the ocean environment. The industrial countries have or will soon have the capacity to begin deep seabed mining; they can enrich themselves further, or at least put off the day of their own mineral depletion, with a first-come, first-served approach. The developing world, on the other hand, benefits from a more controlled "common heritage" approach. So nationalism may block adoption of the proposed treaty. Only forty countries had ratified it by 1989, and 60 must do so for it to go into effect.

Other international agreements affecting the sea are confined to narrower issues, but even so, some have been difficult to implement. MARPOL, the 1973

International Convention for the Prevention of Pollution from Ships, established minimal distances from the land for ocean dumping, limited the dumping of garbage, required ports to provide facilities for receiving trash from incoming ships, and prohibited the dumping of plastics. Only thirty-nine nations had ratified this treaty eighteen years later, and it took fourteen years for the United States to ratify it. Under the treaty, the U.S. ban on the dumping of plastics took effect in 1989, although the largest source of plastics dumping, the armed forces, will not be brought under the treaty until 1994. The London Dumping Convention of 1972 has won wider support; sixty-three nations have signed it. It prohibits ocean dumping of heavy metals, specified carcinogens, and radioactive and other hazardous substances. Yet enforcement of the treaty has been spotty; violators are caught and punished with only as much vigor as each nation chooses to muster. In this connection, as we have noted earlier, even ocean treaties and conventions that have nearly universal support, (such as the moratorium on whaling and the prohibition of driftnet fishing) either have loopholes through which nations can jump or, as with whaling, are often openly flouted. Occasionally, another signatory to such a treaty who is angry about such defiance may engage in a trade sanction against a delinquent country. Generally, however, a country's flouting of environmental agreements does not result in the international community's imposing a meaningful penalty.

Still, ocean conventions and treaties have had more results beneficial to the environment than have international agreements concerning hazardous wastes and air pollution. Regarding hazardous wastes, the most the international community has managed to agree to is a prohibition of transboundary shipment of such goods by stealth. A 1989 United Nations draft treaty forbids transboundary movement of waste without notification by the exporter, without the consent of the importer, or with documents that do not conform to the shipment. A 1990 United Nations system of Prior Informed Consent regarding restricted chemicals (primarily pesticides) requires that prospective importing nations be provided with information about the benefits and risks of a chemical before deciding whether to allow it to be imported. Environmentalists had wanted a stronger draft making it illegal for a country to export to another country a chemical that is banned within the exporting country itself. But the United States, which exports large amounts of banned pesticides, led the successful opposition to that proposal.

International air pollution treaties and conventions have also been weak. Developing countries have largely refused to agree to international controls of air pollution, fearing that such controls will impede their pace of development. Most air pollution agreements have been concluded only among Western European nations, sometimes with the United States and/or Britain not going along, although they were invited to sign. Examples include the 1988 conventions to reduce sulfur and nitrogen emissions. The United States and Western European governments have also had several conferences on reducing greenhouse emissions, but the United States has refused to agree to targets to reduce carbon emissions and has frustrated the attempts of European nations to come to a binding agreement among themselves. The best of the international air pollution agreements was the Montreal commitment by industrial countries to phase out their use of CFCs by 2000. . . . But . . . this agreement will be too little and too late to avert hundreds of thousands of cancer deaths and millions of cancer cases that will result from ozone depletion.

The forces that prevent strong international environmental agreements are many. First, the spirit of militant nationalism that has animated so much of the history of the postwar world has not abated, except among Western European governments. Indeed, the tendency of the world is to move in the opposite direction, with the nations of Eastern Europe and the Soviet Union breaking up into militant ethnic states. Nation states insist on the absolute and sovereign right of self-determination in use of resources, population policy, and development in general, regardless of the wider consequences. Second, the demand among Third World countries for economic development has, if anything, increased in intensity, and whatever seems to stand in the way, as ecological considerations often do, gets rather short shift. Third, largely because their prospects for development are so dim, the countries of the developing world have begun to press even harder for fundamental reform of the world system. . . . Thus every discussion of such environmental issues as food and population is inevitably converted by those who represent the developing world into a discussion of international economic justice as well, which enormously complicates the process of negotiation. In short, environmental issues have become pawns in the larger diplomatic and political struggle between the nations. . . .

If one wished to be optimistic, one could conclude that the world community has taken the first attitudinal and institutional steps toward meeting the challenges of ecological scarcity. A more realistic assessment, however, would be that although modest environmental improvements have been achieved, major impediments to further progress remain. One might even be forced to conclude, more pessimistically, that the world political community as presently constituted is simply incapable of coping with the challenges of ecological scarcity, at least in a timely way.

PLANETARY GOVERNMENT OR THE WAR OF ALL AGAINST ALL

. . . Even before the emergence of ecological scarcity, the world's difficulties and their starkly Hobbesian implications were grave enough. Some saw the "revolution of rising expectations" pushing the world toward a situation in which wants greatly exceeded capacity to meet them, provoking Hobbesian turmoil and violence. . . . The world lives under the blade of a deadly Sword of Damocles. The hair holding this environmental Sword has come loose; pollution and other environmental problems will not obligingly postpone their impact while diplomats haggle, so the Sword is already descending toward our unprotected heads. There is thus no way for the world community to put the environmental issue in the back of its mind and go about its business. The crisis of ecological scarcity is a Sword that must be parried, squarely and soon.

The need for a world government with enough coercive power over fractious nation states to achieve what reasonable people would regard as the planetary common interest has become overwhelming. Yet we must recognize that the very environmental degradation that makes a world government necessary has also made it much more difficult to achieve. The clear danger is that, instead of promoting world cooperation, ecological scarcity will simply intensify the Hobbesian war of all against all—with the destruction of the common planet (for purposes of human habitation) the tragic outcome.

43

ENVIRONMENT AND SECURITY: MUDDLED THINKING

Daniel Deudney

With the end of the Cold War many analysts have begun to treat matters previously regarded as in the realm of low politics with the rhetoric once reserved for the high politics of peace and security. The concept "environmental security" is an example. Daniel Deudney is critical of the "use of language traditionally associated with violence and war to understand environmental problems." He argues that "ecological degradation is not a threat to national security; rather, environmentalism is a threat to national security attitudes and institutions." Deudney is assistant professor of social sciences at the University of Pennsylvania and author of the forthcoming book *Pax Atomica: States and Republics in Sustainable Global Security Systems.*

A striking feature of the growing discussion of environmental issues in the United States is the use of language traditionally associated with violence and war to understand environmental problems and to motivate action. Lester Brown, Jessica Tuchman Mathews, Michael Renner, and others have proposed "redefining national security" to encompass resource and environmental threats. Richard Ullman and others have proposed including natural disasters in the security definition. Hal Harvey has put forth the concept of "natural security," and Senator Albert Gore [now U.S. vice president] [has] proposed a "strategic

From the *Bulletin of the Atomic Scientists.* Copyright © 1991 by the Educational Foundation for Nuclear Science, 6042 South Kimbark, Chicago, Illinois 60637, U.S.A.

environment initiative." Backed by some of the country's wealthiest foundations, numerous conferences and researchers are addressing issues of "environmental security." With Congress's . . . adoption of Senate Armed Services Chairman Sam Nunn's $200 million proposal to use military facilities for environmental monitoring and research, these ideas have begun to shape spending and organizational priorities.

Conceptual ferment in language often reflects important changes in political and social norms. New phrases are coined and old terms are appropriated for new purposes. Great changes like the emergence of capitalism, the growth of democracy, and the end of slavery were accompanied by shifting and expanding political language. Such experimentation in the language used to understand and act upon environmental problems is a natural and encouraging development.

But not all neologisms and linkages are equally plausible or useful. Traditionally, the concept of national security, as opposed to national interest or well-being, has centered upon organized violence. Obviously, security from violence is a primal human need since loss of life prevents the enjoyment of all other goods. And various resource factors, such as access to fuels and ores, have contributed to state capacities to wage war and achieve security from violence. But before melding these "threats," it is worth comparing the national pursuit of security from violence to environmental problems and their solutions.

War and the preparation for war pose threats to the environment and consume resources that could be used to ameliorate environmental degradation. Defoliation in Vietnam, toxic and radioactive waste from nuclear weapons production, the oil spill in the Persian Gulf, and the possibility of "nuclear winter" are direct environmental problems caused by violence and war. Because of these environmental impacts, the war system imposes costs beyond the intentional destruction and loss of life.[1] However, most environmental degradation is not caused by war and preparation for war, and there is no guarantee that the world would spend money saved from military expenditures on environmental restoration. Nor is it clear that the world cannot afford environmental restoration without cutting military expenditures.

DIFFERENT THREATS, SOLUTIONS

Identifying environmental degradation as a threat to national security can be useful if the two phenomena—security from violence and from environmental threats—are similar. Unfortunately, they have little in common. Four major dissimilarities deserve mention:

---

[1]Arthur H. Westing, ed., *Environmental Hazards of War* (London: Sage, 1990).

• Environmental degradation and violence pose very different types of threats. Both may kill people and may reduce human well-being, but not all threats to life and property are threats to security. Disease, aging, and accidents routinely destroy life and property, but we do not think of them as threats to security. And when an earthquake or hurricane causes extensive damage, it is customary to speak of natural disasters, but not to speak about such events as threatening national security. If everything that causes a decline in human well-being is labeled a security threat, the term loses any analytical usefulness.

• The scope and source of threats to environmental well-being and national security from violence are very different. Nothing about the problem of environmental degradation is particularly national in character. Few environmental threats afflict just one nation, and many altogether ignore national borders. But it would be misleading even to call most environmental problems international, because perpetrators and victims are within the same country. There is nothing distinctively national about the causes, harms, or solutions.

• Threats to environmental well-being and national security involve greatly differing degrees of intention. Threats of violence are highly intentional: organizations are mobilized, weapons procured, and wars waged with relatively definite aims in mind. In contrast, environmental degradation is largely unintentional, the side effect of many other activities. With the limited exception of environmental modification for military purposes, no one really sets out to harm the environment.

• Organizations that provide protection from violence differ greatly from those engaged in environmental protection. Citizens typically delegate the goal of achieving national security to organizations far removed from the experience of civil society. Military organizations are secretive, extremely hierarchical, and centralized; they typically deploy expensive, highly specialized, and advanced technologies. The specialized professional group staffing them is trained to kill and destroy.

Responding to environmental problems requires opposite approaches and organizations. Everyone is involved, because certain aspects of virtually all mundane activities—house construction, farming techniques, waste treatment, factory design, land-use planning—must be reformed. And the professional ethos of environmental restoration is stewardship: respectful cultivation and protection of plants, animals, and the land. Because national security from violence and environmental habitability have little in common, the new fashion of linking them may create a conceptual muddle rather than a paradigm shift.

RISKS OF NATIONALIST APPEALS

Another motive for speaking of environmental degradation as a threat to natural security is rhetorical: to make people respond to environmental threats with a sense of urgency. But before harnessing the old horse of national security to pull the heavy new environmental wagon, one must examine its temperament. The sentiments associated with national security are powerful because they relate to war. Historian Michael Howard has observed: "Self-consciousness as a nation implies, by definition, a sense of differentiation from other communities, and the most memorable incidents in the group memory usually are of conflict with, and triumph over, other communities. It is in fact very difficult to create national self-consciousness *without* a war."[2] If the emotional appeals of national security can somehow be connected to environmental issues, then it is also possible that other, less benign associations may be transferred.

Yet the national security mentality engenders an enviable sense of urgency, and a corresponding willingness to accept great personal sacrifice. Unfortunately, these emotions may be difficult to sustain. Crises call for resolution, and the patience of a mobilized populace is rarely long. A cycle of arousal and somnolence is unlikely to establish permanent patterns of environmentally sound behavior, and "crash" solutions are often bad ones. For example, the energy crisis of the 1970s spawned such white elephants as the proposed synfuels program, the "energy mobilization board," and a Byzantine system of price controls.

Finally, the "nation" is not a concept waiting to be defined, but is instead profoundly linked to war and "us against them" thinking. The stronger the nationalism, the stronger the distinction between friend and foe.

In contrast, in the environmental sphere "we"—not "they"—are the "enemy." Existing groups of opponents in world politics do not match the causal lines of environmental degradation. In fact, intense nationalism conflicts with the globalism that has been one of the most important insights of environmentalism. Thinking of the environment as a national security problem risks undercutting the sense of world community and common fate that may be necessary to solve the problem.

If pollution is seen as a threat to national security, there is also a danger that the citizens of one country will resent the pollution from other countries more than the pollution created by their fellow citizens. U.S. citizens, for example, could become much more concerned about deforestation in Brazil than about reversing centuries of North American deforestation. This could increase international tensions, make international agreements more difficult to achieve, and divert attention from solving internal problems. Taken to an absurd extreme—as national security threats sometimes are—seeing environmental degradation in a neighboring country as a national security threat could trigger various types of intervention and imperialism.

Instead of linking national security to the environment, environmentalists should emphasize that global ecological problems call into question the nation-

---

[2]Michael Howard, "War and the Nation-State," *Daedalus* (Fall 1979).

state and its privileged status in world politics. Ecological decay is not a threat to national security, but it challenges the utility of thinking in national terms.

Integrally woven into ecological awareness is a powerful set of values and symbols, ranging from human health and property values to beauty and concern for future generations, which draw upon basic human aspirations and are powerful motivators of human action. This "green" sensibility can make strong claim to being the master metaphor for an emerging post-industrial civilization. Instead of attempting to gain leverage by appropriating "national security" thinking, environmentalists should continue developing and disseminating this rich, emergent world view.

WAR AND THE ENVIRONMENT

Many analysts have begun calling ecological degradation a national security problem because they think environmental stress will cause or exacerbate wars. If states become much more concerned with resources and ecological decay, particularly if they think such decay is a threat to their security, they may well fight resource and pollution wars. For example, Arthur Westing has observed: "Global deficiencies and degradation of natural resources, both renewable and non-renewable, coupled with the uneven distribution of these raw materials, can lead to unlikely—and thus unstable—alliances, to national rivalries, and, of course, to war."[3]

Few ideas seem more intuitively sound, and many ideas about resource war are derived from the cataclysmic world wars of the first half of the twentieth century. Influenced by geopolitical theories that emphasized the importance of land resources for Great Power status, Hitler in significant measure fashioned Nazi war aims to achieve resource autonomy.[4] Lacking indigenous fuel and minerals, and faced with a tightening embargo by the Western colonial powers in Asia, the Japanese invaded Southeast Asia for oil, tin, and rubber.[5] Although the United States had a richer resource base than the Axis powers, fears of shortages and industrial strangulation played a central role in U.S. strategic thinking. During the Cold War, the presence of natural resources in the Third World helped stimulate East-West conflict in this vast area.[6]

[3] Arthur H. Westing, "Global Resources and International Conflict: An Overview," in Arthur H. Westing, ed., *Global Resources and Environmental Conflict: Environmental Factors in Strategic Policy and Action* (New York: Oxford University Press, 1986), p. 1.

[4] See, for example, Brooks Emeny, *The Strategy of Raw Materials* (New York: Macmillan, 1934); Norman Rich, *Hitler's War Aims: Ideology, the Nazi State, and the Course of Expansion* (New York: W. W. Norton, 1973).

[5] James Crowley, *Japan's Quest for Autonomy: National Security and Foreign Policy, 1930–1938* (Princeton, N.J.: Princeton University Press, 1966).

[6] Alfred E. Eckes, Jr., *The United States and the Global Struggle for Minerals* (Austin, Texas: University of Texas Press, 1979).

But scenarios of resource war may be diminishing in plausibility. The robust character of the world trade system means that resource dependency is no longer a major threat to a nation's military security and political autonomy. During the 1930s the world trading system had collapsed, driving states to pursue autarkic economies. In contrast, contemporary states routinely meet their resource needs without controlling the territory containing the resources.[7]

Moreover, it is becoming more difficult for states to exploit foreign resources through territorial conquest. It is very costly for any invader, even one equipped with advanced technology, to subdue a resisting population—as France discovered in Indochina and Algeria, the United States in Vietnam, and the Soviet Union in Afghanistan. Iraq's invasion of Kuwait fits the older pattern but was based upon a truly exceptional imbalance between power (Iraq had the fourth-largest military force in the world) and wealth (Kuwait had the third-largest oil reserves and a tiny military).

In addition, the world is entering what H. E. Goeller and Alvin M. Weinberg have called the "age of substitutability," in which industrial technology makes it possible to fashion virtually everything needed from substances such as iron, aluminum, silicon, and hydrocarbons which are ubiquitous and plentiful. Evidence for this trend is that prices for virtually every raw material have been stagnant or falling for the last several decades despite the continued growth in world output, and despite expectations many voiced during the 1970s that resource scarcity would drive up commodity prices to the benefit of Third World raw material suppliers.

FOUR WAR SCENARIOS

Environmental analysts have outlined a number of ways resource scarcity and environmental stress may lead to violent conflict:

Water Wars   The most frequently mentioned scenario is that disputes over water supplies will become acute as rainfall and runoff patterns are altered by atmospheric warming. Many rivers cross international boundaries, and water is already becoming scarce in several arid regions. But it seems less likely that conflicts over water will lead to interstate war than that the development of jointly owned water resources will reinforce peace. Exploitation of water resources typically requires expensive—and vulnerable—civil engineering systems such as dams and pipelines. Large dams, like nuclear power plants, are potential weapons in the hands of an

[7]Ronnie D. Lipschutz, *When Nations Clash: Raw Materials, Ideology and Foreign Policy* (Cambridge, Mass.: Ballinger, 1989).

enemy.[8] This creates a mutual hostage situation which greatly reduces the incentives for states to employ violence to resolve conflicts. Furthermore, there is evidence that the development of water resources by antagonistic neighbors creates a network of common interests.

Poverty Wars   In a second scenario, declining living standards first cause internal turmoil, then war. If groups at all levels of affluence protect their standard of living by pushing deprivation on other groups, class war and revolutionary upheavals could result. Faced with these pressures, liberal democracy and free market systems could increasingly be replaced by authoritarian systems capable of maintaining minimum order.[9] If authoritarian regimes are more war-prone because they lack democratic control, and if revolutionary regimes are war-prone because of their ideological fervor and isolation, then the world is likely to become more violent. The record of previous depressions supports the proposition that widespread economic stagnation and unmet economic expectations contribute to international conflict.

Although initially compelling, this scenario has major flaws. One is that it is arguably based on unsound economic theory. Wealth is formed not so much by the availability of cheap natural resources as by capital formation through savings and more efficient production. Many resource-poor countries, like Japan, are very wealthy, while many countries with more extensive resources are poor. Environmental constraints require an end to economic growth based on growing use of raw materials, but not necessarily an end to growth in the production of goods and services.

In addition, economic decline does not necessarily produce conflict. How societies respond to economic decline may largely depend upon the rate at which such declines occur. And as people get poorer, they may become less willing to spend scarce resources for military forces. As Bernard Brodie observed about the modern era, "The predisposing factors to military aggression are full bellies, not empty ones."[10] The experience of economic depressions over the last two centuries may be irrelevant, because such depressions were characterized by underutilized production capacity and falling resource prices. In the 1930s, increased military spending stimulated economies, but if economic growth is retarded by environmental constraints, military spending will exacerbate the problem.

---

[8]Wilson Clark and Jake Page, *Energy, Vulnerability, and War* (New York: W. W. Norton, 1981); Amory B. Lovins and L. Hunter Lovins, *Brittle Power: Energy Strategy for National Security* (Andover, Mass.: Brick House, 1982).

[9]See, for example, William Ophuls, *Ecology and the Politics of Scarcity* (San Francisco: Freeman, 1976), p. 152; Susan M. Leeson, "Philosophical Implications of the Ecological Crisis: The Authoritarian Challenge to Liberalism," *Polity,* vol. 11, no. 3 (Spring 1979).

[10]Bernard Brodie, "The Impact of Technological Change on the International System," in Sullivan and Sattler, eds., *Change and the Future of the International System* (N.Y.: Columbia University Press, 1972).

Power Wars A third scenario is that environmental degradation might cause war by altering the relative power of states; that is, newly stronger states may be tempted to prey upon the newly weaker ones, or weakened states may attack and lock in their positions before their power ebbs further. But such alterations might not lead to war as readily as the lessons of history suggest, because economic power and military power are not as tightly coupled as in the past. The economic power positions of Germany and Japan have changed greatly since World War II, but these changes have not been accompanied by war or threat of war. In the contemporary world, whole industries rise, fall, and relocate, causing substantial fluctuations in the economic well-being of regions and peoples, without producing wars. There is no reason to believe that changes in relative wealth and power caused by the uneven impact of environmental degradation would inevitably lead to war.

Even if environmental degradation were to destroy the basic social and economic fabric of a country or region, the impact on international order may not be very great. Among the first casualties in such a country would be the capacity to wage war. The poor and wretched of the earth may be able to deny an outside aggressor an easy conquest, but they are themselves a minimal threat to other states. Contemporary offensive military operations require complex organizational skills, specialized industrial products, and surplus wealth.

In today's world everything is connected, but not everything is tightly coupled. Severe regional disasters may produce scarcely a ripple in the rest of the world. For example, Idi Amin drew Uganda back into savage darkness, the Khmer Rouge murdered an estimated two million Cambodians, and the Sahara has advanced across the Sahel without much perturbing the economies and political systems of the rest of the world.

Pollution Wars A fourth possible route from environmental degradation to interstate conflict and violence is pollution across interstate borders. It is easy to imagine a situation in which one country dumps an intolerable amount of pollution on a neighbor, and coercive efforts to stop the offense eventually lead to armed conflict. But in real life such cases are rare. More typically, activities produce harm both internally and outside a country's border. This creates complex sets of winners and losers, as well as potential internal and interstate coalitions.

Another type of conflict could emerge in the effort to preserve the global commons. Solutions to global phenomena like atmospheric warming and ozone depletion require collective action, but one significant polluter might resist joining an agreement, and the others might attempt to force the "free rider" to cooperate. It is difficult to judge this scenario because we lack historical examples. It seems doubtful, however, that states would find military instruments useful for coercion and compliance. Any state sufficiently industrialized to be a major contributor to these problems is a poor target for military coercion.

THE WRONG PARADIGM

The case for asserting that environmental degradation will cause institutional violence is weak, largely because of factors having little to do with environmental matters. Of course, today there are some [190] independent states and environmental problems are diverse; therefore any generalization will surely have important exceptions. Although many analogies for such conflict can be drawn from historical experience, they fail to take into account the ways in which the current international system differs from earlier ones. Because military aggression is prohibitively costly, even large shifts in the relative power of states are less likely to cause war. War is a poor way to resolve many of the conflicts that might arise from environmental degradation. The vitality of the international trading system and complex interdependency in general also militate against violence. The result is a world system with considerable resilience and "rattle room" to weather significant environmental disruption without significant violent conflict.

The degradation of the natural environment upon which human well-being depends is a challenge of far-reaching significance for societies everywhere. But this emerging problem has little to do with national security from violence. Not only do the causes and solutions to these two problems have little in common, but the nationalist and militarist mindsets closely associated with national security thinking directly conflict with the core of the environmentalist world view. Harnessing their sentiments for a "war on pollution" is unnecessary, dangerous, and probably self-defeating. The prospects for resource and pollution wars are not great but, ironically, could be increased if the national security mindset becomes as pervasive as some environmentalists hope.

The fashionable recourse to national security paradigms to conceptualize the environmental problem represents a profound and disturbing failure of imagination and political awareness. If the nation-state enjoys a more prominent status in world politics than its competence and accomplishments warrant, then it makes little sense to emphasize the links between it and the emerging problem of global habitability.[11] Nationalist sentiment and the war system have a long-established character that are likely to defy any rhetorically conjured redirection toward benign ends. The movement to preserve the habitability of the planet for future generations must directly challenge the tribal power of nationalism and the chronic militarization of public discourse. Ecological degradation is not a threat to national security; rather, environmentalism is a threat to national security attitudes and institutions. When environmentalists dress their programs in the blood-soaked garments of the war system, they betray their core values and create confusion about the real tasks at hand.

---

[11]See George Modelski, *Principles of World Politics* (New York: Free Press, 1972).